EXAM CRAM

The Netwo [barcode: D1173243] et

This Cram Sheet contains the distilled key facts about the CompTIA Network+ exam. Review this information as the last thing you do before you enter the testing center, paying special attention to those areas in which you feel you need the most review. You can transfer any of these facts from your head onto a blank sheet of paper immediately before you begin the exam.

Network Concepts

▶ As data is passed up or down through the OSI model structure, headers are added (going down) or removed (going up) at each layer—a process called encapsulation (when added) or decapsulation (when removed).

TABLE 1 Summary of the OSI Model

OSI Layer	Description
Application	Provides access to the network for applications and certain end-user functions. Displays incoming information and prepares outgoing information for network access.
Presentation	Converts data from the application layer into a format that can be sent over the network. Converts data from the session layer into a format that the application layer can understand. Encrypts and decrypts data. Provides compression and decompression functionality.
Session	Synchronizes the data exchange between applications on separate devices. Handles error detection and notification to the peer layer on the other device.
Transport	Establishes, maintains, and breaks connections between two devices. Determines the ordering and priorities of data. Performs error checking and verification and handles retransmissions if necessary.
Network	Provides mechanisms for the routing of data between devices across single or multiple network segments. Handles the discovery of destination systems and addressing.
Data link	Has two distinct sublayers: LLC and MAC. Performs error detection and handling for the transmitted signals. Defines the method by which the medium is accessed. Defines hardware addressing through the MAC sublayer.
Physical	Defines the network's physical structure. Defines voltage/signal rates and the physical connection methods. Defines the physical topology.

TABLE 2 TCP/IP Model Compared to OSI Model

TCP/IP Model	OSI Model
Application layer	Application layer
	Presentation layer
	Session layer
Transport layer	Transport layer
Internet layer	Network layer
Network interface layer	Data link layer
	Physical layer

TABLE 3 **Comparing IPv4 to IPv6**

Address Feature	IPv4 Address	IPv6 Address
Loopback address	127.0.0.1	0:0:0:0:0:0:0:1 (::1)
Networkwide addresses	IPv4 public address	Global unicast IPv6 address ranges
Private network addresses	10.0.0.0	Site-local address ranges (FEC0::)
	172.16.0.0	
	192.168.0.0	
Autoconfigured addresses	IPv4 automatic private IP addressing (169.254.0.0)	Link-local addresses of FE80:: prefix

TABLE 4 **TCP/UDP Port Assignments for Commonly Used Protocols**

Protocol	Port Assignment	Protocol	Port Assignment	Protocol	Port Assignment
FTP	20	HTTP	80	DHCP	67
FTP	21	POP3	110	TFTP	69
SSH	22	NNTP	119	DNS	53
Telnet	23	NTP	123	BOOTPS DHCP	67, 68
SMTP	25	IMAP4	143		
DNS	53	HTTPS	443	SNMP	161

- ▶ A MAC address is a 6-byte hexadecimal address that enables a device to be uniquely identified on the network. A MAC address combines numbers and the letters A to F. An example of a MAC address is 00:D0:59:09:07:51.
- ▶ A Class A TCP/IP address uses only the first octet to represent the network portion, a Class B address uses two octets, and a Class C address uses three octets.
- ▶ Class A addresses span from 1 to 126, with a default subnet mask of 255.0.0.0.
- ▶ Class B addresses span from 128 to 191, with a default subnet mask of 255.255.0.0.
- ▶ Class C addresses span from 192 to 223, with a default subnet mask of 255.255.255.0.
- ▶ The 127 network ID is reserved for the IPv4 local loopback.

Steps in the Network Troubleshooting Methodology

1. Identify the problem:
   - ▶ Gather information.
   - ▶ Identify symptoms.
   - ▶ Question users.
   - ▶ Determine if anything has changed.
2. Establish a theory of probable cause:
   - ▶ Question the obvious.
3. Test the theory to determine cause:
   - ▶ After theory is confirmed, determine next steps to resolve problem.
   - ▶ If theory is not confirmed, re-establish new theory or escalate.
4. Establish a plan of action to resolve the problem and identify potential effects.
5. Implement the solution or escalate as necessary.
6. Verify full system functionality and if applicable implement preventative measures.
7. Document findings, actions, and outcomes.

Virtual Network Components

- ▶ Virtualization makes it possible to take a single physical device and make it appear as if it is a number of stand-alone entities.
- ▶ A virtual switch works the same as a physical switch but enables multiple switches to exist on the same host, saving the implementation of additional hardware.
- ▶ Network as a Service (NaaS) is a cloud computing model offered by many telecom providers provided on demand in a pay-as-you-go model. OpenStack is the open source NaaS project.

CompTIA Network+

N10-005 Authorized

Emmett Dulaney
Mike Harwood

800 East 96th Street, Indianapolis, Indiana 46240 USA

CompTIA Network+ N10-005 Authorized Exam Cram

ISBN-13: 978-0-7897-4905-5
ISBN-10: 0-7897-4905-X

Library of Congress Cataloging-in-Publication data is on file.

Seventh Printing: August 2014

Trademarks

All terms mentioned in this book that are known to be trademarks or service marks have been appropriately capitalized. Pearson cannot attest to the accuracy of this information. Use of a term in this book should not be regarded as affecting the validity of any trademark or service mark.

Warning and Disclaimer

Every effort has been made to make this book as complete and as accurate as possible, but no warranty or fitness is implied. The information provided is on an "as is" basis. The author and the publisher shall have neither liability nor responsibility to any person or entity with respect to any loss or damages arising from the information contained in this book or from the use of the CD or programs accompanying it.

Bulk Sales

Que Publishing offers excellent discounts on this book when ordered in quantity for bulk purchases or special sales. For more information, please contact

U.S. Corporate and Government Sales
1-800-382-3419
corpsales@pearsontechgroup.com

For sales outside of the U.S., please contact

International Sales
international@pearsoned.com

Publisher
Paul Boger

Associate Publisher
David Dusthimer

Acquisitions Editor
Betsy Brown

Development Editor
Box Twelve Communications, Inc.

Managing Editor
Sandra Schroeder

Project Editor
Seth Kerney

Copy Editor
Apostrophe Editing Services

Indexer
Ken Johnson

Proofreader
Williams Woods Publishing Services

Technical Editor
Chris Crayton

Publishing Coordinator
Vanessa Evans

Multimedia Developer
Tim Warner

Book Designer
Gary Adair

Page Layout
Bronkella Publishing

Contents at a Glance

Table of Contents

About the Authors

Emmett Dulaney (Network+, A+, Security+, ManyOthers+) is the author of numerous books on certifications and operating systems. He is a columnist for CertCities and an associate professor at Anderson University. In addition to the *Network+ Exam Cram*, he is the author of the *CompTIA A+ Complete Study Guide* and the *CompTIA Security+ Study Guide*.

Mike Harwood (MCSE, A+, Network+, Server+, Linux+) has more than 14 years experience in information technology and related fields. He has held a number of roles in the IT field including network administrator, instructor, technical writer, website designer, consultant, and online marketing strategist. Mike has been a regular on air technology contributor for CBC radio and has coauthored numerous computer books, including the *Network+ Exam Cram* published by Pearson.

About the Technical Editor

Christopher A. Crayton is an author, a technical editor, a technical consultant, a security consultant, a trainer and a SkillsUSA state-level technology competition judge. Formerly, he worked as a computer and networking instructor at Keiser College (2001 Teacher of the Year); a network administrator for Protocol, a global electronic customer relationship management (eCRM) company; and at Eastman Kodak Headquarters as a computer and network specialist. Chris has authored several print and online books, including The *A+ Exams Guide*, Second Edition (Cengage Learning, 2008), *Microsoft Windows Vista 70-620 Exam Guide Short Cut* (O'Reilly, 2007), *CompTIA A+ Essentials 220-601 Exam Guide Short Cut* (O'Reilly, 2007), *The A+ Exams Guide, The A+ Certification and PC Repair Handbook* (Charles River Media, 2005), *The Security+ Exam Guide* (Charles River Media, 2003) and *A+ Adaptive Exams* (Charles River Media, 2002). He is also co-author of the *How to Cheat at Securing Your Network* (Syngress, 2007). As an experienced technical editor, Chris has provided many technical edits and reviews for several major publishing companies, including Pearson Education, McGraw-Hill, Cengage Learning, Wiley, O'Reilly, Syngress, and Apress. He holds MCSE, A+ and Network+ certifications.

Dedication

For Karen, Kristin, Evan, and Spencer: the backbone of my network.
—Emmett Dulaney

Acknowledgments

I would like to thank Mike Harwood for creating a great book of which I was honored to join with this edition. Thanks are due to a wonderful team of talented individuals, three of whom deserve special attention: Betsy Brown, Jeff Riley, and Christopher A. Crayton. They represent the best in the business.

—Emmett Dulaney

We Want to Hear from You!

As the reader of this book, *you* are our most important critic and commentator. We value your opinion and want to know what we're doing right, what we could do better, what areas you'd like to see us publish in, and any other words of wisdom you're willing to pass our way.

As an associate publisher for Pearson, I welcome your comments. You can email or write me directly to let me know what you did or didn't like about this book—as well as what we can do to make our books better.

Please note that I cannot help you with technical problems related to the topic of this book. We do have a User Services group, however, where I will forward specific technical questions related to the book.

When you write, please be sure to include this book's title and author as well as your name, email address, and phone number. I will carefully review your comments and share them with the author and editors who worked on the book.

Email: feedback@pearsonitcertification.com

Mail: David Dusthimer
         Associate Publisher
         Pearson
         800 East 96th Street
         Indianapolis, IN 46240 USA

Reader Services

Visit our website and register this book at www.pearsonitcertification.com/register for convenient access to any updates, downloads, or errata that might be available for this book.

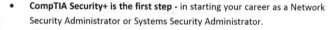

CompTIA Security+

- Designed for IT professionals focused on system security.
- Covers network infrastructure, cryptography, assessments, and audits.
- Security+ is mandated by the U.S. Department of Defense and is recommended by top companies such as Microsoft, HP, and Cisco.

It Pays to Get Certified

In a digital world, digital literacy is an essential survival skill. Certification proves you have the knowledge and skill to solve business problems in virtually any business environment. Certifications are highly valued credentials that qualify you for jobs, increased compensation, and promotion.

Security is one of the highest demand job categories. Growing in importance as the frequency and severity of security threats continues to be a major concern for organizations around the world.

- **Jobs for security administrators are expected to increase by 18%** -the skill set required for these types of jobs map to CompTIA Security+ certification.

- **Network Security Administrators** - can earn as much as $106,000 per year.

- **CompTIA Security+ is the first step** - in starting your career as a Network Security Administrator or Systems Security Administrator.

- **CompTIA Security+ is regularly used in organizations** - such as Hitachi Information Systems, Trendmicro, the McAfee Elite Partner program, the U.S. State Department, and U.S. government contractors such as EDS, General Dynamics, and Northrop Grumman.

How Certification Helps Your Career

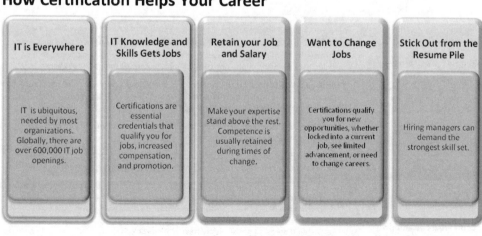

IT is Everywhere	IT Knowledge and Skills Gets Jobs	Retain your Job and Salary	Want to Change Jobs	Stick Out from the Resume Pile
IT is ubiquitous, needed by most organizations. Globally, there are over 600,000 IT job openings.	Certifications are essential credentials that qualify you for jobs, increased compensation, and promotion.	Make your expertise stand above the rest. Competence is usually retained during times of change.	Certifications qualify you for new opportunities, whether locked into a current job, see limited advancement, or need to change careers.	Hiring managers can demand the strongest skill set.

CompTIA Career Pathway

CompTIA offers a number of credentials that form a foundation for your career in technology and allow you to pursue specific areas of concentration. Depending on the path you choose to take, CompTIA certifications help you build upon your skills and knowledge, supporting learning throughout your entire career.

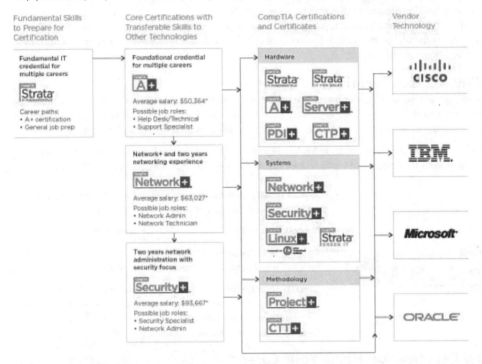

*Source: Computerworld Salary Survey 2010—U.S. salaries only

Steps to Getting Certified and Staying Certified	
Review Exam Objectives	Review the certification objectives to make sure you know what is covered in the exam. http://www.comptia.org/certifications/testprep/examobjectives.aspx
Practice for the Exam	After you have studied for the certification, take a free assessment and sample test to get an idea what type of questions might be on the exam. http://www.comptia.org/certifications/testprep/practicetests.aspx
Purchase an Exam Voucher	Purchase your exam voucher on the CompTIA Marketplace, which is located at: www.comptiastore.com
Take the Test!	Select a certification exam provider and schedule a time to take your exam. You can find exam providers at the following link: http://www.comptia.org/certifications/testprep/testingcenters.aspx
Stay Certified! **Continuing Education**	Effective January 1, 2011, new CompTIA Security+ certifications are valid for three years from the date of your certification. There are a number of ways the certification can be renewed. For more information go to: http://certification.comptia.org/getCertified/steps_to_certification/stayCertified.aspx

Join the Professional Community

	The free IT Pro online community provides valuable content to students and professionals.
Join IT Pro Community http://itpro.comptia.org	• Career IT Job Resources ▪Where to start in IT ▪Career Assessments ▪Salary Trends ▪US Job Board • Forums on Networking, Security, Computing and Cutting Edge Technologies • Access to blogs written by Industry Experts • Current information on Cutting Edge Technologies • Access to various industry resource links and articles related to IT and IT careers

Content Seal of Quality

This courseware bears the seal of **CompTIA Approved Quality Content.** This seal signifies this content covers 100% of the exam objectives and implements important instructional design principles. CompTIA recommends multiple learning tools to help increase coverage of the learning objectives.

Why CompTIA?

- **Global Recognition** – CompTIA is recognized globally as the leading IT non-profit trade association and has enormous credibility. Plus, CompTIA's certifications are vendor-neutral and offer proof of foundational knowledge that translates across technologies.
- **Valued by Hiring Managers -** Hiring managers value CompTIA certification because it is vendor and technology independent validation of your technical skills.

- **Recommended or Required by Government and Businesses** - Many government organizations and corporations either recommend or require technical staff to be CompTIA certified. (e.g. Dell, Sharp, Ricoh, the U.S. Department of Defense and many more)

- **Three CompTIA Certifications ranked in the top 10**. In a study by DICE of 17,000 technology professionals, certifications helped command higher salaries at all experience levels.

How to obtain more information

- **Visit CompTIA online** - www.comptia.org to learn more about getting CompTIA certified.
- **Contact CompTIA** - call 866-835-8020 ext. 5 or email questions@comptia.org
- **Join the IT Pro Community** – http://itpro.comptia.org to join the IT community to get relevant career information.
- **Connect with us :**

Introduction

Welcome to the *Network+ Exam Cram*. This book is designed to prepare you to take—and pass—the CompTIA Network+ exam. The Network+ exam has become the leading introductory-level network certification available today. It is recognized by both employers and industry giants as providing candidates with a solid foundation of networking concepts, terminology, and skills. The Network+ exam covers a broad range of networking concepts to prepare candidates for the technologies they are likely to work with in today's network environments.

About Network+ Exam Cram

Exam Crams are designed to give you the information you need to know to prepare for a certification exam. They cut through the extra information, focusing on the areas you need to get through the exam. With this in mind, the elements within the *Exam Cram* titles are aimed at providing the exam information you need in the most succinct and accessible manner.

In this light, this book is organized to closely follow the actual CompTIA objectives for exam N10-005. As such, it is easy to find the information required for each of the specified CompTIA Network+ objectives. The objective focus design used by this *Exam Cram* is an important feature because the information you need to know is easily identifiable and accessible. To see what we mean, compare the CompTIA objectives to the book's layout, and you can see that the facts are right where you would expect them to be.

Within the chapters, potential exam hot spots are clearly highlighted with Exam Alerts. They have been carefully placed to let you know that the surrounding discussion is an important area for the exam. To further help you prepare for the exam, a Cram Sheet is included that you can use in the final stages of test preparation. Be sure to pay close attention to the bulleted points on the Cram Sheet because they pinpoint the technologies and facts you probably will encounter on the test.

Finally, great effort has gone into the questions that appear throughout the chapter and the practice tests to ensure that they accurately represent the look and feel of the ones you will see on the real Network+ exam. Be sure, before taking the exam, that you are comfortable with both the format and content of the questions provided in this book.

About the Network+ Exam

The Network+ (N10-005 Edition) exam is a revised version of the original exam. The new Network+ objectives are aimed toward those who have at least 9 months of experience in network support and administration. CompTIA believes that new Network+ candidates require more hands-on experience in network administration and troubleshooting, but this should not discourage those who do not. Quite simply, the nature of the questions on the new exam is not dissimilar to the old, and you can get by without actual hands-on experience. Still, a little hands-on experience never hurt anyone and can certainly add to your confidence going into the exam.

You will have a maximum of 90 minutes to answer the 100 questions on the exam. The allotted time is quite generous, so when you finish, you probably will have time to double-check a few of the answers you were unsure of. By the time the dust settles, you need a minimum score of 720 to pass the Network+ exam. This is on a scale of 100 to 900. For more information on the specifics of the Network+ exam, refer to CompTIA's main website at http://certification.comptia.org/.

CompTIA Network+ Exam Topics

Table I-1 lists general exam topics (that is, *objectives*) and specific topics under each general topic (that is, *subobjectives*) for the CompTIA Network+ N10-005 exam. This table also lists the chapter in which each exam topic is covered. Some objectives and subobjectives are addressed in multiple chapters.

TABLE I-1   **CompTIA Network+ Exam Topics**

Chapter	N10-005 Exam Objective	N10-005 Exam Subobjective
1 (Introduction to Networking)	3.0 Network Media and Topologies	3.5 Describe different network topologies.
2 (OSI and TCP/IP Models and Network Protocols)	1.0 Network Concepts 2.0 Network Installation and Configuration 4.0 Network Management	1.1 Compare the layers of the OSI and TCP/IP models. 1.6 Explain the function of common network protocols. 1.7 Summarize DNS concepts and its components. 2.3 Explain the purpose and properties of DHCP. 4.4 Given a scenario, use the appropriate network resource to analyze traffic.

TABLE I-1 **Continued**

Chapter	N10-005 Exam Objective	N10-005 Exam Subobjective
3 (Addressing and Routing)	1.0 Network Concepts 2.0 Network Installation and Configuration	1.3 Explain the purpose and properties of IP addressing. 1.4 Explain the purpose and properties of routing and switching. 1.5 Identify common TCP and UDP default ports. 2.1 Given a scenario, install and configure routers and switches.
4 (Components and Devices)	1.0 Network Technologies 4.0 Network Management	1.2 Classify how applications, devices, and protocols relate to the OSI model layers. 1.9 Identify virtual network components. 4.1 Explain the purpose and features of various network appliances. 3.7 Compare and contrast different LAN technologies.
5 (Installation and Configuration)	2.0 Network Installation and Configuration 3.0 Network Media and Topologies	2.6 Given a set of requirements, plan and implement a basic SOHO network. 3.4 Categorize WAN technology types and properties.
6 (Cabling and Wiring)	3.0 Network Media and Topologies	3.1 Categorize standard media types and associated properties. 3.2 Categorize standard connector types based on network media. 3.7 Compare and contrast different LAN technologies. 3.8 Identify components of wiring distribution.
7 (Wireless)	2.0 Network Installation and Configuration 3.0 Network Media and Topologies 5.0 Network Security	2.2 Given a scenario, install and configure a wireless network. 2.4 Given a scenario, troubleshoot common wireless problems. 3.3 Compare and contrast different wireless standards. 5.1 Given a scenario, implement appropriate wireless security measures.
8 (Network Management)	4.0 Network Management	4.2 Given a scenario, use appropriate hardware tools to troubleshoot connectivity issues. 4.3 Given a scenario, use appropriate software tools to troubleshoot connectivity issues. 4.4 Given a scenario, use the appropriate network monitoring resource to analyze traffic. 4.5 Describe the purpose of configuration management documentation.

TABLE I-1 **Continued**

Chapter	N10-005 Exam Objective	N10-005 Exam Subobjective
9 (Network Optimization)	4.0 Network Management	4.6 Explain different methods and rationales for network performance optimization.
10 (Network Security)	5.0 Network Security	5.2 Explain the methods of network access security. 5.3 Explain methods of user authentication. 5.4 Explain common threats, vulnerabilities, and mitigation techniques. 5.5 Given a scenario, install and configure a basic firewall. 5.6 Categorize different types of network security appliances and methods.
11 (Network Troubleshooting)	1.0 Network Technologies 2.0 Network Installation and Configuration 3.0 Network Media and Topologies	1.8 Given a scenario, implement a given troubleshooting methodology. 2.5 Given a scenario, troubleshoot common router and switch problems. 3.6 Given a scenario, troubleshoot common physical connectivity problems.

Booking and Taking the Network+ Certification Exam

Unfortunately, testing is not free. You're charged $246 for each test you take, whether you pass or fail. In the United States and Canada, tests are administered by Sylvan Prometric or VUE testing services. To book a test with Prometric or to locate a Prometric testing center near you, refer to the website at http://securereg3.prometric.com/ or call 1-888-895-6116. To access the VUE contact information and book an exam, refer to the website at http://www.vue.com or call 1-877-551-7587. When booking an exam, you need to provide the following information:

▶ Your name as you would like it to appear on your certificate.

▶ Your Social Security or Social Insurance number.

▶ Contact phone numbers (to be called in case of a problem).

▶ Mailing address, which identifies the address to which you want your certificate mailed.

▶ Exam number and title.

▶ Email address for contact purposes. This often is the fastest and most effective means to contact you. Many clients require it for registration.

▶ Credit-card information so that you can pay online. You can redeem vouchers by calling the respective testing center.

What to Expect from the Exam

If you haven't taken a certification test, the process can be a little unnerving. Even if you've taken numerous tests, it is not much better. Mastering the inner mental game often can be as much of a battle as knowing the material. Knowing what to expect before heading in can make the process a little more comfortable.

Certification tests are administered on a computer system at a Prometric or VUE authorized testing center. The format of the exams is straightforward: Each question has several possible answers to choose from. The questions in this book provide a good example of the types of questions you can expect on the exam. If you are comfortable with them, the test should hold few surprises. Many of the questions vary in length; some of them are longer scenario questions, whereas others are short and to the point. Carefully read the questions; the longer questions often have a key point that will lead you to the correct answer.

Most of the questions on the Network+ exam require you to choose a single correct answer, but a few require multiple answers. When there are multiple correct answers, a message at the bottom of the screen prompts you to "Choose all that apply." Be sure to read these messages.

A Few Exam Day Details

It is recommended that you arrive at the examination room at least 15 minutes early, although a few minutes earlier certainly would not hurt. This will give you time to prepare and will give the test administrator time to answer any questions you might have before the test begins. Many people suggest that you review the most critical information about the test you're taking just before the test. (*Exam Cram* books provide a reference—the Cram Sheet, located inside the front of this book—that lists the essential information from the book in distilled form.) Arriving a few minutes early will give you some time to compose yourself and mentally review this critical information.

You will be asked to provide two forms of ID, one of which must be a photo ID. Both of the identifications you choose should have a signature. You also might need to sign in when you arrive and sign out when you leave.

Be warned: The rules are clear about what you can and cannot take into the examination room. Books, laptops, note sheets, and so on are not allowed in the examination room. The test administrator will hold these items, to be returned after you complete the exam. You might receive either a wipe board or a pen and a single piece of paper for making notes during the exam. The test administrator will ensure that no paper is removed from the examination room.

After the Test

Whether you want it or not, as soon as you finish your test, your score displays on the computer screen. In addition to the results appearing on the computer screen, a hard copy of the report prints for you. Like the onscreen report, the hard copy displays the results of your exam and provides a summary of how you did on each section and on each technology. If you were unsuccessful, this summary can help you determine the areas you need to brush up on.

When you pass the Network+ exam, you will have earned the Network+ certification, and your certificate will be mailed to you within a few weeks. Should you not receive your certificate and information packet within 5 weeks of passing your exam, contact CompTIA at fulfillment@comptia.org, or call 1-630-268-1818 and ask for the fulfillment department.

Last-Minute Exam Tips

Studying for a certification exam is no different than studying for any other exam, but a few hints and tips can give you the edge on exam day:

- ▶ **Read all the material**: CompTIA has been known to include material not expressly specified in the objectives. This book has included additional information not reflected in the objectives to give you the best possible preparation for the examination.

- ▶ **Watch for the Exam Tips and Notes**: The Network+ objectives include a wide range of technologies. Exam Tips and Notes found throughout each chapter are designed to pull out exam-related hot spots. These can be your best friends when preparing for the exam.

▶ **Use the questions to assess your knowledge**: Don't just read the chapter content; use the exam questions to find out what you know and what you don't. If you struggle, study some more, review, and then assess your knowledge again.

▶ **Review the exam objectives**: Develop your own questions and examples for each topic listed. If you can develop and answer several questions for each topic, you should not find it difficult to pass the exam.

Good luck!

CHAPTER 1

Introduction to Networking

This chapter covers the following official Network+ objectives:

▶ Multiprotocol Label Switching (MPLS)

▶ Point-to-point

▶ Point-to-multipoint

▶ Ring

▶ Star

▶ Mesh

▶ Bus

▶ Peer-to-peer

▶ Client/server

▶ Hybrid

For more information on the official Network+ exam topics, see the "About the Network+ Exam" section in the "Introduction."

A variety of physical and logical network layouts are in use today. As a network administrator, you might work on these different network layouts or topologies. Therefore, you need to understand how they are designed to function.

This chapter reviews general network considerations such as the various topologies used on today's networks, LANs, and WANs, and some of the Institute of Electrical and Electronics Engineers (IEEE) standards.

LANs, WANs, and Network Models

▶ **Peer-to-peer**

▶ **Client/server**

Cram**Saver**

If you can correctly answer these questions before going through this section, save time by skimming the Exam Alerts in this section and then complete the Cram Quiz at the end of the section.

1. True or False: The biggest difference between a LAN and WAN is usually the size of the network.

2. What network model offers no centralized storage of data or centralized control over the sharing of files or resources?

3. In what networking model is the processing power shared between the client systems and the server?

Answers

1. True. A WAN is a network that spans more than one geographic location, often connecting separated LANs.

2. A peer-to-peer network is a decentralized network model offering no centralized storage of data or centralized control over the sharing of files or resources.

3. A distributed network model has the processing power distributed between the client systems and the server.

Networks are classified according to their geographic coverage and size. The two most common network classifications are local area networks (LANs) and wide area networks (WANs).

LANs

A LAN is a data network restricted to a single geographic location and typically encompasses a relatively small area, such as an office building or school. The function of the LAN is to interconnect workstation computers for the purpose of sharing files and resources. Because of its localized nature, the LAN typically is high speed and cheaper to set up than a WAN. Figure 1.1 shows an example of a LAN.

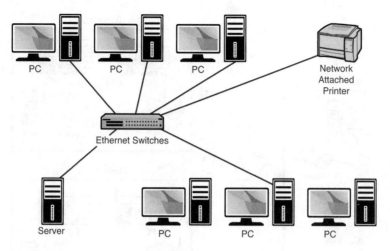

FIGURE 1.1 **A local area network.**

> **Note**
>
> Wireless technologies have introduced a new term—wireless personal area network (WPAN). WPAN refers to the technologies involved in connecting devices in close proximity to exchange data or resources. An example is connecting a laptop with a PDA to synchronize an address book. Because of their small size and the nature of the data exchange, WPAN devices lend themselves well to ad hoc wireless networking. Ad hoc wireless networks are those that have devices connect to each other directly, not through a wireless access point. Ad hoc wireless networks are discussed later in this chapter.

WANs

A WAN is a network that spans more than one geographic location, often connecting separated LANs. WANs are slower than LANs and often require additional and costly hardware such as routers, dedicated leased lines, and complicated implementation procedures. Figure 1.2 shows an example of a WAN.

Occasionally, a WAN will be referenced as a Metropolitan Area Network (MAN) when it is confined to a certain geographic area, such as a university campus or city. No formal guidelines dictate the differences between a MAN and a WAN; technically, a MAN *is* a WAN. Perhaps for this reason, the term MAN is used less frequently than WAN. If any distinction exists, it's that a MAN is smaller than a WAN. A MAN is almost always bigger than a LAN and usually is smaller than or equal to a WAN. MANs use an Internet service provider (ISP) or telecommunications (telco) provider.

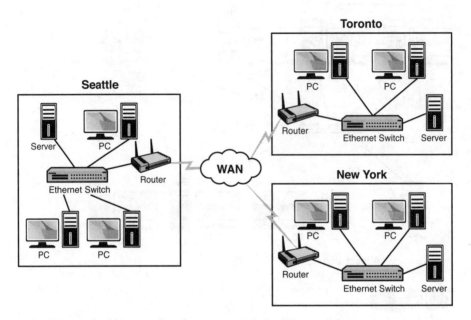

FIGURE 1.2   A wide area network.

Network Models

You can choose from two basic wired network models: peer-to-peer and client/server. The model used for a network is determined by several factors, including how the network will be used, how many users will be on the network, and budgetary considerations.

Peer-to-Peer Networking Model

A peer-to-peer network is a decentralized network model offering no centralized storage of data or centralized control over the sharing of files or resources. All systems on a peer-to-peer network can share the resources on their local computer and use resources of other systems.

Peer-to-peer networks are cheaper and easier to implement than client/server networks, making them an ideal solution for environments in which budgets are a concern. The peer-to-peer model does not work well with large numbers of computer systems. As a peer-to-peer network grows, it becomes increasingly complicated to navigate and access files and resources connected to each computer because they are distributed throughout the network. Furthermore, the lack of centralized data storage makes it difficult to locate and back up key files.

Peer-to-peer networks typically are found in small offices or residential settings where only a limited number of computers will be attached and only a few files and resources shared. A general rule of thumb is to have no more than 10 computers connected to a peer-to-peer network.

Client/Server Networking Model

The client/server networking model is, without question, the most widely implemented model and the one you are most likely to encounter when working in real-world environments. The advantages of the client/server system are that it is a centralized model and it enables centralized network management of all network services, including user management, security, and backup procedures.

A client/server network often requires technically skilled personnel to implement and manage the network. This, and the cost of dedicated server hardware and software, increases the cost of the client/server model. Despite this, the advantages of centralized management, data storage, administration, and security make the client/server network the network model of choice.

Comparing Peer-to-Peer and Client/Server Network Models

Table 1.1 summarizes the characteristics of the peer-to-peer and client/server network models.

> **ExamAlert**
>
> The role of the client computer in the client/server model is to request the data from the server and present that data to the users.

TABLE 1.1 **Comparison of Networking Models**

Attribute	Peer-to-Peer Network Model	Client/Server Network Model
Size	Recommended to a maximum of 10 computers.	The size of the network is limited only by server size, network hardware, and budget. It can have thousands of connected systems.
Administration	Each individual is responsible for the administration of his or her own system. An administrator is not needed.	A skilled network administrator is often required to maintain and manage the network.

TABLE 1.1 **Continued**

Attribute	Peer-to-Peer Network Model	Client/Server Network Model
Security	Each individual is responsible for maintaining security for local files and devices connected to the system.	Security is managed from a central location but often requires a skilled administrator to correctly configure.
Cost	Minimal startup and implementation cost.	Requires dedicated equipment and specialized hardware and administration, increasing the network's cost.
Implementation	Easy to configure and set up.	Often requires complex setup procedures and skilled staff to set up.

Centralized Computing versus Distributed Computing

The terms centralized computing and distributed computing describe where the network processing takes place. In a centralized computing model, one system provides both the data storage and processing power for client systems. This networking model is most often associated with computer mainframes and dumb terminals, where no processing or storage capability exists at the workstation. These network environments are rare, but they do still exist.

A distributed network model has the processing power distributed between the client systems and the server. Most modern networks use the distributed network model, where client workstations share in the processing responsibilities.

Cram Quiz

1. What is the maximum number of computers recommended for inclusion in a peer-to-peer network?

   ○ **A.** 2

   ○ **B.** 5

   ○ **C.** 10

   ○ **D.** 25

2. When a WAN is confined to a certain geographic area, such as a university campus or city, it is known as a

   ○ **A.** LAN

   ○ **B.** MAN

   ○ **C.** VAN

   ○ **D.** VPN

Cram Quiz Answers

1. **C.** The maximum number of computers recommended in a peer-to-peer network is 10.

2. **B.** A WAN can be referred to as a MAN (Metropolitan Area Network) when it is confined to a certain geographic area, such as a university campus or city.

Network Topologies

- ▶ **Multiprotocol Label Switching (MPLS)**
- ▶ **Point-to-point**
- ▶ **Point-to-multipoint**
- ▶ **Ring**
- ▶ **Star**
- ▶ **Mesh**
- ▶ **Bus**
- ▶ **Hybrid**

Cram**Saver**

If you can correctly answer these questions before going through this section, save time by skimming the Exam Alerts in this section and then complete the Cram Quiz at the end of the section.

1. Which topology (star, bus, or ring) would use a hub or switch?

2. With which topology does every node have a direct connection to every other node?

Answers

1. Of the choices given, only a star topology would use a hub or switch.

2. With a mesh topology, every node has a direct connection to every other node.

A *topology* refers to a network's physical and logical layout. A network's *physical* topology refers to the actual layout of the computer cables and other network devices. A network's *logical* topology refers to the way in which the network appears to the devices that use it.

Several topologies are in use on networks today. Some of the more common topologies are the bus, ring, star, mesh, and wireless. The following sections provide an overview of each.

Bus Topology

A *bus topology* uses a trunk or backbone to connect all the computers on the network, as shown in Figure 1.3. Systems connect to this backbone using *T connectors* or taps (known as a vampire tap, if you must pierce the wire). To avoid signal reflection, a physical bus topology requires that each end of the physical bus be terminated, with one end also being grounded. A hub or switch is not needed in this installation.

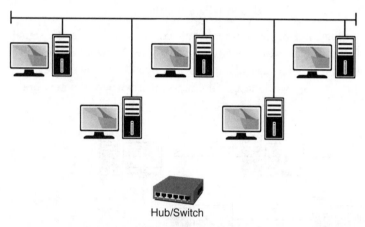

Hub/Switch

FIGURE 1.3 **Physical bus topology.**

ExamAlert

Loose or missing terminators from a bus network disrupt data transmissions.

The most common implementation of a linear bus is the IEEE 802.3 standard (the collection of standards defining this type of wiring). Table 1.2 summarizes the advantages and disadvantages of the bus topology.

TABLE 1.2 **Advantages and Disadvantages of the Bus Topology**

Advantage	Disadvantage
Compared to other topologies, a bus is cheap and easy to implement.	Network disruption might occur when computers are added or removed.
Requires less cable than other topologies.	Because all systems on the network connect to a single backbone, a break in the cable prevents all systems from accessing the network.
Does not use any specialized network equipment.	Difficult to troubleshoot.

Ring Topology

The *ring topology* is actually a logical ring, meaning that the data travels in a circular fashion from one computer to another on the network. It is not a physical ring topology. Figure 1.4 shows the logical layout of a ring network. A hub or switch is not needed in this installation either.

In a true ring topology, if a single computer or section of cable fails, the signal is interrupted. The entire network becomes inaccessible. Network disruption can also occur when computers are added to or removed from the network, making it an impractical network design in environments where the network changes often.

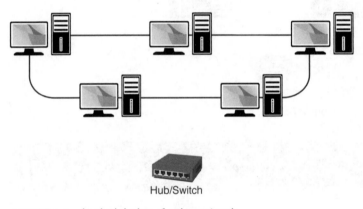

Hub/Switch

FIGURE 1.4   **Logical design of a ring network.**

As just mentioned, if a single system on the ring fails, the whole network fails. This is why ring networks can be set up in a fault-tolerant design, meaning that they have a primary and secondary ring. If one ring fails, data can use the second ring to reach its destination. Naturally, the addition of the second ring adds to the cost of the network and the complexity.

Ring networks are most commonly wired in a star configuration. In a token ring network, a multistation access unit (MSAU) is equivalent to a hub or switch on an Ethernet network. The MSAU internally performs the token circulation. To create the complete ring, the ring in (RI) port on each MSAU is connected to the ring out (RO) port on another MSAU. The last MSAU in the ring is then connected to the first to complete the ring. Table 1.3 summarizes the advantages and disadvantages of the ring topology.

TABLE 1.3 **Advantages and Disadvantages of the Ring Topology**

Advantage	Disadvantage
Cable faults are easily located, making troubleshooting easier.	Expansion to the network can cause network disruption.
Ring networks are moderately easy to install.	A single break in the cable can disrupt the entire network.

Star Topology

In the *star topology*, all computers and other network devices connect to a central device called a *hub* or *switch*. Each connected device requires a single cable to be connected to the hub, creating a point-to-point connection between the device and the hub.

Using a separate cable to connect to the hub or switch allows the network to be expanded without disruption. A break in any single cable does not cause the entire network to fail. Figure 1.5 shows a star topology.

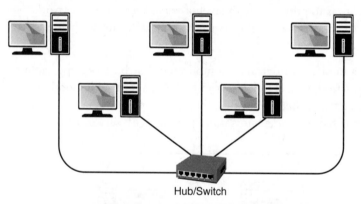

Hub/Switch

FIGURE 1.5 **Star topology.**

Exam Alert

Among the network topologies discussed in this chapter, the star topology is the easiest to expand in terms of the number of devices connected to the network.

The star topology is the most widely implemented network design in use today, but it is not without shortcomings. Because all devices connect to a centralized hub or switch, this creates a single point of failure for the network. If the hub or switch fails, any device connected to it cannot access the network. Because of the number of cables required and the need for network devices, the cost of a star network is often higher than other topologies. Table 1.4 summarizes the advantages and disadvantages of the star topology.

TABLE 1.4 **Advantages and Disadvantages of the Star Topology**

Advantage	Disadvantage
Star networks are easily expanded without disruption to the network.	Requires more cable than most of the other topologies.
Cable failure affects only a single user.	A central connecting device enables a single point of failure.
Easy to troubleshoot and implement.	Requires additional networking equipment to create the network layout.

Mesh Topology

The wired *mesh topology* (see Figure 1.6) incorporates a unique network design in which each computer on the network connects to every other, creating a point-to-point connection between every device on the network. The purpose of the mesh design is to provide a high level of *redundancy*. If one network cable fails, the data always has an alternative path to get to its destination— each node can act as a relay.

The wiring for a mesh network can be complicated. Furthermore, the cabling costs associated with the mesh topology can be high, and troubleshooting a failed cable can be tricky. Because of this, the mesh topology is not the first choice for many wired networks but is more popular with servers or routers.

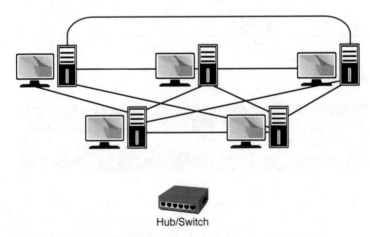

Hub/Switch

FIGURE 1.6 **Mesh topology.**

A variation on a true mesh topology is the hybrid mesh. It creates a redundant point-to-point network connection between only specific network devices (such as the servers). The hybrid mesh is most often seen in WAN implementations but can be used in any network.

Table 1.5 summarizes the advantages and disadvantages of the mesh topology.

> **ExamAlert**
>
> Because of the redundant connections, the mesh topology offers better fault tolerance than other topologies.

TABLE 1.5   **Advantages and Disadvantages of the Mesh Topology**

Advantage	Disadvantage
Provides redundant paths between LAN topologies.	Requires more cable than the other devices
The network can be expanded without disruption to current users.	Complicated implementation

MPLS

> **Tip**
>
> MPLS is a switching technology used to make packet forwarding happen. With this iteration of the exam, CompTIA has moved the discussion of it beneath network technologies; although, it could be a better fit beneath other objectives. To maintain consistency, however, it is discussed beneath that objective as well to make exam preparation easier on you.

Multiprotocol Label Switching (MPLS) is a technology designed to speed up network traffic flow by moving away from the use of traditional routing tables. Instead of routing tables, MPLS uses short labels to direct packets and forward them through the network. This is an important distinction. In a traditional packet-forwarding design, the packet travels from one router to the next, with a forwarding decision made at each hop along the way. The forwarding decision is based on the information in the IP packet header with the routing table. This packet has to be analyzed at each hop along the way. It was just a matter of time before a more efficient packet-forwarding method came into play.

With MPLS routing, the packet is analyzed only a single time. In operation, MPLS creates a channel or path for a given sequence of packets to reach their destination. Each packet has been assigned a label that associates it with this specific path. For routing data packets, all packets with the same label use the same path (known as a label-switched path [LSP]). Because labels refer to paths and not endpoints, packets destined for the same endpoint can use a variety of LSPs to get there. The packet follows the channel to its destination, thereby eliminating the need to check the packet for forwarding information at each hop and reducing the need to check routing tables.

The multiprotocol part of the name refers to the fact that MPLS works with a variety of protocols, including Frame Relay, ATM, and IP.

ExamAlert

Make sure you understand the function of MPLS.

Wireless Topologies

Wireless networks typically are implemented using one of two wireless topologies:

- ▶ Infrastructure, or managed, wireless topology
- ▶ Ad hoc, or unmanaged, wireless topology

The following sections describe these two wireless topologies in greater detail.

Infrastructure Wireless Topology

The *infrastructure wireless topology* is commonly used to extend a wired LAN to include wireless devices. Wireless devices communicate with the wired LAN through a base station known as an *access point (AP)* or *wireless access point*. The AP forms a bridge between a wireless and wired LAN, and all transmissions between wireless stations, or between a system and a wired network client, go through the AP. APs are not mobile and must stay connected to the wired network; therefore, they become part of the wired network infrastructure (thus the name). In infrastructure wireless networks, there might be several access points providing wireless coverage for a large area or only a single access point for a small area, such as a single home or small building.

Note

Although it is called a wireless access point, it is referred to as an AP and not a WAP. WAP is the acronym for wireless application protocol.

Ad Hoc Wireless Topology

In a *wireless ad hoc topology*, devices communicate directly between themselves without using an access point. This peer-to-peer network design is commonly used to connect a small number of computers or wireless devices. For example, an ad hoc wireless network may be set up temporarily between laptops in a boardroom or to connect systems in a home instead of using a wired solution. The ad hoc wireless design provides a quick method to share files and resources between a small number of systems. Figure 1.7 shows an ad hoc wireless network, and Figure 1.8 shows the infrastructure network using the AP.

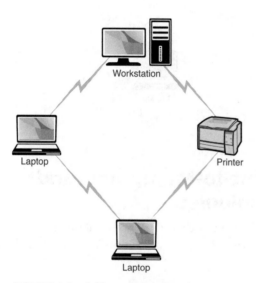

FIGURE 1.7   **Ad hoc wireless topology.**

> ### Tip
>
> The ad hoc, or unmanaged, network design does not use an AP. All wireless devices connect directly to each other.
>
> In an infrastructure wireless network, devices use a wireless AP to connect to the network.

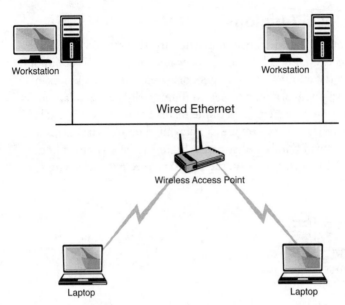

FIGURE 1.8   Infrastructure wireless topology.

Point-to-Point, Point-to-Multipoint, and Wireless Mesh Topologies

When setting up a wireless network, you can choose from several other topologies. These include the point-to-point, point-to-multipoint, and wireless mesh configuration.

Point-to-Point Networks

As the name suggests, in a point-to-point (PtP) wireless configuration, the communication link travels from one node directly to one other node. Wireless point-to-point systems often are used in wireless backbone systems, such as microwave relay communications, or as a replacement for a single wired communication cable. Figure 1.9 shows a point-to-point wireless configuration.

The point-to-point wireless link connects two remote locations (refer to Figure 1.9). Not having to run cable such as fiber makes it an economical way to provide a communication link. However, a typical point-to-point wireless configuration has no redundancy. This means that if the wireless link should fail, communication between the locations is unavailable.

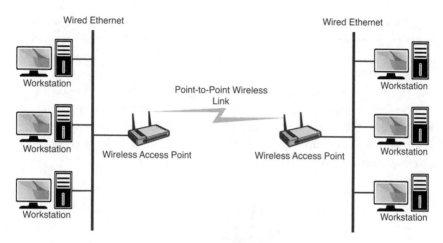

FIGURE 1.9   **A point-to-point wireless topology.**

The point-to-point link is often used for organizations that need a direct link between two remote office buildings. These point-to-point wireless connections typically are easy to install and require no external outdoor casing, cables, or other accessories. Because there is no need for the cabling infrastructure, a point-to-point wireless solution is a cost-effective method to connect two remote locations.

Point-to-Multipoint Networks

A point-to-multipoint (PtMP) wireless connection is designed to link multiple wired networks. Signals in point-to-multipoint networks travel from a central node such as a base station of a cellular system, an access point of a WLAN, or a satellite. The function of the multipoint wireless topology is to interconnect multiple locations, enabling them to access and share resources. Multipoint networks use a base station as the "hub" and client networks as the connection points communicating with the base station. These point-to-multipoint networks are used in wireless Internet service providers (WISPs), large corporate campuses, interconnected branch offices, and more.

The reliability of the PtMP network topology depends on the quality of the central node and each connecting node. The location of the central node is important to ensure the range and strength of the wireless signal.

Wireless Mesh Networks

As discussed earlier, wired mesh networks are costly because of the cabling required to interconnect all computer systems. Wireless mesh networks obviously do not need cables running between systems, making wireless mesh networks fairly common in the networking world. In the wireless mesh network, as with the wired mesh, each network node interconnects to other nodes on the network. With a wireless mesh, the wireless signal starts at a wireless base station (access point) attached to a wired network. A wireless mesh network extends the transmission distance by relaying the signal from one computer to another. Unlike the wired mesh, in which a complex and expensive collection of physical cables is required to create the mesh, the wireless mesh is inexpensive to implement. Figure 1.10 shows a wireless mesh network.

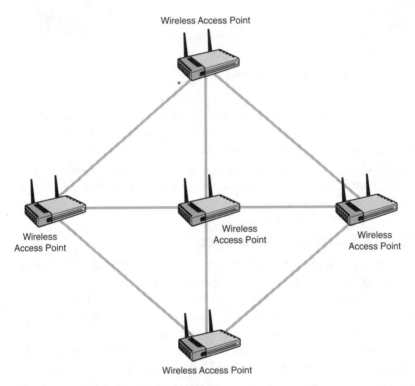

FIGURE 1.10 **A wireless mesh topology.**

> **Note**
>
> A wireless mesh network is created through the connection of wireless access points installed at each network user's locale. Data signals in a wireless mesh rely on all nodes to propagate signals. You can identify wireless mesh networks by the interconnecting signals between each node.

The wireless mesh network has several key advantages. Because a wireless mesh network interconnects with one or more nodes on the network, the data can travel multiple paths to reach its destination. When you add a new node, it provides new paths for other nodes, which in turn improves network performance and decreases congestion. Advantages of the wireless mesh include the following:

▶ **Self-healing**: Wireless mesh networks are known as self-healing, which refers to the network's capability to adapt to network failure and even function should a node be moved from one location to another. Self-healing in a wireless mesh environment is possible because of the interconnected connections and because of the wireless media.

▶ **Scalable**: Wireless mesh networks are highly scalable. Using wireless, you can add new systems to the network without the need for expensive cables.

▶ **Reliability**: Of all network topologies, the mesh network provides the greatest reliability. The redundant number of paths for the data to travel ensures that data can reach its destination.

▶ **Cost**: One disadvantage of the wired mesh is the cost associated with running the cabling and the support costs of such a complex network. Wireless mesh networks are essentially self-configuring and do not have cabling requirements. Therefore, you can add, remove, and relocate systems with little cost or disruption to the network.

Hybrid Topologies

As you might expect, topology designs are not black-and-white. Many topologies found in large networking environments are a hybrid of physical topologies. An example of a hybrid topology is the star bus—a combination of the star topology and the bus topology. Figure 1.11 shows how this might look in a network implementation.

> **ExamAlert**
>
> Another meaning: The term *hybrid topology* also can refer to the combination of wireless and wired networks. For the Network+ exam, however, the term *hybrid* most likely refers to the combination of physical networks.

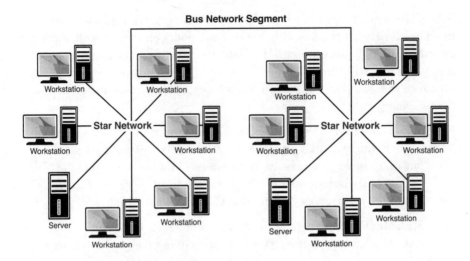

FIGURE 1.11   A star bus topology.

Cram Quiz

1. You have been asked to install a network to give the network users the greatest amount of fault tolerance. Which of the following network topologies would you choose?

   ○ **A.** Star

   ○ **B.** Ring

   ○ **C.** Mesh

   ○ **D.** Bus

2. Which of the following topologies enables network expansion with the least amount of disruption for the current network users?

   ○ **A.** Bus

   ○ **B.** Ring

   ○ **C.** LAN

   ○ **D.** Star

3. You have been asked to connect two office locations. It has been specified that you use a wireless link. Which of the following strategies would you use to connect the two offices?

   ○ **A.** Point-to-point

   ○ **B.** Wireless mesh

   ○ **C.** PtMP

   ○ **D.** Star bus hybrid

4. What topology is represented in the following figure?

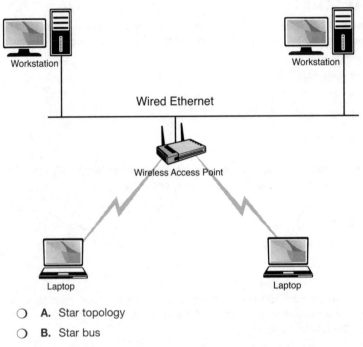

- ○ **A.** Star topology
- ○ **B.** Star bus
- ○ **C.** Ad hoc
- ○ **D.** Infrastructure

5. Which network topology offers the greatest level of redundancy but also has the highest implementation cost?

- ○ **A.** Wireless mesh
- ○ **B.** Wired mesh
- ○ **C.** Hybrid star
- ○ **D.** Bus network

6. Which of the following statements are associated with a bus LAN network? (Choose all correct answers.)

- ○ **A.** A single cable break can cause complete network disruption.
- ○ **B.** All devices connect to a central device.
- ○ **C.** It uses a single backbone to connect all network devices.
- ○ **D.** It uses a dual-ring configuration.

Cram Quiz Answers

1. **C.** A mesh network uses a point-to-point connection to every device on the network. This creates multiple points for the data to transmit around the network and therefore creates a high degree of redundancy. The star, ring, and bus topologies do not offer fault tolerance.

2. **D.** On a star network, each network device uses a separate cable to make a point-to-point connection to a centralized device such as a hub or switch. With such a configuration, you can add a new device to the network by attaching the new device to the hub or switch with its own cable. This process does not disrupt the users who are currently on the network. Answers A and B are incorrect because the addition of new network devices on a ring or bus network can cause a disruption in the network and cause network services to be unavailable during the installation of a new device. A LAN (local area network) is created using any topology and is not a topology in and of itself.

3. **A.** In a point-to-point (PtP) wireless configuration, the communication link travels from one node directly to one other node. Wireless point-to-point systems are often used in wireless backbone systems such as microwave relay communications or as a replacement for a single wired communication cable. You can use the point-to-point link to connect two locations to share data and resources. The other choices are not appropriate options for creating the wanted connection.

4. **D.** The infrastructure wireless topology is commonly used to extend a wired LAN to include wireless devices. Wireless devices communicate with the wired LAN through a base station known as an access point (AP) or wireless access point. The AP forms a bridge between a wireless and wired LAN, and all transmissions between wireless stations or between a system and a wired network client go through the AP.

5. **B.** The wired mesh topology requires each computer on the network to be individually connected to every other device. This configuration provides maximum reliability and redundancy for the network. However, of those listed, it is the most costly to implement because of the multiple wiring requirements.

6. **A, C.** In a bus network, a single break in the network cable can disrupt all the devices on that segment of the network—a significant shortcoming. A bus network also uses a single cable as a backbone to which all networking devices attach. A star network requires networked devices to connect to a centralized device such as a hub or MSAU. It does not use a dual-ring configuration. Therefore, answer B is incorrect.

Going Virtual

▸ **Virtual private networks (VPNs)**

▸ **Virtual local area networks (VLANs)**

Cram**Saver**

If you can correctly answer these questions before going through this section, save time by skimming the Exam Alerts in this section and then completing the Cram Quiz at the end of the section.

1. What type of network configuration enables a remote user to access a private network across the Internet?

2. True or False: VLANs enable you to create multiple broadcast domains on a single switch.

Answers

1. A virtual private network (VPN) can enable a remote user to access a private network across the Internet.

2. True. VLANs enable you to create multiple broadcast domains on a single switch.

Virtualization has become exceedingly popular in recent years as a necessary requirement in a network. The two major areas that CompTIA expects you to know for Network+ study are VPNs and VLANs, both of which are discussed in the following sections. Virtual network components are discussed later in this book.

Virtual Private Networks (VPNs)

In the mid-1990s, Microsoft, IBM, and Cisco began working on a technology called *tunneling*. By 1996, more companies had become interested and involved in the work. From their efforts, virtual private networks (VPNs) became one of the most popular methods of remote access. But before you can know why VPNs became so popular, you must know a bit more about them.

Essentially, a VPN extends a LAN by establishing a remote connection using a public network such as the Internet. A VPN provides a point-to-point dedicated link between two points over a public IP network. Figure 1.12 shows how a VPN enables remote access for a remote client to a private network.

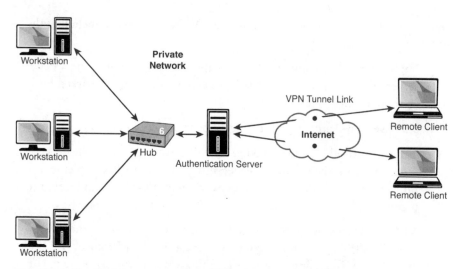

FIGURE 1.12   **Remote access using a VPN.**

For many companies, the VPN link provides the perfect method to expand their networking capabilities and reduce their costs. By using the public network (Internet), a company does not need to rely on expensive private leased lines to provide corporate network access to its remote users. Using the Internet to facilitate the remote connection, the VPN enables network connectivity over a possibly long physical distance. In this respect, a VPN is a form of WAN.

> **Note**
>
> Many companies use a VPN to provide a cost-effective method to establish a connection between remote clients and a private network. There are other times a VPN link is handy. You can also use a VPN to connect one private LAN to another, known as LAN-to-LAN internetworking. For security reasons, you can use a VPN to provide controlled access within an intranet. As an exercise, try drawing what the VPN would look like in these two scenarios.

Components of the VPN Connection

A VPN enables anyone with an Internet connection to use the infrastructure of the public network to dial in to the main network and access resources as if the user were locally logged on to the network. It also enables two networks to securely connect to each other.

Many elements are involved in establishing a VPN connection, including the following:

- ▶ **VPN client**: The computer that initiates the connection to the VPN server. The VPN clients are the laptop computer systems marked "remote client" (refer to Figure 1.12).

- ▶ **VPN server**: Authenticates connections from VPN clients.

- ▶ **Access method**: As mentioned, a VPN is most often established over a public network such as the Internet; however, some VPN implementations use a private intranet. The network used must be IP (Internet protocol)-based.

- ▶ **VPN protocols**: Required to establish, manage, and secure the data over the VPN connection. Point-to-Point Tunneling Protocol (PPTP) and Layer 2 Tunneling Protocol (L2TP) are commonly associated with VPN connections. These protocols enable authentication and encryption in VPNs. Authentication enables VPN clients and servers to correctly establish the identity of people on the network. Encryption enables potentially sensitive data to be guarded from the general public.

VPNs have become popular because they enable the public Internet to be safely used as a WAN connectivity solution.

> **ExamAlert**
>
> VPNs support analog modems, Integrated Services Digital Network (ISDN) wireless connections, and dedicated broadband connections such as cable and DSL. You should remember this for the exam.

VPN Pros and Cons

As with any technology, VPN has both pros and cons. Fortunately with VPN technology, these are clear-cut, and even the cons typically do not prevent an organization from using VPNs in its networks. Using a VPN offers two primary benefits:

- ▶ **Cost**: If you use the infrastructure of the Internet, you don't need to spend money on dedicated private connections to link remote clients to the private network. Furthermore, when you use the public network, you don't need to hire support personnel to support those private links.

▶ **Easy scalability**: VPNs make it easy to expand the network. Employees who have a laptop with wireless capability can simply log on to the Internet and establish the connection to the private network.

Table 1.6 outlines some of the advantages and potential disadvantages of using a VPN.

TABLE 1.6 **Pros and Cons of Using a VPN**

Advantage	Description
Reduced cost	When you use the Internet, you don't need to rent dedicated lines between remote clients and a private network. In addition, a VPN can replace remote-access servers and long-distance dialup network connections that were commonly used in the past by business travelers who needed access to their company intranet. This eliminates long-distance phone charges.
Network scalability	The cost to an organization to build a dedicated private network may be reasonable at first, but it increases exponentially as the organization grows. The Internet enables an organization to grow its remote client base without having to increase or modify an internal network infrastructure.
Reduced support	Using the Internet, organizations do not need to employ support personnel to manage a VPN infrastructure.
Simplified	With a VPN, a network administrator can easily add remote clients. All authentication work is managed from the VPN authentication server, and client systems can be easily config-ured for automatic VPN access.
Disadvantage	**Description**
Security	Using a VPN, data is sent over a public network, so data securi-ty is a concern. VPNs use security protocols to address this shortcoming, but VPN administrators must understand data security over public networks to ensure that data is not tam-pered with or stolen.
Reliability	The reliability of the VPN communication depends on the public network and is not under an organization's direct control. Instead, the solution relies on an ISP and its quality of service.

Virtual Local Area Networks (VLANs)

The word *virtual* is used a lot in the computing world—perhaps too often. For VLANs, the word *virtual* does little to help explain the technology. Perhaps a more descriptive name for the VLAN concept might have been *seg-mented*. For now at least, use *virtual*.

> **Tip**
>
> 802.1Q is the Institute of Electrical and Electronics Engineers (IEEE) specification developed to ensure interoperability of VLAN technologies from the various vendors.

VLANs are used for network segmentation, a strategy that significantly increases the network's performance capability, removes potential performance bottlenecks, and can even increase network security. A VLAN is a group of connected computers that act as if they are on their own network segments, even though they might not be. For instance, suppose that you work in a three-story building in which the advertising employees are spread over all three floors. A VLAN can enable all the advertising personnel to be combined and access network resources as if they were connected on the same physical segment. This virtual segment can be isolated from other network segments. In effect, it would appear to the advertising group that they were on a network by themselves.

> **ExamAlert**
>
> VLANs enable you to create multiple broadcast domains on a single switch. In essence, this is the same as creating separate networks for each VLAN.

VLANs offer some clear advantages. Logically segmenting a network gives administrators flexibility beyond the restrictions of the physical network design and cable infrastructure. VLANs enable easier administration because the network can be divided into well-organized sections. Furthermore, you can increase security by isolating certain network segments from others. For example, you can segment the marketing personnel from finance or the administrators from the students. VLANs can ease the burden on overworked routers and reduce broadcast storms. Table 1.7 summarizes the benefits of VLANs.

TABLE 1.7 **Benefits of VLANs**

Advantage	Description
Increased security	With the creation of logical (virtual) boundaries, network segments can be isolated.
Increased performance	By reducing broadcast traffic throughout the network, VLANs free up bandwidth.
Organization	Network users and resources linked and that communicate frequently can be grouped in a VLAN.
Simplified administration	With a VLAN the network administrator's job is easier when moving users between LAN segments, recabling, addressing new stations, and reconfiguring switches and routers.

VLAN Membership

You can use several methods to determine VLAN membership or how devices are assigned to a specific VLAN. The following sections describe the common methods to determine how VLAN membership is assigned.

▸ **Protocol-based VLANs**: With protocol-based VLAN membership, computers are assigned to VLANs using the protocol in use and the Layer 3 address. For example, this method enables an Internetwork Packet Exchange (IPX) network or a particular IP subnet to have its own VLAN.

The term *Layer 3 address* refers to one of the most important networking concepts, the Open Systems Interconnect (OSI) reference model. This conceptual model, created by the International Organization for Standardization (ISO) in 1978 and revised in 1984, describes a network architecture that enables data to be passed between computer systems. There are seven layers in total, which are discussed in detail in Chapter 2, "OSI and TCP/IP Models and Network Protocols." In brief, Layer 3, known as the network layer, identifies the mechanisms by which data can be moved between two networks or systems, such as transport protocols, which in the case of TCP/IP is IP.

Although VLAN membership may be based on Layer 3 information, this has nothing to do with routing or routing functions. The IP numbers are used only to determine the membership in a particular VLAN, not to determine routing.

▸ **Port-based VLANs**: Port-based VLANs require that specific ports on a network switch be assigned to a VLAN. For example, ports 1 through 4 may be assigned to marketing, ports 5 through 7 may be assigned to sales, and so on. Using this method, a switch determines VLAN membership by taking note of the port used by a particular packet. Figure 1.13 shows how the ports on a server could be used for port-based VLAN membership.

▸ **MAC address-based VLANs**: The Media Access Control (MAC) address is a unique 12-digit hexadecimal number that is stamped into every network interface card. Every device used on a network has this unique address built into it. It cannot be modified in any way. As you may have guessed, the MAC address type of a VLAN assigns membership according to the workstation's MAC address. To do this, the switch must keep track of the MAC addresses that belong to each VLAN. The advantage of this method is that a workstation computer can be moved anywhere in an office without needing to be reconfigured. Because the MAC address does not change, the workstation remains a member of a particular VLAN. Table 1.8 provides examples of the membership of MAC address-based VLANs.

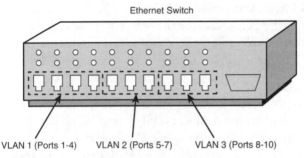

FIGURE 1.13   **Port-based VLAN membership.**

TABLE 1.8   **MAC Address-Based VLANs**

MAC Address	VLAN	Description
44-45-53-54-00-00	1	Sales
44-45-53-54-13-12	2	Marketing
44-45-53-54-D3-01	3	Administration
44-45-53-54-F5-17	1	Sales

VLAN Segmentation

The capability to logically segment a LAN provides a level of administrative flexibility, organization, and security. Whether the LAN is segmented using the protocol, MAC address, or port, the result is the same: The network is segmented. The segmentation is used for several reasons, including security, organization, and performance. To give you a better idea of how this works, Figure 1.14 shows a network that doesn't use a VLAN.

In Figure 1.14, all systems on the network can see each other. That is, the students can see the finance and administrator computers. Figure 1.15 shows how this network may look using a VLAN.

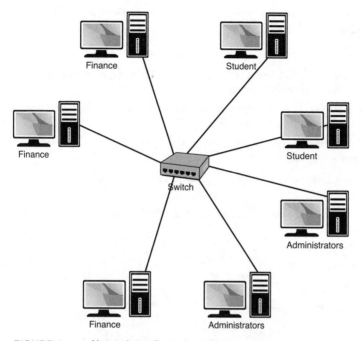

FIGURE 1.14   **Network configuration without using a VLAN.**

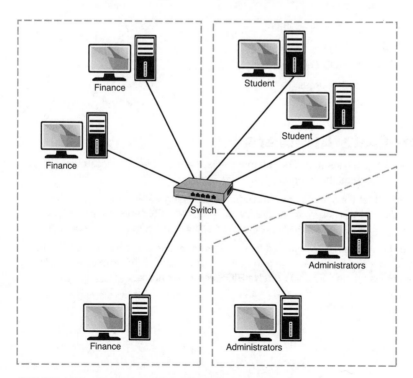

FIGURE 1.15   **Network configuration using a VLAN.**

Cram Quiz

1. Which of the following statements best describes a VPN?

   ○ **A.** It is any protocol that enables remote clients to log in to a server over a network such as the Internet.

   ○ **B.** It provides a system whereby only screen display and keyboard and mouse input travel across the link.

   ○ **C.** It is a secure communication channel across a public network such as the Internet.

   ○ **D.** It is a protocol used to encrypt user IDs and passwords.

2. Which of the following are required to establish a VPN connection? (Choose all correct answers.)

   ○ **A.** VPN server

   ○ **B.** VPN client

   ○ **C.** VPN protocols

   ○ **D.** VPN MAC identification

3. Which of the following are valid ways to assign computers to a VLAN? (Choose the three best answers.)

   ○ **A.** Protocol assignment

   ○ **B.** Port-based assignment

   ○ **C.** NetBIOS computer name

   ○ **D.** MAC address

Cram Quiz Answers

1. **C.** A VPN provides a secure communication path between devices over a public network such as the Internet.

2. **A, B, C.** Many elements are involved in establishing a VPN connection. This includes the VPN client to initiate the session, the VPN server to answer the client requests, and the VPN protocols to secure and establish the connection.

3. **A, B, D.** VLANs can be created by using protocol assignments, by defining the ports on a device as belonging to a VLAN, or by using MAC addresses. VLANs cannot be created by using the NetBIOS computer name.

What Next?

This chapter created a foundation upon which Chapter 2 builds. Chapter 2 examines the Open Systems Interconnect (OSI) reference model, which is a conceptual model describing how network architecture enables data to be passed between computer systems. It also examines how common network devices relate to the model.

CHAPTER 2

OSI and TCP/IP Models and Network Protocols

This chapter covers the following official Network+ objectives:

▶ Compare the layers of the OSI and TCP/IP models.

▶ Explain the function of common networking protocols.

▶ Summarize DNS concepts and its components.

▶ Explain the purpose and properties of DHCP.

▶ Given a scenario, use the appropriate network monitoring resources to analyze traffic.

For more information on the official Network+ exam topics, see the "About the Network+ Exam" section in the "Introduction."

One of the most important networking concepts to understand is the *Open Systems Interconnect (OSI)* reference model. This conceptual model, created by the *International Organization for Standardization (ISO)* in 1978 and revised in 1984, describes a network architecture that enables data to be passed between computer systems. The TCP/IP model performs the same functions, but predates OSI, and does so in only four layers.

This chapter looks at the OSI and TCP/IP models and describes how they relate to real-world networking. It also examines how common network devices relate to the OSI model. Even though the OSI model is conceptual, an appreciation of its purpose and function can help you better understand how protocol suites and network architectures work in practical applications.

The Networking Models

▶ **Compare the layers of the OSI and TCP/IP models.**

Cram**Saver**

If you can correctly answer these questions before going through this section, save time by skimming the Exam Alerts in this section and then completing the Cram Quiz at the end of the section.

1. Which layer of the OSI model converts data from the application layer into a format that can be sent over the network?

2. True or False: Transport protocols, such as UDP, map to the transport layer of the OSI model and are responsible for transporting data across the network.

3. At what layer of the OSI model do FTP and TFTP map?

Answers

1. The presentation layer converts data from the application layer into a format that can be sent over the network. It also converts data from the session layer into a format the application layer can understand.

2. True. Transport protocols map to the transport layer of the OSI model and are responsible for transporting data across the network. UDP is a transport protocol.

3. FTP and TFTP map to the application layer.

For networking, two models commonly are referenced: the OSI model and the TCP/IP model. Both offer a framework, theoretical and actual, for how networking is implemented.

The OSI Seven-Layer Model

As shown in Figure 2.1, the OSI reference model is built, bottom to top, in the following order: physical, data link, network, transport, session, presentation, and application. The physical layer is classified as Layer 1, and the top layer of the model, the application layer, is Layer 7.

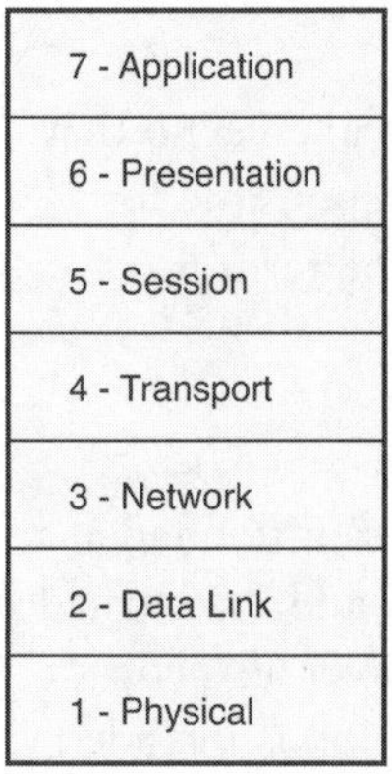

7 - Application
6 - Presentation
5 - Session
4 - Transport
3 - Network
2 - Data Link
1 - Physical

FIGURE 2.1   **The OSI seven-layer model.**

ExamAlert

On the Network+ exam, you might see an OSI layer referenced either by its name, such as data link, or by its layer number. For instance, you might find that a router is referred to as a Layer 3 device. An easy mnemonic that you can use to remember the layers from top to bottom is: All People Seem To Need Data Processing.

Each layer of the OSI model has a specific function. The following sections describe the function of each layer, starting with the physical layer and working up the model.

Physical Layer (Layer 1)

The physical layer of the OSI model identifies the network's physical characteristics, including the following specifications:

▸ **Hardware**: The type of media used on the network, such as type of cable, type of connector, and pinout format for cables.

▸ **Topology**: The physical layer identifies the topology to be used in the network. Common topologies include ring, mesh, star, and bus.

In addition to these characteristics, the physical layer defines the voltage used on a given medium and the frequency at which the signals that carry the data operate. These characteristics dictate the speed and bandwidth of a given medium, as well as the maximum distance over which a certain media type can be used.

Data Link Layer (Layer 2)

The data link layer is responsible for getting data to the physical layer so that it can transmit over the network. The data link layer is also responsible for error detection, error correction, and hardware addressing. The term *frame* describes the logical grouping of data at the data link layer.

The data link layer has two distinct sublayers:

> ▸ **Media Access Control (MAC) layer**: The MAC address is defined at this layer. The MAC address is the physical or hardware address burned into each network interface card (NIC). The MAC sublayer also controls access to network media. The MAC layer specification is included in the IEEE 802.1 standard.

> ▸ **Logical Link Control (LLC) layer**: The LLC layer is responsible for the error and flow-control mechanisms of the data link layer. The LLC layer is specified in the IEEE 802.2 standard.

Network Layer (Layer 3)

The primary responsibility of the network layer is *routing*—providing mechanisms by which data can be passed from one network system to another. The network layer does not specify how the data is passed, but rather provides the mechanisms to do so. Functionality at the network layer is provided through routing protocols, which are software components.

Protocols at the network layer are also responsible for *route selection*, which refers to determining the best path for the data to take throughout the network. In contrast to the data link layer, which uses MAC addresses to communicate on the LAN, network layer protocols use software configured addresses and special routing protocols to communicate on the network. The term *packet* describes the logical grouping of data at the network layer.

When working with networks, routes can be configured in two ways: *statically* or *dynamically*. In a static routing environment, routes are manually added to the routing tables. In a dynamic routing environment, routing protocols such as *Routing Information Protocol (RIP)* and *Open Shortest Path First (OSPF)* are used. These protocols communicate routing information between networked devices on the network.

Transport Layer (Layer 4)

The basic function of the transport layer is to provide mechanisms to transport data between network devices. Primarily it does this in three ways:

▶ **Error checking**: Protocols at the transport layer ensure that data is correctly sent or received.

▶ **Service addressing**: Protocols such as TCP/IP support many network services. The transport layer ensures that data is passed to the right service at the upper layers of the OSI model.

▶ **Segmentation**: To traverse the network, blocks of data need to be broken into packets of a manageable size for the lower layers to handle. This process, called *segmentation*, is the responsibility of the transport layer.

Protocols that operate at the transport layer can either be connectionless, such as *User Datagram Protocol (UDP)*, or connection-oriented, such as *Transmission Control Protocol (TCP)*. For a further discussion of these protocols, and of the difference between connection-oriented and connectionless protocols, refer to the later section "Connectionless and Connection-Oriented Protocols."

The transport layer is also responsible for *data flow control*, which refers to how the receiving device can accept data transmissions. Two common methods of flow control are used:

▶ **Buffering**: When buffering flow control is used, data is temporarily stored and waits for the destination device to become available. Buffering can cause a problem if the sending device transmits data much faster than the receiving device can manage.

▶ **Windowing**: In a windowing environment, data is sent in groups of segments that require only one acknowledgment. The size of the window (that is, how many segments fit into one acknowledgment) is defined when the session between the two devices is established. As you can imagine, the need to have only one acknowledgment for every, say, five segments can greatly reduce overhead.

Session Layer (Layer 5)

The session layer is responsible for managing and controlling the synchronization of data between applications on two devices. It does this by establishing, maintaining, and breaking sessions. Whereas the transport layer is responsible for setting up and maintaining the connection between the two nodes, the session layer performs the same function on behalf of the application.

Presentation Layer (Layer 6)

The presentation layer's basic function is to convert the data intended for or received from the application layer into another format. Such conversion is necessary because of how data is formatted so that it can be transported across the network. Applications cannot necessarily read this conversion. Some common data formats handled by the presentation layer include the following:

▸ **Graphics files**: JPEG, TIFF, GIF, and so on are graphics file formats that require the data to be formatted in a certain way.

▸ **Text and data**: The presentation layer can translate data into different formats, such as American Standard Code for Information Interchange (ASCII) and Extended Binary Coded Decimal Interchange Code (EBCDIC).

▸ **Sound/video**: MPEG, MP3, and MIDI files all have their own data formats to and from which data must be converted.

Another important function of the presentation layer is *encryption*, which is the scrambling of data so that it can't be read by anyone other than the intended recipient. Given the basic role of the presentation layer—that of data-format translator—it is the obvious place for encryption and decryption to take place.

Application Layer (Layer 7)

In simple terms, the function of the application layer is to take requests and data from the users and pass them to the lower layers of the OSI model. Incoming information is passed to the application layer, which then displays the information to the users. Some of the most basic application-layer services include file and print capabilities.

The most common misconception about the application layer is that it represents applications used on a system such as a web browser, word processor, or spreadsheet. Instead, the application layer defines the processes that enable applications to use network services. For example, if an application needs to open a file from a network drive, the functionality is provided by components that reside at the application layer.

ExamAlert

Be sure you understand the OSI model and its purpose. You will almost certainly be asked questions on it during the exam.

OSI Model Summary

Table 2.1 summarizes the seven layers of the OSI model and describes some of the most significant points of each layer.

TABLE 2.1 **OSI Model Summary**

OSI Layer	Major Function
Physical (Layer 1)	Defines the physical structure of the network and the topology.
Data link (Layer 2)	Provides error detection and correction. Uses two distinct sublayers: the Media Access Control (MAC) and Logical Link Control (LLC) layers. Identifies the method by which media are accessed. Defines hardware addressing through the MAC sublayer.
Network (Layer 3)	Handles the discovery of destination systems and addressing. Provides the mechanism by which data can be passed and routed from one network system to another.
Transport (Layer 4)	Provides connection services between the sending and receiving devices and ensures reliable data delivery. Manages flow control through buffering or windowing. Provides segmentation, error checking, and service identification.
Session (Layer 5)	Synchronizes the data exchange between applications on separate devices.
Presentation (Layer 6)	Translates data from the format used by applications into one that can be transmitted across the network. Handles encryption and decryption of data. Provides compression and decompression functionality. Formats data from the application layer into a format that can be sent over the network.
Application (Layer 7)	Provides access to the network for applications.

The TCP/IP Four-Layer Model

The OSI model does a fantastic job to outline how networking should occur and the responsibility of each layer. Unfortunately, TCP/IP predates this model and has to perform the same functionality with only four layers. Figure 2.2 shows how these four layers line up with the seven layers of the OSI model.

TCP/IP Model	OSI Model
Application Layer	Application Layer Presentation Layer Session Layer
Transport Layer	Transport Layer
Internet Layer	Network Layer
Network Interface Layer	Data Link Layer Physical Layer

FIGURE 2.2   The TCP/IP model compared to the OSI model.

The Network Interface layer is sometimes referred to as the Network Access or Link layer and this is where Ethernet, FDDI, or any other physical technology can run. The Internet layer is where IP runs (along with ICMP, ARP, and others). The Transport layer is where TCP and its counterpart UDP operates. The Application layer enables any number of protocols to be plugged in, such as HTTP, SMTP, SNMP, DNS, and many others.

Identifying the OSI Layers at Which Various Network Components Operate

When you understand the OSI model, you can relate network connectivity devices to the appropriate layer of the OSI model. Knowing at which OSI level a device operates enables you to better understand how it functions on the network. Table 2.2 identifies various network devices and maps them to the OSI model.

ExamAlert

For the Network+ exam, you are expected to identify at which layer of the OSI model certain network devices operate.

TABLE 2.2   **Mapping Network Devices to the OSI Model**

Device	OSI Layer
Hub	Physical (Layer 1)
Bridge	Data link (Layer 2)
Switch	Data link (Layer 2) or network (Layer 3)
Router	Network (Layer 3)
NIC	Data link (Layer 2)
Access point (AP)	Data link (Layer 2)

Cram Quiz

1. At which OSI layer does an AP operate?

   - ○ **A.** Network
   - ○ **B.** Physical
   - ○ **C.** Data link
   - ○ **D.** Session

2. Which of the following are sublayers of the data link layer? (Choose two.)

   - ○ **A.** MAC
   - ○ **B.** LCL
   - ○ **C.** Session
   - ○ **D.** LLC

3. At which two OSI layers can a switch operate? (Choose two.)

   - ○ **A.** Layer 1
   - ○ **B.** Layer 2
   - ○ **C.** Layer 3
   - ○ **D.** Layer 4

4. Which of the following OSI layers is responsible for establishing connections between two devices?

   - ○ **A.** Network
   - ○ **B.** Transport
   - ○ **C.** Session
   - ○ **D.** Data link

Cram Quiz Answers

1. **C.** A wireless access point (AP) operates at the data link layer of the OSI model. An example of a network layer device is a router. An example of a physical layer device is a hub. Session layer components normally are software, not hardware.

2. **A, D.** The data link layer is broken into two distinct sublayers: Media Access Control (MAC) and Logical Link Control (LLC). LCL is not a valid term. Session is another of the OSI model layers.

3. **B, C.** A switch uses the MAC addresses of connected devices to make its forwarding decisions. Therefore, it is called a data link, or Layer 2, network device. It can also operate at layer 3 or be a multilayer switch. Devices or components that operate at Layer 1 typically are media-based, such as cables or connectors. Layer 4 components typically are software-based, not hardware-based.

4. **B.** The transport layer is responsible for establishing a connection between networked devices. The network layer is most commonly associated with route discovery and datagram delivery. Protocols at the session layer synchronize the data exchange between applications on separate devices. Protocols at the data link layer perform error detection and handling for the transmitted signals and define the method by which the medium is accessed.

Protocols

▶ **Explain the function of common networking protocols**

Cram**Saver**

If you can correctly answer these questions before going through this section, save time by skimming the Exam Alerts in this section and then completing the Cram Quiz at the end of the section.

1. With TCP, a data session is established through a three-step process. This is known as a three-way _____.

2. What FTP command uploads multiple files to the remote host?

3. The SSH protocol is a more secure alternative to what protocol?

Answers

1. This is known as a three-way handshake.

2. The mput command uploads multiple files to the remote host in FTP.

3. SSH is a more secure alternative to Telnet.

When computers were restricted to standalone systems, there was little need for mechanisms to communicate between them. However, it wasn't long before the need to connect computers for the purpose of sharing files and printers became a necessity. Establishing communication between network devices required more than a length of cabling; a method or a set of rules was needed to establish how systems would communicate. Protocols provide that method.

Note

Protocols are presented in this chapter but ports used by these protocols are covered in a later chapter.

It would be nice if a single protocol facilitated communication between all devices, but this is not the case. You can use a number of protocols on a network, each of which has its own features, advantages, and disadvantages. What protocol you choose can have a significant impact on the network's functioning and performance. This section explores some of the more common protocols you can expect to work with as a network administrator.

> **Note**
>
> In this chapter and throughout the book, the term request for comment (RFC) is used. RFCs are standards published by the Internet Engineering Task Force (IETF) and describe methods, behaviors, research, or innovations applicable to the operation of the Internet and Internet-connected systems. Each new RFC has an associated reference number. Looking up this number gives you information on the specific technology. For more information on RFCs, look for the Internet Engineering Task Force online.

Connection-Oriented Protocols Versus Connectionless Protocols

Before getting into the characteristics of the various network protocols and protocol suites, you must first identify the difference between connection-oriented and connectionless protocols.

In a *connection-oriented* communication, data delivery is guaranteed. The sending device re-sends any packet that the destination system does not receive. Communication between the sending and receiving devices continues until the transmission has been verified. Because of this, connection-oriented protocols have a higher overhead and place greater demands on bandwidth.

> **ExamAlert**
>
> Connection-oriented protocols such as the Transmission Control Protocol (TCP) can accommodate lost or dropped packets by asking the sending device to retransmit them. They can do this because they wait for all the packets in a message to be received before considering the transmission complete. On the sending end, connection-oriented protocols also assume that a lack of acknowledgment is sufficient reason to retransmit.

In contrast to connection-oriented communication, connectionless protocols offer only a best-effort delivery mechanism. Basically, the information is just sent; there is no confirmation that the data has been received. If an error occurs in the transmission, there is no mechanism to re-send the data, so transmissions made with connectionless protocols are not guaranteed. Connectionless communication requires far less overhead than connection-oriented communication, so it is popular in applications such as streaming audio and video, where a small number of dropped packets might not represent a significant problem.

> **ExamAlert**
>
> As you work through the various protocols, keep an eye out for those that are connectionless and those that are connection-oriented. Also, look for protocols such as TCP that guarantee delivery of data and those such as UDP that are a fire-and-forget or best-delivery method.

Internet Protocol (IP)

IP, which is defined in RFC 791, is the protocol used to transport data from one node on a network to another. IP is connectionless, which means that it doesn't guarantee the delivery of data; it simply makes its best effort to do so. To ensure that transmissions sent via IP are completed, a higher-level protocol such as TCP is required.

> **ExamAlert**
>
> IP operates at the network layer of the OSI model.

In addition to providing best-effort delivery, IP also performs fragmentation and reassembly tasks for network transmissions. Fragmentation is necessary because the maximum transmission unit (MTU) size is limited in IP. In other words, network transmissions that are too big to traverse the network in a single packet must be broken into smaller chunks and reassembled at the other end. Another function of IP is addressing. IP addressing is a complex subject. Refer to Chapter 3, "Addressing and Routing," for a complete discussion of IP addressing.

Transmission Control Protocol (TCP)

TCP, which is defined in RFC 793, is a connection-oriented protocol and the transport protocol. Being connection-oriented means that TCP establishes a mutually acknowledged session between two hosts before communication takes place. TCP provides reliability to IP communications. Specifically, TCP adds features such as flow control, sequencing, and error detection and correction. For this reason, higher-level applications that need guaranteed delivery use TCP rather than its lightweight and connectionless brother, UDP.

How TCP Works

When TCP wants to open a connection with another host, it follows this procedure:

1. It sends a message called a *SYN* to the target host.

2. The target host opens a connection for the request and sends back an acknowledgment message called an *ACK* (or SYN ACK).

3. The host that originated the request sends back another acknowledgment, saying that it has received the ACK message and that the session is ready to be used to transfer data.

When the data session is completed, a similar process is used to close the session. This three-step session establishment and acknowledgment process is called the *TCP three-way handshake.*

> **ExamAlert**
>
> TCP operates at the transport layer of the OSI model.

TCP is a reliable protocol because it has mechanisms that can accommodate and handle errors. These mechanisms include timeouts, which cause the sending host to automatically retransmit data if its receipt is not acknowledged within a given time period.

User Datagram Protocol (UDP)

UDP, which is defined in RFC 768, is the brother of TCP. Like TCP, UDP is the transport protocol, but the big difference is that UDP does not guarantee delivery like TCP does. In a sense, UDP is a "fire and forget" protocol; it assumes that the data sent will reach its destination intact. The checking of whether data is delivered is left to upper-layer protocols. UDP operates at the transport layer of the OSI model.

Unlike TCP, with UDP no session is established between the sending and receiving hosts, which is why UDP is called a connectionless protocol. The upshot of this is that UDP has much lower overhead than TCP. A TCP packet header has 14 fields, whereas a UDP packet header has only four fields. Therefore, UDP is much more efficient than TCP. In applications that don't need the added features of TCP, UDP is much more economical in terms of bandwidth and processing effort.

> **Note**
>
> Additional discussion of TCP/UDP ports appears in Chapter 3.

> **ExamAlert**
>
> Remember that TCP is a connection-oriented protocol and UDP is a connection-less protocol.

File Transfer Protocol (FTP)

As its name suggests, FTP provides for the uploading and downloading of files from a remote host running FTP server software. As well as uploading and downloading files, FTP enables you to view the contents of folders on an FTP server and rename and delete files and directories if you have the necessary permissions. FTP, which is defined in RFC 959, uses TCP as a transport protocol to guarantee delivery of packets.

FTP has security mechanisms used to authenticate users. However, rather than create a user account for every user, you can configure FTP server software to accept anonymous logons. When you do this, the username is anonymous, and the password normally is the user's email address. Most FTP servers that offer files to the general public operate in this way.

In addition to being popular as a mechanism for distributing files to the general public over networks such as the Internet, FTP is also popular with organizations that need to frequently exchange large files with other people or organizations. For example, the chapters in this book were sent between the author and Que Publishing using FTP. Such a system is necessary because the files exchanged were sometimes larger than can be easily accommodated using email.

> **ExamAlert**
>
> Remember that FTP is an application layer protocol.

All the common network operating systems offer FTP server capabilities; although, whether you use them depends on whether you need FTP services. All popular workstation operating systems offer FTP client functionality; although, it is common to use third-party utilities such as CuteFTP and SmartFTP instead.

FTP assumes that files uploaded or downloaded are straight text (that is, ASCII) files. If the files are not text, which is likely, the transfer mode must be changed to binary. With sophisticated FTP clients, such as CuteFTP, the transition between transfer modes is automatic. With more basic utilities, you must manually perform the mode switch.

Unlike some of the other protocols discussed in this chapter that perform tasks transparent to the user, FTP is an application layer service frequently called upon. Therefore, it can be useful to know some of the commands supported by FTP. If you use a client such as CuteFTP, you might never need to use these commands, but they are useful to know in case you use a command-line FTP client. Table 2.3 lists some of the most commonly used FTP commands.

ExamAlert

You might be asked to identify the appropriate FTP command to use in a given situation.

TABLE 2.3 **Commonly Used FTP Commands**

Command	Description
ls	Lists the files in the current directory on the remote system
cd	Changes the working directory on the remote host
lcd	Changes the working directory on the local host
put	Uploads a single file to the remote host
get	Downloads a single file from the remote host
mput	Uploads multiple files to the remote host
mget	Downloads multiple files from the remote host
binary	Switches transfers into binary mode
ascii	Switches transfers into ASCII mode (the default)

Secure File Transfer Protocol (SFTP)

One of the big problems associated with FTP is that it is considered insecure. Even though simple authentication methods are associated with FTP, it is still susceptible to relatively simple hacking approaches. In addition, FTP transmits data between sender and receiver in an unencrypted format. By using a packet sniffer, a hacker could easily copy packets from the network and read the contents. In today's high-security computing environments, you need a more robust solution.

That solution is the Secure File Transfer Protocol (SFTP), which, based on Secure Shell (SSH) technology, provides robust authentication between sender and receiver. It also provides encryption capabilities, which means that even if packets are copied from the network, their contents remain hidden from prying eyes.

SFTP is implemented through client and server software available for all commonly used computing platforms.

> **ExamAlert**
>
> In an industry dominated by acronyms, it should come as no surprise that eventually two protocols will have the same acronym. In this case, the SFTP acronym is used to describe both Secure File Transfer Protocol and Simple File Transfer Protocol. If you research additional information for the Network+ exam, make sure that you read about the right protocol.

Trivial File Transfer Protocol (TFTP)

A variation on FTP is TFTP, which is also a file transfer mechanism. However, TFTP does not have the security capability or the level of functionality that FTP has. TFTP, which is defined in RFC 1350, is most often associated with simple downloads, such as those associated with transferring firmware to a device such as a router and booting diskless workstations.

Another feature that TFTP does not offer is directory navigation. Whereas in FTP commands can be executed to navigate and manage the file system, TFTP offers no such capability. TFTP requires that you request not only exactly what you want but also the particular location. Unlike FTP, which uses TCP as its transport protocol to guarantee delivery, TFTP uses UDP.

> **ExamAlert**
>
> TFTP is an application layer protocol that uses UDP, which is a connectionless transport layer protocol. For this reason, TFTP is called a *connectionless file transfer method*.

Simple Mail Transfer Protocol (SMTP)

SMTP, which is defined in RFC 821, is a protocol that defines how mail messages are sent between hosts. SMTP uses TCP connections to guarantee error-free delivery of messages. SMTP is not overly sophisticated and requires that the destination host always be available. For this reason, mail systems spool incoming mail so that users can read it later. How the user then reads the mail depends on how the client accesses the SMTP server.

> **Note**
>
> SMTP can be used to both send and receive mail. Post Office Protocol version 3 (POP3) and Internet Message Access Protocol version 4 (IMAP4) can be used only to receive mail.

Hypertext Transfer Protocol (HTTP)

HTTP, which is defined in RFC 2068, is the protocol that enables text, graphics, multimedia, and other material to be downloaded from an HTTP server. HTTP defines what actions can be requested by clients and how servers should answer those requests.

In a practical implementation, HTTP clients (that is, web browsers) make requests in an HTTP format to servers running HTTP server applications (that is, web servers). Files created in a special language such as Hypertext Markup Language (HTML) are returned to the client, and the connection is closed.

> **ExamAlert**
>
> Make sure you understand that HTTP is a connection-oriented protocol that uses TCP as a transport protocol.

HTTP uses a uniform resource locator (URL) to determine what page should be downloaded from the remote server. The URL contains the type of request (for example, http://), the name of the server contacted (for example, www.microsoft.com), and optionally the page requested (for example, /support). The result is the syntax that Internet-savvy people are familiar with: http://www.microsoft.com/support.

Hypertext Transfer Protocol Secure (HTTPS)

One of the downsides of using HTTP is that HTTP requests are sent in clear text. For some applications, such as e-commerce, this method to exchange information is unsuitable—a more secure method is needed. The solution is HTTPS, which uses a system known as Secure Socket Layer (SSL), which encrypts the information sent between the client and host.

For HTTPS to be used, both the client and server must support it. All popular browsers now support HTTPS, as do web server products, such as Microsoft Internet Information Services (IIS), Apache, and almost all other web server applications that provide sensitive applications. When you access an application that uses HTTPS, the URL starts with https rather than http—for example, https://www.mybankonline.com.

Post Office Protocol Version 3/Internet Message Access Protocol Version 4 (POP3/IMAP4)

Both POP3, which is defined in RFC 1939, and IMAP4, the latest version which is defined in RFC 1731, are mechanisms for downloading, or pulling, email from a server. They are necessary because although the mail is transported around the network via SMTP, users cannot always immediately read it, so it must be stored in a central location. From this location, it needs to be downloaded or retrieved, which is what POP3 and IMAP4 enable you to do.

POP3 and IMAP4 are popular, and many people now access email through applications such as Microsoft Outlook, Netscape Communicator, and Eudora, which are POP3 and IMAP4 clients.

One of the problems with POP3 is that the password used to access a mailbox is transmitted across the network in clear text. This means that if people want to, they could determine your POP3 password with relative ease. This is an area in which IMAP4 offers an advantage over POP3. It uses a more sophisticated authentication system, which makes it more difficult for people to determine a password.

> **ExamAlert**
>
> POP3 and IMAP4 can be used to download, or pull, email from a server, but they cannot be used to send mail. That function is left to SMTP, which can both send and receive.

> **Note**
>
> Although accessing email by using POP3 and IMAP4 has many advantages, such systems rely on servers to hold the mail until it is downloaded to the client system. In today's world, a more sophisticated solution to anytime/anywhere email access is needed. For many people, that solution is web-based mail. Having an Internet-based email account enables you to access your mail from anywhere and from any device that supports a web browser. Recognizing the obvious advantages of such a system, all the major email systems have, for some time, included web access gateway products.

Telnet

Telnet, which is defined in RFC 854, is a virtual terminal protocol. It enables sessions to be opened on a remote host, and then commands can be executed on that remote host. For many years, Telnet was the method by which clients accessed multiuser systems such as mainframes and minicomputers. It also was the connection method of choice for UNIX systems. Today, Telnet is still commonly used to access routers and other managed network devices.

One of the problems with Telnet is that it is not secure. As a result, remote session functionality is now almost always achieved by using alternatives such as SSH.

> **ExamAlert**
>
> Telnet is used to access UNIX and Linux systems.

Secure Shell (SSH)

Created by students at the Helsinki University of Technology, Secure Shell (SSH) is a secure alternative to Telnet. SSH provides security by encrypting data as it travels between systems. This makes it difficult for hackers using packet sniffers and other traffic-detection systems. It also provides more robust authentication systems than Telnet.

Two versions of SSH are available: SSH1 and SSH2. Of the two, SSH2 is considered more secure. The two versions are incompatible. If you use an SSH client program, the server implementation of SSH that you connect to must be the same version.

Although SSH, like Telnet, is associated primarily with UNIX and Linux systems, implementations of SSH are available for all commonly used computing platforms, including Windows and Macintosh. As discussed earlier, SSH is the foundational technology for Secure File Transfer Protocol (SFTP).

> **ExamAlert**
>
> Remember that SSH is a more secure alternative to Telnet.

Internet Control Message Protocol (ICMP)

ICMP, which is defined in RFC 792, is a protocol that works with the IP layer to provide error checking and reporting functionality. In effect, ICMP is a tool that IP uses in its quest to provide best-effort delivery.

ICMP can be used for a number of functions. Its most common function is probably the widely used and incredibly useful ping utility, which can send a stream of ICMP echo requests to a remote host. If the host can respond, it does so by sending echo reply messages back to the sending host. In that one simple process, ICMP enables the verification of the protocol suite configuration of both the sending and receiving nodes and any intermediate networking devices.

However, ICMP's functionality is not limited to the use of the ping utility. ICMP also can return error messages such as `Destination unreachable` and `Time exceeded`. (The former message is reported when a destination cannot be contacted and the latter when the Time To Live [TTL] of a datagram has been exceeded.)

In addition to these and other functions, ICMP performs *source quench*. In a source quench scenario, the receiving host cannot handle the influx of data at the same rate as the data is sent. To slow down the sending host, the receiving host sends ICMP source quench messages, telling the sender to slow down. This action prevents packets from dropping and having to be re-sent.

ICMP is a useful protocol. Although ICMP operates largely in the background, the ping utility makes it one of the most valuable of the protocols discussed in this chapter.

Address Resolution Protocol (ARP)/Reverse Address Resolution Protocol (RARP)

ARP, which is defined in RFC 826, is responsible for resolving IP addresses to Media Access Control (MAC) addresses. When a system attempts to contact another host, IP first determines whether the other host is on the same network it is on by looking at the IP address. If IP determines that the destination is on the local network, it consults the ARP cache to see whether it has a corresponding entry. The ARP cache is a table on the local system that stores mappings between data link layer addresses (the MAC address or physical address) and network layer addresses (IP addresses). Following is a sample of the ARP cache:

```
Interface: 192.168.1.66 --- 0x8
  Internet Address        Physical Address        Type
  192.168.1.65            00-1c-c0-17-41-c8        dynamic
  192.168.1.67            00-22-68-cb-e2-f9        dynamic
  192.168.1.254           00-18-d1-95-f6-02        dynamic
  224.0.0.2               01-00-5e-00-00-02        static
  239.255.255.250         01-00-5e-7f-ff-fa        static
```

If the ARP cache doesn't have an entry for the host, a broadcast on the local network asks the host with the target IP address to send back its MAC address. The communication is sent as a broadcast because without the target system's MAC address, the source system cannot communicate directly with the target system.

Because the communication is a broadcast, every system on the network picks it up. However, only the target system replies because it is the only device whose IP address matches the request. The target system, recognizing that the ARP request is targeted at it, replies directly to the source system. It can do this because the ARP request contains the MAC address of the system that sent it. If the destination host is determined to be on a different subnet than the sending host, the ARP process is performed against the default gateway and then repeated for each step of the journey between the sending and receiving host. Table 2.4 lists the common switches used with the arp command.

ExamAlert

ARP links IP addressing to Ethernet addressing (MAC addressing).

TABLE 2.4 **Commonly Used** arp **Command Switches**

Switch	Description
-a	Displays the entries in the ARP cache
-s	Manually adds a permanent entry to the ARP cache
-d	Deletes an entry from the ARP cache

When you work with the ARP cache, you can dynamically or statically make entries. With dynamic entries, the ARP cache is automatically updated. The ARP cache is maintained with no intervention from the user. Dynamic entries are the ones most used. Static entries are configured manually using the arp

-s command. The static entry becomes a permanent addition to the ARP cache until it is removed using the arp -d command.

Reverse Address Resolution Protocol (RARP) performs the same function as ARP, but in reverse. In other words, it resolves MAC addresses to IP addresses. RARP makes it possible for applications or systems to learn their own IP address from a router or Domain Name Service (DNS) server. Such a resolution is useful for tasks such as performing reverse lookups in DNS. RARP is defined in RFC 903.

> **Tip**
>
> The function of ARP is to resolve a system's IP address to the interface's MAC address on that system. Do not confuse ARP with DNS or WINS, which also perform resolution functions, but for different things.

Network Time Protocol (NTP)

NTP, which is defined in RFC 958, is the part of the TCP/IP protocol suite that facilitates the communication of time between systems. The idea is that one system configured as a time provider transmits time information to other systems that can be both time receivers and time providers for other systems.

Time synchronization is important in today's IT environment because of the distributed nature of applications. Two good examples of situations in which time synchronization is important are email and directory services systems. In each of these cases, having time synchronized between devices is important because without it there would be no way to keep track of changes to data and applications.

In many environments, external time sources such as radio clocks, global positioning system (GPS) devices, and Internet-based time servers are used as sources of NTP time. In others, the system's BIOS clock is used. Regardless of what source is used, the time information is communicated between devices by using NTP.

> **Note**
>
> Specific guidelines dictate how NTP should be used. You can find these "rules of engagement" at http://support.ntp.org/bin/view/Servers/RulesOfEngagement.

NTP server and client software is available for a wide variety of platforms and devices. If you want a way to ensure time synchronization between devices, look to NTP as a solution.

Network News Transfer Protocol (NNTP)

Network News Transfer Protocol (NNTP) is a protocol associated with posting and retrieving messages to and from newsgroups. A *newsgroup* is a discussion forum hosted on a remote system. By using NNTP client software, like that included with many common email clients, users can post, reply to, and retrieve messages.

Although web-based discussion forums are slowly replacing newsgroups, demand for newsgroup access remains high. The distinction between web-based discussion forums and NNTP newsgroups is that messages are retrieved from the server to be read. In contrast, on a web-based discussion forum, the messages are not downloaded. They are simply viewed from a remote location.

NNTP, which is defined in RFC 977, is an application layer protocol that uses TCP as its transport mechanism.

Secure Copy Protocol (SCP)

Secure Copy Protocol (SCP) is another protocol based on SSH technology. SCP provides a secure means to copy files between systems on a network. By using SSH technology, it encrypts data as it travels across the network, thereby securing it from eavesdropping. It is intended as a more secure substitute for Remote Copy Protocol (RCP). SCP is available as a command-line utility, or as part of application software for most commonly used computing platforms.

Lightweight Directory Access Protocol (LDAP)

Lightweight Directory Access Protocol (LDAP) is a protocol that provides a mechanism to access and query directory services systems. In the context of the Network+ exam, these directory services systems are most likely to be Novell Directory Services (NDS) and Microsoft's Active Directory. Although LDAP supports command-line queries executed directly against the directory database, most LDAP interactions are via utilities such as an authentication program (network logon) or locating a resource in the directory through a search utility.

Internet Group Management Protocol (IGMP)

Internet Group Management Protocol (IGMP) is the protocol within the TCP/IP protocol suite that manages multicast groups. It enables, for example, one computer on the Internet to target content to a specific group of computers that will receive content from the sending system. This is in contrast to unicast messaging, in which data is sent to a single computer or network device and not to a group, or a broadcast message goes to all systems.

Multicasting is a mechanism by which groups of network devices can send and receive data between the members of the group at one time, instead of separately sending messages to each device in the group. The multicast grouping is established by each device configured with the same multicast IP address. These multicast IP addresses are from the IPv4 Class D range, including 224.0.0.0 to 239.255.255.255 address ranges.

IGMP is used to register devices into a multicast group, as well as to discover what other devices on the network are members of the same multicast group. Common applications for multicasting include groups of routers on an internetwork and videoconferencing clients.

Transport Layer Security

The *Transport Layer Security (TLS) protocol* is a security protocol designed to ensure privacy between communicating client/server applications. When a server and client communicate, TLS ensures that no one can eavesdrop and intercept or otherwise tamper with the data message. TLS is the successor to SSL.

TLS is composed of two layers:

- ▶ **TLS record protocol**: Uses a reliable transport protocol such as TCP and ensures that the connection made between systems is private using data encryption.

- ▶ **TLS handshake protocol**: Used for authentication between the client and server.

> Note
>
> Chapter 10, "Network Security," covers authentication, encryption, and more on security protocols.

Session Initiation Protocol (SIP)/ Real-Time Transport Protocol (RTP)

Long-distance calls are expensive, in part because it is costly to maintain phone lines and employ technicians to keep those phones ringing. Voice over IP (VoIP) provides a cheaper alternative for phone service. VoIP technology enables regular voice conversations to occur by traveling through IP packets and via the Internet. VoIP avoids the high cost of regular phone calls by using the existing infrastructure of the Internet. No monthly bills or expensive long-distance charges are required. But how does it work?

Like every other type of network communication, VoIP requires protocols to make the magic happen. For VoIP, one such protocol is Session Initiation Protocol (SIP), which is an application layer protocol designed to establish and maintain multimedia sessions, such as Internet telephony calls. This means that SIP can create communication sessions for such features as audio/videoconferencing, online gaming, and person-to-person conversations over the Internet. SIP does not operate alone; it uses TCP or UDP as a transport protocol. Remember, TCP enables guaranteed delivery of data packets, whereas UDP is a fire-and-forget transfer protocol.

> **ExamAlert**
>
> SIP operates at the application layer of the OSI model and is used to maintain a multimedia session.

> **Note**
>
> SIP also includes a suite of security services, which include denial-of-service prevention, authentication (both user-to-user and proxy-to-user), integrity protection, and encryption and privacy services.

The Real-time Transport Protocol (RTP) is the Internet-standard protocol for the transport of real-time data, including audio and video. RTP can use either TCP or UDP as a transport mechanism. However, UDP is used more often because applications using RTP are less sensitive to packet loss but typically are sensitive to delays. UDP, then, is a faster protocol because packet delivery is not guaranteed. RTP is often used with VoIP. VoIP data packets live in RTP packets, which are inside UDP-IP packets.

ExamAlert

Remember that RTP is used to transport real-time data and is often used with VoIP.

RTP has two parts:

▶ The data part supports applications with real-time properties such as continuous media (such as audio and video), including timing reconstruction, loss detection, security, and content identification.

▶ The control part (RTCP) supports real-time conferencing of groups of any size within an internet.

TCP/IP Protocol Suite Summary

Table 2.5 summarizes the details of each of the protocols discussed in the preceding sections. You can use this table for review before you take the Network+ exam.

TABLE 2.5 **TCP/IP Protocol Suite Summary**

Protocol	Full Name	Description	OSI Layer
IP	Internet Protocol	A connectionless protocol used to move data around a network.	Network layer (3)
TCP	Transmission Control Protocol	A connection-oriented protocol that offers flow control, sequencing, and retransmission of dropped packets.	Transport layer (4)
UDP	User Datagram Protocol	A connectionless alternative to TCP used for applications that do not require the functions offered by TCP.	Transport layer (4)
FTP	File Transfer Protocol	Uploads and downloads files to and from a remote host. Also accommodates basic file-management tasks.	Application layer (7)
SFTP	Secure File Transfer Protocol	Securely uploads and downloads files to and from a remote host. Based on SSH security.	Application layer (7)
TFTP	Trivial File Transfer Protocol	A file transfer protocol that does not have the security or error checking of FTP. TFTP uses UDP as a transport protocol and therefore is connectionless.	Application layer (7)

TABLE 2.5 **Continued**

Protocol	Full Name	Description	OSI Layer
SMTP	Simple Mail Transfer Protocol	A mechanism for transporting email across networks.	Application layer (7)
HTTP	Hypertext Transfer Protocol	Retrieves files from a web server.	Application layer (7)
HTTPS	Hypertext Transfer Protocol Secure	A secure protocol for retrieving files from a web server.	Application layer (7)
POPv3/ IMAPv4	Post Office Protocol version 3/ Internet Message Access Protocol version 4	Retrieves email from a server on which it is stored. Can only retrieve mail. IMAP and POP cannot send mail.	Application layer (7)
Telnet	Telnet	Enables sessions to be opened on a remote host.	Application layer (7)
SSH	Secure Shell	Enables secure sessions to be opened on a remote host.	Application layer (7)
ICMP	Internet Control Message Protocol	Used on IP-based networks for error reporting, flow control, and route testing.	Network layer (3)
ARP	Address Resolution Protocol	Resolves IP addresses to MAC addresses to enable communication between devices.	Data link layer (2)
RARP	Reverse Address Resolution Protocol	Resolves MAC addresses to IP addresses.	Data link layer (2)
NTP	Network Time Protocol	Communicates time synchronization information between devices.	Application layer (7)
NNTP	Network News Transport Protocol	Facilitates the access and downloading of messages from newsgroup servers.	Application layer (7)
SCP	Secure Copy Protocol	Enables files to be copied securely between two systems. Uses SSH technology to provide encryption services.	Application layer (7)
LDAP	Lightweight Directory Access Protocol	Accesses and queries directory services systems such as Novell Directory Services and Microsoft Active Directory.	Application layer (7)
IGMP	Internet Group Management Protocol	Provides a mechanism for systems within the same multicast group to register and communicate with each other.	Network layer (3)

TABLE 2.5 **Continued**

Protocol	Full Name	Description	OSI Layer
TLS	Transport Layer Security	A security protocol designed to ensure privacy between communicating client/server applications.	Application layer (7)
SIP	Session Initiation Protocol	An application layer protocol designed to establish and maintain multimedia sessions such as Internet telephony calls.	Application layer (7)
RTP	Real-time Transport Protocol	The Internet-standard protocol for transporting real-time data.	Application layer (7)

Cram Quiz

1. TCP is an example of what kind of transport protocol?

   ○ **A.** Connection-oriented

   ○ **B.** Connection-reliant

   ○ **C.** Connection-dependent

   ○ **D.** Connectionless

2. Which of the following are considered transport protocols? (Choose the two best answers.)

   ○ **A.** TCP

   ○ **B.** IP

   ○ **C.** UDP

   ○ **D.** THC

3. What is the function of ARP?

   ○ **A.** It resolves MAC addresses to IP addresses.

   ○ **B.** It resolves NetBIOS names to IP addresses.

   ○ **C.** It resolves IP addresses to MAC addresses.

   ○ **D.** It resolves hostnames to IP addresses.

4. What is the function of NTP?

   ○ **A.** It provides a mechanism for the sharing of authentication information.

   ○ **B.** It is used to access shared folders on a Linux system.

   ○ **C.** It is used to communicate utilization information to a central manager.

   ○ **D.** It is used to communicate time synchronization information between systems.

5. Which of the following protocols offers guaranteed delivery?

   ○ **A.** FTP

   ○ **B.** IPX

   ○ **C.** IP

   ○ **D.** TCP

Cram Quiz Answers

1. **A.** TCP is an example of a connection-oriented transport protocol. UDP is an example of a connectionless protocol. Connection-reliant and connection-dependent are not terms commonly associated with protocols.

2. **A, C.** Both TCP and UDP are transport protocols. IP is a network protocol, and THC is not a valid protocol.

3. **C.** ARP resolves IP addresses to MAC addresses. Answer A describes the function of RARP, Answer B describes the process of WINS, and Answer D describes the process of DNS resolution.

4. **D.** NTP is used to communicate time synchronization information between devices. NFS (Network File System) is a protocol typically associated with accessing shared folders on a Linux system. Utilization information is communicated to a central management system most commonly by using the SNMP protocol.

5. **D.** TCP is a connection-oriented protocol that guarantees delivery of data. FTP is a protocol used to transfer large blocks of data. IPX stands for Internetwork Packet Exchange. IP is a network layer protocol responsible for tasks such as addressing and route discovery.

Domain Name Service (DNS)

▶ **Summarize DNS concepts and its components**

Cram**Saver**

If you can correctly answer these questions before going through this section, save time by skimming the Exam Alerts in this section and then completing the Cram Quiz at the end of the section.

1. Prior to the widespread use of DNS, what local file was used for name resolution?

2. Within DNS, what is the domain name, along with any subdomains, called?

Answers

1. The HOSTS file was a static file stored locally and used for name resolution.

2. The domain name, along with any subdomains, is called the fully qualified domain name (FQDN) because it includes all the components from the top of the DNS namespace to the host.

DNS performs an important function on TCP/IP-based networks. It resolves hostnames, such as www.quepublishing.com, to IP addresses, such as 209.202.161.67. Such a resolution system makes it possible for people to remember the names of and refer to frequently used hosts using easy-to-remember hostnames rather than hard-to-remember IP addresses.

Note

Like other TCP/IP-based services, DNS is a platform-independent protocol. Therefore, it can be used on Linux, UNIX, Windows, NetWare, and almost every other platform.

In the days before the Internet, the network that was to become the Internet used a text file called HOSTS to perform name resolution. The HOSTS file

was regularly updated with changes and distributed to other servers.
Following is a sample of some entries from a HOSTS file:

```
192.168.3.45     server1  s1             #The main
                                         file and
                                         print server
192.168.3.223    mail     mailserver     #The email server
127.0.0.1        localhost
```

ExamAlert

You might be asked to identify the purpose and function of the HOSTS file.

Note

A comment in the HOSTS file is preceded by a hash symbol (#).

As you can see, the host's IP address is listed, along with the corresponding
hostname. You can add to a HOSTS file aliases of the server names, which in
this example are s1 and mailserver. All the entries must be added manually,
and each system to perform resolutions must have a copy of the file.

Even when the Internet was growing at a relatively slow pace, such a mechanism was both cumbersome and prone to error. It was obvious that as the network grew, a more automated and dynamic method of performing name resolution was needed. DNS became that method.

Tip

HOSTS file resolution is still supported by most platforms. If you need to resolve
just a few hosts that will not change often or at all, you can still use the HOSTS file
for this.

DNS solves the problem of name resolution by offering resolution through
servers configured to act as name servers. The name servers run DNS server
software, which enables them to receive, process, and reply to requests from
systems that want to resolve hostnames to IP addresses. Systems that ask DNS
servers for a hostname-to-IP address mapping are called *resolvers* or *DNS
clients*. Figure 2.3 shows the DNS resolution process. In this example, the
client asks to reach the first server at mycoltd.com; the router turns to the
DNS server for an IP address associated with that server; and after the address
is returned, the client can establish a connection.

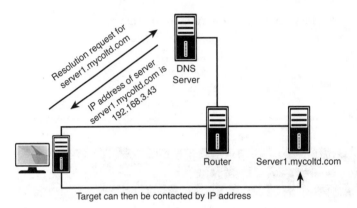

FIGURE 2.3   The DNS resolution process.

Because the DNS namespace (which is discussed in the following section) is large, a single server cannot hold all the records for the entire namespace. As a result, there is a good chance that a given DNS server might not resolve the request for a certain entry. In this case, the DNS server asks another DNS server if it has an entry for the host.

> **Note**
>
> One of the problems with DNS is that, despite all its automatic resolution capabilities, entries and changes to those entries must still be manually performed. A strategy to solve this problem is to use Dynamic DNS (DDNS), a newer system that enables hosts to be dynamically registered with the DNS server. By making changes in real time to hostnames, addresses, and related information, there is less likelihood of not finding a server or site that has been recently added or changed,

> **ExamAlert**
>
> You might be asked to identify the difference between DNS and DDNS.

The DNS Namespace

DNS operates in the *DNS namespace*. This space has logical divisions hierarchically organized. At the top level are domains such as .com (commercial) and .edu (education), as well as domains for countries, such as .uk (United Kingdom) and .de (Germany). Below the top level are subdomains or second-level domains associated with organizations or commercial companies, such as Red Hat and Microsoft. Within these domains, hosts or other subdomains can be assigned. For example, the server ftp.redhat.com would be in the redhat.com domain. Figure 2.4 shows a DNS hierarchical namespace.

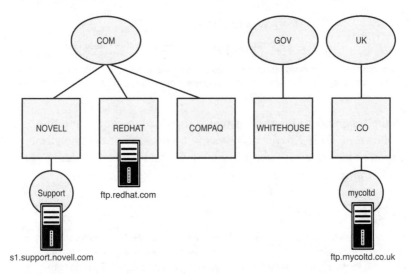

FIGURE 2.4   **A DNS hierarchical namespace.**

> **Note**
>
> The domain name, along with any subdomains, is called the fully qualified domain name (FQDN) because it includes all the components from the top of the DNS namespace to the host. For this reason, many people refer to DNS as *resolving FQDNs to IP addresses*. An example of an FQDN is www.comptia.org, where www is the host, comptia is the second-level domain, and .org is the top-level domain.

The lower domains are largely open to use in whatever way the domain name holder sees fit. However, the top-level domains are relatively closely controlled. Table 2.6 lists a selection of the most widely used top-level DNS domain names. Recently, a number of top-level domains were added, mainly to accommodate the increasing need for hostnames.

TABLE 2.6   **Selected Top-Level Domains in the DNS Namespace**

Top-Level Domain Name	Intended Purpose
com	Commercial organizations
edu	Educational organizations/establishments
gov	U.S. government organizations/establishments
net	Network providers/centers
org	Not-for-profit and other organizations

TABLE 2.6 **Continued**

Top-Level Domain Name	Intended Purpose
mil	Military
arpa	Reverse DNS lookup
de	A country-specific domain—in this case, Germany*

*In addition to country-specific domains, many countries have created subdomains that follow roughly the same principles as the original top-level domains (such as co.uk and gov.nz).

Although the assignment of domain names is supposed to conform to the structure shown in Table 2.6, the assignment of names is not as closely controlled as you might think. It's not uncommon for some domain names to be used for other purposes, such as .org or .net being used for business.

> **Note**
>
> Although the primary function of DNS is to resolve hostnames to IP addresses, you can also have DNS perform IP address-to-hostname resolution. This process is called *reverse lookup*, which is accomplished by using pointer (PTR) records.

Types of DNS Entries

Although the most common entry in a DNS database is an A (address) record, which maps a hostname to an IP address, DNS can hold numerous other types of entries as well. Some are the MX record, which can map entries that correspond to mail exchanger systems, and CNAME (canonical record name), which can create alias records for a system. A system can have an A record and then multiple CNAME entries for its aliases. A DNS table with all these types of entries might look like this:

```
fileserve.mycoltd.com   IN   A     192.168.33.2
email.mycoltd.com       IN   A     192.168.33.7
fileprint.mycoltd.com   IN CNAME fileserver.mycoltd.com
mailer.mycoltd.com      IN   MX  10    email.mycoltd.com
```

As you can see, rather than map to an actual IP address, the CNAME and MX record entries map to another host, which DNS in turn can resolve to an IP address.

DNS Records

Each DNS name server maintains information about its zone, or domain, in a series of records, known as DNS resource records. There are several DNS resource records; each contains information about the DNS domain and the systems within it. These records are text entries stored on the DNS server. Some of the DNS resource records include the following:

- **Start of Authority (SOA):** A record of information containing data on DNS zones and other DNS records. A DNS zone is the part of a domain for which an individual DNS server is responsible. Each zone contains a single SOA record.

- **Name Server (NS):** Stores information that identifies the name servers in the domain that store information for that domain.

- **Canonical Name (CNAME):** Stores additional hostnames, or aliases, for hosts in the domain. A CNAME specifies an alias or nickname for a canonical hostname record in a domain name service (DNS) database. CNAME records give a single computer multiple names (aliases).

- **Pointer (PTR):** A pointer to the canonical name, which is used to perform a reverse DNS lookup, in which case the name is returned when the query originates with an IP address.

- **IPv6 Address (AAAA):** Stores information for IPv6 (128-bit) addresses. It is most commonly used to map hostnames to an IP address for a host.

- **Mail Exchange (MX):** Stores information about where mail for the domain should be delivered.

DNS in a Practical Implementation

In a real-world scenario, whether you use DNS is almost a nonissue. If you have Internet access, you will most certainly use DNS, but you are likely to use the DNS facilities of your Internet service provider (ISP) rather than have your own internal DNS server. However, if you operate a large, complex, multiplatform network, you might find that internal DNS servers are necessary. The major network operating system vendors know that you might need DNS facilities in your organization, so they include DNS server applications with their offerings.

It is common practice for workstations to be configured with the IP addresses of two DNS servers for fault tolerance. Figure 2.5 shows an example of this.

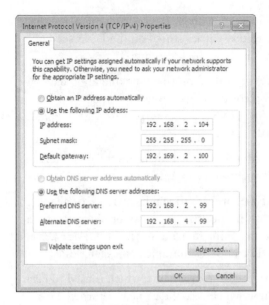

FIGURE 2.5   The DNS entries on a Windows 7 system.

The importance of DNS, particularly in environments in which the Internet is heavily used, cannot be overstated. If DNS facilities are not accessible, the Internet effectively becomes unusable, unless you can remember the IP addresses of all your favorite sites.

Windows Internet Name Service (WINS)

On Windows networks, you can use a system called WINS to enable Network Basic Input/Output System (NetBIOS) names to be resolved to IP addresses. NetBIOS name resolution is necessary on Windows networks so that systems can locate and access each other by using the NetBIOS computer name rather than the IP address. It's a lot easier for a person to remember a computer called secretary than to remember its IP address, 192.168.2.34. The NetBIOS name needs to be resolved to an IP address and subsequently to a MAC address (by ARP).

NetBIOS name resolution can be performed three ways on a network. The simplest way is to use a WINS server on the network that automatically performs the NetBIOS name resolution. If a WINS server is not available, NetBIOS name resolution can be performed statically using an LMHOSTS file. Using an LMHOSTS file requires that you manually configure at least one text file with the entries. As you can imagine, this can be a time-consuming process, particularly if the systems on the network frequently change. The third method, and the default, is that systems resolve NetBIOS names using broadcasts. This approach has two problems. First, the broadcasts create additional network traffic, and second, the broadcasts cannot traverse routers unless the router is configured to forward them. This means that resolutions between network segments are impossible.

Cram Quiz

1. During a discussion with your ISP's technical support representative, he mentions that you might have been using the wrong FQDN. Which TCP/IP-based network service is he referring to?

   ○ **A.** DHCP

   ○ **B.** WINS

   ○ **C.** SNMP

   ○ **D.** DNS

2. Which DNS record stores additional hostnames, or aliases, for hosts in the domain?

   ○ **A.** ALSO

   ○ **B.** ALIAS

   ○ **C.** CNAME

   ○ **D.** PTR

Cram Quiz Answers

1. **D.** DNS is a system that resolves hostnames to IP addresses. The term FQDN is used to describe the entire hostname. None of the other services use FQDNs.

2. **C.** The CNAME record stores additional hostnames, or aliases, for hosts in the domain.

Simple Network Management Protocol (SNMP)

▶ Given a scenario, use the appropriate network monitoring resources to analyze traffic

> **Note**
>
> This chapter addresses SNMP. Chapter 8, "Network Management," covers the objectives related to log files and traffic.

> **CramSaver**
>
> If you can correctly answer these questions before going through this section, save time by skimming the Exam Alerts in this section and then complete the Cram Quiz at the end of the section.
>
> 1. What protocol, in the TCP/IP suite, facilitates network management functionality?
>
> 2. Although the SNMP manager resides on a PC, each device that is part of the SNMP structure also needs to have SNMP functionality enabled. What is the software component that performs this called?
>
> **Answers**
>
> 1. SNMP is a protocol that facilitates network management functionality.
>
> 2. Although the SNMP manager resides on a PC, each device that is part of the SNMP structure also needs to have SNMP functionality enabled. This is performed through a software component called an agent.

SNMP enables network devices to communicate information about their state to a central system. It also enables the central system to pass configuration parameters to the devices.

> **ExamAlert**
>
> SNMP is a protocol that facilitates network management functionality. It is not, in itself, a network management system (NMS), simply the protocol that makes NMS possible.

Components of SNMP

In an SNMP configuration, a central system known as a *manager* acts as the central communication point for all the SNMP-enabled devices on the network. On each device to be managed and monitored via SNMP, software called an SNMP agent is set up and configured with the manager's IP address. Depending on the configuration, the SNMP manager then communicates with and retrieves information from the devices running the SNMP agent software. In addition, the agent can communicate the occurrence of certain events to the SNMP manager as they happen. These messages are known as *traps*. Figure 2.6 shows how an SNMP system works.

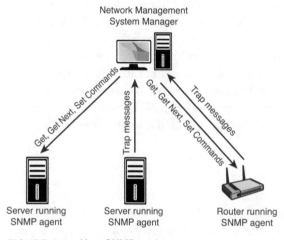

FIGURE 2.6   **How SNMP works.**

As Figure 2.6 illustrates, there are a number of components to SNMP. The following discussion looks at the management system, the agents, the management information base, and communities.

SNMP Management Systems

An SNMP management system is a computer running a special piece of software called a Network Management System (NMS). These software applications can be free, or they can cost thousands of dollars. The difference between the free applications and those that cost a great deal of money normally boils down to functionality and support. All NMS applications, regardless of cost, offer the same basic functionality. Today, most NMS applications use graphical maps of the network to locate a device and then query it. The queries are built into the application and are triggered by pointing and click-ing. You can actually issue SNMP requests from a command-line utility, but with so many tools available, this is simply unnecessary.

> **Note**
>
> Some people call SNMP managers or NMSs *trap managers*. This reference is mis-leading, however, because NMS can do more than just accept trap messages from agents.

Using SNMP and an NMS, you can monitor all the devices on a network, including switches, hubs, routers, servers, and printers, as well as any device that supports SNMP, from a single location. Using SNMP, you can see the amount of free disk space on a server in Jakarta or reset the interface on a router in Helsinki—all from the comfort of your desk in San Jose. Such power, though, brings with it some considerations. For example, because an NMS enables you to reconfigure network devices, or at least get information from them, it is common practice to implement an NMS on a secure worksta-tion platform such as a Linux or Windows server and to place the NMS PC in a secure location.

SNMP Agents

Although the SNMP manager resides on a PC, each device that is part of the SNMP structure also needs to have SNMP functionality enabled. This is per-formed through a software component called an *agent*.

An SNMP agent can be any device that can run a small software component that facilitates communication with an SNMP manager. SNMP agent functionality is supported by almost any device designed to be connected to a network.

In addition to providing a mechanism for managers to communicate with them, agents can tell SNMP managers when a threshold is surpassed. When this happens, on a device running an SNMP agent, a trap is sent to the NMS, and the NMS then performs an action, depending on the configuration. Basic NMS systems might sound an alarm or flash a message on the screen. Other, more advanced products might send a pager message, dial a cell phone, or send an email message.

Management Information Bases (MIBs)

Although the SNMP trap system might be the most commonly used aspect of SNMP, manager-to-agent communication is not just a one-way street. In addition to reading information from a device using the SNMP commands `Get` and `Get Next`, SNMP managers can issue the `Set` command. Having just three commands might make SNMP seem like a limited mechanism, but this is not the case. The secret of SNMP's power is in how it uses those three commands.

To demonstrate how SNMP commands work, imagine that you and a friend each have a list on which the following four words are written: four, book, sky, and table. If you, as the manager, ask your friend for the first value, she, acting as the agent, can reply "four." This is analogous to an SNMP `Get` command. Now, if you ask for the next value, she would reply "book." This is analogous to an SNMP `Get Next` command. If you then say "set green," and your friend changes the word *book* to *green*, you have performed the equivalent of an SNMP `Set` command. Sound simplistic? Well, if you can imagine expanding the list to include 100 values, you can see how you could navigate and set any parameter in the list, using just those three commands. The key, though, is to make sure that you and your friend have exactly the same list—which is where Management Information Bases (MIBs) come in.

SNMP uses databases of information called MIBs to define what parameters are accessible, which of the parameters are read-only, and which can be set. MIBs are available for thousands of devices and services, covering every imaginable need.

To ensure that SNMP systems offer cross-platform compatibility, MIB creation is controlled by the International Organization for Standardization (ISO). An organization that wants to create a MIB can apply to the ISO. The ISO then assigns the organization an ID under which it can create MIBs as it sees fit. The assignment of numbers is structured within a conceptual model called the *hierarchical name tree*.

SNMP Communities

Another feature of SNMP that enables manageability is communities. *SNMP communities* are logical groupings of systems. When a system is configured as part of a community, it communicates only with other devices that have the same community name. In addition, it accepts `Get`, `Get Next`, or `Set` commands only from an SNMP manager with a community name it recognizes. Typically, two communities are defined by default: a public community, intended for read-only use, and a private community, intended for read-and-write operations.

Whether you use SNMP depends on how many devices you have and how distributed your network infrastructure is. Even in environments that have just a few devices, SNMP can be useful because it can act as your eyes and ears, notifying you if a problem on the network occurs.

SNMPv3

SNMP is now on its third version, and this version has some significant differences. One of the most noticeable changes is that, unlike SNMPv1 and SNMPv2, SNMPv3 supports authentication and encryption:

▸ **Authentication**: Authentication protocols ensure that the message is from a valid source.

▸ **Encryption**: Encryption protocols ensure that data cannot be read by unintended sources.

ExamAlert

You might be asked to know the differences between SNMPv2 and SNMPv3.

Cram Quiz

1. What are SNMP databases called?

   ○ **A.** HOSTS

   ○ **B.** MIBs

   ○ **C.** WINS

   ○ **D.** Agents

2. What are logical groupings of SNMP systems known as?

   ○ **A.** Communities

   ○ **B.** Pairs

   ○ **C.** Mirrors

   ○ **D.** Nodes

3. What are two features supported in SNMPv3 and not previous versions?

   ○ **A.** Authentication

   ○ **B.** Dynamic mapping

   ○ **C.** Platform independence

   ○ **D.** Encryption

Cram Quiz Answers

1. **B.** SNMP uses databases of information called MIBs to define what parameters are accessible, which of the parameters are read-only, and which can be set.

2. **A.** SNMP communities are logical groupings of systems. When a system is configured as part of a community, it communicates only with other devices that have the same community name.

3. **A** and **D.** SNMPv3 supports authentication and encryption.

Dynamic Host Configuration Protocol (DHCP)

▶ **Explain the purpose and properties of DHCP.**

Cram**Saver**

If you can correctly answer these questions before going through this section, save time by skimming the Exam Alerts in this section and then complete the Cram Quiz at the end of the section.

1. What is the name used for ranges of IP addresses available within DHCP?

2. What is the name of the packet on a system configured to use DHCP broadcasts when it comes onto the network?

Answers

1. Within DHCP, ranges of IP addresses are known as scopes.

2. When a system configured to use DHCP comes onto the network, it broadcasts a special packet that looks for a DHCP server. This packet is known as the `DHCPDISCOVER` packet.

One method to assign IP addresses to hosts is to use static addressing. This involves manually assigning an address from those available to you and allowing the host to always use that address. The problems with this method include the difficulty in managing addresses for a multitude of machines and efficiently and effectively issuing them.

Dynamic Host Configuration Protocol (DHCP), which is defined in RFC 2131, enables ranges of IP addresses, known as *scopes*, to be defined on a system running a DHCP server application. When another system configured as a DHCP client is initialized, it asks the server for an address. If all things are as they should be, the server assigns an address from the scope to the client for a predetermined amount of time, known as the *lease*.

At various points during the lease (normally the 50 percent and 85 percent points), the client attempts to renew the lease from the server. If the server cannot perform a renewal, the lease expires at 100 percent, and the client stops using the address.

In addition to an IP address and the subnet mask, the DHCP server can supply many other pieces of information; although, exactly what can be provided depends on the DHCP server implementation. In addition to the address information, the default gateway is often supplied, along with DNS information.

In addition to having DHCP supply a random address from the scope, you can configure it to supply a specific address to a client. Such an arrangement is known as a *reservation*. Reservations are a means by which you can still use DHCP for a system but at the same time guarantee that it always has the same IP address. DHCP can also be configured for exclusions. In this scenario, certain IP addresses are not given out to client systems.

The advantages of using DHCP are numerous. First, administrators do not need to manually configure each system. Second, human error such as the assignment of duplicate IP addresses is eliminated. Third, DHCP removes the need to reconfigure systems if they move from one subnet to another, or if you decide to make a wholesale change in the IP addressing structure. The downsides are that DHCP traffic is broadcast-based and thus generates network traffic—albeit a small amount. Finally, the DHCP server software must be installed and configured on a server, which can place additional processor load (again, minimal) on that system. From an administrative perspective, after the initial configuration, DHCP is about as maintenance-free as a service can get, with only occasional monitoring normally required.

Exam**Alert**

DHCP is a protocol-dependent service and is not platform-dependent. This means that you can use, say, a Linux DHCP server for a network with Windows clients or a Novell DHCP server with Linux clients. Although the DHCP server offerings in the various network operating systems might slightly differ, the basic functionality is the same across the board. Likewise, the client configuration for DHCP servers running on a different operating system platform is the same as for DHCP servers running on the same base operating system platform.

The DHCP Process

To better understand how DHCP works, spend a few minutes looking at the processes that occur when a DHCP-enabled client connects to the network. When a system configured to use DHCP comes onto the network, it broadcasts a special packet that looks for a DHCP server. This packet is known as the DHCPDISCOVER packet. The DHCP server, which is always on the lookout for DHCPDISCOVER broadcasts, picks up the packet and compares the request with the scopes it has defined. If it finds that it has a scope for the network from which the packet originated, it chooses an address from the scope, reserves it, and sends the address, along with any other information, such as the lease duration, to the client. This is known as the DHCPOFFER packet. Because the client still does not have an IP address, this communication is also achieved via broadcast.

When the client receives the offer, it looks at the offer to determine if it is suitable. If more than one offer is received, which can happen if more than one DHCP server is configured, the offers are compared to see which is best. *Best* in this context can involve a variety of criteria but normally is the length of the lease. When the selection process completes, the client notifies the server that the offer has been accepted, through a packet called a DHCPRE-QUEST packet. At this point the server finalizes the offer and sends the client an acknowledgment. This last message, which is sent as a broadcast, is known as a DHCPACK packet. After the client system receives the DHCPACK, it initializes the TCP/IP suite and can communicate on the network.

DHCP and DNS Suffixes

In DNS, *suffixes* define the DNS servers to be used and the order in which to use them. DHCP settings can push a domain suffix search list to DNS clients. When such a list is specifically given to a client, the client uses only that list for name resolution. With Linux clients, this can occur by specifying entries in the resolve.conf file.

ExamAlert

Make sure you know that DHCP can provide DNS suffixes to clients.

Cram Quiz

1. One of the programmers has asked that DHCP always issue his workstation the same IP address. What feature of DHCP enables you to accomplish this?

   ○ **A.** Stipulation

   ○ **B.** Rider

   ○ **C.** Reservation

   ○ **D.** Provision

2. Which of the following is NOT a common packet sent during the normal DHCP process?

   ○ **A.** DHCPACK

   ○ **B.** DHCPPROVE

   ○ **C.** DHCPDISCOVER

   ○ **D.** DHCPOFFER

Cram Quiz Answers

1. **C.** Reservations are specific addresses reserved for clients.

2. **B.** DHCPPROVE is not a common packet. The other choices presented (DHCPACK, DHCPDISCOVER, and DHCPOFFER) are part of the normal process.

What Next?

The TCP/IP suite is the most widely implemented protocol on networks today. As such, it is an important topic on the Network+ exam. Chapter 3 deals with the individual protocols within the protocol suite. It looks at the functions of the individual protocols and their purposes. It starts by discussing one of the more complex facets of TCP/IP: addressing.

CHAPTER 3

Addressing and Routing

This chapter covers the following official Network+ objectives:

▶ Explain the purpose and properties of IP addressing.

▶ Explain the purpose and properties of routing and switching.

▶ Identify common TCP and UDP default ports.

▶ Given a scenario, install and configure routers and switches.

For more information on the official Network+ exam topics, see the "About the Network+ Exam" section in the "Introduction."

Without question, the TCP/IP suite is the most widely implemented protocol on networks today. As such, it is an important topic on the Network+ exam. To pass the exam, you definitely need to understand the material presented in this chapter.

This chapter deals with the individual protocols within the protocol suite. It looks at the functions of the individual protocols and their purposes. It starts by discussing one of the more complex facets of TCP/IP: addressing.

IP Addressing

▶ **Explain the purpose and properties of IP addressing.**

Cram**Saver**

If you can correctly answer these questions before going through this section, save time by skimming the Exam Alerts in this section and then complete the Cram Quiz at the end of the section.

1. How many octets does a Class A address use to represent the network portion?

2. What is the range that Class C addresses span in the first octet?

3. What are the reserved IPv4 ranges for private networks?

Answers

1. A Class A address uses only the first octet to represent the network portion, a Class B address uses two octets, and a Class C address uses three octets.

2. Class C addresses span from 192 to 223, with a default subnet mask of 255.255.255.0.

3. A private network is any network to which access is restricted. Reserved IP addresses are 10.0.0.0, 172.16.0.0 to 172.31.0.0, and 192.168.0.0.

IP addressing is one of the most challenging aspects of TCP/IP. It can leave even the most seasoned network administrators scratching their heads. Fortunately, the Network+ exam requires only a fundamental knowledge of IP addressing. The following sections look at how IP addressing works for both IPv4 and the newest version of IP: IPv6.

To communicate on a network using TCP/IP, each system must be assigned a unique address. The address defines both the number of the network to which the device is attached and the number of the node on that network. In other words, the IP address provides two pieces of information. It's a bit like a street name and house number in a person's home address.

Each device on a logical network segment must have the same network address as all the other devices on the segment. All the devices on that network segment must then have different node addresses.

In IP addressing, another set of numbers, called a subnet mask, defines which portion of the IP address refers to the network address and which refers to the node address.

IP addressing is different in IPv4 and IPv6. The discussion begins by looking at IPv4.

IPv4

An IPv4 address is composed of four sets of 8 binary bits, which are called *octets*. The result is that IP addresses contain 32 bits. Each bit in each octet is assigned a decimal value. The leftmost bit has a value of 128, followed by 64, 32, 16, 8, 4, 2, and 1, left to right.

Each bit in the octet can be either a 1 or a 0. If the value is 1, it is counted as its decimal value, and if it is 0, it is ignored. If all the bits are 0, the value of the octet is 0. If all the bits in the octet are 1, the value is 255, which is 128 + 64 + 32 + 16 + 8 + 4 + 2 + 1.

By using the set of 8 bits and manipulating the 1s and 0s, you can obtain any value between 0 and 255 for each octet.

Table 3.1 shows some examples of decimal-to-binary value conversions.

TABLE 3.1 **Decimal-to-Binary Value Conversions**

Decimal Value	Binary Value	Decimal Calculation
10	00001010	8 + 2 = 10
192	11000000	128 + 64 = 192
205	11001101	128 + 64 + 8 + 4 + 1 = 205
223	11011111	128 + 64 + 16 + 8 + 4 + 2 + 1 = 223

IP Address Classes

IP addresses are grouped into logical divisions called *classes*. The IPv4 address space has five address classes (A through E); although, only three (A, B, and C) assign addresses to clients. Class D is reserved for multicast addressing, and Class E is reserved for future development.

Of the three classes available for address assignments, each uses a fixed-length subnet mask to define the separation between the network and the node address. A Class A address uses only the first octet to represent the network portion; a Class B address uses two octets; and a Class C address uses the first three octets. The upshot of this system is that Class A has a small number of network addresses, but each Class A address has a large number of possible host addresses. Class B has a larger number of networks, but each Class B address has a smaller number of hosts. Class C has an even larger number of networks, but each Class C address has an even smaller number of hosts. The exact numbers are provided in Table 3.2.

> **ExamAlert**
>
> Be prepared for questions asking you to identify IP class ranges, such as the IP range for a Class A network.

TABLE 3.2 **IPv4 Address Classes and the Number of Available Network/Host Addresses**

Address Class	Range	Number of Networks	Number of Hosts Per Network	Binary Value of First Octet
A	1 to 126	126	16,777,214	0xxxxxxx
B	128 to 191	16,384	65,534	10xxxxxx
C	192 to 223	2,097,152	254	110xxxxx
D	224 to 239	N/A	N/A	1110xxxx
E	240 to 255	N/A	N/A	1111xxxx

> **Note**
>
> Notice in Table 3.2 that the network number 127 is not included in any of the ranges. The 127.0.0.1 network ID is reserved for the IPv4 local loopback. The local loopback is a function of the protocol suite used in the troubleshooting process.

> **ExamAlert**
>
> For the Network+ exam, you should be prepared to identify into which class a given address falls. You should also be prepared to identify the IPv4 loopback address. The actual loopback address is 127.0.0.1.

Subnet Mask Assignment

Like an IP address, a *subnet mask* is most commonly expressed in 32-bit dotted-decimal format. Unlike an IP address, though, a subnet mask performs just one function—it defines which parts of the IP address refer to the network address and which refer to the node address. Each class of the IP address used for address assignment has a default subnet mask associated with it. Table 3.3 lists the default subnet masks.

TABLE 3.3 **Default Subnet Masks Associated with IP Address Classes**

Address Class	Default Subnet Mask
A	255.0.0.0
B	255.255.0.0
C	255.255.255.0

ExamAlert

You will likely see questions about address class and the corresponding default subnet mask. Review Table 3.3 before taking the exam.

Subnetting

Now that you have looked at how IP addresses are used, you can learn the process of subnetting. *Subnetting* is a process by which the node portions of an IP address create more networks than you would have if you used the default subnet mask.

To illustrate subnetting, for example, suppose that you have been assigned the Class B address 150.150.0.0. Using this address and the default subnet mask, you could have a single network (150.150) and use the rest of the address as node addresses. This would give you a large number of possible node addresses, which in reality is probably not useful. With subnetting, you use bits from the node portion of the address to create more network addresses. This reduces the number of nodes per network, but you probably will still have more than enough.

Following are two main reasons for subnetting:

▶ It enables you to more effectively use IP address ranges.

▶ It makes IP networking more secure and manageable by providing a mechanism to create multiple networks rather than having just one. Using multiple networks confines traffic to the network that it needs to be on, which reduces overall network traffic levels. Multiple subnets also create more broadcast domains, which in turn reduces networkwide broadcast traffic. A difference exists between broadcast domains and collision domains: The latter is all the connected nodes, whereas the former is all the logical nodes that can reach each other. As such, collision domains are typically subsets of broadcast domains.

ExamAlert

Subnetting does not increase the number of IP addresses available. It increases the number of network IDs and, as a result, decreases the number of node IDs per network. It also creates more broadcast domains. Broadcasts are not forwarded by routers, so they are limited to the network on which they originate.

Identifying the Differences Between IPv4 Public and Private Networks

IP addressing involves many considerations, not the least of which are public and private networks.

▶ A *public network* is a network to which anyone can connect. The best (and perhaps only pure) example of such a network is the Internet.

▶ A *private network* is any network to which access is restricted. A corporate network and a network in a school are examples of private networks.

Note

The Internet Assigned Numbers Authority (IANA) is responsible for assigning IP addresses to public networks. However, because of the workload involved in maintaining the systems and processes to do this, IANA has delegated the assignment process to a number of regional authorities. For more information, visit http://www.iana.org/ipaddress/ip-addresses.htm.

The main difference between public and private networks, other than access to a private network is tightly controlled and access to a public network is not, is that the addressing of devices on a public network must be carefully considered. Addressing on a private network has a little more latitude.

As already discussed, for hosts on a network to communicate by using TCP/IP, they must have unique addresses. This number defines the logical network that each host belongs to and the host's address on that network. On a private network with, say, three logical networks and 100 nodes on each network, addressing is not a difficult task. On a network on the scale of the Internet, however, addressing is complex.

If you connect a system to the Internet, you need to get a valid registered IP address. Most commonly, you obtain this address from your ISP. Alternatively, if you wanted a large number of addresses, for example, you could contact the organization responsible for address assignment in your area. You can determine who the regional numbers authority for your area is by visiting the IANA website.

Because of the nature of their business, ISPs have large blocks of IP addresses that they can assign to their clients. If you need a registered IP address, getting one from an ISP is almost certainly a simpler process than going through a regional numbers authority. Some ISPs' plans actually include blocks of registered IP addresses, working on the principle that businesses want some kind of permanent presence on the Internet. Of course, if you discontinue your service with the ISP, you can no longer use the provided IP address.

Private Address Ranges

To provide flexibility in addressing and to prevent an incorrectly configured network from polluting the Internet, certain address ranges are set aside for private use. These address ranges are called *private ranges* because they are designated for use only on private networks. These addresses are special because Internet routers are configured to ignore any packets they see that use these addresses. This means that if a private network "leaks" onto the Internet, it won't get any farther than the first router it encounters. So a private address cannot be on the Internet because it cannot be routed to public networks.

Three ranges are defined in RFC 1918: one each from Classes A, B, and C. You can use whichever range you want; although, the Class A and B address ranges offer more addressing options than Class C. Table 3.4 defines the address ranges for Class A, B, and C addresses.

TABLE 3.4   **Private Address Ranges**

Class	Address Range	Default Subnet Mask
A	10.0.0.0 to 10.255.255.255	255.0.0.0
B	172.16.0.0 to 172.31.255.255	255.255.0.0
C	192.168.0.0 to 192.168.255.255	255.255.255.0

ExamAlert

You can expect questions on private IP address ranges and their corresponding default subnet masks.

Classless Interdomain Routing (CIDR)

Classless interdomain routing (CIDR) is a method to assign addresses outside the standard Class A, B, and C structure that is used by IPv6. Specifying the number of bits in the subnet mask offers more flexibility than the three standard class definitions.

Using CIDR, addresses are assigned using a value known as the *slash*. The actual value of the slash depends on how many bits of the subnet mask are used to express the network portion of the address. For example, a subnet mask that uses all 8 bits from the first octet and 4 from the second would be described as /12, or "slash 12." A subnet mask that uses all the bits from the first three octets would be called /24. Why the slash? In actual addressing terms, the CIDR value is expressed after the address, using a slash. So the address 192.168.2.1/24 means that the node's IP address is 192.168.2.1, and the subnet mask is 255.255.255.0.

> **Note**
>
> You can find a great CIDR calculator that can compute values from ranges at http://www.subnet-calculator.com/cidr/php.

> **ExamAlert**
>
> You will likely see IP addresses in their CIDR format on the exam. Be sure that you understand CIDR addressing for the exam.

Default Gateways

Default gateways are the means by which a device can access hosts on other networks for which it does not have a specifically configured route. Most workstation configurations actually default to just using default gateways rather than having any static routes configured. This enables workstations to communicate with other network segments, or with other networks, such as the Internet.

> **ExamAlert**
>
> You will be expected to identify the purpose and function of a default gateway.

When a system wants to communicate with another device, it first determines whether the host is on the local network or a remote network. If the host is on a remote network, the system looks in the routing table to determine whether it has an entry for the network on which the remote host resides. If it does, it uses that route. If it does not, the data is sent to the default gateway.

> **Note**
>
> Although it might seem obvious, it's worth mentioning that the default gateway must be on the same network as the nodes that use it.

In essence, the default gateway is simply the path out of the network for a given device. Figure 3.1 shows how a default gateway fits into a network infrastructure.

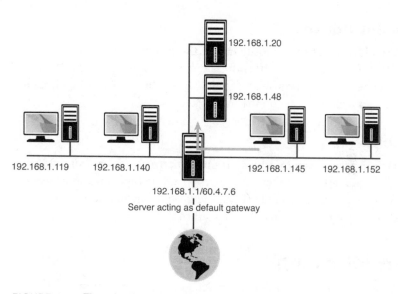

FIGURE 3.1   **The role of a default gateway.**

On the network, a default gateway could be a router or a computer with network interfaces for all segments to which it is connected. These interfaces have local IP addresses for the respective segments. If a system is not configured with any static routes or a default gateway, it is limited to operating on its own network segment.

> **ExamAlert**
>
> If a system is not configured with any static routes or a default gateway, it is limited to operating on its own network segment.

IPv4 Address Types

IPv4 has three primary address types: unicast, broadcast, and multicast. You need to distinguish between these three types of IPv4 addresses.

Unicast Address

With a *unicast address*, a single address is specified. Data sent with unicast addressing is delivered to a specific node identified by the address. It is a point-to-point address link.

Broadcast Address

A broadcast address is at the opposite end of the spectrum from a unicast address. A *broadcast address* is an IP address that you can use to target all systems on a subnet or network instead of single hosts. In other words, a broadcast message goes to everyone on the network.

Multicast

Multicasting is a mechanism by which groups of network devices can send and receive data between the members of the group at one time, instead of separately sending messages to each device in the group. The multicast grouping is established by configuring each device with the same multicast IP address.

IPv6 Addressing

Internet Protocol Version 4 (IPv4) has served as the Internet's protocol for almost 30 years. When IPv4 was in development 30 years ago, it would have been impossible for its creators to imagine or predict the future demand for IP devices and therefore IP addresses.

> **Note**
>
> Does the IETF assign protocol numbers using multiples of 2? Well, no. There was an IPv5. It was an experimental protocol that never went anywhere. But although IPv5 may have fallen into obscurity, because the name had been used, we got IPv6.

Where have all the IPv4 addresses gone?

IPv4 uses a 32-bit addressing scheme. This gives IPv4 a total of 4,294,967,296 possible unique addresses that can be assigned to IP devices. More than 4 billion addresses might sound like a lot, and it is. However, the number of IP-enabled devices increases daily at a staggering rate. Not all these addresses can be used by public networks. Many of these addresses are reserved and are unavailable for public use. This reduces the number of addresses that can be allocated as public Internet addresses.

The IPv6 project started in the mid-1990s, well before the threat of IPv4 limitations. Now network hardware and software are equipped for and ready to deploy IPv6 addressing. IPv6 offers a number of improvements. The most notable is its capability to handle growth in public networks. IPv6 uses a 128-bit addressing scheme, enabling a huge number of possible addresses:

340,282,366,920,938,463,463,374,607,431,768,211,456

Identifying IPv6 Addresses

As previously discussed, IPv4 uses a dotted-decimal format: 8 bits converted to its decimal equivalent and separated by periods. An example of an IPv4 address is 192.168.2.1.

Because of the 128-bit structure of the IPv6 addressing scheme, it looks quite a bit different. An IPv6 address is divided along 16-bit boundaries, and each 16-bit block is converted into a four-digit hexadecimal number and separated by colons. The resulting representation is called colon-hexadecimal. Now look at how it works. Figure 3.2 shows the IPv6 address 2001:0:4137:9e50:2811:34ff:3f57:febc from a Windows 7 system.

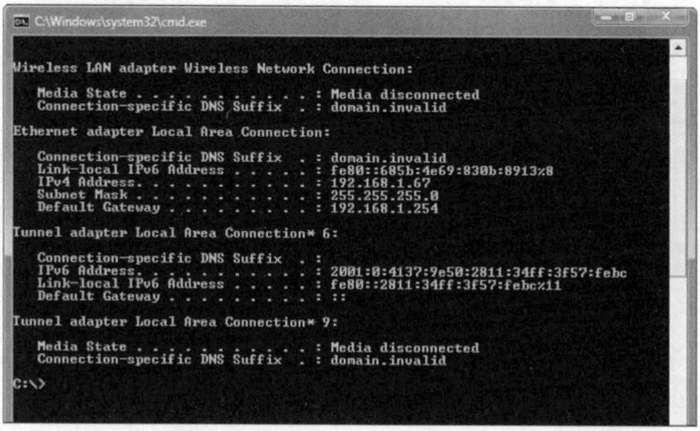

FIGURE 3.2   An IPv6 address in a Windows 7 dialog screen.

An IPv6 address can be simplified by removing the leading 0s within each 16-bit block. Not all the 0s can be removed, however, because each address block must have at least a single digit. Removing the 0 suppression, the address representation becomes

2001:0000:4137:9e50:2811:34ff:3f57:febc

Some of the IPv6 addresses you will work with have sequences of 0s. When this occurs, the number is often abbreviated to make it easier to read. In the preceding example you saw that a single 0 represented a number set in hexadecimal form. To further simplify the representation of IPv6 addresses, a contiguous sequence of 16-bit blocks set to 0 in colon hexadecimal format can be compressed to ::, known as the *double colon*.

For example, the IPv6 address of

2001:0000:0000:0000:3cde:37d1:3f57:fe93

can be compressed to

2001::3cde:37d1:3f57:fe93.

Of course, there are limits on how the IPv6 0s can be reduced. 0s within the IPv6 address cannot be eliminated when they are not first in the number sequence. For instance, 2001:4000:0000:0000:0000:0000:0000:0003 cannot be compressed as 2001:4::3. This would actually appear as 2001:4000::3.

When you look at an IPv6 address that uses a double colon, how do you know exactly what numbers are represented? The formula is to subtract the number of blocks from 8 and then multiply that number by 16. For example, the address 2001:4000::3 uses three blocks: 2001, 4000, and 3. So the formula is as follows:

(8 − 3) * 16 = 80

Therefore, the total number of bits represented by the double colon in this example is 80.

> **Note**
>
> You can remove 0s only once in an IPv6 address. Using a double colon more than once would make it impossible to determine the number of 0 bits represented by each instance of ::.

IPv6 Address Types

Another difference between IPv4 and IPv6 is in the address types. IPv4 addressing was discussed in detail earlier. IPv6 addressing offers several types of addresses, as detailed in this section.

Unicast IPv6 Addresses

As you might deduce from the name, a unicast address specifies a single interface. Data packets sent to a unicast destination travel from the sending host to the destination host. It is a direct line of communication. A few types of addresses fall under the unicast banner:

Global Unicast Addresses

Global unicast addresses are the equivalent of IPv4 public addresses. These addresses are routable and travel throughout the network.

Link-Local Addresses

Link-local addresses are designated for use on a single local network. Link-local addresses are automatically configured on all interfaces. This automatic configuration is comparable to the 169.254.0.0/16 APIPA automatically assigned IPv4 addressing scheme. The prefix used for a link-local address is fe80::/64. On a single-link IPv6 network with no router, link-local addresses are used to communicate between devices on the link.

Site-Local Addresses

Site-local addresses are equivalent to the IPv4 private address space (10.0.0.0/8, 172.16.0.0/12, and 192.168.0.0/16). As with IPv4, in which private address ranges are used in private networks, IPv6 uses site-local addresses that do not interfere with global unicast addresses. In addition, routers do not forward site-local traffic outside the site. Unlike link-local addresses, site-local addresses are not automatically configured and must be assigned through either stateless or stateful address configuration processes. The prefix used for the site-local address is FEC0::/10.

Multicast Addresses

As with IPv4 addresses, multicasting sends and receives data between groups of nodes. It sends IP messages to that group rather than to every node on the LAN (broadcast) or just one other node (unicast).

Anycast Addresses

Anycast addresses represent the middle ground between unicast addresses and multicast addresses. Anycast delivers messages to any one node in the multicast group.

> **Note**
>
> You might encounter the terms *stateful* and *stateless* configuration. *Stateless* refers to IP autoconfiguration, in which administrators need not manually input configuration information. In a *stateful* configuration network, devices obtain address information from a server.

> **ExamAlert**
>
> Earlier you read that IPv4 reserves 127.0.0.1 as the loopback address. IPv6 has the same reservation. IPv6 addresses 0:0:0:0:0:0:0:0 and 0:0:0:0:0:0:0:1 are reserved as the loopback addresses.

> **ExamAlert**
>
> Remember that fe80:: is a private link-local address.

Comparing IPv4 and IPv6 Addressing

Table 3.5 compares IPv4 and IPv6 addressing.

> **Note**
>
> Automatic Private IP Addressing (APIPA) appears in the table and is discussed in detail in the section "Automatic Private IP Addressing (APIPA)" later in this chapter.

TABLE 3.5 **Comparing IPv4 and IPv6 Addressing**

Address Feature	IPv4 Address	IPv6 Address
Loopback address	127.0.0.1	0:0:0:0:0:0:0:1 (::1)
Network-wide addresses	IPv4 public address ranges	Global unicast IPv6 addresses
Private network addresses	10.0.0.0 172.16.0.0 192.168.0.0	Site-local address ranges (FEC0::)
Autoconfigured addresses	IPv4 automatic private IP addressing (169.254.0.0)	Link-local addresses of the FE80:: prefix

> **ExamAlert**
>
> Make sure you know the information provided in Table 3.5.

Assigning IP Addresses

Now that you understand the need for each system on a TCP/IP-based network to have a unique address, the following sections examine how those systems receive their addresses.

Static Addressing

Static addressing refers to the manual assignment of IP addresses to a system. This approach has two main problems:

- ▶ Statically configuring one system with the correct address is simple, but in the course of configuring, say, a few hundred systems, mistakes are likely to be made. If the IP addresses are entered incorrectly, the system probably cannot connect to other systems on the network.

- ▶ If the IP addressing scheme for the organization changes, each system must again be manually reconfigured. In a large organization with hundreds or thousands of systems, such a reconfiguration could take a considerable amount of time. These drawbacks of static addressing are so significant that nearly all networks use dynamic IP addressing.

Dynamic Addressing

Dynamic addressing refers to the automatic assignment of IP addresses. On modern networks, the mechanism used to do this is Dynamic Host Configuration Protocol (DHCP). DHCP, part of the TCP/IP suite, enables a central system to provide client systems with IP addresses. Automatically assigning addresses with DHCP alleviates the burden of address configuration and reconfiguration that occurs with static IP addressing.

The basic function of the DHCP service is to automatically assign IP addresses to client systems. To do this, ranges of IP addresses, known as *scopes*, are defined on a system running a DHCP server application. When another system configured as a DHCP client is initialized, it asks the server for an address. If all things are as they should be, the server assigns an address to the client for a predetermined amount of time, which is known as the *lease*, from the scope.

A DHCP server typically can be configured to assign more than just IP addresses. It often is used to assign the subnet mask, the default gateway, and Domain Name Service (DNS) information.

Using DHCP means that administrators do not need to manually configure each client system with a TCP/IP address. This removes the common problems associated with statically assigned addresses, such as human error. The potential problem of assigning duplicate IP addresses is also eliminated. DHCP also removes the need to reconfigure systems if they move from one subnet to another, or if you decide to make a wholesale change in the IP addressing structure.

> **Note**
>
> Even when a network is configured to use DHCP, several mission-critical network systems continue to use static addressing: DHCP server, DNS server, web server, and more. They do not have dynamic IP addressing because their IP addresses can never change. If they do, client systems may be unable to access the resources from that server.

Configuring a client for TCP/IP can be relatively complex, or it can be simple. Any complexity involved is related to the possible need to manually configure TCP/IP. The simplicity is because TCP/IP configuration can occur automatically via DHCP or through APIPA. At the least, a system needs an IP address and subnet mask to log on to a network. The default gateway and DNS server IP information is optional, but network functionality is limited without them. The following list briefly explains the IP-related settings used to connect to a TCP/IP network:

▸ **IP address**: Each system must be assigned a unique IP address so that it can communicate on the network.

▸ **Subnet mask**: Enables the system to determine what portion of the IP address represents the network address and what portion represents the node address.

▸ **Default gateway**: Enables the system to communicate on a remote network, without the need for explicit routes to be defined.

▸ **DNS server addresses**: Enable dynamic hostname resolution to be performed. It is common practice to have two DNS server addresses defined so that if one server becomes unavailable, the other can be used.

> **Exam Alert**
>
> At the very minimum, an IP address and subnet mask are required to connect to a TCP/IP network. With just this minimum configuration, connectivity is limited to the local segment, and DNS resolution is not possible.

BOOT Protocol (BOOTP)

BOOTP was originally created so that diskless workstations could obtain information needed to connect to the network, such as the TCP/IP address, subnet mask, and default gateway. Such a system was necessary because diskless workstations had no way to store the information.

When a system configured to use BOOTP is powered up, it broadcasts for a BOOTP server on the network. If such a server exists, it compares the MAC address of the system issuing the BOOTP request with a database of entries. From this database, it supplies the system with the appropriate information. It can also notify the workstation about a file that it must run on BOOTP.

In the unlikely event that you use BOOTP, you should be aware that, like DHCP, it is a broadcast-based system. Therefore, routers must be configured to forward BOOTP broadcasts.

Automatic Private IP Addressing (APIPA)

Automatic Private IP Addressing (APIPA) was introduced with Windows 98 and has been included in all subsequent Windows versions. The function of APIPA is that a system can give itself an IP address if it is incapable of receiving an address dynamically from a DHCP server. Then APIPA assigns the system an address from the 169.254.0.0 address range and configures an appropriate subnet mask (255.255.0.0). However, it doesn't configure the system with a default gateway address. As a result, communication is limited to the local network.

> **Exam Alert**
>
> If a system that does not support APIPA cannot get an address from a DHCP server, it typically assigns itself an IP address of 0.0.0.0. Keep this in mind when troubleshooting IP addressing problems on non-APIPA platforms.

The idea behind APIPA is that systems on a segment can communicate with each other if DHCP server failure occurs. In reality, the limited usability of APIPA makes it little more than a last resort. For example, imagine that a system is powered on while the DHCP server is operational and receives an IP address of 192.168.100.2. Then the DHCP server fails. Now, if the other systems on the segment are powered on and cannot get an address from the DHCP server because it is down, they would self-assign addresses in the 169.254.0.0 address range via APIPA. The systems with APIPA addresses would talk to each other, but they couldn't talk to a system that received an address from the DHCP server. Likewise, any system that receives an IP address via DHCP cannot talk to systems with APIPA-assigned addresses. This, and the absence of a default gateway, is why APIPA is of limited use in real-world environments.

> **Exam**Alert
>
> Be prepared to answer APIPA questions. Know what it is and how you can tell if you have been assigned an APIPA address and why.

Identifying MAC Addresses

Many times this book refers to MAC addresses and how certain devices use them. However, it has not yet discussed why MAC addresses exist, how they are assigned, and what they consist of.

> **Note**
>
> A MAC address is sometimes called a *physical address* because it is physically embedded in the interface.

A MAC address is a 6-byte (48-bit) hexadecimal address that enables a NIC to be uniquely identified on the network. The MAC address forms the basis of network communication, regardless of the protocol used to achieve network connection. Because the MAC address is so fundamental to network communication, mechanisms are in place to ensure that duplicate addresses cannot be used.

To combat the possibility of duplicate MAC addresses being assigned, the Institute of Electrical and Electronics Engineers (IEEE) took over the assignment of MAC addresses. But rather than be burdened with assigning individual addresses, the IEEE decided to assign each manufacturer an ID and then let the manufacturer further allocate IDs. The result is that in a MAC address, the first 3 bytes define the manufacturer, and the last 3 are assigned by the manufacturer.

For example, consider the MAC address of the computer on which this book is being written: 00:D0:59:09:07:51. The first 3 bytes (00:D0:59) identify the manufacturer of the card; because only this manufacturer can use this address, it is known as the *Organizational Unique Identifier (OUI)*. The last 3 bytes (09:07:51) are called the *Universal LAN MAC address*: They make this interface unique. You can find a complete listing of organizational MAC address assignments at http://standards.ieee.org/regauth/oui/oui.txt.

> ### Exam**Alert**
>
> Because MAC addresses are expressed in hexadecimal, only the numbers 0 through 9 and the letters A through F can be used in them. If you get an exam question about identifying a MAC address and some of the answers contain letters and numbers other than 0 through 9 and the letters A through F, you can immediately discount those answers.

You can discover the NIC's MAC address in various ways, depending on what system or platform you work on. Table 3.6 defines various platforms and methods you can use to view an interface's MAC address.

TABLE 3.6 **Methods of Viewing the MAC Addresses of NICs**

Platform	Method
Windows 2003/2008/XP/Vista/7	Enter `ipconfig /all` at a command prompt.
Linux/some Unix	Enter the `ifconfig -a` command.
Novell NetWare	Enter the `config` command.
Cisco router	Enter the `sh int interface name` command.

> ### Exam**Alert**
>
> Be sure you know the commands used to identify the MAC address in various operating system formats.

Network Address Translation (NAT) and Port Address Translation (PAT)

This chapter has defined many acronyms and continues with two more: NAT and PAT.

NAT

The basic principle of NAT is that many computers can "hide" behind a single IP address. The main reason you need to do this (as pointed out earlier in the section "IP Addressing") is because there simply aren't enough IPv4 addresses to go around. Using NAT means that only one registered IP address is needed on the system's external interface, acting as the gateway between the internal and external networks.

> **Note**
>
> Don't confuse NAT with proxy servers. The proxy service is different from NAT, but many proxy server applications do include NAT functionality.

NAT enables you to use whatever addressing scheme you like on your internal networks; although, it is common practice to use the private address ranges, which were discussed earlier.

When a system is performing NAT, it funnels the requests given to it to the Internet. To the remote host, the request looks like it is originating from a single address. The system performing the NAT function keeps track of who asked for what and makes sure that when the data is returned, it is directed to the correct system. Servers that provide NAT functionality do so in different ways. For example, you can statically map a specific internal IP address to a specific external one (known as the *one-to-one NAT method*) so that outgoing requests are always tagged with the same IP address. Alternatively, if you have a group of public IP addresses, you can have the NAT system assign addresses to devices on a first-come, first-served basis. Either way, the basic function of NAT is the same.

There is a transition technology known as Teredo that gives full IPv6 connectivity for IPv6-capable hosts, which are on the IPv4 Internet but lack direct native connection to an IPv6 network. The distinguishing feature of Teredo is that it can do this from behind network address translation (NAT) devices (such as home routers). You can find more information on this at http://ipv6.com/articles/nat/NAT-In-Depth.htm.

PAT

NAT enables administrators to conserve public IP addresses and, at the same time, secure the internal network. Port Address Translation (PAT) is a variation on NAT. With PAT, all systems on the LAN are translated to the same IP address, but with a different port number assignment. PAT is used when multiple clients want to access the Internet. However, with not enough available public IP addresses, you need to map the inside clients to a single public IP address. When packets come back into the private network, they are routed to their destination with a table within PAT that tracks the public and private port numbers.

When PAT is used, there is a typically only a single IP address exposed to the public network, and multiple network devices access the Internet through this exposed IP address. The sending devices, IP address, and port number are not exposed. For example, an internal computer with the IP address of 192.168.2.2 wants to access a remote Web server at address 204.23.85.49. The request goes to the PAT router where the sender's private IP and port number are modified, and a mapping is added to the PAT table. The remote web server sees the request coming from the IP address of the PAT router and not the computer actually making the request. The web server sends the reply to the address and port number of the router. When received, the router checks its table to see the packet's actual destination and forwards it.

> **ExamAlert**
>
> PAT enables nodes on a LAN to communicate with the Internet without revealing their IP address. All outbound IP communications are translated to the router's external IP address. Replies come back to the router that then translates them back into the private IP address of the original host for final delivery.

Static NAT is a simple form of NAT. Static Network Address Translation (SNAT) directly maps a private IP address to a static unchanging public IP address. This enables an internal system, such as a mail server, to have an unregistered (private) IP address and still be reachable over the Internet. For example, if a network uses a private address of 192.168.2.1 for a mail server, it can be statically linked to a public IP address such as 213.23.213.85.

Cram Quiz

1. What is the IPv6 equivalent of 127.0.0.1? (Choose two.)

   ○ **A.** 0:0:0:0:0:0:0:1

   ○ **B.** 0:0:0:0:0:0:0:24

   ○ **C.** ::1

   ○ **D.** ::24

2. Which of the following is a Class B address?

   ○ **A.** 129.16.12.200

   ○ **B.** 126.15.16.122

   ○ **C.** 211.244.212.5

   ○ **D.** 193.17.101.27

3. You are the administrator for a network with two Windows Server systems and 65 Windows 7 systems. At 10 a.m., three users call to report that they are experiencing network connectivity problems. Upon investigation, you determine that the DHCP server has failed. How can you tell that the DHCP server failure is the cause of the connectivity problems experienced by the three users?

   ○ **A.** When you check their systems, they have an IP address of 0.0.0.0.

   ○ **B.** When you check their systems, they have an IP address in the 192.168.x.x address range.

   ○ **C.** When you check their systems, they have a default gateway value of 255.255.255.255.

   ○ **D.** When you check their systems, they have an IP address from the 169.254.x.x range.

4. Which of the following address types are associated with IPv6? (Choose three.)

   ○ **A.** Broadcast

   ○ **B.** Multicast

   ○ **C.** Unicast

   ○ **D.** Anycast

5. Which of the following IP addresses is not from a private address range?

   ○ **A.** 192.168.200.117

   ○ **B.** 172.16.3.204

   ○ **C.** 127.45.112.16

   ○ **D.** 10.27.100.143

6. You have been assigned to set up a new network with TCP/IP. For the external interfaces, you decide to obtain registered IP addresses from your ISP, but for the internal network, you choose to configure systems by using one of the private address ranges. Of the following address ranges, which one would you not consider?

   ○ **A.** 192.168.0.0 to 192.168.255.255

   ○ **B.** 131.16.0.0 to 131.16.255.255

   ○ **C.** 10.0.0.0 to 10.255.255.255

   ○ **D.** 172.16.0.0 to 172.31.255.255

7. You ask your ISP to assign a public IP address for the external interface of your Windows 2008 server, which is running a proxy server application. In the email message you get that contains the information, the ISP tells you that you have been assigned the IP address 203.15.226.12/24. When you fill out the subnet mask field on the IP configuration dialog box on your system, what subnet mask should you use?

   ○ **A.** 255.255.255.255

   ○ **B.** 255.255.255.0

   ○ **C.** 255.255.240.0

   ○ **D.** 255.255.255.240

8. Examine the diagram shown here. What is the most likely reason that user Spencer cannot communicate with user Evan?

   ○ **A.** The default gateways should have different values.

   ○ **B.** Spencer's IP address is not a loopback address.

   ○ **C.** The subnet values should be the same.

   ○ **D.** There is no problem identifiable by the values given.

User: Evan
IP address: 192.168.1.121
Subnet mask: 255.255.255.0
Default gateway: 192.168.1.1

User: Spencer
IP address: 192.168.1.127
Subnet mask: 255.255.248.0
Default gateway: 192.168.1.1

Cram Quiz Answers

1. **A** and **C.** The IPv4 address 127.0.0.1 is reserved as the loopback address, and IPv6 has the same reservation. IPv6 addresses 0:0:0:0:0:0:0:0 and 0:0:0:0:0:0:0:1 are reserved as the loopback addresses. The address 0:0:0:0:0:0:0:1 can be shown using the :: notation with the 0s removed, resulting in ::1.

2. **A.** Class B addresses fall into the range 128 to 191. Answer A is the only address listed that falls into that range. Answer B is a Class A address, and answers C and D are Class C IP addresses.

3. **D.** When a Windows 7 system that is configured to obtain an IP address via DHCP fails to obtain an address, it uses APIPA to assign itself an address from the 169.254.x.x address range. An address of 0.0.0.0 normally results from a system that does not support APIPA. APIPA does not use the 192.168.x.x address range. The IP address 255.255.255.255 is the broadcast address. A DHCP failure would not lead to a system assigning itself this address.

4. **B, C,** and **D.** A key difference between IPv4 and IPv6 is in the address types. IPv6 addressing has three main types of addresses: unicast, multicast, and any-cast. IPv4 uses broadcast addressing, but IPv6 doesn't.

5. **C.** The 127.x.x.x network range is reserved for the loopback function. It is not one of the recognized private address ranges. The private address ranges as defined in RFC 1918 are 10.x.x.x, 172.16.x.x to 172.31.x.x, and 192.168.x.x.

6. **B.** The 131.16 range is from the Class B range and is not one of the recognized private IP address ranges. All the other address ranges are valid private IP address ranges.

7. **B.** In CIDR terminology, the number of bits to be included in the subnet mask is expressed as a slash value. If the slash value is 24, the first three octets form the subnet mask, so the value is 255.255.255.0.

8. **C.** The most likely problem, given the IP values for each user's workstation, is that the subnet value is not correct on Spencer's machine and should be 255.255.255.0.

Understanding TCP/UDP Port Functions

▶ **Identify common TCP and UDP default ports.**

Cram**Saver**

If you can correctly answer these questions before going through this section, save time by skimming the Exam Alerts in this section and then complete the Cram Quiz at the end of the section.

1. What is the default port used by NTP?

2. True or False: Although FTP is a TCP-based protocol, TFTP uses UDP.

Answers

1. By default, NTP uses port 123.

2. True. Although FTP is a TCP-based protocol, TFTP uses UDP.

Each TCP/IP or application has a port associated with it. When a communication is received, the target port number is checked to determine which protocol or service it is destined for. The request is then forwarded to that protocol or service. For example, consider HTTP, whose assigned port number is 80. When a web browser forms a request for a web page, that request is sent to port 80 on the target system. When the target system receives the request, it examines the port number. When it sees that the port is 80, it forwards the request to the web server application.

TCP/IP has 65,535 ports available, with 0 to 1023 labeled as the well-known ports. Although a detailed understanding of the 65,535 ports is not necessary for the Network+ exam, you need to understand the numbers of some well-known ports. Network administration often requires you to specify port assignments when you work with applications and configuring services. Table 3.7 shows some of the most common port assignments.

Exam**Alert**

You should concentrate on the information provided in Table 3.7 and answer any port-related questions you might receive. The exam may present you with a situation in which you can't access a particular service; you may have to determine whether a port is open or closed on a firewall.

TABLE 3.7 **TCP/IP Port Assignments for Commonly Used Protocols**

Protocol	Port Assignment
TCP Ports	
FTP	20
FTP	21
SSH	22
Telnet	23
SMTP	25
DNS	53
HTTP	80
POP3	110
NNTP	119
NTP	123
IMAP4	143
HTTPS	443
RDP	3389
UDP Ports	
TFTP	69
DNS	53
DHCP (and BOOTP server)	67
DHCP (and BOOTP client)	68
SNMP	161
RDP	3389

ExamAlert

The term *well-known ports* identifies the ports ranging from 0 to 1023. When CompTIA says to "identify the well-known ports," this is what it refers to.

Note

You might have noticed in Table 3.7 that two ports are associated with FTP. Port 20 is considered the data port, whereas port 21 is considered the control port. In practical use, FTP connections use port 21. Port 20 is rarely used in modern implementations.

Cram Quiz

1. As the network administrator, you decide to block port 80. Which of the following services will be unavailable for network users?

   ○ **A.** DNS

   ○ **B.** POP3

   ○ **C.** FTP

   ○ **D.** HTTP

2. Which of the following is the most commonly used port for FTP in modern implementations?

   ○ **A.** 20

   ○ **B.** 21

   ○ **C.** 23

   ○ **D.** 27

Cram Quiz Answers

1. **D.** The HTTP service uses port 80, so blocking port 80 prevents users from using the HTTP service. Answer A is incorrect because DNS uses port 53. Answer B is incorrect because POP3 uses port 110. Answer C is incorrect because FTP uses port 21.

2. **B.** The most commonly used port for FTP in modern implementations is 21.

Managing TCP/IP Routing

▶ **Explain the purpose and properties of routing and switching.**

Cram**Saver**

If you can correctly answer these questions before going through this section, save time by skimming the Exam Alerts in this section and then complete the Cram Quiz at the end of the section.

   1. What are the most common distance-vector routing protocols?

   2. What are the most common link-state protocols?

   3. What is convergence?

Answers

   1. Distance-vector routing protocols include RIP, RIPv2, BGP, and EIGRP.

   2. Link-state protocols include OSPF and IS-IS.

   3. Convergence represents the time it takes routers to detect change on the network.

Because today's networks branch out between interconnected offices all over the world, networks may have any number of separate physical network segments connected using routers. Routers are devices that direct data between networks. Essentially, when a router receives data, it must determine the destination for the data and send it there. To accomplish this, the network router uses two key pieces of information: the gateway address and the routing tables.

The Default Gateway

A default gateway is the router's IP address, which is the pathway to any and all remote networks. To get a packet of information from one network to another, the packet is sent to the default gateway, which helps forward the packet to its destination network. Computers that live on the other side of routers are said to be on remote networks. Without default gateways, Internet communication is not possible because your computer doesn't have a way to send a packet destined for any other network. On the workstation, it is common for the default gateway option to be configured automatically through DHCP configuration.

Routing Tables

Before a data packet is forwarded, a chart is reviewed to determine the best possible path for the data to reach its destination. This chart is the computer's routing table. Maintaining an accurate routing table is essential for effective data delivery. Every computer on a TCP/IP network has a routing table stored locally. Figure 3.3 shows the routing table on a Windows 7 system.

> **Note**
>
> The route print command can be used to view the routing table on a client system.

As shown in Figure 3.3, the information in the routing table includes the following:

- ▸ **Destination**: The host IP address.

- ▸ **Network mask**: The subnet mask value for the destination parameter.

- ▸ **Gateway**: Where the IP address is sent. This may be a gateway server, router, or another system acting as a gateway.

- ▸ **Interface**: The address of the interface that's used to send the packet to the destination.

- ▸ **Metric**: A measurement of the directness of a route. The lower the metric, the faster the route. If multiple routes exist for data to travel, the one with the lowest metric is chosen.

Routing tables play an important role in the network routing process. They are the means by which the data is directed through the network. For this reason, a routing table needs to be two things. It must be up to date and complete. The router can get the information for the routing table in two ways: through static routing or dynamic routing.

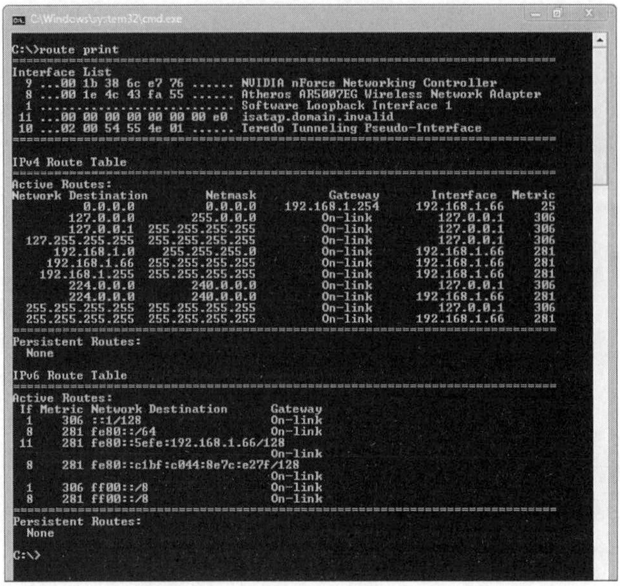

FIGURE 3.3 The routing table on a Windows 7 system.

Static Routing

In environments that use *static routing*, routes and route information are manually entered into the routing tables. Not only can this be a time-consuming task, but also errors are more common. In addition, when a change occurs to the network's layout, or topology, statically configured routers must be manually updated with the changes. Again, this is a time-consuming and potentially error-laden task. For these reasons, static routing is suited to only the smallest environments, with perhaps just one or two routers. A far more practical solution, particularly in larger environments, is to use dynamic routing.

You can add a static route to a routing table using the route add command. To do this, specify the route, the network mask, and the destination IP address of the network card your router will use to get the packet to its destination network.

The syntax for the route add command is as follows:

```
route add 192.168.2.1 mask (255.255.255.0) 192.168.2.4
```

Adding a static address is not permanent; in other words, it will most likely be gone when the system reboots. To make it persistent (the route is still in the routing table on boot), you can use the switch with the command.

> **Exam Alert**
>
> The `route add` command adds a static route to the routing table. The `route add` command with the `-p` switch makes the static route persistent. You may want to try this on your own before taking the Network+ exam.

Dynamic Routing

In a *dynamic routing* environment, routers use special routing protocols to communicate. The purpose of these protocols is simple: They enable routers to pass on information about themselves to other routers so that other routers can build routing tables. Two types of routing protocols are used: the older distance-vector protocols and the newer link-state protocols.

Distance-Vector Routing

With distance-vector router communications, each router on the network communicates all the routes it knows about to the routers to which it is directly attached. In this way, routers communicate only with their router neighbors and are unaware of other routers that may be on the network.

The communication between distance-vector routers is known as *hops*. On the network, each router represents one hop, so a network using six routers has five hops between the first and last router.

The `tracert` command is used in a Windows environment to see how many hops a packet takes to reach a destination. To try this at the command prompt, enter `tracert comptia.org`. Figure 3.4 shows an example of the output on a Windows 7 workstation.

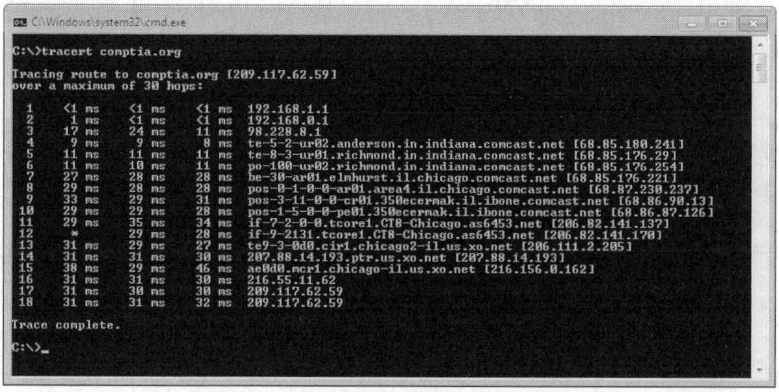

FIGURE 3.4   The results of running tracert on a Windows 7 system.

Several distance-vector protocols are in use today, including Routing Information Protocol (RIP and RIPv2), Enhanced Interior Gateway Routing Protocol (EIGRP), and Border Gateway Protocol (BGP):

▶ **RIP**: As mentioned, RIP is a distance-vector routing protocol. RIP is limited to a maximum of 15 hops. One of the downsides of the protocol is that the original specification required router updates to be transmitted every 30 seconds. On smaller networks this is acceptable; however, this can result in a huge traffic load on larger networks. The original RIP specification also did not support router authentication, leaving it vulnerable to attacks.

▶ **RIPv2**: The second version of RIP dealt with the shortcomings of the original design. Authentication was included to enable secure transmissions, also, it changed from a networkwide broadcast discovery method to a multicast method to reduce overall network traffic. However, to maintain compatibility with RIP, RIPv2 still supports a limit of 15 hops.

▶ **BGP**: A routing protocol often associated with the Internet. BGP can be used between gateway hosts on the Internet. BGP examines the routing table, which contains a list of known routers, the addresses they can reach, and a cost metric associated with the path to each router so that the best available route is chosen. BGP communicates between the routers using TCP.

▶ **EIGRP**: A protocol that enables routers to exchange information more efficiently than earlier network protocols. EIGRP uses its neighbors to help determine routing information. Routers configured to use EIGRP keep copies of their neighbors' routing information and query these tables to help find the best possible route for transmissions to follow. EIGRP uses Diffusing Update Algorithm (DUAL) to determine the best route to a destination.

> **ExamAlert**
>
> Be sure you can identify the differences between the distance-vector protocols discussed here.

Distance-vector routing protocols operate by having each router send updates about all the other routers it knows about to the routers directly connected to it. The routers use these updates to compile their routing tables. The updates are sent automatically every 30 or 60 seconds. The interval depends on the routing protocol used. Apart from the periodic updates, routers can also be configured to send a *triggered update* if a change in the network topology is detected. The process by which routers learn of a change in the network topology is called *convergence*.

Routing loops can occur on networks with slow convergence. Routing loops occur when the routing tables on the routers are slow to update and a redundant communication cycle is created between routers. Two strategies can combat potential routing loops:

- ▶ **Split horizon**: Works by preventing the router from advertising a route back to the other router from which it was learned. This prevents two nodes from bouncing packets back and forth between them, creating a loop.

- ▶ **Poison reverse (also called split horizon with poison reverse)**: Dictates that the route *is* advertised back on the interface from which it was learned, but it has a hop count of infinity, which tells the node that the route is unreachable.

ExamAlert

If a change in the routing is made, it takes some time for the routers to detect and accommodate this change. This is known as convergence.

Although distance-vector protocols can maintain routing tables, they have three problems:

- ▶ The periodic update system can make the update process slow.

- ▶ The periodic updates can create large amounts of network traffic—much of the time unnecessarily, because the network's topology should rarely change.

- ▶ Perhaps the most significant problem is that because the routers know about only the next hop in the journey, incorrect information can be propagated between routers, creating routing loops.

ExamAlert

Know that "next hop" in routing is the next closest router that a packet can go through.

Link-State Routing

A router that uses a link-state protocol differs from a router that uses a distance-vector protocol because it builds a map of the entire network and then holds that map in memory. On a network that uses a link-state protocol, routers send link-state advertisements (LSAs) that contain information about the networks to which they connect. The LSAs are sent to every router on the network, thus enabling the routers to build their network maps.

When the network maps on each router are complete, the routers update each other at a given time, just like with a distance-vector protocol; however, the updates occur much less frequently with link-state protocols than with distance-vector protocols. The only other circumstance under which updates are sent is if a change in the topology is detected, at which point the routers use LSAs to detect the change and update their routing tables. This mechanism, combined with the fact that routers hold maps of the entire network, makes convergence on a link-state-based network quickly occur.

Although it might seem like link-state protocols are an obvious choice over distance-vector protocols, routers on a link-state-based network require more powerful hardware and more RAM than those on a distance-vector-based network. Not only do the routing tables need to be calculated, but they must also be stored. A router that uses distance-vector protocols need only maintain a small database of the routes accessible by the routers to which it is directly connected. A router that uses link-state protocols must maintain a database of all the routers in the entire network.

Link-state protocols include the following:

▶ **Open Shortest Path First (OSPF)**: A link-state routing protocol based on the SPF (Shortest Path First) algorithm to find the least-cost path to any destination in the network. In operation, each router using OSPF sends a list of its neighbors to other routers on the network. From this information, routers can determine the network design and the shortest path for data to travel.

▶ **Intermediate System-to-Intermediate System (IS-IS)**: A link-state protocol that discovers the shortest path for data to travel using the shortest path first (SPF) algorithm. IS-IS routers distribute topology information to other routers, enabling them to make the best path decisions.

So what's the difference between the two? OSPF (a network layer protocol) is more often used in medium to large enterprise networks because of its special tunneling features. IS-IS is more often used in large ISP networks because of its stability features and that it can support more routers.

IGP Versus EGP

Now that routing protocols have been discussed, you need to understand the difference between Interior Gateway Protocols (IGPs) and Exterior Gateway Protocols (EGPs). An IGP identifies the protocols used to exchange routing information between routers within a LAN or interconnected LANs. IGP is not a protocol itself but describes a category of link-state routing protocols that support a single, confined geographic area such as a LAN. IGPs fall into two categories: distance-vector protocols, which include RIP and IGRP, and link-state protocols, which include OSPF and IS-IS.

Whereas IGPs are geographically confined, EGPs are used to route information outside the network, such as on the Internet. On the Internet, an EGP is required. An EGP is a distance-vector protocol commonly used between hosts on the Internet to exchange routing table information. BGP is an example of an EGP.

ExamAlert

Be prepared to identify both the link-state and distance-vector routing protocols used on TCP/IP networks.

Routing Metrics

Following are a number of metrics related to routing that you should know for the exam:

- ▶ *Hop counts* are the number of hops necessary to reach a node. A hop count of infinity means the route is unreachable.

- ▶ The *Maximum Transmission Unit (MTU)* defines the largest data unit that can be passed without fragmentation.

- ▶ *Bandwidth* specifies the maximum packet size permitted for Internet transmission.

- ▶ *Costs* are the numbers associated with traveling from point A to point B (often hops). The lower the total costs (the less links in the route), the more that route should be favored.

- ▶ *Latency* is the amount of time it takes for a packet to travel from one location to another.

Cram Quiz

1. Which of the following best describes the function of the default gateway?

   ○ **A.** It provides the route for destinations outside the local network.

   ○ **B.** It enables a single Internet connection to be used by several users.

   ○ **C.** It identifies the local subnet and formulates a routing table.

   ○ **D.** It is used to communicate in a multiple-platform environment.

2. What is the term used for the number of hops necessary to reach a node?

   ○ **A.** Jump list

   ○ **B.** Link stops

   ○ **C.** Connections

   ○ **D.** Hop count

Cram Quiz Answers

1. **A.** The default gateway enables systems on one local subnet to access those on another. Answer B does not accurately describe the role of the default gateway. Answers C and D don't describe the main function of a default gateway, which is to provide the route for destinations outside the local network.

2. **D.** The hop count is the number of hops necessary to reach a node.

Configuring Routers and Switches

▶ **Given a scenario, install and configure routers and switches.**

The next chapter focuses on actual hardware components of a network, but the reason for the hardware is to carry out the operations discussed in this chapter. This section looks at a few of the more advanced features that routers and switches perform.

Power over Ethernet (PoE)

The purpose of Power over Ethernet (PoE) is pretty much described in its name. Essentially, PoE is a technology that enables electrical power to transmit over twisted-pair Ethernet cable. The power transfers, along with data, to provide power to remote devices. These devices may include remote switches, wireless access points, voice over IP (VoIP) equipment, and more.

One of the key advantages of PoE is the centralized management of power. For instance, without PoE, all remote devices need to be independently powered. In the case of a power outage, each of these devices requires an uninterruptible power supply (UPS) to continue operating. A UPS is a battery pack that enables devices to operate for a period of time. With PoE supplying power, a UPS is required only in the main facility. In addition, centralized power management enables administrators to power up or down remote equipment.

> **Note**
>
> VLAN and spanning tree were outlined in the CompTIA objectives for this chapter. Spanning tree is covered next. VLANs are discussed in Chapter 1, "Introduction to Networking."

The Spanning Tree Protocol (STP)

An Ethernet network can have only a single active path between devices on a network. When multiple active paths are available, switching loops can occur. Switching loops are simply the result of having more than one path between two switches in a network. Spanning Tree Protocol (STP) is designed to prevent these loops from occurring.

STP is used with network bridges and switches. With the help of Spanning Tree Algorithm (STA), STP avoids or eliminates loops on a Layer 2 bridge.

> **Note**
>
> As a heads-up, talking about STP refers to Layer 2 of the OSI model. Both bridges and switches work at Layer 2. Routers work at Layer 3.

STA enables a bridge or switch to dynamically work around loops in a network's topology. Both STA and STP were developed to prevent loops in the network and provide a way to route around any failed network bridge or ports. If the network topology changes, or if a switch port or bridge fails, STA creates a new spanning tree, notifies the other bridges of the problem, and routes around it. STP is the protocol, and STA is the algorithm STP uses to correct loops.

If a particular port has a problem, STP can perform a number of actions, including blocking the port, disabling the port, or forwarding data destined for that port to another port. It does this to ensure that no redundant links or paths are found in the spanning tree and that only a single active path exists between any two network nodes.

STP uses bridge protocol data units (BPDUs) to identify the status of ports and bridges across the network. BPDUs are simple data messages exchanged between switches. BPDUs contain information on ports and provide the status of those ports to other switches. If a BPDU message finds a loop in the network, it is managed by shutting down a particular port or bridge interface.

Redundant paths and potential loops can be avoided within ports in several ways:

- ▶ **Blocking**: A blocked port accepts BPDU messages but does not forward them.

- ▶ **Disabled**: The port is offline and does not accept BPDU messages.

- ▶ **Forwarding**: The port is part of the active spanning tree topology and forwards BPDU messages to other switches.

- ▶ **Learning**: In a learning state, the port is not part of the active spanning tree topology but can take over if another port fails. Learning ports receive BPDUs and identify changes to the topology when made.

- ▶ **Listening**: A listening port receives BPDU messages and monitors for changes to the network topology.

Most of the time, ports are in either a forwarding or blocked state. When a disruption to the topology occurs or a bridge or switch fails for some reason, listening and learning states are used.

ExamAlert

STP actively monitors the network, searching for redundant links. When it finds some, it shuts them down to prevent switching loops. STP uses STA to create a topology database to find and then remove the redundant links. With STP operating from the switch, data is forwarded on approved paths, which limits the potential for loops.

Trunking

In computer networking, the term *trunking* refers to the use of multiple network cables or ports in parallel to increase the link speed beyond the limits of any one cable or port. Sound confusing? If you have network experience, you might have heard the term *link aggregation*, which is essentially the same thing. It is just using multiple cables to increase the throughput. The higher-capacity trunking link is used to connect switches to form larger networks.

VLAN trunking—or *VLAN (trunking)*, as CompTIA lists it—is the application of trunking to the virtual LAN—now common with routers, firewalls, VMWare hosts, and wireless access points. VLAN trunking provides a simple and cheap way to offer a nearly unlimited number of virtual network connections. The requirements are only that the switch, the network adapter, and the OS drivers all support VLANs. The *VLAN Trunking Protocol (VTP)* is a proprietary protocol from Cisco for just such a purpose.

Port Mirroring

You need some way to monitor network traffic and monitor how well a switch works. This is the function of port mirroring. To use port mirroring, administrators configure a copy of all inbound and outbound traffic to go to a certain port. A protocol analyzer examines the data sent to the port and therefore does not interrupt the flow of regular traffic.

> **ExamAlert**
>
> Port mirroring enables administrators to monitor the traffic outbound and inbound to the switch.

Port Authentication

Port authentication is what it sounds like—authenticating users on a port-by-port basis. One standard that specifies port authentication is the 802.1X standard, often associated with wireless security. Systems that attempt to connect to a LAN port must be authenticated. Those who are authenticated can access the LAN; those who are not authenticated get no further. Chapter 10 provides more information on the 802.1X standard and port authentication.

Cram Quiz

1. Port mirroring enables administrators to monitor which traffic to the switch?

   ○ **A.** Inbound only

   ○ **B.** Outbound only

   ○ **C.** Inbound and outbound

   ○ **D.** Neither inbound nor outbound

2. Which of the following is NOT used to avoid redundant paths and potential loops within ports?

   ○ **A.** Blocking

   ○ **B.** Learning

   ○ **C.** Forwarding

   ○ **D.** Jamming

Cram Quiz Answers

1. **C.** Port mirroring enables administrators to monitor the traffic outbound and inbound to the switch.

2. **D.** The common methods to avoid redundant paths and potential loops within ports include blocking, disabled, forwarding, learning, and listening. Jamming is not one of the methods employed.

What Next?

Chapter 4, "Components and Devices," introduces you to commonly used networking devices. All but the most basic of networks require devices to provide connectivity and functionality. Understanding how these networking devices operate and identifying the functions they perform are essential skills for any network administrator and are requirements for a Network+ candidate.

CHAPTER 4

Components and Devices

This chapter covers the following official Network+ objectives:

▶ Classify how applications, devices, and protocols relate to the OSI model layers.

▶ Identify virtual network components.

▶ Explain the purpose and features of various network appliances.

This chapter covers CompTIA Network+ objectives 1.2, 1.9, and 4.1 For more information on the official Network+ exam topics, see the "About the Network+ Exam" section in the "Introduction."

All but the most basic of networks require devices to provide connectivity and functionality. Understanding how these networking devices operate and identifying the functions they perform are essential skills for any network administrator and are requirements for a Network+ candidate.

This chapter introduces commonly used networking devices. Though you are not likely to encounter all the devices mentioned in this chapter on the exam, you can expect to work with at least some of them.

Common Network Devices

▶ **Classify how applications, devices, and protocols relate to the OSI model layers.**

Cram**Saver**

If you can correctly answer these questions before going through this section, save time by skimming the Exam Alerts in this section and then complete the Cram Quiz at the end of the section.

1. What is the difference between an active and passive hub?
2. What is the major difference between a hub and a switch?
3. What are the types of ports found on hubs and switches?

Answers

1. Hubs can be either active or passive. Hubs are considered active when they regenerate a signal before forwarding it to all the ports on the device.
2. Rather than forwarding data to all the connected ports, a switch forwards data only to the port on which the destination system is connected.
3. Hubs and switches have two types of ports: Medium-Dependent Interface (MDI) and Medium-Dependent Interface Crossed (MDI-X).

The best way to think about this chapter is as a catalog of networking devices. The first half looks at devices that you can commonly find in a network of any substantial size. The devices are discussed in alphabetical order to simplify study and include everything from bridges to wireless access points.

Bridges

Bridges are used to divide larger networks into smaller sections. Bridges accomplish this by sitting between two physical network segments and managing the flow of data between the two. By looking at the MAC address of the devices connected to each segment, bridges can elect to forward the data (if they believe that the destination address is on another interface) or block it from crossing (if they can verify that it is on the interface from which it came). Figure 4.1 shows how a bridge can be used to segregate a network.

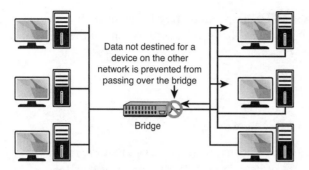

FIGURE 4.1   **How a bridge is used to segregate a network.**

> **Note**
>
> Bridges can also be used to connect two physical LANs into a larger logical LAN.

When bridges were introduced, the MAC addresses of the devices on the connected networks had to be manually entered. This was a time-consuming process that had plenty of opportunity for error. Today, almost all bridges can build a list of the MAC addresses on an interface by watching the traffic on the network. Such devices are called *learning bridges* because of this functionality.

> **Note**
>
> The last 64 bits of an IPv6 address are known as *EUI-64* (Extended Unique Identifier, 64-bit) and are derived from the MAC address. There is a formula for converting a 48-bit MAC address into a 64-bit EUI-64 format, but you do not need to know it for the Network+ exam.

Bridge Placement and Eliminating Bridging Loops

You must consider two issues when using bridges:

- ▶ **Bridge placement**: Bridges should be positioned in the network using the 80/20 rule. This rule dictates that 80% of the data should be local and the other 20% should be destined for devices on the other side of the bridge.

- ▶ **Eliminating bridging loops**: Bridging loops can occur when more than one bridge is implemented on the network. In this scenario, the bridges can confuse each other by leading one another to believe that a device is located on a certain segment when it is not. To combat the bridging loop problem, the IEEE 802.1d Spanning Tree Protocol enables bridge interfaces to be assigned a value that is then used to control the bridge-learning process.

Types of Bridges

Three types of bridges are used in networks:

▶ **Transparent bridge**: Derives its name from the fact that the devices on the network are unaware of its existence. A transparent bridge does nothing except block or forward data based on the MAC address.

▶ **Source route bridge**: Used in token ring networks. The source route bridge derives its name from the fact that the entire path that the packet is to take through the network is embedded in the packet.

▶ **Translational bridge**: Used to convert one networking data format to another, such as from token ring to Ethernet and vice versa.

Exam Alert

Today, bridges are falling out of favor. Ethernet switches offer similar functionality; they can provide logical divisions, or segments, in the network. Switches are sometimes called *multiport bridges* because of how they operate.

As discussed in Chapter 2, "OSI and TCP/IP Models and Network Protocols," the term *frame* is used to describe the logical grouping of data at the data link layer. A bridge works at Layer 2 (the data link layer) of the OSI model.

DHCP Server

Without question, the easiest way to assign TCP/IP information to client systems is to use a Dynamic Host Configuration Protocol (DHCP) server. On a network running TCP/IP, each computer must have a unique IP address to be recognized and be part of the network. Briefly, a *protocol* is a method to communicate between computers.

Computers on a network using TCP/IP require specific network settings to connect to the network. First among these settings is the IP address. An IP address consists of four *octets*, or four sets of 8 bits—for example, 192.168.2.1. Each computer on the network must have one of these numbers to perform network functions through TCP/IP. The number must be unique to the PC and must be within a certain range to allow the PC to connect to other systems.

There was a time when these IP addresses were entered manually into the network settings of each client workstation. Manually set, or static, IP addresses were difficult to maintain in large networks. Adding to the time it takes to individually set the IP addresses is that each address must be unique. Duplicate IP addresses will prevent a successful connection to the network, meaning that all network services will be unavailable to the workstations with the duplicate addresses. When you set static IP addresses, it is essential to carefully track assigned IP addresses to prevent duplicating addresses and to make future expansion and troubleshooting easier.

In larger networks, the assignment of manual addresses can be a nightmare, especially when IP addressing schemes can be changed and computers can be moved, retired, or replaced. That's where DHCP comes in. DHCP assigns IP addresses, eliminating the need to individually assign IP addresses and making the job of network administrators considerably easier. When a DHCP server runs on a network, the workstation boots up and requests an IP address from the server. The server responds to the request and automatically assigns an IP address to the computer for a given period of time, known as a *lease*. The workstation acknowledges the receipt of the IP address, and the workstation has all the information it needs to become part of the network. This communication between the server and the workstation happens completely automatically and is invisible to the computer user.

Because of their capability to efficiently distribute IP addresses to network workstations, DHCP servers are widely used in client/server environments. People working with networks will most certainly encounter DHCP servers. The critical nature of DHCP services means that companies often choose to run more than one DHCP server. Mechanisms built in to DHCP enable this to happen.

> ### Exam**Alert**
>
> Be prepared to identify the role of a DHCP server for the exam.

Firewalls

A *firewall* is a networking device, either hardware- or software-based, that controls access to your organization's network. This controlled access is designed to protect data and resources from an outside threat. To do this, firewalls typically are placed at a network's entry/exit points—for example, between an internal network and the Internet. After it is in place, a firewall can control access into and out of that point.

Although firewalls typically protect internal networks from public networks, they are also used to control access between specific network segments within a network. An example is placing a firewall between the Accounts and Sales departments.

As mentioned, firewalls can be implemented through software or through a dedicated hardware device. Organizations implement software firewalls through network operating systems (NOSs) such as Linux/UNIX, Windows servers, and Mac OS servers. The firewall is configured on the server to allow or block certain types of network traffic. In small offices and for regular home use, a firewall is commonly installed on the local system and is configured to control traffic. Many third-party firewalls are available.

Hardware firewalls are used in networks of all sizes today. Hardware firewalls are often dedicated network devices that can be implemented with little configuration. They protect all systems behind the firewall from outside sources. Hardware firewalls are readily available and often are combined with other devices today. For example, many broadband routers and wireless access points have firewall functionality built in. In such a case, the router or AP might have a number of ports available to plug systems into.

> **ExamAlert**
>
> Remember that a firewall can protect internal networks from public networks and control access between specific network segments.

> **Note**
>
> Firewalls are discussed in greater detail in Chapter 10, "Network Security."

Hubs

At the bottom of the networking food chain, so to speak, are hubs. Hubs are used in networks that use twisted-pair cabling to connect devices. Hubs also can be joined to create larger networks. *Hubs* are simple devices that direct data packets to all devices connected to the hub, regardless of whether the data package is destined for the device. This makes them inefficient devices and can create a performance bottleneck on busy networks.

In its most basic form, a hub does nothing except provide a pathway for the electrical signals to travel along. Such a device is called a *passive* hub. Far more common nowadays is an *active* hub, which, as well as providing a path for the data signals, regenerates the signal before it forwards it to all the connected devices. In addition, an active hub can buffer data before forwarding it. However, a hub does not perform any processing on the data it forwards, nor does it perform any error checking.

Hubs come in a variety of shapes and sizes. Small hubs with five or eight connection ports are commonly called *workgroup hubs*. Others can accommodate larger numbers of devices (normally up to 32). These are called *high-density devices*.

> ### ExamAlert
> Because hubs don't perform any processing, they do little except enable communication between connected devices. For today's high-demand network applications, something with a little more intelligence is required. That's where switches come in.

A bridge works at Layer 1 (the physical layer) of the OSI model.

Media Converters

Network technologies change rapidly, and administrators are always on the lookout for cost-effective ways to increase network performance. The demand for higher speeds and greater distances keeps administrators on their toes. The process to incorporate new technology with older infrastructure is made easier with media converters.

Network media converters are used to interconnect different types of cables within an existing network. For example, the media converter can be used to connect newer Gigabit Ethernet technologies with older 100BaseT networks.

The ability to combine networks and increase networking flexibility while decreasing the cost of having to retrofit the network to accommodate new technology is important. Converters come in many shapes and sizes to connect to a variety of networks. This includes coax, twisted-pair, single mode, and multimode fiber. Converters can be designed to work with any network type, including Ethernet, Fast Ethernet, Gigabit Ethernet, Asynchronous Transfer Mode (ATM), Fiber Distributed Data Interface (FDDI), and token ring.

> **ExamAlert**
>
> Using media converters, companies do not need to dismantle the current wiring infrastructures. Media converters enable you to use existing infrastructure while keeping pace with changing technologies.

Modems

A *modem*, short for modulator/demodulator, is a device that converts the digital signals generated by a computer into analog signals that can travel over conventional phone lines. The modem at the receiving end converts the signal back into a format that the computer can understand. Modems can be used as a means to connect to an ISP or as a mechanism for dialing up a LAN.

Modems can be internal add-in expansion cards or integrated with the motherboard, external devices that connect to a system's serial or USB port, or proprietary devices designed for use on other devices, such as portables and handhelds.

Network Cards

A network card, also called a network interface card (NIC), is a device that enables a computer to connect to the network.

When specifying or installing a NIC, you must consider the following issues:

▶ **System bus compatibility**: If the network interface you are installing is an internal device, bus compatibility must be verified. The most common bus system in use is the Peripheral Component Interconnect Express (PCIe) bus, but some older systems might still use PCI or Industry Standard Architecture (ISA) expansion cards.

▶ **System resources**: Network cards, like other devices, need Interrupt Request (IRQ) and memory I/O addresses. If the network card does not correctly operate after installation, there might be a device conflict.

▶ **Media compatibility**: Today, the assumption is that networks use twisted-pair cabling, so if you need a card for coaxial or fiber-optic connections, you must specify this. Wireless network cards are also available.

Types of Network Interfaces

Network interfaces come as add-in expansion cards or as ExpressCards used with laptop systems. In some cases, rather than having an add-in NIC, the network interface is embedded into the motherboard.

A network interface typically has at least two LEDs that indicate certain conditions:

> ▶ **Link light**: This LED indicates whether a network connection exists between the card and the network. An unlit link light indicates that something is awry with the network cable or connection.

> ▶ **Activity light**: This LED indicates network activity. Under normal conditions, the light should flicker sporadically and often. Constant flickering might indicate a busy network or a problem somewhere on the network that is worth investigating.

> ▶ **Speed light**: This LED indicates that the interface is connected at a certain speed. This feature normally is found on Ethernet NICs that operate at 10Mbps/100Mbps/1000Mbps—and then only on certain cards.

Some network cards combine the functions of certain lights by using dual-color LEDs. ExpressCards sometimes have no lights, or the lights are incorporated into the media adapter that comes with the card.

Installing Network Cards

At some point in your networking career, it is likely that you will have to install a NIC into a system. For that reason, an understanding of the procedures and considerations related to NIC installations is useful. The following are some of the main points to consider.

> **ExamAlert**
>
> When installing any component in a system, you need to observe proper and correct procedures to guard against electrostatic discharge (ESD). ESD can cause components to immediately fail or degrade and fail at some point in the future. Proper ESD precautions include wearing an antistatic wrist strap and properly grounding yourself.

▶ **Drivers**: Almost every NIC is supplied with a driver disc, but the likelihood of the drivers on the disk being the latest drivers is slim. A device driver is software that enables communication between the hardware and the operating system. All hardware devices require device drivers to function. Always make sure that you have the latest drivers by visiting the website of the NIC manufacturer. The drivers play an important role in the correct functioning of the NIC, so spend a few extra minutes making sure the drivers are correctly installed and configured.

▶ **NIC configuration utilities**: In days gone by, NICs were configured with small groups of pins known as *jumpers*, or with small plastic blocks of switches known as *dip switches*. Unless you are working with old equipment, you are unlikely to encounter dip switches.

Although these methods were efficient and easy to use, they have largely been abandoned in favor of software configuration utilities. These allow you to configure the card's settings (if any) and to test whether the card is properly working. Other utilities can be used through the operating system to obtain statistical information, help, and a range of other features.

▶ **System resources**: To function correctly, NICs must have certain system resources allocated to them: the interrupt request (IRQ) and memory addresses. In some cases, you might need to manually assign the values for these. In most cases, you can rely on plug-and-play, which automatically assigns resources for devices.

▶ **Physical slot availability**: Most modern PCs have at least three or four usable expansion slots. Not only that, but the increasing trend toward component integration on the motherboard means that devices such as serial and parallel ports and sound cards are now built in to the system board and therefore don't use up valuable slots. If you work on older systems or systems that have a lot of add-in hardware, you might be short of slots. Check to make sure that a slot is available before you begin.

▶ **Built-in network interfaces**: A built-in network interface is a double-edged sword. The upsides are that it doesn't occupy an expansion slot, and hardware compatibility with the rest of the system is almost guaranteed. The downside is that a built-in component cannot be upgraded. For this reason, you might install an add-in NIC and at the same time disable the onboard network interface. Disabling the onboard interface normally is a straightforward process; you go into the BIOS setup screen or, on some systems, use a system configuration utility. In either case, consult the documentation that came with the system, or look for information on the manufacturer's website.

As time goes on, NIC and operating system manufacturers are making it increasingly easy to install NICs in systems of all sorts and sizes. By understanding the card's requirements and the correct installation procedure, you should simply and efficiently install cards. A network card works at Layer 2 (the data link layer) of the OSI model.

Routers

In a common configuration, routers create larger networks by joining two network segments. A small office, home office (SOHO) router connects a user to the Internet. A SOHO router typically serves 1 to 10 users on the system. A router can be a dedicated hardware device or a computer system with more than one network interface and the appropriate routing software. All modern network operating systems include the functionality to act as a router.

> **Note**
>
> Routers normally create, add, or divide networks or network segments at the network layer of the OSI reference model because they normally are IP-based devices. Chapter 2 covers the OSI reference model in greater detail.

A router derives its name from the fact that it can route data it receives from one network to another. When a router receives a packet of data, it reads the packet's header to determine the destination address. After the router has determined the address, it looks in its routing table to determine whether it knows how to reach the destination; if it does, it forwards the packet to the next hop on the route. The next hop might be the final destination, or it might be another router. Figure 4.2 shows, in basic terms, how a router works.

> **Note**
>
> You can find more information on network routing in Chapter 3, "Addressing and Routing."

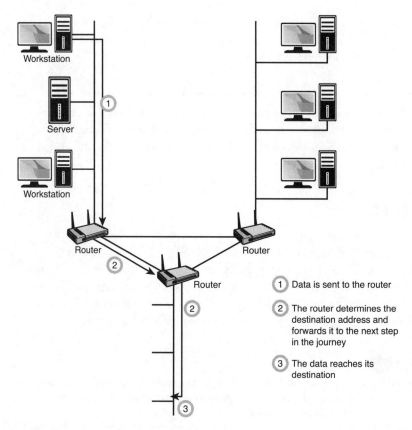

FIGURE 4.2　**How a router works.**

A router works at Layer 3 (the network layer) of the OSI model.

Switches

Like hubs, *switches* are the connectivity points of an Ethernet network. Devices connect to switches via twisted-pair cabling, one cable for each device. The difference between hubs and switches is in how the devices deal with the data they receive. Whereas a hub forwards the data it receives to all the ports on the device, a switch forwards it to only the port that connects to the destination device. It does this by *learning* the MAC address of the devices attached to it and then by matching the destination MAC address in the data it receives. Figure 4.3 shows how a switch works. In this case, it has learned the MAC addresses of the devices attached to it; when the workstation sends a message intended for another workstation, it forwards the message on and ignores all the other workstations.

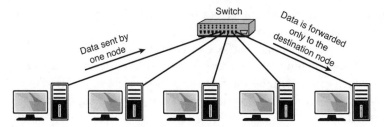

FIGURE 4.3 **How a switch works.**

By forwarding data to only the connection that should receive it, the switch can greatly improve network performance. By creating a direct path between two devices and controlling their communication, the switch can greatly reduce the traffic on the network and therefore the number of collisions. As you might recall, collisions occur on Ethernet networks when two devices attempt to transmit at exactly the same time. In addition, the lack of collisions enables switches to communicate with devices in full-duplex mode. In a full-duplex configuration, devices can send data to and receive data from the switch at the same time. Contrast this with half-duplex communication, in which communication can occur in only one direction at a time. Full-duplex transmission speeds are double that of a standard half-duplex connection. So, a 100Mbps connection becomes 200Mbps, and a 1000Mbps connection becomes 2000Mbps.

The net result of these measures is that switches can offer significant performance improvements over hub-based networks, particularly when network use is high.

Irrespective of whether a connection is at full or half duplex, the method of switching dictates how the switch deals with the data it receives. The following is a brief explanation of each method:

> **Cut-through**: In a cut-through switching environment, the packet begins to be forwarded as soon as it is received. This method is fast, but it creates the possibility of errors being propagated through the network, because no error checking occurs.

> **Store-and-forward**: Unlike cut-through, in a store-and-forward switching environment, the entire packet is received and error-checked before being forwarded. The upside of this method is that errors are not propagated through the network. The downside is that the error-checking process takes a relatively long time, and store-and-forward switching is considerably slower as a result.

▸ **FragmentFree**: To take advantage of the error checking of store-and-forward switching, but still offer performance levels nearing that of cut-through switching, FragmentFree switching can be used. In a FragmentFree-switching environment, enough of the packet is read so that the switch can determine whether the packet has been involved in a collision. As soon as the collision status has been determined, the packet is forwarded.

Hub and Switch Cabling

In addition to acting as a connection point for network devices, hubs and switches can be connected to create larger networks. This connection can be achieved through standard ports with a special cable or by using special ports with a standard cable.

The ports on a hub to which computer systems are attached are called *Medium-Dependent Interface Crossed (MDI-X)*. The crossed designation is derived from the fact that two of the wires within the connection are crossed so that the send signal wire on one device becomes the receive signal of the other. Because the ports are crossed internally, a standard or *straight-through* cable can be used to connect devices.

Another type of port, called a *Medium-Dependent Interface (MDI)* port, is often included on a hub or switch to facilitate the connection of two switches or hubs. Because the hubs or switches are designed to see each other as simply an extension of the network, there is no need for the signal to be crossed. If a hub or switch does not have an MDI port, hubs or switches can be connected by using a *crossover* cable between two MDI-X ports. The crossover cable uncrosses the internal crossing. Crossover cables are discussed in Chapter 6, "Cabling and Wiring."

> **ExamAlert**
>
> In a crossover cable, wires 1 and 3 and wires 2 and 6 are crossed.

A switch can work at either Layer 2 (the data link layer) or Layer 3 (the network layer) of the OSI model.

Wireless Access Points

Wireless access points (APs) are a transmitter and receiver (transceiver) device used to create a wireless LAN (WLAN). APs typically are a separate network device with a built-in antenna, transmitter, and adapter. APs use the wireless infrastructure network mode to provide a connection point between WLANs and a wired Ethernet LAN. APs also typically have several ports, giving you a way to expand the network to support additional clients.

Depending on the size of the network, one or more APs might be required. Additional APs are used to allow access to more wireless clients and to expand the range of the wireless network. Each AP is limited by a transmission range—the distance a client can be from an AP and still obtain a usable signal. The actual distance depends on the wireless standard used and the obstructions and environmental conditions between the client and the AP.

> **ExamAlert**
>
> An AP can operate as a bridge connecting a standard wired network to wireless devices or as a router passing data transmissions from one access point to another.

Saying that an AP is used to extend a wired LAN to wireless clients doesn't give you the complete picture. A wireless AP today can provide different services in addition to just an access point. Today, the APs might provide many ports that can be used to easily increase the network's size. Systems can be added to and removed from the network with no effect on other systems on the network. Also, many APs provide firewall capabilities and DHCP service. When they are hooked up, they give client systems a private IP address and then prevent Internet traffic from accessing those systems. So, in effect, the AP is a switch, DHCP server, router, and firewall.

APs come in all different shapes and sizes. Many are cheaper and designed strictly for home or small-office use. Such APs have low-powered antennas and limited expansion ports. Higher-end APs used for commercial purposes have high-powered antennas, enabling them to extend how far the wireless signal can travel.

> **Note**
>
> APs are used to create a wireless LAN and to extend a wired network. APs are used in the infrastructure wireless topology. Chapter 1, "Introduction to Networking," discusses wireless topologies.

An access point works at Layer 2 (the data link layer) of the OSI model.

Encryption Devices

The term *encryption devices* is used to loosely encompass any device capable of encrypting data for the purpose of making it more difficult to intercept. On the lower end, this can encompass devices used by individual users (encrypted flash drives, for example). On the higher end, a server can encrypt data for the network.

ExamAlert

Because the Network+ exam focuses on networking and the objective focuses on the OSI model, the presentation layer is responsible for encrypting/decrypting data sent across the network.

Cram Quiz

1. Users are complaining that the network's performance is unsatisfactory. It takes a long time to pull files from the server, and, under heavy loads, workstations can become disconnected from the server. The network is heavily used, and a new videoconferencing application is about to be installed. The network is a 1000BaseT system created with Ethernet hubs. Which device are you most likely to install to alleviate the performance problems?

   ○ **A.** Switch

   ○ **B.** Router

   ○ **C.** Bridge

   ○ **D.** Gateway

2. Which of the following devices forwards data packets to all connected ports?

   ○ **A.** Router

   ○ **B.** Switch

   ○ **C.** Bridge

   ○ **D.** Hub

3. Of the following routing methods, which is likely to require the most administration time in the long term?

   ○ **A.** Static

   ○ **B.** Link state

   ○ **C.** Distance vector

   ○ **D.** Dynamic

4. Which of the following statements best describes a gateway?

   ○ **A.** It is a device that enables data to be routed from one network to another.

   ○ **B.** It refers to any device that resides at the entrance of a network.

   ○ **C.** It is a device, system, or application that translates data from one format into another.

   ○ **D.** It is a network device that can forward or block data based on the MAC address embedded in the packet.

5. You are experiencing performance problems on your Ethernet-based network. By using a network performance-monitoring tool, you determine that the network has a large number of collisions. To reduce the collisions, you decide to install a network bridge. What kind of bridge are you most likely to implement?

- ○ **A.** Collision bridge
- ○ **B.** Transparent bridge
- ○ **C.** Visible bridge
- ○ **D.** Translational bridge

Cram Quiz Answers

1. **A.** Replacing Ethernet hubs with switches can yield significant performance improvements. Of the devices listed, switches are also the only ones that can be substituted for hubs. A router is used to separate networks, not as a connectivity point for workstations. A bridge could be used to segregate the network and therefore improve performance, but a switch is a more obvious choice in this example. A gateway is a device, system, or application that translates data from one format into another.

2. **D.** Hubs are inefficient devices that send data packets to all connected devices. Switches pass data packets to the specific destination device. This method significantly increases network performance.

3. **A.** Static routing takes more time to administer in the long term because any changes to the network routing table must be manually entered. Distance vector and link state are both dynamic routing methods. Dynamic routing might take more time to configure initially, but in the long term, it requires less administration time. It can automatically adapt to changes in the network layout.

4. **C.** A gateway can be a device, system, or application that translates data from one format into another. Answers A and B more closely describe a router. Answer D describes a bridge. A bridge is a device that is used to segregate a network. It makes forwarding or blocking decisions based on the MAC address embedded in the packet.

5. **B.** A transparent bridge can be used to segment a network, reducing the number of collisions and overall network traffic. It is called transparent because the other devices on the network do not need to be aware of the device and operate as if it weren't there. A translational bridge is used in environments where it is necessary to translate one data format into another. Such a conversion is unnecessary in this scenario. There is no such thing as a collision bridge or a visible bridge.

Specialized Network Devices

▶ **Explain the purpose and features of various network appliances.**

Cram**Saver**

If you can correctly answer these questions before going through this section, save time by skimming the Exam Alerts in this section and then complete the Cram Quiz at the end of the section.

1. What acts as a translator between the LAN and WAN data formats?

2. What is the term that describes the mechanisms used to control bandwidth usage on the network?

3. True or False: A load balancer must be a hardware device specially configured to balance the load.

Answers

1. A CSU/DSU acts as a translator between the LAN and WAN data formats.

2. Bandwidth shaping describes the mechanisms used to control bandwidth usage on the network.

3. False. A load balancer can be either a hardware device or software specially configured to balance the load.

Any network is composed of many different pieces of hardware. Some, such as firewalls and DHCP servers, are in most networks. Other devices are more specialized and are not found in every network environment. CompTIA includes the following as specialized networking devices (in alphabetical order):

▶ Bandwidth shaper

▶ Content filter

▶ Load balancer

▶ Multilayer and content switch

▶ Proxy server

▶ VPN concentrator

The following sections take a quick look at what these devices are designed to do.

Bandwidth Shaper

The demand for bandwidth on networks has never been higher. Internet and intranet applications demand a large amount of bandwidth. Administrators must ensure that despite all these demands, adequate bandwidth is available for mission-critical applications while few resources are dedicated to spam or peer-to-peer downloads. To do this, you need to monitor network traffic to ensure that data flows as you need it to.

The term *traffic shaping* describes the mechanisms used to control bandwidth usage on the network. With this, administrators can control who uses bandwidth, for what purpose, and what time of day bandwidth can be used. Traffic shaping establishes priorities for data traveling to and from the Internet and within the network.

A bandwidth shaper, as shown in Figure 4.4, essentially performs two key functions—monitoring and shaping. Monitoring includes identifying where bandwidth usage is high and the time of day. After that information is obtained, administrators can customize or shape bandwidth usage for the best needs of the network.

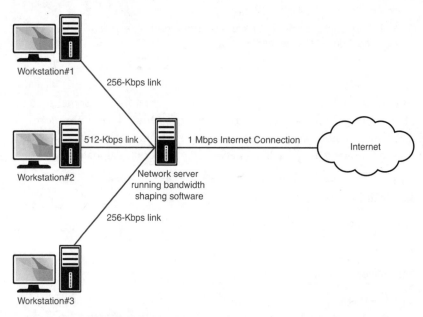

FIGURE 4.4   **A bandwidth shaper.**

Content Filter

A content filter is any software that controls what a user is allowed to peruse and is most often associated with websites. Using a content filter, an employer can block access to pornographic sites to all users, some users, or even just an individual user. The filter can be applied as software on client machines (known as *client-side filters*), on a proxy server on the network (a *server-side filter*), at the ISP, or even within the search engine itself. The latter is most commonly used on home machines and an example would be Content Advisor in Internet Explorer.

Load Balancer

Network servers are the workhorses of the network. They are relied on to hold and distribute data, maintain backups, secure network communications, and more. The load of servers is often a lot for a single server to maintain. This is where load balancing comes into play. Load balancing is a technique in which the workload is distributed between several servers. This feature can take networks to the next level; it increases network performance, reliability, and availability.

> **ExamAlert**
>
> Remember that load balancing increases redundancy and therefore data availability. Also, load balancing increases performance by distributing the workload.

A load balancer can be either a hardware device or software specially configured to balance the load.

> **Note**
>
> Multilayer switches (discussed next) and DNS servers can serve as load balancers.

Multilayer and Content Switches

It used to be that networking devices and the functions they performed were separate; bridges, routers, hubs, and more, existed but were separate devices. Over time, the functions of some individual network devices became integrated into a single device. This is true of multilayer switches.

A multilayer switch is one that can operate at both Layer 2 and Layer 3 of the OSI model, which means that the multilayer device can operate as both a switch and a router. Also called a Layer 3 switch, the multilayer switch is a high-performance device that actually supports the same routing protocols that routers do. It is a regular switch directing traffic within the LAN; in addition, it can forward packets between subnets.

> **ExamAlert**
>
> A multilayer switch operates as both a router and a switch.

A content switch is another specialized device. A content switch is not as common on today's networks, mostly due to cost. A content switch examines the network data it receives, decides where the content is intended to go, and forwards it. The content switch can identify the application that data is targeted for by associating it with a port. For example, if data uses the SMTP port, it could be forwarded to an SMTP server.

Content servers can help with load balancing because they can distribute requests across servers and target data to only the servers that need it, or distribute data between application servers. For example, if multiple mail servers are used, the content switch can distribute requests between the servers, thereby sharing the load evenly. This is why the content switch is sometimes called a load-balancing switch.

> **ExamAlert**
>
> A content switch can distribute incoming data to specific application servers and help distribute the load.

Proxy Server

Proxy servers typically are part of a firewall system. They have become so integrated with firewalls that the distinction between the two can sometimes be lost.

However, proxy servers perform a unique role in the network environment—a role that is separate from that of a firewall. For the purposes of this book, a proxy server is defined as a server that sits between a client computer and the Internet, looking at the web page requests the client sends. For example, if a client computer wants to access a web page, the request is sent to the proxy server rather than directly to the Internet. The proxy server first determines whether the request is intended for the Internet or for a web server locally. If the request is intended for the Internet, the proxy server sends the request *as if it originated the request*. When the Internet web server returns the information, the proxy server returns the information to the client. Although a delay might be induced by the extra step of going through the proxy server, the process is largely transparent to the client that originated the request. Because each request a client sends to the Internet is channeled through the proxy server, the proxy server can provide certain functionality over and above just forwarding requests.

One of the most notable extra features is that proxy servers can greatly improve network performance through a process called *caching*. When a caching proxy server answers a request for a web page, the server makes a copy of all or part of that page in its cache. Then, when the page is requested again, the proxy server answers the request from the cache rather than going back to the Internet. For example, if a client on a network requests the web page www.comptia.org, the proxy server can cache the contents of that web page. When a second client computer on the network attempts to access the same site, that client can grab it from the proxy server cache, and accessing the Internet is unnecessary. This greatly increases the response time to the client and can significantly reduce the bandwidth needed to fulfill client requests.

Nowadays, speed is everything, and the ability to quickly access information from the Internet is a crucial concern for some organizations. Proxy servers and their capability to cache web content accommodate this need for speed.

An example of this speed might be found in a classroom. If a teacher asks 30 students to access a specific Uniform Resource Locator (URL), without a proxy server, all 30 requests would be sent into cyberspace and subjected to delays or other issues that could arise. The classroom scene with a proxy server is quite different. Only one request of the 30 finds its way to the Internet; the other 29 are filled by the proxy server's cache. Web page retrieval can be almost instantaneous.

However, this caching has a potential drawback. When you log on to the Internet, you get the latest information, but this is not always so when information is retrieved from a cache. For some web pages, it is necessary to go directly to the Internet to ensure that the information is up to date. Some proxy servers can update and renew web pages, but they are always one step behind.

The second key feature of proxy servers is allowing network administrators to filter client requests. If a server administrator wants to block access to certain

websites, a proxy server enables this control, making it easy to completely disallow access to some websites. This is okay, but what if it were necessary to
block numerous websites? This is when maintaining proxy servers gets a bit
more complicated.

Determining which websites users can or cannot access typically is done
through something called an *access control list (ACL)*. The ACL is a list of
allowed or nonallowed websites; as you might imagine, compiling such a list
can be a monumental task. Given that millions of websites exist, and new ones
are created daily, how can you target and disallow access to the "questionable"
ones? One approach is to reverse the situation and deny access to all pages
except those that appear in an "allowed" list. This approach has high administrative overhead and can greatly limit the productive benefits available from
Internet access.

> **ExamAlert**
>
> Remember that the ACL is a list of allowed or nonallowed websites.

Understandably, it is impossible to maintain a list that contains the locations
of all sites with questionable content. In fairness, that is not what proxy
servers were designed to do. However, by maintaining a list, proxy servers can
better provide a greater level of control than an open system. Along the way,
proxy servers can make the retrieval of web pages far more efficient.

VPN Concentrator

A VPN concentrator can be used to increase remote-access security. This
device, discussed more in Chapter 10, can establish a secure connection (tunnel) between the sending and receiving network devices. VPN concentrators
add an additional level to VPN security. They can not only create the tunnel,
but they also can authenticate users, encrypt the data, regulate the data transfer, and control traffic.

> **Note**
>
> See Chapter 10 for more information on VPN concentrators.

Network Devices Summary

The information in this chapter is important for the Network+ exam. To summarize the coverage of network devices to this point, Table 4.1 lists some of the key points about each device. You should learn this information well.

TABLE 4.1 **Network Devices Summary**

Device	Description	Key Points
Hub	Connects devices on an Ethernet twisted-pair network	A hub does not perform any tasks besides signal regeneration.
Switch	Connects devices on a twisted-pair network	A switch forwards data to its destination by using the MAC address embedded in each packet.
Bridge	Connects LANs to reduce overall network traffic	A bridge enables data to pass through it or prevents data from passing through it by reading the MAC address.
Router	Connects networks	A router uses the software-configured network address to make forwarding decisions.
Gateway	Translates from one data format into another	Gateways can be hardware- or software-based. Any device that translates data formats is called a gateway.
CSU/DSU	Translates digital signals used on a LAN into those used on a WAN	CSU/DSU functionality is sometimes incorporated into other devices, such as a router with a WAN connection.
Modem	Provides serial communication capabilities across phone lines	Modems modulate the digital signal into analog at the sending end and perform the reverse function at the receiving end.
Network card	Enables systems to connect to the network	Network interfaces can be add-in expansion cards, ExpressCards, or built-in interfaces.
Media converter	Interconnects older technology with new	A media converter is a hardware device that connects newer Gigabit Ethernet technologies with older 100BaseT networks or older copper standards with fiber.

TABLE 4.1 **Continued**

Device	Description	Key Points
Firewall	Provides controlled data access between networks	Firewalls can be hardware- or software-based. They are an essential part of a network's security strategy.
DHCP server	Automatically distributes IP information	DHCP assigns all IP information, including IP address, subnet mask, DNS, gateway, and more.
Multilayer switch	Functions as a switch or router	Operates on Layers 2 and 3 of the OSI model as a switch and can perform router functionality.
Content switch	Forwards data by application	Content switches can identify and forward data by its port and application.
Load balancer	Distributes network load	Load balancing increases redundancy by distributing the load to multiple servers.
Multifunction devices	Combines network services	These are hardware devices that combine multiple network services into a single device, reducing cost and easing administrative difficulty.
DNS server	Provides name resolution from hostnames to IP addresses	A DNS server answers clients' requests to translate hostnames into IP addresses.
Bandwidth shaper	Manages network bandwidth	The bandwidth shaper monitors and controls bandwidth usage.
Proxy server	Manages client Internet requests	Serves two key network functions: increases network performance by caching, and filters outgoing client requests.

ExamAlert

You will be expected to know the function of the devices mentioned in this chapter. Review Table 4.1. Make sure you understand each device and how and why it is used on the network.

Cram Quiz

1. Several users on your network are downloading from peer-to-peer networks, tying up bandwidth during peak hours. Which of the following is used to manage network bandwidth?

   ○ **A.** Load leveler

   ○ **B.** Load toner

   ○ **C.** Bandwidth toner

   ○ **D.** Bandwidth shaper

2. Which of the following devices passes data based on the MAC address?

   ○ **A.** Hub

   ○ **B.** Switch

   ○ **C.** MSAU

   ○ **D.** Router

Cram Quiz Answers

1. **D.** The term bandwidth shaping describes the mechanisms used to control bandwidth usage on the network. With this, administrators have complete control over who uses bandwidth, for what purpose, and the time of day bandwidth can be used. Bandwidth shaping establishes priorities for data traveling to and from the Internet and within the network.

2. **B.** When determining the destination for a data packet, the switch learns the MAC address of all devices attached to it and then matches the destination MAC address in the data it receives. None of the other devices listed passes data based solely on the MAC address.

Virtual Network Components

▶ **Identify virtual network components.**

Cram**Saver**

If you can correctly answer these questions before going through this section, save time by skimming the Exam Alerts in this section and then complete the Cram Quiz at the end of the section.

1. On a virtual desktop what is the term that encompasses the software and hardware needed to create the virtual environment?

2. True or False: NaaS is similar to the Software as a Service (SaaS) cloud computing model in that it is provided on demand in a pay-as-you-go model.

Answers

1. The virtual desktop is often called a virtual desktop interface (VDI) and that term encompasses the software and hardware needed to create the virtual environment.

2. True. NaaS is similar to the Software as a Service (SaaS) cloud computing model in that it is provided on demand in a pay-as-you-go model.

Virtualization is the current rage due to the cost-savings and performance it provides. Virtualization can be implemented through open source solutions (such as Xen and VirtualBox) as well as proprietary solutions (such as VMware), allowing you to take a single physical device and make it appear to users as if it is a number of stand-alone entities.

The following sections take a look at some of the possibilities that exist in the virtual world.

Virtual Desktops

Traditionally, workstations can have multiple operating systems installed on them, but run only one at a time. By running virtualization software, the same workstation can be running Windows 7 along with Windows Server 2008 and Red Hat Enterprise Linux (or almost any other operating system) at the same time, allowing a developer to be testing code in various environments as well as cutting and pasting between them within a virtual machine (VM).

From a networking standpoint, each of the virtual desktops typically need full network access and configuring the permissions for each can sometimes be tricky. The virtual desktop is often called a *virtual desktop interface (VDI)* and that term encompasses the software and hardware needed to create the virtual environment.

> **ExamAlert**
>
> Equate VDI with hosting an operating system within a virtual machine.

Remote administration often uses virtual desktops, allowing a remote administrator to work on the workstation with or without the knowledge of the user sitting in front of the machine.

Virtual Servers

Just as workstations can be virtualized, so can servers: A single server can host multiple logical machines. Using only one server to perform the functions of many, the cost-savings that can accumulate in terms of hardware, utilities, and infrastructure can add up.

Tales of security woes that can occur with attackers jumping out of one virtual machine and accessing another have been exaggerated. Although such threats are possible, most software solutions include sufficient protection to reduce the possibility to a small one.

Virtual Switches

As the name implies, a virtual switch works the same as a physical switch but allows multiple switches to exist on the same host (thus saving the implementation of additional hardware). Virtual switches are regularly used with VLAN implementations.

> **Note**
>
> Open vSwitch is an open source virtual switch licensed beneath the Apache 2.0 license. It can be found at http://openvswitch.org.

One key difference between physical and virtual switches is that the virtual switch can provide a direct channel to the virtual Ethernet adapters for configuration information (intelligently directing information), avoiding the need for unicast addresses or IGMP snooping to learn multicast group membership.

> **Note**
>
> A good source of information to peruse for additional information on virtualization possibilities is the VMware Virtual Networking Concepts at http://www.vmware.com/files/pdf/virtual_networking_concepts.pdf.

Virtual PBX

A virtual private branch exchange (PBX) is a phone system that handles such features as call routing, voicemail, faxing, and so on. What makes it virtual is that it is hosted by a company other than yours—the service is contracted out to a vendor. Callers do not know that they have not reached your company; they are instead routed through a vendor.

A benefit to using vendors for providing virtual PBX service is that they are responsible for the equipment and software. VoIP is used for routing the voice traffic.

> **ExamAlert**
>
> Think of a virtual PBX as a cost-savings method that incorporates VoIP.

Onsite Versus Offsite

Just as workstations, servers, switches, and PBXs can be made virtual, so, too, can the datacenter. Instead of hosting the datacenter onsite, it is possible to have all of it hosted elsewhere (offsite) and remotely accessed. The advantage of doing this is that another location/vendor is responsible for maintaining hardware and software. A disadvantage can be your reliance on them to provide the contracted service.

An example of this in operation involves a large electronic monitoring company. All the data comes in to servers in Colorado, but operators work with the data from workstations in Indiana. The servers are in a secure facility where the data can be physically protected and secured, whereas the operators work where the cost of living and the cost of office space is among the cheapest in the country.

Network as a Service (NaaS)

Just as vendors can offer virtual PBX services, they can also offer an entire network, freeing the company from the need for true administration. Known as *Network as a Service (Naas)*, this stops the company from needing to worry about bandwidth, connectivity, scalability, and all the issues normally associated with networking.

NaaS is similar to the Software as a Service (SaaS) cloud computing model in that it is provided on demand in a pay-as-you-go model. Many of the telecom providers currently offer this service, and Cisco is supporting the OpenStack open source project (originally started by Rackspace Hosting and NASA) to support virtual public and private clouds. More information on OpenStack can be found at http://www.openstack.org.

Exam Alert

Know that OpenStack is an open source NaaS implementation.

Cram Quiz

1. Which of the following is an open source virtual switch?

   ○ **A.** VirtualBox

   ○ **B.** VMware

   ○ **C.** Xen

   ○ **D.** Open vSwitch

2. When a vendor offers to provide all networking for a client—freeing the company from needing to worry about bandwidth, connectivity, scalability, and all the issues normally associated with networking—what is it known as?

   ○ **A.** SaaS

   ○ **B.** NaaS

   ○ **C.** SAN

   ○ **D.** NAS

Cram Quiz Answers

1. **D.** Open vSwitch is an open source virtual switch licensed beneath the Apache 2.0 license. It can be found at http://openvswitch.org. The other options listed (some proprietary and some open source) are for virtual desktops.

2. **B.** Known as *Network as a Service (Naas)*, this alleviates the company's concerns about bandwidth, connectivity, scalability, and all the issues normally associated with networking.

What Next?

Chapter 5, "Installation and Configuration," looks at the creation of a network of varying size. It starts by examining small (SOHO) networks and then looks at the WAN. It also covers Internet access technologies.

CHAPTER 5

Installation and Configuration

This chapter covers the following official Network+ objectives:

▶ Given a set of requirements, plan and implement a basic SOHO network.

▶ Categorize WAN technology types and properties.

This chapter covers CompTIA Network+ objectives 2.6, and 3.4. For more information on the official Network+ exam topics, see the "About the Network+ Exam" section in the "Introduction."

If you think of networking as something that can be represented on a plane, there would be two ends of the spectrum. At one end of the spectrum, there would be small networks of only a few nodes and devices connected together. These are known as small office, home office (SOHO) networks and are easy to assemble.

At the other end of the spectrum is the WAN: An amalgamation of multiple local area networks creating an entity that is only as strong as its weakest link. This chapter examines both ends of the spectrum, starting with the simplest first and building from there. It concludes by looking at Internet access technologies because few networks today—if any—do not connect to the Internet.

Creating a SOHO Network

▶ **Given a set of requirements, plan and implement a basic SOHO network.**

Cram**Saver**

If you can correctly answer these questions before going through this section, save time by skimming the Exam Alerts in this section and then complete the Cram Quiz at the end of the section.

1. What is the point of demarcation with a small office?

2. True or False: Cable modems and DSL modems are commonly used in SOHO implementations for Internet access.

Answers

1. The point of demarcation is always the point where the service provider stops being responsible for the wiring and it becomes your responsibility.

2. True. Cable modems and DSL modems are commonly used in SOHO implementations for Internet access.

A small office/home office (SOHO) network is typically defined as one that serves 1 to 10 users; although, no hard and fast rule exists for this. The commonality between all implementations falling into this category is that usually a small number of users exists, and the physical environment is typically small. A number of SOHO-labeled solutions are available, including small routers and firewalls. Appropriately, a SOHO router typically serves 1 to 10 users on the system.

Just as when configuring any other type of network, you need to be mindful of your requirements and limitations. The limitations for cable length, device types, environment, equipment, and compatibility do not change just because the network created is smaller.

Exam**Alert**

For the Network+ exam, CompTIA also lists cable length, environment limitations, equipment limitations, and compatibility requirements as topics. These items do not change just because the network may be small and are addressed throughout this book.

In this section, you look at some of the basic configuration elements not covered elsewhere, and you can skip over them if you have significant previous experience in building networks.

Figure 5.1 shows a common configuration for a home or small network. A connection to the Internet is made possible through a high-speed link using either DSL or a cable modem. A router connects to the modem (in small networks, this can be the same device) and enables the workstations to network and share that connection.

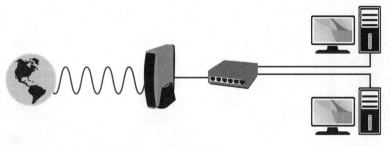

FIGURE 5.1   **A simple network configuration.**

Far more common than a wire-only router today is the implementation of a wireless router. Cisco makes a series of popular broadband routers for this market that incorporate a four-port wired switch.

Note

More on wireless routers? Chapter 7, "Wireless," covers wireless technologies in detail.

Although wireless is quickly replacing wired connectivity in many implementations, there are still plenty of times when wired must be used. You can run traditional cabling through the wall and use a wall jack (as shown in Figure 5.2) or take the route of running the wire on the outside of the wall and use a surface jack (as shown in Figure 5.3).

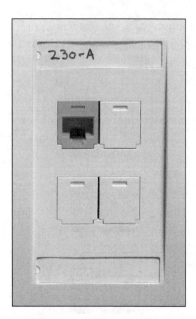

FIGURE 5.2 **A wall jack.**

FIGURE 5.3 **A surface jack.**

In Figures 5.2 and 5.3 multiple ports can be housed in the same jack. In Figure 5.3, a telephone port occupies the same jack as the Ethernet port, while both have ample room for expansion. You can purchase cables already assembled in a variety of lengths, but they can become expensive and difficult to snake through existing walls. A more common solution is to purchase cable in bulk, such as the CAT6 cable from Belden shown in Figure 5.4, and make your own.

FIGURE 5.4   **Bulk twisted-pair cable.**

The modem connecting the network to the Internet service provider can differ slightly based on the manufacturer, but most follow an identical format. On the back, there is a connection for power and for the incoming line (either coax if cable or RJ-11 if DSL). In addition to that, there is an Ethernet port for connecting to the router, hub, or a single workstation. In some cases, there will be a USB port that can be used in place of the Ethernet port if you want to connect directly to a single PC.

> **ExamAlert**
>
> Make sure you understand how a SOHO network can connect to the Internet.

On the front of the modem, there is typically a button for on/off/standby and a number of lights. The lights are the first place to turn to when troubleshooting. A typical sequence of lights on a cable modem is power, receive, send, online, and activity.

The *point of demarcation* (often referred to as *demarcation point* or merely *demarc*) in a small network such as this is the point where the service provider stops being responsible for the line and it becomes your responsibility. With a telephone provider, this is usually the box on the outside of the home/business. With a cable provider, this is typically at the splitter nearest where the cable originates—coming out of the ground, off the pole, and so on. Figure 5.5 shows a point of demarcation for a home in the form of a Network Interface Device (NID), and Figure 5.6 shows the equivalent for a small office. In both cases, the provider is responsible to provide and maintain service to the point and the customer is responsible for everything from there on.

ExamAlert

Make sure you know what a demarcation point is.

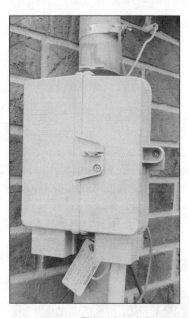

FIGURE 5.5   **The point of demarc for a home.**

FIGURE 5.6   **The point of demarc for a small office.**

> **Note**
>
> Many SOHO routers (and some of the personal firewall solutions on end-user work-stations) close down the ICMP ports by default. This can frustrate you when you try to see if a brand-new station/server/router is up and running.

Cram Quiz

1. On a typical cable modem, which panel light is found beneath the power light?

   ○ **A.** Receive

   ○ **B.** Send

   ○ **C.** Online

   ○ **D.** Activity

2. Which of the following is true of many SOHO routers?

   ○ **A.** They close down the DHCP ports by default.

   ○ **B.** They close down the NAT ports by default.

   ○ **C.** They close down the ICMP ports by default.

   ○ **D.** They leave open the DHCP, NAT, and ICMP ports by default.

Cram Quiz Answers

1. **A.** A typical sequence of lights on a cable modem is power, receive, send, online, and activity.

2. **C.** Many SOHO routers close down the ICMP ports by default.

WAN Technologies

▶ **Categorize WAN technology types and properties.**

Cram**Saver**

If you can correctly answer these questions before going through this section, save time by skimming the Exam Alerts in this section and then complete the Cram Quiz at the end of the section.

1. What are T-lines used for, and what is the maximum speed of T1 and T3?

2. What are the X.25 transmission speed restrictions?

3. What is the difference between circuit switching and packet switching?

Answers

1. T-carrier lines create point-to-point network connections for private networks. T1 lines offer transmission speeds of up to 1.544Mbps, whereas T3 lines offer transmission speeds of 44.736Mbps.

2. X.25 is restricted to transmission rates of 56Kbps or 64Kbps with digital implementations.

3. Circuit switching offers a dedicated transmission channel that is reserved until it is disconnected. Packet switching enables packets to be routed around network congestion.

Many of today's network environments are not restricted to a single location or LAN. Instead, many networks span great distances, becoming wide area networks (WANs). When they do, hardware and software are needed to connect these networks. This section reviews the characteristics of various WAN technologies. Before discussing the specific WAN technologies, look at an important element of WAN technologies: switching methods.

Switching Methods

For systems to communicate on a network, the data needs a communication path or multiple paths on which to travel. To allow entities to communicate, these paths move the information from one location to another and back. This is the function of *switching*, which provides communication pathways between two endpoints and manages how data flows between them. Following are two of the more common switching methods used today:

▶ Packet switching

▶ Circuit switching

Packet Switching

In packet switching, messages are broken into smaller pieces called *packets*. Each packet is assigned source, destination, and intermediate node addresses. Packets are required to have this information because they do not always use the same path or route to get to their intended destination. Referred to as *independent routing*, this is one of the advantages of packet switching. Independent routing enables better use of available bandwidth by letting packets travel different routes to avoid high-traffic areas. Independent routing also enables packets to take an alternative route if a particular route is unavailable for some reason.

In a packet-switching system, when packets are sent onto the network, the sending device is responsible for choosing the best path for the packet. This path might change in transit, and the receiving device can receive the packets in a random or nonsequential order. When this happens, the receiving device waits until all the data packets are received, and then it reconstructs them according to their built-in sequence numbers.

Two types of packet-switching methods are used on networks:

▶ **Virtual-circuit packet switching**: A logical connection is established between the source and the destination device. This logical connection is established when the sending device initiates a conversation with the receiving device. The logical communication path between the two devices can remain active for as long as the two devices are available or can be used to send packets once. After the sending process has completed, the line can be closed.

▶ **Datagram packet switching**: Unlike virtual-circuit packet switching, datagram packet switching does not establish a logical connection between the sending and transmitting devices. The packets in datagram packet switching are independently sent, meaning that they can take different paths through the network to reach their intended destination. To do this, each packet must be individually addressed to determine its source and destination. This method ensures that packets take the easiest possible routes to their destination and avoid high-traffic areas. Datagram packet switching is mainly used on the Internet.

Circuit Switching

In contrast to the packet-switching method, circuit switching requires a dedicated physical connection between the sending and receiving devices. The most commonly used analogy to represent circuit switching is a telephone conversation in which the parties involved have a dedicated link between them for the duration of the conversation. When either party disconnects, the circuit is broken, and the data path is lost. This is an accurate representation of how circuit switching works with network and data transmissions. The sending system establishes a physical connection, and the data is transmitted between the two. When the transmission is complete, the channel is closed.

Some clear advantages to the circuit-switching technology make it well suited for certain applications such as PSTN and ISDN. The primary advantage is that after a connection is established, a consistent and reliable connection exists between the sending and receiving device. This allows for transmissions at a guaranteed rate of transfer.

Like all technologies, circuit switching has its downsides. As you might imagine, a dedicated communication line can be inefficient. After the physical connection is established, it is unavailable to any other sessions until the transmission completes. Again, using the phone call analogy, this would be like a caller trying to reach another caller and getting a busy signal. Circuit switching therefore can be fraught with long connection delays.

Comparing Switching Methods

Table 5.1 provides an overview of the various switching technologies.

TABLE 5.1 **Comparison of Switching Methods**

Switching Method	Pros	Cons	Key Features
Packet switching	Packets can be routed around network congestion. Packet switching makes efficient use of network bandwidth.	Packets can become lost while taking alternative routes to the destination. Messages are divided into packets that contain source and destination information.	The two types of packet switching are datagram and virtual circuit. Virtual circuit uses a logical connection between the source and the destination device. With datagram circuit switching, packets are independently sent and can take different paths through the network to reach their intended destination.
Circuit switching	Offers a dedicated transmission channel that is reserved until it is disconnected.	Dedicated channels can cause delays because a channel is unavailable until one side disconnects. Uses a dedicated physical link between the sending and receiving devices.	Offers the capability of storing messages temporarily to reduce network congestion.

Integrated Services Digital Network (ISDN)

ISDN has long been an alternative to the slower modem WAN connections but at a higher cost. ISDN enables the transmission of voice and data over the same physical connection.

ISDN connections are considerably faster than regular modem connections. To access ISDN, a special phone line is required. This line usually is paid for through a monthly subscription. You can expect these monthly costs to be significantly higher than those for traditional dialup modem connections.

To establish an ISDN connection, you dial the number associated with the receiving computer, much as you do with a conventional phone call or modem dialup connection. A conversation between the sending and receiving devices is then established. The connection is dropped when one end disconnects or hangs up. The line pickup of ISDN is fast, enabling a connection to be established, or brought up, much more quickly than a conventional phone line.

ISDN has two defined interface standards: Basic Rate Interface (BRI) and Primary Rate Interface (PRI).

BRI

BRI ISDN uses three separate channels; two bearer (B) channels of 64Kbps each and a delta channel of 16Kbps. B channels can be divided into four D channels, which ENABLE businesses to have eight simultaneous Internet connections. The B channels carry the voice or data, and the D channels are used for signaling.

> **Exam Alert**
>
> BRI ISDN channels can be used separately using 64Kbps transfer or combined to provide 128Kbps transfer rates.

PRI

PRI is a form of ISDN that generally is carried over a T1 line and can provide transmission rates of up to 1.544Mbps. PRI is composed of 23 B channels, each providing 64Kbps for data/voice capacity, and one 64kbps D channel, which is used for signaling.

Comparing BRI and PRI ISDN

Table 5.2 compares BRI to PRI ISDN.

> **Exam Alert**
>
> ISDN is considered a leased line because access to ISDN is leased from a service provider.

TABLE 5.2 **BRI to PRI ISDN Comparison**

Characteristic	BRI	PRI
Speed	128Kbps	1.544Mbps
Channels	2B+D	23B+D
Transmission carrier	ISDN	T1

> **Exam Alert**
>
> Be ready to answer questions about the characteristics of both BRI and PRI; the exam includes the information provided in Table 5.2.

T-carrier Lines

T-carrier lines are high-speed dedicated digital lines that can be leased from telephone companies. This creates an always-open, always-available line between you and whomever you choose to connect to when you establish the service.

T-carrier lines can support both voice and data transmissions and are often used to create point-to-point private networks. Because they are a dedicated link, they can be a costly WAN option. Four types of T-carrier lines are available:

▶ **T1**: Offers transmission speeds of 1.544Mbps and can create point-to-point dedicated digital communication paths. T1 lines have commonly been used for connecting LANs. In North America, DS (digital signal) notation is used with T-lines to describe the circuit. For all practical purposes, DS1 is synonymous with T1.

▶ **T2**: Offers transmission speeds of 6.312Mbps. They accomplish this by using 96 64Kbps B channels.

▶ **T3**: Offers transmission speeds of up to 44.736Mbps, using 672 64Kbps B channels. Digital signal 3 (DS3) is a more accurate name in North America, but T3 is what most refer to the link as.

> **ExamAlert**
>
> When you take the exam, think of DS3 and T3 as synonymous.

▶ **T4**: Offers impressive transmission speeds of up to 274.176Mbps by using 4,032 64Kbps B channels.

> **ExamAlert**
>
> Of these T-carrier lines, the ones commonly associated with networks and the ones most likely to appear on the exam are the T1 and T3 lines.

> **Note**
>
> Because of the cost of a T-carrier solution, you can lease portions of a T-carrier service. This is known as *fractional T*. You can subscribe and pay for service based on 64Kbps channels.

T-carrier is the designation for the technology used in the United States and Canada. In Europe, they are called E-carriers and in Japan, J-carriers. Table 5.3 describes the T/E/J carriers.

TABLE 5.3 **Comparing T/E/J Carriers**

Name	Transmission Speed
T1	1.544Mbps
T1C	. 3.152Mbps
T2	6.312Mbps
T3	44.736Mbps
T4	274.176Mbps
J0	64Kbps
J1	1.544Mbps
J1C	3.152Mbps
J2	6.312Mbps
J3	32.064Mbps
J3C	97.728Mbps
J4	397.200Mbps
E0	64Kbps
E1	2.048Mbps
E2	8.448Mbps
E3	34.368Mbps
E4	139.264Mbps
E5	565.148Mbps

> **ExamAlert**
>
> Ensure that you review the speeds of the T1 and T3 carriers.

T3 Lines

For a time, the speeds offered by T1 lines were sufficient for all but a few organizations. As networks and the data they support expanded, T1 lines did not provide enough speed for many organizations. T3 service answered the call by providing transmission speeds of 44.736Mbps.

T3 lines are dedicated circuits that provide high capacity and generally are used by large companies, ISPs, or long-distance companies. T3 service offers all the strengths of a T1 service (just a whole lot more), but the cost associated with T3 limits its use to the few organizations that have the money to pay for it.

SONET/OCx Levels

In 1984, the U.S. Department of Justice and AT&T reached an agreement stating that AT&T was a monopoly that needed to be divided into smaller, directly competitive companies. This created a challenge for local telephone companies, which were faced with the task of connecting to an ever-growing number of independent long-distance carriers, each of which had a different interfacing mechanism. Bell Communications Research answered the challenge by developing Synchronous Optical Network (SONET), a fiber-optic WAN technology that delivers voice, data, and video at speeds starting at 51.84Mbps. Bell's main goals in creating SONET were to create a standardized access method for all carriers within the newly competitive U.S. market and to unify different standards around the world. SONET is capable of transmission speeds from 51.84Mbps to 2.488Gbps and beyond.

One of Bell's biggest accomplishments with SONET was that it created a new system that defined data rates in terms of Optical Carrier (OCx) levels. Table 5.4 lists the OCx levels you should be familiar with.

> **ExamAlert**
>
> Before taking the exam, review the information provided in Table 5.4.

TABLE 5.4 **OCx Levels and Transmission Rates**

OCx Level	Transmission Rate
OC-1	51.84Mbps
OC-3	155.52Mbps
OC-12	622.08Mbps
OC-24	1.244Gbps
OC-48	2.488Gbps
OC-96	4.976Gbps
OC-192	9.953Gbps
OC-768	39.813Gbps

> **Note**
>
> Optical carrier (OCx) levels represent the range of digital signals that can be carried on SONET fiber-optic networks. Each OCx level defines the speed at which it operates.
>
> Synchronous Digital Hierarchy (SDH) is the European counterpart to SONET.

> **ExamAlert**
>
> When you take the exam, equate SDH with SONET.

A passive optical network (PON) is one in which unpowered optical splitters are used to split the fiber so it can service a number of different locations and brings the fiber either to the curb, the building, or the home. It is known as a passive system because there is no power to the components and consists of an optical line termination (OLT) at the split and a number of optical network units (ONUs) at the end of each run (typically near the end user). It can be combined with wavelength division multiplexing and is then known as WDM-PON.

A form of multiplexing optical signals is dense wavelength division multiplexing (DWDM). This method replaces SONET/SDH regenerators with erbium doped fiber amplifiers (EDFAs) and can also amplify the signal and enable it to travel a greater distance. The main components of a DWDM system include the following:

▶ Terminal multiplexer

▶ Line repeaters

▶ Terminal demultiplexer

> **Note**
>
> Chapter 7 discusses several other methods of multiplexing.

> **ExamAlert**
>
> Make sure you understand that DWDM works with SONET/SDH.

X.25 and Frame Relay

X.25 was one of the original packet-switching technologies, but today it has been replaced in many applications by Frame Relay. Various telephone companies, along with network providers, developed X.25 in the mid-1970s to transmit digital data over analog signals on copper lines. Because so many different entities had their hands in the development and implementation of X.25, it works well on many different kinds of networks with different types of traffic. X.25 is one of the oldest standards, and therein lie both its greatest advantage and its greatest disadvantage. On the upside, X.25 is a global standard that can be found all over the world. On the downside, its maximum transfer speed is 56Kbps—which is reasonable when compared to other technologies in the mid-1970s but slow and cumbersome today. However, in the 1980s a digital version of X.25 was released, increasing throughput to a maximum of 64Kbps. This too is slow by today's standards.

Because X.25 is a packet-switching technology, it uses different routes to get the best possible connection between the sending and receiving device at a given time. As conditions on the network change, such as increased network traffic, so do the routes that the packets take. Consequently, each packet is likely to take a different route to reach its destination during a single communication session. The device that makes it possible to use the X.25 service is called a *packet assembler/disassembler (PAD)*, which is required at each end of the X.25 connection.

Frame Relay

Frame Relay is a WAN protocol that operates at the physical and data link layers of the OSI model. Frame Relay enables data transmission for intermittent traffic between LANs and between endpoints in a WAN.

Frame Relay was designed to provide standards for transmitting data packets in high-speed bursts over digital networks, using a public data network service. Frame Relay is a packet-switching technology that uses variable-length packets. Essentially, Frame Relay is a streamlined version of X.25. It uses smaller packet sizes and fewer error-checking mechanisms than X.25, and consequently it has less overhead than X.25.

A Frame Relay connection is built by using permanent virtual circuits (PVCs) that establish end-to-end communication. This means that Frame Relay is not dependent on the best-route method of X.25. Frame Relay can be implemented on several WAN technologies, including 56Kbps, T1, T3, and ISDN lines.

To better understand how it works, look at some of the components of Frame Relay technology. All devices in the Frame Relay WAN fall into two primary categories:

▶ **Data terminal equipment (DTE):** In the Frame Relay world, the term DTE refers to terminating equipment located within a company's network. Termination equipment includes such hardware as end-user systems, servers, routers, bridges, and switches.

▶ **Data circuit-terminating equipment (DCE)**: DCE refers to the equipment owned by the carrier. This equipment provides the switching services for the network and therefore is responsible for actually transmitting the data through the WAN.

As previously mentioned, Frame Relay uses virtual circuits to create a communication channel. These virtual circuits establish a bidirectional communication link from DTE devices. Two types of virtual circuits are used with Frame Relay:

▶ **Permanent virtual circuit (PVC)**: A permanent dedicated virtual link shared in a Frame Relay network, replacing a hard-wired dedicated end-to-end line.

▶ **Switched virtual circuit (SVC)**: Represents a temporary virtual circuit established and maintained only for the duration of a data transfer session.

Figure 5.7 shows the components of a Frame Relay network.

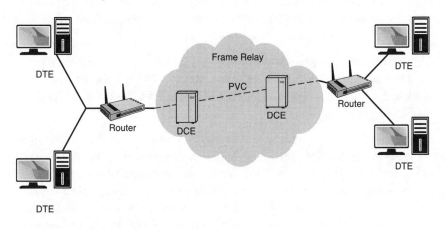

FIGURE 5.7   **A Frame Relay network.**

Asynchronous Transfer Mode (ATM)

Introduced in the early 1990s, ATM was heralded as a breakthrough technology for networking because it was an end-to-end solution, ranging in use from a desktop to a remote system. Although it was promoted as both a LAN and WAN solution, ATM did not live up to its hype due to associated implementation costs and a lack of standards. The introduction of Gigabit Ethernet, which offered great transmission speeds and compatibility with existing network infrastructure, further dampened the momentum of the ATM bandwagon. ATM has, however, found a niche with some ISPs and is also commonly used as a network backbone.

ATM is a packet-switching technology that provides transfer speeds ranging from 1.544Mbps to 622Mbps. It is well suited for a variety of data types, such as voice, data, and video. Using fixed-length packets, or cells, that are 53 bytes long, ATM can operate more efficiently than variable-length-packet packet-switching technologies such as Frame Relay. Having a fixed-length packet allows ATM to be concerned only with the header information of each packet. It does not need to read every bit of a packet to determine its beginning and end. ATM's fixed cell length also makes it easily adaptable to other technologies as they develop. Each cell has 48 bytes available for data, with 5 bytes reserved for the ATM header.

ATM is a circuit-based network technology because it uses a virtual circuit to connect two networked devices. Like Frame Relay, ATM is a circuit-based network technology that also uses PVCs and SVCs. PVCs and SVCs were discussed in the preceding section.

ATM is compatible with the most widely used and implemented networking media types available today, including single-mode and multimode fiber, coaxial cable, unshielded twisted pair, and shielded twisted pair. Although ATM can be used over various media, the limitations of some of the media types make them impractical choices for deployment in an ATM network. ATM can also operate over other media, including FDDI, T1, T3, SONET, OC-3, and Fibre Channel.

Summary of WAN Technologies

Table 5.5 provides an overview of the technologies discussed so far.

TABLE 5.5 **Comparing WAN Technologies**

WAN Technology	Speed	Supported Media	Switching Method Used	Key Characteristics
ISDN	BRI: 64kbps to 128kbps PRI: 64kbps to 1.5Mbps	Copper/ fiber-optic	Can be used for circuit-switching or packet-switching connections	ISDN can be used to transmit all types of traffic, including voice, video, and data. BRI uses 2B+D channels; PRI uses 23B+D channels. B channels are 64kbps. ISDN uses the public network and requires dial-in access.
T-carrier (T1, T3)	T1: 1.544Mbps T3: 44.736Mbps	Copper/ fiber-optic	Circuit switching	T-carrier is used to create point-to-point network connections for private networks.
ATM	1.544Mbps to 622Mbps	Copper/ fiber-optic	Cell switching	ATM uses fixed cells that are 53 bytes long.
X.25	56kbps/64kbps	Copper/ fiber-optic	Packet switching	X.25 is limited to 56kbps. X.25 provides a packet-switching network over standard phone lines.
Frame Relay	56kbps to 1.544Mbps	Copper/ fiber-optic	PVCs and SVCs	Frame Relay is a packet-oriented protocol, and it uses variable-length packets.
SONET/OCx	51.8Mbps to 2.4Gbps	Fiber-optic	N/A	SONET defines synchronous data transfer over optical cable.

ExamAlert

For the Network+ exam, be sure you can identify the characteristics of the various WAN technologies from Table 5.5.

Cram Quiz

1. Your company currently uses a standard PSTN communication link to transfer files between LANs. Until now, the transfer speeds have been sufficient for the amount of data that needs to be transferred. Recently, a new application was purchased that requires a minimum transmission speed of 1.5Mbps. You have been given the task to find the most cost-effective solution to accommodate the new application. Which of the following technologies would you use?

   ○ **A.** T3

   ○ **B.** X.25

   ○ **C.** T1

   ○ **D.** BRI ISDN

2. Which of the following best describes the process to create a dedicated circuit between two communication endpoints and direct traffic between those two points?

   ○ **A.** Multiplexing

   ○ **B.** Directional addressing

   ○ **C.** Addressing

   ○ **D.** Circuit switching

3. Which of the following statements are true of ISDN? (Choose the two best answers.)

   ○ **A.** BRI ISDN uses two B+1 D channels.

   ○ **B.** BRI ISDN uses 23 B+1 D channels.

   ○ **C.** PRI ISDN uses two B+1 D channels.

   ○ **D.** PRI ISDN uses 23 B+1 D channels.

4. You have been hired to establish a WAN connection between two offices: one in Vancouver and one in Seattle. The transmission speed can be no less than 2Mbps. Which of the following technologies could you choose?

   ○ **A.** T1

   ○ **B.** PSTN

   ○ **C.** T3

   ○ **D.** ISDN

5. On an ISDN connection, what is the purpose of the D channel?

  ○ **A.** It carries the data signals.

  ○ **B.** It carries signaling information.

  ○ **C.** It enables multiple channels to be combined to provide greater bandwidth.

  ○ **D.** It provides a temporary overflow capacity for the other channels.

6. Which of the following circuit-switching strategies does ATM use? (Choose the two best answers.)

  ○ **A.** SVC

  ○ **B.** VCD

  ○ **C.** PVC

  ○ **D.** PCV

7. Due to recent cutbacks, your boss approaches you, demanding an alternative to the company's costly dedicated T1 line. Only small amounts of data require transfer over the line. Which of the following are you likely to recommend?

  ○ **A.** ISDN

  ○ **B.** FDDI

  ○ **C.** The PSTN

  ○ **D.** X.25

8. Which of the following technologies requires a logical connection between the sending and receiving devices?

  ○ **A.** Circuit switching

  ○ **B.** Virtual-circuit packet switching

  ○ **C.** Message switching

  ○ **D.** High-density circuit switching

Cram Quiz Answers

1. **C.** A T1 line has a transmission capability of 1.544Mbps and is considerably cheaper than a T3 line. X.25 and BRI ISDN cannot provide the required transmission speed.

2. **D.** Circuit switching is the process of creating a dedicated circuit between two communications endpoints and directing traffic between those two points. None of the other answers are valid types of switching.

3. **A, D.** BRI ISDN uses two B+1 D channels, which are two 64Kbps data channels, and PRI ISDN uses 23 B+1 D channels. The D channel is 16Kbps for BRI and 64Kbps for PRI.

4. **C.** The only possible answer capable of transfer speeds above 2Mbps is a T3 line. None of the other technologies listed can provide the transmission speed required.

5. **B.** The D channel on an ISDN link carries signaling information, whereas the B, or bearer, channels carry the data.

6. **A, C.** ATM uses two types of circuit switching: PVC and SVC. VCD and PCV are not the names of switching methods.

7. **C.** When little traffic will be sent over a line, the PSTN is the most cost-effective solution; although, it is limited to 56Kbps. All the other WAN connectivity methods accommodate large amounts of data and are expensive compared to the PSTN.

8. **B.** When virtual-circuit switching is used, a logical connection is established between the source and the destination device.

Internet Access Technologies

▶ **Categorize WAN technology types and properties.**

Cram**Saver**

If you can correctly answer these questions before going through this section, save time by skimming the Exam Alerts in this section and then complete the Cram Quiz at the end of the section.

1. What is VHDSL commonly used for?

2. True or False: DSL using regular phone lines transfers data over the same copper wire.

3. What is the difference between a one-way and a two-way satellite system?

Answers

1. VHDSL supports high-bandwidth applications such as VoIP and HDTV.

2. True. DSL using regular phone lines transfers data over the same copper wire.

3. A *one-way satellite system* requires a satellite card and a satellite dish installed at the end user's site. This system works by sending outgoing requests on one link using a phone line, with inbound traffic returning on the satellite link. A *two-way satellite system*, on the other hand, provides data paths for both upstream and downstream data.

Internet access has become an integral part of modern business. You have several ways to obtain Internet access. Which type you choose often depends on the cost and what technologies are available in your area. This section explores some of the more common methods of obtaining Internet access.

Note

The term *broadband* often refers to high-speed Internet access. Both DSL and cable modem are common broadband Internet technologies. Broadband routers and broadband modems are network devices that support both DSL and cable.

DSL Internet Access

DSL is an Internet access method that uses a standard phone line to provide high-speed Internet access. DSL is most commonly associated with high-speed Internet access; because it is a relatively inexpensive Internet access, it is often found in homes and small businesses. With DSL, a different frequency can be used for digital and analog signals, which means that you can talk on the phone while you upload data.

For DSL services, two types of systems exist: Asymmetric Digital Subscriber Line (ADSL) and High-Rate Digital Subscriber Line (HDSL). ADSL provides a high data rate in only one direction. It enables fast download speeds but significantly slower upload speeds. ADSL is designed to work with existing analog telephone service (POTS) service. With fast download speeds, ADSL is well suited for home-use Internet access where uploading large amounts of data isn't a frequent task.

In contrast to ADSL, HDSL provides a bidirectional high data rate service that can accommodate services, such as videoconferencing, that require high data rates in both directions. A variant of HDSL is VHDSL (Very High-Rate Digital Subscriber Line), which provides an HDSL service at very high data transfer rates.

DSL arrived on the scene in the late 1990s and brought with it a staggering number of flavors. Together, all these variations are known as xDSL:

- **Asymmetric DSL (ADSL)**: Probably the most common of the DSL varieties is ADSL, which uses different channels on the line. One channel is used for plain old telephone service (POTS) and is responsible for analog traffic. The second channel provides upload access, and the third channel is used for downloads. With ADSL, downloads are faster than uploads, which is why it is called asymmetric DSL.

- **Symmetric DSL (SDSL)**: Offers the same speeds for uploads and downloads, making it most suitable for business applications such as web hosting, intranets, and e-commerce. It is not widely implemented in the home/small business environment and cannot share a phone line.

- **ISDN DSL (IDSL)**: A symmetric type of DSL commonly used in environments in which SDSL and ADSL are unavailable. IDSL does not support analog phones.

- **Rate-Adaptive DSL (RADSL)**: A variation on ADSL that can modify its transmission speeds based on signal quality. RADSL supports line sharing.

▶ **Very High Bit Rate DSL (VHDSL or VDSL)**: An asymmetric version of DSL and, as such, can share a telephone line. VHDSL supports high-bandwidth applications such as VoIP and HDTV. VHDSL can achieve data rates up to approximately 10Mbps, making it the fastest available form of DSL. To achieve high speeds, VHDSL uses fiber-optic cabling.

▶ **High Bit Rate DSL (HDSL)**: A symmetric technology that offers identical transmission rates in both directions. HDSL does not allow line sharing with analog phones.

Why are there are so many DSL variations? The answer is quite simply that each flavor of DSL is aimed at a different user, business, or application. Businesses with high bandwidth needs are more likely to choose a symmetric form of DSL, whereas budget-conscious environments such as home offices are likely to opt for an option that enables phone line sharing at the expense of bandwidth. In addition, some of the DSL variants are simply older technologies. Although the name persists, they have been replaced with newer DSL implementations. When you work in a home/small office environment, you should expect to work with an ADSL system.

Table 5.6 summarizes the maximum speeds of the various DSL options. Maximum speeds are rarely obtained.

TABLE 5.6 **DSL Speeds**

DSL Variation	Upload Speed[*]	Download Speed[*]
ADSL	1Mbps	3Mbps
SDSL	1.5Mbps	1.5Mbps
IDSL	144Kbps	144Kbps
RADSL	1Mbps	7Mbps
VHDSL	1.6Mbps	13Mbps
HDSL	768Kbps	768Kbps

[*]Speeds may vary greatly, depending on the technologies used and the quality of the connection.

Note

DSL using regular phone lines transfers data over the same copper wire. The data and voice signals are sent over different frequencies, but sometimes the signals interfere with each other. This is why you use DSL filters. A DSL filter works by minimizing this interference, making for a faster and cleaner DSL connection.

DSL Troubleshooting Procedures

Troubleshooting DSL is similar to troubleshooting any other Internet connection. The following are a few things to check when users are experiencing problems with a DSL connection:

▶ **Physical connections**: The first place to look when troubleshooting a DSL problem is the network cable connections. From time to time, these cables can come loose or inadvertently be detached, and they are often overlooked as the cause of a problem. DSL modems typically have a minimum of three connections: one for the DSL line, one for the local network, and one for the power. Make sure that they are all plugged in appropriately.

▶ **The NIC**: While you're checking the cable at the back of the system, take a quick look to see whether the network card LED is lit. If it is not, something could be wrong with the card. It might be necessary to swap out the network card and replace it with one that is known to be working.

▶ **Drivers**: Ensure that the network card is installed and has the correct drivers. Many times, simply using the most up-to-date driver can resolve connectivity issues.

▶ **Protocol configuration**: The device you are troubleshooting might not have a valid IP address. Confirm the IP address by using the appropriate tool for the operating system being used—for example, `winipcfg`, `ipconfig`, or `ifconfig`. If the system requires the automatic assignment of an IP address, confirm that the system is automatically set to obtain an IP address. It might be necessary to use the `ipconfig /release` and `ipconfig /renew` commands to get a new IP address.

▶ **DSL LEDs**: Each DSL box has an LED on it. The light sequences are often used to identify connectivity problems or problems with the box itself. Refer to the manufacturer's website for specific information about error codes and LEDs, but remember the basics. A link light should be on to indicate that the physical connection is complete, and a flashing LED indicates that the connection is active.

> **ExamAlert**
>
> When troubleshooting remote connectivity on a cable or DSL modem, use the LEDs that are always present on these devices to aid in your troubleshooting process.

Ultimately, if none of these steps cures or indicates the cause of the problem, you might have to call the DSL provider for assistance.

Cable Internet Access

Cable Internet access is an always-on Internet access method available in areas that have digital cable television. Cable Internet access is attractive to many small businesses and home office users because it is both inexpensive and reliable. Most cable providers do not restrict how much use is made of the access. Connectivity is achieved by using a device called a *cable modem*. It has a coaxial connection for connecting to the provider's outlet and an Unshielded Twisted Pair (UTP) connection for connecting directly to a system or to a hub or switch.

Cable providers often supply the cable modem, with a monthly rental agreement. Many cable providers offer free or low-cost installation of cable Internet service, which includes installing a network card in a PC. Some providers also do not charge for the network card. Cable Internet costs are comparable to DSL subscription.

Most cable modems offer the ability to support a 30Mbps (or more) Ethernet connection for the home LAN; although, you wouldn't expect the Internet connection to reach these speeds. The actual speed of the connection can vary somewhat, depending on the utilization of the shared cable line in your area. In day-to-day application, data rates range from 1.5Mbps to 7Mbps.

> **ExamAlert**
>
> A cable modem generally is equipped with a medium-dependent interface crossed (MDI-X) port, so you can use a straight-through UTP cable to connect the modem to a system.

One of the biggest disadvantages of cable access is (by DSL providers, at least) that you share the available bandwidth with everyone else in your cable area. As a result, during peak times, performance of a cable link might be poorer than in low-use periods. In residential areas, busy times are evenings and weekends, and particularly right after school. In general, though, performance with cable systems is good, and in low-usage periods, it can be fast.

> **Note**
>
> Although the debate between cable and DSL goes on, for regular users, it doesn't make that much difference which one you choose. Although cable modem technology delivers *shared bandwidth* within the local neighborhood, its speeds are marginally higher but influenced by this shared bandwidth. DSL delivers *dedicated local bandwidth* but is sensitive to distance that impacts overall performance. With the monthly costs about the same, it is too close to call.

Cable Troubleshooting Procedures

In general, cable Internet access is a low-maintenance system with few problems. When problems do occur, you can try various troubleshooting measures:

▶ **Check the user's end**: Before looking at the cable modem, make sure that the system is configured correctly and that all cables are plugged in. If a hub or switch is used to share the cable Internet access among a group of computers, make sure that the hub or switch is on and correctly functioning.

▶ **Check the physical connections**: Like DSL modems, cable modems have three connections: one for the cable signal, one for the local network, and one for the power. Make sure that they are all appropriately plugged in.

▶ **Ensure that the protocol configuration on the system is valid**: If an IP address is assigned via DHCP, the absence of an address is a sure indicator that connectivity is at fault. Try obtaining a new IP address by using the appropriate command for the operating system platform you use. If the IP addresses are statically configured, make sure that they are correctly set. Trying to use any address other than that specified by the ISP might prevent a user from connecting to the network.

▶ **Check the indicator lights on the modem**: Most cable modems have indicator lights that show the modem's status. Under normal conditions, a single light labeled Ready or Online should be lit. Most cable providers give the user a modem manual that details the functions of the lights and what they indicate in certain states. Generally, any red light is bad. Flashing LEDs normally indicate traffic on the connection.

▶ **Cycle the power on the modem**: Cycling the power on the modem is a surefire way to reset it.

▶ **Call the technical support line**: If you are sure that the connectors are all in place and the configuration of the system is correct, the next step is to call the technical support line of the cable provider. If the provider experiences problems that affect many users, you might get a message while you're on hold, informing you of that. If not, you eventually get to speak to someone who can help you troubleshoot the problem. One of the good things about cable access is that the cable company can remotely monitor and reset the modem. The cable company should tell you whether the modem is correctly functioning.

Unless the modem is faulty, which is not that common, by this point the user should be back on the Internet, or at least you should fully understand why the user cannot connect. If the problem is with the cable provider's networking equipment, you and the user simply have to wait for the system to come back on.

Broadband Security Considerations

Whether you use DSL or cable Internet access, you should keep a few things in mind. Each of these technologies offers always-on service. This means that even when you are away from your computer, it still connects to the Internet. As you can imagine, this creates a security risk. The longer you are online, the better the chances that someone can remotely access your system.

The operating systems in use today all have some security holes that attackers wait to exploit. These attacks often focus on technologies such as email or open TCP/UDP ports. Combining OS security holes with an always-on Internet technology is certainly a dangerous mix.

Today, DSL and cable Internet connections must be protected by mechanisms such as firewalls. The firewall offers features such as packet filtering and network address translation (NAT). The firewall can be a third-party software application installed on the system, or it can be a hardware device.

In addition to a firewall, it is equally important to ensure that the operating system you use is completely up to date in terms of service packs and security updates. Today's client systems typically offer automatic update features that alert you when a new security update is available.

If you diligently follow a few security measures, both DSL and cable Internet can provide safe Internet access.

POTS Internet Access

Although it's somewhat slow, one of the most popular means to connect to the Internet or a remote network may still be the good old telephone line and modem. Because the same line used for a household phone is used for dialup access, it is called the POTS (plain old telephone system) method of access. Although many parts of the world are served by broadband providers offering services such as those discussed so far in this chapter, some people still must (or choose to) connect with a modem.

Internet access through a phone system requires two things: a modem and a dialup access account through an ISP. Modems are devices that convert the digital signals generated by a computer system into analog signals that can travel across a phone line. A computer can have either an internal or external modem. External modems tend to be less problematic to install and troubleshoot because they don't require reconfiguration of the host system. Internal modems use one of the serial port assignments (that is, a COM port) and therefore must be configured not to conflict with other devices.

The second piece of the puzzle, the dialup ISP account, can easily be obtained by contacting one of the many local, regional, or national ISPs. Most ISPs offer a range of plans normally priced based on the amount of time the user is allowed to spend online. Almost without exception, ISPs offer 56Kbps access, the maximum possible under current standards. Most ISPs also provide email accounts, access to newsgroup servers, and often small amounts of web space.

It is a good idea to carefully research an ISP choice. Free services exist, but they generally restrict users to a certain number of online hours per month or use extensive banner advertising to pay for the services.

Another big consideration for dialup Internet access is how many lines the ISP has. ISPs never have the same number of lines as subscribers; instead, they work on a first-come, first-served basis for dialup clients. This means that sometimes users get busy signals when they try to connect. Before signing up for a dialup Internet access account, ask the company what its ratio of lines to subscribers is, and use that figure as part of your comparison criteria.

With a modem and an ISP account, you are ready to connect. But what happens if things don't go as you plan? Welcome to the interesting and sometimes challenging world of troubleshooting dialup connections.

POTS Troubleshooting Procedures

Troubleshooting a dialup connection problem can be tricky and time-consuming, because you must consider many variables. Of the remote connectivity mechanisms discussed in this chapter, you are far more likely to have problems with a POTS connection than with any of the others. The following are some places to start your troubleshooting under various conditions.

> **Note**
>
> In some cases, users may not even use an ISP; instead, they may directly dial another system on the corporate network. In that case, all the troubleshooting steps in this section apply. The exception is that you must rely on the technical support capabilities of the person responsible for the remote system rather than the ISP if you have a problem.

If the user cannot dial out, try the following:

- ▶ **Check physical connections**: The most common problem with modem connections is that something has become unplugged; modems rarely fail after they initially work. For an external modem, you also need to verify that the modem has power and that it is connected to the correct COM port.

- ▶ **Check that the line has a dial tone**: You can do this by plugging a normal phone into the socket to see whether you can dial out. Also, a modem generally has a speaker, and you can set up the modem to use the speaker so that you can hear what is going on.

If the user can dial out but cannot connect to the network, try the following:

- ▶ **Make sure that the user is dialing the correct number**: This suggestion sounds obvious, but sometimes numbers change or are incorrectly entered.

- ▶ **Call the ISP**: You can call the ISP to determine whether it is having problems.

- ▶ **Check the modem speaker**: Find out whether you get busy signals from the ISP by turning on the modem speaker.

If the user can dial out and can get a connection but is then disconnected, try the following:

- ▶ **Make sure that the modem connection is correctly configured**: The most common modem configuration is 8 data bits, 1 stop bit, and no parity (commonly called *eight-one-none*).

▶ **Check the username and password**: Make sure that the correct username and password combination is configured for the dialup connection.

▶ **Verify that the connection settings are correct**: Pay particular attention to things such as the IP address. Nearly all ISPs assign IP addresses through DHCP, and trying to connect with a statically configured IP address is not permitted.

▶ **Make sure that the user has not exceeded a preset connection time limit**: Some ISPs restrict the number of monthly access hours. If the user has such a plan, check to ensure that some time credit is left.

▶ **Try specifying a lower speed for the connection**: Modems are designed to negotiate a connection speed with which both devices are comfortable. Sometimes, during the negotiation process, the line can be dropped. Initially setting a lower speed might get you a connection. You can then increase the modem speed to accommodate a better connection.

The Public Switched Telephone Network (PSTN)

The *PSTN*, often considered a POTS, is the entire collection of interconnected telephone wires throughout the world. Discussions of the PSTN include all the equipment that goes into connecting two points, such as the cable, the networking equipment, and the telephone exchanges.

> **ExamAlert**
>
> If money is a major concern, the PSTN is the method of choice for creating a WAN.

The modern PSTN is largely digital, with analog connections existing primarily between homes and local phone exchanges. Modems are used to convert the computer system's digital signals into analog so that they can be sent over the analog connection.

Using the PSTN to establish WAN connections is a popular choice; although, the significant drawback is the limited transfer speeds. Transfer on the PSTN is limited to 56Kbps with a modem and 128Kbps with an ISDN connection, and it's difficult to share large files or videoconferencing at such speeds. However, companies that need to send only small amounts of data remotely can use the PSTN as an inexpensive alternative for remote access, particularly when other resources such as the Internet are unavailable.

Satellite Internet Access

Many people take DSL and cable Internet access for granted, but these technologies are not offered everywhere. Many rural areas do not have cable Internet access. For areas where cheaper broadband options are unavailable, a limited number of Internet options are available. One of the primary options is Internet via satellite.

Satellite access provides a viable Internet access solution for those who cannot get other methods of broadband. Satellite Internet offers an always-on connection with theoretical speeds advertised anywhere from 512Kbps upload speeds to 2048Kbps download speeds, considerably faster than a 56Kbps dialup connection. Satellite Internet access does have a few drawbacks, though, such as cost and high latency. Latency is the time it takes for the signal to travel back and forth from the satellite.

Although satellite Internet is slower and more costly than DSL or cable, it offers some attractive features, the first of which is its portability. Quite literally, wherever you go, you have Internet access with no phone lines or other cables. For businesses with remote users and clients, the benefit is clear. But the technology has a far-reaching impact; it is not uncommon to see recreational vehicles (RVs) with a satellite dish on the roof. They have 24/7 unlimited access to the Internet as they travel.

Many companies offer satellite Internet services; a quick Internet search reveals quite a few. These Internet providers offer different Internet packages that vary greatly in terms of price, access speeds, and service. Some target businesses, whereas others aim for the private market.

Two different types of broadband Internet satellite services are deployed: one-way and two-way systems. A *one-way satellite system* requires a satellite card and a satellite dish installed at the end user's site. This system works by sending outgoing requests on one link using a phone line, with inbound traffic returning on the satellite link. A *two-way satellite system*, on the other hand, provides data paths for both upstream and downstream data. Like a one-way system, a two-way system uses a satellite card and a satellite dish installed at the end user's site; bidirectional communication occurs directly between the end user's node and the satellite.

Home satellite systems are asymmetric; that is, download speeds are faster than upload speeds. A home satellite system is likely to use a modem for the uplink traffic, with downloads coming over the satellite link. The exact speeds you can expect with satellite Internet depend on many factors. As with other wireless technologies, atmospheric conditions can significantly affect the performance of satellite Internet access. One additional consideration for satellite Internet is increased *propagation time*—how long it takes the signal to travel back and forth from the satellite. In networking terms, this time is long and therefore is an important consideration for business applications.

Home Satellite Troubleshooting Procedures

Your ability to troubleshoot satellite Internet connections might be limited. Home satellite Internet is a line-of-sight wireless technology, and the installation configuration must be precise. Because of this requirement, many satellite companies insist that the satellite be set up and configured by trained staff members. If you install a satellite system in a way that does not match the manufacturer's recommendations, you might void any warranties.

Given this limitation, troubleshooting satellite connections often requires you to concentrate less on connectivity issues and more on physical troubleshooting techniques. Perhaps more than for any other Internet technology, calls to technical support occur early in the troubleshooting process. Satellite Internet has a few aspects that you should be aware of:

▶ **Rain fade**: Refers to signal loss due to moisture interference. The general rule is that the smaller the dish, the more susceptible it is to rain fade. Home and small businesses use small dishes.

▶ **Latency**: Refers to the time lapse between sending or requesting information and the time it takes to return. As you might expect, satellite communication experiences high latency due to the distance it has to travel.

▶ **Line of sight**: Despite the distance, satellite is basically a line-of-sight technology. This means that the path between the satellite dish and the satellite should be as unobstructed as possible.

Wireless Internet Access

Not too long ago, it would have been inconceivable to walk into your local coffee shop with your laptop under your arm and surf the Web while drinking a latte. Putting aside that beverages and laptops don't mix, wireless Internet access is becoming more common.

Wireless Internet access is provided by a Wireless Internet Service Provider (WISP). The WISP provides public wireless Internet access known as *hotspots*. Hotspots offer Internet access for mobile network devices such as laptops, handheld computers, and cell phones in airports, coffee shops, conference rooms, and so on. A hotspot is created using one or many wireless access points near the hotspot location.

Client systems might need to install special application software for billing and security purposes; others require no configuration other than obtaining the network name (Service Set Identifier [SSID]). Hotspots do not always require a fee for service because companies use them as a marketing tool to lure Internet users to their businesses.

Hotspots are not everywhere, but finding them is not difficult. Typically, airports, hotels, and coffee shops advertise that they offer Internet access for customers or clients. In addition, WISPs list their hotspot sites online so that they are easily found.

Establishing a connection to a wireless hotspot is a straightforward process. If not equipped with built-in wireless capability, laptops require an external wireless adapter card. With the physical requirements of the wireless card taken care of, connect as follows:

1. When you arrive at the hotspot site, power up your laptop. In some instances, you might need to reboot your system if it were on standby to clear out old configuration settings.

2. The card might automatically detect the network. If this is the case, configuration settings, such as the SSID, are automatically detected, and the wireless Internet is available. If Internet access is free, there is little else to do; if it is a paid-for service, you need to enter a method of payment. One thing to remember is to verify that you use encryption for secure data transfer.

3. If for some reason the wireless settings are not automatically detected, you need to open your wireless NIC's configuration utility and manually set the configurations. These settings can include setting the mode to infrastructure, inputting the correct SSID, and setting the level of encryption used.

In addition to using a WISP, some companies such as hotels and cafes provide wireless Internet access by connecting a wireless router to a DSL or cable Internet connection. The router becomes the wireless access point to which the users connect, and it enables clients to connect to the Internet through the broadband connection. The technology is based on the 802.11 standards, typically 802.11b/g/n, and client systems require only an internal or external wireless adapter.

> **Note**
>
> Want more wireless? Chapter 7 covers wireless technologies in detail.

Cellular

Just as POTS can serve as a means to connect to the Internet, so, too, can the cellular network. When the cellular network is used for this purpose, it is often marketed as a "mobile data service" and uses a wireless NIC to connect the laptop or desktop to the network.

One technology that enables this is Long Term Evolution (LTE), which is often referred to as 4G because it is the fourth generation in a long series of products offering similar services. Another technology is Worldwide Interoperability for Microwave Access (WiMax), which is based on 802.16. Table 5.7 shows peak upload and download speeds for both LTE and WiMax. Actual implementations by carriers vary but are always below the theoretical possibilities.

TABLE 5.7 **LTE and WiMax Speeds**

	Peak Upload Speed	Peak Download Speed
LTE	50Mbit/s	100Mbit/s
WiMax	56Mbit/s	1Gbit/s

> **Note**
>
> It is important to know that there have been several versions of both LTE and WiMax. While discussing them in association with 4G here (technically, LTE Advanced and WiMax Advanced), versions also existed for 3G (LTE and Mobile WiMax). As of this writing, WiMax Release 2 is expected to be commercially released in the near future.

Evolved High Speed Packet Access (HSPA+) is known as a 3G transitional technology that supports legacy architecture. It can offer theoretical upload speeds of 22Mbit/s and downloads of 84Mbit/s.

> **ExamAlert**
>
> When you take the exam, associate HSPA+ with 3G cellular networking and LTE/WiMax with 4G.

Cram Quiz

1. Which of the following technologies require dialup access? (Choose the two best answers.)

   ○ **A.** FDDI

   ○ **B.** ISDN

   ○ **C.** Packet switching

   ○ **D.** The PSTN

2. Which of the following is an advantage of ISDN over the PSTN?

   ○ **A.** ISDN is more reliable.

   ○ **B.** ISDN is cheaper.

   ○ **C.** ISDN is faster.

   ○ **D.** ISDN uses 53Kbps fixed-length packets.

3. Which of the following technologies is known as a 3G transitional technology that supports legacy architecture?

   ○ **A.** HSPA+

   ○ **B.** LTE

   ○ **C.** WiMax

   ○ **D.** PON

4. What is the theoretical download speed possible with WiMax?

   ○ **A.** 84Mbit/s

   ○ **B.** 100Mbit/s

   ○ **C.** 1Gbit/s

   ○ **D.** 10Gbit/s

5. Which of the following is the time lapse between sending or requesting information and the time it takes to return?

   ○ **A.** Echo

   ○ **B.** Attenuation

   ○ **C.** Bandwidth

   ○ **D.** Latency

6. Which of the following provides public hotspots for wireless Internet access?

   ○ **A.** WISP

   ○ **B.** WASP

   ○ **C.** WSP+

   ○ **D.** WPST

7. What is the speed usually offered with dialup service?

   ○ **A.** 1Gbps

   ○ **B.** 256Kbps

   ○ **C.** 144Kbps

   ○ **D.** 56Kbps

Cram Quiz Answers

1. **B** and **D.** Both the PSTN and ISDN require dialup connections to establish communication sessions.

2. **C.** One clear advantage that ISDN has over the PSTN is its speed. ISDN can combine 64Kbps channels for faster transmission speeds than the PSTN can provide. ISDN is no more or less reliable than the PSTN. ISDN is more expensive than the PSTN. Answer D describes ATM.

3. **A.** HSPA+ (Evolved High Speed Packet Access) is known as a 3G transitional technology that supports legacy architecture.

4. **C.** The theoretical download speed possible with WiMax is 1Gbit/s. The speed possible with HSPA+ is 84Mbits/s, whereas that possible with LTE is 100Mbit/s.

5. **D.** Latency refers to the time lapse between sending or requesting information and the time it takes to return.

6. **A.** Wireless Internet access is provided by a Wireless Internet Service Provider (WISP). The WISP provides public wireless Internet access known as hotspots. Hotspots offer Internet access for mobile network devices such as laptops, handheld computers, and cell phones in airports, coffee shops, conference rooms, and so on.

7. **D.** Almost without exception, ISPs offer 56Kbps access, the maximum possible under current standards.

What Next?

For the Network+ exam and for routinely working with an existing network or implementing a new one, you need to identify the characteristics of network media and their associated cabling. Chapter 6, "Cabling and Wiring," focuses on the media and connectors used in today's networks and how they fit into wiring closets.

CHAPTER 6

Cabling and Wiring

This chapter covers the following official Network+ objectives:

▶ Categorize standard media types and associate properties.

▶ Categorize standard connector types based on network media.

▶ Compare and contrast different LAN technologies.

▶ Identify components of wiring distribution.

This chapter covers CompTIA Network+ objectives 3.1, 3.2, 3.7, and 3.8. For more information on the official Network+ exam topics, see the "About the Network+ Exam" section in the "Introduction."

When working with an existing network or implementing a new one, you need to identify the characteristics of network media and their associated cabling. This chapter focuses on the media and connectors used in today's networks and how they fit into wiring closets.

In addition to media and connectors, this chapter identifies the characteristics of the IEEE 802.3 standard and its variants.

General Media Considerations

▶ Categorize standard media types and associated properties.

▶ Categorize standard connector types based on network media.

▶ Identify components of wiring distribution.

CramSaver

If you can correctly answer these questions before going through this section, save time by skimming the Exam Alerts in this section and then complete the Cram Quiz at the end of the section.

1. What is the difference between RJ-11 and RJ-45 connectors?

2. What are the two most common connectors used with fiber-optic cabling?

3. What are F-type connectors used for?

4. What hardware is located at the demarcation point?

5. What is BPL?

Answers

1. RJ-11 connectors are used with standard phone lines and are similar in appearance to RJ-45 connectors used in networking. However, RJ-11 connectors are smaller. RJ-45 connectors are used with UTP cabling.

2. Fiber-optic cabling uses a variety of connectors, but SC and ST are more commonly used than others. ST connectors offer a twist-type attachment, whereas SCs have a push-on connector. LC and MT-RJ are other types of fiber-optic connectors.

3. F-type connectors are used to connect coaxial cable to devices such as Internet modems.

4. The hardware at the demarcation point is the smart jack, also known as the Network Interface Device (NID).

5. Broadband over Power Lines (BPL) enables electrical wiring to be used to build a network.

In addition to identifying the characteristics of network media and their associated cabling, the Network+ exam requires knowledge of some general terms and concepts that are associated with network media. Before looking at the individual media types, it is a good idea to first have an understanding of some general media considerations.

Broadband Versus Baseband Transmissions

Networks employ two types of signaling methods:

▶ **Baseband transmissions**: Baseband transmissions use digital signaling over a single wire. Communication on baseband transmissions is bidirectional, allowing signals to be sent and received, but not at the same time. To send multiple signals on a single cable, baseband uses something called *Time Division Multiplexing* (TDM). TDM divides a single channel into time slots. The key thing about TDM is that it doesn't change how baseband transmission works—only how data is placed on the cable.

> **Exam Alert**
>
> Most networks use baseband transmissions. (Notice the word "base.") Examples are 10GBaseT and 10GBaseLR.

▶ **Broadband transmissions**: In terms of LAN network standards, broadband transmissions use analog transmissions. For broadband transmissions to be sent and received, the medium must be split into two channels. (Alternatively, two cables can be used: one to send and one to receive transmissions.) Multiple channels are created using *Frequency Division Multiplexing* (FDM). FDM allows broadband media to accommodate traffic going in different directions on a single medium at the same time.

> **Exam Alert**
>
> Be prepared to identify the characteristics of baseband and broadband.

Broadband over Power Lines

You can transmit data over lines used for electric power through the utilization of *Broadband over Power Lines* (BPL). Implementations are traditionally limited to the premises (such as a home network) because transformers prevent the signal from being useful after the data passes through. This limits the execution and keeps it from being implementable in large networks. It can, however, provide Internet access by connecting the network to a high speed modem.

The HomePlug Powerline Alliance (https://www.homeplug.org) provides the specification used for most implementations. HomePlug has worked with the IEEE to create the following current standards:

▶ **IEEE 1901**: For high-speed communication devices

▶ **IEEE 1905**: For hybrid home networks (those containing Blu-Ray players, set top boxes, and so on)

> **Note**
>
> You can find more information on the current standard at
> http://standards.ieee.org/develop/project/1905.1.html.

> **Exam Alert**
>
> For the exam, equate HomePlug with Broadband over Power Lines.

Simplex, Half Duplex, and Full Duplex Modes

Simplex, half duplex, and full duplex are referred to as dialog modes, and they determine the direction in which data can flow through the network media:

▶ *Simplex mode* enables one-way communication of data through the network, with the full bandwidth of the cable used for the transmitting signal. One-way communication is of little use on LANs, making it unusual at best for network implementations.

▶ Far more common is *half-duplex mode*, which accommodates transmitting and receiving on the network, but not at the same time. Many networks are configured for half-duplex communication.

▶ The preferred dialog mode for network communication is *full-duplex mode*. To use full duplex, both the network card and the hub or switch must support full duplexing. Devices configured for full duplexing can simultaneously transmit and receive. This means that 100Mbps network cards theoretically can transmit at 200Mbps using full-duplex mode.

Media Interference

Depending on where network cabling (commonly called media) is installed, *interference* can be a major consideration. Two types of media interference can

adversely affect data transmissions over network media: electromagnetic interference (EMI) and crosstalk.

EMI is a problem when cables are installed near electrical devices, such as air
conditioners or fluorescent light fixtures. If a network medium is placed close
enough to such a device, the signal within the cable might become corrupt.
Network media vary in their resistance to the effects of EMI. Standard
unshielded twisted-pair (UTP) cable is susceptible to EMI, whereas fiber
cable, with its light transmissions, is resistant to EMI. When deciding on a
particular medium, consider where it will run and the impact EMI can have
on the installation.

A second type of interference is *crosstalk*. Crosstalk refers to how the data signals on two separate media interfere with each other. The result is that the
signal on both cables can become corrupt. As with EMI, media varies in its
resistance to crosstalk, with fiber-optic cable being the most resistant.

> **ExamAlert**
>
> Remember that fiber-optic uses optical signals, not electrical, giving it a greater
> resistance to EMI and crosstalk.

Attenuation

Attenuation refers to the weakening of data signals as they travel through a
medium. Network media vary in their resistance to attenuation. Coaxial cable
generally is more resistant than UTP; STP is slightly more resistant than
UTP; and fiber-optic cable does not suffer from attenuation. That's not to say
that a signal does not weaken as it travels over fiber-optic cable, but the correct term for this weakening is *chromatic dispersion* rather than attenuation.

You need to understand attenuation or chromatic dispersion and the maximum distances specified for network media. Exceeding a medium's distance
without using repeaters can cause hard-to-troubleshoot network problems. A
repeater is a network device that amplifies data signals as they pass, enabling
them to travel farther. Most attenuation-related or chromatic dispersion-relat-
ed difficulties on a network require using a network analyzer to detect them.

Data Transmission Rates

One of the more important media considerations is the supported data transmission rate or speed. Different media types are rated to certain maximum

speeds, but whether they are used to this maximum depends on the networking standard used and the network devices connected to the network.

> **Note**
>
> The transmission rate of media is sometimes incorrectly called the bandwidth. Actually, the term bandwidth refers to the width of the range of electrical frequencies or the number of channels that the medium can support.

Transmission rates normally are measured by the number of data bits that can traverse the medium in a single second. In the early days of data communications, this measurement was expressed in bits per second (bps), but today's networks are measured in Mbps (megabits per second) and Gbps (gigabits per second).

The different network media vary greatly in the transmission speeds they support. Many of today's application-intensive networks require more than the 10Mbps or 100Mbps offered by the older networking standards. In some cases, even 1Gbps, which is found in many modern LANs, is simply not enough to meet current network needs. For this reason, many organizations now deploy 10Gbps implementations.

Types of Network Media

Whatever type of network is used, some type of network medium is needed to carry signals between computers. Two types of media are used in networks: cable-based media, such as twisted pair, and the media types associated with wireless networking, such as radio waves.

In networks using cable-based media, there are three basic choices:

▶ Twisted pair

▶ Coaxial

▶ Fiber-optic

Twisted-pair and coaxial cables both use copper wire to conduct the signals electronically; fiber-optic cable uses a glass or plastic conductor and transmits the signals as light.

For many years, coaxial was the cable of choice for most LANs. Today, twisted pair has proven to be the cable medium of choice, thus retiring coaxial to the confines of storage closets. Fiber-optic cable has also seen its popularity rise, but because of cost it has been primarily restricted to use as a network backbone where segment length and higher speeds are needed. That said, fiber is now increasingly common in server room environments as a server-to-switch connection method, and in building-to-building connections in metropolitan area networks (MANs).

> **Note**
>
> For more information on MANs, see Chapter 1, "Introduction to Networking."

The following sections summarize the characteristics of each of these cable types.

Twisted-Pair Cabling

Twisted-pair cabling has been around for a long time. It was originally created for voice transmissions and has been widely used for telephone communication. Today, in addition to telephone communication, twisted pair is the most widely used medium for networking.

The popularity of twisted pair can be attributed to the fact that it is lighter, more flexible, and easier to install than coaxial or fiber-optic cable. It is also cheaper than other media alternatives and can achieve greater speeds than its coaxial competition. These factors make twisted pair the ideal solution for most network environments.

Two main types of twisted-pair cabling are in use today: *Unshielded Twisted Pair* (UTP) and *Shielded Twisted Pair* (STP). UTP is significantly more common than STP and is used for most networks. Shielded twisted pair is used in environments in which greater resistance to EMI and attenuation is required. The greater resistance comes at a price, however. The additional shielding, plus the need to ground that shield (which requires special connectors), can significantly add to the cost of a cable installation of STP.

STP provides the extra shielding by using an insulating material that is wrapped around the wires within the cable. This extra protection increases the distances that data signals can travel over STP but also increases the cost of the cabling. Figure 6.1 shows UTP and STP cabling.

UTP Cable   Shielding

STP Cable

FIGURE 6.1   **UTP and STP cabling.**

There are several categories of twisted-pair cabling. The early categories are most commonly associated with voice transmissions. The categories are specified by the Electronic Industries Association/Telecommunications Industry Association (EIA/TIA). EIA/TIA is an organization that focuses on developing standards for electronic components, electronic information, telecommunications, and Internet security. These standards are important to ensure uniformity of components and devices.

> **Note**
>
> When learning about cabling, you need to understand the distinction between hertz and bits per second in relation to bandwidth. When you talk about bandwidth and a bits-per-second rating, you refer to a rate of data transfer.

EIA/TIA has specified a number of categories of twisted-pair cable, some of which are now obsolete. Those still in use today include the following:

▶ **Category 3**: Data-grade cable that can transmit data up to 10Mbps with a possible bandwidth of 16MHz. For many years, Category 3 was the cable of choice for twisted-pair networks. As network speeds pushed the 100Mbps speed limit, Category 3 became ineffective.

▶ **Category 4**: Data-grade cable that has potential data throughput of 16Mbps. Category 4 cable was often implemented in the IBM Token-Ring Network. Category 4 cable is no longer used.

▶ **Category 5**: Data-grade cable that typically was used with Fast Ethernet operating at 100Mbps with a transmission range of 100 meters. Although Category 5 was a popular media type, this cable is an outdated standard. Newer implementations use the 5e standard. Category 5 provides a minimum of 100MHz of bandwidth. Category 5, despite being used primarily for 10/100 Ethernet networking, can go faster. The IEEE 802.11ae standard specifies 1000Mbps over Category 5 cable.

▶ **Category 5e**: Data-grade cable used on networks that run at 10/100Mbps and even up to 1000Mbps. Category 5e cabling can be used up to 100 meters, depending on the implementation and standard used. Category 5e cable provides a minimum of 100MHz of bandwidth.

▶ **Category 6**: High-performance UTP cable that can transmit data up to 10Gbps. Category 6 has a minimum of 250MHz of bandwidth and specifies cable lengths up to 100 meters with 10/100/1000Mbps transfer, along with 10Gbps over shorter distances. Category 6 cable typically is made up of four twisted pairs of copper wire, but its capabilities far exceed those of other cable types. Category 6 twisted pair uses a *longitudinal separator*, which separates each of the four pairs of wires from each other. This extra construction significantly reduces the amount of crosstalk in the cable and makes the faster transfer rates possible.

▶ **Category 6a**: Also called augmented 6. Offers improvements over Category 6 by offering a minimum of 500MHz of bandwidth. It specifies transmission distances up to 100 meters with 10Gbps networking speeds.

Tip

If you work on a network that is a few years old, you might need to determine which category of cable it uses. The easiest way to do this is to simply read the cable. The category number should be clearly printed on it.

Table 6.1 summarizes the categories and the speeds they support in common network implementations.

TABLE 6.1 **Twisted-Pair Cable Categories**

Category	Common Application
3	16Mbps
4	20Mbps
5	100Mbps
5e	1000Mbps
6	10/100/1000Mbps plus 10Gbps
6a	10Gbps and beyond networking

> **Note**
>
> The numbers shown in Table 6.1 refer to speeds these cables are commonly used to support. Ratified standards for these cabling categories might actually specify lower speeds than those listed, but cable and network component manufacturers are always pushing the performance envelope in the quest for greater speeds. The ratified standards define minimum specifications. For more information on cabling standards, visit the TIA website at http://www.tiaonline.org/.

Coaxial Cables

Coaxial cable, or *coax* as it is commonly called, has been around for a long time. Coax found success in both TV signal transmission and network implementations. As shown in Figure 6.2, coax is constructed with a copper core at the center (the main wire) that carries the signal, insulation (made of plastic), ground (braided metal shielding), and insulation on the outside (an outer plastic covering).

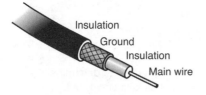

FIGURE 6.2 **Coaxial cabling.**

Coaxial cable is constructed in this way to add resistance to *attenuation* (the loss of signal strength as the signal travels over distance), *crosstalk* (the degradation of a signal, caused by signals from other cables running close to it), and EMI. Two types of coax are used in networking: thin coax, also known as thinnet, and thick coax, also known as thicknet. Neither is particularly popular anymore, but you are most likely to encounter thin coax. Thick coax was used primarily for backbone cable. It could be run through plenum spaces because it offered significant resistance to EMI and crosstalk and could run in lengths up to 500 meters. Thick coax offers speeds up to 10Mbps, far too slow for today's network environments.

Thin coax is much more likely to be seen than thick coax in today's networks, but it isn't common. Thin coax is only .25 inches in diameter, making it fairly easy to install. Unfortunately, one of the disadvantages of all thin coax types is that they are prone to cable breaks, which increase the difficulty when installing and troubleshooting coaxial-based networks.

Several types of thin coax cable exist, each of which has a specific use. Table 6.2 summarizes these categories.

TABLE 6.2 **Thin Coax Categories**

Cable Type	Description
RG-59 /U	Used to generate low-power video connections. The RG-59 cable cannot be used over long distances because of its high-frequency power losses. In such cases, RG-6 cables are used instead.
RG-58 /U	Has a solid copper core. Used for radio communication and thin Ethernet (10Base2).
RG-58 A/U	Has a stranded wire core. Used for radio communication and thin Ethernet (10Base2).
RG-58 C/U	Used for military specifications.
RG-6	Often used for cable TV and cable modems.

Fiber-Optic Cables

In many ways, fiber-optic media addresses the shortcomings of copper-based media. Because fiber-based media use light transmissions instead of electronic pulses, threats such as EMI, crosstalk, and attenuation become nonissues. Fiber is well suited for the transfer of data, video, and voice transmissions. In addition, fiber-optic is the most secure of all cable media. Anyone trying to access data signals on a fiber-optic cable must physically tap into the medium. Given the composition of the cable, this is a particularly difficult task.

Unfortunately, despite the advantages of fiber-based media over copper, it still does not enjoy the popularity of twisted-pair cabling. The moderately difficult installation and maintenance procedures of fiber often require skilled technicians with specialized tools. Furthermore, the cost of a fiber-based solution limits the number of organizations that can afford to implement it. Another sometimes hidden drawback of implementing a fiber solution is the cost of retrofitting existing network equipment. Fiber is incompatible with most electronic network equipment. This means you have to purchase fiber-compatible network hardware.

> **ExamAlert**
>
> Fiber-optic cable, although still more expensive than other types of cable, is well suited for high-speed data communications. It eliminates the problems associated with copper-based media, such as near-end crosstalk, EMI, and signal tampering.

As shown in Figure 6.3, fiber-optic cable is composed of a core (glass fiber) that is surrounded by *cladding* (silica). A silicone coating is next, followed by a buffer jacket. There are strength members next and then a protective sheath (polyurethane outer jacket) surrounds everything.

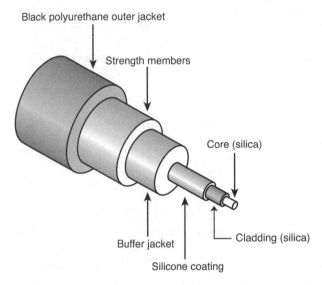

FIGURE 6.3   **Fiber-optic cabling.**

Two types of fiber-optic cable are available:

▶ **Multimode fiber**: Many beams of light travel through the cable, bouncing off the cable walls. This strategy actually weakens the signal, reducing the length and speed at which the data signal can travel.

▶ **Single-mode fiber**: Uses a single direct beam of light, thus allowing for greater distances and increased transfer speeds.

Some of the common types of fiber-optic cable include the following:

▶ 62.5-micron core/125-micron cladding multimode

▶ 50-micron core/125-micron cladding multimode

▶ 8.3-micron core/125-micron cladding single mode

In the ever-increasing search for bandwidth that can keep pace with the demands of modern applications, fiber-optic cables are sure to play a key role.

Plenum Cables

Plenum is the mysterious space that resides between the false, or drop, ceiling and the true ceiling. This space typically is used for air conditioning and heating ducts. It might also hold a myriad of cables, including telephone, electrical, and networking. The cables that occupy this space must be plenum-rated. Plenum cables are coated with a nonflammable material, often Teflon or Kynar, and they do not give off toxic fumes if they catch fire. As you might imagine, plenum-rated cables cost more than regular cables, but they are mandatory when cables are not run through a conduit. As a bonus, plenum-rated cables suffer from less attenuation than non-plenum cables.

Types of Media Connectors

A variety of connectors are used with the associated network media. Media connectors attach to the transmission media and allow the physical connection into the computing device. For the Network+ exam, you need to identify the connectors associated with a specific medium. The following sections describe the connectors and associated media.

BNC Connectors

BNC connectors are associated with coaxial media and 10Base2 networks. BNC connectors are not as common as they previously were, but they still are used on some networks, older network cards, and older hubs. Common BNC connectors include a barrel connector, T-connector, and terminators. Figure 6.4 shows two terminators (top and bottom) and two T-connectors (left and right).

Terminators

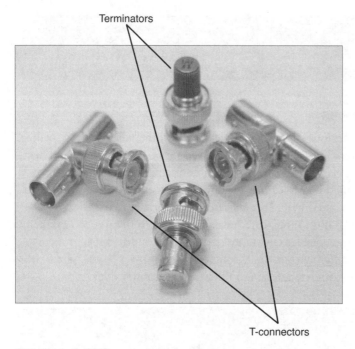

T-connectors

FIGURE 6.4   **BNC connectors.**

RJ-11 Connectors

RJ- (registered jack) 11 connectors are small plastic connectors used on telephone cables. They have capacity for six small pins. However, in many cases, not all the pins are used. For example, a standard telephone connection uses only two pins, and a cable used for a DSL modem connection uses four.

RJ-11 connectors are somewhat similar to RJ-45 connectors, which are discussed next, although they are a little smaller. Both RJ-11 and RJ-45 connectors have a small plastic flange on top of the connector to ensure a secure connection. Figure 6.5 shows two views of an RJ-11 connector.

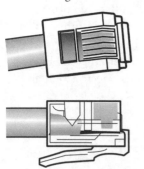

FIGURE 6.5   **RJ-11 connectors.**

RJ-45 Connectors

RJ-45 connectors, as shown in Figure 6.6, are the ones you are most likely to encounter in your network travels. RJ-45 connectors are used with twisted-pair cabling, the most prevalent network cable in use today. RJ-45 connectors resemble the aforementioned RJ-11 phone jacks, but they support up to eight wires instead of the six supported by RJ-11 connectors. RJ-45 connectors are also larger than RJ-11 connectors.

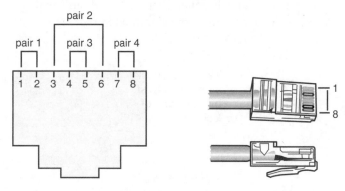

FIGURE 6.6   **RJ-45 connectors.**

F-Type Connectors and RG-59 and RG-6 Cables

F-Type connectors, as shown in Figure 6.7, are screw-on connections used to attach coaxial cable to devices. This includes RG-59 and RG-6 cables. In the world of modern networking, F-Type connectors are most commonly associated with connecting Internet modems to cable or satellite Internet service providers' (ISPs') equipment. However, F-Type connectors are also used to connect to some proprietary peripherals.

FIGURE 6.7   **F-Type connector.**

F-Type connectors have a "nut" on the connection that provides something to grip as the connection is tightened by hand. If necessary, this nut can also be lightly gripped with pliers to aid disconnection.

ExamAlert

For the Network+ exam, you will be expected to identify the connectors discussed in this chapter by their appearance.

Fiber Connectors

A variety of connectors are associated with fiber cabling, and there are several ways of connecting them. These include bayonet, snap-lock, and push-pull connectors. Figure 6.8 shows the fiber connectors identified in the Network+ objectives.

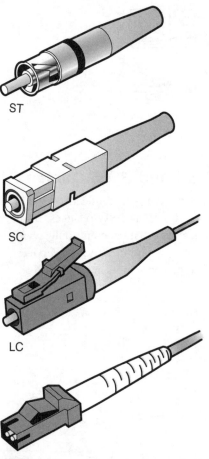

The ST connector uses a half-twist bayonet type of lock.

ST

The SC uses a push-pull connector similar to common audio and video plugs and sockets.

SC

LC connectors have a flange on top, similar to an RJ-45 connector, that aids secure connection.

LC

MT-RJ is a popular connector for two fibers in a very small form factor.

MT-RJ

FIGURE 6.8 Fiber connectors.

> **ExamAlert**
>
> As with the other connectors discussed in this section, be prepared to identify fiber connectors by their appearance and by how they are physically connected.

RS-232 Standard Connectors

RS-232 (Recommended Standard 232) is a TIA/EIA standard for serial transmission between computers and peripheral devices such as modems, mice, and keyboards. The RS-232 standard was introduced way back in the 1960s and is still used today. However, peripheral devices are more commonly connected using USB or wireless connections. RS-232 commonly uses a 25-pin DB-25 connector or a nine-pin DB-9 connector. Figure 6.9 shows an example of RS-232 standard connectors with the numbers identifying the pin sequences used by all.

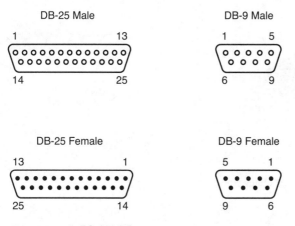

FIGURE 6.9   **RS-232 DB connectors.**

Of course, serial connectors need to attach to a serial cable. Serial cables often use four to six wires to attach to the connectors. Similar to other cable types, they can come in both an unshielded and shielded type. Shielding reduces interference and EMI for the cable. The distance that a length of serial cable can run varies somewhat. It depends on the characteristics of the serial port and, of course, the quality of the serial cable. The RS-232 standard specifies serial cable distances up to 50 feet and a transfer speed up to 20kbps. Other serial standards increase this range and speed.

Universal Serial Bus (USB) Connectors

Universal Serial Bus (USB) ports are now an extremely common sight on both desktop and laptop computer systems. Like IEEE 1394, USB is associated more with connecting consumer peripherals such as MP3 players and digital cameras than with networking. However, many manufacturers now make wireless network cards that plug directly into a USB port. Most desktop and laptop computers have between two and four USB ports, but USB hubs are available that provide additional ports if required.

A number of connectors are associated with USB ports, but the two most popular are Type A and Type B. Type A connectors are the more common of the two and are the type used on PCs. Although many peripheral devices also use a Type A connector, an increasing number now use a Type B. Figure 6.10 shows a Type A connector and a Type B connector.

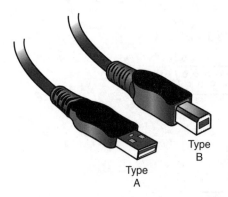

Type
B

Type
A

FIGURE 6.10   **Type A and Type B connectors.**

Media Converters

When you have two dissimilar types of network media, a *media converter* is used to allow them to connect. Depending upon the conversion being done, the converter can be a small device barely larger than the connectors themselves, or a large device within a sizable chassis.

Reasons for not using the same media throughout the network, and thus reasons for needing a converter, can range from cost (gradually moving from coax to fiber), disparate segments (connecting the office to the factory), or needing to run a particular media in a setting (the need for fiber to reduce EMI problems in a small part of the building).

Figure 6.11 shows an example of a media converter. The one shown converts between 10/100/1000TX and 1000LX (with an SC-type connector).

FIGURE 6.11   **1000TX to 1000LX Media Converter.**

The following converters are commonly implemented and ones that CompTIA includes on the Network+ exam.

ExamAlert

Make sure you know that the possibilities listed here exist.

▶ Singlemode fiber to Ethernet

▶ Singlemode to multimode fiber

▶ Multimode fiber to Ethernet

▶ Fiber to Coaxial

Note

Media converters were also discussed in Chapter 4, "Components and Devices."

568A and 568B Wiring Standards

568A and 568B are telecommunications standards from TIA and EIA. These 568 standards specify the pin arrangements for the RJ-45 connectors on UTP or STP cables. The number 568 refers to the order in which the wires within the Category 5 cable are terminated and attached to the connector.

The 568A and 568B standards (often referred to as *T568A* and *T568B* for termination standard) are quite similar; the difference is the order in which the pins are terminated. The signal is the same for both. Both are used for patch cords in an Ethernet network.

Network media may not always come with connectors attached, or you might need to make custom length cables. This is when you need to know something about how these standards actually work. Before you can crimp on the connectors, you need to know in which order the individual wires will be attached to the connector. Figure 6.12 shows the pin number assignments for the T568A and T568B standards.

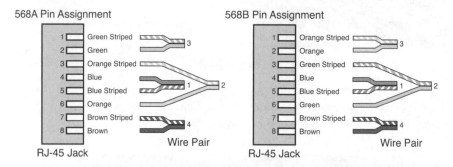

FIGURE 6.12 **Pin assignments for the T568A and T568B standards.**

Straight-Through Versus Crossover Cables

Two types of cables are used to connect devices to hubs and switches: crossover cables and straight-through cables. The difference between the two types is that in a crossover cable, two of the wires are crossed; in a straight-through cable, all the wires run straight through.

Specifically, in a crossover cable, wires 1 and 3 and wires 2 and 6 are crossed. Wire 1 at one end becomes wire 3 at the other end, wire 2 at one end becomes wire 6 at the other end, and vice versa in both cases. You can see the differences between the two cables in Figures 6.13 and 6.14. Figure 6.13 shows the pinouts for a straight-through cable, and Figure 6.14 shows the pinouts for a crossover cable.

Exam Alert

The crossover cable can be used to directly network two PCs without using a hub or switch. This is done because the cable performs the function of the switch.

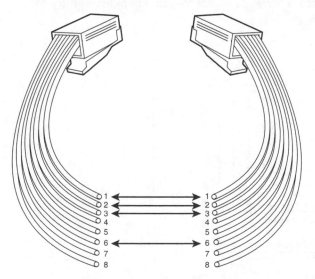

FIGURE 6.13 **Pinouts for a straight-through twisted-pair cable.**

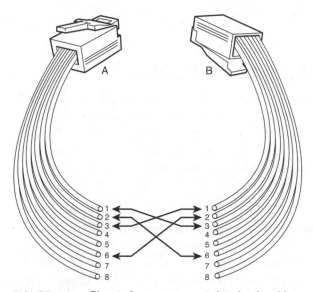

FIGURE 6.14 **Pinouts for a crossover twisted-pair cable.**

To make a crossover Ethernet cable, you need to use both the 568A and 568B standards. One end of the cable can be wired according to the 568A standard, and the other with the 568B standard.

A *T1 crossover* cable, the pinouts of which are shown in Figure 6.15, is used to connect two T1 CSU/DSU devices in a back-to-back configuration. RJ-45 connectors are used on both ends.

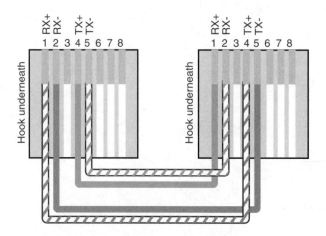

PRI (T1/E1) CrossOver/Loopback Cable

FIGURE 6.15   Pinouts for a T1 crossover cable.

Rollover and Loopback Cables

The rollover cable is a Cisco proprietary cable used to connect a computer system to a router or switch console port. The rollover cable resembles an Ethernet UTP cable; however, it is not possible to use it on anything but Cisco equipment. Like UTP cable, the rollover cable has eight wires inside and an RJ-45 connector on each end that connect to the router and the computer port.

As far as pinouts are concerned, pin 1 on one end of the rollover cable connects to pin 8 at the other end of the cable. Similarly, pin 2 connects to pin 7, and so on. The ends are simply reversed. As soon as one end of the rollover cable is connected to the PC and the other to the Cisco terminal, the Cisco equipment can be accessed from the computer system using a program such as HyperTerminal.

> **ExamAlert**
>
> Remember that the rollover cable is a proprietary cable used to connect a PC to a Cisco router.

A loopback cable, also known as a plug, is used to test and isolate network problems. If made correctly, the loopback plug causes the link light on a device such as a network interface card (NIC) to come on. This is a quick and cheap way to test simple network cabling problems. The loopback plug redirects outgoing data signals to the system. The system then believes that it is both sending and receiving data.

The loopback cable is basically a troubleshooting tool used to test the device to see if it is sending and receiving properly. It uses UTP cable and RJ-45 connectors.

> **ExamAlert**
>
> Know a loopback cable is a basic troubleshooting tool.

Components of Wiring Distribution

So far, this chapter has examined various types of media and the associated connectors. This section looks at wiring in the closet, the place in networks where you connect the cables and networking devices. These rooms have many names, including the wiring closet, the telecommunications room, and the network operations center (NOC). These telecommunications rooms contain the key network devices, such as the hubs, routers, switches, and servers. These rooms also contain the network media, such as patch cables that connect network devices to horizontal cables and the rest of the network.

Network Cross-Connects

The cable that runs throughout a network can be divided into two distinct sections:

- ▶ **Horizontal cabling**: Connects client systems to the network.
- ▶ **Vertical (backbone) cabling**: Runs between floors to connect different locations on the network.

Both of these cable types have to be consolidated and distributed from a location—a wiring closet.

Following are three types of cable distribution:

▸ **Vertical or main cross-connect**: The location where outside cables enter the building for distribution. This can include Internet and phone cabling.

▸ **Horizontal cross-connect**: The location where the vertical and horizontal connections meet.

▸ **Intermediate cross-connect**: Typically used in larger networks. Provides an intermediate cross-connect between the main and horizontal cross-connects.

The term *cross-connect* refers to the point where the cables running throughout the network meet and are connected.

Horizontal Cabling

Within the telecommunications room, horizontal cabling connects the telecommunications room to the end user, as shown in Figure 6.16. Specifically, the horizontal cabling extends from the telecommunications outlet, or a network outlet with RJ-45 connectors, at the client end. It includes all cable from that outlet to the telecommunications room to the horizontal cross-connect—the distribution point for the horizontal cable. The horizontal cross-connect includes all connecting hardware, such as patch panels and patch cords. The horizontal cross-connect is the termination point for all network horizontal cables.

Horizontal cabling runs within walls and ceilings and therefore is called *permanent cable* or *structure cable*. The length of cable running from the horizontal connects and the telecommunication outlet on the client side should not exceed 90 meters. Patch cables used typically should not exceed 5 meters. This is due to the 100-meter distance limitation of most UTP cable.

> **Note**
>
> Horizontal wiring includes all cabling run from the wall plate or network connection to the telecommunications closet. The outlets, cable, and cross-connects in the closet are all part of the horizontal wiring, which gets its name because the cable typically runs horizontally above ceilings or along the floor.

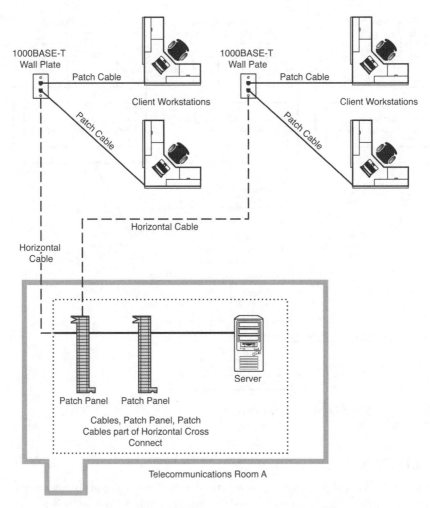

FIGURE 6.16 **Horizontal cabling.**

Vertical Cables

Vertical cable, or backbone cable, refers to the media used to connect telecommunications rooms, server rooms, and remote locations and offices. Vertical cable may be used to connect locations outside the local LAN that require high-speed connections. Therefore, vertical cable is often fiber-optic cable or high-speed UTP cable. Figure 6.17 shows the relationship between horizontal cable and vertical cable.

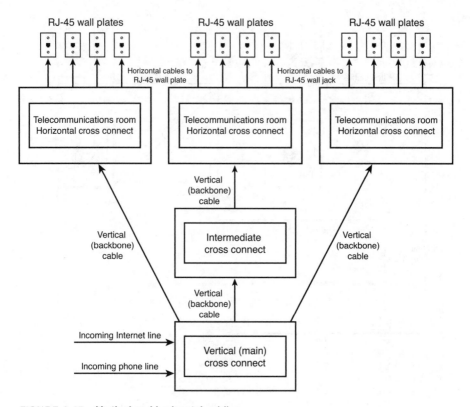

FIGURE 6.17 **Vertical and horizontal cabling.**

Patch Panels

If you've ever looked in a telecommunications room, you have probably seen a distribution block, more commonly called a patch panel. A *patch panel* is a freestanding or wall-mounted unit with a number of RJ-45 port connections on the front. In a way, it looks like a wall-mounted hub without the light-emitting diodes (LEDs). The patch panel provides a connection point between network equipment such as hubs and switches and the ports to which PCs are connected, which normally are distributed throughout a building.

> **Note**
>
> Not all environments use patch panels. In some environments, cables run directly between systems and a hub or switch. This is an acceptable method of connectivity, but it is not as easy to make tidy as a structured cabling system that uses a patch panel system and wall or floor sockets.

Also found in a wiring closet is the punchdown block. The wires from a telephony or UTP cable are attached to the punchdown block using a *punch-down tool*. To use the punchdown tool, you place the wires in the tip of the tool and push it into the connectors attached to the punchdown block. The wire insulation is stripped, and the wires are firmly embedded into the metal connector. Because the connector strips the insulation on the wire, it is known rather grandiosely as an *insulation displacement connector (IDC)*. Figure 6.18 shows a punchdown tool placing wires into an IDC of a patch panel.

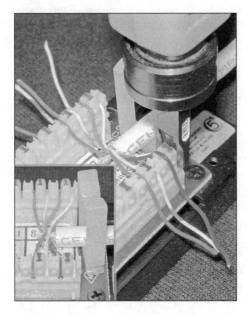

FIGURE 6.18 **Punchdown tool inserting wires into an IDC.**

Using a punchdown tool is much faster than using wire strippers to prepare each individual wire and then twisting the wire around a connection pole or tightening a screw to hold the wire in place. In many environments, cable tasks are left to a specialized cable contractor. In others, the administrator is the one who must connect wires to a patch panel.

110 Blocks (T568A, T568B)

Two main types of punchdown blocks are used: type 66 and type 110. Type 66 is an older design used to connect wiring for telephone systems and other low-speed network systems and is not as widely used as type 110. The 66 block has 50 rows of IDC contacts to accommodate 25-pair twisted-pair cable. Block 66 was used primarily for voice communication. Although it is approved for Category 5, it may not be suitable due to crosstalk problems.

In the network wiring closet, the 110 block is used to connect network cable to patch panels. 110 connections can also be used at the other end of the network cable at the RJ-45 wall jack. 110 blocks are preferred over the older 66 blocks, the 110 block improves on the 66 block by supporting higher frequencies and less crosstalk. Therefore, it supports higher-speed networks and higher grade twisted-pair cable. The termination will be T568A or T568B, depending upon which wiring standard is used, and both were illustrated in Figure 6.12.

MDF and IDF Wiring Closets

The preceding section looked at wiring closets. Two types of wiring closets are Main Distribution Frame (MDF) and Intermediate Distribution Frame (IDF). The main wiring closet for a network typically holds the majority of the network gear, including routers, switches, wiring, servers, and more. This is also typically the wiring closet where outside lines run into the network. This main wiring closet is known as the MDF. One of the key components in the MDF is a primary patch panel. The network connector jacks attached to this patch panel lead out to the building for network connections.

In some networks, multiple wiring closets are used. When this is the case, the MDF connects to these secondary wiring closets, or IDFs, using a backbone cable. This backbone cable may be UTP, fiber, or even coaxial. In today's high-speed networks, UTP Gigabit Ethernet or high-speed fiber are the media of choice. Figure 6.19 shows the relationship between the MDF and the IDF.

ExamAlert

Be prepared to identify the difference between an IDF and an MDF.

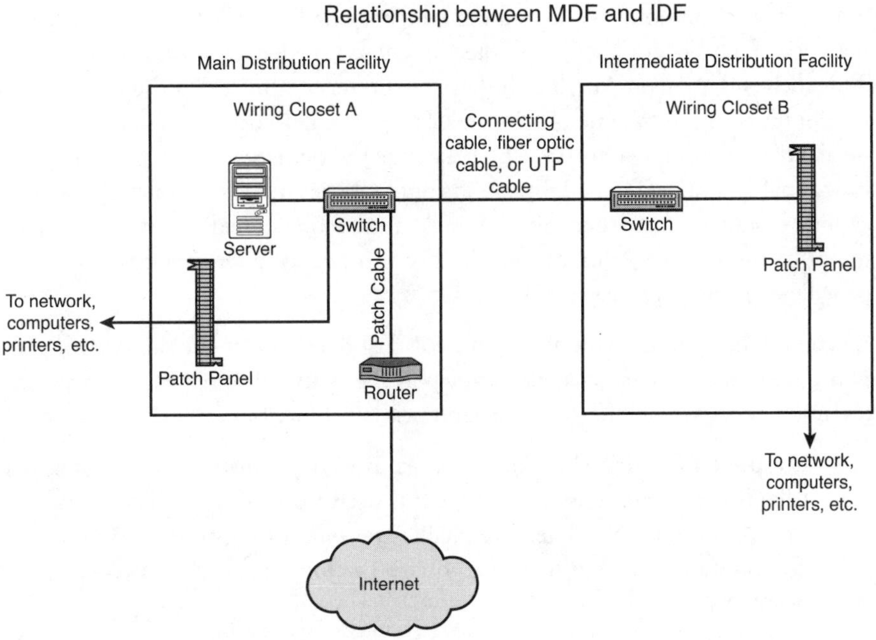

Relationship between MDF and IDF

FIGURE 6.19 The relationship between MDFs and IDFs.

Demarc, Demarc Extension, and Smart Jacks

A network's demarcation point is the connection point between the operator's part of the network and the customer's portion of the network. This point is important for network administrators because it distinguishes the portion of the network that the customer is responsible for from the section the owner is responsible for. For example, for those who have high-speed Internet, the boundary between the customer's premises and the ISP typically is mounted on the wall on the side of the home. However, high-speed service providers support everything from the cable modem back to their main distribution center. This is why, if a modem fails, it is replaced by the ISP and not by the customer. This is true for the wiring to that point as well.

As mentioned, knowing the location of the demarcation point is essential, because it marks the point between where the customer (or administrator) is responsible and where the owner is. It also identifies the point at which the customer is responsible should a problem occur and who should pay for that problem. The ISP is responsible for ensuring that the network is functional up to the demarcation point. The customer/administrator is responsible for ensuring that everything from that point is operational.

The demarcation point is the point at which the ISP places its services in your network. There is not always a choice of where this demarcation is placed. This means that a company might have six floors of offices and the demarcation point is in the basement—impractical for the network. This is when you need a demarcation extension, which extends the demarcation point to a more functional location. This might sound simple, but it involves knowledge of cabling distances and other infrastructure needs. The demarcation extension might be the responsibility of the administrator, or for a fee, owners might provide extension services.

As you might imagine, you need some form of hardware at the demarcation point. This is the smart jack, also known as the Network Interface Device (NID). The smart jack performs several primary functions:

▶ **Loopback feature**: The loopback feature is built into the smart jack. Like the Ethernet loopback cable, it is used for testing purposes. In this case, the loopback feature enables remote testing so that technicians do not always need to be called to visit the local network to isolate problems.

▶ **Signal amplification**: The smart jack can amplify signals. This feature is similar to that of the function of repeaters in an Ethernet network.

▶ **Surge protection**: Lighting and other environmental conditions can cause electrical surges that can quickly damage equipment. Many smart jacks include protection from environmental situations.

▶ **Remote alarms**: Smart jacks typically include an alarm that allows the owner to identify if something goes wrong with the smart jack and therefore the connections at the demarcation point.

> **ExamAlert**
>
> Demarc is the telephone company or ISP term for where their facilities or wires end and where yours begin.

CSUs/DSUs

A Channel Service Unit/Data Service Unit (CSU/DSU) acts as a translator between the LAN data format and the WAN data format. Such a conversion is necessary because the technologies used on WAN links are different from those used on LANs. Some consider a CSU/DSU a type of digital modem. But unlike a normal modem, which changes the signal from digital to analog, a CSU/DSU changes the signal from one digital format to another.

A CSU/DSU has physical connections for the LAN equipment, normally via a serial interface, and another connection for a WAN.

> ### Exam**Alert**
>
> Traditionally, the CSU/DSU has been in a box separate from other networking equipment. However, the increasing use of WAN links means that some router manufacturers are now including CSU/DSU functionality in routers or are providing the expansion capability to do so.

Verify Wiring Installation and Termination

After a segment of network cable has been placed where it needs to go, whether run through the plenum or connecting a patch cable, the final task is wiring termination. Termination is the process to connect the network cable to the wall jack, plug, or patch panel. Termination generally is a straightforward process. You can quickly see if the wiring and termination worked if the LED on the connected network card is lit. Also, if you connect a client system, you can ping other devices on the network if all works.

If you run the wiring and complete termination, but a system cannot access the network and the link light is not lit, you should look for a few things when troubleshooting the wiring installation and termination.

Verify that the termination and wiring installation link light on the device (switch/NIC) is not lit:

> ▶ If you connect a patch cable to a PC or switch, and no link light is lit, verify that the patch cable is good by switching it with a known working one.
>
> ▶ If it is a homemade patch cable, ensure that the RJ-45 connector is properly attached.
>
> ▶ Ensure that the RJ-45 connector is properly seated in the wall jack and NIC or switch port.
>
> ▶ If no link light is lit when you connect to a switch, change to another port on the switch. Sometimes a single port can be faulty.
>
> ▶ Verify that the correct patch cable is used. It is possible that a rollover cable or crossover cable has been accidentally used.
>
> ▶ Verify that the cables used are the correct standard. For example, the patch cable should be a 568A or 568B.

If the link light on a device is lit and intermittent problems occur, check the following:

- ▶ Try replacing the cable with a known working one.

- ▶ Verify where the network cable is run. Ensure that a plenum-rated cable is used if it runs through ceilings or ductwork.

- ▶ Look for heavy bends or partial breaks in the network cable.

- ▶ Verify that shielded cabling is used in areas of potentially high interference.

- ▶ Check the length of the cable run. Remember, the total run of cable should be about 100 meters. If the patch cable or the cable between the wall jack and the wiring closet is too long, intermittent signals can occur.

Cram Quiz

1. Which of following connectors is commonly used with fiber cabling?
   - ○ **A.** RJ-45
   - ○ **B.** BNC
   - ○ **C.** SC
   - ○ **D.** RJ-11

2. Which of the following describes the loss of signal strength as a signal travels through a particular medium?
   - ○ **A.** Attenuation
   - ○ **B.** Crosstalk
   - ○ **C.** EMI
   - ○ **D.** Chatter

3. What kind of cable would you associate with an F-type connector?
   - ○ **A.** Fiber-optic
   - ○ **B.** UTP
   - ○ **C.** Coaxial
   - ○ **D.** STP

4. A user calls to report that he is experiencing periodic problems connecting to the network. Upon investigation, you find that the cable connecting the user's PC to the switch is close to a fluorescent light fitting. What condition is most likely causing the problem?
   - ○ **A.** Crosstalk
   - ○ **B.** EMI
   - ○ **C.** Attenuation
   - ○ **D.** Faulty cable

5. Which of the following is not a type of fiber-optic connector used in network implementations?
   - ○ **A.** MT-RJ
   - ○ **B.** SC
   - ○ **C.** BNC
   - ○ **D.** LC

6. Which of the following fiber connectors uses a twist-type connection method?

   ○ **A.** ST

   ○ **B.** SC

   ○ **C.** BNC

   ○ **D.** SA

7. Which Broadband over Power Lines standard exists for high-speed communication devices?

   ○ **A.** MLME

   ○ **B.** IEEE 754

   ○ **C.** IEEE 1901

   ○ **D.** Wibree

8. In a crossover cable, which wire is wire 1 crossed with?

   ○ **A.** 2

   ○ **B.** 3

   ○ **C.** 4

   ○ **D.** 5

9. What are the two main types of punchdown blocks? (Choose two.)

   ○ **A.** 110

   ○ **B.** 220

   ○ **C.** 66

   ○ **D.** 12

10. What device acts as a translator between the LAN data format and the WAN data format?

    ○ **A.** CSMA/CD

    ○ **B.** T568B

    ○ **C.** MTRJ

    ○ **D.** CSU/DSU

Cram Quiz Answers

1. **C.** SC connectors are used with fiber-optic cable. RJ-45 connectors are used with UTP cable, BNC is used for thin coax cable, and RJ-11 is used for regular phone connectors.

2. **A.** The term used to describe the loss of signal strength for media is attenuation. Crosstalk refers to the interference between two cables, EMI is electromagnetic interference, and chatter is not a valid media interference concern.

3. **C.** F-type connectors are used with coaxial cables. They are not used with fiber-optic, Unshielded Twisted Pair (UTP), or Shielded Twisted Pair (STP) cabling.

4. **B.** EMI is a type of interference that is often seen when cables run too close to electrical devices. Crosstalk is when two cables interfere with each other. Attenuation is a loss of signal strength. Answer D is incorrect also. It may be that a faulty cable is causing the problem. However, the question asked for the most likely cause. Because the cable is running near fluorescent lights, the problem is more likely associated with EMI.

5. **C.** BNC is a connector type used with coaxial cabling. It is not used as a connector for fiber-optic cabling. MT-RJ, SC, and LC are all recognized types of fiber-optic connectors.

6. **A.** ST fiber connectors use a twist-type connection method. SC connectors use a push-type connection method. The other choices are not valid fiber connectors.

7. **C.** The IEEE 1901 standard applies to high-speed communication devices and Broadband over Power Lines (BPL). The other choices are not valid for Broadband over Power Lines.

8. **B.** In a crossover cable, wires 1 and 3 and wires 2 and 6 are crossed.

9. **A,C.** The two main types of punchdown blocks are type 66 and type 110. Type 66 is an older design used to connect wiring for telephone systems and other low-speed network systems and is not as widely used as type 110.

10. **D.** A Channel Service Unit/Data Service Unit (CSU/DSU) acts as a translator between the LAN data format and the WAN data format. Such a conversion is necessary because the technologies used on WAN links are different from those used on LANs.

Comparing and Contrasting LAN Technologies

▶ **Compare and contrast different LAN technologies.**

CramSaver

If you can correctly answer these questions before going through this section, save time by skimming the Exam Alerts in this section and then complete the Cram Quiz at the end of the section.

1. What are the characteristics/limitations of 1000BaseCX?

2. Which IEEE standard defines 10Gbps networks?

3. What type of connectors can be used with 100BaseTX networks?

Answers

1. 1000BaseCX offers 1000Mbps transfer speeds over shielded copper cable. Distances are restricted to 25 meters.

2. 10Gbps networks are defined by the IEEE 802.3ae standard.

3. 100BaseTX networks use RJ-45 connectors.

The Institute of Electrical and Electronics Engineers (IEEE) developed a series of networking standards to ensure that networking technologies developed by respective manufacturers are compatible. This means that the cabling, networking devices, and protocols are all interchangeable when designed under the banner of a specific IEEE standard. Table 6.3 summarizes the IEEE 802 networking standards.

TABLE 6.3 **IEEE 802 Networking Standards**

Specification	Name
802.1	Internetworking
802.2	The LLC (Logical Link Control) sublayer
802.3	CSMA/CD (Carrier Sense Multiple Access with Collision Detection) for Ethernet networks
802.4	A token-passing bus
802.5	Token ring networks
802.6	Metropolitan area network (MAN)
802.7	Broadband Technical Advisory Group

Specification	Name
802.8	Fiber-Optic Technical Advisory Group
802.9	Integrated voice and data networks
802.10	Standards for Interoperable LAN/MAN Security (SILS) (network security)
802.11	Wireless networks
802.12	100Mbps technologies, including 100BaseVG-AnyLAN

Each of these IEEE specifications outlines specific characteristics for LAN networking, including the speed, topology, cabling, and access method. The following sections outline the key features of the standards you are likely to encounter on the Network+ exam.

IEEE 802.2 Standard

The 802.2 standard, called Logical Link Control (LLC), manages data flow control and error control for the other IEEE LAN standards. Data flow control regulates how much data can be transmitted in a certain amount of time. Error control refers to the recognition and notification of damaged signals. The LLC layer is discussed more in Chapter 2, "OSI and TCP/IP Models and Networking Protocols."

IEEE 802.3x Standard Characteristics

The IEEE 802.3 standards define a range of networking systems based on the original Ethernet standard. The variations for each standard include speed, access method, physical topology, and implementation considerations. The next sections review some of the characteristics specified within each standard.

Speed

Many factors contribute to the speed of a network. The standard defines the maximum speed of a networking system. The speed is measured in either megabits per second (Mbps), or gigabits per second (Gbps, where 1Gbps is equivalent to 1000Mbps).

> Note
>
> The term bandwidth has become a gray area in the networking world. In everyday use it is sometimes used to describe the amount of data that can travel over a network connection in a given time period. This is technically not accurate; it more closely defines data throughput.

Some networks are faster than others. For example, a token ring (802.5) network has a maximum speed of 16Mbps. Many Ethernet networks (802.3 variants) operate at 1000Mbps and beyond. However, the maximum speed attainable on a network can be affected by many factors. Networks that achieve 100% of their potential bandwidth are few and far between.

Access Methods

Access methods govern how systems access the network media and send data. Access methods are necessary to ensure that systems on the network can communicate with each other. Without an access method, two systems could communicate at the exclusion of every other system. Access methods ensure that everyone gets an opportunity to use the network.

Several access methods are used in networks; the most popular are CSMA/CD and CSMA/CA. Look at CSMA/CD first and then CSMA/CA.

Carrier Sense Multiple Access/Collision Detection (CSMA/CD), which is defined in the IEEE 802.3 standard, is the most common media access method because it is associated with 802.3 Ethernet networking, which is by far the most popular networking system.

On a network that uses CSMA/CD, when a system wants to send data to another system, it first checks to see whether the network medium is free. It must do this because each piece of network medium used in a LAN can carry only one signal at a time. If the sending node detects that the medium is free, it transmits, and the data is sent to the destination. It seems simple.

> **ExamAlert**
>
> A node is *any* device connected to the network. A node might be a client computer, server computer, printer, router, or gateway.

Now, if it always worked like this, you wouldn't need the CD part of CSMA/CD. Unfortunately, in networking, as in life, things do not always go as planned. The problem arises when two systems attempt to transmit at exactly the same time. It might seem unlikely that two systems would pick the exact same moment to send data, but you are dealing with communications that occur many times in a single second—and most networks have more than two machines. Imagine that 200 people are in a room. The room is silent, but then two people decide to say something at exactly the same time. Before they start to speak, they check (listen) to see whether someone else is speaking;

because no one else is speaking, they begin to talk. The result is two people speaking at the same time, which is similar to a network collision.

Collision detection works by detecting fragments of the transmission on the network media that result when two systems try to talk at the same time. The two systems wait for a randomly calculated amount of time before attempting to transmit again. This amount of time—a matter of milliseconds—is known as the *backoff* period or jam signal.

> **Exam Alert**
>
> Know that collisions do occur with CSMA. You can detect them (CD) or attempt to avoid them (CA).

When the backoff period has elapsed, the system attempts to transmit again. If the system doesn't succeed on the second attempt, it keeps retrying until it gives up and reports an error.

> **Exam Alert**
>
> CSMA/CD is known as a contention media access method because systems contend for access to the media.

The upside of CSMA/CD is that it has relatively low overhead, meaning that not much is involved in the workings of the system. The downside is that as more systems are added to the network, more collisions occur, and the network becomes slower. The performance of a network that uses CSMA/CD degrades exponentially as more systems are added. Its low overhead means that CSMA/CD systems theoretically can achieve greater speeds than high-overhead systems, such as token passing. However, because collisions take place, the chance of all that speed translating into usable bandwidth is relatively low.

> **Exam Alert**
>
> On a network that uses CSMA/CD, every node has equal access to the network media.

Despite its problems, CSMA/CD is an efficient system. As a result, rather than replace it with some other technology, workarounds have been created that reduce the likelihood of collisions. One such strategy is the use of network switches that create multiple collision domains and therefore reduce the impact of collisions on performance.

Instead of collision detection, as with CSMA/CD, the Carrier Sense Multiple Access with Collision Avoidance (CSMA/CA) access method uses signal avoidance rather than detection. In a networked environment, CSMA/CA is the access mechanism used in Apple's LocalTalk network and with the 802.11 wireless standards.

On CSMA/CA networks, each computer signals its intent to transmit data signals before any data is actually sent. When a networked system detects a potential collision, it waits before sending the transmission, allowing systems to avoid transmission collisions. The CSMA/CA access method uses a random backoff time that determines how long to wait before trying to send data on the network. When the backoff time expires, the system again "listens" to verify a clear channel on which to transmit. If the medium is still busy, another backoff interval is initiated that is less than the first. The process continues until the wait time reaches zero, and the medium is clear.

CSMA/CA uses a broadcast method to signal its intention to transmit data. Network broadcasts create a considerable amount of network traffic and can cause network congestion, which could slow down the entire network. Because CSMA/CD and CSMA/CA differ only in terms of detection and avoidance, they have similar advantages and disadvantages.

> **ExamAlert**
>
> Know that CSMA/CA uses broadcasts.

> **Note**
>
> The CSMA/CA access method uses a "listen before talking" strategy. Any system wanting to transmit data must first verify that the channel is clear before transmitting, thereby avoiding potential collisions.

Bonding

Bonding, also known as *channel bonding*, enables you to use multiple channels at the same time to increase performance. Chapter 7, "Wireless," for example, discusses how wireless technologies use bonding to help increase transmission rates.

Topology

As discussed in Chapter 1, topologies dictate both the physical and logical layouts of the network. Remember that topologies include bus, star, ring, mesh, and wireless. Each of the IEEE LAN standards can be implemented by using the topology specified within the standard. Some standards, such as 802.3 (Ethernet), have multiple physical topologies but always use the same logical topology. Token Ring has two possible physical topologies and a single logical topology.

Media

Each IEEE specification defines what media are available to transport the signal around the network. The term *media*, which is the plural of *medium*, generically describes the methods by which data is transported from one point to another. Common network media types include twisted-pair cable, coaxial cable, infrared, radio frequency, and fiber-optic cable.

802.3 Ethernet Standards

Now that you know some of the characteristics defined by the IEEE standards, examine the standards. Make sure that you are completely familiar with the information provided in each of the following sections before you take the Network+ exam.

10BaseT

The 10BaseT LAN standard specifies an Ethernet network that commonly uses unshielded twisted-pair cable. However, in some implementations that require a greater resistance to interference and attenuation, shielded twisted pair (STP) can be used. STP has extra shielding to combat interference.

10BaseT uses baseband transmission and has a maximum physical segment length of 100 meters. Repeaters are sometimes used to extend the maximum segment length; although, the repeating capability is now often built into networking devices used in twisted-pair networks. 10BaseT specifies transmission speeds of 10Mbps and can use several categories of UTP cable, including Categories 3, 4, 5, and 6 (all of which use RJ-45 connectors). 10BaseT takes advantage of the multiple wires inside twisted-pair cable to create independent transmit and receive paths, which means that full-duplex mode can optionally be supported. The maximum number of computers supported on a 10BaseT network is 1,024.

All 10BaseT networks use a point-to-point network design, with one end of the connection attaching to the network card and the other to a hub or switch. These point-to-point connections result in a physical star topology.

> **Note**
>
> You can link two 10BaseT computer systems directly, without using a hub, by using a specially constructed crossover cable. Crossover cables are also sometimes used to establish other same-device connections, such as when connecting two hubs or two switches to create a larger network.

Table 6.4 summarizes the characteristics of the 10BaseT standard.

TABLE 6.4 **Summary of 10BaseT Characteristics**

Characteristic	Description
Transmission method	Baseband
Speed	10Mbps
Total distance/segment	100 meters
Cable type	Category 3, 4, 5, or 6 UTP or STP
Connector	RJ-45

> **ExamAlert**
>
> Know the distances associated with each technology discussed in the remainder of this chapter.

100BaseTX/100BaseFX

There was a time when 10Mbps networks were considered fast enough, but those days are long gone. Today, companies and home users alike demand more bandwidth than is available with 10Mbps network solutions. For such networks, Fast Ethernet (also known as *100BaseT*) is the most commonly used network design. Three Fast Ethernet standards are specified in the IEEE 802.3u standard: 100BaseT4, 100BaseTX, and 100BaseFX—the latter two of which the Network+ exam includes in their objectives.

> **Note**
>
> 100BaseT4 is not a common implementation of Fast Ethernet. As a result, it is not included in the Network+ objectives.

100BaseTX is known as Fast Ethernet networking design and is one of three 802.3u standards. As its name suggests, 100BaseTX transmits network data at speeds up to 100Mbps, the speeds at which most LANs operate today. 100BaseTX is most often implemented with UTP cable, but it can use STP; therefore, it suffers from the same 100-meter distance limitations as other UTP-based networks. 100BaseTX uses Category 5 UTP cable, and, like 10BaseT, it uses independent transmit and receive paths and therefore can support full-duplex operation. 100BaseTX is, without question, the most common Fast Ethernet standard.

> **Tip**
>
> Repeaters are sometimes needed when you connect segments that use 100BaseTX, or 100BaseFX.

100BaseFX is the IEEE standard for running Fast Ethernet over fiber-optic cable. Due to the expense of fiber implementations, 100BaseFX is largely limited to use as a network backbone. 100BaseFX can use two-strand multimode fiber or single-mode fiber media. The maximum segment length for half-duplex multimode fiber is 412 meters, but this maximum increases to an impressive 10,000 meters for full-duplex single-mode fiber. 100BaseFX often uses SC or ST fiber connectors. Table 6.5 shows how 100BaseFX compares with other 100Base technologies.

Table 6.5 summarizes the characteristics of the 802.3u Fast Ethernet specifications.

TABLE 6.5 **Summary of 802.3u Fast Ethernet Characteristics**

Characteristic	100BaseTX	100BaseFX
Transmission method	Baseband	Baseband
Speed	100Mbps	100Mbps
Distance	100 meters	412 meters (multimode half duplex); 10,000 meters (single mode full duplex)
Cable type	Category UTP, STP	Fiber-optic
Connector type	RJ-45	SC, ST

1000BaseX

Gigabit Ethernet, *1000BaseX*, is another variation on the 802.3 standard and is given its own identifier: 802.3z. Gigabit Ethernet offers transfer rates of up to 1000Mbps and is most often associated with fiber cable, but not always.

1000BaseX refers collectively to three distinct standards: 1000BaseLX, 1000BaseSX, and 1000BaseCX.

Both 1000BaseSX and 1000BaseLX are laser standards used over fiber. *SX* refers to *short wavelength laser*, and *LX* refers to *long wavelength laser*. Both the SX and LX wave lasers can be supported over two types of multimode fiber-optic cable: fibers of 62.5-micron and 50-micron diameters. Only LX wave lasers support the use of single-mode fiber.

The differences between 1000BaseLX and 1000BaseSX have to do with cost and transmission distance. 1000BaseLX can transmit over 316 meters in half duplex for both multimode fiber and single-mode fiber, 550 meters for full-duplex multimode fiber, and 5,000 meters for full-duplex single-mode fiber. Although 1000BaseSX is less expensive than 1000BaseLX, it cannot match the distances achieved by 1000BaseLX.

1000BaseCX moves away from fiber cable and uses shielded copper wire. Segment lengths in 1000BaseCX are severely restricted; the maximum cable distance is 25 meters. Because of the restricted cable lengths, 1000BaseCX networks are not widely implemented. Table 6.6 summarizes the characteristics of Gigabit Ethernet 802.3z standards.

TABLE 6.6 **Summary of IEEE 802.3z Gigabit Ethernet Characteristics**

Characteristic	1000BaseSX	1000BaseLX	1000BaseCX
Transmission method	Baseband	Baseband	Baseband
Speed	1000Mbps	1000Mbps	1000Mbps
Distance	Half duplex 275 (62.5-micron multimode fiber); half duplex 316 (50-micron multimode fiber); full duplex 275 (62.5-micron multimode fiber); full duplex 550 (50-micron multimode fiber)	Half duplex 316 (multimode and single-mode fiber); full duplex 550 (multimode fiber); full duplex 5000 (single-mode fiber)	25 meters for both full-duplex and half-duplex operations
Cable type	62.5/125 and 50/125 multimode fiber	62.5/125 and 50/125 multimode fiber; two 10-micron single-mode optical fibers	Shielded copper cable
Connector type	Fiber connectors	Fiber connectors	Nine-pin shielded connector

1000BaseT

1000BaseT, sometimes called 1000BaseTX, is another Gigabit Ethernet standard, and it is given the IEEE 802.3ab designation. The 802.3ab standard specifies Gigabit Ethernet over Category 5 UTP cable. The standard allows for full-duplex transmission using the four pairs of twisted cable. To reach speeds of 1000Mbps over copper, a data transmission speed of 250Mbps is achieved over each pair of twisted-pair cable. Table 6.7 summarizes the characteristics of 1000BaseT.

TABLE 6.7 **Summary of 1000BaseT Characteristics**

Characteristic	Description
Transmission method	Baseband
Speed	1000Mbps
Total distance/segment	75 meters
Cable type	Category 5 or better
Connector type	RJ-45

10 Gigabit Ethernet

In the never-ending quest for faster data transmission rates, network standards are always pushed to the next level. In today's networking environments, that level is 10 Gigabit Ethernet, also called 10GbE. As the name suggests, 10GbE can provide data transmission rates of up to 10 gigabits per second. That's 10000 Mbps, or 100 times faster than most modern LAN implementations. A number of 10GbE implementations exist. This section explores the standards highlighted in the Network+ objectives.

Designed primarily as a WAN and MAN connectivity medium, 10GbE was ratified as the IEEE 802.3ae standard. Many networking hardware manufacturers now market 10GbE equipment. Although 10GbE network implementations are expensive, companies such as ISPs that require extremely high-speed networks have been relatively quick to implement 10GbE.

10GBaseSR/SW

The IEEE 802.3ae 10 Gigabit Ethernet specification includes a serial interface referred to as 10GBaseS (the S stands for short wavelength) that is designed for transmission on multimode fiber. Two Ethernet standards that fall in the S category are 10GBaseSR and 10GBaseSW. Both SR and SW are designed for deployment over short-wavelength multimode fiber. The distance range for both classifications ranges from as little as 2 meters to 300 meters. The difference between the two classifications is that SR is designed for use over dark fiber. In the networking world, dark fiber refers to "unlit" fiber or fiber that is not in use and connected to any other equipment. The 10GBaseSW standard is designed for longer-distance data communications and connects to Synchronous Optical Network (SONET) equipment. SONET is a fiber-optic transmission system for high-speed digital traffic.

> **Note**
>
> 10GBaseSR/SW is designed for LAN or MAN implementations, with a maximum distance of 300 meters using 50-micron multimode fiber cabling. 10BaseSR also can be implemented with 62.5-micron multimode fiber cabling but is limited to 33 meters.

10GBaseLR/LW

The 10GBaseLR/LW Ethernet standards are not used over multimode fiber. Instead, they offer greater distances using single-mode fiber. Both the LR and LW standards are designed to be used over long-wavelength single-mode fiber, giving it a potential transmission range of anywhere from 2 meters to 10 kilometers. This transmission range makes the standards available for LAN, MAN, and WAN deployments. As with the previous standards, the LR standard is used with dark fiber, whereas the LW standard is designed to connect to SONET equipment.

10GBaseER/EW

When it comes to WANs that require greater transmission distances, the Ethernet 10GBaseER/EW standards come into play. Both the ER and EW Gigabit standards are deployed with extra-long wavelength single-mode fiber. This medium provides transmission distances ranging from 2 meters to 40 kilometers. As with the previous two standards, ER is deployed over dark fiber, whereas the EW standard is used primarily with SONET equipment. Table 6.8 outlines the characteristics of the 10GBase Ethernet standards.

TABLE 6.8 **Summary of 802.3ae Characteristics**

Fiber	62.5-Micron Multimode Fiber	50-Micron Multimode Fiber	Single-Mode Fiber
SR/SW	Up to 33m	300 m	Not used
LR/LW	Not used	Not used	10km
ER/EW	Not used	Not used	40km

Exam Alert

10 Gigabit Ethernet is defined in the IEEE 802.3ae standard.

Note

Providing a common ground between the 802.3ae standards is 10GBaseLX4. It is a hybrid of the other standards in that it can be used over both single-mode and multimode fiber. In application the LX4 standard can reach distances ranging from 2 to 300 meters using multimode fiber and anywhere from 2 to 10 kilometers using single-mode fiber.

10GBaseT

The final standard outlined in the Network+ objectives is the 802.3an Ethernet standard. The 802.3an standard brings 10-gigabit speed to regular copper cabling. Although transmission distances may not be that of fiber, it allows a potential upgrade from 1000-gigabit networking to 10-gigabit networking using the current wiring infrastructure.

The 10GBaseT standard specifies 10-gigabit transmissions over UTP or STP twisted-pair cables. The standard calls for a cable specification of Category 6 or Category 6a. With Category 6, the maximum transmission range is 55 meters; with the augmented Category 6a cable, transmission range increases to 100 meters. Category 6 and 6a cables are specifically designed to reduce attenuation and crosstalk, making 10-gigabit speeds possible. 802.3an specifies regular RJ-45 networking connectors. Table 6.9 outlines the characteristics of the 802.3an standard.

TABLE 6.9 **Summary of 802.3an Characteristics**

Characteristic	Description
Transmission method	Baseband
Speed	10 gigabit
Total distance/segment	100 meters Category 6a cable; 55 meters Category 6 cable
Cable type	Category 6, 6a UTP or STP
Connector	RJ-45

Cram Quiz

1. You troubleshoot a network using 1000BaseCX cable, and you suspect that the maximum length has been exceeded. What is the maximum length of 1000BaseCX cable?

   ○ **A.** 1,000 meters

   ○ **B.** 100 meters

   ○ **C.** 25 meters

   ○ **D.** 10,000 meters

2. Which of the following 10 Gigabit Ethernet standards has the greatest maximum transmission distance?

   ○ **A.** 10GBaseSR

   ○ **B.** 10GBaseER

   ○ **C.** 10GBaseLR

   ○ **D.** 10GBaseXR

3. Your manager has asked you to specify a high-speed 10GbE link to provide connectivity between two buildings 3km from each other. Which of the following IEEE standards are you likely to recommend?

   ○ **A.** 10GBaseLR

   ○ **B.** 10GBaseSR

   ○ **C.** 10GBaseT4

   ○ **D.** 10GBaseFL

4. In a 100BaseTX network environment, what is the maximum distance between the device and the networking equipment, assuming that no repeaters are used?

   ○ **A.** 1,000 meters

   ○ **B.** 100 meters

   ○ **C.** 500 meters

   ○ **D.** 185 meters

Cram Quiz Answers

1. **C.** The 1000BaseCX standard specifies Gigabit Ethernet transfer over Category 5 UTP cable. It uses STP twisted-pair cable and has a 25-meter length restriction.

2. **B.** The 10GBaseER standard specifies a maximum transmission distance of 40,000 meters. The 10GBaseSR standard specifies a maximum transmission distance of 300 meters, whereas 10GBaseLR specifies a maximum transmission distance of 10,000 meters. 10GBaseXR is not a recognized 10 Gigabit Ethernet standard.

3. **A.** 10GBaseLR can be used over distances up to 10km. 10GBaseSR can only be used up to a maximum distance of 300 meters. 10GBaseT4 and 10GBaseFL are not recognized 10-Gigabit Ethernet standards.

4. **B.** 100BaseT networks use UTP cabling, which has a maximum cable length of 100 meters. Answer A is incorrect because this distance could be achieved only with UTP cabling by using repeaters. Answer C specifies the maximum cable length for 10Base5 networks. Answer D specifies the maximum cable length for 10Base2 networks.

What Next?

Although this chapter focused on wiring solutions, Chapter 7 looks at wireless. Client systems communicate with a wireless access point using wireless LAN adapters. Such adapters are built into or can be added to laptops, PDAs, or desktop computers. Wireless LAN adapters provide the communication point between the client system and the airwaves via an antenna.

CHAPTER 7
Wireless

This chapter covers the following official Network+ objectives:

▶ Given a scenario, install and configure a wireless network.

▶ Given a scenario, troubleshoot common wireless problems.

▶ Compare and contrast different wireless standards.

▶ Given a scenario, implement appropriate wireless security measures.

This chapter covers CompTIA Network+ objectives 2.2, 2.4, 3.3, and 5.1 For more information on the official Network+ exam topics, see the "About the Network+ Exam" section in the "Introduction."

One of the bigger changes in the networking world since the release of the previous Network+ exam is in wireless networking. Networks of all shapes and sizes incorporate wireless segments into their networks. Home wireless networking has also grown significantly in the last few years.

Wireless networking enables users to connect to a network using radio waves instead of wires. Network users within range of a wireless access point (AP) can move around an office freely without needing to plug into a wired infrastructure. The benefits of wireless networking clearly have led to its growth.

This chapter explores the many facets of wireless networking, starting with some of the concepts and technologies that make wireless networking possible.

Understanding Wireless Basics

▶ Given a scenario, install and configure a wireless network.

Cram**Saver**

If you can correctly answer these questions before going through this section, save time by skimming the Exam Alerts in this section and then complete the Cram Quiz at the end of the section.

1. What is the network name needed to connect to a wireless AP?

2. True or False: A wireless access point (AP) is both a transmitter and receiver (transceiver) device used for wireless LAN (WLAN) radio signals.

Answers

1. SSID (Service Set Identifier).

2. True. A wireless access point (AP) is both a transmitter and receiver (transceiver) device used for wireless LAN (WLAN) radio signals.

Today, wireless local area networks (WLANs) provide a flexible and secure data communications system that augments an Ethernet LAN or, in some cases, replaces it. Wireless transmissions send and receive data using radio frequency (RF) signals, freeing you from wired solutions.

In a common wireless implementation, a wireless transceiver (transmitter/receiver), known as an access point, connects to the wired network from a fixed location using standard cabling. The wireless access point receives and then transmits data between the wireless LAN and the wired network infrastructure.

Client systems communicate with a wireless access point using wireless LAN adapters. Such adapters are built into or can be added to laptops, PDAs, or desktop computers. Wireless LAN adapters provide the communication point between the client system and the airwaves via an antenna.

Note

This chapter discusses ad hoc and infrastructure wireless network topologies. If you need a refresher on these topologies, they are discussed in Chapter 1, "Introduction to Networking."

Wireless Access Points (APs)

A wireless access point (AP) is both a transmitter and receiver (transceiver) device used for wireless LAN (WLAN) radio signals. An AP typically is a separate network device with a built-in antenna, transmitter, and adapter. APs use the wireless infrastructure network mode to provide a connection point between WLANs and a wired Ethernet LAN. APs also typically have several ports, giving you a way to expand the network to support additional clients.

Depending on the size of the network, one or more APs might be required. Additional APs are used to allow access to more wireless clients and to expand the range of the wireless network. Each AP is limited by a transmission range—the distance a client can be from an AP and still get a usable signal. The actual distance depends on the wireless standard being used and the obstructions and environmental conditions between the client and the AP. Factors affecting wireless transmission ranges are covered later in this chapter.

> **ExamAlert**
>
> An AP can operate as a bridge, connecting a standard wired network to wireless devices, or as a router, passing data transmissions from one access point to another.

> **Tip**
>
> If you use a wireless device that loses its connection, you might be too far from the AP.

You can use an AP in an infrastructure wireless network design. Used in the infrastructure mode, the AP receives transmissions from wireless devices within a specific range and transmits those signals to the network beyond. This network might be a private Ethernet network or the Internet. In infrastructure wireless networking, multiple access points might cover a large area or only a single access point for a small area, such as a single home or small building.

Working with APs

When working with wireless APs, you need to understand many terms and acronyms. This section defines some of the more common wireless acronyms you see both on the exam and in wireless networking documentation.

> **ExamAlert**
>
> Several of the acronyms provided in the following list are sure to be on the exam. Be sure you can identify the function of each before taking the exam.

▶ **Service Set Identifier (SSID)**—A network name needed to connect to a wireless AP. It is like a workgroup name used with Windows networking. 802.11 wireless networks use the SSID to identify all systems belonging to the same network. Client stations must be configured with the SSID to be authenticated to the AP. The AP might broadcast the SSID, allowing all wireless clients in the area to see the AP's SSID. For security reasons, APs can be configured not to broadcast the SSID or to cloak it. This means that an administrator needs to give client systems the SSID instead of allowing it to be discovered automatically.

> **Tip**
>
> One element of wireless security involves configuring the AP not to broadcast the SSID. This configuration is made on the AP.

▶ **Basic Service Set (BSS)**—Refers to a wireless network that uses a single AP and one or more wireless clients connecting to the AP. Many home offices are an example of a BSS design. The BSS is an example of the infrastructure wireless topology. Chapter 1 discusses wireless topologies and other networks.

▶ **Extended Service Set (ESS)**—Refers to two or more connected BSSs that use multiple APs. The ESS is used to create WLANs or larger wireless networks and is a collection of APs and clients. Connecting BSS systems enables clients to roam between areas and maintain the wireless connection without having to reconfigure between BSSs.

▶ **Extended Service Set Identifier (ESSID)**—Although the terms ESSID and SSID are used interchangeably, there is a difference between the two. SSID is the name used with BSS networks. ESSID is the network name used with an ESS wireless network design. With an ESS, not all APs necessarily use the same name.

▶ **Basic Service Set Identifier (BSSID)**—The MAC address of the Basic Service Set (BSS) AP. The BSSID is not to be confused with the SSID, which is the name of the wireless network.

▶ **Basic Service Area (BSA)**—When troubleshooting or designing wireless networks, the BSA is an important consideration. The BSA refers to the AP's coverage area. The BSA for an AP depends on many factors, including the strength of the AP antenna, interference in the area, and whether an omnidirectional or directional antenna is used.

Troubleshooting AP Coverage

Like any other network medium, APs have a limited transmission distance. This limitation is an important consideration when you decide where an AP should be placed on the network. When troubleshooting a wireless network, pay close attention to how far the client systems are from the AP.

When faced with a problem in which client systems cannot consistently access the AP, you could try moving the access point to better cover the area, but then you may disrupt access for users in other areas. So what can be done to troubleshoot AP coverage?

Depending on the network environment, the quick solution may be to throw money at the problem and purchase another access point, cabling, and other hardware to expand the transmission area. However, you can try a few things before installing another wireless access point. The following list starts with the least expensive solution and progresses to the most expensive:

▶ **Increase transmission power**: Some access points have a setting to adjust the transmission power output. By default, most of these settings are set to the maximum output; however, this is worth verifying just in case. You can decrease the transmission power if you're trying to reduce the dispersion of radio waves beyond the immediate network. Increasing the power gives clients stronger data signals and greater transmission distances.

▶ **Relocate the AP**: When wireless client systems suffer from connectivity problems, the solution may be as simple as relocating the AP. You could relocate it across the room, a few feet away, or across the hall. Finding the right location can likely take a little trial and error.

▶ **Adjust or replace antennas**: If the access point distance is insufficient for some network clients, it might be necessary to replace the default antenna used with both the AP and the client with higher-end antennas. Upgrading an antenna can make a big difference in terms of transmission range. Unfortunately, not all APs have replaceable antennas.

▶ **Signal amplification**: RF amplifiers add significant distance to wireless signals. An RF amplifier increases the strength and readability of the data transmission. The amplifier improves both the received and transmitted signals, resulting in an increase in wireless network performance.

▶ **Use a repeater**: Before installing a new AP, you might want to think about a wireless repeater. When set to the same channel as the AP, the repeater takes the transmission and repeats it. So, the AP transmission gets to the repeater, and then the repeater duplicates the signal and passes it on. This is an effective strategy to increase wireless transmission distances.

> **ExamAlert**
>
> Be prepared to answer questions on access point coverage and possible reasons to relocate APs.

Wireless Antennas

A wireless antenna is an integral part of overall wireless communication. Antennas come in many different shapes and sizes, with each one designed for a specific purpose. Selecting the right antenna for a particular network implementation is a critical consideration and one that could ultimately decide how successful a wireless network will be. In addition, using the right antenna can save you money on networking costs because you need fewer antennas and access points.

Many small home network adapters and access points come with a nonupgradable antenna, but higher-grade wireless devices require you to choose an antenna. Determining which antenna to select takes careful planning and requires an understanding of what range and speed you need for a network. The antenna is designed to help wireless networks do the following:

▶ Work around obstacles

▶ Minimize the effects of interference

▶ Increase signal strength

▶ Focus the transmission, which can increase signal speed

The following sections explore some of the characteristics of wireless antennas.

Antenna Ratings

When a wireless signal is low and is affected by heavy interference, it might be possible to upgrade the antenna to create a more solid wireless connection. To determine an antenna's strength, refer to its *gain value*. But how do you determine the gain value?

Suppose that a huge wireless tower is emanating circular waves in all directions. If you could see these waves, you would see them forming a sphere around the tower. The signals around the antenna flow equally in all directions, including up and down. An antenna that does this has a 0dBi gain value and is called an isotropic antenna. The isotropic antenna rating provides a base point for measuring actual antenna strength.

> **Note**
>
> The *dB* in dBi stands for decibels and the *i* stands for the hypothetical isotropic antenna.

An antenna's gain value represents the difference between the 0dBi isotropic and the antenna's power. For example, a wireless antenna advertised as 15dBi is 15 times stronger than the hypothetical isotropic antenna. The higher the decibel figure, the higher the gain.

When looking at wireless antennas, remember that a higher gain value means stronger send and receive signals. In terms of performance, the rule of thumb is that every 3dB of gain added doubles an antenna's effective power output.

Antenna Coverage

When selecting an antenna for a particular wireless implementation, you need to determine the type of coverage the antenna uses. In a typical configuration, a wireless antenna can be either *omnidirectional* or *directional*. Which one you choose depends on the wireless environment.

An omnidirectional antenna is designed to provide a 360-degree dispersed wave pattern. This type of antenna is used when coverage in all directions from the antenna is required. Omnidirectional antennas are advantageous when a broad-based signal is required. For example, if you provide an even signal in all directions, clients can access the antenna and its associated access point from various locations. Because of the dispersed nature of omnidirectional antennas, the signal is weaker overall and therefore accommodates shorter signal distances. Omnidirectional antennas are great in an environment that has a clear line of sight between the senders and receivers. The power is evenly spread to all points, making omnidirectional antennas well suited for home and small office applications.

Directional antennas are designed to focus the signal in a particular direction. This focused signal enables greater distances and a stronger signal between two points. The greater distances enabled by directional antennas give you a viable alternative for connecting locations, such as two offices, in a point-to-point configuration.

Directional antennas are also used when you need to tunnel or thread a signal through a series of obstacles. This concentrates the signal power in a specific direction and enables you to use less power for a greater distance than an omnidirectional antenna. Table 7.1 compares omnidirectional and directional wireless antennas.

TABLE 7.1 **Comparing Omnidirectional and Directional Antennas**

Characteristic	Omnidirectional	Directional	Advantage/Disadvantage
Wireless area coverage	General coverage area	Focused coverage area.	Omnidirectional allows 360-degree coverage, giving it a wide coverage area. Directional provides a targeted path for signals to travel.
Wireless transmission range	Limited	Long point-to-point range.	Omnidirectional antennas provide a 360-degree coverage pattern and, as a result, far less range. Directional antennas focus the wireless transmission; this focus enables greater range.
Wireless coverage shaping	Restricted	The directional wireless range can be increased and decreased.	Omnidirectional antennas are limited to their circular pattern range. Directional antennas can be adjusted to define a specific pattern, wider or more focused.

> **Note**
>
> In the wireless world, polarization refers to the direction in which the antenna radiates wavelengths. This direction can either be vertical, horizontal, or circular. Today, vertical antennas are perhaps the most common. As far as the configuration is concerned, the sending and receiving antennas should be set to the same polarization.

Wireless Signal Quality

Because wireless signals travel through the atmosphere, they are subjected to all sorts of environmental and external factors. This includes storms and the number of walls, ceilings, and so on that the signal must pass through. Just how weakened the signal becomes depends on the building material used and the level of RF interference. All these elements decrease the power of the wireless signal.

> **ExamAlert**
>
> Wireless signals degrade depending on the construction material used. Signals passing through concrete and steel are particularly weakened.

If you are troubleshooting a wireless connection that has a particularly weak signal, you can do a few things to help increase the signal's power:

▶ **Antenna**: Perhaps the first and most obvious thing to do is to make sure that the antenna on the AP is positioned for best reception. It often takes a little trial and error to get the placement right. Today's wireless access cards commonly ship with diagnostic software that displays signal strength and makes it easy to find the correct position.

▶ **Device placement**: One factor that can degrade wireless signals is RF interference. Because of this, you need to try to keep wireless devices away from appliances that output RF noise. This includes microwaves, electrical devices, and certain cordless devices using the same frequency, such as phones.

▶ **Network location**: Although there may be limited choice, as much as possible try to reduce the number of obstructions that the signal must pass through. Every obstacle strips a little more power from the signal. The type of material a signal must pass through also can have a significant impact on signal integrity.

> ▶ **Boost the signal**: If all else fails, you can purchase devices, such as wireless repeaters, that can amplify the wireless signal. The device takes the signal and amplifies it to make it stronger. This also increases the distance that the client system can be placed from the AP.

To successfully manage wireless signals, you need to know which wireless standard you use. The standards used today specify range distances, RF ranges, and speeds. It may be that the wireless standard cannot do what you need it to.

Troubleshooting Scenario and Solution

Suppose users connecting to a wireless access point experience random problems such as lost connections, poor speed, and network errors. Check to see whether the wireless devices operate within the accepted range of the wireless access point. Also find out whether any environmental considerations have not been fully taken into account, such as construction materials and heavy machinery, which can interfere with the signal's quality.

Wireless Radio Channels

Radio frequency (RF) channels are an important part of wireless communication. A *channel* is the band of RF used for the wireless communication. Each IEEE wireless standard specifies the channels that can be used. The 802.11a standard specifies radio frequency ranges between 5.15 and 5.875GHz. In contrast, 802.11b and 802.11g standards operate in the 2.4 to 2.497GHz range. IEEE wireless standards are discussed later in this chapter.

> **Note**
>
> Hertz (Hz) is the standard of measurement for radio frequency. Hertz is used to measure the frequency of vibrations and waves, such as sound waves and electromagnetic waves. One hertz is equal to one cycle per second. Radio frequency is measured in kilohertz (KHz), 1,000 cycles per second; megahertz (MHz), one million cycles per second; or gigahertz (GHz), one billion cycles per second.

As far as channels are concerned, 802.11a has a wider frequency band, enabling more channels and therefore more data throughput. As a result of the wider band, 802.11a supports up to eight nonoverlapping channels. 802.11b/g standards use the smaller band and support only up to three nonoverlapping channels.

It is recommended that nonoverlapping channels be used for communication. In the United States, 802.11b/g use 11 channels for data communication, as mentioned; three of these—channels 1, 6, and 11—are nonoverlapping. Most manufacturers set their default channel to one of the nonoverlapping channels to avoid transmission conflicts. With wireless devices you can select which channel your WLAN operates on to avoid interference from other wireless devices that operate in the 2.4GHz frequency range.

When troubleshooting a wireless network, be aware that overlapping channels can disrupt the wireless communications. For example, in many environments, APs are inadvertently placed close together—perhaps two access points in separate offices located next door to each other or between floors. Signal disruption results if channel overlap exists between the access points. The solution is to try to move the access point to avoid the overlap problem, or to change channels to one of the other nonoverlapping channels. For example, you could switch from channel 6 to channel 11.

Typically, you would change the channel of a wireless device only if it overlapped with another device. If a channel must be changed, it must be changed to another, nonoverlapping channel. Table 7.2 shows the channel ranges for 802.11b/g wireless standards. Table 7.3 shows the channel ranges for 802.11a. 802.11n has the option of using both channels used by 802.11a and b/g and operating at 2.4GHz/5GHz. You can think of 802.11n as an amendment that improves upon the previous 802.11 standards by adding multiple-input multiple-output antennas (MIMO) and a huge increase in the data rate.

ExamAlert

When troubleshooting a wireless problem in Windows, you can use the `ipconfig` command to see the status of IP configuration. Similarly, the `ifconfig` command can be used in Linux. In addition, Linux users can use the `iwconfig` command to view the state of your wireless network. Using `iwconfig`, you can view such important information as the link quality, AP MAC address, data rate, and encryption keys, which can be helpful in ensuring that the parameters in the network are consistent.

Tip

IEEE 802.11b/g wireless systems communicate with each other using radio frequency signals in the band between 2.4GHz and 2.5GHz. Neighboring channels are 5MHz apart. Applying two channels that allow the maximum channel separation decreases the amount of channel crosstalk and provides a noticeable performance increase over networks with minimal channel separation.

Tables 7.2 and 7.3 outline the available wireless channels. When deploying a wireless network, it is recommended that you use channel 1, grow to use channel 6, and add channel 11 when necessary because these three channels do not overlap.

> **ExamAlert**
>
> 802.11n is the standard today and you will be hard pressed to purchase (or even find) older technologies. It is, however, recommended that you know the older technologies for the exam.

TABLE 7.2 **RF Channels for 802.11b/g**

Channel	Frequency Band
1	2412MHz
2	2417MHz
3	2422MHz
4	2427MHz
5	2432MHz
6	2437MHz
7	2442MHz
8	2447MHz
9	2452MHz
10	2457MHz
11	2462MHz

> **Note**
>
> One thing to remember when looking at Table 7.2 is that the RF channels listed (2412 for channel 1, 2417 for 2, and so on) are actually the center frequency that the transceiver within the radio and access point uses. There is only 5MHz separation between the center frequencies, and an 802.11b signal occupies approximately 30MHz of the frequency spectrum. As a result, data signals fall within about 15MHz of each side of the center frequency and overlap with several adjacent channel frequencies. This leaves you with only three channels (channels 1, 6, and 11 for the United States) that you can use without causing interference between access points.

TABLE 7.3 **RF Channels for 802.11a**

Channel	Frequency
36	5180MHz
40	5200MHz
44	5220MHz
48	5240MHz
52	5260MHz
56	5280MHz
60	5300MHz
64	5320MHz

Data Rate Versus Throughput

When talking about wireless transmissions, you need to distinguish between *throughput* and *data rate*. From time to time these terms are used interchangeably, but technically speaking, they are different. As shown later in this chapter, each wireless standard has an associated speed. For instance, 802.11n lists a speed of up to 100Mbps. This represents the speed at which devices using this standard can send and receive data. However, in network data transmissions, many factors prevent the actual speeds from reaching this end-to-end theoretical maximum. For instance, data packets include overhead such as routing information, checksums, and error recovery data. Although this might all be necessary, it can impact overall speed.

The number of clients on the network can also impact the data rate; the more clients, the more collisions. Depending on the network layout, collisions can have a significant impact on end-to-end transmission speeds. Wireless network signals degrade as they pass through obstructions such as walls or doors; the signal speed deteriorates with each obstruction.

All these factors leave you with the actual throughput of wireless data transmissions. Throughput represents the actual speed to expect from wireless transmissions. In practical application, wireless transmissions are approximately one-half or less of the data rate. This means that you could hope for about 40 to 50Mbps for 802.11n. Depending on the wireless setup, the transmission rate could be much less.

> **Exam Alert**
>
> Data rate refers to the theoretical maximum of a wireless standard, such as 100Mbps. Throughput refers to the actual speeds achieved after all implementation and interference factors.

Beacon Management Frame

Within wireless networking is a frame type known as the beacon management frame (beacon). Beacons are an important part of the wireless network because it is their job to advertise the presence of the access point so that systems can locate it. Wireless clients automatically detect the beacons and attempt to establish a wireless connection to the access point.

The beacon frame is sent by the access point in an infrastructure network design. Client stations send beacons only if connected in an ad hoc network design. The beacon frame has several parts, all of which the client system uses to learn about the AP before attempting to join the network:

- ▶ **Channel information**: Includes which channel the AP uses.

- ▶ **Supported data rates**: Includes the data transfer rates identified by the AP configuration.

- ▶ **Service Set Identifier (SSID)**: This beacon includes the name of the wireless network.

- ▶ **Time stamp**: Includes synchronization information. The client system uses the time stamp to synchronize its clock with the AP.

These beacons are transmitted from the AP about every 10 milliseconds. The beacon frames add overhead to the network. Therefore, some APs let you reduce the number of beacons that are sent. With home networks, constant beacon information is unnecessary.

Passive and Active Scanning

Before a client system can attempt to connect to an access point, it must locate it. The two methods of AP discovery follows

- ▶ **Passive scanning**: The client system listens for the beacon frames to discover the AP. After it is detected, the beacon frame provides the information necessary for the system to access the AP.

▶ **Active scanning**: The client station transmits another type of management frame known as a probe request. The probe request goes out from the client system, looking for a specific SSID or any SSID within its area. After the probe request is sent, all APs in the area with the same SSID reply with another frame, the probe response. The information contained in the probe response is the same information included with the beacon frame. This information enables the client to access the system.

Spread-Spectrum Technology

Spread spectrum refers to the manner in which data signals travel through a radio frequency. With spread spectrum, data does not travel straight through a single RF band; this type of transmission is known as *narrowband transmission*. Spread spectrum, on the other hand, requires that data signals either alternate between carrier frequencies or constantly change their data pattern. Although the shortest distance between two points is a straight line (narrowband), spread spectrum is designed to trade bandwidth efficiency for reliability, integrity, and security. Spread-spectrum signal strategies use more bandwidth than in the case of narrowband transmission, but the trade-off is a data signal that is clearer and easier to detect. The two types of spread-spectrum radio are *frequency hopping* and *direct sequence*.

Frequency-Hopping Spread-Spectrum (FHSS) Technology

FHSS requires the use of narrowband signals that change frequencies in a predictable pattern. The term *frequency hopping* refers to data signals hopping between narrow channels. For example, consider the 2.4GHz frequency band used by 802.11b/g. This range is divided into 70 narrow channels of 1MHz each. Somewhere between 20 and several hundred milliseconds, the signal hops to a new channel following a predetermined cyclical pattern.

Because data signals using FHSS switch between RF bands, they have a strong resistance to interference and environmental factors. The FHSS signal strategy makes it well suited for installations designed to cover a large geographic area and where using directional antennas to minimize the influence of environmental factors is not possible.

FHSS is not the preferred spread-spectrum technology for today's wireless standards. However, FHSS is used for some lesser-used standards and for cellular deployments for fixed broadband wireless access (BWA), where the use of DSSS (discussed next) is virtually impossible because of its limitations.

Direct-Sequence Spread-Spectrum (DSSS) Technology

With DSSS transmissions, the signal is spread over a full transmission frequency spectrum. For every bit of data sent, a redundant bit pattern is also sent. This 32-bit pattern is called a *chip*. These redundant bits of data provide both security and delivery assurance. The reason transmissions are so safe and reliable is simply because the system sends so many redundant copies of the data, and only a single copy is required to have complete transmission of the data or information. DSSS can minimize the effects of interference and background noise.

As for a comparison between the two, DSSS has the advantage of providing better security and signal delivery than FHSS, but it is a sensitive technology, affected by many environmental factors.

Orthogonal Frequency Division Multiplexing

Orthogonal Frequency Division Multiplexing (OFDM) is a transmission technique that transfers large amounts of data over 52 separate, evenly spaced frequencies. OFDM splits the radio signal into these separate frequencies and simultaneously transmits them to the receiver. Splitting the signal and transferring over different frequencies reduces the amount of crosstalk interference. OFDM is associated with 802.11a, 802.11g amendments, and 802.11n wireless standards.

Infrared Wireless Networking

Infrared has been around for a long time; perhaps your first experience with it was the TV remote. The commands entered onto the remote control travel over an infrared light wave to the receiver on the TV. Infrared technology has progressed, and today infrared development in networking is managed by the Infrared Data Association (IrDA).

Infrared wireless networking uses infrared beams to send data transmissions between devices. Infrared wireless networking offers higher transmission rates, reaching 10Mbps to 16Mbps.

As expected, infrared light beams cannot penetrate objects; therefore, the signal is disrupted when something blocks the light. Infrared can be either a directed (line-of-sight) or diffuse technology. A directed infrared system provides a limited range of approximately 3 feet and typically is used for personal area networks. Diffused infrared can travel farther and is more difficult to block with a signal object. Diffused infrared wireless LAN systems do not require line of sight, but usable distance is limited to room distances.

Infrared provides a secure, low-cost, convenient cable-replacement technology. It is well suited for many specific applications and environments. Some key infrared points follows

- ▶ It provides adequate speeds—up to 16Mbps.

- ▶ Infrared devices use less power and therefore don't drain batteries as much.

- ▶ Infrared is a secure medium. Infrared signals typically are a direct-line implementation in a short range and therefore do not travel far outside the immediate connection. This eliminates the problem of eavesdropping or signal tampering.

- ▶ Infrared is a proven technology. Infrared devices have been available for some time and as such are a proven, nonproprietary technology with an established user and support base.

- ▶ It has no radio frequency interference issues or signal conflicts.

- ▶ It replaces cables for many devices, such as keyboards, mice, and other peripherals.

- ▶ It uses a dispersed mode or a direct line-of-sight transmission.

- ▶ Transmissions travel over short distances.

Establishing Communications Between Wireless Devices

When you work with wireless networks, you must have a basic understanding of the communication that occurs between wireless devices. If you use an infrastructure wireless network design, the network has two key parts: the wireless client, also known as the station (STA), and the AP. The AP acts as a bridge between the STA and the wired network.

> **Exam Alert**
>
> When a single AP is connected to the wired network and to a set of wireless stations, it is called a *Basic Service Set (BSS)*. An *Extended Service Set (ESS)* describes the use of multiple BSSs that form a single subnetwork. Ad hoc mode is sometimes called an *Independent Basic Service Set (IBSS)*.

As with other forms of network communication, before transmissions between devices can occur, the wireless access point and the client must begin to talk to each other. In the wireless world, this is a two-step process involving *association* and *authentication*.

The association process occurs when a wireless adapter is turned on. The client adapter immediately begins scanning the wireless frequencies for wireless APs or, if using ad hoc mode, other wireless devices. When the wireless client is configured to operate in infrastructure mode, the user can choose a wireless AP with which to connect. This process may also be automatic, with the AP selection based on the SSID, signal strength, and frame error rate. Finally, the wireless adapter switches to the assigned channel of the selected wireless AP and negotiates the use of a port.

If at any point the signal between the devices drops below an acceptable level, or if the signal becomes unavailable for any reason, the wireless adapter initiates another scan, looking for an AP with stronger signals. When the new AP is located, the wireless adapter selects it and associates with it. This is known as *reassociation*.

> **Exam Alert**
>
> The 802.11 standards enable a wireless client to roam between multiple APs. An AP transmits a beacon signal every so many milliseconds. It includes a time stamp for client synchronization and an indication of supported data rates. A client system uses the beacon message to identify the strength of the existing connection to an AP. If the connection is too weak, the roaming client attempts to associate itself with a new AP. This enables the client system to roam between distances and APs.

With the association process complete, the authentication process begins. After the devices associate, keyed security measures are applied before communication can take place. On many APs, authentication can be set to either *shared key authentication* or *open authentication*. The default setting typically is open authentication. Open authentication enables access with only the SSID and/or the correct WEP key for the AP. The problem with open authentication is that if you don't have other protection or authentication mechanisms in place, your wireless network is totally open to intruders. When set to shared key mode, the client must meet security requirements before communication with the AP can occur.

After security requirements are met, you have established IP-level communication. This means that wireless standard requirements have been met, and Ethernet networking takes over. There is basically a switch between 802.11 to 802.3 standards. The wireless standards create the physical link to the network, enabling regular networking standards and protocols to use the link. This is how the physical cable is replaced, but to the networking technologies there is no difference between regular cable media and wireless media.

Several components combine to enable wireless communications between devices. Each of these must be configured on both the client and the AP:

- **Service Set Identifier (SSID)**: Whether your wireless network uses infrastructure mode or ad hoc mode, an SSID is required. The SSID is a configurable client identification that enables clients to communicate with a particular base station. Only client systems configured with the same SSID as the AP can communicate with it. SSIDs provide a simple password arrangement between base stations and clients in a BSS network. ESSIDs are used for the ESS wireless network.

- **Wireless channel**: RF channels are an important part of wireless communications. A channel is the frequency band used for the wireless communication. Each standard specifies the channels that can be used. The 802.11a standard specified radio frequency ranges between 5.15 and 5.875GHz. In contrast, the 802.11b and 802.11g standards operate in the 2.4 to 2.497GHz ranges. Fourteen channels are defined in the IEEE 802.11b/g channel set, 11 of which are available in North America. The number of channels used by 802.11n varies, with its big advantage being the ability to use multiple antennas.

- **Security features**: IEEE 802.11 provides security using two methods: authentication and encryption. Authentication verifies the client system. In infrastructure mode, authentication is established between an AP and each station. Wireless encryption services must be the same on the client and the AP for communication to occur.

Configuring the Wireless Connection

Now that you have reviewed key wireless settings, take a look at an actual wireless connection configuration. Figure 7.1 shows an example of a simple wireless router. In addition to providing only wireless access, it also includes a four-port wired switch.

FIGURE 7.1   **A wireless broadband router for a small network.**

Most of the broadband routers similar to the one shown in Figure 7.1 differ based upon the following features:

▸ **Wireless bands**: The routers can provide only 2.4 GHz, only 5 GHz, or be either selectable (choosing one of the two) or simultaneous (using both).

▸ **Switch speed**: The ports on the switch can usually support either Fast Ethernet (10/100Mbps) or Gigabit Ethernet (10/100/1000Mbps).

▸ **Security supported**: The SSID, security mode, and passphrase may be configurable for each band, and some routers include a push-button feature for accessing setup. Some enable you to configure MAC address filtering and Guest access. MAC address filtering enables you to limit access to only those specified hosts . Guest access uses a different password and network name and enables visitors to use the Internet without having access to the rest of the network (thus avoiding your data and computers).

ExamAlert

Make sure you understand the purpose of MAC address filtering.

▶ **Antennae**: The antennae may be a single external pole, two poles, or be entirely internal. The model shown in Figure 7.1 uses an internal antenna, as shown in Figure 7.2.

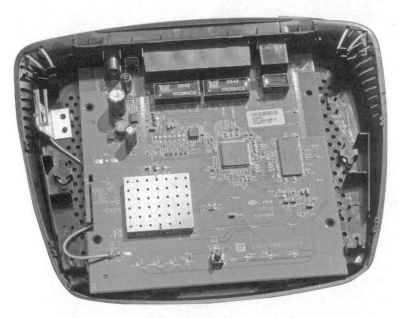

FIGURE 7.2 **The antenna is the wire and metal component on the left.**

Note

The wireless antenna for the laptop is often built into the areas around the screen. Figure 7.3 shows the area behind which the antennae are located on an HP EliteBook.

FIGURE 7.3   The antenna in a laptop is often built into the space behind the screen.

As shown in Figure 7.4, the settings for a wireless router are typically clearly laid out. For instance, you can see that the wireless connection uses an SSID password of Gigaset602 and wireless channel 11.

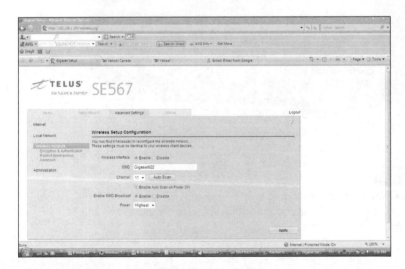

FIGURE 7.4   Wireless configuration information.

You can adjust many settings for troubleshooting or security reasons (refer to Figure 7.4). Following are some of the settings that can be adjusted on a wireless access point:

▶ **SSID**: Figure 7.4 shows the SSID of Gigaset602. This name is used for anyone who wants to access the Internet through this wireless access point. The SSID is a configurable client identification that enables clients to communicate with a particular base station. In an application, only clients configured with the same SSID can communicate with base stations having the same SSID. SSID provides a simple password arrangement between base stations and clients.

As far as troubleshooting is concerned, if a client cannot access a base station, ensure that both use the same SSID. Incompatible SSIDs are sometimes found when clients move computers, such as laptops, between different wireless networks. They obtain an SSID from one network. If the system is not rebooted, the old SSID doesn't enable communication with a different base station.

▶ **Channel**: The channel in Figure 7.4 is set to use channel 11. To access this network, all systems must use this channel. If needed, you can change the channel using the drop-down menu. The menu lists channels 1 through 11.

▶ **SSID Broadcast**: In their default configuration, wireless access points typically broadcast the SSID name into the air at regular intervals. This feature is intended to allow clients to easily discover the network and roam between WLANs. The problem with SSID broadcasting is that it makes it a little easier to get around security. SSIDs are not encrypted or protected in any way. Anyone can snoop and get a look at the SSID and attempt to join the network.

> **Note**
>
> For home and small office use, roaming is not needed. This feature can be disabled for home use to improve the security of your WLAN. As soon as your wireless clients are manually configured with the right SSID, they no longer require these broadcast messages.

▶ **Authentication**: When configuring authentication security for the AP, you have several options, including WEP-Open, WEP-Shared, and WPA-psk. WEP-Open is the simplest of the authentications methods because it does not perform any type of client verification. It is a weak form of authentication because it requires no proof of identity. WEP-Shared requires that a WEP key be configured on both the client system and the access point. This makes authentication with WEP-Shared mandatory, so it is more secure for wireless transmission. WPA-psk (Wi-Fi Protected Access with Pre-Shared Key) is a stronger form of encryption in which keys are automatically changed and authenticated between devices after a specified period of time, or after a specified number of packets have been transmitted.

▶ **Wireless Mode**: To access the network, the client must use the same wireless mode as the AP. Today most users configure the network for 802.11n for faster speeds.

▶ **DTIM Period (seconds)**: Wireless transmissions can broadcast to all systems—that is, they can send messages to all clients on the wireless network. Multiple broadcast messages are known as multicast or broadcast traffic. Delivery Traffic Indication Message (DTIM) is a feature used to ensure that when the multicast or broadcast traffic is sent, all systems are awake to hear the message. The DTIM setting specifies how often the DTIM is sent within the beacon frame. For example, if the DTIM setting by default is 1, this means that the DTIM is sent with every beacon. If the DTIM is set to 3, the DTIM is sent every three beacons as a DTIM wake-up call.

▶ **Maximum Connection Rate**: The transfer rate typically is set to Auto by default. This enables the maximum connection speed. However, it is possible to decrease the speed to increase the distance that the signal travels and boost signal strength due to poor environmental conditions.

▶ **Network Type**: This is where the network can be set to use the ad hoc or infrastructure network design.

Cram Quiz

1. Which of the following wireless protocols operate at 2.4GHz? (Select two.)

   ○ **A.** 802.11a

   ○ **B.** 802.11b

   ○ **C.** 802.11g

   ○ **D.** 802.11n

2. Under what circumstance would you change the default channel on an access point?

   ○ **A.** When channel overlap occurs between access points

   ○ **B.** To release and renew the SSID

   ○ **C.** To increase WEP security settings

   ○ **D.** To decrease WEP security settings

3. A client on your network has had no problems accessing the wireless network in the past, but recently she moved to a new office. Since the move she cannot access the network. Which of the following is most likely the cause of the problem?

   ○ **A.** The SSIDs on the client and the AP are different.

   ○ **B.** The SSID has been erased.

   ○ **C.** The client has incorrect WEP settings.

   ○ **D.** The client system has moved too far from the access point.

Cram Quiz Answers

1. **B, C,** and **D.** Wireless standards specify an RF range on which communications are sent. The 802.11b and 802.11g standards use the 2.4GHz range. 802.11a uses the 5GHz range. 802.11n can operate at 2.4GHz and 5GHz. For more information, see the section "802.11 Wireless Standards."

2. **A.** Ordinarily, the default channel used with a wireless device is adequate; however, you might need to change the channel if overlap occurs with another nearby access point. The channel should be changed to another, nonoverlapping channel. Changing the channel would not impact the WEP security settings. For more information, see the section "Wireless Radio Channels."

3. **D.** An AP has a limited distance that it can send data transmissions. When a client system moves out of range, it can't access the AP. Many strategies exist to increase transmission distances, including RF repeaters, amplifiers, and buying more powerful antennas. The problem is not likely related to the SSID or WEP settings because the client had access to the network before, and no settings were changed. For more information, see the section "Wireless Troubleshooting Checklist."

802.11 Wireless Standards

▶ Compare and contrast different wireless standards.

CramSaver

If you can correctly answer these questions before going through this section, save time by skimming the Exam Alerts in this section and then complete the Cram Quiz at the end of the section.

1. What is the access method employed by the 802.11 wireless standards?

2. What technology can be considered the biggest development for 802.11n and the key to the new speeds?

Answers

1. All the 802.11 wireless standards employ the CSMA/CA access method.

2. Multiple input multiple output (MIMO) antenna technology is the biggest development for 802.11n and the key to the new speeds.

802.11 represents the IEEE designation for wireless networking. Several wireless networking specifications exist under the 802.11 banner. The Network+ objectives focus on 802.11a, 802.11b, 802.11g, and 802.11n. All these standards use the Ethernet protocol and the CSMA/CA access method.

ExamAlert

The exam will have questions on the characteristics of the wireless standards. Remember, 802.11 wireless standards use the CSMA/CA access method.

The 802.11 wireless standards can differ in terms of speed, transmission ranges, and frequency used, but in terms of actual implementation they are similar. All standards can use either an infrastructure or ad hoc network design, and each can use the same security protocols. Ad hoc and infrastructure wireless topologies were discussed in Chapter 1.

▶ **IEEE 802.11**: There were actually two variations on the initial 802.11 wireless standard. Both offered 1 or 2Mbps transmission speeds and the same RF of 2.4GHz. The difference between the two was in how data traveled through the RF media. One used FHSS, and the other used DSSS. The original 802.11 standards are far too slow for modern networking needs and are now no longer deployed.

▸ **IEEE 802.11a**: In terms of speed, the 802.11a standard was far ahead of the original 802.11 standards. 802.11a specified speeds of up to 54Mbps in the 5GHz band, but most commonly, communication takes place at 6Mbps, 12Mbps, or 24Mbps. 802.11a is incompatible with the 802.11b and 802.11g wireless standards.

▸ **IEEE 802.11b**: The 802.11b standard provides for a maximum transmission speed of 11Mbps. However, devices are designed to be backward compatible with previous 802.11 standards that provided for speeds of 1, 2, and 5.5Mbps. 802.11b uses a 2.4GHz RF range and is compatible with 802.11g.

▸ **IEEE 802.11g**: 802.11g offers wireless transmission over distances of 150 feet and speeds up to 54Mbps compared with the 11Mbps of the 802.11b standard. Like 802.11b, 802.11g operates in the 2.4GHz range and therefore is compatible with it.

▸ **IEEE 802.11n**: The newest of the wireless standards listed in the Network+ objectives is 802.11n, which is a popular wireless standard today. The goal of the 802.11n standard was to significantly increase throughput in both the 2.4GHz and the 5GHz frequency range. The baseline goal of the standard was to reach speeds of 100Mbps, but given the right conditions, it is estimated that the 802.11n speeds can reach a staggering 600Mbps. In practical operation, 802.11n speeds are much slower.

Exam Alert

Be prepared to answer questions on the specific characteristics of wireless standards.

The Magic Behind 802.11n

802.11n takes the best from the 802.11 standards and mixes in some new features to take wireless to the next level. First among these new technologies is multiple input multiple output (MIMO) antenna technology.

MIMO is unquestionably the biggest development for 802.11n and the key to the new speeds. Essentially, MIMO uses multiplexing to increase the range and speed of wireless networking. Multiplexing is a technique that combines multiple signals for transmission over a single line or medium. MIMO enables the transmission of multiple data streams traveling on different antennas in the same channel at the same time. A receiver reconstructs the streams, which have multiple antennas as well. By using multiple paths, MIMO provides a significant capacity gain over conventional single-antenna systems, along with more reliable communication.

In addition to all these improvements, 802.11n enables channel bonding that essentially doubles the data rate again. What is channel bonding? The 802.11b and 802.11g wireless standards use a single channel to send and receive information. With channel bonding, you can use two channels at the same time. As you might guess, the ability to use two channels at once increases performance. It is expected that bonding can help increase wireless transmission rates from the 54Mbps offered with the 802.11g standards to a theoretical maximum of 600Mbps. 802.11n uses the OFDM transmission strategy.

> **Note**
>
> In wireless networking a single channel is 20MHz in width. When two channels are bonded, they are a total of 40MHz. 802.11n systems can use either the 20MHz channels or the 40MHz channel.

A Summary of 802.11 Wireless Standards

Table 7.4 highlights the characteristics of the various 802.11 wireless standards.

TABLE 7.4 **802.11 Wireless Standards**

IEEE Standard	Frequency/ Medium	Speed	Topology	Transmission Range	Access Method
802.11	2.4GHz RF	1 to 2Mbps	Ad hoc/ infrastructure	20 feet indoors.	CSMA/CA
802.11a	5GHz	Up to 54Mbps	Ad hoc/ infrastructure	25 to 75 feet indoors; range can be affected by building materials.	CSMA/CA
802.11b	2.4GHz	Up to 11Mbps	Ad hoc/ infrastructure	Up to 150 feet indoors; range can be affected by building materials.	CSMA/CA

TABLE 7.4 **Continued**

IEEE Standard	Frequency/ Medium	Speed	Topology	Transmission Range	Access Method
802.11g	2.4GHz	Up to 54Mbps	Ad hoc/ infrastructure	Up to 150 feet indoors; range can be affected by building materials.	CSMA/CA
802.11n	2.4GHz/ 5GHz	Up to 600Mbps	Ad hoc/ infrastructure	175+ feet indoors; range can be affected by building materials.	CSMA/CA

FHSS, DSSS, OFDM, and 802.11 Standards

FHSS, DSS, and OFDM were mentioned earlier in the section on "Spread Spectrum Technology." The discussion here is not on the technology itself, but instead on the standards that apply to them.

The original 802.11 standard had two variations, both offering the same speeds but differing in the RF spread spectrum used. One of the 802.11 standards used FHSS. This 802.11 variant used the 2.4GHz radio frequency band and operated at a 1 or 2Mbps data rate. Since this original standard, wireless implementations have favored DSSS.

The second 802.11 variation used DSSS and specified a 2Mbps peak data rate with optional fallback to 1Mbps in noisy environments. 802.11, 802.11b, and 802.11g use DSSS. This means that the underlying modulation scheme is similar between each standard, enabling all DSSS systems to coexist with 2, 11, and 54Mbps 802.11 standards. As a comparison, it is like the migration from the older 10Mbps Ethernet networking to the more commonly implemented 1000Mbps standard. The speed was different, but the underlying technologies were similar, enabling an easier upgrade.

Table 7.5 compares wireless standards and the spread spectrum used.

TABLE 7.5 **Comparison of IEEE 802.11 Standards**

IEEE Standard	RF Used	Spread Spectrum	Data Rate (in Mbps)
802.11	2.4GHz	DSSS	1 or 2
802.11	2.4GHz	FHSS	1 or 2
802.11a	5GHz	OFDM	54
802.11b	2.4GHz	DSSS	11
802.11g	2.4GHz	DSSS	54
802.11n	2.4/5GHz	OFDM	600 (theoretical)

Cram Quiz

1. You are installing a wireless network solution, and you require a standard that can operate using either 2.4GHz or 5GHz frequencies. Which of the following standards would you choose?

   ○ **A.** 802.11a

   ○ **B.** 802.11b

   ○ **C.** 802.11g

   ○ **D.** 802.11n

2. You are installing a wireless network solution that uses a feature known as MIMO. Which wireless networking standard are you using?

   ○ **A.** 802.11a

   ○ **B.** 802.11b

   ○ **C.** 802.11g

   ○ **D.** 802.11n

Cram Quiz Answers

1. **D.** The IEEE standard 802.11n can use either the 2.4GHz or 5GHz radio frequencies. 802.11a uses 5GHz, and 802.11b and 802.11g use 2.4GHz. For more information, see the section "802.11 Wireless Standards."

2. **D.** MIMO is used by the 802.11n standard and takes advantage of multiplexing to increase the range and speed of wireless networking. Multiplexing is a technique that combines multiple signals for transmission over a single line or medium. MIMO enables the transmission of multiple data streams traveling on different antennas in the same channel at the same time. A receiver reconstructs the streams, which have multiple antennas. For more information, see the section "The Magic Behind 802.11n."

Securing Wireless Networks

▶ **Given a scenario, implement appropriate wireless security measures.**

Cram**Saver**

If you can correctly answer these questions before going through this section, save time by skimming the Exam Alerts in this section and then complete the Cram Quiz at the end of the section.

1. What does WPA use to scramble encryption keys using a hashing algorithm?

2. WPA2 uses CCMP. What is the strength of CCMP in terms of bits?

Answers

1. WPA uses a temporal key integrity protocol (TKIP), which scrambles encryption keys using a hashing algorithm.

2. CCMP uses 128-bit AES encryption with a 48-bit initialization vector.

Many different strategies and protocols are used to secure LAN and WAN transmissions. What about network transmissions that travel over the airwaves?

In the last few years, wireless networking has changed the look of modern networks, bringing with it an unparalleled level of mobility and a host of new security concerns.

Wireless LANs (WLANs) require new protocols and standards to handle security for radio communications. As it stands today, wireless communications represent a significant security concern. You should be aware of a few wireless security standards when working with wireless, including Wired Equivalent Privacy (WEP), Wi-Fi Protected Access (WPA), and 802.1X. To make the subject easy to understand, imagine the analogy of an entry; in the absence of any wireless security, the knob resembles that in Figure 7.5.

FIGURE 7.5 Wireless networking, in the absence of security, is like a door knob without a lock.

Wired Equivalent Privacy (WEP)

Wired equivalent privacy (WEP) was the first attempt to keep wireless networks safe. WEP was designed to be easy to configure and implement. Originally, it was hoped that WEP would provide the same level of security to wireless networks as was available to wired. For a time it was the best and only option for securing wireless networks.

WEP is an IEEE standard introduced in 1997, designed to secure 802.11 networks. With WEP enabled, each data packet transmitted over the wireless connection would be encrypted. Originally, the data packet was combined with a secret 40-bit number key as it passed through an encryption algorithm known as RC4. The packet was scrambled and sent across the airwaves. On the receiving end, the data packet passed through the RC4 backward, and the host received the data as it was intended. WEP originally used a 40-bit number key, but later it specified 128-bit encryption, making WEP that much more robust.

WEP is a protocol designed to provide security by encrypting data from the sending and receiving devices. In a short period of time, however, it was discovered that WEP encryption was not nearly as secure as hoped. Part of the problem was that when the 802.11 standards were written, security was not the major concern it is today. As a result, WEP security was easy to crack with freely available hacking tools. From this point, wireless communication was regarded as a potentially insecure transmission medium.

The two types of WEP security are static and dynamic. Dynamic and static WEP differ in that dynamic WEP changes security keys periodically, making it more secure. Static WEP uses the same security key on an ongoing basis. The primary security risks are associated with static WEP, which uses a shared password to protect communications. Security weaknesses discovered in static WEP mean that WLANs protected by it are vulnerable to several types of threats. Freely available hacking tools make breaking into static WEP-protected wireless networks a trivial task. Unsecured WLANs are obviously exposed to these same threats as well; the difference is that less expertise, time, and resources are required to carry out the attacks. To continue the analogy, think of WEP security as a door knob that now has a lock added to it, as shown in Figure 7.6.

FIGURE 7.6   The lock adds minimal security, and the door can still be opened rather easily.

Wi-Fi Protected Access (WPA)

Security weaknesses associated with WEP gave administrators a valid reason
to be concerned about wireless security. The need for increased wireless security was important for wireless networking to reach its potential and to reas-
sure those who had sensitive data that it was safe to use wireless communications. In response, Wi-Fi Protected Access (WPA) was created. WPA was
designed to improve on the security weaknesses of WEP and to be backward
compatible with older devices that used the WEP standard. WPA addressed
two main security concerns:

▶ **Enhanced data encryption**: WPA uses a temporal key integrity protocol (TKIP), which scrambles encryption keys using a hashing algorithm.
  Then the keys are issued an integrity check to verify that they have not
  been modified or tampered with during transit.

▶ **Authentication**: Using Extensible Authentication Protocol (EAP),
  WEP regulates access to a wireless network based on a computer's hard-
  ware-specific MAC address, which is relatively simple to be sniffed and
  stolen. EAP is built on a more secure public-key encryption system to
  ensure that only authorized network users can access the network.

> **Note**
>
> Temporal Key Integrity Protocol (TKIP) was designed to address the shortcomings
> of the WEP security protocol. TKIP is an encryption protocol defined in IEEE
> 802.11i. TKIP was designed not only to increase security but also to use existing
> hardware, making it easy to upgrade to TKIP encryption. TKIP is built on the origi-
> nal WEP security standard but enhances it by "wrapping" additional code at both
> the end and the beginning of the data packet. This code modifies the code for
> additional security. Because TKIP is based on WEP, it too uses the RC4 stream
> encryption method. But unlike WEP, TKIP encrypts each data packet with a
> stronger encryption key than is available with regular WEP.
>
> TKIP provides strong encryption for home users and nonsensitive data. However, it
> may not provide the level of security necessary to protect corporate or more sensi-
> tive data while in transmission.

Continuing with the analogy, WPA remains backward compatible by still
using the same door knob as before but has now added a "helper" to increase
security (see Figure 7.7).

FIGURE 7.7   A "helper" has been added to the lock on the door knob to increase security.

WPA2

The *802.11i* standard provides for security enhancements to the wireless standard with particular focus on authentication. The standard is often referenced as WPA2, the name given it by the Wi-Fi Alliance. The difference between WPA and WPA2 is that the former implements most—but not all—of 802.11i to communicate with older wireless cards (which might still need an update through their firmware to be compliant) and it used the RC4 encryption algorithm with TKIP, whereas WPA2 implements the full standard and is not compatible with older cards.

WPA also mandates the use of TKIP, whereas WPA2 favors *Counter Mode with Cipher Block Chaining Message Authentication Code Protocol (CCMP)*. CCMP uses 128-bit AES encryption with a 48-bit initialization vector. With the larger initialization vector, it increases the difficulty in cracking and minimizes the risk of replay.

As a simplified timeline useful for exam study, think of WEP as coming first. It was fraught with errors, and WPA (with TKIP) was used as an intermediate solution, implementing a portion of the 802.11i standard. The final solution—a full implementation of the 802.11i standard—is WPA2 (with CCMP).

Rounding out the analogy, WPA2 basically adds two locks to the door, as shown in Figure 7.8.

FIGURE 7.8   Adding two actual locks to the door effectively increases security.

WPA Enterprise

WPA Enterprise, also more properly known as 802.1X for the IEEE standard defining it, specifies port-based network access control. 802.1X was not specifically designed for wireless networks; rather, it provides authenticated access for both wired and wireless networks. Port-based network access control uses the physical characteristics of a switched local area network (LAN) infrastructure to authenticate devices attached to a LAN port and to prevent access to that port in cases where the authentication process fails. The 802.1X framework has three main components:

▶ **Supplicant**: The system or node requesting access and authentication to a network resource

▶ **Authenticator**: A control mechanism that allows or denies traffic that wants to pass through a port

▶ **Authentication server**: Validates the credentials of the supplicant that is trying to access the network or resource

During a port-based network access control interaction, a LAN port adopts one of two roles: authenticator or supplicant. In the role of authenticator, a LAN port enforces authentication before it allows user access to the services that can be accessed through that port. In the role of supplicant, a LAN port requests access to the services that can be accessed through the authenticator's port. An authentication server, which can be either a separate entity or collocated with the authenticator, checks the supplicant's credentials on behalf of the authenticator. The authentication server then responds to the authenticator, indicating whether the supplicant is authorized to access the authenticator's services.

The authenticator's port-based network access control defines two logical access points to the LAN through one physical LAN port. The first logical access point, the uncontrolled port, enables data exchange between the authenticator and other computers on the LAN, regardless of the computer's authorization state. The second logical access point, the controlled port, enables data exchange between an authenticated LAN user and the authenticator.

In a wireless network environment, the supplicant typically is a network host. The authenticator could be the wireless network switch or AP.

ExamAlert

Always equate WPA Enterprise with 802.1X: For exam purposes, the two are synonymous.

Cram Quiz

1. You are asked to configure the security settings for a new wireless network. You want the setting that offers the greatest level of security. Which of the following would you choose?

    - ○ **A.** WEP-Open
    - ○ **B.** WEP-Closed
    - ○ **C.** WEP-Shared
    - ○ **D.** WEP-Unshared

2. Which of the following best describes 802.1X?

    - ○ **A.** A port-based access control
    - ○ **B.** A wireless standard specifying 11Mbps data transfer
    - ○ **C.** A wireless standard specifying 54Mbps data transfer
    - ○ **D.** An integrity-based access control

3. In the 802.1X security framework, which of the following best describes the role of the supplicant?

    - ○ **A.** Authenticating usernames and passwords
    - ○ **B.** Encrypting usernames and passwords
    - ○ **C.** The system or node requesting access and authentication to a network resource
    - ○ **D.** A control mechanism that allows or denies traffic that wants to pass through a port

Cram Quiz Answers

1. **C.** Both WEP-Open and WEP-Shared are forms of wireless security. WEP-Open is the simpler of the two authentication methods because it does not perform any type of client verification. It is a weak form of authentication because no proof of identity is required. WEP-Shared requires that a WEP key be configured on both the client system and the access point. This makes authentication with WEP-Shared mandatory and therefore more secure for wireless transmission.

2. **A.** 802.1X is an IEEE standard specifying port-based network access control. Port-based network access control uses the physical characteristics of a switched local area network (LAN) infrastructure to authenticate devices attached to a LAN port and to prevent access to that port in cases where the authentication process fails. For more information, see the section "WPA Enterprise."

3. **C.** The 802.1X security framework has three main components. The supplicant is the system or node requesting access and authentication to a network resource. The authenticator usually is a switch or AP that acts as a control mechanism, allowing or denying traffic that wants to pass through a port. Finally, the authentication server validates the credentials of the supplicant that is trying to access the network or resource. For more information, see the section "WPA Enterprise."

Wireless Troubleshooting Checklist

▶ **Given a scenario, troubleshoot common wireless problems.**

Cram**Saver**

If you can correctly answer these questions before going through this section, save time by skimming the Exam Alerts in this section and then complete the Cram Quiz at the end of the section.

1. You have noticed that connections between nodes on one network are inconsistent and suspect there may be another network using the same channel. What should you try first?

2. True or False: Weather conditions should not have a noticeable impact on wireless signal integrity.

Answers

1. If connections are inconsistent, try changing the channel to another, nonoverlapping channel.

2. False. Weather conditions can have a huge impact on wireless signal integrity.

Poor communication between wireless devices has many different potential causes. The following is a review checklist of wireless troubleshooting:

▶ **Wireless enabled**: Some laptops make it incredibly easy to turn wireless on and off. A user may accidentally press a button that they are not aware of and then suddenly cannot access the network. Although this is a simple problem to fix, it is one that you need to identify as quickly as possible. Figure 7.9 shows the wireless light on an HP EliteBook. This light is also a button that toggles wireless on and off. When the light is blue, wireless is enabled, and when it is not blue (orange), it is disabled.

▶ **Auto transfer rate**: By default, wireless devices are configured to use the strongest, fastest signal. If you experience connectivity problems between wireless devices, try using the lower transfer rate in a fixed mode to achieve a more stable connection. For example, you can manually choose the wireless transfer rate. Also, instead of using the highest transfer rate available, try a lesser speed. The higher the transfer rate, the shorter the connection distance.

FIGURE 7.9   A light also serves as a button, enabling wireless to be quickly turned on and off.

▶ **Router placement**: If signal strength is low, try moving the access point to a new location. Moving it just a few feet can make a difference.

▶ **Antenna**: The default antenna shipped with wireless devices may not be powerful enough for a particular client system. Better-quality antennas can be purchased for some APs, which can boost the distance the signal can go.

▶ **Building obstructions**: Wireless RF communications are weakened if they have to travel through obstructions such as metal and concrete.

▶ **Conflicting devices**: Any device that uses the same frequency range as the wireless device can cause interference. For example, 2.4GHz phones can cause interference with devices using the 802.11g standard.

▶ **Wireless channels**: If connections are inconsistent, try changing the channel to another, nonoverlapping channel.

▶ **Protocol issues**: If an IP address is not assigned to the wireless client, an incorrect SSID or incorrect WEP settings can prevent a system from obtaining IP information.

- ▸ **SSID**: The SSID number used on the client system must match the one used on the AP. You might need to change it if you're switching a laptop between different WLANs.

- ▸ **WEP**: If WEP is enabled, the encryption type must match what is set in the AP.

Factors Affecting Wireless Signals

Because wireless signals travel through the atmosphere, they are susceptible to different types of interference than standard wired networks. Interference weakens wireless signals and therefore is an important consideration when working with wireless networking.

Interference Types

Wireless interference is an important consideration when you plan a wireless network. Interference is unfortunately inevitable, but the trick is to minimize the levels of interference. Wireless LAN communications typically are based on radio frequency signals that require a clear and unobstructed transmission path.

The following are some factors that cause interference:

- ▸ **Physical objects**: Trees, masonry, buildings, and other physical structures are some of the most common sources of interference. The density of the materials used in a building's construction determines the number of walls the RF signal can pass through and still maintain adequate coverage. Concrete and steel walls are particularly difficult for a signal to pass through. These structures weaken or at times completely prevent wireless signals.

> **ExamAlert**
>
> Be sure you understand that physical objects are a common source of interference.

- ▸ **Radio frequency interference**: Wireless technologies such as 802.11n can use an RF range of 2.4GHz, and so do many other devices, such as cordless phones, microwaves, and so on. Devices that share the channel can cause noise and weaken the signals.

- ▸ **Electrical interference**: Electrical interference comes from devices such as computers, refrigerators, fans, lighting fixtures, or any other motorized devices. The impact that electrical interference has on the signal depends on the proximity of the electrical device to the wireless access point. Advances in wireless technologies and in electrical devices have reduced the impact that these types of devices have on wireless transmissions.

▶ **Environmental factors**: Weather conditions can have a huge impact on wireless signal integrity. Lightning, for example, can cause electrical interference, and fog can weaken signals as they pass through.

Many wireless implementations are found in the office or at home. Even when outside interference such as weather is not a problem, every office has plenty of wireless obstacles. Table 7.6 highlights a few examples to be aware of when implementing a wireless network indoors.

TABLE 7.6 **Wireless Obstacles Found Indoors**

Obstruction	Obstacle Severity	Sample Use
Wood/wood paneling	Low	Inside a wall or hollow door
Drywall	Low	Inside walls
Furniture	Low	Couches or office partitions
Clear glass	Low	Windows
Tinted glass	Medium	Windows
People	Medium	High-volume traffic areas that have considerable pedestrian traffic
Ceramic tile	Medium	Walls
Concrete blocks	Medium/high	Outer wall construction
Mirrors	High	Mirror or reflective glass
Metals	High	Metal office partitions, doors, metal office furniture
Water	High	Aquariums, rain, fountains

ExamAlert

Be sure you understand the severity of obstructions given in Table 7.6.

Cram Quiz

1. You purchase a new wireless access point that uses no WEP security by default. You change the security settings to use 128-bit encryption. How must the client systems be configured?

   - ○ **A.** All client systems must be set to 128-bit encryption.
   - ○ **B.** The client system inherits security settings from the AP.
   - ○ **C.** WEP does not support 128-bit encryption.
   - ○ **D.** The client WEP settings must be set to autodetect.

2. You experience connectivity problems with your SOHO network. What can you change in an attempt to solve this problem?

   - ○ **A.** Shorten the SSID.
   - ○ **B.** Remove all encryption.
   - ○ **C.** Lower the transfer rate.
   - ○ **D.** Raise the transfer rate.

Cram Quiz Answers

1. **A.** On a wireless connection between an access point and the client, each system must be configured to use the same WEP security settings. In this case, they must both be configured to use 128-bit encryption. For more information, see the section "Wireless Troubleshooting Checklist."

2. **C.** If you experience connectivity problems between wireless devices, try using the lower transfer rate in a fixed mode to achieve a more stable connection. For example, you can manually choose the wireless transfer rate. The higher the transfer rate, the shorter the connection distance. For more information, see the section "Wireless Troubleshooting Checklist."

What Next?

Chapter 8, "Network Management," focuses on two important parts of the role of a network administrator: documentation and connectivity tools. Documentation, although not glamorous, is an essential part of the job. You need to understand and appreciate why administrators must spend valuable time sitting down writing and reviewing documentation.

CHAPTER 8

Network Management

This chapter covers the following official Network+ objectives:

▶ Describe the purpose of configuration management documentation.

▶ Given a scenario, use appropriate software tools to troubleshoot connectivity issues.

▶ Given a scenario, use the appropriate networking monitoring resources to analyze traffic.

▶ Given a scenario, use appropriate hardware tools to troubleshoot connectivity issues.

This chapter covers CompTIA Network+ objectives 4.2, 4.3, 4.4, and 4.5. For more information on the official Network+ exam topics, see the "About the Network+ Exam" section in the "Introduction."

This chapter focuses on two important parts of the role of a network administrator: documentation and the tools to use to monitor or troubleshoot connectivity. Documentation, although not glamorous, is an essential part of the job. This chapter looks at several aspects of network documentation.

Administrators have several daily tasks, and new ones are frequently cropping up. In this environment, tasks such as documentation sometimes fall to the background. This is when you need to understand why administrators need to spend valuable time writing and reviewing documentation. Having a well-documented network offers a number of advantages:

▶ **Troubleshooting**: When something goes wrong on the network, including the wiring, up-to-date documentation is a valuable reference to guide the troubleshooting effort. The documentation saves you money and time in isolating potential problems.

▶ **Training new administrators**: In many network environments, new administrators are hired, and old ones leave. In this scenario, documentation is critical. New administrators do not have the time to try to figure out where cabling is run, what cabling is used, potential trouble spots, and more. Up-to-date information helps new administrators quickly see the network layout.

▶ **Contractors and consultants**: Consultants and contractors occasionally may need to visit the network. This may be done to make future recommendations for the network or to add wiring or other components. In such cases, up-to-date documentation is needed. If it were missing, it would be much more difficult for these people to do their jobs, and more time and money would likely be required.

Recognizing the importance of documentation is one thing; knowing what to document and when to document it is another. This chapter looks at types of management documentation and how network administrators use documentation.

Documentation Management

▶ **Describe the purpose of configuration management documentation.**

Cram**Saver**

If you can correctly answer these questions before going through this section, save time by skimming the Exam Alerts in this section and then complete the Cram Quiz at the end of the section.

1. Which network topology focuses on the direction in which data flows within the physical environment?

2. In computing, what are historical readings used as a measurement for future calculations referred to as?

3. True or False: Both logical and physical network diagrams provide an overview of the network layout and function.

Answers

1. The logical network refers to the direction in which data flows on the network within the physical topology. The logical diagram is not intended to focus on the network hardware but rather on how data flows through that hardware.

2. Keeping and reviewing baselines is an essential part of the administrator's role.

3. True. Both logical and physical network diagrams provide an overview of the network layout and function.

Quality network documentation does not happen by accident; rather, it requires careful planning. When creating network documentation, you must keep in mind who you are creating the documentation for and that it is a communication tool. Documentation is used to take technical information and present it in a manner that someone new to the network can understand. When planning network documentation, you must decide what you need to document.

Note

Imagine that you have just taken over a network as administrator. What information would you like to see? This is often a clear gauge of what to include in your network documentation.

All networks differ and so does the documentation required for each network. However, certain elements are always included in quality documentation:

▶ **Network topology**: Networks can be complicated. If someone new is looking over the network, it is critical to document the entire topology.

This includes both the wired and wireless topologies used on the network. Network topology documentation typically consists of a diagram or diagrams labeling all critical components used to create the network. These diagrams include such components as routers, switches, hubs, gateways, and firewalls.

▶ **Wiring layout**: Network wiring can be confusing. Much of it is hidden in walls and ceilings, making it hard to know where the wiring is and what kind is used on the network. This makes it critical to keep documentation on network wiring up to date.

▶ **Server configuration**: A single network typically uses multiple servers spread over a large geographic area. Documentation must include schematic drawings of where servers are located on the network and the services each provides. This includes server function, server IP address, operating system (OS), software information, and more. Essentially, you need to document all the information you need to manage or administer the servers.

▶ **Network equipment**: The hardware used on a network is configured in a particular way—with protocols, security settings, permissions, and more. Trying to remember these would be a difficult task. Having up-to-date documentation would make it easier to recover from a failure.

▶ **Key applications**: Documentation also includes information on all the key applications used on the network, such as up-to-date information on their updates, vendors, install dates, and more.

▶ **Detailed account of network services**: Network services are a key ingredient in all networks. Services such as Domain Name Service (DNS), Dynamic Host Configuration Protocol (DHCP), Remote Access Service (RAS), and more are an important part of documentation. You should describe in detail which server maintains these services, the backup servers for these services, maintenance schedules, how they are structured, and more.

▶ **Network procedures**: Finally, documentation should include information on network policy and procedures. This includes many elements, ranging from who can and cannot access the server room, to network firewalls, protocols, passwords, physical security, and so on.

ExamAlert

Be sure you know the types of information that should be included in network documentation.

Wiring Schematics

Network wiring schematics are an essential part of network documentation, particularly for midsize to large networks, where the cabling is certainly complex. For such networks, it becomes increasingly difficult to visualize network cabling and even harder to explain it to someone else. A number of software tools exist to help administrators clearly document network wiring in detail.

Several types of wiring schematics exist. They can be general, as shown in Figure 8.1, or they can be supplemented with the details found in Table 8.1, as shown in Figure 8.2.

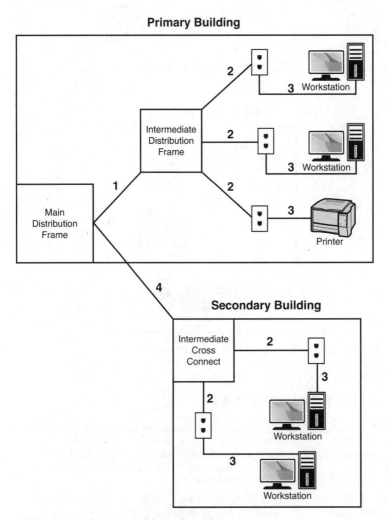

FIGURE 8.1   A general wiring schematic.

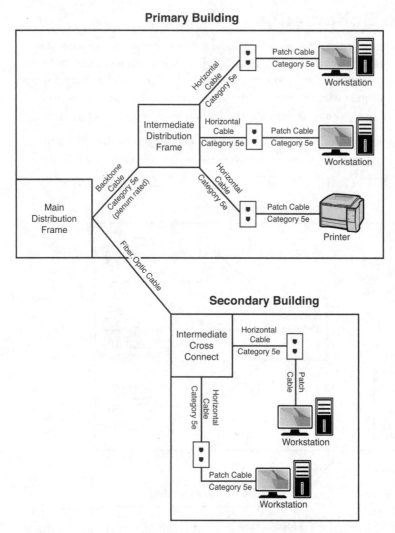

FIGURE 8.2   A wiring schematic that has a corresponding detail table.

TABLE 8.1   **Wiring Schematic Details**

Cable	Description	Installation Notes
1	Cat5E 350MHz nonplenum-rated cable	Cable runs 50 feet from the MDF to IDF. Cable placed through the ceiling and through a mechanical room. Cable was installed 01/15/2011, upgrading a non-plenum Cat5 cable.
2	Cat5E 350MHz nonplenum cable	Horizontal cable runs 45 feet to 55 feet from IDF to wall jack. Cable 5E replaced Cat5 cable February 2012. Section of cable run through the ceiling and over fluorescent lights.

TABLE 8.1 **Continued**

Cable	Description	Installation Notes
3	Category 5e UTP cable	All patch cable connectors were attached in-house. Patch cable connecting the printer runs 45 feet due to printer placement.
4	8.3-micron core/ 125-micron cladding single mode	Connecting fiber cable runs 2 kilometers between the primary and secondary buildings.

Figures 8.1 and 8.2 provide a simplified look at network wiring schematics. Imagine how complicated these diagrams would look on a network with one, two, or even six thousand computers. Quality network documentation software makes this easier; however, the task of network wiring can be a large one for administrators. Administrators need to ensure that someone can pick up the wiring documentation diagrams and have a good idea of the network wiring.

ExamAlert

Reading schematics and determining where wiring runs is an important part of the administrator's role. Expect to see a schematic on your exam.

Troubleshooting Using Wiring Schematics

Some network administrators do not take the time to maintain quality documentation. This will haunt them when it comes time to troubleshoot some random network problems. Without any network wiring schematics, the task will be frustrating and time-consuming. The information shown in Figure 8.2 might be simplified, but you could use that documentation to evaluate the network wiring and make recommendations. In the hypothetical information provided in Figure 8.2 and Table 8.1, several potential problems with the network wiring exist. Any administrator could walk in and review the network documentation and isolate the potential problems. Now it's your turn. Can you find some problems in those schematics?

Need a hint? Cable 1 runs through the ceiling and a mechanical room and is not plenum-rated. This could cause interference for a regular UTP cable. Cable 2 has sections running through the ceiling and over fluorescent lights. In this case the cable needs to be shielded somehow. Perhaps shielded twisted pair (STP) needs to be used. Finally, Cable 3 might be a problem. The cable connectors were attached in-house, meaning that some of the cables may not be made as well as cable purchased with connectors attached. There may be intermittent problems that can be traced to a poorly made cable.

> **Exam Alert**
>
> When looking at a wiring schematic, pay close attention to where the cable is run and the type of cable used. If a correct cable is not used, there could be a problem.

> **Note**
>
> Network wiring schematics are a work in progress. Although changes to wiring do not happen daily, they do occur when the network expands or old cabling is replaced. It is imperative to remember that when changes occur to the network, the schematics and their corresponding references must be updated to reflect the changes. Out-of-date schematics can be frustrating to work with.

Physical and Logical Network Diagrams

In addition to the wiring schematics, documentation should include diagrams of the physical and logical network design. Recall from Chapter 1, "Introduction to Networking," that network topologies can be defined on a physical or logical level. The *physical topology* refers to how a network is physically constructed—how it looks. The *logical topology* refers to how a network looks to the devices that use it—how it functions.

Network infrastructure documentation isn't reviewed daily; however, this documentation is essential for someone unfamiliar with the network to manage or troubleshoot the network. When it comes to documenting the network, you need to document all aspects of the infrastructure. This includes the physical hardware, physical structure, protocols, and software used.

> **Exam Alert**
>
> You should be able to identify a physical and logical diagram. You need to know the types of information that should be included in each diagram.

The physical documentation of the network should include the following elements:

- ▶ **Cabling information**: A visual description of all the physical communication links, including all cabling, cable grades, cable lengths, WAN cabling, and more.

- ▶ **Servers**: The server names and IP addresses, types of servers, and domain membership.

> ▶ **Network devices**: The location of the devices on the network. This includes the printers, hubs, switches, routers, gateways, and more.

> ▶ **Wide area network**: The location and devices of the WAN and components.

> ▶ **User information**: Some user information, including the number of local and remote users.

As you can see, many elements can be included in the physical network diagram. Figure 8.3 shows a physical segment of a network.

Exam Alert

You should recognize the importance of maintaining documentation on cabling management, asset management, and change management.

Networks are dynamic, and changes can happen regularly, which is why the physical network diagrams must be updated as well. Networks have different policies and procedures on how often updates should occur. Best practice is that the diagram should be updated whenever significant changes to the network occur, such as the addition of a bridge, a change in protocols, or the addition of a new server. These changes impact how the network operates, and the documentation should reflect the changes.

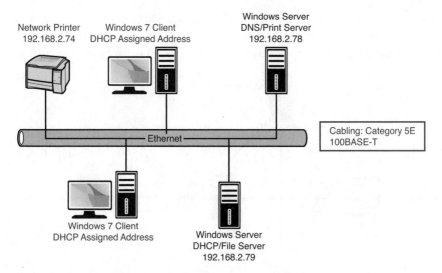

FIGURE 8.3 **A physical network diagram.**

ExamAlert

There are no hard and fast rules about when to change or update network documentation. However, most administrators will want to update whenever functional changes to the network occur.

The logical network refers to the direction in which data flows on the network within the physical topology. The logical diagram is not intended to focus on the network hardware but rather on how data flows through that hardware. In practice, the physical and logical topologies can be the same. In the case of the bus physical topology, data travels along the length of the cable from one computer to the next. So the diagram for the physical and logical bus would be the same.

This is not always the case. For example, a topology can be in the physical shape of a star, but data is passed in a logical ring. The function of data travel is performed inside a switch in a ring formation. So the physical diagram appears to be a star, but the logical diagram shows data flowing in a ring formation from one computer to the next. Simply put, it is difficult to tell from looking at a physical diagram how data is flowing on the network.

In today's network environments, the star topology is a common network implementation. Ethernet uses a physical star topology but a logical bus topology. In the center of the physical Ethernet star topology is a switch. It is what happens inside the switch that defines the logical bus topology. The switch passes data between ports as if they were on an Ethernet bus segment.

In addition to data flow, logical diagrams may include additional elements, such as the network domain architecture, server roles, protocols used, and more. Figure 8.4 shows how a logical topology may look in the form of network documentation.

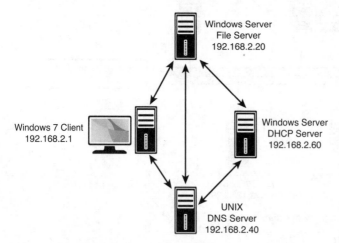

FIGURE 8.4 **A logical topology diagram.**

Baselines

Baselines play an integral part in network documentation because they let you monitor the network's overall performance. In simple terms, a *baseline* is a measure of performance that indicates how hard the network is working and where network resources are spent. The purpose of a baseline is to provide a basis of comparison. For example, you can compare the network's performance results taken in March to results taken in June or from one year to the next. More commonly, you would compare the baseline information at a time when the network is having a problem to information recorded when the network was operating with greater efficiency. Such comparisons help you determine if there has been a problem with the network, how significant that problem is, and even where the problem lies.

To be of any use, baselining is not a one-time task; rather, baselines should be taken periodically to provide an accurate comparison. You should take an initial baseline after the network is set up and operational, and then again when major changes are made to the network. Even if no changes are made to the network, periodic baselining can prove useful as a means to determine if the network is still correctly operating.

All network operating systems (NOSs), including Windows, Mac OS, UNIX, and Linux, have built-in support for network monitoring. In addition, many third-party software packages are available for detailed network monitoring. These system-monitoring tools provided in a NOS give you the means to take performance baselines, either of the entire network or for an individual segment within the network. Because of the different functions of these two baselines, they are called a system baseline and a component baseline.

To create a network baseline, network monitors provide a graphical display of network statistics. Network administrators can choose a variety of network measurements to track. They can use these statistics to perform routine troubleshooting tasks, such as locating a malfunctioning network card, downed server, or denial-of-service attack.

Collecting network statistics is a process called *capturing*. Administrators can capture statistics on all elements of the network. For baseline purposes, one of the most common statistics to monitor is bandwidth usage. By reviewing bandwidth statistics, administrators can see where the bulk of network bandwidth is used. Then they can adapt the network for bandwidth use. If too much bandwidth is used by a particular application, administrators can actively control its bandwidth usage. Without comparing baselines, however, it is difficult to see what is normal network bandwidth usage and what is unusual.

> **Exam Alert**
>
> Remember that baselines need to be taken periodically and under the same conditions to be effective. They are used to compare current performance with past performance to help determine if the network is functioning properly or if troubleshooting is required.

Policies, Procedures, Configurations, and Regulations

Well-functioning networks are characterized by documented policies, procedures, configurations, and regulations. Because they are unique to every network, policies, procedures, configurations, and regulations should be clearly documented.

Policies

By definition, policies refer to an organization's documented rules about what is to be done, or not done, and why. Policies dictate who can and cannot access particular network resources, server rooms, backup tapes, and more.

Although networks might have different policies depending on their needs, some common policies include the following:

▶ **Network usage policy**: Who can use network resources such as PCs, printers, scanners, and remote connections. In addition to who can use these resources, the usage policy dictates what can be done with these resources after they are accessed. No outside systems will be networked without permission from the network administrator.

▶ **Internet usage policy**: This policy specifies the rules for Internet use on the job. Typically, usage should be focused on business-related tasks. Incidental personal use is allowed during specified times.

▶ **Email usage policy**: Email must follow the same code of conduct as expected in any other form of written or face-to-face communication. All emails are company property and can be accessed by the company. Personal emails should be immediately deleted.

▶ **Personal software policy**: No outside software should be installed on network computer systems. All software installations must be approved by the network administrator. No software can be copied or removed from a site.

▶ **User account policy**: All users are responsible for keeping their password and account information secret. All staff are required to log off and sometimes lock their systems after they finish using them. Attempting to log on to the network with another user account is considered a serious violation.

▶ **Ownership policy**: The company owns all data, including users' email, voice mail, and Internet usage logs, and the company reserves the right to inspect these at any time. Some companies even go so far as controlling how much personal data can be stored on a workstation.

This list is just a snapshot of the policies that guide the behavior for administrators and network users. Network policies should be clearly documented and available to network users. Often, these policies are reviewed with new staff members or new administrators. As they are updated, they are rereleased to network users. Policies are regularly reviewed and updated.

Exam Alert

You may be asked about network policies. Network policies dictate network rules and provide guidelines for network conduct. Policies are often updated and reviewed and are changed to reflect changes to the network and perhaps changes in business requirements.

Procedures

Network procedures differ from policies in that they describe how tasks are to be performed. For example, each network administrator has backup procedures specifying the time of day backups are done, how often they are done, and where they are stored. A network is full of a number of procedures for practical reasons and, perhaps more important, for security reasons.

Administrators must be aware of several procedures when on the job. The number and exact type of procedures depends on the network. The network's overall goal is to ensure uniformity and ensure that network tasks follow a framework. Without this procedural framework, different administrators might approach tasks differently, which could lead to confusion on the network.

Network procedures might include the following:

▸ **Backup procedures**: Backup procedures specify when they are to be performed, how often a backup occurs, who does the backup, what data is to be backed up, and where and how it will be stored. Network administrators should carefully follow backup procedures.

▸ **Procedures for adding new users**: When new users are added to a network, administrators typically have to follow certain guidelines to ensure that the users have access to what they need, but no more. This is called the principle of least privilege.

▸ **Security procedures**: Some of the more critical procedures involve security. Security procedures are numerous but may include specifying what the administrator must do if security breaches occur, security monitoring, security reporting, and updating the OS and applications for potential security holes.

▸ **Network monitoring procedures**: The network needs to be constantly monitored. This includes tracking such things as bandwidth usage, remote access, user logons, and more.

▸ **Software procedures**: All software needs to be periodically monitored and updated. Documented procedures dictate when, how often, why, and for whom these updates are done.

▸ **Procedures for reporting violations**: Users do not always follow outlined network policies. This is why documented procedures should exist to properly handle the violations. This might include a verbal warning upon the first offense, followed by written reports and account lockouts thereafter.

▸ **Remote-access procedures**: Many workers remotely access the network. This remote access is granted and maintained using a series of defined procedures. These procedures might dictate when remote users can access the network, how long they can access it, and what they can access.

These represent just a few of the procedures that administrators must follow on the job. It is crucial that all these procedures are well-documented, accessible, reviewed, and updated as needed to be effective.

Configuration Documentation

One other critical form of documentation is configuration documentation. Many administrators feel they could never forget the configuration of a router, server, or switch, but it often happens. Although it's often a thankless, time-consuming task, documenting the network hardware and software configurations is critical for continued network functionality.

Two primary types of network configuration documentation are required: software documentation and hardware documentation. Both include all configuration information so that should a computer or other hardware fail, both the hardware and software can be replaced and reconfigured as quickly as possible. The documentation is important because often the administrator who configured the software or hardware is unavailable, and someone else has to re-create the configuration using nothing but the documentation. To be effective in this case, the documentation must be as current as possible. Older configuration information might not help.

Note

Organizing and completing the initial set of network documentation is a huge task, but it is just the beginning. Administrators must constantly update all documentation to keep it from becoming obsolete. Documentation is perhaps one of the less glamorous aspects of the administrator's role, but it's one of the most important.

Regulations

The terms *regulation* and *policy* are often used interchangeably; however, there is a difference. As mentioned, policies are written by an organization for its employees. Regulations are actual legal restrictions with legal consequences. These regulations are set not by the organizations but by applicable laws in the area. Improper use of networks and the Internet can certainly lead to legal violations and consequences. The following is an example of network regulation from an online company:

"Transmission, distribution, uploading, posting or storage of any material in violation of any applicable law or regulation is prohibited. This includes, without limitation, material protected by copyright, trademark, trade secret or other intellectual property right used without proper authorization, material kept in violation of state laws or industry regulations such as social security numbers or credit card numbers, and material that is obscene, defamatory, libelous, unlawful, harassing, abusive, threatening, harmful, vulgar, constitutes an illegal threat, violates export control laws, hate propaganda, fraudulent material or fraudulent activity, invasive of privacy or publicity rights, profane, indecent or otherwise objectionable material of any kind or nature. You may not transmit, distribute, or store material that contains a virus, 'Trojan Horse,' adware or spyware, corrupted data, or any software or information to promote or utilize software or any of Network Solutions services to deliver unsolicited e-mail. You further agree not to transmit any material that encourages conduct that could constitute a criminal offense, gives rise to civil liability or otherwise violates any applicable local, state, national or international law or regulation."

ExamAlert

For the exam and for real-life networking, remember that regulations often are enforceable by law.

Cram Quiz

You have been given a physical wiring schematic that shows the following:

Description	Installation Notes
Cat5E 350MHz plenum-rated cable	Cable runs 50 feet from the MDF to the IDF.
	Cable placed through the ceiling and through a mechanical room.
	Cable was installed 01/15/2012, upgrading a nonplenum Cat5 cable.
Cat5E 350MHz nonplenum cable	Horizontal cable runs 45 feet to 55 feet from the IDF to a wall jack.
	Cable 5E replaced Cat5 cable February 2011.
	Section of cable run through ceiling and over fluorescent lights.
Category 5E UTP cable	Patch cable connecting printer runs 15 feet due to printer placement.
8.3-micron core/125-micron	Connecting fiber cable runs 2 kilometers cladding single mode between the primary and secondary buildings.

1. Given this information, what cable recommendation might you make, if any?

   ○ **A.** Nonplenum cable should be used between the IDF and MDF.

   ○ **B.** The horizontal cable run should use plenum cable.

   ○ **C.** The patch cable connecting the printer should be shorter.

   ○ **D.** Leave the network cabling as is.

2. You have been called in to inspect a network configuration. You are given only one network diagram, shown in the following figure. Using the diagram, what recommendation might you make?

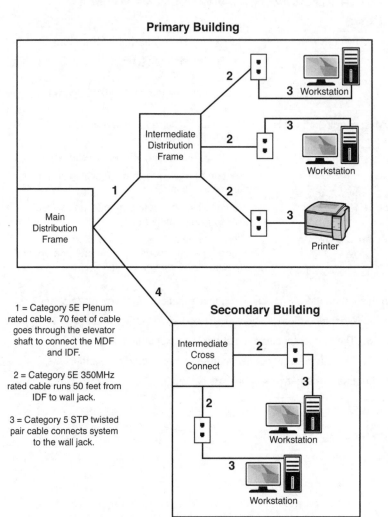

Primary Building

1 = Category 5E Plenum rated cable. 70 feet of cable goes through the elevator shaft to connect the MDF and IDF.

2 = Category 5E 350MHz rated cable runs 50 feet from IDF to wall jack.

3 = Category 5 STP twisted pair cable connects system to the wall jack.

Secondary Building

○ **A.** Cable 1 does not need to be plenum-rated.

○ **B.** Cable 2 should be STP cable.

○ **C.** Cable 3 should be STP cable.

○ **D.** None. The network looks good.

Cram Quiz Answers

1. **B.** In this scenario, a section of horizontal cable runs through the ceiling and over fluorescent lights. This cable run might be a problem because such devices can cause EMI. Alternatively, plenum cable is used in this scenario. STP may have worked as well.

2. **B.** In this diagram, Cable 1 is plenum-rated and should be fine. Cable 3 is patch cable and does not need to be STP-rated. Cable 2, however, goes through walls and ceilings. Therefore, it would be recommended to have a better grade of cable than regular UTP. STP provides greater resistance to EMI.

Monitoring Network Performance

▶ Given a scenario, use appropriate software tools to troubleshoot connectivity issues.

▶ Given a scenario, use the appropriate networking monitoring resources to analyze traffic.

Cram**Saver**

If you can correctly answer these questions before going through this section, save time by skimming the Exam Alerts in this section and then complete the Cram Quiz at the end of the section.

1. What can be used to capture network data?

2. True or False: Port scanners detect open and often unsecured ports.

Answers

1. Packet sniffers can be used by both administrators and hackers to capture network data.

2. True. Port scanners detect open and often unsecured ports.

When networks were smaller and few stretched beyond the confines of a single location, network management was a simple task. In today's complex, multisite, hybrid networks, however, the task of maintaining and monitoring network devices and servers has become a complicated but essential part of the network administrator's role. Nowadays, the role of network administrator often stretches beyond the physical boundary of the server room and reaches every node and component on the network. Whether an organization has 10 computers on a single segment or a multisite network with several thousand devices attached, the network administrator must monitor all network devices, protocols, and usage—preferably from a central location.

Given the sheer number and diversity of possible devices, software, and systems on any network, it is clear why network management is such a significant consideration. Despite that a robust network management strategy can improve administrator productivity and reduce downtime, many companies choose to neglect network management because of the time involved in setting up the system or because of the associated costs. If these companies understood the potential savings, they would realize that neglecting network management provides false economies.

Network management and network monitoring are essentially methods to control, configure, and monitor devices on a network. Imagine a scenario in which you are a network administrator working out of your main office in Spokane, Washington, and you have satellite offices in New York, Dallas, Vancouver, and London. Network management allows you to access systems in the remote locations or have the systems notify you when something goes awry. In essence, network management is about seeing beyond your current boundaries and acting on what you see.

Network management is not one thing. Rather, it's a collection of tools, systems, and protocols that, when used together, enables you to perform tasks such as reconfiguring a network card in the next room or installing an application in the next state.

Common Reasons to Monitor Networks

The capabilities demanded from network management vary somewhat among organizations, but essentially, several key types of information and functionality are required, such as fault detection and performance monitoring. Some of the types of information and functions that network management tools can provide include the following:

▶ **Fault detection**: One of the most vital aspects of network management is knowing if anything is not working or is not working correctly. Network management tools can detect and report on a variety of faults on the network. Given the number of possible devices that constitute a typical network, determining faults without these tools could be an impossible task. In addition, network management tools might not only detect the faulty device, but also shut it down. This means that if a network card is malfunctioning, you can remotely disable it. When a network spans a large area, fault detection becomes even more invaluable because it enables you to be alerted to network faults and to manage them, thereby reducing downtime.

▶ **Performance monitoring**: Another feature of network management is the ability to monitor network performance. Performance monitoring is an essential consideration that gives you some crucial information. Specifically, performance monitoring can provide network usage statistics and user usage trends. This type of information is essential when you plan network capacity and growth. Monitoring performance also helps you determine if there are any performance-related concerns, such as whether the network can adequately support the current user base.

▶ **Security monitoring**: Good server administrators have a touch of paranoia built into their personality. A network management system enables you to monitor who is on the network, what they are doing, and how long they have been doing it. More important, in an environment in which corporate networks are increasingly exposed to outside sources, the ability to identify and react to potential security threats is a priority. Reading log files to learn of an attack is a poor second to knowing that an attack is in progress and being able to react accordingly.

▶ **Maintenance and configuration**: Want to reconfigure or shut down the server located in Australia? Reconfigure a local router? Change the settings on a client system? Remote management and configuration are key parts of the network management strategy, enabling you to centrally manage huge multisite locations.

Many tools are available to help monitor the network and ensure that it is properly functioning. Some tools, such as a packet sniffer, can be used to monitor traffic by administrators and those who want to obtain data that doesn't belong to them. The following sections look at several monitoring tools.

Packet Sniffers

Packet sniffers are commonly used on networks. They are either a hardware device or software that basically eavesdrops on transmissions traveling throughout the network. The packet sniffer quietly captures data and saves it to be reviewed later. Packet sniffers can also be used on the Internet to capture data traveling between computers. Internet packets often have long distances to travel, going through various servers, routers, and gateways. Anywhere along this path, packet sniffers can quietly sit and collect data. Given the capability of packet sniffers to sit and silently collect data packets, it's easy to see how they could be exploited.

You should use two key defenses against packet sniffers to protect your network:

▶ Use a switched network, which most today are. In a switched network, data is sent from one computer system and is directed from the switch only to intended targeted destinations. In an older network using traditional hubs, the hub does not switch the traffic to isolated users but to all users connected to the hub's ports. This shotgun approach to network transmission makes it easier to place a packet sniffer on the network to obtain data.

▶ Ensure that all sensitive data is encrypted as it travels. Ordinarily, encryption is used when data is sent over a public network such as the Internet, but it may also be necessary to encrypt sensitive data on a LAN. Encryption can be implemented in a number of ways. For example, connections to web servers can be protected using the Secure Socket Layer (SSL) protocol and HTTPS. Communications to mail servers can also be encrypted using SSL. For public networks, the IPSec protocol can provide end-to-end encryption services.

> **Note**
>
> Chapter 10, "Network Security," provides more information on encryption protocols.

Throughput Testing

In the networking world, *throughput* refers to the rate of data delivery over a communication channel. In this case, throughput testers test the rate of data delivery over a network. Throughput is measured in bits per second (bps). Testing throughput is important for administrators to make them aware of exactly what the network is doing. With throughput testing, you can tell if a high-speed network is functioning close to its expected throughput.

A throughput tester is designed to quickly gather information about network functionality—specifically, the average overall network throughput. Many software-based throughput testers are available online—some for free and some for a fee. Figure 8.5 shows a software-based throughput tester.

As you can see, throughput testers do not need to be complicated to be effective. A throughput tester tells you how long it takes to send data to a destination point and receive an acknowledgment that the data was received. To use the tester, enter the beginning point and then the destination point. The tester sends a predetermined number of data packets to the destination and then reports on the throughput level. The results typically display in kilobits per second (Kbps), megabits per second (Mbps), or gigabits per second (Gbps). Table 8.2 shows the various data rate units.

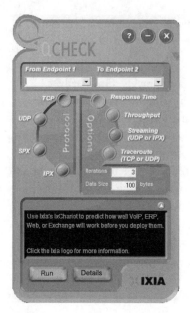

FIGURE 8.5   A software throughput tester.

TABLE 8.2   **Data Rate Units**

Data Transfer	Abbreviation	Rate
Kilobits per second	Kbps or Kbit/s	1,000 bits per second
Megabits per second	Mbps or Mbit/s	1,000,000 bits per second
Gigabits per second	Gbps or Gbit/s	1,000,000,000 bits per second
Kilobytes per second	KBps	1,000 bytes per second, or 8 kilobits per second
Megabytes per second	MBps	1,000,000 bytes per second, or 8 megabits per second
Gigabytes per second	GBps	1,000,000,000 bytes per second, or 8 gigabits per second

Administrators can periodically conduct throughput tests and keep them on file to create a picture of network performance. If you suspect a problem with the network functioning, you can run a test to compare with past performance to see exactly what is happening.

One thing worth mentioning is the difference between throughput and bandwidth. These terms are often used interchangeably, but they have different meanings. When talking about measuring throughput, you measure the amount of data flow under real-world conditions—measuring with possible

EMI influences, heavy traffic loads, improper wiring, and even network colli-sions. Take all this into account, take a measurement, and you have the net-work throughput. Bandwidth, on the other hand, refers to the maximum amount of information that can be sent through a particular medium under ideal conditions.

ExamAlert

Be sure you know the difference between throughput and bandwidth.

Port Scanners

Port scanners are software-based security utilities designed to search a net-work host for open ports on a TCP/IP-based network. As a refresher, in a TCP/IP-based network, a system can be accessed through one of 65,535 avail-able port numbers. Each network service is associated with a particular port.

Note

Chapter 3, "Addressing and Routing," includes a list of some of the most common TCP/IP suite protocols and their port assignments.

Many of the thousands of ports are closed by default; however, many others, depending on the OS, are open by default. These are the ports that can cause trouble. Like packet sniffers, port scanners can be used by both administrators and hackers. Hackers use port scanners to try to find an open port that they can use to access a system. Port scanners are easily obtained on the Internet either for free or for a modest cost. After it is installed, the scanner probes a computer system running TCP/IP, looking for a UDP or TCP port that is open and listening.

When a port scanner is used, several port states may be reported:

▶ **Open/Listening**: The host sent a reply indicating that a service is lis-tening on the port. There was a response from the port.

▶ **Closed or Denied or Not Listening**: No process is listening on that port. Access to this port will likely be denied.

▶ **Filtered or Blocked**: There was no reply from the host, meaning that the port is not listening or the port is secured and filtered.

Because others can potentially review the status of our ports, it is critical that administrators know which ports are open and potentially vulnerable. As mentioned, many tools and utilities are available for this. The quickest way to get an overview of the ports used by the system and their status is to issue the netstat -a command from the command line. The following is a sample of the output from the netstat -a command and active connections for a computer system:

```
Proto      Local Address          Foreign Address          State
  TCP      0.0.0.0:135            mike-PC:0                LISTENING
  TCP      0.0.0.0:10114          mike-PC:0                LISTENING
  TCP      0.0.0.0:10115          mike-PC:0                LISTENING
  TCP      0.0.0.0:20523          mike-PC:0                LISTENING
  TCP      0.0.0.0:20943          mike-PC:0                LISTENING
  TCP      0.0.0.0:49152          mike-PC:0                LISTENING
  TCP      0.0.0.0:49153          mike-PC:0                LISTENING
  TCP      0.0.0.0:49154          mike-PC:0                LISTENING
  TCP      0.0.0.0:49155          mike-PC:0                LISTENING
  TCP      0.0.0.0:49156          mike-PC:0                LISTENING
  TCP      0.0.0.0:49157          mike-PC:0                LISTENING
  TCP      127.0.0.1:5354         mike-PC:0                LISTENING
  TCP      127.0.0.1:27015        mike-PC:0                LISTENING
  TCP      127.0.0.1:27015        mike-PC:49187            ESTABLISHED
  TCP      127.0.0.1:49187        mike-PC:27015            ESTABLISHED
  TCP      192.168.0.100:49190    206.18.166.15:http       CLOSED
  TCP      192.168.1.66:139       mike-PC:0                LISTENING
  TCP      [::]:135               mike-PC:0                LISTENING
  TCP      [::]:445               mike-PC:0                LISTENING
  TCP      [::]:2869              mike-PC:0                LISTENING
  TCP      [::]:5357              mike-PC:0                LISTENING
  TCP      [::]:10115             mike-PC:0                LISTENING
  TCP      [::]:20523             mike-PC:0                LISTENING
  TCP      [::]:49152             mike-PC:0                LISTENING
  TCP      [::]:49153             mike-PC:0                LISTENING
  TCP      [::]:49154             mike-PC:0                LISTENING
  TCP      [::]:49155             mike-PC:0                LISTENING
  TCP      [::]:49156             mike-PC:0                LISTENING
  TCP      [::]:49157             mike-PC:0                LISTENING
  UDP      0.0.0.0:123            *:*
  UDP      0.0.0.0:500            *:*
  UDP      0.0.0.0:3702           *:*
  UDP      0.0.0.0:3702           *:*
```

As you can see from the output, the system has many listening ports. Not all these suggest that a risk exists, but the output does let you know that there are many listening ports and that they might be vulnerable. To test for actual vulnerability, you use a port scanner. For example, you can use a free online scanner to probe the system. Many free online scanning services are available. Although a network administrator might use these free online tools out of curiosity, for better security testing, you should use a quality scanner.

> **Tip**
>
> To find out more about port scanners and to conduct an online scan of your computer system, go to www.grc.com and use the ShieldsUP! utility.

> **ExamAlert**
>
> Administrators use the detailed information revealed from a port scan to ensure network security. Port scans identify closed, open, and listening ports. However, port scanners also can be used by people who want to compromise security by finding open and unguarded ports.

Network Performance, Load, and Stress Testing

To testing the network, administrators often perform three distinct types of tests:

- Performance tests
- Load tests
- Stress tests

These test names are sometimes used interchangeably. Although there is some overlap, they are actually different types of network tests, each with different goals.

Performance Tests

A performance test is, as the name suggests, all about measuring the network's current performance level. The goal is to take ongoing performance tests and evaluate and compare them, looking for potential bottlenecks. For performance tests to be effective, they need to be taken under the same type of network load each time, or the comparison is invalid. For example, a performance test taken at 3 a.m. will be different from one taken at 3 p.m.

ExamAlert

The goal of performance testing is to establish baselines for the comparison of network functioning. The results of a performance test are meaningless unless you can compare them to previously documented performance levels.

Load Tests

Load testing has some overlap with performance testing. Sometimes called volume or endurance testing, load tests involve artificially placing the network under a larger workload. For example, the network traffic might be increased throughout the entire network. After this is done, performance tests can be done on the network with the increased load. Load testing is sometimes done to see if bugs exist in the network that are not currently visible but that may become a problem as the network grows. For example, the mail server might work fine with current requirements. However, if the number of users in the network grew by 10%, you would want to determine if the increased load would cause problems with the mail server. Load tests are all about finding a potential problem before it happens.

Performance tests and load tests are actually quite similar; however, the information outcomes are different. Performance tests identify the current level of network functioning for measurement and benchmarking purposes. Load tests are designed to give administrators a look into the future of their network load and to see if the current network infrastructure can handle it.

ExamAlert

Performance tests are about network functioning today. Load tests look forward to see if performance may be hindered in the future by growth or other changes to the network.

Stress Tests

Whereas load tests do not try to break the system under intense pressure, stress tests sometimes do. They push resources to the limit. Although these tests are not done often, they are necessary and—for administrators, at least—entertaining. Stress testing has two clear goals:

▸ It shows you exactly what the network can handle. Knowing a network's breaking point is useful information when you consider network expansion.

▸ It enables administrators to test their backup and recovery procedures. If a test knocks out network resources, administrators can verify that their recovery procedures work. Stress testing enables administrators to observe network hardware failure.

Stress tests assume that someday something will go wrong, and administrators will know exactly what to do when it happens.

Tracking Event Logs

In a network environment, all NOSs and most firewalls, proxy servers, and other network components have logging features. These logging features are essential for network administrators to review and monitor. Many different types of logs can be used. The following sections review some of the most common log file types.

On a Windows server system, as with the other operating systems, events and occurrences are logged to files for later review. Windows server and desktop systems such as Windows 7/Vista/XP and 2000 use Event Viewer to view many of the key log files. The logs in Event Viewer can be used to find information on, for example, an error on the system or a security incident. Information is recorded into key log files; although, you will also see additional log files under certain conditions, such as if the system is a domain controller or is running a DHCP server application.

Event logs refer generically to all log files used to track events on a system. Event logs are crucial for finding intrusions and diagnosing current system problems. In a Windows environment, for example, three primary event logs are used: security, application, and system.

ExamAlert

Be sure you know the types of information included in the different types of log files.

Security Logs

A system's security log contains events related to security incidents such as successful and unsuccessful logon attempts and failed resource access. Security logs can be customized, meaning that administrators can fine-tune exactly what they want to monitor. Some administrators choose to track nearly every security event on the system. Although this might be prudent, it can often create huge log files that take up too much space. Figure 8.6 shows a security log from a Windows system.

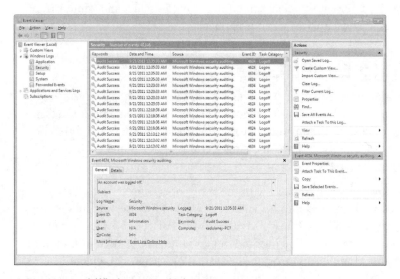

FIGURE 8.6   A Windows security log.

Figure 8.6 shows that some successful logons and logoffs occurred. A potential security breach would show some audit failures for logon or logoff attempts. To save space and prevent the log files from growing too big, administrators might choose to audit just failed logon attempts and not successful ones.

Each event in a security log contains additional information to make it easy to get the details on the event:

▶ **Date**: The exact date the security event occurred.

▶ **Time**: The time the event occurred.

▶ **User**: The name of the user account that was tracked during the event.

▶ **Computer**: The name of the computer used when the event occurred.

▶ **Event ID**: The Event ID tells you what event has occurred. You can use this ID to obtain additional information about the particular event. For example, you can take the ID number, enter it at the Microsoft support website, and gather information about the event. Without the ID, it would be difficult to find this information.

To be effective, security logs should be regularly reviewed.

Application Log

This log contains information logged by applications that run on a particular system rather than the operating system itself. Vendors of third-party applications can use the application log as a destination for error messages generated by their applications.

The application log works in much the same way as the security log. It tracks both successful events and failed events within applications. Figure 8.7 shows the details provided in an application log.

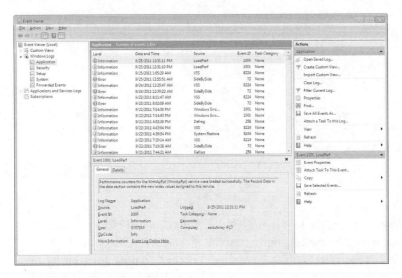

FIGURE 8.7   **An application log.**

Figure 8.7 shows three types of events occurred: general application information events, a warning event, and an error event. Vigilant administrators would likely want to check the event ID of both the event and warning failures to isolate the cause.

System Logs

System logs record information about components or drivers in the system, as shown in Figure 8.8. This is the place to look when you're troubleshooting a problem with a hardware device on your system or a problem with network connectivity. For example, messages related to the client element of DHCP appear in this log. The system log is also the place to look for hardware device errors, time synchronization issues, or service startup problems.

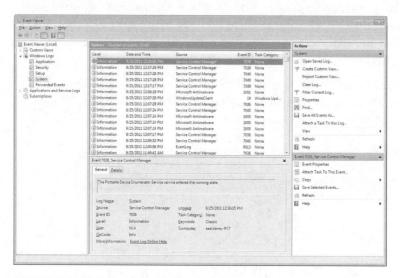

FIGURE 8.8   **A system log.**

Syslog

In addition to the specific logs mentioned previously, most UNIX/Linux-based systems include the capability to write messages (either directly or through applications) to log files via syslog. This can be done for security or management reasons and provides a central means by which devices that otherwise could not write to a central repository can easily do so (often by using the logger utility).

History Logs

History logs are most often associated with the tracking of Internet surfing habits. They maintain a record of all sites that a user visits. Network administrators might review these for potential security or policy breaches, but generally these are not commonly reviewed.

Another form of history log is a compilation of events from other log files. For instance, one history log might contain all significant events over the past year from the security log on a server. History logs are critical because they provide a detailed account of alarm events that can be used to track trends and locate problem areas in the network. This information can help you revise maintenance schedules, determine equipment replacement plans, and anticipate and prevent future problems.

> **Note**
>
> Application logs and system logs can often be viewed by any user. Security logs can be viewed only by users who use accounts with administrative privileges.

Log Management

While discussing these logs, it becomes clear that monitoring them can be a huge issue. That is where log management (LM) comes in. LM describes the process of managing large volumes of system-generated computer log files. LM includes the collection, retention, and disposal of all system logs. Although LM can be a huge task, it is essential to ensure the proper functioning of the network and its applications. It also helps you keep an eye on network and system security.

Configuring systems to log all sorts of events is the easy part. Trying to find the time to review the logs is an entirely different matter. To assist with this process, third-party software packages are available to help with the organization and reviewing of log files. To find this type of software, enter **log management** into a web browser, and you will have many options to choose from. Some have trial versions of their software that you may want to try to get a better idea of how LM works.

Cram Quiz

1. Which of the following involves pushing the network beyond its limits, often taking down the network to test its limits and recovery procedures?

    ○ **A.** Crash and burn

    ○ **B.** Stress test

    ○ **C.** Recovery test

    ○ **D.** Load test

2. You suspect that an intruder has gained access to your network. You want to see how many failed logon attempts there were in one day to help determine how the person got in. Which of the following might you do?

    ○ **A.** Review the history logs.

    ○ **B.** Review the security logs.

    ○ **C.** Review the logon logs.

    ○ **D.** Review the performance logs.

3. Which utility can be used to write syslog entries on a Linux-based operating system?

    ○ **A.** memo

    ○ **B.** record

    ○ **C.** logger

    ○ **D.** trace

4. Which of the following is **not** a standard component of an entry in a Windows-based security log?

    ○ **A.** Event ID

    ○ **B.** Date

    ○ **C.** Computer

    ○ **D.** Domain

    ○ **E.** User

5. You have just used a port scanner for the first time. On one port, it reports that there is not a process listening and access to this port will likely be denied. Which state is the port most likely to be considered to be in?

    ○ **A.** Listening

    ○ **B.** Closed

    ○ **C.** Filtered

    ○ **D.** Blocked

Cram Quiz Answers

1. **B.** Whereas load tests do not try to break the system under intense pressure, stress tests sometimes do. Stress testing has two goals. The first is to see exactly what the network can handle. It's useful to know the network's breaking point in case the network ever needs to be expanded. Secondly, stress testing allows administrators to test their backup and recovery procedures.

2. **B.** The security logs can be configured to show failed or successful logon attempts as well as object access attempts. In this case, the administrator can review the security logs and failed logon attempts to get the desired information. The failed logs will show the date and time when the failed attempts occurred.

3. **C.** The syslog feature exists in most UNIX/Linux-based distributions and entries can be written using logger. The other options are not possibilities for writing syslog entries.

4. **D.** The standard components of an entry in a Windows-based security log include the date, time, user, computer, and Event ID. The domain is not a standard component of a log entry.

5. **B.** When a port is closed, no process is listening on that port and access to this port will likely be denied. When the port is Open/Listening, the host sends a reply indicating that a service is listening on the port. When the port is Filtered or Blocked, there is no reply from the host, meaning that the port is not listening or the port is secured and filtered.

Networking Tools

▶ **Given a scenario, use appropriate hardware tools to troubleshoot connectivity issues.**

▶ **Given a scenario, use appropriate software tools to troubleshoot connectivity issues.**

CramSaver

If you can correctly answer these questions before going through this section, save time by skimming the Exam Alerts in this section and then complete the Cram Quiz at the end of the section.

1. What tools are used to attach twisted-pair network cable to connectors within a patch panel?

2. What are the two parts of a toner probe?

Answers

1. Punchdown tools are used to attach twisted-pair network cable to connectors within a patch panel.

2. A toner probe has two parts: the tone generator, or toner, and the tone locator, or probe.

A large part of network administration involves having the right tools for the job and knowing when and how to use them. Selecting the correct tool for a networking job sounds like an easy task, but network administrators can choose from a mind-boggling number of tools and utilities.

Given the diverse range of tools and utilities available, it is unlikely that you will encounter all the tools available—or even all those discussed in this chapter. For the Network+ exam, you are required to have general knowledge of the tools available and what they are designed to do.

Until networks become completely wireless, network administrators can expect to spend some of their time using a variety of media-related troubleshooting and installation tools. Some of these tools (such as the tone generator and locator) may be used to troubleshoot media connections, and others (such as wire crimpers and punchdown tools) are used to create network cables and connections.

The Basic Tools

Although many costly, specialized networking tools and devices are available to network administrators, the most widely used tools cost only a few dollars: the standard screwdrivers we use on almost a daily basis. As a network administrator, you can expect to take the case off a system to replace a network interface card (NIC) or perhaps remove the cover from a hub to replace a fan with amazing regularity. Advanced cable testers and specialized tools will not help you when a screwdriver is needed.

Wire Crimpers, Strippers, and Snips

Wire crimpers are tools you might regularly use. Like many things, making your own cables can be fun at first, but the novelty soon wears off. Basically, a wire crimper is a tool that you use to attach media connectors to the ends of cables. For instance, you use one type of wire crimper to attach RJ-45 connectors on unshielded twisted-pair (UTP) cable. You use a different type of wire crimper to attach British Naval Connectors (BNCs) to coaxial cabling.

> **Tip**
>
> When making cables, always order more connectors than you need; a few mishaps will probably occur along the way.

In a sense, you can think of a wire crimper as a pair of special pliers. You insert the cable and connector separately into the crimper, making sure that the wires in the cable align with the appropriate connectors. Then, by squeezing the crimper's handles, you force metal connectors through the cable's wires, making the connection between the wire and the connector.

When you crimp your own cables, you need to be sure to test them before putting them on the network. It takes only a momentary lapse to make a mistake when creating a cable, and you can waste time later trying to isolate a problem in a faulty cable.

Two other commonly used wiring tools are strippers and snips. Wire strippers come in a variety of shapes and sizes. Some are specifically designed to strip the outer sheathing from coaxial cable, and others are designed to work best with UTP cable. All strippers are designed to cleanly remove the sheathing from wire to make sure a clean contact can be made.

Many administrators do not have specialized wire strippers unless they do a lot of work with copper-based wiring. However, standard wire strippers are good things to have on hand.

Wire snips are tools designed to cleanly cut the cable. Sometimes network administrators buy cable in bulk and use wire snips to cut the cable into desired lengths. The wire strippers are then used to prepare the cable for the attachment of the connectors.

> **ExamAlert**
>
> Punchdown tools are used to attach twisted-pair network cable to connectors within a patch panel. Specifically, they connect twisted-pair wires to the insulation displacement connector (IDC).

Voltage Event Recorder

A voltage event recorder, as shown in Figure 8.9, is used to monitor the quality of power used on the network or by network hardware. You plug it into a wall socket, and it finds potential power-related concerns such as power sags, spikes, surges, or other power variations. The administrator then reviews the recorder's findings. Such power irregularities can cause problems for hardware and, in the case of serious spikes, can destroy hardware.

FIGURE 8.9   **A voltage event recorder.**

Environmental Monitors

When discussing environmental monitoring, you often refer to the temperature of the server and network equipment rooms. In general, the heat tolerance range for computer equipment is surprisingly wide. For example, consider a typical server system, which can happily operate in a range between 50°F and 93°F (10° and 33.8° Celsius). That is a spread of 43°F (23.8°C), plenty of room in a normal heated environment. But the problem is that if you maintain a computer room at either the upper or lower end of these levels, the equipment will run, but for how long, no one knows.

Although no specific figures relate to the recommended temperature of server rooms, the accepted optimum is around 70° to 72°F (21° to 22°C). At this temperature, the equipment in the room should be able to operate, and those working in the room should not get too cold. Human beings generally require a higher temperature than computer equipment, which is why placing servers in an office space with staff is not ideal.

Many people assume that the biggest problem with servers and network equipment is overheating. To some extent, this is true; servers in particular generate a great deal of heat and can overheat to the point where components fail. But this is only one heat-related issue. A more significant, and more gradual, problem is that of temperature consistency.

Heat causes components to expand, and cooling causes them to contract. Even the slightest temperature shift causes the printed circuit boards and chips to shift, and if they shift too much or too often, the chance of their becoming separated from their connections is greatly increased. This is known as chip creep. Keeping the heat at a moderate and constant level reduces the expansion and contraction of the boards and increases the components' reliability.

ExamAlert

Never wedge open a door to an environmentally controlled room, no matter how cold you get. An open door not only defeats the purpose of the controlled environment, it can damage air-conditioning units.

Environmental monitors are part of how administrators keep their equipment rooms at the right temperature. The environmental monitor sits in the equipment room and constantly documents changes in room temperature and humidity. If radical changes in temperature are detected, an alert is sent to the administrator. This can sometimes occur if someone leaves a door to the server room open, the air conditioning breaks, or some piece of network hardware is producing a lot of heat. Although network environmental monitors might not often be needed, just having them installed gives administrators peace of mind.

Keeping It Cool

Fortunately, the solution to the heat problem is relatively simple. You use an air conditioning unit. The only problem is, you can't use just any old A/C unit. Having a late 1960s window unit may be better than nothing, but you need high-quality protection.

High-quality air conditioning systems fall under the domain of industrial heating, ventilation, and air conditioning (HVAC) equipment. Server environment-specific air conditioning units are designed to maintain a constant temperature. High-quality units guarantee an accuracy of plus or minus 1°F. Most units have an audible alarm, but some also can communicate with management systems so that the server room temperature can be monitored remotely. Although the icy blast of a server room air conditioning system may not be welcomed by those who have to work in it for an extended period of time, the discomfort is far outweighed by the benefit to the server equipment.

Calculating the correct size and type of air conditioning unit can be a tricky proposition. Air conditioning systems are rated on how many cubic feet they can cool. Using this figure, and estimating the increase in temperature caused by the hardware in the room, you will have the basic information you need to choose an A/C unit. Of course, the calculation should take into account potential future growth. In some cases, a standby A/C unit is also installed. Whether such a system is required depends on how much fault tolerance you need and are willing to pay for.

Toner Probes

A *toner probe* is a device that can save a network installer many hours of frustration. This device has two parts: the tone generator, or toner, and the tone locator, or probe. The toner sends the tone, and at the other end of the cable, the probe receives the toner's signal. This tool makes it easier to find the beginning and end of a cable. You might hear the tone generator and tone locator referred to as the *fox and hound*.

As you might expect, the purpose of the tone probe is to generate a signal that is transmitted on the wire you are attempting to locate. At the other end, you press the probe against individual wires. When it makes contact with the wire that has the signal on it, the locator emits an audible signal or tone.

The tone locator probe is a useful device, but it does have some drawbacks. First, it often takes two people to operate one at each end of the cable. Of course, one person could just keep running back and forth, but if the cable is run over great distances, this can be a problem. Second, using the toner probe is time-consuming because it must be attached to each cable independently.

> **Note**
>
> Many problems that can be discovered with a tone generator are easy to prevent by simply taking the time to properly label cables. If the cables are labeled at both ends, you will not need to use such a tool to locate them.

> **Exam Alert**
>
> Toner probes are specifically used to locate cables hidden in floors, ceilings, or walls and to track cables from the patch panels to their destinations.

Protocol Analyzer

Protocol analyzers are used to do just that—analyze network protocols such as TCP, UDP, HTTP, and FTP. Protocol analyzers can be hardware- or software-based. In use, protocol analyzers help diagnose computer networking problems, alert you to unused protocols, identify unwanted or malicious network traffic, and help isolate network traffic-related problems.

Like packet sniffers, protocol analyzers capture the communication stream between systems. But unlike the sniffer, the protocol analyzer captures more than network traffic; it reads and decodes the traffic. Decoding allows the administrator to view the network communication in English. From this, administrators can get a better idea of the traffic that is flowing on the network. As soon as unwanted or damaged traffic is spotted, analyzers make it easy to isolate and repair. For example, if there is a problem with specific TCP/IP communication, such as a broadcast storm, the analyzer can find the source of the TCP/IP problem and isolate the system causing the storm. Protocol analyzers also provide many real-time trend statistics that help you justify to management the purchase of new hardware.

You can use protocol analyzers for two key reasons:

- ▶ **Identify protocol patterns**: By creating a historical baseline of analysis, administrators can spot trends in protocol errors. That way, when a protocol error occurs, it can be researched in the documentation to see if that error has occurred before and what was done to fix it.

▶ **Decoding information**: Capturing and decoding network traffic allows administrators to see what exactly is going on with the network at a protocol level. This helps find protocol errors as well as potential intruders.

> **Exam Alert**
>
> Protocol analyzers enable administrators to examine the bandwidth that a particular protocol is using.

Media/Cable Testers

A media tester, also called a cable tester, defines a range of tools designed to test whether a cable properly works. Any tool that facilitates the testing of a cable can be deemed a cable tester. However, a specific tool called a media tester enables administrators to test a segment of cable, looking for shorts, improperly attached connectors, or other cable faults. All media testers tell you whether the cable correctly works and where the problem in the cable might be.

A *cable certifier* is a type of tester that enables you to certify cabling by testing it for speed and performance to see that the implementation will live up to the ratings. Most stress and test the system based on noise and error testing. You need to know that the gigabit cable you think you have run is actually providing that speed to the network.

TDR and OTDR

A time domain reflectometer (TDR) is a device used to send a signal through a particular medium to check the cable's continuity. Good-quality TDRs can locate many types of cabling faults, such as a severed sheath, damaged conductors, faulty crimps, shorts, loose connectors, and more. Although network administrators will not need to use a tool such as this every day, it could significantly help in the troubleshooting process. TDRs help ensure that data sent across the network is not interrupted by poor cabling that may cause faults in data delivery.

> **Exam Alert**
>
> TDRs work at the physical layer of the OSI model, sending a signal through a length of cable, looking for cable faults.

Because the majority of network cabling is copper-based, most tools designed to test cabling are designed for copper-based cabling. However, when you test fiber-optic cable, you need an optical tester.

An optical cable tester performs the same basic function as a wire media tester, but on optical media. The most common problem with an optical cable is a break in the cable that prevents the signal from reaching the other end. Due to the extended distances that can be covered with fiber-optic cables, degradation is rarely an issue in a fiber-optic LAN environment.

Ascertaining whether a signal reaches the other end of a fiber-optic cable is relatively easy, but when you determine that there is a break, the problem becomes locating the break. That's when you need a tool called an optical time domain reflectometer (OTDR). By using an OTDR, you can locate how far along in the cable the break occurs. The connection on the other end of the cable might be the source of the problem, or perhaps there is a break halfway along the cable. Either way, an OTDR can pinpoint the problem.

Unless you work extensively with fiber-optic cable, you're unlikely to have an OTDR or even a fiber-optic cable tester in your toolbox. Specialized cabling contractors will have them, though, so knowing they exist is important.

Multimeter

One of the simplest cable-testing devices is a *multimeter*. By using the continuity setting, you can test for shorts in a length of coaxial cable. Or if you know the correct cable pinouts and have needlepoint probes, you can test twisted-pair cable.

A basic multimeter combines several electrical meters into a single unit that can measure voltage, current, and resistance. Advanced models can also measure temperature.

A multimeter has a display, terminals, probes, and a dial to select various measurement ranges. A digital multimeter has a numeric digital display, and an analog has a dial display. Inside a multimeter, the terminals are connected to different resistors, depending on the range selected.

Network multimeters can do much more than test electrical current:

> ▶ **Ping specific network devices**: A multimeter can ping and test response times of key networking equipment, such as routers, DNS servers, DHCP servers, and more.

- ▶ **Verify network cabling**: You can use a network multimeter to isolate cable shorts, split pairs, and other faults.

- ▶ **Locate and identify cable**: Quality network multimeters enable administrators to locate cables at patch panels and wall jacks using digital tones.

- ▶ **Documentation ability**: Multimeter results can be downloaded to a PC for inspection. Most network multimeters provide a means such as USB ports to link to a PC.

Network Qualification Tester

One more tool worth mentioning is the network qualification tester. This tool gives administrators a quick glance at the network's bandwidth and whether its current configuration can grow to support VoIP or Gigabit Ethernet, for example.

If a network is running slowly, the network qualification tester can tell you why the network is struggling. For example, it can identify crosstalk within a cable and how it is impacting network performance. Most quality network qualification testers can test twisted-pair and coaxial cable with other models available for fiber-optic cable.

> **ExamAlert**
>
> Network qualification testers enable administrators to identify the current speeds the network cabling can support and to isolate cabling from network problems.

Butt Set

A butt set is most often associated with telephony, but it can be used on some data networks as well. A butt set enables the administrator or technician to butt into a communication line and use it. In the case of a phone line, a technician can use the line normally—that is, make a call, answer a call, or listen in to a call.

The butt set for telephony looks somewhat like a regular phone handset with wires attached. The wires from the handset connect to the phone wire, and that's it. The technician can test and access the phone line. This device can be used to test network telephony but has limited use on actual network cable. Some network butt sets enable the access of data on the cable, but many other tools can do the same thing with better results.

Wireless Detection

Wireless media require their own types of tools. One such tool is a Wi-Fi detector. The intent of such a device is to reveal Wi-Fi hot spots and detect wireless network access with LED visual feedback. Such devices can be configured to scan specific frequencies. When working with 802.11b/g/n networks, you will most certainly require scanning for 2.4GHz RF signals.

Such devices can be used in the troubleshooting process to see where and how powerful RF signals are. Given the increase in wireless technologies, RF detectors are sure to increase in popularity.

Cram Quiz

1. You recently installed a new server in a wiring closet. The server shuts down periodically; you suspect power-related problems. Which of the following tools might you use to isolate a power problem?

   ○ **A.** Voltage multimeter

   ○ **B.** Voltage regulator

   ○ **C.** Voltage monitor

   ○ **D.** Voltage event recorder

2. While you were away, an air conditioning unit malfunctioned in a server room, and some equipment overheated. Which of the following would have alerted you to the problem?

   ○ **A.** Multimeter

   ○ **B.** Environmental monitor

   ○ **C.** TDR

   ○ **D.** OTDR

3. What tool would you use when working with an IDC?

   ○ **A.** Wire crimper

   ○ **B.** Media tester

   ○ **C.** OTDR

   ○ **D.** Punchdown tool

4. As a network administrator, you work in a wiring closet where none of the cables have been labeled. Which of the following tools are you most likely to use to locate the physical ends of the cable?

   ○ **A.** Toner probe

   ○ **B.** Wire crimper

   ○ **C.** Punchdown tool

   ○ **D.** ping

5. You are installing a new system into an existing star network, and you need a cable that is 45 feet long. Your local vendor does not stock cables of this length, so you are forced to make your own. Which of the following tools do you need to complete the task?

   ○ **A.** Optical tester

   ○ **B.** Punchdown tool

   ○ **C.** Crimper

   ○ **D.** UTP splicer

Cram Quiz Answers

1. **D.** Voltage event recorders are used to monitor the quality of power used on the network or by network hardware. Voltage event recorders identify potential power-related concerns such as power sags, spikes, surges, and other power variations.

2. **B.** Environmental monitors are used in server and network equipment rooms to ensure that the temperature does not fluctuate too greatly. In the case of a failed air conditioner, the administrator is alerted to the drastic changes in temperature. Multimeters, TDRs, and OTDRs are used to work with copper-based media.

3. **D.** You use a punchdown tool when working with an IDC. All the other tools are associated with making and troubleshooting cables; they are not associated with IDCs.

4. **A.** The toner probe tool, along with the tone locator, can be used to trace cables. Crimpers and punchdown tools are not used to locate a cable. The ping utility would be of no help in this situation.

5. **C.** When attaching RJ-45 connectors to UTP cables, the wire crimper is the tool you use. None of the other tools listed are used in the construction of UTP cable.

Working with Command-Line Utilities

▶ Given a scenario, use appropriate software tools to troubleshoot connectivity issues.

CramSaver

If you can correctly answer these questions before going through this section, save time by skimming the Exam Alerts in this section and then complete the Cram Quiz at the end of the section.

1. What TCP/IP command can be used to troubleshoot DNS problems?

2. What is the Linux, Macintosh, and UNIX equivalent of the `ipconfig` command?

3. What utility is the part of the TCP/IP suite and has the function of resolving IP addresses to MAC addresses?

Answers

1. The `nslookup` command is a TCP/IP diagnostic tool used to troubleshoot DNS problems. On Linux, UNIX, and Macintosh systems, you can also use the `dig` command for the same purpose.

2. The `ifconfig` command is the Linux, Macintosh, and UNIX equivalent of the `ipconfig` command.

3. The function of `arp` is to resolve IP addresses to MAC addresses.

For anyone working with TCP/IP networks, troubleshooting connectivity is something that simply must be done. This section describes the tools used in the troubleshooting process and identifies scenarios in which they can be used.

You can use many utilities when troubleshooting TCP/IP. Although the actual utilities available vary from platform to platform, the functionality between platforms is quite similar. Table 8.3 lists the TCP/IP troubleshooting tools covered on the Network+ exam, along with their purpose.

TABLE 8.3 **Common TCP/IP Troubleshooting Tools and Their Purposes**

Tool	Description
tracert/traceroute	Used to track the path a packet takes as it travels across a network. tracert is used on Windows systems; traceroute is used on UNIX, Linux, and Macintosh systems.
ping	Used to test connectivity between two devices on a network.
arp	Used to view and work with the IP address to MAC address resolution cache.
arp ping	Uses ARP to test connectivity between systems rather than using Internet Control Message Protocol (ICMP), as done with a regular ping.
netstat	Used to view the current TCP/IP connections on a system.
nbtstat	Used to view statistics related to NetBIOS name resolution and to see information about current NetBIOS over TCP/IP connections.
ipconfig	Used to view and renew TCP/IP configuration on a Windows system.
ifconfig	Used to view TCP/IP configuration on a UNIX, Linux, or Macintosh system.
nslookup/dig	Used to perform manual DNS lookups. nslookup can be used on Windows, UNIX, Macintosh, and Linux systems. dig can be used on UNIX, Linux, and Macintosh systems.
host	Used on Linux/UNIX systems to perform a reverse lookup on an IP address.
route	Used to view and configure the routes in the routing table.

The following sections look in more detail at these utilities and the output they produce.

> **Note**
>
> Many of the utilities discussed in this chapter have a help facility that you can access by typing the command followed by /? or -?. On a Windows system, for example, you can get help on the netstat utility by typing netstat /?. Sometimes, using a utility with an invalid switch also brings up the help screen.

> **ExamAlert**
>
> Be prepared to identify what tool to use in a given scenario. Remember, there might be more than one tool that could be used. You will be expected to pick the best one for the situation described.

The Trace Route Utility (`tracert`/`traceroute`)

The trace route utility does exactly what its name implies—it traces the route between two hosts. It does this by using ICMP echo packets to report information at every step in the journey. Each of the common network operating systems provides a trace route utility, but the name of the command and the output vary slightly on each. However, for the purposes of the Network+ exam, you should not concern yourself with the minor differences in the output format. Table 8.4 shows the trace route command syntax used in various operating systems.

Note

The phrase trace route utility is used in this section to refer generically to the various route-tracing applications available on common operating systems. In a live environment, you should become familiar with the version of the tool used on the operating systems you are working with.

TABLE 8.4 **Trace Route Utility Commands**

Operating System	Trace Route Command Syntax
Windows systems	`tracert IP address`
Linux/UNIX	`traceroute IP address`
Macintosh	`traceroute IP address`

`trace route` provides a lot of useful information, including the IP address of every router connection it passes through and, in many cases, the name of the router. (Although this depends on the router's configuration.) Trace route also reports the length, in milliseconds, of the round-trip the packet made from the source location to the router and back. This information can help identify where network bottlenecks or breakdowns might be. The following is an example of a successful tracert command on a Windows Server system:

```
C:\>tracert 24.7.70.37
Tracing route to c1-p4.sttlwa1.home.net [24.7.70.37]
 over a maximum of 30 hops:
  1    30 ms    20 ms    20 ms   24.67.184.1
  2    20 ms    20 ms    30 ms   rd1ht-ge3-0.ok.shawcable.net
[24.67.224.7]
  3    50 ms    30 ms    30 ms   rc1wh-atm0-2-1.vc.shawcable.net
  [204.209.214.193]
  4    50 ms    30 ms    30 ms   rc2wh-pos15-0.vc.shawcable.net
  [204.209.214.90]
  5    30 ms    40 ms    30 ms   rc2wt-pos2-0.wa.shawcable.net
  [66.163.76.37]
  6    30 ms    40 ms    30 ms   c1-pos6-3.sttlwa1.home.net [24.7.70.37]
Trace complete.
```

Similar to the other common operating systems covered on the Network+ exam, the tracert display on a Windows-based system includes several columns of information. The first column represents the hop number. You may recall that hop is the term used to describe a step in the path a packet takes as it crosses the network. The next three columns indicate the round-trip time, in milliseconds, that a packet takes in its attempts to reach the destination. The last column is the hostname and the IP address of the responding device.

Of course, not all trace route attempts are successful. The following is the output from a tracert command on a Windows Server system that doesn't manage to get to the remote host:

```
C:\>tracert comptia.org

Tracing route to comptia.org [216.119.103.72]
over a maximum of 30 hops:
  1    27 ms    28 ms    14 ms   24.67.179.1
  2    55 ms    13 ms    14 ms   rd1ht-ge3-0.ok.shawcable.net
  [24.67.224.7]
  3    27 ms    27 ms    28 ms   rc1wh-atm0-2-1.shawcable.net
  [204.209.214.19]
  4    28 ms    41 ms    27 ms   rc1wt-pos2-0.wa.shawcable.net
  [66.163.76.65]
  5    28 ms    41 ms    27 ms   rc2wt-pos1-0.wa.shawcable.net
  [66.163.68.2]
  6    41 ms    55 ms    41 ms   c1-pos6-3.sttlwa1.home.net
[24.7.70.37]
  7    54 ms    42 ms    27 ms   home-gw.st6wa.ip.att.net
  [192.205.32.249]
  8     *         *         *     Request timed out.
```

```
 9      *        *        *        Request timed out.
10      *        *        *        Request timed out.
11      *        *        *        Request timed out.
12      *        *        *        Request timed out.
13      *        *        *        Request timed out.
14      *        *        *        Request timed out.
15      *        *        *        Request timed out.
```

In this example, the trace route request gets to only the seventh hop, at which point it fails. This failure indicates that the problem lies on the far side of the device in step 7 or on the near side of the device in step 8. In other words, the device at step 7 is functioning but might not make the next hop. The cause of the problem could be a range of things, such as an error in the routing table or a faulty connection. Alternatively, the seventh device might be operating at 100 percent, but device 8 might not be functioning at all. In any case, you can isolate the problem to just one or two devices.

Note

In some cases, the owner of a router might configure it to not return ICMP traffic like that generated by `ping` or `traceroute`. If this is the case, the `ping` or `traceroute` will fail just as if the router did not exist or was not operating.

ExamAlert

Although we have used the Windows `tracert` command to provide sample output in these sections, the output from `traceroute` on a UNIX, Linux, or Macintosh system is extremely similar.

The trace route utility can also help you isolate a heavily congested network. In the following example, the trace route packets fail in the midst of the `tracert` from a Windows Server system, but subsequently they continue. This behavior can be an indicator of network congestion:

```
C:\>tracert comptia.org

Tracing route to comptia.org [216.119.103.72]over a maximum of 30
hops:
  1     96 ms     96 ms     55 ms   24.67.179.1
  2     14 ms     13 ms     28 ms   rd1ht-ge3-0.ok.shawcable.net
  [24.67.224.7]
  3     28 ms     27 ms     41 ms   rc1wh-atm0-2-1.shawcable.net
  [204.209.214.19]
  4     28 ms     41 ms     27 ms   rc1wt-pos2-0.wa.shawcable.net
  [66.163.76.65]
  5     41 ms     27 ms     27 ms   rc2wt-pos1-0.wa.shawcable.net
```

```
[66.163.68.2]
  6     55 ms     41 ms     27 ms     c1-pos6-3.sttlwal.home.net
[24.7.70.37]
  7     54 ms     42 ms     27 ms     home-gw.st6wa.ip.att.net
[192.205.32.249]
  8     55 ms     41 ms     28 ms     gbr3-p40.st6wa.ip.att.net
[12.123.44.130]
  9      *         *         *        Request timed out.
 10      *         *         *        Request timed out.
 11      *         *         *        Request timed out.
 12      *         *         *        Request timed out.
 13     69 ms     68 ms     69 ms     gbr2-p20.sd2ca.ip.att.net
[12.122.11.254]
 14     55 ms     68 ms     69 ms     gbr1-p60.sd2ca.ip.att.net
[12.122.1.109]
 15     82 ms     69 ms     82 ms     gbr1-p30.phmaz.ip.att.net
[12.122.2.142]
 16     68 ms     69 ms     82 ms     gar2-p360.phmaz.ip.att.net
[12.123.142.45]
 17    110 ms     96 ms     96 ms     12.125.99.70
 18    124 ms     96 ms     96 ms     light.crystaltech.com [216.119.107.1]
 19     82 ms     96 ms     96 ms     216.119.103.72
Trace complete.
```

Generally speaking, trace route utilities enable you to identify the location of a problem in the connectivity between two devices. After you determine this location, you might need to use a utility such as ping to continue troubleshooting. In many cases, as in the examples provided in this chapter, the routers might be on a network such as the Internet and therefore not within your control. In that case, you can do little except inform your ISP of the problem.

ping

Most network administrators are familiar with the ping utility and are likely to use it on an almost daily basis. The basic function of the ping command is to test the connectivity between the two devices on a network. All the command is designed to do is determine whether the two computers can see each other and to notify you of how long the round-trip takes to complete.

Although ping is most often used on its own, a number of switches can be used to assist in the troubleshooting process. Table 8.5 shows some of the commonly used switches with ping on a Windows system.

TABLE 8.5   ping **Command Switches**

Option	Description
ping -t	Pings a device on the network until stopped
ping -a	Resolves addresses to hostnames
ping -n count	Specifies the number of echo requests to send
ping -r count	Records the route for *count* hops
ping -s count	Timestamp for *count* hops
ping -w timeout	Timeout in milliseconds to wait for each reply

ExamAlert

You will likely be asked about ping, its switches used, and how ping can be used in a troubleshooting scenario.

ping works by sending ICMP echo request messages to another device on the network. If the other device on the network hears the ping request, it automatically responds with an ICMP echo reply. By default, the ping command on a Windows-based system sends four data packets; however, using the -t switch, a continuous stream of ping requests can be sent.

ping is perhaps the most widely used of all network tools; it is primarily used to verify connectivity between two network devices. On a good day, the results from the ping command are successful, and the sending device receives a reply from the remote device. Not all ping results are that successful. To use ping effectively, you must interpret the results of a failed ping command.

The Destination Host Unreachable Message

The Destination host unreachable error message means that a route to the destination computer system cannot be found. To remedy this problem, you might need to examine the routing information on the local host to confirm that the local host is correctly configured, or you might need to make sure that the default gateway information is correct. The following is an example of a ping failure that gives the Destination host unreachable message:

```
Pinging 24.67.54.233 with 32 bytes of data:
Destination host unreachable.
Destination host unreachable.
Destination host unreachable.
Destination host unreachable.
```

```
Ping statistics for 24.67.54.233:
    Packets: Sent = 4, Received = 0, Lost = 4 (100% loss),
Approximate round trip times in milli-seconds:
    Minimum = 0ms, Maximum =  0ms, Average =  0ms
```

The Request Timed Out Message

The Request timed out error message is common when you use the ping command. Essentially, this error message indicates that your host did not receive the ping message back from the destination device within the designated time period. Assuming that the network connectivity is okay on your system, this typically indicates that the destination device is not connected to the network, is powered off, or is not correctly configured. It could also mean that some intermediate device is not operating correctly. In some rare cases, it can also indicate that the network has so much congestion that timely delivery of the ping message could not be completed. It might also mean that the ping is being sent to an invalid IP address or that the system is not on the same network as the remote host, and an intermediary device is not correctly configured. In any of these cases, the failed ping should initiate a troubleshooting process that might involve other tools, manual inspection, and possibly reconfiguration. The following example shows the output from a ping to an invalid IP address:

```
C:\>ping 169.76.54.3
Pinging 169.76.54.3 with 32 bytes of data:

Request timed out.
Request timed out.
Request timed out.
Request timed out.

Ping statistics for 169.76.54.3:
    Packets: Sent = 4, Received = 0, Lost = 4 (100%
Approximate round trip times in milli-seconds:
    Minimum = 0ms, Maximum =  0ms, Average =  0ms
```

During the ping request, you might receive some replies from the remote host that are intermixed with Request timed out errors. This is often the result of a congested network. An example follows; notice that this example, which was run on a Windows 7 system, uses the -t switch to generate continuous pings:

```
C:\>ping -t 24.67.184.65
Pinging 24.67.184.65 with 32 bytes of data:

Reply from 24.67.184.65: bytes=32 time=55ms TTL=127
Reply from 24.67.184.65: bytes=32 time=54ms TTL=127
Reply from 24.67.184.65: bytes=32 time=27ms TTL=127
```

```
Request timed out.
Request timed out.
Request timed out.
Reply from 24.67.184.65: bytes=32 time=69ms TTL=127
Reply from 24.67.184.65: bytes=32 time=28ms TTL=127
Reply from 24.67.184.65: bytes=32 time=28ms TTL=127
Reply from 24.67.184.65: bytes=32 time=68ms TTL=127
Reply from 24.67.184.65: bytes=32 time=41ms TTL=127

Ping statistics for 24.67.184.65:
    Packets: Sent = 11, Received = 8, Lost = 3 (27% loss),
Approximate round trip times in milli-seconds:
    Minimum = 27ms, Maximum =  69ms, Average =   33ms
```

In this example, three packets were lost. If this continued on your network, you would need to troubleshoot to find out why packets were dropped.

The Unknown Host Message

The Unknown host error message is generated when the hostname of the destination computer cannot be resolved. This error usually occurs when you ping an incorrect hostname, as shown in the following example, or try to use ping with a hostname when hostname resolution (via DNS or a HOSTS text file) is not configured:

```
C:\>ping www.comptia.ca
Unknown host www.comptia.ca
```

If the ping fails, you need to verify that the ping is sent to the correct remote host. If it is, and if name resolution is configured, you have to dig a little more to find the problem. This error might indicate a problem with the name resolution process, and you might need to verify that the DNS or WINS server is available. Other commands, such as nslookup or dig, can help in this process.

The Expired TTL Message

The *Time To Live* (TTL) is a key consideration in understanding the ping command. The function of the TTL is to prevent circular routing, which occurs when a ping request keeps looping through a series of hosts. The TTL counts each hop along the way toward its destination device. Each time it counts one hop, the hop is subtracted from the TTL. If the TTL reaches 0, it has expired, and you get a message like the following:

```
Reply from 24.67.180.1: TTL expired in transit
```

If the TTL is exceeded with ping, you might have a routing problem on the network. You can modify the TTL for ping on a Windows system by using the `ping -i` command.

Troubleshooting with `ping`

Although `ping` does not completely isolate problems, you can use it to help identify where a problem lies. When troubleshooting with `ping`, follow these steps:

1. Ping the IP address of your local loopback using the command `ping 127.0.0.1`. If this command is successful, you know that the TCP/IP protocol suite is installed correctly on your system and is functioning. If you cannot ping the local loopback adapter, TCP/IP might need to be reloaded or reconfigured on the machine you are using.

> **ExamAlert**
>
> The loopback is a special function within the TCP/IP protocol stack that is supplied for troubleshooting purposes. The Class A IP address 127.*X.X.X* is reserved for the loopback. Although convention dictates that you use 127.0.0.1, you can use any address in the 127.*X.X.X* range, except for the network number itself (127.0.0.0) and the broadcast address (127.255.255.255). You can also ping by using the default hostname for the local system, which is called localhost (for example, `ping localhost`). The same function can be performed in IPv6 by using the address ::1.

2. Ping the assigned IP address of your local network interface card (NIC). If the ping is successful, you know that your NIC is functioning on the network and has TCP/IP correctly installed. If you cannot ping the local NIC, TCP/IP might not be correctly bound to the NIC, or the NIC drivers might be improperly installed.

3. Ping the IP address of another known good system on your local network. By doing so, you can determine whether the computer you are using can see other computers on the network. If you can ping other devices on your local network, you have network connectivity.

   If you cannot ping other devices on your local network, but you could ping the IP address of your system, you might not be connected to the network correctly.

4. After you confirm that you have network connectivity for the local network, you can verify connectivity to a remote network by sending a ping to the IP address of the default gateway.

5. If you can ping the default gateway, you can verify remote connectivity by sending a ping to the IP address of a system on a remote network.

> **ExamAlert**
>
> You might be asked to relate the correct procedure for using ping for a connectivity problem.

Using just the `ping` command in these steps, you can confirm network connectivity on not only the local network, but also on a remote network. The whole process requires as much time as it takes to enter the command, and you can do it all from a single location.

If you are an optimistic person, you can perform step 5 first. If that works, all the other steps will also work, saving you the need to test them. If your step 5 trial fails, you can go to step 1 and start the troubleshooting process from the beginning.

> **Note**
>
> All but one of the ping examples used in this section show the `ping` command using the IP address of the remote host. It is also possible to ping the Domain Name Service (DNS) name of the remote host (for example, `ping www.comptia.org`, `ping server1`); of course, you can do this only if your network uses a DNS server. On a Windows-based network, you can also ping by using the Network Basic Input/Output System (NetBIOS) computer name.

ARP

Address Resolution Protocol (ARP) is used to resolve IP addresses to MAC addresses. This is significant because on a network, devices find each other using the IP address, but communication between devices requires the MAC address.

> **ExamAlert**
>
> Remember that the function of ARP is to resolve IP addresses to Layer 2 or MAC addresses.

When a computer wants to send data to another computer on the network, it must know the MAC address (physical address) of the destination system. To discover this information, ARP sends out a discovery packet to obtain the MAC address. When the destination computer is found, it sends its MAC address to the sending computer. The ARP-resolved MAC addresses are stored temporarily on a computer system in the ARP cache. Inside this ARP cache is a list of matching MAC and IP addresses. This ARP cache is checked before a discovery packet is sent to the network to determine if there is an existing entry.

Entries in the ARP cache are periodically flushed so that the cache doesn't fill up with unused entries. The following code shows an example of the arp command with the output from a Windows server system:

```
C:\>arp -a
Interface: 24.67.179.22 on Interface 0x3
  Internet Address       Physical Address      Type
  24.67.179.1            00-00-77-93-d8-3d      dynamic
```

As you might notice, the type is listed as dynamic. Entries in the ARP cache can be added statically or dynamically. Static entries are added manually and do not expire. The dynamic entries are added automatically when the system accesses another on the network.

As with other command-line utilities, several switches are available for the arp command. Table 8.6 shows the available switches for Windows-based systems.

TABLE 8.6 arp **Switches**

Switch	Description
-a or -g	Displays both the IP and MAC addresses and whether they are dynamic or static entries
inet_addr	Specifies a specific Internet address
-N if_addr	Displays the ARP entries for a specified network interface
eth_addr	Specifies a MAC address
if_addr	Specifies an Internet address
-d	Deletes an entry from the ARP cache
-s	Adds a static permanent address to the ARP cache

arp ping

Earlier in this chapter we talked about the ping command and how it is used to test connectivity between devices on a network. Using the ping command is often an administrator's first step to test connectivity between network devices. If the ping fails, it is assumed that the device you are pinging is offline. But this may not always be the case.

Most companies now use firewalls or other security measures that may block ICMP requests. This means that a ping request will not work. Blocking ICMP is a security measure; if a would-be hacker cannot hit the target, he may not attack the host.

> **ExamAlert**
>
> One type of attack is called an ICMP flood attack (also known as a ping attack). The attacker sends continuous ping packets to a server or network system, eventually tying up that system's resources, making it unable to respond to requests from other systems.

If ICMP is blocked, you have still another option to test connectivity with a device on the network: the arp ping. As mentioned, the ARP utility is used to resolve IP addresses to MAC addresses. The arp ping utility does not use the ICMP protocol to test connectivity like ping does, rather it uses the ARP protocol. However, ARP is not routable, and the arp ping cannot be routed to work over separate networks. The arp ping works only on the local subnet.

Just like with a regular ping, an arp ping specifies an IP address; however, instead of returning regular ping results, the arp ping responds with the MAC address and name of the computer system. So, when a regular ping using ICMP fails to locate a system, the arp ping uses a different method to find the system. With arp ping, you can directly ping a MAC address. From this, you can determine if duplicate IP addresses are used and, as mentioned, determine if a system is responding.

arp ping is not built into Windows, but you can download a number of programs that allow you to ping using ARP. Linux, on the other hand, has an arp ping utility ready to use. Figure 8.10 shows the results of an arp ping from a shareware Windows utility.

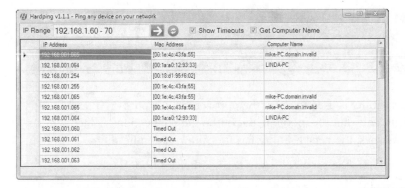

FIGURE 8.10   **An example of an arp ping.**

The `netstat` Command

The `netstat` command displays the protocol statistics and current TCP/IP connections on the local system. Used without any switches, the `netstat` command shows the active connections for all outbound TCP/IP connections. In addition, several switches are available that change the type of information `netstat` displays. Table 8.7 shows the various switches available for the netstat utility.

TABLE 8.7   `netstat` **Switches**

Switch	Description
-a	Displays the current connections and listening ports
-e	Displays Ethernet statistics
-n	Lists addresses and port numbers in numeric form
-p	Shows connections for the specified protocol
-r	Shows the routing table
-s	Lists per-protocol statistics
interval	Specifies how long to wait before redisplaying statistics

The netstat utility is used to show the port activity for both TCP and UDP connections, showing the inbound and outbound connections. When used without switches, the netstat utility has four information headings.

▸ **Proto**: Lists the protocol being used, either UDP or TCP

▸ **Local address:** Specifies the local address and port being used

▸ **Foreign address**: Identifies the destination address and port being used

▸ **State**: Specifies whether the connection is established

In its default usage, the `netstat` command shows outbound connections that have been established by TCP. The following shows sample output from a `netstat` command without using any switches:

```
C:\>netstat
Active Connections
   Proto  Local Address          Foreign Address          State
   TCP    laptop:2848            MEDIASERVICES1:1755      ESTABLISHED
   TCP    laptop:1833            www.dollarhost.com:80    ESTABLISHED
   TCP    laptop:2858            194.70.58.241:80         ESTABLISHED
   TCP    laptop:2860            194.70.58.241:80         ESTABLISHED
   TCP    laptop:2354            www.dollarhost.com:80    ESTABLISHED
   TCP    laptop:2361            www.dollarhost.com:80    ESTABLISHED
   TCP    laptop:1114            www.dollarhost.com:80    ESTABLISHED
   TCP    laptop:1959            www.dollarhost.com:80    ESTABLISHED
   TCP    laptop:1960            www.dollarhost.com:80    ESTABLISHED
   TCP    laptop:1963            www.dollarhost.com:80    ESTABLISHED
   TCP    laptop:2870            localhost:8431           TIME_WAIT
   TCP    laptop:8431            localhost:2862           TIME_WAIT
   TCP    laptop:8431            localhost:2863           TIME_WAIT
   TCP    laptop:8431            localhost:2867           TIME_WAIT
   TCP    laptop:8431            localhost:2872           TIME_WAIT
```

As with any other command-line utility, the netstat utility has a number of switches. The following sections briefly explain the switches and give sample output from each.

netstat -e

The `netstat -e` command shows the activity for the NIC and displays the number of packets that have been both sent and received. Here's an example:

```
C:\WINDOWS\Desktop>netstat -e
Interface Statistics

                        Received            Sent

Bytes                   17412385        40237510
Unicast packets            79129           85055
Non-unicast packets          693             254
Discards                       0               0
Errors                         0               0
Unknown protocols            306
```

As you can see, the `netstat -e` command shows more than just the packets that have been sent and received:

▶ **Bytes**: The number of bytes that the NIC has sent or received since the computer was turned on.

▶ **Unicast packets**: Packets sent and received directly by this interface.

▶ **Non-unicast packets**: Broadcast or multicast packets that the NIC picked up.

▶ **Discards**: The number of packets rejected by the NIC, perhaps because they were damaged.

▶ **Errors**: The errors that occurred during either the sending or receiving process. As you would expect, this column should be a low number. If it is not, this could indicate a problem with the NIC.

▶ **Unknown protocols**: The number of packets that the system could not recognize.

netstat -a

The `netstat -a` command displays statistics for both TCP and User Datagram Protocol (UDP). Here is an example of the `netstat -a` command:

```
C:\WINDOWS\Desktop>netstat -a

Active Connections

  Proto  Local Address          Foreign Address            State
  TCP    laptop:1027            LAPTOP:0                   LISTENING
  TCP    laptop:1030            LAPTOP:0                   LISTENING
  TCP    laptop:1035            LAPTOP:0                   LISTENING
  TCP    laptop:50000           LAPTOP:0                   LISTENING
  TCP    laptop:5000            LAPTOP:0                   LISTENING
  TCP    laptop:1035            msgr-ns41.msgr.hotmail.com:1863
ESTABLISHED
  TCP    laptop:nbsession       LAPTOP:0                   LISTENING
  TCP    laptop:1027            localhost:50000            ESTABLISHED
  TCP    laptop:50000           localhost:1027             ESTABLISHED
  UDP    laptop:1900            *:*
  UDP    laptop:nbname          *:*
  UDP    laptop:nbdatagram      *:*
  UDP    laptop:1547            *:*
  UDP    laptop:1038            *:*
  UDP    laptop:1828            *:*
  UDP    laptop:3366            *:*
```

As you can see, the output includes four columns, which show the protocol, the local address, the foreign address, and the port's state. The TCP connections show the local and foreign destination addresses and the connection's current state. UDP, however, is a little different. It does not list a state status because, as mentioned throughout this book, UDP is a connectionless protocol and does not establish connections. The following list briefly explains the information provided by the `netstat -a` command:

- ▶ **Proto**: The protocol used by the connection.

- ▶ **Local Address**: The IP address of the local computer system and the port number it is using. If the entry in the local address field is an asterisk (*), the port has not yet been established.

- ▶ **Foreign Address**: The IP address of a remote computer system and the associated port. When a port has not been established, as with the UDP connections, *:* appears in the column.

- ▶ **State**: The current state of the TCP connection. Possible states include established, listening, closed, and waiting.

netstat -r

The netstat -r command is often used to view a system's routing table. A system uses a routing table to determine routing information for TCP/IP traffic. The following is an example of the netstat -r command from a Windows 7 system:

```
C:\WINDOWS\Desktop>netstat -r
Route table

========================================================================
=====
========================================================================
=====
Active Routes:
Network Destination          Netmask          Gateway           Interface
Metric
          0.0.0.0          0.0.0.0       24.67.179.1      24.67.179.22
1
     24.67.179.0    255.255.255.0      24.67.179.22      24.67.179.22
1
     24.67.179.22  255.255.255.255        127.0.0.1         127.0.0.1
1
   24.255.255.255  255.255.255.255      24.67.179.22      24.67.179.22
1
        127.0.0.0        255.0.0.0        127.0.0.1         127.0.0.1
1
        224.0.0.0        224.0.0.0      24.67.179.22      24.67.179.22
1
  255.255.255.255  255.255.255.255      24.67.179.22                 2
1
Default Gateway:       24.67.179.1
========================================================================
=====
Persistent Routes:
  None
```

Exam Alert

The netstat -r command output shows the same information as the output from the route print command.

netstat -s

The netstat -s command displays a number of statistics related to the
TCP/IP protocol suite. Understanding the purpose of every field in the output is beyond the scope of the Network+ exam, but for your reference, sample
output from the netstat -s command is shown here:

```
C:\>netstat -s

IP Statistics

  Packets Received                      = 389938
  Received Header Errors                = 0
  Received Address Errors               = 1876
  Datagrams Forwarded                   = 498
  Unknown Protocols Received            = 0
  Received Packets Discarded            = 0
  Received Packets Delivered            = 387566
  Output Requests                       = 397334
  Routing Discards                      = 0
  Discarded Output Packets              = 0
  Output Packet No Route                = 916
  Reassembly Required                   = 0
  Reassembly Successful                 = 0
  Reassembly Failures                   = 0
  Datagrams Successfully Fragmented     = 0
  Datagrams Failing Fragmentation       = 0
  Fragments Created                     = 0

ICMP Statistics

                            Received      Sent
  Messages                  40641         41111
  Errors                    0             0
  Destination Unreachable   223           680
  Time Exceeded             24            0
  Parameter Problems        0             0
  Source Quenches           0             0
  Redirects                 0             38
  Echos                     20245         20148
  Echo Replies              20149         20245
  Timestamps                0             0
  Timestamp Replies         0             0
  Address Masks             0             0
  Address Mask Replies      0             0
```

```
TCP Statistics

    Active Opens                           = 13538
    Passive Opens                          = 23132
    Failed Connection Attempts             = 9259
    Reset Connections                      = 254
    Current Connections                    = 15
    Segments Received                      = 330242
    Segments Sent                          = 326935
    Segments Retransmitted                 = 18851

UDP Statistics

    Datagrams Received      = 20402
    No Ports                = 20594
    Receive Errors          = 0
    Datagrams Sent          = 10217
```

nbtstat

The nbtstat utility is used to view protocol statistics and information for NetBIOS over TCP/IP connections. nbtstat is commonly used to troubleshoot NetBIOS name resolution problems. Because nbtstat resolves NetBIOS names, it's available only on Windows systems.

A number of case-sensitive switches are available for the nbtstat command, as shown in Table 8.8.

TABLE 8.8   nbtstat **Switches**

Switch	Description
nbtstat -a	(Adapter status) Outputs the NetBIOS name table and MAC addresses of the card for the specified computer.
nbtstat -A (IP address)	(Adapter status) Lists the remote machine's name table given its IP address.
nbtstat -c (cache)	Lists the contents of the NetBIOS name cache.
nbtstat -n (names)	Lists local NetBIOS names.
nbtstat -r (resolved)	Lists names resolved by broadcast or WINS.
nbtstat -R (Reload)	Purges and reloads the remote cache name table.
nbtstat -S (Sessions)	Summarizes the current NetBIOS sessions and their status.
nbtstat -s (sessions)	Lists the sessions table, converting destination IP addresses into computer NetBIOS names.

TABLE 8.8 **Continued**

Switch	Description
nbtstat -RR (ReleaseRefresh)	Sends Name Release packets to WINS and then starts Refresh.
nbtstat RemoteName	Remote host machine name.
nbtstat IP address	Dotted-decimal representation of the IP address.
nbtstat interval	Redisplays selected statistics, pausing *interval* seconds between each display. Press Ctrl+C to stop redisplaying statistics.

For example, the following is the output from the nbtstat -n command:

```
C:\>nbtstat -n
Lana # 0:
Node IpAddress: [169.254.196.192] Scope Id: []

            NetBIOS Local Name Table

       Name              Type         Status
    ---------------------------
       LAPTOP        <00>  UNIQUE     Registered
       KCS           <00>  GROUP      Registered
       LAPTOP        <03>  UNIQUE     Registered
```

The ipconfig **Command**

The ipconfig command is a technician's best friend when it comes to viewing the TCP/IP configuration of a Windows system. Used on its own, the ipconfig command shows basic information such as the name of the local network interface, the IP address, the subnet mask, and the default gateway. Combined with the /all switch, it shows a detailed set of information, as shown in the following example:

```
C:\>ipconfig /all
Windows 2008 IP Configuration
    Host Name . . . . . . . . . . . . . : server
    Primary DNS Suffix  . . . . . . . : write
    Node Type . . . . . . . . . . . . : Broadcast
    IP Routing Enabled. . . . . . . . : Yes
    WINS Proxy Enabled. . . . . . . . : No
    DNS Suffix Search List. . . . . . : write
                                        ok.anyotherhost.net
Ethernet adapter Local Area Connection:

Connection-specific DNS Suffix  . : ok.anyotherhost.net
Description . . . . . . . . . . . : D-Link DFE-530TX PCI Fast
Ethernet
```

```
Physical Address. . . . . . . . . : 00-80-C8-E3-4C-BD
DHCP Enabled. . . . . . . . . . . : Yes
Autoconfiguration Enabled . . . . : Yes
IP Address. . . . . . . . . . . . : 24.67.184.65
Subnet Mask . . . . . . . . . . . : 255.255.254.0
Default Gateway . . . . . . . . . : 24.67.184.1
DHCP Server . . . . . . . . . . . : 24.67.253.195
DNS Servers . . . . . . . . . . . : 24.67.253.195
                                    24.67.253.212
Lease Obtained.. . . . . : Thursday, February 07, 2011 3:42:00 AM
Lease Expires .. . . . . : Saturday, February 09, 2011 3:42:00 AM
```

As you can imagine, you can use the output from the ipconfig /all command in a massive range of troubleshooting scenarios. Table 8.9 lists some of the most common troubleshooting symptoms, along with where to look for clues about solving them in the ipconfig /all output.

> **Tip**
>
> When looking at ipconfig information, you should be sure that all information is present and correct. For example, a missing or incorrect default gateway parameter limits communication to the local segment.

TABLE 8.9 **Common Troubleshooting Symptoms That** ipconfig **Can Help Solve**

Symptom	Field to Check in the Output
The user cannot connect to any other system.	Ensure that the TCP/IP address and subnet mask are correct. If the network uses DHCP, ensure that DHCP is enabled.
The user can connect to another system on the same subnet but cannot connect to a remote system.	Ensure the default gateway is configured correctly.
The user is unable to browse the Internet.	Ensure the DNS server parameters are correctly configured.
The user cannot browse across remote subnets.	Ensure the WINS or DNS server parameters are correctly configured, if applicable.

> **ExamAlert**
>
> You should be prepared to identify the output from an ipconfig command in relationship to a troubleshooting scenario.

Using the /all switch might be the most popular, but there are a few others. These include the switches listed in Table 8.10.

ExamAlert

ipconfig and its associated switches are widely used by network administrators and therefore should be expected to make an appearance on the exam.

TABLE 8.10   ipconfig **Switches**

Switch	Description
?	Displays the ipconfig help screen
/all	Displays additional IP configuration information
/release	Releases the IPv4 address of the specified adapter
/release6	Releases the IPv6 address of the specified adapter
/renew	Renews the IPv4 address of a specified adapter
/renew6	Renews the IPv6 address of a specified adapter
/flushdns	Purges the DNS cache
/registerdns	Refreshes the DHCP lease and reregisters the DNS names
/displaydns	Used to display the information in the DNS cache

Tip

The ipconfig /release and ipconfig /renew commands work only when your system is using DHCP.

ExamAlert

The ipconfig command on the Windows 7/Vista and Windows Server operating systems provides additional switches and functionality geared toward Active Directory and Dynamic DNS. You do not need to be concerned with these switches for the exam, but you can view information on them by using the ipconfig /? command.

ifconfig

ifconfig performs the same function as ipconfig, but on a Linux, UNIX, or Macintosh system. Because Linux relies more heavily on command-line utilities than Windows, the Linux and UNIX version of ifconfig provides much more functionality than `ipconfig`. On a Linux or UNIX system, you can get information about the usage of the `ifconfig` command by using `ifconfig –help`. The following output provides an example of the basic `ifconfig` command run on a Linux system:

```
eth0      Link encap:Ethernet  HWaddr 00:60:08:17:63:A0
          inet addr:192.168.1.101  Bcast:192.168.1.255
Mask:255.255.255.0
          UP BROADCAST RUNNING  MTU:1500  Metric:1
          RX packets:911 errors:0 dropped:0 overruns:0 frame:0
          TX packets:804 errors:0 dropped:0 overruns:0 carrier:0
          collisions:0 txqueuelen:100
          Interrupt:5 Base address:0xe400

lo        Link encap:Local Loopback
          inet addr:127.0.0.1  Mask:255.0.0.0
          UP LOOPBACK RUNNING  MTU:3924  Metric:1
          RX packets:18 errors:0 dropped:0 overruns:0 frame:0
          TX packets:18 errors:0 dropped:0 overruns:0 carrier:0
          collisions:0 txqueuelen:0
```

Although the `ifconfig` command displays the IP address, subnet mask, and default gateway information for both the installed network adapter and the local loopback adapter, it does not report DHCP lease information. Instead, you can use the `pump -s` command to view detailed information on the DHCP lease, including the assigned IP address, the address of the DHCP server, and the time remaining on the lease. The `pump` command can also be used to release and renew IP addresses assigned via DHCP and to view DNS server information.

nslookup

`nslookup` is a utility used to troubleshoot DNS-related problems. Using `nslookup`, you can, for example, run manual name resolution queries against DNS servers, get information about your system's DNS configuration, or specify what kind of DNS record should be resolved.

When `nslookup` is started, it displays the current hostname and the IP address of the locally configured DNS server. You then see a command prompt that allows you to specify further queries. This is known as *interactive* mode. Table 8.11 lists the commands you can enter in interactive mode.

TABLE 8.11 nslookup **Switches**

Switch	Description
All	Prints options, as well as current server and host information
[no]debug	Prints debugging information
[no]d2	Prints exhaustive debugging information
[no]defname	Appends the domain name to each query
[no]recurse	Asks for a recursive answer to the query
[no]search	Uses the domain search list
[no]vc	Always uses a virtual circuit
domain=NAME	Sets the default domain name to *NAME*
srchlist=N1[/N2/.../N6]	Sets the domain to *N1* and the search list to *N1*, *N2*, and so on
root=NAME	Sets the root server to *NAME*
Retry=X	Sets the number of retries to *X*
timeout=X	Sets the initial timeout interval to *X* seconds
Type=X	Sets the query type (for example, A, ANY, CNAME, MX, NS, PTR, SOA, or SRV)
querytype=X	Same as type
Class=X	Sets the query class (for example, IN [Internet], ANY)
[no]msxfr	Uses Microsoft fast zone transfer
ixfrver=X	The current version to use in an IXFR transfer request
server NAME	Sets the default server to *NAME*, using the current default server
Exit	Exits the program

Instead of using interactive mode, you can also execute nslookup requests directly at the command prompt. The following listing shows the output from the nslookup command when a domain name is specified to be resolved:

```
C:\>nslookup comptia.org
Server:  nsc1.ht.ok.shawcable.net
Address:  64.59.168.13

Non-authoritative answer:
Name:    comptia.org
Address:  208.252.144.4
```

As you can see from the output, nslookup shows the hostname and IP address of the DNS server against which the resolution was performed, along with the hostname and IP address of the resolved host.

dig

dig is used on a Linux, UNIX, or Macintosh system to perform manual DNS lookups. dig performs the same basic task as nslookup, but with one major distinction: The dig command does not have an interactive mode and instead uses only command-line switches to customize results.

dig generally is considered a more powerful tool than nslookup, but in the course of a typical network administrator's day, the minor limitations of nslookup are unlikely to be too much of a factor. Instead, dig is often simply the tool of choice for DNS information and troubleshooting on UNIX, Linux, or Macintosh systems. Like nslookup, dig can be used to perform simple name resolution requests. The output from this process is shown in the following listing:

```
; <<>> DiG 8.2 <<>> examcram.com
;; res options: init recurs defnam dnsrch
;; got answer:
;; ->>HEADER<<- opcode: QUERY, status: NOERROR, id: 4
;; flags: qr rd ra; QUERY: 1, ANSWER: 1, AUTHORITY: 2, ADDITIONAL: 0
;; QUERY SECTION:
;;      examcram.com, type = A, class = IN

;; ANSWER SECTION:
examcram.com.          7h33m IN A    63.240.93.157

;; AUTHORITY SECTION:
examcram.com.          7h33m IN NS    usrxdns1.pearsontc.com.
examcram.com.          7h33m IN NS    oldtxdns2.pearsontc.com.

;; Total query time: 78 msec
;; FROM: localhost.localdomain to SERVER: default - 209.53.4.130
;; WHEN: Sat Oct 16 20:21:24 2004
;; MSG SIZE  sent: 30  rcvd: 103
```

As you can see, dig provides a number of pieces of information in the basic output—more so than nslookup. Network administrators can gain information from three key areas of the output—ANSWER SECTION, AUTHORITY SECTION, and the last four lines of the output.

The ANSWER SECTION of the output provides the name of the domain or host being resolved, along with its IP address. The A in the results line indicates the record type that is being resolved.

The AUTHORITY SECTION provides information on the authoritative DNS servers for the domain against which the resolution request was performed.

This information can be useful in determining whether the correct DNS servers are considered authoritative for a domain.

The last four lines of the output show how long the name resolution request took to process and the IP address of the DNS server that performed the resolution. It also shows the date and time of the request, as well as the size of the packets sent and received.

The `host` Command

The `host` command is used on Linux/UNIX systems to perform a reverse lookup on an IP address. A reverse lookup involves looking up an IP address and resolving the hostname from that. Users running Microsoft Windows operating systems could use the `nslookup` command to perform a reverse lookup on an IP address, and Linux users can use the `host` command or `nslookup`.

Here's an example of the `host` command:

```
host 24.67.108.119
```

This command returns the hostname associated with the IP address 24.67.108.119.

The `route` Utility

The route utility is an often-used and very handy tool. With the `route` command, you display and modify the routing table on your Windows and Linux systems. Figure 8.11 shows the output from a `route print` command on a Windows system.

> **Note**
>
> The discussion here focuses on the Windows `route` command, but other operating systems have equivalent commands. On a Linux system, for example, the command is also `route`, but the usage and switches are different.

In addition to displaying the routing table, the Windows version of the `route` command has a number of other switches, as detailed in Table 8.12. For complete information about all the switches available with the `route` command on a Windows system, type `route` at the command line. To see a list of the `route` command switches on a Linux system, use the command `route - help`.

FIGURE 8.11   The output from a route print command on a Windows system.

TABLE 8.12   **Switches for the route Command in Windows**

Switch	Description
add	Enables you to add a static route to the routing table.
delete	Enables you to remove a route from the routing table.
change	Enables you to modify an existing route.
-p	When used with the add command, makes the route permanent. If the -p switch is not used when a route is added, the route is lost upon reboot.
print	Enables you to view the system's routing table.
-f	Removes all gateway entries from the routing table.

Cram Quiz

1. What command can you issue from the command line to view the status of the system's ports?

   ○ **A.** `netstat -p`

   ○ **B.** `netstat -o`

   ○ **C.** `netstat -a`

   ○ **D.** `netstat -y`

2. Which of the following tools can you use to perform manual DNS lookups on a Linux system? (Choose two.)

   ○ **A.** `dig`

   ○ **B.** `nslookup`

   ○ **C.** `tracert`

   ○ **D.** `dnslookup`

3. Which of the following commands generates a `Request timed out` error message?

   ○ **A.** `ping`

   ○ **B.** `netstat`

   ○ **C.** `ipconfig`

   ○ **D.** `nbtstat`

4. Which of the following commands would you use to add a static entry to the ARP table of a Windows 7 system?

   ○ **A.** `arp -a IP ADDRESS MAC ADDRESS`

   ○ **B.** `arp -s MAC ADDRESS IP ADDRESS`

   ○ **C.** `arp -s IP ADDRESS MAC ADDRESS`

   ○ **D.** `arp -i IP ADDRESS MAC ADDRESS`

5. Which command created the following output?

   ```
   Server:   nen.bx.ttfc.net
   Address:  209.55.4.155

   Name:     examcram.com
   Address:  63.240.93.157
   ```

   ○ **A.** `nbtstat`

   ○ **B.** `ipconfig`

   ○ **C.** `tracert`

   ○ **D.** `nslookup`

Cram Quiz Answers

1. **C.** Administrators can quickly determine the status of common ports by issuing the `netstat -a` command from the command line. This command output lists the ports used by the system and whether they are open and listening.

2. **A** and **B.** Both the `dig` and `nslookup` commands can be used to perform manual DNS lookups on a Linux system. You cannot perform a manual lookup with the `tracert` command. There is no such command as `dnslookup`.

3. **A.** The `ping` command generates a `Request timed out` error when it cannot receive a reply from the destination system. None of the other commands listed produce this output.

4. **C.** This command would correctly add a static entry to the ARP table. None of the other answers are valid ARP switches.

5. **D.** The output was produced by the `nslookup` command. The other commands listed produce different output.

What Next?

For network administration, nothing is more important than fault tolerance and disaster recovery—the topics of the next chapter. Because both fault tolerance and disaster recovery are such an essential part of network administration, they are well represented on the Network+ exam.

CHAPTER 9

Network Optimization

This chapter covers the following official Network+ objective:

▶ Explain the different methods and rationale for network performance optimization.

This chapter covers CompTIA Network+ objective 4.6. For more information on the official Network+ exam topics, see the "About the Network+ Exam" section in the "Introduction."

For network administration, nothing is more important than *fault tolerance* and *disaster recovery*. First and foremost, it is the responsibility of the network administrator to safeguard the data held on the servers and to ensure that, when requested, this data is ready to go.

Because both fault tolerance and disaster recovery are such an important part of network administration, they are well represented on the CompTIA Network+ exam. Therefore, this chapter is important in terms of both real-world application and the exam.

Uptime and Fault Tolerance

▶ Explain the different methods and rationale for network performance optimization.

CramSaver

If you can correctly answer these questions before going through this section, save time by skimming the Exam Alerts in this section and then completing the Cram Quiz at the end of the section.

1. Which RAID implementation uses two disks in a mirrored configuration?

2. Which RAID implementation employs disk striping with parity and requires a minimum of three disks?

3. What technology involves grouping servers for the purposes of fault tolerance and load balancing?

4. What protocol enables multiple hosts on the same network to share a set of IP addresses?

Answers

1. RAID 1 uses two disks in a mirrored configuration.

2. RAID 5 is disk striping with parity, requiring three disks at a minimum

3. Server clustering involves grouping servers for the purposes of fault tolerance and load balancing.

4. Common Address Redundancy Protocol (CARP).

All devices on the network, from routers to cabling, and especially servers, must have one prime underlying trait: availability. Networks play such a vital role in the operation of businesses that their availability must be measured in dollars. The failure of a single desktop PC affects the productivity of a single user. The failure of an entire network affects the productivity of the entire company and potentially the company's clients as well. A network failure might have an even larger impact than that as new e-commerce customers look somewhere else for products, and existing customers start to wonder about the site's reliability.

Every minute that a network is not running can potentially cost an organization money. The exact amount depends on the role that the server performs and how long it is unavailable. For example, if a small departmental server supporting 10 people goes down for 1 hour, this might not be a big deal. If the server that runs the company's e-commerce website goes down for even 10 minutes, it can cost hundreds of thousands of dollars in lost orders.

The importance of data availability varies between networks, but it dictates to what extent a server/network implements fault tolerance measures. The projected capability for a network or network component to weather failure is defined as a number or percentage. Because no solution is labeled as providing 100 percent availability indicates that no matter how well you protect your networks, some aspect of the configuration will fail sooner or later.

So how expensive is failure? For equipment replacement costs, it's not that high. For how much it costs to fix the problem, it is a little more expensive. The actual cost of downtime is the biggest factor. For businesses, downtime impacts functionality and productivity of operations. The longer the downtime, the greater the business loss.

Assuming that you know you can never really obtain 100 percent uptime, what should you aim for? Consider this. If you were responsible for a server system that was available 99.5 percent of the time, you might be satisfied. But if you realized that you would also have 43.8 hours of downtime each year—that's one full workweek and a little overtime—you might not be so smug. Table 9.1 compares various levels of downtime.

TABLE 9.1 **Levels of Availability and Related Downtime**

Level of Availability	Availability %	Downtime Per Year
Commercial availability	99.5%	43.8 hours
High availability	99.9%	8.8 hours
Fault-resilient clusters	99.99%	53 minutes
Fault-tolerant	99.999%	5 minutes
Continuous	100%	0

These figures make it simple to justify spending money to implement fault tolerance measures. Even to reach the definition of commercial availability, you need to have a range of measures in place. After the commercial availability level, the strategies that take you to each subsequent level are likely to be increasingly expensive, even though they might be easy to justify.

For example, if you estimate that each hour of server downtime costs the company $1,000, the elimination of 35 hours of downtime—from 43.8 hours for commercial availability to 8.8 hours for high availability—justifies some serious expenditure on technology. Although this first jump is an easily justifiable one, subsequent levels might not be so easy to sell. Working on the same basis, moving from high availability to fault-resilient clusters equates to less than $10,000, but the equipment, software, and skills required to move to the next level can far exceed this figure. In other words, increasing fault tolerance is a law of diminishing returns. As your need to reduce the possibility of downtime increases, so does the investment required to achieve this goal.

The role played by the network administrator in all this can be somewhat challenging. In some respects, you must function as if you sell insurance. Informing management of the risks and potential outcomes of downtime can seem a little sensational, but the reality is that the information must be provided if you are to avoid post-event questions about why management was not made aware of the risks. At the same time, a realistic evaluation of exactly the risks presented is needed, along with a realistic evaluation of the amount of downtime each failure might bring.

Having established that you need to guard against equipment failure, you can now look at which pieces of equipment are more liable to fail than others. In terms of component failure, the hard disk is responsible for 50 percent of all system downtime. It should come as no surprise that hard disks have garnered the most attention for fault tolerance. Redundant array of inexpensive disks (RAID), which is discussed in detail in this chapter, is a set of standards that enables servers to cope with the failure of one or more hard disks.

> **Note**
>
> Although this chapter discusses various methods of fault tolerance designed to reduce the susceptibility to server failure and downtime, none of these methods is a substitute for a complete and robust backup strategy. No matter how many of these measures are in place, backing up data to an external medium is still the most essential fault-tolerance measure.

In fault tolerance, RAID is only half the story. Measures are in place to cope with failures of most other components as well. In some cases, fault tolerance is an elegant solution, and in others, it is a simple case of duplication. The next discussion begins with RAID and then moves to other fault tolerance measures.

Types of Fault Tolerance

For computers, *fault tolerance* refers to the capability of the computer system or network to provide continued data availability if hardware failure occurs. Every component within a server, from the CPU fan to the power supply, has a chance to fail. Some components such as processors rarely fail, whereas hard disk failures are well documented.

Almost every component has fault tolerance measures. These measures typically require redundant hardware components that can easily or automatically take over when a hardware failure occurs.

Of all the components inside computer systems, the hard disks require the most redundancy. Not only are hard disk failures more common than for any other component, but they also maintain the data, without which there would be little need for a network.

Hard Disks Are Half the Problem

The failure of any component in a computer system is undesirable, but the failure of the component that holds your data is particularly troubling. Hard disks are far more likely to fail than any other component, followed closely by system fans. Why these two? They both have moving parts that can wear out. This is why you spend so much effort ensuring that there are fault-tolerance measures for hard disks.

ExamAlert

The primary function of fault-tolerance measures is to enable a system or network to continue operating if unexpected hardware or software errors occur.

Disk-Level Fault Tolerance

Deciding to have *hard disk fault tolerance* on the server is the first step; the second is deciding which fault tolerance strategy to use. Hard disk fault tolerance is implemented according to different RAID levels. Each RAID level offers differing amounts of data protection and performance. The RAID level appropriate for a given situation depends on the importance placed on the data, the difficulty of replacing that data, and the associated costs of a respective RAID implementation. Often, the costs of data loss and replacement outweigh the costs associated with implementing a strong RAID fault tolerance solution. RAID can be deployed through dedicated hardware, which is more costly, or can be software-based. Today's network operating systems, such as UNIX and Windows server products, have built-in support for RAID.

RAID 0

Although it's given RAID status, *RAID 0* does not actually provide any fault tolerance. Using RAID 0 might even be less fault-tolerant than storing all your data on a single hard disk.

RAID 0 combines unused disk space on two or more hard drives into a single logical volume, with data written to equally sized stripes across all the disks. Using multiple disks, reads and writes are performed simultaneously across all drives. This means that disk access is faster, making the performance of RAID 0 better than other RAID solutions and significantly better than a single hard disk. The downside of RAID 0 is that if any disk in the array fails, the data is lost and must be restored from backup.

Because of its lack of fault tolerance, RAID 0 is rarely implemented. Figure 9.1 shows an example of RAID 0 striping across three hard disks. In this case, the data written is symbolized by each letter of the alphabet. ("A" is one set of data, "B" is another, and so on.)

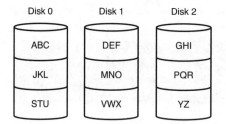

FIGURE 9.1 **RAID 0 striping without parity.**

RAID 1

One of the more common RAID implementations is *RAID 1*, which requires two hard disks and uses *disk mirroring* to provide fault tolerance. When information is written to the hard disk, it is automatically and simultaneously written to the second hard disk. Both of the hard disks in the mirrored configuration use the same hard disk controller; the partitions used on the hard disk need to be approximately the same size to establish the mirror. In the mirrored configuration, if the primary disk were to fail, the second mirrored disk would contain all the required information, and there would be little disruption to data availability. RAID 1 ensures that the server continues operating in the case of primary disk failure.

A RAID 1 solution has some key advantages. First, it is cheap in terms of cost per megabyte of storage because only two hard disks are required to provide fault tolerance. Second, no additional software is required to establish RAID 1 because modern network operating systems have built-in support for it. RAID levels using striping are often incapable of including a boot or system partition in fault-tolerance solutions. Finally, RAID 1 offers load balancing over multiple disks, which increases read performance over that of a single disk. Write performance, however, is not improved.

Because of its advantages, RAID 1 is well suited as an entry-level RAID solution, but it has a few significant shortcomings that exclude its use in many environments. It has limited storage capacity; two 100GB hard drives provide only 100GB of storage space. Organizations with large data storage needs can quickly exceed a mirrored solution capacity. RAID 1 also has a single point of failure, the hard disk controller. If it were to fail, the data would be inaccessible on either drive. Figure 9.2 shows an example of RAID 1 disk mirroring.

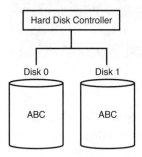

FIGURE 9.2 **RAID 1 disk mirroring.**

An extension of RAID 1 is *disk duplexing*. Disk duplexing is the same as mirroring, with the exception of one key detail: It places the hard disks on separate hard disk controllers, eliminating the single point of failure.

> **ExamAlert**
>
> Be aware of the differences between disk duplexing and mirroring for the exam.

RAID 5

RAID 5, also known as *disk striping with parity*, uses *distributed parity* to write information across all disks in the array. Unlike the striping used in RAID 0, RAID 5 includes parity information in the striping, which provides fault tolerance. This parity information can re-create the data if a failure occurs. RAID 5 requires a minimum of three disks, with the equivalent of a single disk used for the parity information. This means that if you have three 1TB hard disks, you have 2TB of storage space, with the other 1TB used for parity. To increase storage space in a RAID 5 array, you need to add only another disk to the array. Depending on the sophistication of the RAID setup you use, the RAID controller can incorporate the new drive into the array automatically, or you need to rebuild the array and restore the data from backup.

Many factors have made RAID 5 a popular fault-tolerant design. RAID 5 can continue to function if a single drive failure occurs. If a hard disk in the array were to fail, the parity would re-create the missing data and continue to function with the remaining drives. The read performance of RAID 5 is improved over a single disk.

> **Exam Alert**
>
> RAID 5 can continue operation if a hard disk fails. However, administrators must remember to replace the failed hard disk and restore the RAID 5 configuration. If a second hard disk fails before the failed one is replaced, data loss could occur.

The RAID 5 solution has only a few drawbacks:

▶ The costs of implementing RAID 5 are initially higher than other fault-tolerance measures requiring a minimum of three hard disks. Given the costs of hard disks today, this is a minor concern. However, when it comes to implementing a RAID 5 solution, hardware RAID 5 is more expensive than a software-based RAID 5 solution.

▶ RAID 5 suffers from poor write performance because the parity must be calculated and then written across several disks. The performance lag is minimal and doesn't have a noticeable difference on the network.

▶ When a new disk is placed in a failed RAID 5 array, there is a regeneration time when the data is being rebuilt on the new drive. This process requires extensive resources from the server.

Figure 9.3 shows an example of RAID 5 striping with parity, which is computed on a rotating basis for each disk by looking at the values on the other two disks.

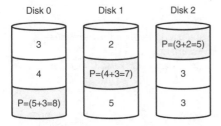

FIGURE 9.3   **RAID 5 striping with parity.**

RAID 10

Sometimes RAID levels are combined to take advantage of the best of each. One such strategy is *RAID 10*, which combines RAID levels 1 and 0. In this configuration, four disks are required. As you might expect, the configuration consists of a *mirrored stripe set*. To some extent, RAID 10 takes advantage of the performance capability of a stripe set while offering the fault tolerance of a mirrored solution. In addition to the benefits of each, though, RAID 10 inherits the shortcomings of each strategy. In this case, the high overhead and decreased write performance are the disadvantages. Figure 9.4 shows an example of a RAID 10 configuration. Table 9.2 summarizes the various RAID levels.

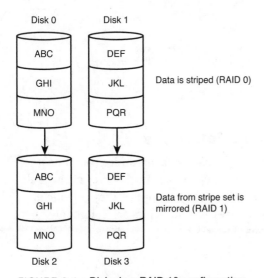

FIGURE 9.4   **Disks in a RAID 10 configuration.**

> **Note**
>
> RAID levels 2, 3, and 4 are omitted from this discussion because they are infrequently and rarely used in modern network environments.

TABLE 9.2 **Summary of RAID Levels**

RAID Level	Description	Advantage	Disadvantage	Required Disks
RAID 0	Disk striping	Increased read and write performance. RAID 0 can be implemented with two or more disks.	Does not offer any fault tolerance.	Two or more
RAID 1	Disk mirroring	Provides fault tolerance. Can also be used with separate disk controllers, reducing the single point of failure. This is called disk duplexing.	RAID 1 has 50% overhead and suffers from poor write performance.	Two
RAID 5	Disk striping with distributed parity	Can recover from a single disk failure. Increased read performance over a poor-write single disk. Disks can be added to the array to increase storage capacity.	May slow down the network during regeneration time, and performance may suffer.	Minimum of three
RAID 10	Striping with mirrored volumes	Increased performance with striping. Offers mirrored fault tolerance.	High overhead, as with mirroring.	Four

Server and Services Fault Tolerance

In addition to providing fault tolerance for individual hardware components, some organizations go the extra mile and include the entire server in the fault-tolerant design. Such a design keeps servers and the services they provide up and running. For server fault tolerance, two key strategies are commonly employed: standby servers and server clustering.

Standby Servers

Standby servers are a fault-tolerance measure in which a second server is identically configured to the first one. The second server can be stored remotely or locally and set up in a *failover configuration*. In a failover configuration, the secondary server connects to the primary and is ready to take over the server functions at a moment's notice. If the secondary server detects that the primary has failed, it automatically cuts in. Network users will not notice the transition, because little or no disruption in data availability occurs.

The primary server communicates with the secondary server by issuing special notification notices called *heartbeats*. If the secondary server stops receiving the heartbeat messages, it assumes that the primary has died and therefore assumes the *primary server configuration*.

Server Clustering

Companies that want maximum data availability and that have the funds to pay for it can choose to use *server clustering*. As the name suggests, server clustering involves grouping servers for the purposes of fault tolerance and load balancing. In this configuration, other servers in the cluster can compensate for the failure of a single server. The failed server has no impact on the network, and the end users have no idea that a server has failed.

> **ExamAlert**
>
> The term *server cluster* is synonymous with *server farm*.

The clear advantage of server clusters is that they offer the highest level of fault tolerance and data availability. The disadvantage is equally clear—cost. The cost of buying a single server can be a huge investment for many organizations; having to buy duplicate servers is far too costly. In addition to hardware costs, additional costs can be associated with recruiting administrators who have the skills to configure and maintain complex server clusters. Clustering provides the following advantages:

- ▶ **Increased performance**: More servers equals more processing power. The servers in a cluster can provide levels of performance beyond the scope of a single system by combining resources and processing power.

- ▶ **Load balancing**: Rather than having individual servers perform specific roles, a cluster can perform a number of roles, assigning the appropriate resources in the best places. This approach maximizes the power of the systems by allocating tasks based on which server in the cluster can best service the request.

▶ **Failover**: Because the servers in the cluster are in constant contact with each other, they can detect and cope with the failure of an individual system. How transparent the failover is to users depends on the clustering software, the type of failure, and the capability of the application software used to cope with the failure.

▶ **Scalability**: The capability to add servers to the cluster offers a degree of scalability simply not possible in a single-server scenario. It is worth mentioning, though, that clustering on PC platforms is still in its relative infancy, and the number of machines that can be included in a cluster is still limited.

To make server clustering happen, you need certain ingredients: servers, storage devices, network links, and software that makes the cluster work.

ExamAlert

Server clustering increases load balancing by distributing the workload over multiple systems and increases availability by having failover servers if a system crash occurs.

Link Redundancy

Although a failed network card might not actually stop the server or a system, it might as well. A network server that cannot be used on the network results in server downtime. Although the chances of a failed network card are relatively low, attempts to reduce the occurrence of downtime have led to the development of a strategy that provides fault tolerance for network connections.

Through a process called *adapter teaming*, groups of network cards are configured to act as a single unit. The teaming capability is achieved through software, either as a function of the network card driver or through specific application software. The process of adapter teaming is not widely implemented; although, the benefits it offers are many, so it's likely to become a more common sight. The result of adapter teaming is increased bandwidth, fault tolerance, and the ability to more effectively manage network traffic. These features are broken into three sections:

▶ **Adapter fault tolerance**: The basic configuration enables one network card to be configured as the primary device and others as secondary. If the primary adapter fails, one of the other cards can take its place without the need for intervention. When the original card is replaced, it resumes the role of primary controller.

▸ **Adapter load balancing**: Because software controls the network adapters, workloads can be distributed evenly among the cards so that each link is used to a similar degree. This distribution enables a more responsive server because one card is not overworked while another is underworked.

▸ **Link aggregation**: This provides vastly improved performance by allowing more than one network card's bandwidth to be *aggregated—* combined into a single connection. For example, through link aggregation, four 1000Mbps (1Gbps) network cards can provide a total of 4000Mbps of bandwidth. Link aggregation requires that both the network adapters and the switch used support it. In 1999, the IEEE ratified the 802.3ad standard for link aggregation, allowing compatible products to be produced.

Common Address Redundancy Protocol (CARP)

Common Address Redundancy Protocol (CARP) is a protocol that enables multiple hosts on the same network to share a set of IP addresses and thus provides failover redundancy. It is commonly used with routers and firewalls and can provide load balancing.

The hosts within the redundant group are known as the *group of redundancy*. CARP requires a minimum of one common virtual host ID and a set of virtual host IP addresses (one for each machine taking part in the group).

> **Exam Alert**
>
> CARP is an open source protocol enabling multiple hosts to share a set of IP addresses.

Using Uninterruptible Power Supplies (UPSs)

No discussion of fault tolerance can be complete without a look at power-related issues and the mechanisms used to combat them. When you design a fault-tolerant system, your planning should definitely include uninterruptible power supplies (UPSs). A *UPS* serves many functions and is a major part of server consideration and implementation.

On a basic level, a UPS is a box that holds a battery and built-in charging circuit. During times of good power, the battery is recharged; when the UPS is needed, it's ready to provide power to the server. Most often, the UPS is required to provide enough power to give the administrator time to shut down the server in an orderly fashion, preventing any potential data loss from a dirty shutdown.

Why Use a UPS?

Organizations of all shapes and sizes need UPSs as part of their fault tolerance strategies. A UPS is as important as any other fault-tolerance measure. Three key reasons make a UPS necessary:

▶ **Data availability**: The goal of any fault-tolerance measure is data availability. A UPS ensures access to the server if a power failure occurs—or at least as long as it takes to save a file.

▶ **Protection from data loss**: Fluctuations in power or a sudden power-down can damage the data on the server system. In addition, many servers take full advantage of caching, and a sudden loss of power could cause the loss of all information held in cache.

▶ **Protection from hardware damage**: Constant power fluctuations or sudden power-downs can damage hardware components within a computer. Damaged hardware can lead to reduced data availability while the hardware is repaired.

Power Threats

In addition to keeping a server functioning long enough to safely shut it down, a UPS safeguards a server from inconsistent power. This inconsistent power can take many forms. A UPS protects a system from the following power-related threats:

▶ **Blackout**: A total failure of the power supplied to the server.

▶ **Spike**: A short (usually less than 1 second) but intense increase in voltage. Spikes can do irreparable damage to any kind of equipment, especially computers.

▶ **Surge**: Compared to a spike, a surge is a considerably longer (sometimes many seconds) but usually less intense increase in power. Surges can also damage your computer equipment.

▶ **Sag**: A short-term voltage drop (the opposite of a spike). This type of voltage drop can cause a server to reboot.

▶ **Brownout**: A drop in voltage that usually lasts more than a few minutes.

Many of these power-related threats can occur without your knowledge; if you don't have a UPS, you cannot prepare for them. For the cost, it is worth buying a UPS, if for no other reason than to sleep better at night.

Cram Quiz

1. Which of the following is a common phrase used for server clustering?

   ○ **A.** Server farm

   ○ **B.** Server band

   ○ **C.** Server stack

   ○ **D.** Cluster range

2. In the server room you find a box with five 2TB hard disks. If you were to implement a RAID 5 solution using all five disks, how much storage space would you have for the actual data?

   ○ **A.** 10TGB

   ○ **B.** 8TB

   ○ **C.** 4TB

   ○ **D.** 6TB

3. With CARP, what are the hosts within a redundant group known as?

   ○ **A.** Range of possibles

   ○ **B.** Redundancy scope

   ○ **C.** Redundancy pool

   ○ **D.** Group of redundancy

4. Which of the following RAID levels offers the greatest read-and-write performance?

   ○ **A.** RAID 0

   ○ **B.** RAID 1

   ○ **C.** Disk duplexing

   ○ **D.** RAID 5

   ○ **E.** RAID 10

5. Which of the following power-related problems is associated with a short-term voltage drop?

   ○ **A.** Surge

   ○ **B.** Brownout

   ○ **C.** Sag

   ○ **D.** Spike

6. As a network administrator, you have been asked to implement a RAID solution that offers high performance. Fault tolerance is not a concern. Which RAID level are you likely to use?

    ◯ **A.** RAID 0

    ◯ **B.** RAID 1

    ◯ **C.** RAID 2

    ◯ **D.** RAID 5

    ◯ **E.** RAID 10

Cram Quiz Answers

1. **A.** A common phrase used for server clustering is a server farm.

2. **B.** RAID 5 uses distributed parity. The parity information is spread across all disks and requires the equivalent space of a single hard disk. This example has five 2TB disks, giving a total of 10TB of storage. 2TB is required for the parity information, leaving 8TB for saving actual data.

3. **D.** The hosts that are within the redundant group are known as the group of redundancy.

4. **A.** Although not a fault-tolerant RAID level, RAID 0 offers the best performance of any RAID level. Other RAID levels do offer some performance improvements over a single disk, but their fault-tolerance considerations inhibit the write operations.

5. **C.** A sag is a short-term voltage drop. A brownout is also a voltage drop, but it lasts longer than a sag. A surge is an increase in power that lasts a few seconds. A spike is a power increase that lasts a few milliseconds.

6. **A.** RAID 0 offers the highest level of performance but does not offer any fault tolerance. If the performance of RAID 0 is required and so is fault tolerance, RAID 10 is a better choice. RAID 1 offers fault tolerance but no increase in performance.

Disaster Recovery

▶ Explain the different methods and rationale for network performance optimization.

Cram**Saver**

If you can correctly answer these questions before going through this section, save time by skimming the Exam Alerts in this section and then complete the Cram Quiz at the end of the section.

1. What is the difference between an incremental backup and a differential backup?

2. When someone speaks of GFS rotation, what are they referring to?

3. What are hot, warm, and cold sites used for?

Answers

1. With incremental backups, all data that has changed since the last full or incremental backup is backed up. The restore procedure requires several tapes: the latest full backup and all incremental tapes since the last full backup. An incremental backup uses the archive bit and clears it after a file is saved to disk. With a differential backup, all data changed since the last full backup is backed up. The restore procedure requires the latest full backup tape and the latest differential backup tape. A differential backup uses the archive bit to determine which files must be backed up but does not clear it.

2. It is important with backups to use an offsite tape rotation scheme to store current copies of backups in a secure offsite location. One of the most commonly used with tapes and other rewritable media is the grandfather, father, son (GFS) rotation.

3. Hot, warm, and cold sites are designed to provide alternative locations for network operations if a disaster occurs.

Even the most fault-tolerant networks can fail, which is an unfortunate fact. When those costly and carefully implemented fault-tolerance strategies fail, you are left with *disaster recovery*.

Disaster recovery can take many forms. In addition to disasters such as fire, flood, and theft, many other potential business disruptions can fall under the banner of disaster recovery. For example, the failure of the electrical supply to your city block might interrupt the business functions. Such an event, although not a disaster per se, might invoke the disaster recovery methods.

The cornerstone of every disaster recovery strategy is the preservation and recoverability of data. When talking about preservation and recoverability, you must talk about backups. When talking about backups, you likely talk about tape backups. Implementing a regular backup schedule can save you a lot of grief when fault tolerance fails or when you need to recover a file that has been accidentally deleted. When it's time to design a backup schedule, you can use three key types of backups: full, differential, and incremental.

Full Backups

The preferred method of backup is the *full backup* method, which copies all files and directories from the hard disk to the backup media. There are a few reasons why doing a full backup is not always possible. First among them is likely the time involved in performing a full backup.

> **ExamAlert**
>
> A full backup is the fastest way to restore data of all the methods discussed here, because only one tape, or set of tapes, is required for a full restore.

Depending on the amount of data to be backed up, full backups can take an extremely long time and can use extensive system resources. Depending on the configuration of the backup hardware, this can considerably slow down the network. In addition, some environments have more data than can fit on a single tape. This makes doing a full backup awkward because someone might need to be there to change the tapes.

The main advantage of full backups is that a single tape or tape set holds all the data you need backed up. If a failure occurs, a single tape might be all that is needed to get all data and system information back. The upshot of all this is that any disruption to the network is greatly reduced.

Unfortunately, its strength can also be its weakness. A single tape holding an organization's data can be a security risk. If the tape were to fall into the wrong hands, all the data could be restored on another computer. Using passwords on tape backups and using a secure offsite and onsite location can minimize the security risk.

Differential Backups

Companies that don't have enough time to complete a full backup daily can use the *differential backup*. Differential backups are faster than a full backup because they back up only the data that has changed since the last full backup. This means that if you do a full backup on a Saturday and a differential backup on the following Wednesday, only the data that has changed since Saturday is backed up. Restoring the differential backup requires the last full backup and the latest differential backup.

Differential backups know what files have changed since the last full backup because they use a setting called the *archive bit*. The archive bit flags files that have changed or have been created and identifies them as ones that need to be backed up. Full backups do not concern themselves with the archive bit because all files are backed up, regardless of date. A full backup, however, does clear the archive bit after data has been backed up to avoid future confusion. Differential backups notice the archive bit and use it to determine which files have changed. The differential backup does not reset the archive bit information.

> **ExamAlert**
>
> If you experience trouble with any type of backup, you should clean the tape drive and then try the backup again. Also visually inspect the tape for physical damage.

Incremental Backups

Some companies have a finite amount of time they can allocate to backup procedures. Such organizations are likely to use *incremental backups* in their backup strategy. Incremental backups save only the files that have changed since the last full or incremental backup. Like differential backups, incremental backups use the archive bit to determine which files have changed since the last full or incremental backup. Unlike differentials, however, incremental backups clear the archive bit, so files that have not changed are not backed up.

> **ExamAlert**
>
> Both full and incremental backups clear the archive bit after files have been backed up.

The faster backup time of incremental backups comes at a price—the amount of time required to restore. Recovering from a failure with incremental backups requires numerous tapes—all the incremental tapes and the most recent full backup. For example, if you have a full backup from Sunday and an incremental for Monday, Tuesday, and Wednesday, you need four tapes to restore the data. Each tape in the rotation is an additional step in the restore process and an additional failure point. One damaged incremental tape, and you cannot restore the data. Table 9.3 summarizes the various backup strategies.

TABLE 9.3 **Backup Strategies**

Backup Type	Advantage	Disadvantage	Data Backed Up	Archive Bit
Full	Backs up all data on a single tape or tape set. Restoring data requires the fewest tapes.	Depending on the amount of data, full backups can take a long time.	All files and directories are backed up.	Does not use the archive bit, but resets it after data has been backed up.
Differential	Faster backups than a full backup.	Uses more tapes than a full backup. The restore process takes longer than a full backup.	All files and directories that have changed since the last full backup.	Uses the archive bit to determine the files that have changed but does not reset the archive bit.
Incremental	Faster backup times.	Requires multiple disks; restoring data takes more time than the other backup methods.	The files and directories that have changed since the last full or incremental backup.	Uses the archive bit to determine the files that have changed, and resets the archive bit.

Tape Rotations

After you select a backup type, you are ready to choose a backup rotation. Several backup rotation strategies are in use—some good, some bad, and some really bad. The most common, and perhaps the best rotation strategy is grandfather, father, son (GFS).

The GFS backup rotation is the most widely used—and for good reason. For example, a GFS rotation may require 12 tapes: four tapes for daily backups (son), five tapes for weekly backups (father), and three tapes for monthly backups (grandfather).

Using this rotation schedule, you can recover data from days, weeks, or months earlier. Some network administrators choose to add tapes to the monthly rotation so that they can retrieve data even further back, sometimes up to a year. In most organizations, however, data that is a week old is out of date, not 6 months or a year.

Backup Best Practices

Many details go into making a backup strategy a success. The following are issues to consider as part of your backup plan:

▸ **Offsite storage**: Consider storing backup tapes offsite so that if a disaster occurs in a building, a current set of tapes is still available offsite. The offsite tapes should be as current as any onsite and should be secure.

▸ **Label tapes**: The goal is to restore the data as quickly as possible, and trying to find the tape you need can be difficult if it isn't marked. Furthermore, this can prevent you from recording over a tape you need.

▸ **New tapes**: Like old cassette tapes, the tape cartridges used for the backups wear out over time. One strategy used to prevent this from becoming a problem is to periodically introduce new tapes into the rotation schedule.

▸ **Verify backups**: Never assume that the backup was successful. Seasoned administrators know that checking backup logs and performing periodic test restores are part of the backup process.

▸ **Cleaning**: You need to occasionally clean the tape drive. If the inside gets dirty, backups can fail.

> **Exam Alert**
>
> A backup strategy must include offsite storage to account for theft, fire, flood, or other disasters.

Hot and Cold Spares

The impact that a failed component has on a system or network depends largely on the predisaster preparation and on the recovery strategies used. Hot and cold spares represent a strategy for recovering from failed components.

Hot Spares and Hot Swapping

Hot spares enable system administrators to quickly recover from component failure. In a common use, a hot spare enables a RAID system to automatically fail over to a spare hard drive should one of the other drives in the RAID array fail. A hot spare does not require any manual intervention. Instead, a redundant drive resides in the system at all times, just waiting to take over if another drive fails. The hot spare drive takes over automatically, leaving the failed drive to be removed later. Even though hot-spare technology adds an extra level of protection to your system, after a drive has failed and the hot spare has been used, the situation should be remedied as soon as possible.

Hot swapping is the ability to replace a failed component while the system is running. Perhaps the most commonly identified hot-swap component is the hard drive. In certain RAID configurations, when a hard drive crashes, hot swapping allows you to simply take the failed drive out of the server and install a new one.

The benefits of hot swapping are clear in that it allows a failed component to be recognized and replaced without compromising system availability. Depending on the system's configuration, the new hardware normally is recognized automatically by both the current hardware and the operating system. Nowadays, most internal and external RAID subsystems support the hot-swapping feature. Some hot-swappable components include power supplies and hard disks.

Cold Spares and Cold Swapping

The term *cold spare* refers to a component, such as a hard disk, that resides within a computer system but requires manual intervention in case of component failure. A hot spare engages automatically, but a cold spare might require configuration settings or some other action to engage it. A cold spare configuration typically requires a reboot of the system.

The term cold spare has also been used to refer to a redundant component stored outside the actual system but is kept in case of component failure. To replace the failed component with a cold spare, you need to power down the system.

Cold swapping refers to replacing components only after the system is completely powered off. This strategy is by far the least attractive for servers because the services provided by the server are unavailable for the duration of the cold-swap procedure. Modern systems have come a long way to ensure that cold swapping is a rare occurrence. For some situations and for some components, however, cold swapping is the only method to replace a failed component. The only defense against having to shut down the server is to have redundant components reside in the system.

> **Note**
>
> The term *warm swap* is applied to a device that can be replaced while the system is still running but that requires some kind of manual intervention to disable the device before it can be removed. Using a PCI hot plug technically is a warm-swap strategy because it requires that the individual PCI slot be powered down before the PCI card is replaced. Of course, a warm swap is not as efficient as a hot swap, but it is much better than a cold swap.

Hot, Warm, and Cold Sites

A disaster recovery plan might include the provision for a recovery site that can be quickly brought into play. These sites fall into three categories: hot, warm, and cold. The need for each of these types of sites depends largely on the business you are in and the funds available. Disaster recovery sites represent the ultimate in precautions for organizations that need them. As a result, they don't come cheap.

The basic concept of a disaster recovery site is that it can provide a base from which the company can be operated during a disaster. The disaster recovery site normally is not intended to provide a desk for every employee. It's intended more as a means to allow key personnel to continue the core business functions.

In general, a cold recovery site is a site that can be up and operational in a relatively short amount of time, such as a day or two. Provision of services, such as telephone lines and power, is taken care of, and the basic office furniture might be in place. But there is unlikely to be any computer equipment, even though the building might have a network infrastructure and a room ready to act as a server room. In most cases, cold sites provide the physical location and basic services.

Cold sites are useful if you have some forewarning of a potential problem. Generally, cold sites are used by organizations that can weather the storm for a day or two before they get back up and running. If you are the regional office of a major company, it might be possible to have one of the other divisions take care of business until you are ready to go. But if you are the only office in the company, you might need something a little hotter.

For organizations with the dollars and the desire, hot recovery sites represent the ultimate in fault-tolerance strategies. Like cold recovery sites, hot sites are designed to provide only enough facilities to continue the core business function, but hot recovery sites are set up to be ready to go at a moment's notice.

A hot recovery site includes phone systems with connected phone lines. Data networks also are in place, with any necessary routers and switches plugged in and turned on. Desks have installed and waiting desktop PCs, and server areas are replete with the necessary hardware to support business-critical functions. In other words, within a few hours, the hot site can become a fully functioning element of an organization.

The issue that confronts potential hot-recovery site users is simply that of cost. Office space is expensive in the best of times, but having space sitting idle 99.9 percent of the time can seem like a tremendously poor use of money. A popular strategy to get around this problem is to use space provided in a disaster recovery facility, which is basically a building, maintained by a third-party company, in which various businesses rent space. Space is usually apportioned according to how much each company pays.

Sitting between the hot and cold recovery sites is the warm site. A warm site typically has computers but is not configured ready to go. This means that data might need to be upgraded or other manual interventions might need to be performed before the network is again operational. The time it takes to get a warm site operational lands right in the middle of the other two options, as does the cost.

> **ExamAlert**
>
> A hot site that mirrors the organization's production network can assume network operations at a moment's notice. Warm sites have the equipment needed to bring the network to an operational state but require configuration and potential database updates. A cold site has the space available with basic service but typically requires equipment delivery.

Cram Quiz

1. Which two types of tape backup methods clear the archive bit after the backup has been completed?

   ○ **A.** Full
   ○ **B.** Differential
   ○ **C.** Incremental
   ○ **D.** GFS

2. You come to work on Thursday morning to find that the server has failed and you need to restore the data from backup. You finished a full backup on Sunday and incremental backups on Monday, Tuesday, and Wednesday. How many tapes are required to restore the backup?

   ○ **A.** Four
   ○ **B.** Two
   ○ **C.** Three
   ○ **D.** Five

3. Which of the following recovery sites might require the delivery of computer equipment and an update of all network data?

   ○ **A.** Cold site
   ○ **B.** Warm site
   ○ **C.** Hot site
   ○ **D.** None of the above

4. As part of your network administrative responsibilities, you have completed your monthly backups. As part of backup best practices, where should the tapes be stored?

   ○ **A.** In a secure location in the server room
   ○ **B.** In a secure location somewhere in the building
   ○ **C.** In an offsite location
   ○ **D.** In a secure offsite location

5. As network administrator, you have been tasked with designing a disaster recovery plan for your network. Which of the following might you include in a disaster recovery plan?

   ○ **A.** RAID 5
   ○ **B.** Offsite tape storage
   ○ **C.** Mirrored hard disks
   ○ **D.** UPS

Cram Quiz Answers

1. **A, C.** The archive bit is reset after a full backup and an incremental backup. Answer B is incorrect because the differential backup does not reset the archive bit. Answer D is wrong because GFS is a rotation strategy, not a backup method.

2. **A.** Incremental backups save all files and directories that have changed since the last full or incremental backup. To restore, you need the latest full backup and all incremental tapes. In this case, you need four tapes to complete the restore process.

3. **A.** A cold site provides an alternative location but typically not much more. A cold site often requires the delivery of computer equipment and other services. A hot site has all network equipment ready to go if a massive failure occurs. A warm site has most equipment ready but still needs days or weeks to have the network up and running.

4. **D.** Although not always done, it is a best practice to store tape backups in a secure offsite location in case of fire or theft. Answer A is incorrect because if the server room is damaged by fire or flood, the tapes and the data on the server can be compromised by the same disaster. Similarly, answer B is incorrect because storing the backups onsite does not eliminate the threat of a single disaster destroying the data on the server and tapes. Answer C is incorrect because of security reasons. The offsite tapes must be secured.

5. **B.** Offsite tape storage is part of a disaster recovery plan. The other answers are considered fault-tolerance measures because they are implemented to ensure data availability.

Network Optimization Strategies

▶ Explain the different methods and rationale for network performance optimization.

Cram**Saver**

If you can correctly answer these questions before going through this section, save time by skimming the Exam Alerts in this section and then complete the Cram Quiz at the end of the section.

1. What are the two categories of QoS that applications generally can be broken into?

2. What term involves delaying the flow of data traffic designated as less important compared to other traffic streams?

Answers

1. Applications generally can be broken into either latency-sensitive or latency-insensitive.

2. Traffic shaping involves delaying the flow of data traffic designated as less important compared to other traffic streams.

Today's networks are all about speed. Network users expect data and application delivery quickly. Just look at how impatient many people get waiting for web pages to load. Networks, however, are saturated and congested with traffic, making it necessary to have strategies to ensure that you use bandwidth in the best possible way. These strategies are collectively referred to as quality of service (QoS).

Quality of Service (QoS)

QoS describes the strategies used to manage and increase the flow of network traffic. QoS features enable administrators to predict bandwidth use, monitor that use, and control it to ensure that bandwidth is available to the applications that need it. These applications generally can be broken into two categories:

▶ **Latency-sensitive**: These applications need bandwidth for quick delivery where network lag time impacts their effectiveness. This includes voice and video transfer. For example, voice over IP (VoIP) would be difficult to use if there were a significant lag time in the conversation.

▶ **Latency-insensitive**: Controlling bandwidth also involves managing latency-insensitive applications. This includes bulk data transfers such as huge backup procedures and File Transfer Protocol (FTP) transfers.

With bandwidth limited, and networks becoming increasingly congested, it becomes more difficult to deliver latency-sensitive traffic. If network traffic continues to increase and you can't always increase bandwidth, the choice is to prioritize traffic to ensure timely delivery. This is where QoS comes into play. QoS ensures the delivery of applications, such as videoconferencing (and related video applications), VoIP telephony, and unified communications without adversely affecting network throughput. QoS achieves more efficient use of network resources by differentiating between latency-insensitive traffic such as fax data and latency-sensitive streaming media.

One important strategy for QoS is priority queuing. Essentially what happens is that traffic is placed in order based on its importance on delivery time. All data is given access, but the more important and latency-sensitive data is given higher priority.

> **ExamAlert**
>
> Be sure you understand QoS and the methods used to ensure QoS on networks. Know that it is used with high-bandwidth applications such as VoIP, video applications, and unified communications.

Traffic Shaping

Traffic shaping is a QoS strategy designed to enforce prioritization policies on the transmission of data throughout the network. It is intended to reduce latency by controlling the amount of data that flows into and out of the network. Traffic is categorized, queued, and directed according to network policies.

Methods Used for Traffic Shaping

You can shape and limit network traffic using several different strategies. Which one you choose depends on the network's needs and the amount of traffic. Following are some common traffic-shaping methods:

▶ **Shaping by application**: Administrators can configure a traffic shaper by categorizing specific types of network traffic and assigning that category a bandwidth limit. For example, traffic can be categorized using FTP. The rule can specify that no more than 4Mbps be dedicated for

FTP traffic. This same principle can apply to Telnet sessions, streaming audio, or any other application coming through the network.

▸ **Shaping network traffic per user**: Every network has users who use more bandwidth than others. Some of this might be work-related, but more often than not, it is personal use. In such a case, you might need to establish traffic shaping on a per-user basis. Traffic shapers allow administrators to delegate a certain bandwidth to a user. For instance, Bob from accounting is allowed no more than 256Kbps. This doesn't limit what the user can access, just the speed at which that content can be accessed.

▸ **Priority shaping**: One important consideration when looking at traffic shaping is determining which traffic is mission-critical and which is less so. In addition to setting hard or burstable traffic limits on a per-application or per-user basis, traffic shaping devices can also be used to define the relative importance, or priority, of different types of traffic. For example, in an academic network where teaching and research are most important, recreational uses of the network (such as network games or peer-to-peer file-sharing application traffic) can be allowed bandwidth only when higher-priority applications don't need it.

> ### ExamAlert
>
> Remember that traffic shaping involves delaying the flow of data traffic that is designated as less important compared to other traffic streams.

Caching Engines

Caching is an important consideration when optimizing network traffic. For example, as discussed in Chapter 4, "Components and Devices," proxy servers use caching to limit the number of client requests that go to the Internet. Instead, the requests are filled from the proxy server's cache. Recall from Chapter 4 that when a caching proxy server has answered a request for a web page, the server makes a copy of all or part of that page in its cache. Then, when the page is requested again, the proxy server answers the request from the cache rather than going back out to the Internet. For example, if a client on a network requests the web page www.comptia.org, the proxy server can cache the contents of that web page. When a second client computer on the network attempts to access the same site, that client can grab it from the proxy server cache; accessing the Internet is not necessary. This greatly reduces the network traffic that has to be filtered to the Internet, a significant gain in terms of network optimization.

When it comes to determining what to cache, an administrator can establish many rules:

▶ What websites to cache

▶ How long the information is cached

▶ When cached information is updated

▶ The size of cached information

▶ What type of content is cached

▶ Who can access the cache

The rules for caching vary from network to network, depending on the network's needs. In networks where a large number of people access similar websites, caching can greatly increase network performance. The advantages of properly configured caching are clear—reduced bandwidth, and latency and increased throughput. One possible disadvantage of caching is receiving out-of-date files because you obtain content from the caching engine and not the website itself.

Exam Alert

Caching improves network performance by locally caching content, thereby limiting surges in traffic.

Cram Quiz

1. Caching improves network performance by caching content where?

   ○ **A.** Locally.

   ○ **B.** On a remote server.

   ○ **C.** In archives.

   ○ **D.** Caching does not improve network performance.

2. Which of the following would most likely use latency-sensitive QoS?

   ○ **A.** FTP

   ○ **B.** DNS

   ○ **C.** SNMP

   ○ **D.** VoIP

Cram Quiz Answers

1. **A.** Caching improves network performance by locally caching content, thereby limiting surges in traffic.

2. **D.** Latency-sensitive applications include those for voice and video transfer. For example, voice over IP (VoIP) would be difficult to use if there were a significant lag time in the conversation.

What Next?

One of the primary goals of today's network administrators is to design, implement, and maintain secure networks. This is not always easy and is the topic of Chapter 10, "Network Security." No network can ever be labeled "secure." Security is an ongoing process involving a myriad of protocols, procedures, and practices.

CHAPTER 10

Network Security

This chapter covers the following official Network+ objectives:

▶ Explain the methods of network access security.

▶ Explain methods of user authentication.

▶ Explain common threats, vulnerabilities, and mitigation techniques.

▶ Given a scenario, install and configure a basic firewall.

▶ Categorize different types of network security appliances and methods.

This chapter covers CompTIA Network+ objectives 5.2, 5.3, 5.4, 5.5, and 5.6. For more information on the official Network+ exam topics, see the "About the Network+ Exam" section in the "Introduction."

One of the primary goals of today's network administrators is to design, implement, and maintain secure networks. This is not always easy. No network can ever be labeled "secure." Security is an ongoing process involving a myriad of protocols, procedures, and practices. This chapter focuses on some of the elements administrators use to keep their networks as secure as possible.

Tunneling, Encryption, and Access Control

▶ Explain the methods of network access security.

Cram**Saver**

If you can correctly answer these questions before going through this section, save time by skimming the Exam Alerts in this section and then complete the Cram Quiz at the end of the section.

1. True or False: VPNs require a secure protocol to safely transfer data over the Internet.

2. How many phases are there to L2TP authentication?

Answers

1. True. VPNs require a secure protocol such as IPSec or SSL to safely transfer data over the Internet.

2. L2TP offers two-phase authentication—once for the computer and once for the user.

Chapter 1, "Introduction to Networking," introduced the topic of tunneling and two virtual private networking solutions: Point-to-Point Tunneling Protocol (PPTP) and Layer 2 Tunneling Protocol (L2TP). Ascend, 3Com, Microsoft, and U.S. Robotics developed PPTP, and Cisco introduced the Layer 2 Forwarding (L2F) protocol.

VPN encapsulates encrypted data inside another datagram that contains routing information. The connection between two computers establishes a switched connection dedicated to the two computers. The encrypted data is encapsulated inside Point-to-Point Protocol (PPP), and that connection is used to deliver the data.

A VPN enables users with an Internet connection to use the infrastructure of the public network to dial in to the main network and access resources as if they were logged on to the network locally. It also enables two networks to be connected to each other securely.

Internet Security Association and Key Management Protocol (ISAKMP)

ISAKMP, which is documented in RFC 2408, is a framework defining the procedures for authentication, creation and management of security associations (SAs), key generation techniques, and threat mitigation. In short, it outlines how secure communications should take place, but is not a protocol, or application, itself.

> **ExamAlert**
>
> Be sure you understand that ISAKMP is a framework and not an implementable entity.

Point-to-Point Tunneling Protocol (PPTP)

PPTP, which is documented in RFC 2637, is often mentioned together with PPP. Although it's used in dialup connections, as PPP is, PPTP provides different functionality. It creates a secure *tunnel* between two points on a network, over which other connectivity protocols, such as PPP, can be used. This tunneling functionality is the basis of VPNs.

> **ExamAlert**
>
> VPNs are created and managed using PPTP, which builds on the functionality of PPP. This makes it possible to create dedicated point-to-point tunnels through a public network such as the Internet.

To establish a PPTP session between a client and server, a TCP connection known as a *PPTP control connection* is required to create and maintain the communication tunnel. The PPTP control connection exists between the IP address of the PPTP client and the IP address of the PPTP server, using TCP port 1723 on the server and a dynamic port on the client. It is the function of the PPTP control connection to pass the PPTP control and management messages used to maintain the PPTP communication tunnel between the remote system and the server. PPTP provides authenticated and encrypted communications between two endpoints such as a client and server. PPTP does not use a public key infrastructure but does use a user ID and password.

PPTP uses the same authentication methods as PPP, including MS-CHAP, CHAP, PAP, and EAP, which are discussed later in this chapter.

Layer 2 Tunneling Protocol (L2TP)

L2TP is a combination of PPTP and Cisco L2F technology. L2TP, as the name suggests, uses tunneling to deliver data. It authenticates the client in a two-phase process: It authenticates the computer and then the user. By authenticating the computer, it prevents the data from being intercepted, changed, and returned to the user in what is known as a *man-in-the-middle attack*. L2TP ensures both parties that the data they receive is exactly the data sent by the originator.

Exam Alert

Remember for the exam that L2TP offers two-phase authentication—once for the computer and once for the user. This helps prevent man-in-the-middle attacks.

Note

You create an L2TP tunnel without using encryption, but this is not a true VPN and, obviously, lacks a certain amount of security.

Exam Alert

Unlike IPSec, which operates at the network layer of the OSI model, L2TP operates at the data link layer, making it protocol-independent. This means that an L2TP connection can even support protocols other than TCP/IP, such as AppleTalk and Novell's legacy IPX.

L2TP and PPTP are both tunneling protocols, so you might wonder which you should use. Following is a quick list of some of the advantages of each, starting with PPTP:

▶ PPTP has been around longer; it offers more interoperability than L2TP.

▶ PPTP is an industry standard.

▶ PPTP is easier to configure than L2TP because L2TP uses digital certificates.

▶ PPTP has less overhead than L2TP.

Following are some of the advantages of L2TP:

▶ L2TP offers greater security than PPTP.

▶ L2TP supports common public key infrastructure technology.

▶ L2TP provides support for header compression.

IPSec

The IP Security (IPSec) protocol is designed to provide secure communications between systems. This includes system-to-system communication in the same network, as well as communication to systems on external networks. IPSec is an IP layer security protocol that can both encrypt and authenticate network transmissions. In a nutshell, IPSec is composed of two separate protocols: Authentication Header (AH) and Encapsulating Security Payload (ESP). AH provides the authentication and integrity checking for data packets, and ESP provides encryption services.

> **ExamAlert**
>
> IPSec relies on two underlying protocols: AH and ESP. AH provides authentication services, and ESP provides encryption services.

Using both AH and ESP, data traveling between systems can be secured, ensuring that transmissions cannot be viewed, accessed, or modified by those who should not have access to them. It might seem that protection on an internal network is less necessary than on an external network; however, much of the data you send across networks has little or no protection, allowing unwanted eyes to see it.

> **Note**
>
> The Internet Engineering Task Force (IETF) created IPSec, which you can use on both IPv4 and IPv6 networks.

IPSec provides three key security services:

▶ **Data verification**: Verifies that the data received is from the intended source

▶ **Protection from data tampering**: Ensures that the data has not been tampered with or changed between the sending and receiving devices

▶ **Private transactions**: Ensures that the data sent between the sending and receiving devices is unreadable by any other devices

IPSec operates at the network layer of the Open Systems Interconnect (OSI) model and provides security for protocols that operate at the higher layers. Thus, by using IPSec, you can secure practically all TCP/IP-related communications.

> **Tip**
>
> IPSec can be used only on TCP/IP networks. If you use another network protocol, you need to use a security protocol such as L2TP.

Site-to-Site and Client-to-Site

The scope of a tunnel can vary, with the two most common variations being *site-to-site* and *client-to-site*. In a site-to-site implementation, as the name implies, whole networks are connected together. An example of this would be divisions of a large company. Because the networks are supporting the VPN, each gateway does the work and the individual clients do not need to have any VPN.

In a client-to-site scenario, individual clients (such as telecommuters or travelers) connect to the network remotely. Because the individual client makes a direct connection to the network, each client doing so must have VPN client software installed.

> **ExamAlert**
>
> Be sure you understand that site-to-site and client-to-site are two types of VPNs.

Overview of Access Control

Access control describes the mechanisms used to filter network traffic to determine who is and who is not allowed to access the network and network resources. Firewalls, proxy servers, routers, and individual computers all can maintain access control to some degree. By limiting who can and cannot access the network and its resources, it is easy to understand why access control plays a critical role in security strategy. Several types of access control strategies exist, as discussed in the following sections.

Exam Alert

Be sure you can identify the purpose and types of access control.

Mandatory Access Control (MAC)

Mandatory access control (MAC) is the most secure form of access control. In systems configured to use mandatory access control, administrators dictate who can access and modify data, systems, and resources. MAC systems are commonly used in military installations, financial institutions, and, because of new privacy laws, medical institutions.

MAC secures information and resources by assigning sensitivity labels to objects and users. When users request access to an object, their sensitivity level is compared to the object's. A label is a feature applied to files, directories, and other resources in the system. It is similar to a confidentiality stamp. When a label is placed on a file, it describes the level of security for that specific file. It permits access by files, users, programs, and so on that have a similar or higher security setting.

Discretionary Access Control (DAC)

Unlike mandatory access control, discretionary access control (DAC) is not forced from the administrator or operating system. Instead, access is controlled by an object's owner. For example, if a secretary creates a folder, he decides who will have access to that folder. This access is configured using permissions and an access control list.

DAC uses an access control list (ACL) to determine access. The ACL is a table that informs the operating system of the rights each user has to a particular system object, such as a file, directory, or printer. Each object has a security attribute that identifies its ACL. The list has an entry for each system user with access privileges. The most common privileges include the ability to read a file (or all the files in a directory), to write to the file or files, and to execute the file (if it is an executable file or program).

Microsoft Windows Servers/7/Vista/XP, Linux, UNIX, and Mac OS X are among the operating systems that use ACLs. The list is implemented differently by each operating system.

In Windows Server products, an ACL is associated with each system object. Each ACL has one or more access control entries (ACEs) consisting of the name of a user or group of users. The user can also be a role name, such as "secretary" or "research." For each of these users, groups, or roles, the access privileges are stated in a string of bits called an access mask. Generally, the system administrator or the object owner creates the ACL for an object.

Rule-Based Access Control (RBAC)

Rule-based access control controls access to objects according to established rules. The configuration and security settings established on a router or firewall are a good example.

When a firewall is configured, rules are set up that control access to the network. Requests are reviewed to see if the requestor meets the criteria to be allowed access through the firewall. For instance, if a firewall is configured to reject all addresses in the 192.166.x.x IP address range, and the requestor's IP is in that range, the request would be denied.

In a practical application, rule-based access control is a variation on MAC. Administrators typically configure the firewall or other device to allow or deny access. The owner or another user does not specify the conditions of acceptance, and safeguards ensure that an average user cannot change settings on the devices.

> **Note**
>
> It seems that rule-based access control and role-based access control sometimes share the same acronym on the Internet. This can make things tricky; however, remember that role-based access control should be represented as RoBAC.

Role-Based Access Control (RoBAC)

In role-based access control (RoBAC), access decisions are determined by the roles that individual users have within the organization. Role-based access requires the administrator to have a thorough understanding of how a particular organization operates, the number of users, and each user's exact function in that organization.

Because access rights are grouped by role name, the use of resources is restricted to individuals who are authorized to assume the associated role. For example, within a school system, the role of teacher can include access to certain data, including test banks, research material, and memos. School administrators might have access to employee records, financial data, planning projects, and more.

The use of roles to control access can be an effective means of developing and enforcing enterprise-specific security policies and for streamlining the security management process.

Roles should receive just the privilege level necessary to do the job associated with that role. This general security principle is known as the least privilege concept. When people are hired in an organization, their role is clearly defined. A network administrator creates a user account for the new employee and places that user account in a group with people who have the same role in the organization.

Least privilege is often too restrictive to be practical in business. For instance, using teachers as an example, some more experienced teachers might have more responsibility than others and might require increased access to a particular network object. Customizing access to each individual is a time-consuming process.

> **ExamAlert**
>
> You may be asked about the concept of least privilege. This refers to assigning network users the privilege level necessary to do the job associated with their role—nothing more and nothing less.

Remote-Access Protocols and Services

Today, there are many ways to establish remote access into networks. Some of these include such things as VPNs or Plain Old Telephone System (POTS) dialup access. Regardless of the technique used for remote access or the speed at which access is achieved, certain technologies need to be in place for the magic to happen. These technologies include the protocols to allow access to the server and to secure the data transfer after the connection is established. Also necessary are methods of access control that make sure only authorized users are using the remote-access features.

All the major operating systems include built-in support for remote access. They provide both the access methods and security protocols necessary to secure the connection and data transfers.

Remote Access Service (RAS)

RAS is a remote-access solution included with Windows Server products. RAS is a feature-rich, easy-to-configure, easy-to-use method of configuring remote access.

Any system that supports the appropriate dial-in protocols, such as PPP, can connect to a RAS server. Most commonly, the clients are Windows systems that use the dialup networking feature, but any operating system that supports dialup client software will work. Connection to a RAS server can be made over a standard phone line, using a modem, over a network, or via an ISDN connection.

RAS supports remote connectivity from all the major client operating systems available today, including all newer Windows OSs:

- ▶ Windows Server products

- ▶ Windows 7/XP/Vista Home-based clients

- ▶ Windows 7/XP/Vista Professional-based clients

- ▶ UNIX-based/Linux clients

- ▶ Macintosh-based clients

Although the system is called RAS, the underlying technologies that enable the RAS process are dialup protocols such as PPP.

PPP

PPP is the standard remote-access protocol in use today. PPP is actually a family of protocols that work together to provide connection services.

Because PPP is an industry standard, it offers interoperability between different software vendors in various remote-access implementations. PPP provides a number of security enhancements compared to regular SLIP, the most important being the encryption of usernames and passwords during the authentication process. PPP enables remote clients and servers to negotiate data encryption methods and authentication methods and support new technologies. PPP even enables administrators choose which LAN protocol to use over a remote link.

> **Note**
>
> PPP can use a variety of LAN protocols to establish a remote link.

During the establishment of a PPP connection between the remote system and the server, the remote server needs to authenticate the remote user. It does so by using the PPP authentication protocols. PPP accommodates a number of authentication protocols, and it's possible on many systems to configure more than one authentication protocol. The protocol used in the authentication process depends on the security configurations established between the remote user and the server. PPP authentication protocols include

CHAP, MS-CHAP, MS-CHAP v2, EAP, and PAP. Each of these authentication methods is discussed in the section "Remote Authentication Protocols."

> **ExamAlert**
>
> If you work on a network that uses SLIP, and you run into connectivity problems, try upgrading to PPP because it is more flexible and secure.

PPPoE

Point-to-Point Protocol over Ethernet (PPPoE) is a protocol used to connect multiple network users on an Ethernet local area network to a remote site through a common device. For example, using PPPoE, you can have all users on a network share the same link, such as a DSL, cable modem, or wireless connection to the Internet. PPPoE is a combination of PPP and the Ethernet protocol, which supports multiple users in a local area network (hence the name). The PPP information is encapsulated within an Ethernet frame.

With PPPoE, a number of different users can share the same physical connection to the Internet. In the process, PPPoE provides a way to keep track of individual user Internet access times. Because PPPoE e for individual authenticated access to high-speed data networks, it is an efficient way to create a separate connection to a remote server for each user. This strategy enables Internet service providers (ISPs) or administrators to bill or track access on a per-user basis rather than a per-site basis.

Users accessing PPPoE connections require the same information as required with standard dialup phone accounts, including a username and password combination. As with a dialup PPP service, an ISP will most likely automatically assign configuration information such as the IP address, subnet mask, default gateway, and DNS server.

The PPPoE communication process has two stages: the discovery stage and the PPP session stage. The discovery stage uses four steps to establish the PPPoE connection: initiation, offer, request, and session confirmation. These steps represent back-and-forth communication between the client and the PPPoE server. After these steps have been negotiated, the PPP session can be established using familiar PPP authentication protocols.

Network Access Control

Network Access Control (NAC) is a method to restrict access to the network based on identify or posture (discussed later in this chapter). This was created by Cisco to enforce privileges and make decisions on a client device based on information gathered from it (such as the vendor and version of the antivirus software running). If the wanted information is not found (such as that the antivirus definitions are a year old), the client can be placed in a quarantine area to keep them from infecting the rest of the network.

A *posture assessment* is any evaluation of a system's security based on settings and applications found. In addition to looking at such values as settings in the Registry or dates of files, NACs can also check *802.1x* values—the group of networking protocols associated with authentication of devices attempting to connect to the network. 802.1x works with EAP (discussed later in this chapter).

> **ExamAlert**
>
> Be able to identify posture assessment.

Remote-Control Protocols

CompTIA lists three protocols that are associated with remote-control access: Remote Desktop Protocol (RDP), Secure Shell (SSH), and Citrix Independent Computing Architecture (ICA). RDP is used in a Windows environment. Terminal Services provides a way for a client system to connect to a server, such as Windows Server 2008/2003/2000, and, by using RDP, operate on the server as if they were local client applications. Such a configuration is known as *thin client computing*, whereby client systems use the resources of the server instead of their local processing power.

Windows Server products and Windows 7 (as well as Vista and XP) have built-in support for remote desktop connections. The underlying protocol used to manage the connection is RDP. RDP is a low-bandwidth protocol used to send mouse movements, keystrokes, and bitmap images of the screen on the server to the client computer. RDP does not actually send data over the connection—only screenshots and client keystrokes.

SSH is a tunneling protocol originally created for UNIX systems. It uses encryption to establish a secure connection between two systems and provides alternative, security-equivalent applications for such utilities as Telnet, FTP, and other communications-oriented applications. Although it is available with Windows and other operating systems, it is the preferred method of security for Telnet and other cleartext-oriented programs in the UNIX environment. SSH uses port 22 and TCP for connections.

ExamAlert

Be sure you know the port associated with SSH.

Citrix ICA enables clients to access and run applications on a server, using the server's resources. Only the user interface, keystrokes, and mouse movements transfer between the client system and the server. In effect, even though you work at the remote computer, the system functions as if you were actually sitting at the computer itself. As with Terminal Services and RDP, ICA is an example of thin client computing.

ExamAlert

Three protocols described in this chapter enable access to remote systems and enable users to run applications on the system, using that system's resources. Only the user interface, keystrokes, and mouse movements transfer between the client system and the remote computer.

MAC Filtering

Filtering network traffic using a system's MAC address typically is done using an ACL. This list keeps track of all MAC addresses and is configured to allow or deny access to certain systems based on the list. As an example, look at the MAC ACL from a router. Figure 10.1 shows the MAC ACL screen.

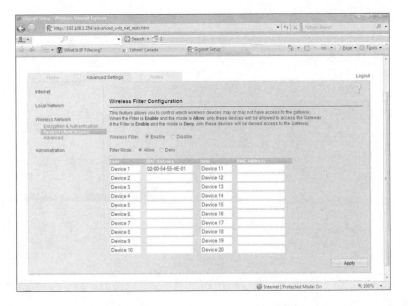

FIGURE 10.1 **A MAC ACL.**

Specific MAC addresses can be either denied or accepted, depending on the configuration (refer to Figure 10.1). In this example, only the system with the MAC address of 02-00-54-55-4E-01 can authenticate to this router.

ExamAlert

When configuring security for wireless networks, filtering by MAC address is a common practice. Typically, in MAC filtering security, MAC addresses can be added to an "allow" ACL or "deny" ACL.

TCP/IP Filtering

Another type of filtering that can be used with an ACL is TCP/IP filtering. The ACL determines what types of IP traffic will be let through the router. IP traffic that is not permitted according to the ACL is blocked. Depending on the type of IP filtering used, the ACL can be configured to allow or deny several types of IP traffic:

▶ Protocol type: TCP, UDP, ICMP, SNMP, IP

▶ Port number used by protocols (for TCP/UPD)

▶ Message source address

▶ Message destination address

Cram Quiz

1. Which of the following protocols is used in thin-client computing?

    ○ **A.** RDP

    ○ **B.** PPP

    ○ **C.** PPTP

    ○ **D.** RAS

2. Which of the following statements best describes the function of PPP?

    ○ **A.** It is a secure technology that enables information to be securely downloaded from a website.

    ○ **B.** It is a dialup protocol used over serial links.

    ○ **C.** It is a technology that enables a secure tunnel to be created through a public network.

    ○ **D.** It provides a public key/private key exchange mechanism.

3. Your company wants to create a secure tunnel between two networks over the Internet. Which of the following protocols would you use to do this?

    ○ **A.** PAP

    ○ **B.** CHAP

    ○ **C.** PPTP

    ○ **D.** SLAP

4. Because of a recent security breach, you have been asked to design a security strategy that will allow data to travel encrypted through both the Internet and intranet. Which of the following protocols would you use?

    ○ **A.** IPSec

    ○ **B.** SST

    ○ **C.** CHAP

    ○ **D.** FTP

Cram Quiz Answers

1. **A.** RDP is used in thin-client networking, where only screen, keyboard, and mouse input is sent across the line. PPP is a dialup protocol used over serial links. PPTP is a technology used in VPNs. RAS is a remote-access service.

2. **B.** PPP is a protocol that can be used for dialup connections over serial links. Answer A describes SSL, answer C describes a VPN, and answer D describes PKI.

3. **C.** To establish the VPN connection between the two networks, you can use PPTP. PAP and CHAP are not used to create a point-to-point tunnel; they are authentication protocols. SLAP is not a secure dialup protocol.

4. **A.** IPSec is a nonproprietary security standard used to secure transmissions both on the internal network and when data is sent outside the local LAN. IPSec provides encryption and authentication services for data communications. Answer B is not a valid protocol. Answer C, CHAP, is a remote-access authentication protocol. Answer D is incorrect because FTP is a protocol used for large data transfers, typically from the Internet.

Authentication, Authorization, and Accounting (AAA)

▶ **Explain methods of user authentication.**

Cram**Saver**

If you can correctly answer these questions before going through this section, save time by skimming the Exam Alerts in this section and then complete the Cram Quiz at the end of the section.

1. What does the acronym AAA stand for?
2. What are some of the policies that can usually be set for passwords?

Answers

1. AAA refers to authentication, authorization, and accounting services.
2. Common password policies typically include a minimum length of password, password expiration, prevention of password reuse, and prevention of easy-to-guess passwords.

You need to understand the difference between authentication, authorization, and accounting. Although these terms are sometimes used interchangeably, they refer to distinct steps that must be negotiated successfully to determine whether a particular request for a resource results in that resource actually being returned.

Authentication refers to the mechanisms used to verify the identity of the computer or user attempting to access a particular resource. Authentication is usually done with a set of credentials—most commonly a username and password.

Authentication is a significant consideration for network and system security.

Authorization determines if the person, previously identified and authenticated, is allowed access to a particular resource. This is commonly determined through group association. In other words, a particular group may have a specific level of security clearance. Figure 10.2 shows an example of authentication and authorization.

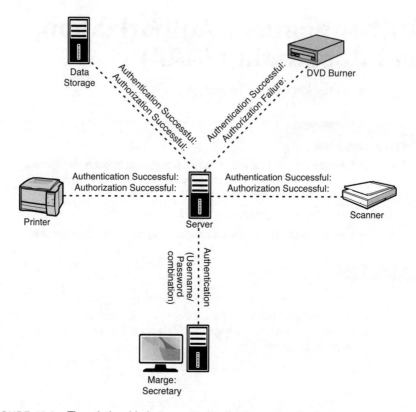

FIGURE 10.2   The relationship between authentication and authorization.

Marge is authenticated to the network but is not authorized to use the DVD duplicator (refer to Figure 10.2).

A bank transaction at an ATM is another good example of authentication and authorization. When a bank card is placed in the ATM, the magnetic strip is read, making it apparent that someone is trying to access a particular account. If the process ended there and access were granted, it would be a significant security problem, because anyone holding the card could gain immediate access. To authenticate the client, after the card is placed in the ATM, a secret code or personal identification number (PIN) is required. This authentication ensures that it is the owner of the card who is trying to gain access to the bank account.

With the correct code, the client is verified and authenticated, and access is granted. Authorization addresses the specifics of which accounts or features the user is allowed to access after being authenticated, such as a checking or savings account.

Accounting refers to the tracking mechanisms used to keep a record of events on a system. One tool often used for this purpose is auditing. Auditing is the process of monitoring occurrences and keeping a log of what has occurred on a system. A system administrator determines which events should be audited. Tracking events and attempts to access the system helps prevent unauthorized access and provides a record that administrators can analyze to make security changes as necessary. It also provides administrators with solid evidence if they need to look into improper user conduct.

> **ExamAlert**
>
> Be sure you can identify the purpose of authentication, authorization, and accounting.

The first step in auditing is to identify what system events to monitor. After the system events are identified, in a Windows environment, the administrator can choose to monitor the success or failure of a system event. For instance, if "logon" is the event being audited, the administrator might choose to log all unsuccessful logon attempts, which might indicate that someone is attempting to gain unauthorized access. Conversely, the administrator can choose to audit all successful attempts to monitor when a particular user or user group is logging on. Some administrators prefer to log both events. However, overly ambitious audit policies can reduce overall system performance.

> **ExamAlert**
>
> In a Windows environment, two pieces of information are required to access the network: a valid username and a valid password. Both are required to gain access.

Passwords and Password Policies

Although biometrics and smart cards are becoming more common, they still have a long way to go before they attain the level of popularity that username and password combinations enjoy. Apart from that usernames and passwords do not require any additional equipment, which practically every other method of authentication does, the username and password process is familiar to users, easy to implement, and relatively secure. For that reason, they are worthy of more detailed coverage than the other authentication systems previously discussed.

Passwords are a relatively simple form of authentication in that only a string of characters can be used to authenticate the user. However, how the string of characters is used and which policies you can put in place to govern them make usernames and passwords an excellent form of authentication.

Password Policies

All popular network operating systems include password policy systems that enable the network administrator to control how passwords are used on the system. The exact capabilities vary between network operating systems. However, generally they enable the following:

- **Minimum length of password**: Shorter passwords are easier to guess than longer ones. Setting a minimum password length does not prevent a user from creating a longer password than the minimum; although, each network operating system has a limit on how long a password can be.

- **Password expiration**: Also known as the maximum password age, password expiration defines how long the user can use the same password before having to change it. A general practice is that a password be changed every 30 days. In high-security environments, you might want to make this value shorter, but you should generally not make it any longer. Having passwords expire periodically is a crucial feature because it means that if a password is compromised, the unauthorized user will not indefinitely have access.

- **Prevention of password reuse**: Although a system might cause a password to expire and prompt the user to change it, many users are tempted to simply use the same password again. A process by which the system remembers the last, say, 10 passwords is most secure because it forces the user to create completely new passwords. This feature is sometimes called enforcing password history.

- **Prevention of easy-to-guess passwords**: Some systems can evaluate the password provided by a user to determine whether it meets a required level of complexity. This prevents users from having passwords such as `password`, `12345678`, their name, or their nickname.

> **ExamAlert**
>
> You need to identify an effective password policy. For example, a robust password policy would include forcing users to change their passwords on a regular basis.

Password Strength

No matter how good a company's password policy, it is only as effective as the passwords created within it. A password that is hard to guess, or strong, is more likely to protect the data on a system than one that is easy to guess, or weak.

To understand the difference between a strong password and a weak one, consider this: A password of six characters that uses only numbers and letters and that is not case-sensitive has 10,314,424,798,490,535,546,171,949,056 possible combinations. That might seem like a lot, but to a password-cracking program, it's actually not much security. A password that uses eight case-sensitive characters, with letters, numbers, and special characters, has so many possible combinations that a standard calculator can't display the actual number.

There has always been a debate over how long a password should be. It should be sufficiently long that it is hard to break but sufficiently short that the user can easily remember it (and type it). In a normal working environment, passwords of eight characters are sufficient. Certainly, they should be no fewer than six characters. In environments in which security is a concern, passwords should be 10 characters or more.

Users should be encouraged to use a password that is considered strong. A strong password has at least eight characters; has a combination of letters, numbers, and special characters; uses mixed case; and does not form a proper word. Examples are 3Ecc5T0h and e1oXPn3r. Such passwords might be secure, but users are likely to have problems remembering them. For that reason, a popular strategy is to use a combination of letters and numbers to form phrases or long words. Examples include d1eTc0La and tAb1eT0p. These passwords might not be quite as secure as the preceding examples, but they are still strong and a whole lot better than the name of the user's pet.

Kerberos Authentication

Kerberos is an Internet Engineering Task Force (IETF) standard for providing authentication. It is an integral part of network security. Networks, including the Internet, can connect people from all over the world. When data travels from one point to another across a network, it can be lost, stolen, corrupted, or misused. Much of the data sent over networks is sensitive, whether it is medical, financial, or otherwise. A key consideration for those responsible for the network is maintaining the confidentiality of the data. In the networking world, Kerberos plays a significant role in data confidentiality.

In a traditional authentication strategy, a username and password are used to access network resources. In a secure environment, it might be necessary to provide a username and password combination to access each network service or resource. For example, a user might be prompted to type in her username and password when accessing a database, and again for the printer and again for Internet access. This is a time-consuming process, and it can also present a security risk. Each time the password is entered, there is a chance that someone will see it being entered. If the password is sent over the network without encryption, it might be viewed by malicious eavesdroppers.

Kerberos was designed to fix such problems by using a method requiring only a single sign-on. This single sign-on enables a user to log into a system and access multiple systems or resources without the need to repeatedly re-enter the username and password. Additionally, Kerberos is designed to have entities authenticate themselves by demonstrating possession of secret information.

Kerberos is one part of a strategic security solution that provides secure authentication services to users, applications, and network devices by eliminating the insecurities caused by passwords stored or transmitted across the network. Kerberos is used primarily to eliminate the possibility of a network "eavesdropper" tapping into data over the network—particularly usernames and passwords. Kerberos ensures data integrity and blocks tampering on the network. It employs message privacy (encryption) to ensure that messages are not visible to eavesdroppers on the network.

For the network user, Kerberos eliminates the need to repeatedly demonstrate possession of private or secret information.

ExamAlert

Kerberos is a nonproprietary protocol and is used for cross-platform authentication. It's the main authentication protocol used with Windows servers.

Kerberos is designed to provide strong authentication for client/server applications by using secret-key cryptography. Cryptography is used to ensure that a client can prove its identity to a server (and vice versa) across an insecure network connection. After a client and server have used Kerberos to prove their identity, they can also encrypt all their communications to ensure privacy and data integrity.

ExamAlert

Kerberos enables secure authentication over an insecure network such as the Internet.

The key to understanding Kerberos is to understand the secret key cryptography it uses. Kerberos uses *symmetric key cryptography*, in which both client and server use the same encryption key to cipher and decipher data.

In secret key cryptography, a plain-text message can be converted into cipher-text (encrypted data) and then converted back into plain text using one key. Thus, two devices share a secret key to encrypt and decrypt their communications. Figure 10.3 shows the symmetric key process.

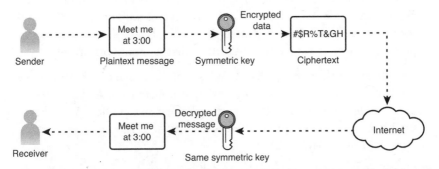

FIGURE 10.3 **The symmetric key process.**

ExamAlert

Another cryptography method in use is asymmetric key cryptography, or public key cryptography. In this method, a device has both a public and private key. The private key is never shared. The public key is used to encrypt the communication, and the private key is used for decrypting.

Kerberos authentication works by assigning a unique key (called a *ticket*) to each client that successfully authenticates to a server. The ticket is encrypted and contains the user's password, which is used to verify the user's identity when a particular network service is requested. Each ticket is time-stamped. It expires after a period of time, and a new one is issued. Kerberos works in the same way that you go to a movie. First, you go to the ticket counter, tell the person what movie you want to see, and get your ticket. After that, you go to a turnstile and hand the ticket to someone else, and then you're "in." In simplistic terms, that's Kerberos.

> **ExamAlert**
>
> You should know that the security tokens used in Kerberos are known as tickets.

Public Key Infrastructure

A Public Key Infrastructure (PKI) is a collection of software, standards, and policies combined to enable users from the Internet or other unsecured public networks to securely exchange data. PKI uses a public and private cryptographic key pair obtained and shared through a trusted authority. Services and components work together to develop the PKI. Some of the key components of a PKI include the following:

▶ **Certificates**: A form of electronic credentials that validates users, computers, or devices on the network. A certificate is a digitally signed statement that associates the credentials of a public key to the identity of the person, device, or service that holds the corresponding private key.

▶ **Certificate authorities (CAs):** CAs issue and manage certificates. They validate the identity of a network device or user requesting data. CAs can be either independent third parties, known as a public CA, or they can be organizations running their own certificate-issuing server software, known as private CAs.

▶ **Certificate templates:** Templates used to customize certificates issued by a Certificate Server. This customization includes a set of rules and settings created on the CA and used for incoming certificate requests.

▶ **Certificate Revocation List (CRL):** A list of certificates that were revoked before they reached the certificate expiration date. Certificates are often revoked due to security concerns such as a compromised certificate.

Public Keys and Private Keys

A cornerstone concept of the PKI infrastructure is public and private keys. Recall from Figure 10.3 that symmetric key cryptography is a system in which both client and server use the same encryption key to cipher and decipher data. The term key is used for good reason—public and private keys are used to lock (encrypt) and unlock (decrypt) data. These keys are actually long numbers, making it next to impossible for someone to access a particular key.

When keys are used to secure data transmissions, the computer generates two different types of keys:

▶ **Public key**: A nonsecret key that forms half of a cryptographic key pair used with a public key algorithm. The public key is freely given to all potential receivers.

▶ **Private key:** The secret half of a cryptographic key pair used with a public key algorithm. The private part of the public key cryptography system is never transmitted over a network.

Keys can be used in two different ways to secure data communications:

▶ Public (asymmetric) key encryption uses both a private and public key to encrypt and decrypt messages. The public key is used to encrypt a message or verify a signature, and the private key is used to decrypt the message or to sign a document. Figure 10.4 shows a public (asymmetric) key encryption.

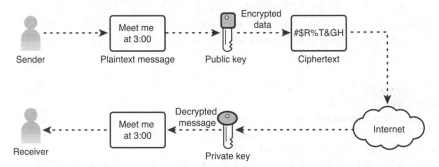

FIGURE 10.4 **Public (asymmetric) key encryption.**

▶ Private (symmetric) key encryption uses a single key for both encryption and decryption. If a person possesses the key, he or she can both encrypt and decrypt messages. Unlike public keys, this single secret key cannot be shared with anyone except people who should be permitted to decrypt as well as encrypt messages.

ExamAlert

Be prepared to answer questions on both public and private keys.

Where Is PKI Used?

The following list discusses areas in which PKI is normally used. Knowing what PKI is used for gives you a better idea of whether it is needed in a particular network.

▶ **Web security**: As you know, the Internet is an unsecured network. PKI increases web security by offering server authentication, which enables client systems to validate that the server they communicate with is indeed the intended sever. Without this information, it is possible for people to place themselves between the client and the server and intercept client data by pretending to be the server. PKI also offers client authentication, which validates the client's identity.

▶ **Confidentiality**: PKI provides secure data transmissions using encryption strategies between the client and the server. In application, PKI works with the Secure Socket Layer (SSL) protocol and the Transport Layer Security (TLS) protocol to provide secure HTTP transfers, referred to as Hypertext Transport Protocol Secure (HTTPS). To take advantage of the SSL and TLS protocols, both the client system and the server require certificates issued by a mutually trusted certificate authority (CA).

> **Note**
>
> SSL was first created for use with the Netscape web browser and is used with a limited number of TCP/IP protocols (such as HTTP and FTP). TLS is not only an enhancement to SSL, but also a replacement for it, working with almost every TCP/IP protocol. Because of this TLS is popular with VPNs and VoIP applications. Just as Kleenex is often used to represent any paper tissue whether it is made by Kimberly-Clark, SSL is often the term used to signify the confidentiality function whether it is actually SSL in use or TLS, the latest version of which is 1.2.

SSL VPN, also marketed as WebVPN an OpenVPN, can be used to connect locations that would run into trouble with firewalls and NAT when used with IPSec. It is known as an SSL VPN whether the encryption is done with SSL or TLS. The National Institute of Standards and Technology (NIST) publishes the Guide to SSL VPNs which can be accessed at http://csrc.nist.gov/publications/nistpubs/800-113/SP800-113.pdf.

▶ **Digital signatures**: Digital signatures are the electronic equivalent of a sealed envelope and are intended to ensure that a file has not been altered in transit. Any file with a digital signature is used to verify not only the publishers of the content or file, but also to verify the content integrity at the time of download. On the network, PKI enables you to issue certificates to internal developers/contractors and enables any employee to verify the origin and integrity of downloaded applications.

▶ **Secure email**: Today's organizations rely heavily on email to provide external and internal communications. Some of the information sent via email is not sensitive and does not need security, but for communications that contain sensitive data, a method is needed to secure email content. PKI can be deployed as a method for securing email transactions. In application, a private key is used to digitally sign outgoing emails, and the sender's certificate is sent with the email so that the recipient of the email can verify the sender's signature.

> **ExamAlert**
>
> Certificatess are the cornerstones of the PKI. A certificate is essentially a form of electronic credential that validates users, computers, or devices on the network. A certificate is a digitally signed statement that associates the credentials of a public key to the identity of the person, device, or service that holds the corresponding private key.

RADIUS and TACACS+

Among the potential issues network administrators face when implementing remote access are utilization and the load on the remote-access server. As a network's remote-access implementation grows, reliance on a single remote-access server might be impossible, and additional servers might be required. RADIUS can help in this scenario.

> **ExamAlert**
>
> RADIUS is a protocol that enables a single server to become responsible for all remote-access authentication, authorization, and auditing (or accounting) services.

RADIUS functions as a client/server system. The remote user dials in to the remote-access server, which acts as a RADIUS client, or network access server (NAS), and connects to a RADIUS server. The RADIUS server performs authentication, authorization, and auditing (or accounting) functions and returns the information to the RADIUS client (which is a remote-access server running RADIUS client software); the connection is either established or rejected based on the information received.

Terminal Access Controller Access Control System+ (TACACS+) is a security protocol designed to provide centralized validation of users who are attempting to gain access to a router or Network Access Server (NAS). Like RADIUS, TACACS+ is a set of security protocols designed to provide authentication, authorization, and accounting (AAA) of remote users. TACACS uses TCP port 49 by default.

Although both RADIUS and TACACS+ offer AAA services for remote users, some noticeable differences exist:

▶ TACACS+ relies on TCP for connection-oriented delivery. RADIUS uses connectionless UDP for data delivery.

▶ RADIUS combines authentication and authorization, whereas TACACS+ can separate their functions.

> **ExamAlert**
>
> Both RADIUS and TACACS+ provide authentication, authorization, and accounting services. One notable difference between TACACS+ and RADIUS is that TACACS+ relies on the connection-oriented TCP, whereas RADIUS uses the connectionless UDP.

Remote Authentication Protocols

One of the most significant decisions an administrator needs to make when designing a remote-access strategy is the method by which remote users will be authenticated. Authentication is simply the way in which the client and server negotiate a user's credentials when the user tries to gain access to the network. The exact protocol used by an organization depends on its security policies. The authentication methods may include the following:

▶ **Microsoft Challenge Handshake Authentication Protocol (MS-CHAP)**: Authenticates remote Windows workstations, providing the functionality to which LAN-based users are accustomed while integrating the hashing algorithms used on Windows networks. MS-CHAP works with PPP, PPTP, and L2TP network connections. MS-CHAP uses a challenge/response mechanism to keep the password from being sent during the authentication process. MS-CHAP uses the Message Digest 5 (MD5) hashing algorithm and the Data Encryption Standard (DES) encryption algorithm to generate the challenge and response. It provides mechanisms for reporting connection errors and for changing the user's password.

▶ **Microsoft Challenge Handshake Authentication Protocol version 2 (MS-CHAP v2)**: Brings with it enhancements over its predecessor, MS-CHAP. These enhancements include support for two-way authentication and a few changes in how the cryptographic key is analyzed. As far as authentication methods are concerned, MS-CHAP version 2 is the most secure. MS-CHAP works with PPP, PPTP, and L2TP network connections.

▶ **Extensible Authentication Protocol (EAP)**: An extension of PPP that supports authentication methods that go beyond the simple submission of a username and password. EAP was developed in response to an increasing demand for authentication methods that use other types of security devices such as token cards, smart cards, and digital certificates.

▶ **Challenge Handshake Authentication Protocol (CHAP)**: A widely supported authentication method that works much the same way as MS-CHAP. A key difference between the two is that CHAP supports non-Microsoft remote-access clients. CHAP enables for authentication without actually having the user send his password over the network. Because it's an industry standard, it enables Windows Server 2008/2003 and Windows 7/Vista to behave as a remote client to almost any third-party PPP server.

▶ **Password Authentication Protocol (PAP)**: Use PAP only if necessary. PAP is a simple authentication protocol in which the username and password are sent to the remote-access server in clear text, making it possible for anyone listening to network traffic to steal both. PAP typically is used only when connecting to older UNIX-based remote-access servers that do not support any additional authentication protocols.

▶ **Unauthenticated access**: Users are allowed to log on without authentication.

Choosing the correct authentication protocol for remote clients is an important part of designing a secure remote-access strategy. After they are authenticated, users have access to the network and servers. It is recommended that administrators start with the most secure protocol, MS-CHAP v2, and step down the list.

> **ExamAlert**
>
> You should be familiar with the different remote-access authentication methods and know where and when they may be used.

Secured Versus Unsecured Protocols

As you know, any network needs a number of protocols to function. This includes both LAN and WAN protocols. Not all protocols are created the same. Some are designed for secure transfer, and others are not. Table 10.1 lists several protocols and describes their use.

TABLE 10.1 **Protocol Summary**

Protocol	Name	Description
FTP	File Transfer Protocol	A protocol for uploading and downloading files to and from a remote host. Also accommodates basic file management tasks.
SFTP	Secure File Transfer Protocol	A protocol for securely uploading and downloading files to and from a remote host. Based on SSH security.
HTTP	Hypertext Transfer Protocol	A protocol for retrieving files from a web server. Data is sent in clear text.
HTTPS	Hypertext Transfer Protocol Secure	A secure protocol for retrieving files from a web server. HTTPS uses SSL to encrypt data between the client and host.
Telnet	Telnet	Enables sessions to be opened on a remote host.
SSH	Secure Shell	A secure alternative to Telnet that enables secure sessions to be opened on a remote host.
TLS	Transport Layer Security	A cryptographic protocol whose purpose is to verity that secure communications between a server and a client remain secure. TLS is an enhancement/replacement for SSL.
ISAKMP	Internet Security Association and Key Management Protocol	Provides an independent framework for authentication and key exchange. The actual implementation is usually done by IPSec but could be handled by any implementation capable of negotiating, modifying, and deleting security associations.
RSH	A UNIX utility used to run a command on a remote machine	Replaced by SSH because RSH sends all data in clear text.
SCP	Secure Copy Protocol	Enables files to be securely copied between two systems. Uses Secure Shell (SSH) technology to provide encryption services.
RCP	Remote Copy Protocol	Copies files between systems, but transport is not secured.
SNMPv1/2	Simple Network Management Protocol versions 1 and 2	A network monitoring system used to monitor the network's condition. Both SNMPv1 and v2 are not secured.
SNMPv3	Simple Network Management Protocol version 3	An enhanced SNMP service offering both encryption and authentication services.

> **Exam Alert**
>
> You will most certainly be asked questions on secure protocols and when they might be used. Review Table 10.1 before taking the Network+ exam.

Adding Physical Security to the Mix

Physical security is a combination of good sense and procedure. The purpose of physical security is to restrict access to network equipment to only people who need it.

The extent to which physical security measures can be implemented to protect network devices and data depends largely on their location. For instance, if a server is installed in a cabinet located in a general office area, the only practical physical protection is to make sure that the cabinet door is locked and that access to keys for the cabinet is controlled. It might be practical to use other antitheft devices, but that depends on the exact location of the cabinet.

On the other hand, if your server equipment is located in a cupboard or dedicated room, access restrictions for the room are easier to implement and can be more effective. Again, access should be limited to only those who need it. Depending on the size of the room, this factor might introduce a number of other factors.

Servers and other key networking components are those to which you need to apply the greatest level of physical security. Nowadays, most organizations choose to locate servers in a cupboard or a specific room.

Access to the server room should be tightly controlled, and all access doors must be secured by some method, whether it is a lock and key or a retinal scanning system. Each method of server room access control has certain characteristics. Whatever the method of server room access, it should follow one common principle—control. Some access control methods provide more control than others.

Lock and Key

If access is controlled by lock and key, the number of people with a key should be restricted to only those people who need access. Spare keys should be stored in a safe location, and access to them should be controlled.

Following are some of the features of lock-and-key security:

▶ **Inexpensive**: Even a good lock system costs only a few hundred dollars.

▶ **Easy to maintain**: With no back-end systems and no configuration, using a lock and key is the easiest access control method.

▶ **Less control than other methods**: Keys can be lost, copied, and loaned to other people. There is no record of access to the server room and no way to prove that the key holder is entitled to enter.

> **Tip**
>
> If you use a lock and key for security, make sure that all copies of the original key are stamped DO NOT COPY. That way, it is more difficult for someone to get a copy because reputable key cutters will not make copies of such keys.

Swipe Card and PIN Access

If budgets and policies permit, swipe card and PIN entry systems are good choices for managing physical access to a server room. Swipe card systems use a credit-card-sized plastic card read by a reader on the outside of the door. To enter the server room, you must swipe the card (run it through the reader), at which point it is read by the reader, which validates it. Usually, the swipe card's use to enter the room is logged by the card system, making it possible for the logs to be checked. In higher-security installations, it is common to have a swipe card reader on the inside of the room as well so that a person's exit can be recorded.

Although swipe card systems have relatively few disadvantages, they do need specialized equipment so that they can be coded with users' information. They also have the same drawbacks as keys in that they can be lost or loaned to other people. Of course, the advantage that swipe cards have over key systems is that swipe cards are hard to copy.

PIN pads can be used alone or with a swipe card system. PIN pads have the advantage of not needing any kind of card or key that can be lost. For the budget conscious, PIN pad systems that do not have any logging or monitoring capability can be purchased for a reasonable price. Following are some of the characteristics of swipe card and PIN pad systems:

▶ **Moderately expensive**: Some systems, particularly those with management capabilities, are quite expensive.

▶ **Enhanced controls and logging**: Each time people enter the server room, they must key in a number or use a swipe card. This process enables systems to log who enters and when.

▶ **Some additional knowledge required**: Swipe card systems need special software and hardware that can configure the cards. Someone has to learn how to do this.

Biometrics

Although they might still seem like the realm of James Bond, biometric security systems are becoming far more common. Biometric systems work by using some unique characteristic of a person's identity—such as a fingerprint, a palm print, or even a retina scan—to validate that person's identity.

Although the price of biometric systems has been falling over recent years, they are not widely deployed in small to midsized networks. Not only are the systems themselves expensive, but also their installation, configuration, and maintenance must be considered. Following are some of the characteristics of biometric access control systems:

▶ **Very effective**: Because each person entering the room must supply proof-of-person evidence, verification of the person entering the server area is as close to 100% reliable as you can get.

▶ **Nothing to lose**: Because there are no cards or keys, nothing can be lost.

▶ **Expensive**: Biometric security systems and their attendant scanners and software are still relatively expensive and can be afforded only by organizations that have a larger budget; although, prices are sure to drop as more people turn to this method of access control.

Two-factor and Multifactor Authentication

When two or more access methods are included as part of the authentication process, you're implementing a *multifactor* system. A system that uses any two items—such as smart cards and passwords—is referred to as a *two-factor authentication* system. A multifactor system can consist of a two-factor system, three-factor system, and so on. As long as there is more than one factor involved in the authentication process, it is considered a multifactor system.

For obvious reasons, the two or more factors employed should not be from the same category. Although you do increase difficulty in gaining system access by requiring the user to enter two sets of username/password combinations, it is preferred to pair a single username/password combination with a biometric identifier or other check.

ExamAlert

Be sure you understand that two-factor authentication is a subset of multifactor authentication.

Cram Quiz

1. Which of the following protocols is used with HTTPS?

   ○ **A.** SSH

   ○ **B.** SSL

   ○ **C.** Proxy

   ○ **D.** IPSec

2. Which of the following is not an authentication protocol?

   ○ **A.** IPSec

   ○ **B.** CHAP

   ○ **C.** PAP

   ○ **D.** EAP

3. Which of the following is the strongest password?

   ○ **A.** password

   ○ **B.** WE300GO

   ○ **C.** 100KalivE

   ○ **D.** lovethemusic

4. You are onsite as a consultant. The client's many remote-access users experience connection problems. Basically, when users try to connect, the system cannot service their authentication requests. What kind of server might you recommend to alleviate this problem?

   ○ **A.** RADIUS server

   ○ **B.** IPSec server

   ○ **C.** Proxy server

   ○ **D.** Kerberos server

5. Which of the following services or protocols use SSH technology to provide additional security to communications? (Choose two.)

   ○ **A.** SCP

   ○ **B.** SFTP

   ○ **C.** SNMP

   ○ **D.** SMTP

Cram Quiz Answers

1. **B.** HTTPS uses SSL to create secure connections over the Internet. Answer A is incorrect because SSH provides a secure multiplatform replacement for Telnet. Answer C is invalid because it is a service and not a protocol. Answer D is incorrect because IPSec is designed to encrypt data during communication between two computers.

2. **A.** IPSec is not an authentication protocol. All the other protocols listed are authentication protocols.

3. **C.** Strong passwords include a combination of letters and numbers and upper- and lowercase letters. Answer C is by far the strongest password. Answer A is not a strong password because it is a standard word, contains no numbers, and is all lowercase. Answer B mixes letters and numbers, and it is not a recognized word, so it is a strong password, but it is not as strong as answer C. Answer D is too easy to guess and contains no numbers.

4. **A.** By installing a RADIUS server, you can move the workload associated with authentication to a dedicated server. A proxy server would not improve the dialup connection's performance. There is no such thing as a Kerberos server or an IPSec server.

5. **A** and **B.** Secure Shell (SSH) technology is used by both Secure Copy Protocol (SCP) and Secure File Transfer Protocol (SFTP). Answers C and D are incorrect because Simple Network Management Protocol (SNMP) and Simple Mail Transfer Protocol (SMTP) do not use SSH technology for additional security.

Managing Common Security Threats

▶ **Explain common threats, vulnerabilities, and mitigation techniques.**

Cram**Saver**

If you can correctly answer these questions before going through this section, save time by skimming the Exam Alerts in this section and then complete the Cram Quiz at the end of the section.

1. What are some of the more common potential risks to computer systems?

2. What type of malware covertly gathers system information through the user's Internet connection without his or her knowledge, usually for advertising purposes?

Answers

1. Viruses, Trojan horses, and worms all present a potential risk to computer systems.

2. Spyware covertly gathers system information through the user's Internet connection without his or her knowledge, usually for advertising purposes.

Malicious software, or malware, is a serious problem in today's computing environments. It is often assumed that malware is composed of viruses. Although this typically is true, many other forms of malware by definition are not viruses, but are equally undesirable.

Malware encompasses many different types of malicious software:

▶ **Viruses**: Software programs or code loaded onto a computer without the user's knowledge. After it is loaded, the virus performs some form of undesirable action on the computer.

▶ **Macro viruses**: Although they are still a form of virus, macro viruses are specifically designed to damage office or text documents.

▶ **Worms**: Worms are a nasty form of software that automatically and silently propagate without modifying software or alerting the user. After they are inside a system, they can carry out their intended harm, whether it is to damage data or relay sensitive information.

▶ **Trojan horses**: Trojan horses appear as helpful or harmless programs but when installed carry and deliver a malicious payload. A Trojan horse virus might, for example, appear to be a harmless or free online game but when activated is actually malware.

▶ **Spyware**: Spyware covertly gathers system information through the user's Internet connection without his or her knowledge, usually for advertising purposes. Spyware applications typically are bundled as a hidden component of freeware or shareware programs that can be downloaded from the Internet.

Viruses

Viruses and their effects are well documented and are feared by users and administrators alike. The damage from viruses varies greatly, from disabling an entire network to damaging applications on a single system. Regardless of the impact, viruses can be destructive, causing irreplaceable data loss and consuming hours of productivity.

As mentioned, not all the malware encountered is by definition a virus. To be considered a virus, the malware must possess the following characteristics:

▶ It must be able to replicate itself.

▶ It requires a host program as a carrier.

▶ It must be activated or executed in order to run.

Many different types of viruses exist:

▶ **Resident virus**: A resident virus installs itself into the operating system and stays there. It typically places itself in memory and from there infects and does damage. The resident loads with the operating system on boot.

▶ **Variant virus**: Like any other applications, from time to time viruses are enhanced to make them harder to detect and to modify the damage they do. Modifications to existing viruses are called variants because they are rereleased versions of known viruses.

▶ **Polymorphic virus**: One particularly hard-to-handle type of virus is the polymorphic. It can change its characteristics to avoid detection. Polymorphic viruses are some of the most difficult types to detect and remove.

▶ **Overwriting/nonoverwriting virus**: Viruses can be designed to over-write files or code and replace them with modified data. In many cases the application can function as normal so that the user does not know the program has been modified. Nonoverwriting viruses amend an application by adding files or code.

▶ **Stealth virus**: A stealth virus can hide itself to avoid detection. Such viruses often fool detection programs by appearing as legitimate pro-grams or hiding within legitimate programs.

▶ **Macro virus**: Macro viruses are designed to infect and corrupt docu-ments. Because documents are commonly shared, these viruses can spread at an alarming rate.

> **Exam Alert**
>
> Be prepared to identify the types of viruses and the differences between a virus, Trojan horse, and worm.

Worms and Trojan Horses

Trojan horses, as the name implies, are about hiding. Trojan horses come hid-den in other programs. For example, a Trojan horse can be hidden in a share-ware game. The game looks harmless, but when it is downloaded and execut-ed, the Trojan is operating in the background, corrupting and damaging the system.

Trojan horses are different from viruses because they do not replicate them-selves and do not require a host program to run. They are commonly found on P2P sharing networks where interesting and helpful-looking programs are actually disguised Trojan horses. Trojan horses are also spread when programs are shared using email communications or removable media. In the past, many executable jokes sent through email, such as cartoons and amusing games, were the front end of a Trojan horse.

Worms are different and have the potential to spread faster than any other form of malware. Worms can be differentiated from viruses. Although they can replicate, they do not require a host and do not require user intervention to propagate. Worms can spread at an alarming rate because they often exploit security holes in applications or operating systems. As soon as a security hole is found, worms automatically begin to replicate, looking for new hosts with the same vulnerability. Worms look for an Internet connection and then use that connection to replicate without any user intervention. Table 10.2 describes the differences between worms, Trojan horses, and viruses.

TABLE 10.2 **Comparing Malware Types**

Malware Type	Replication	Host Required?	User Intervention Required?
Virus	Can self-replicate	Requires a host program to propagate	Needs to be activated or executed by a user.
Trojan horse	Does not replicate itself	Does not require a host program	The user must execute the program in which the Trojan horse is hidden.
Worm	Self-replicates without user intervention	Self-contained and does not require a host	Replicates and activates without requiring user intervention.

> **ExamAlert**
>
> Know the malware types that appear in Table 10.2.

Denial of Service and Distributed Denial of Service Attacks

Denial of service (DoS) attacks are designed to tie up network bandwidth and resources and eventually bring the entire network to a halt. This type of attack is done simply by flooding a network with more traffic than it can handle. A DoS attack is not designed to steal data but rather to cripple a network and, in doing so, cost a company huge amounts of dollars.

The effects of DoS attacks include the following:

▶ Saturating network resources, which then renders those services unusable

▶ Flooding the network media, preventing communication between computers on the network

▶ Causing user downtime because of an inability to access required services

▶ Causing potentially huge financial losses for an organization due to network and service downtime.

Types of Denial of Service Attacks

Several different types of DoS attacks exist, and each seems to target a different area. For instance, they might target bandwidth, network service, memory, CPU, or hard drive space. When a server or other system is overrun by malicious requests, one or more of these core resources breaks down, causing the system to crash or stop responding.

Fraggle

In a Fraggle attack, spoofed UDP packets are sent to a network's broadcast address. These packets are directed to specific ports, such as port 7 or port 19, and, after they are connected, can flood the system.

Smurf

The *Smurf attack* is similar to a Fraggle attack. However, a ping request is sent to a broadcast network address, with the sending address spoofed so that many ping replies overload the victim and prevent it from processing the replies.

Ping of Death

In a *ping of death* attack, an oversized ICMP datagram is used to crash IP devices that were manufactured before 1996.

SYN flood

In a typical TCP session, communication between two computers is initially established by a three-way handshake, referred to as a SYN, SYN/ACK, ACK. At the start of a session, the client sends a SYN message to the server. The server acknowledges the request by sending a SYN/ACK message back to the client. The connection is established when the client responds with an ACK message.

In a *SYN attack*, the victim is overwhelmed with a flood of SYN packets. Every SYN packet forces the targeted server to produce a SYN-ACK response and then wait for the ACK acknowledgment. However, the attacker doesn't respond with an ACK or spoofs its destination IP address with a non-existent address so that no ACK response occurs. The result is that the server begins filling up with half-open connections. When all the server's available resources are tied up on half-open connections, it stops acknowledging new incoming SYN requests, including legitimate ones.

Buffer Overflow

A *buffer overflow* is a type of denial of service attack that occurs when more data is put into a buffer than it can hold, thereby overflowing it (as the name implies).

ICMP flood

An *ICMP flood*, also known as a ping flood, is a denial of service attack in which large numbers of ICMP messages are sent to a computer system to overwhelm it. The result is a failure of the TCP/IP protocol stack, which cannot tend to other TCP/IP requests.

Other Common Attacks

This section details some of the more common attacks used today.

Password Attacks

Password attacks are one of the most common types of attacks. Typically, usernames are easy to obtain. Matching the username with the password allows the intruder to gain system access to the level associated with that particular user. This access is why it is vital to protect administrator passwords. Obtaining a password with administrator privileges provides the intruder with unrestricted access to the system or network.

Social Engineering

Social engineering is a common form of cracking. It can be used by both outsiders and people within an organization. *Social engineering* is a hacker term for tricking people into revealing their password or some form of security information. It might include trying to get users to send passwords or other information over email, shoulder surfing, or any other method that tricks users into divulging information. Social engineering is an attack that attempts to take advantage of human behavior.

Eavesdropping

As the name implies, *eavesdropping* involves an intruder who obtains sensitive information such as passwords, data, and procedures for performing functions by intercepting, listening to, and analyzing network communications. An intruder can eavesdrop by wiretapping, using radio, or using auxiliary ports on terminals. Intruders can also eavesdrop using software that monitors packets sent over the network. In most cases, it is difficult to detect eavesdropping, making it essential to ensure that sensitive data is not sent over the network in clear text.

Back Door Attacks

In a *back door attack*, an attacker gains access to a computer or program by bypassing standard security mechanisms. For instance, a programmer might install a back door so that the program can be accessed for troubleshooting or other purposes. Sometimes, as discussed earlier, nonessential services are installed by default, and it is possible to gain access using one of these unused services.

Man-in-the-Middle Attack

In a *man-in-the-middle attack*, the intruder places himself between the sending and receiving devices and captures the communication as it passes by. The interception of the data is invisible to those actually sending and receiving the data. The intruder can capture the network data and manipulate it, change it, examine it, and then send it on. Wireless communications are particularly susceptible to this type of attack. A rogue access point is an example of a man-in-the-middle attack. If the attack is done with ftp (using the `port` command), then it is known as an *FTP bounce* attack.

Spoofing

Spoofing is a technique in which the real source of a transmission, file, or email is concealed or replaced with a fake source. This technique enables an attacker, for example, to misrepresent the original source of a file available for download. Then he can trick users into accepting a file from an untrusted source, believing it is coming from a trusted source.

Rogue Access Points

A *rogue access point* describes a situation in which a wireless access point has been placed on a network without the administrator's knowledge. The result is that it is possible to remotely access the rogue access point because it likely does not adhere to company security policies. So all security can be compromised by a cheap wireless router placed on the corporate network. An *evil twin* attack is one in which a rogue wireless access point poses as a legitimate wireless service provider to intercept information users transmit.

Advertising Wireless Weaknesses

These attacks start with *war driving*—driving around with a laptop looking for open wireless access points with which to communicate and looking for weak implementations that can be cracked (*WEP cracking* or *WPA cracking*). They then lead to *war chalking*—those who discover a way in to the network leave signals (often written in chalk) on, or outside, the premise to notify others that the vulnerability is there. The marks can be on the sidewalk, the side of the building, a nearby signpost, and so on.

Phishing

Often users receive a variety of emails offering products, services, information, or opportunities. Unsolicited email of this type is called *phishing* (pronounced "fishing"). This technique involves a bogus offer sent to hundreds of thousands or even millions of email addresses. The strategy plays the odds. For every 1,000 emails sent, perhaps one person replies. Phishing can be dangerous because users can be tricked into divulging personal information such as credit card numbers or bank account information.

> **ExamAlert**
>
> Be ready to identify the types of attacks just described. You can expect a question on the exam about these types of attacks.

An Ounce of Prevention

The threat from malicious code is a real concern. You need to take precautions to protect your systems. Although you might not eliminate the threat, you can significantly reduce it.

One of the primary tools used in the fight against malicious software is antivirus software. Antivirus software is available from a number of companies, and each offers similar features and capabilities. The following is a list of the common features and characteristics of antivirus software:

▸ **Real-time protection**: An installed antivirus program should continuously monitor the system looking for viruses. If a program is downloaded, an application opened, or a suspicious email received, the real-time virus monitor detects and removes the threat. The virus application sits in the background, largely unnoticed by the user.

▸ **Virus scanning**: An antivirus program must scan selected drives and disks, either locally or remotely. You can manually run scanning or schedule it to run at a particular time.

▸ **Scheduling**: It is a best practice to schedule virus scanning to occur automatically at a predetermined time. In a network environment, this typically is off hours, when the overhead of the scanning process won't impact users.

- **Live updates**: New viruses and malicious software are released with alarming frequency. It is recommended that the antivirus software be configured to regularly receive virus updates.

- **Email vetting**: Emails represent one of the primary sources of virus delivery. It is essential to use antivirus software that provides email scanning for both inbound and outbound email.

- **Centralized management**: If used in a network environment, it is a good idea to use software that supports managing the virus program from the server. Virus updates and configurations need to be made only on the server, not on each individual client station.

Managing the threat from viruses is considered a proactive measure, with antivirus software only part of the solution. A complete virus protection strategy requires many aspects to help limit the risk of viruses:

- **Develop in-house policies and rules**: In a corporate environment or even a small office, you need to establish what information can be placed on a system. For example, should users download programs from the Internet? Can users bring in their own storage media, such as USB flash drives?

- **Monitoring virus threats**: With new viruses coming out all the time, you need to check whether new viruses have been released and what they are designed to do.

- **Educate users**: One of the keys to a complete antivirus solution is to train users in virus prevention and recognition techniques. If users know what to look for, they can prevent a virus from entering the system or network. Back up copies of important documents. It should be mentioned that no solution is absolute, so care should be taken to ensure that the data is backed up. In the event of a malicious attack, redundant information is available in a secure location.

- **Automate virus scanning and updates**: You can configure today's antivirus software to automatically scan and update itself. Because such tasks can be forgotten and overlooked, it is recommended that you have these processes scheduled to run at predetermined times.

- **Patches and updates**: All applications, including productivity software, virus checkers, and especially the operating system, release patches and updates often designed to address potential security weaknesses. Administrators must keep an eye out for these patches and install them when they are released.

Cram Quiz

1. What type of virus can hide itself to avoid detection?
   - ○ **A.** Macro
   - ○ **B.** Stealth
   - ○ **C.** Partite
   - ○ **D.** Worm

2. Which of the following is an attack in which a rogue wireless access point poses as a legitimate wireless service provider to intercept information users transmit?
   - ○ **A.** Pharming
   - ○ **B.** Phishing
   - ○ **C.** Evil twin
   - ○ **D.** Social Engineering

3. Which of the following is a type of denial of service attack that occurs when more data is put into a buffer than it can hold?
   - ○ **A.** Dictionary attack
   - ○ **B.** Buffer overflow
   - ○ **C.** Worm
   - ○ **D.** Trojan horse

4. Which of the following is an attack in which something that appears as a helpful or harmless program carries and delivers a malicious payload?
   - ○ **A.** Worm
   - ○ **B.** Phish
   - ○ **C.** Evil twin
   - ○ **D.** Trojan horse

5. Which of the following is an attack in which users are tricked into revealing their passwords or some form of security information?
   - ○ **A.** Pharming
   - ○ **B.** Phishing
   - ○ **C.** Evil twin
   - ○ **D.** Social Engineering

Cram Quiz Answers

1. **B.** A stealth virus can hide itself to avoid detection. Such viruses often fool detection programs by appearing as legitimate programs or hiding within legitimate programs.

2. **C.** An evil twin attack is one in which a rogue wireless access point poses as a legitimate wireless service provider to intercept information users transmit.

3. **B.** A buffer overflow is a type of denial of service (DoS) attack that occurs when more data is put into a buffer than it can hold.

4. **D.** Trojan horses appear as helpful or harmless programs but, when installed, carry and deliver a malicious payload.

5. **D.** Social engineering is a term for tricking people (users) into revealing their passwords or some form of security information.

Firewalls and Other Appliances

▶ Given a scenario, install and configure a basic firewall.

▶ Categorize different types of network security appliances and methods.

Cram**Saver**

If you can correctly answer these questions before going through this section, save time by skimming the Exam Alerts in this section and then complete the Cram Quiz at the end of the section.

1. What are some of the services a firewall often provides?

2. What is the primary difference between an IDS and an IPS?

3. What is the scope of a firewall?

Answers

1. A firewall often provides such services as NAT, proxy, and packet filtering.

2. An IDS is a passive security measure, and the IPS is a reactive security measure.

3. A firewall can be either host-based, on a single system, or network-based, protecting systems networkwide.

In today's network environments, firewalls protect systems from both external and internal threats. Although firewalls initially became popular in corporate environments, most home networks with a broadband Internet connection now also implement a firewall to protect against Internet-borne threats.

Essentially a firewall is an application, device, system, or group of systems that controls the flow of traffic between two networks. The most common use of a firewall is to protect a private network from a public network such as the Internet. However, firewalls are also increasingly used to separate a sensitive area of a private network from less-sensitive areas.

At its most basic, a firewall is a device (a computer system running firewall software or a dedicated hardware device) that has more than one network interface. It manages the flow of network traffic between those interfaces. How it manages the flow and what it does with certain types of traffic depends on its configuration. Figure 10.5 shows a firewall configuration.

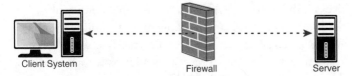

FIGURE 10.5   **A firewall separating a client and server.**

Strictly speaking, a firewall performs no action on the packets it receives besides the basic functions just described. However, in a real-world implementation, a firewall is likely to offer other functionality, such as Network Address Translation (NAT) and proxy server services. Without NAT, any host on the internal network that needs to send or receive data through the firewall needs a registered IP address. Although such environments exist, most people have to settle and use a private address range on the internal network. Therefore, they rely on the firewall system to translate the outgoing request into an acceptable public network address.

Although the fundamental purpose of a firewall is to protect one network from another, you need to configure the firewall to allow some traffic through. If you don't need to allow traffic to pass through a firewall, you can dispense with it and completely separate your network from others.

A firewall can employ a variety of methods to ensure security. In addition to the role just described, modern firewall applications can perform a range of other functions, often through the addition of add-on modules:

▶ **Content filtering**: Most firewalls can be configured to provide some level of content filtering. This can be done for both inbound and outbound content. For instance, the firewall can be configured to monitor inbound content, restricting certain locations or particular websites. Firewalls can also limit outbound traffic by prohibiting access to certain websites by maintaining a list of URLs and IP addresses. This is often done when organizations want to control employee access to Internet sites.

▶ **Signature identification**: A signature is a unique identifier for a particular application. In the antivirus world, a signature is an algorithm that uniquely identifies a specific virus. Firewalls can be configured to detect certain signatures associated with malware or other undesirable applications and block them before they enter the network.

▶ **Virus scanning services**: As web pages are downloaded, content within the pages can be checked for viruses. This feature is attractive to companies concerned about potential threats from Internet-based sources.

▶ **Network Address Translation (NAT)**: To protect the identity of machines on the internal network, and to allow more flexibility in internal TCP/IP addressing structures, many firewalls translate the originating address of data into a different address. This address is then used on the Internet. The most common type of NAT is port address translation (PAT), enabling multiple devices on the network to share one single public address (or a few). NAT is a popular function because it works around the limited availability of TCP/IP addresses in IPv4. When the migration to IPv6 becomes complete, the need for NAT will lessen.

▶ **URL filtering**: By using a variety of methods, the firewall can choose to block certain websites from being accessed by clients within the organization. This blocking allows companies to control what pages can be viewed and by whom.

▶ **Bandwidth management**: Although it's required in only certain situations, bandwidth management can prevent a certain user or system from hogging the network connection. The most common approach to bandwidth management is to divide the available bandwidth into sections and then make just a certain section available to a user or system.

These functions are not strictly firewall activities. However, the flexibility offered by a firewall, coupled with its placement at the edge of a network, makes a firewall the ideal base for controlling access to external resources.

ExamAlert

Security is represented well in the Network+ objectives. You can expect to see exam questions on the types of firewalls and their characteristics. For example, you should know the differences between software and hardware firewalls and understand stateful inspection versus packet filtering firewalls.

Stateful and Stateless Firewalls

When talking about firewalls, two terms often come up: stateful and stateless. These two terms differentiate how firewalls operate. A stateless firewall, sometimes called a packet-filtering firewall, monitors specific data packets and restricts or allows access to the network based on certain criteria. Stateless firewalls look at each data packet in isolation and therefore are unaware if that particular data packet is part of a larger data stream. Essentially, stateless firewalls do not see the big picture or "state" of data flow, only the individual packets. Today, stateful firewalls are more likely to be used. Stateful firewalls monitor data traffic streams from one end to the other. A stateful firewall refuses unsolicited incoming traffic that does not comply with dynamic or preconfigured firewall exception rules. A stateful firewall tracks the state of network connections, watching data traffic, including monitoring source and destination addresses and TCP and UDP port numbers.

ExamAlert

A stateless firewall examines the information within a data packet and rejects or accepts the packet based on the source or destination address or port number listed in the packet header. Stateful firewalls have features allowing them not only to examine individual packets but also to examine packet streams at the application layer (DNS, SMTP, POP3, SNMP).

Packet-Filtering Firewalls

Packet filtering enables the firewall to examine each packet that passes through it and determine what to do with it based on the configuration. A packet-filtering firewall deals with packets at the data link layer (Layer 2) and network layer (Layer 3) of the Open Systems Interconnect (OSI) model. The following are some of the criteria by which packet filtering can be implemented:

▶ **IP address**: By using the IP address as a parameter, the firewall can allow or deny traffic based on the source or destination IP address. For example, you can configure the firewall so that only certain hosts on the internal network can access hosts on the Internet. Alternatively, you can configure it so that only certain hosts on the Internet can gain access to a system on the internal network.

▶ **Port number**: The TCP/IP suite uses port numbers to identify which service a certain packet is destined for. By configuring the firewall to allow certain types of traffic, you can control the flow. You might, for example, open port 80 on the firewall to allow Hypertext Transfer Protocol (HTTP) requests from users on the Internet to reach the corporate web server. Depending on the application, you might also open the HTTP Secure (HTTPS) port, port 443, to allow access to a secure web server application.

Windows Firewall in Windows 7 enables you to configure which programs are allowed through the private network and the public network by checking boxes associated with the programs/features. Figure 10.6 shows an example of the configuration options.

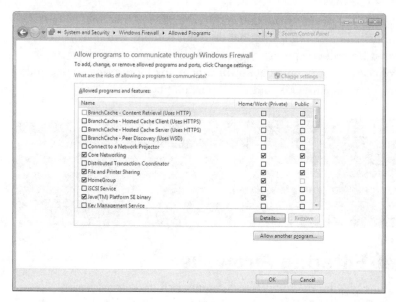

FIGURE 10.6   **Configuration of the software-based Windows Firewall in Windows 7.**

▶ **Protocol ID**: Because each packet transmitted with IP has a protocol identifier, a firewall can read this value and then determine what kind of packet it is. If you filter based on protocol ID, you specify which protocols you will and will not allow to pass through the firewall.

▶ **Implicit deny**: An *implicit deny* means that if the proviso in question has not been explicitly granted, then it is denied. If you explicitly say that you will allow traffic in from ports 21, 80, and 443, then all those not mentioned are implicitly denied access. The entity (traffic/data in this case) is denied access based on its not appearing on the list of entities accepted. Although an implicit deny can apply to firewall configuration, the same principle can apply to an access control list (ACL), MAC address, or any similar configuration option.

▶ **MAC address**: This is perhaps the least used of the packet-filtering methods discussed, but you can configure a firewall to use the hardware-configured MAC address as the determining factor in whether access to the network is granted. This is not a particularly flexible method, and therefore it is suitable only in environments in which you can closely control who uses which MAC address. The Internet is not such an environment.

Circuit-Level Firewalls

Circuit-level firewalls are similar in operation to packet-filtering firewalls, but they operate at the transport and session layers of the OSI model. The biggest difference between a packet-filtering firewall and a circuit-level firewall is that a circuit-level firewall validates TCP and UDP sessions before opening a connection, or circuit, through the firewall. When the session is established, the firewall maintains a table of valid connections and lets data pass through when session information matches an entry in the table. The table entry is removed, and the circuit is closed when the session is terminated. Circuit-level firewalls that operate at the session layer, or Layer 5 of the OSI model, provided enough protection in terms of firewalls in their day. As attacks become more sophisticated and include application layer attacks, circuit-level firewalls might not provide enough protection by themselves.

Application Layer Firewalls

As the name suggests, application layer firewalls operate at the application layer of the OSI model. In operation, application layer firewalls can inspect data packets traveling to or from an application. This allows the firewall to inspect, modify, block, and even redirect data traffic as it sees fit. Application layer firewalls are sometimes called proxy firewalls because they can proxy in each direction. This means that the source and destination systems do not come in direct contact with each other. Instead, the firewall proxy serves as a middle point.

> **ExamAlert**
>
> Application layer firewalls offer a proxy service between the sending and receiving devices. Using proxy services, the firewall can filter the content to and from source and destination.

Comparing Firewall Types

The following list provides a quick comparison of the types of firewalls previously discussed:

▶ Packet-filtering firewalls operate at Layers 2 and 3 of the OSI model and are designed to monitor traffic based on such criteria as source, port, or destination service in individual IP packets. They're usually fast and transparent to users.

▶ Session layer firewalls are also known as circuit-level firewalls. Typically these firewalls use NAT to protect the internal network. These gateways have little or no connection to the application layer and therefore cannot filter more complicated connections. These firewalls can protect traffic on only a basic rule base such as source destination port.

▶ Application layer firewalls control browser, Telnet, and FTP traffic, prevent unwanted traffic, and perform logging and auditing of traffic passing through them.

Firewall Wrap-Up

Firewalls have become a necessity for organizations of all sizes. They are a common sight in businesses and homes alike. As the Internet becomes an increasingly hostile place, firewalls and the individuals who understand them are likely to become an essential part of the IT landscape.

ExamAlert

The three firewall methods described in this chapter are often combined into a single firewall application. Packet filtering is the basic firewall function. Circuit-level functionality provides NAT, and an application firewall provides proxy functionality. This is a good point to remember for the exam.

Note

When working with firewalls, you may hear the terms host-based and network-based firewalls. Network-based firewall systems monitor traffic on the entire network segment. Typically, a firewall server monitors and controls traffic to the entire network. An administrator monitors and controls the firewall services from a central location. A host-based firewall is installed on an individual system and monitors and controls inbound and outbound traffic for just that system.

Demilitarized Zones (Perimeter Network)

An important firewall-related concept is the *demilitarized zone* (DMZ), sometimes called a *perimeter network*. A DMZ is part of a network where you place servers that must be accessible by sources both outside and inside your network. However, the DMZ is not connected directly to either network, and it must always be accessed through the firewall. The military term DMZ is used because it describes an area that has little or no enforcement or policing.

Using DMZs gives your firewall configuration an extra level of flexibility, protection, and complexity. Figure 10.7 shows a DMZ configuration.

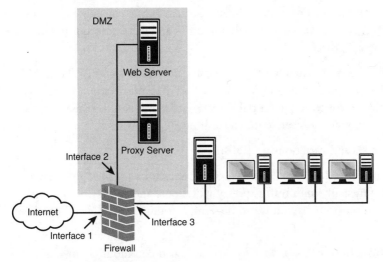

FIGURE 10.7 **A DMZ configuration.**

By using a DMZ, you can create an additional step that makes it more difficult for an intruder to gain access to the internal network. In Figure 10.7, for example, an intruder who tried to come in through Interface 1 would have to spoof a request from either the web server or proxy server into Interface 2 before it could be forwarded to the internal network. Although it is not impossible for an intruder to gain access to the internal network through a DMZ, it is difficult.

> **ExamAlert**
>
> Be prepared to identify the purpose of a DMZ.

Other Security Devices

A firewall is just one device you can use to help keep your networks secure. It is not, however, the only measure you can take. In many cases additional security strategies are required. Three mentioned in the CompTIA Network+ objectives are IDS/IPS, VPN concentrator, and vulnerability scanners.

An intrusion prevention system (IPS) is a network device that continually scans the network, looking for inappropriate activity. It can shut down any potential threats. The IPS looks for any known signatures of common attacks and automatically tries to prevent those attacks. An IPS is considered a reactive security measure because it actively monitors and can take steps to correct a potential security threat.

An intrusion detection system (IDS) is a passive detection system. The IDS can detect the presence of an attack and then log that information. It also can alert an administrator to the potential threat. The administrator then analyzes the situation and takes corrective measures if needed.

Following are several variations on IDSs:

▶ **Behavior-based**: A *behavior-based system* looks for variations in behavior such as unusually high traffic, policy violations, and so on. By looking for deviations in behavior, it can recognize potential threats and quickly respond.

▶ **Signature-based**: A *signature-based system*, also commonly known as *misuse-detection IDS (MD-IDS)*, is primarily focused on evaluating attacks based on attack signatures and audit trails. Attack signatures describe a generally established method of attacking a system. For example, a TCP flood attack begins with a large number of incomplete TCP sessions. If the MD-IDS knows what a TCP flood attack looks like, it can make an appropriate report or response to thwart the attack. This IDS uses an extensive database to determine the signature of the traffic.

▶ **Network-Based Intrusion Detection System (NIDS)**: The NIDS examines all network traffic to and from network systems. If it is software, it is installed on servers or other systems that can monitor inbound traffic. If it is hardware, it may be connected to a hub or switch to monitor traffic.

▶ **Host-Based Intrusion Detection System (HIDS)**: HIDS refers to applications such as spyware or virus applications that are installed on individual network systems. The HIDS monitors and creates logs on the local system.

> **ExamAlert**
>
> The four types of IDS/IPS tested on the exam are behavior-based, signature-based, network-based, and host-based.

▶ **Protocol-Based Intrusion Detection System (PIDS)**: The PIDS monitors and analyzes protocols communicating between network devices. A PIDS is often installed on a web server and analyzes traffic HTTP and HTTPS communications.

▶ **Application Protocol-Based Intrusion Detection System (APIDS)**: The APIDS monitors application-specific protocols.

In addition to IPS and IDS, you can use VPN concentrators to increase remote-access security. As mentioned in Chapter 1, "Introduction to Networking," a VPN provides a way to transfer network data securely over a public network. The data transfer is private, but the network is public or "virtual private." You can create a VPN using a hardware device known as a VPN concentrator. This device sits between the VPN client and the VPN server, creates the tunnel, authenticates users using the tunnel, and encrypts data traveling through the tunnel. When the VPN concentrator is in place, it can establish a secure connection (tunnel) between the sending and receiving network devices.

VPN concentrators add an additional level to VPN security. Depending on the exact concentrator, they can

▶ Create the tunnel.

▶ Authenticate users who want to use the tunnel.

▶ Encrypt and decrypt data.

▶ Regulate and monitor data transfer across the tunnel.

▶ Control inbound and outbound traffic as a tunnel endpoint or router.

The VPN concentrator invokes various standard protocols to accomplish these functions. These protocols were discussed earlier in this chapter.

Honeypots and Honeynets

When talking about network security, honeypots and honeynets are often mentioned. Honeypots are a rather clever approach to network security but perhaps a bit expensive. A honeypot is a system set up as a decoy to attract and deflect attacks from hackers. The server decoy appears to have everything a regular server does—OS, applications, and network services. The attacker thinks he is accessing a real network server, but he is in a network trap.

The honeypot has two key purposes. It can give administrators valuable infor-mation on the types of attacks being carried out. In turn, the honeypot can secure the real production servers according to what it learns. Also, the hon-eypot deflects attention from working servers, allowing them to function without being attacked.

A honeypot can

▶ Deflect the attention of attackers from production servers.

▶ Deter attackers if they suspect their actions may be monitored with a honeypot.

▶ Allow administrators to learn from the attacks to protect the real servers.

▶ Identify the source of attacks, whether from inside the network or outside.

ExamAlert

Think of a honeypot as a trap that allows the intruder in but doesn't allow access to sensitive data.

One step up from the honeypot is the honeynet. The honeynet is an entire network set up to monitor attacks from outsiders. All traffic into and out of the network is carefully tracked and documented. This information is shared with network professionals to help isolate the types of attacks launched against networks and to proactively manage those security risks. Honeynets function as a production network, using network services, applications, and more. Attackers don't know that they are actually accessing a monitored network.

Vulnerability Scanners

In a vulnerability test, you run a software program that contains a database of known vulnerabilities against your system to identify weaknesses. It is highly recommended that you obtain such a vulnerability scanner and run it on your network to check for any known security holes. It is always preferable for you to find them on your own network before someone outside the organization does by running such a tool against you.

The vulnerability scanner may be a port scanner (such as NMAP: http://nmap.org/), a network enumerator, a web application, or even a worm, but in all cases it runs tests on its target against a gamut of known vulnerabilities.

Although Nessus (http://www.nessus.org/nessus/) and Retina (http://www.eeye.com/Retina) are two of the better known vulnerability scanners, SAINT and OpenVAS (which was originally based on Nessus) are also widely used.

ExamAlert

For the exam, CompTIA wants you to know that Nessus and nmap are two popular vulnerability scanners.

Cram Quiz

1. What is the basic reason for implementing a firewall?
   - ○ **A.** It reduces the costs associated with Internet access.
   - ○ **B.** It provides NAT functionality.
   - ○ **C.** It provides a mechanism to protect one network from another.
   - ○ **D.** It allows Internet access to be centralized.

2. Which of the following statements best describes a VPN?
   - ○ **A.** It is any protocol that enables remote clients to log in to a server over a network such as the Internet.
   - ○ **B.** It provides a system whereby only screen display and keyboard and mouse input travel across the link.
   - ○ **C.** It is a secure communication channel across a public network such as the Internet.
   - ○ **D.** It is a protocol used to encrypt user IDs and passwords.

3. While reviewing the security logs for your server, you notice that a user on the Internet has attempted to access your internal mail server. Although it appears that the user's attempts were unsuccessful, you are concerned about the possibility that your systems might be compromised. Which of the following solutions are you most likely to implement?
   - ○ **A.** A more secure password policy
   - ○ **B.** A firewall system at the connection point to the Internet
   - ○ **C.** File-level encryption
   - ○ **D.** Kerberos authentication

4. You have enabled HTTPS because of concerns about the security of your web server application, which runs on a web server system in the DMZ of your corporate network. However, remote users are now unable to connect to the application. Which of the following is the most likely reason for the problem?
   - ○ **A.** Port 80 is being blocked on the corporate firewall.
   - ○ **B.** Port 443 is being blocked on the corporate firewall.
   - ○ **C.** Remote users need to enable HTTPS support in their web browsers.
   - ○ **D.** Port 110 is being blocked on the corporate firewall.

5. Which of the following is not a commonly implemented feature of a firewall system?

- ○ **A.** NAT
- ○ **B.** Packet filtering
- ○ **C.** Proxy
- ○ **D.** NAS

6. When a system running TCP/IP receives a data packet, which of the following does it use to determine which service to forward the packet to?

- ○ **A.** Port number
- ○ **B.** Packet ID number
- ○ **C.** Data IP number
- ○ **D.** IP protocol service type

Cram Quiz Answers

1. **C.** Implementing a firewall gives you protection between networks, typically from the Internet to a private network. All the other answers describe functions offered by a proxy server. Some firewall systems do offer NAT functionality, but NAT is not a firewall feature; it is an added benefit of these systems.

2. **C.** A VPN provides a secure communication path between devices over a public network such as the Internet.

3. **B.** To prevent unauthorized access to a private network from the Internet, you can use a firewall server to restrict outside access. Implementing a more secure password policy (answer A) is a good idea, but it is not the best choice. Implementing a file-level encryption system (answer C) is a good idea, but it is not the best choice. Kerberos (answer D) is an authentication system, not a method to prevent unauthorized access to the system.

4. **B.** The most likely explanation is that port 443, the HTTPS default port, is being blocked by a corporate firewall. Port 80 (answer A) is used by HTTP. All modern web browsers automatically support HTTPS; therefore, answer C is incorrect. Port 110 (answer D) is used by POP3.

5. **D.** A firewall can provide several services to the network, including NAT, proxy services, and packet filtering. NAS is not a function of a firewall server; the acronym stands for network attached storage.

6. **A.** The service for which a data packet is destined is determined by the port number to which it is sent.

What Next?

The final chapter of this book focuses on all areas of troubleshooting, including troubleshooting best practices and some of the tools and utilities you use to assist in the troubleshooting process.

No matter how well a network is designed and how many preventive maintenance schedules are in place, troubleshooting is always necessary. Because of this, network administrators must develop those troubleshooting skills.

CHAPTER 11

Network Troubleshooting

This chapter covers the following official Network+ objectives:

▶ Given a scenario, implement the following network troubleshooting methodology.

▶ Given a scenario, troubleshoot common router and switch problems.

▶ Given a scenario, troubleshoot common physical and connectivity problems.

This chapter covers CompTIA Network+ objectives 1.8, 2.5, and 3.6. For more information on the official Network+ exam topics, see the "About the Network+ Exam" section in the "Introduction."

Many duties and responsibilities fall under the umbrella of network administration. Of these, one of the most practiced is that of troubleshooting. No matter how well a network is designed and how many preventive maintenance schedules are in place, troubleshooting is always necessary. Because of this, network administrators must develop those troubleshooting skills.

This chapter focuses on all areas of troubleshooting, including troubleshooting best practices and some of the tools and utilities you can use to assist in the troubleshooting process.

Troubleshooting Steps and Procedures

▶ **Given a scenario, implement the following network troubleshooting methodology.**

CramSaver

If you can correctly answer these questions before going through this section, save time by skimming the Exam Alerts in this section and then complete the Cram Quiz at the end of the section.

1. What are the key sources from which you can gain information about a computer problem?

2. What is the final step in the network troubleshooting methodology CompTIA expects test takers to follow?

Answers

1. It is important to get as much information as possible about the problem. You can glean information from three key sources: the computer (in the form of logs and error messages), the computer user experiencing the problem, and your own observation.

2. Document the findings, the actions, and the outcomes.

Regardless of the problem, effective network troubleshooting follows some specific steps. These steps provide a framework in which to perform the troubleshooting process. When you follow them, they can reduce the time it takes to isolate and fix a problem. The following sections discuss the common troubleshooting steps and procedures as identified by the CompTIA Network+ objectives:

1. Identify the problem.

 ▶ Information gathering.

 ▶ Identify symptoms.

 ▶ Question users.

 ▶ Determine if anything has changed.

2. Establish a theory of probable cause.

   ▸ Question the obvious.

3. Test the theory to determine cause:

   ▸ When the theory is confirmed, determine the next steps to resolve the problem.

   ▸ If theory is not confirmed, re-establish a new theory or escalate.

4. Establish a plan of action to resolve the problem and identify potential effects.

5. Implement the solution or escalate as necessary.

6. Verify full system functionality and if applicable implement preventive measures.

7. Document findings, actions, and outcomes.

> **ExamAlert**
>
> You should expect questions asking you to identify the troubleshooting steps in exact order.

Identify the Problem

The first step in the troubleshooting process is to establish exactly what the problem is. This stage of the troubleshooting process is all about information gathering, identifying symptoms, questioning users, and determining if anything has changed. To get this information, you need knowledge of the operating system used, good communication skills, and a little patience. You need to get as much information as possible about the problem. You can glean information from three key sources: the computer (in the form of logs and error messages), the computer user experiencing the problem, and your own observation.

After you have listed the symptoms, you can begin to identify some of the potential causes of those symptoms.

> **ExamAlert**
>
> You don't need to know where error messages are stored on an operating system. You need only to know that the troubleshooting process requires you to read system-generated log errors.

Identify Symptoms

Some computer problems are isolated to a single user in a single location; others affect several thousand users spanning multiple locations. Establishing the affected area is an important part of the troubleshooting process, and it often dictates the strategies you use to resolve the problem.

> **ExamAlert**
>
> You might be provided with either a description of a scenario or a description augmented by a network diagram. In either case, you should carefully read the description of the problem, step by step. In most cases, the correct answer is fairly logical, and the wrong answers can be easily identified.

Problems that affect many users are often connectivity issues that disable access for many users. Such problems often can be isolated to wiring closets, network devices, and server rooms. The troubleshooting process for problems that are isolated to a single user often begins and ends at that user's workstation. The trail might indeed lead you to the wiring closet or server, but that is probably not where the troubleshooting process began. Understanding who is affected by a problem can give you the first clues about where the problem exists. For example, a change in DHCP scope by a new administrator might affect several users, whereas a user playing with the TCP/IP settings of a single computer can affect only that person.

Determine if Anything Has Changed

Whether there is a problem with a workstation's access to a database or an entire network, they were working at some point. Although many people claim that their computer "just stopped working," that is unlikely. Far more likely is that changes to the system or network have caused the problem. Look for newly installed applications, applied patches or updates, new hardware, a physical move of the computer, or a new username and password. Establishing any recent changes to a system can often lead you in the right direction to isolate and troubleshoot a problem.

Establish a Theory of Probable Cause

A single problem on a network can have many different causes, but with appropriate information gathering, you can eliminate many of them. When you look for a probable cause, it is often best to look at the easiest solution first and then work from there. Even in the most complex of network designs, the easiest solution is often the right one. For instance, if a single user cannot log on to a network, it is best to confirm network settings before replacing the NIC. Remember, though, that at this point you need to determine only the most probable cause, and your first guess might be incorrect. It might take a few tries to determine the correct cause of the problem.

> **Exam Alert**
>
> Avoid discounting a possible answer because it seems too easy. Many of the troubleshooting questions are based on possible real-world scenarios, some of which do have easy or obvious solutions.

Test the Theory to Determine Cause

After questioning the obvious, you need to establish a theory. After you formulate a theory, you should attempt to confirm it. An example could be a theory that users can no longer print because they downloaded new software that changed the print drivers, or that they can no longer run the legacy application they used to run after the latest service pack was installed.

If the theory can be confirmed, then you must plot a course of action—a list of the next steps to take to resolve the problem. If the theory cannot be confirmed (in the example given, no new software was downloaded and no service pack was applied), you must establish a new theory or consider escalating the problem.

Establish a Plan of Action

After identifying a cause, but before implementing a solution, you should establish a plan for the solution. This is particularly a concern for server systems in which taking the server offline is a difficult and undesirable prospect. After identifying the cause of a problem on the server, it is absolutely necessary to plan for the solution. The plan must include the details of when the server or network should be taken offline and for how long, what support services are in place, and who will be involved in correcting the problem.

Planning is an important part of the whole troubleshooting process and can involve formal or informal written procedures. Those who do not have experience troubleshooting servers might wonder about all the formality, but this attention to detail ensures the least amount of network or server downtime and the maximum data availability.

> **Tip**
>
> If part of an action plan includes shutting down a server or another similar event that can impact many users, it is a best practice to let users know when they will be shut out of the network. This allows them to properly shut off any affected applications and not be frustrated by not being able to access the network or other services.

With the plan in place, you should be ready to implement a solution—that is, apply the patch, replace the hardware, plug in a cable, or implement some other solution. In an ideal world, your first solution would fix the problem; although, unfortunately this is not always the case. If your first solution does not fix the problem, you need to retrace your steps and start again.

You must attempt only one solution at a time. Trying several solutions at once can make it unclear which one corrected the problem.

Implement the Solution or Escalate

After the corrective change has been made to the server, network, or workstation, you must test the results—never assume. This is when you find out if you were right and the remedy you applied actually worked. Don't forget that first impressions can deceive, and a fix that seems to work on first inspection might not actually have corrected the problem.

The testing process is not always as easy as it sounds. If you are testing a connectivity problem, it is not difficult to ascertain whether your solution was successful. However, changes made to an application or to databases you are unfamiliar with are much more difficult to test. It might be necessary to have people who are familiar with the database or application run the tests with you in attendance.

Determine if Escalation Is Necessary

Sometimes the problems you encounter fall outside the scope of your knowledge. Few organizations expect their administrators to know everything, but organizations do expect administrators to fix any problem. To do this, you often need additional help.

> **Note**
>
> System administration is often as much about knowing whom and what to refer to in order to get information about a problem as it is about actually fixing the problem.

Technical escalation procedures do not follow a specific set of rules; rather, the procedures to follow vary from organization to organization and situation to situation. Your organization might have an informal arrangement or a formal one requiring documented steps and procedures to be carried out. Whatever the approach, general practices should be followed for appropriate escalation.

Unless otherwise specified by the organization, the general rule is to start with the closest help and work out from there. If you work in an organization that has an IT team, talk with others on your team; every IT professional has had different experiences, and someone else may know about the issue at hand. If you are still struggling with the problem, it is common practice to notify a supervisor or head administrator, especially if the problem is a threat to the server's data or can bring down the server.

Suppose that, as a server administrator, you notice a problem with a hard disk in a RAID 1 array on a Linux server. You know how to replace drives in a failed RAID 1 configuration, but you have no experience working with software RAID on a Linux server. This situation would most certainly require an escalation of the problem. The job of server administrator in this situation is to notice the failed RAID 1 drive and to recruit the appropriate help to repair the RAID failure within Linux.

> **Note**
>
> When you're confronted with a problem, it is yours until it has been solved or passed to someone else. Of course, the passing on of an issue requires that both parties know that it has been passed on.

Verify Full System Functionality

Sometimes, you might apply a fix that corrects one problem but creates another. Many such circumstances are hard to predict—but not always. For instance, you might add a new network application, but the application requires more bandwidth than your current network infrastructure can support. The result would be that overall network performance would be compromised.

Everything done to a network can have a ripple effect and negatively affect another area of the network. Actions such as adding clients, replacing hubs, and adding applications can all have unforeseen results. It is difficult to always know how the changes you make to a network might affect the network's functioning. The safest thing to do is assume that the changes you make will affect the network in some way and realize that you have to figure out how. This is when you might need to think outside the box and try to predict possible outcomes.

It is imperative that you verify full system functionality before you are satisfied with the solution. After you obtain that level of satisfaction, you should look at the problem and ascertain if any preventative measures should be implemented to keep the same problem from occurring again.

Document the Findings, Actions, and Outcomes

Although it is often neglected in the troubleshooting process, documentation is as important as any of the other troubleshooting procedures. Documenting a solution involves keeping a record of all the steps taken during the fix—not necessarily just the solution.

For the documentation to be of use to other network administrators in the future, it must include several key pieces of information. When documenting a procedure, you should include the following information:

▶ **When**: When was the solution implemented? You must know the date because if problems occur after your changes, knowing the date of your fix makes it easier to determine whether your changes caused the problems.

▶ **Why**: Although it is obvious when a problem is being fixed why it is being done, a few weeks later, it might become less clear why that solution was needed. Documenting why the fix was made is important because if the same problem appears on another system, you can use this information to reduce the time needed to find the solution.

▶ **What**: The successful fix should be detailed, along with information about any changes to the configuration of the system or network that were made to achieve the fix. Additional information should include version numbers for software patches or firmware, as appropriate.

▶ **Results**: Many administrators choose to include information on both successes and failures. The documentation of failures might prevent you from going down the same road twice, and the documentation of successful solutions can reduce the time it takes to get a system or network up and running.

▶ **Who**: It might be that information is left out of the documentation or someone simply wants to ask a few questions about a solution. In both cases, if the name of the person who made a fix is in the documentation, he or she can easily be tracked down. Of course, this is more of a concern in environments that have a large IT staff or if system repairs are performed by contractors instead of company employees.

Cram Quiz

1. A user reports that she can no longer access a legacy database. What should be one of the first questions you ask?

   ○ **A.** What has changed since the last time you accessed that database?

   ○ **B.** How many help calls have you placed in the past few months?

   ○ **C.** Who originally installed or created that database?

   ○ **D.** How long have you worked here?

2. You've spent 2 hours trying to fix a problem and then realize that it falls outside of your area of expertise and ability to fix. What should you do in most organizations?

   ○ **A.** Let the user immediately know that she needs to call someone else; then exit the scene so another person can help.

   ○ **B.** Formulate a workaround; then document the problem and bring it up at the next meeting.

   ○ **C.** Escalate the issue with a supervisor or manager.

   ○ **D.** Continue working on the problem, trying as many solutions as you can find, until you solve the problem.

3. You get numerous calls from users who cannot access an application. Upon investigation, you find that the application crashed. You restart the application, and it appears to run okay. What is the next step in the troubleshooting process?

   ○ **A.** Email the users to let them know that they can use the application again.

   ○ **B.** Test the application to ensure that it correctly operates.

   ○ **C.** Document the problem and the solution.

   ○ **D.** Reload the application executables from the CD, and restart it.

4. A user tells you that she is having a problem accessing her email. What is the first step in the troubleshooting process?

   ○ **A.** Document the problem.

   ○ **B.** Make sure that the user's email address is valid.

   ○ **C.** Discuss the problem with the user.

   ○ **D.** Visit the user's desk to reload the email client software.

5. You have successfully fixed a problem with a server and have tested the application and let the users back onto the system. What is the next step in the troubleshooting process?

   ○ **A.** Document the problem.

   ○ **B.** Restart the server.

   ○ **C.** Document the problem and the solution.

   ○ **D.** Clear the error logs of any reference to the problem.

Cram Quiz Answers

1. **A.** Establishing any recent changes to a system can often lead you in the right direction to isolate and troubleshoot a problem.

2. **C.** When a problem is outside of your ability to fix, you must escalate the issue. Unless otherwise specified by the organization, the general rule is to start with the closest help and work out from there. None of the other options are acceptable choices.

3. **B.** After you fix a problem, you should test it fully to ensure that the network correctly operate before you allow users to log back on. The steps described in answers A and C are valid but only after the application has been tested. Answer D is incorrect because you would reload the executable only as part of a systematic troubleshooting process. Because the application loads, it is unlikely that the executable has become corrupted.

4. **C.** Not enough information is provided for you to come up with a solution. In this case, the next troubleshooting step would be to talk to the user and gather more information about exactly what the problem is. All the other answers are valid troubleshooting steps but only after the information gathering has been completed.

5. **C.** After you have fixed a problem, tested the fix, and let users back on to the system, you should create detailed documentation that describes the problem and the solution. Answer A is incorrect because you must document both the problem and the solution. You do not need to restart the server, so Answer B is incorrect. Answer D would be performed only after the system's documentation has been created.

Troubleshooting the Network

▶ Given a scenario, troubleshoot common router and switch problems.

▶ Given a scenario, troubleshoot common physical and connectivity problems.

CramSaver

If you can correctly answer these questions before going through this section, save time by skimming the Exam Alerts in this section and then complete the Cram Quiz at the end of the section.

1. What commonly used protocol is designed to prevent switching loops?

2. What can occur when a network is overwhelmed with constant broadcasts or multicast traffic?

Answers

1. Switching loops are simply the result of having more than one path between two switches in a network. Spanning Tree Protocol (STP) is designed to prevent these loops from occurring.

2. A broadcast storm occurs when a network is overwhelmed with constant broadcasts or multicast traffic.

You will no doubt find yourself troubleshooting wiring and infrastructure problems much less frequently than you'll troubleshoot client connectivity problems—and thankfully so. Wiring- and infrastructure-related problems can be difficult to trace, and sometimes a costly solution is needed to remedy the situation. When you troubleshoot these problems, a methodical approach is likely to pay off.

ExamAlert

Wiring problems are related to the actual cable used in a network. For the purposes of the exam, infrastructure problems are classified as those related to network devices such as hubs, switches, and routers.

Common Problems to Be Aware Of

In the eyes of CompTIA and the Network+ exam, there are some problems that you should be aware of more than others. Although subsequent sections look at problems in particular areas, you should pay special attention to those that fall within this section as you study for the exam.

Switching Loop

An Ethernet network can have only a single active path between devices on a network. When multiple active paths are available, switching loops can occur. Switching loops are simply the result of having more than one path between two switches in a network. Spanning Tree Protocol (STP) is designed to prevent these loops from occurring. If the packet in the loop is a broadcast message, the loop can create a full broadcast storm (as discussed at the end of this list). Switching loops occur at the data link layer (Layer 2) of the OSI model.

> **ExamAlert**
>
> You should be able to associate STP with switching loops.

Routing Loop

As the name suggests, a routing loop occurs when data packets continue to be routed in an endless circle. In a proper operation, a router forwards packets according to the information in the routing table. If the routing table is correct, the packet takes the optimal path from the source to the destination. It is not common, but if the information in the routing table is incorrect through a manual misconfiguration or faulty route detection, routing loops can form. A routing loop is a path through the internetwork for a network ID that loops back onto itself. Routing loops are detectable because they can quickly bog down a network, and the destination system does not receive some packets.

Route Problems

Route problems typically occur when routing tables contain information that does not reflect the correct topology of the internetwork. Out-of-date or incorrect routing tables mean that packets cannot be correctly routed through the network, and route problems occur. Verify the routing table to ensure that it is correct. Sometimes static routes are entered and cause problems when the network topology is changed.

Proxy ARP

As mentioned in Chapter 9, "Network Optimization," ARP is used to resolve IP addresses to MAC addresses. This is important because on a network, devices find each other using the IP address, but communication between devices requires the MAC address. In a proxy ARP configuration, one system or network device answers ARP requests for another system. It is proxy ARP because one network system is proxying for another's ARP communications.

Broadcast Storms

Recall from Chapter 3, "Addressing and Routing," that a broadcast address is an IP address that you can use to target all systems on a subnet or network instead of single hosts. In other words, a broadcast message goes to everyone on the network. A broadcast storm occurs when a network is overwhelmed with constant broadcast or multicast traffic. Broadcast storms can eventually lead to a complete loss of network connectivity as the network is bogged down with the broadcast storm. As with other network problems, you may suspect a broadcast storm when network response times are poor and people are complaining about the slow network. These broadcast storms can be caused by faulty hardware such as a NIC that continually sends data, switching loops, or even faulty applications running on the network. Baselines work well for identifying broadcast storms.

Port Configuration

On the router, the port configuration dictates what traffic is allowed to flow through. The router can be configured to enable individual port traffic in, out, or both and is referred to as port forwarding. If a port is blocked (such as 80 for HTTP or 21 for FTP), the data will not be allowed through, and users will be affected.

> **ExamAlert**
>
> Think of port configuration and port forwarding as the same when it comes to the router.

Mismatched MTU/MUT Black Hole

A condition known as a *black hole* can occur when a router does not send back an expected message that the data has been received. It is known as a black hole from the view that data is being sent, but is essentially being lost.

> **ExamAlert**
>
> Identify a black hole.

This condition occurs when the packet the router receives is larger than the configured size of the Maximum Transmission Unit (MTU) and the Do Not Fragment flag is configured on that packet. When this occurs, the router is supposed to send a Destination Unreachable message back to the host. If the packet is not received, the host does not know that the packet did not go through.

Although there are a number of solutions to this problem, the best is to verify that there is not a mismatch between the maximum size packet clients can send and that the router can handle. You can use ping to check that packets of a particular size can move through the router by using the –l parameter to set a packet size and the –f parameter to set the do not fragment bit.

On some operating systems, you can toggle the ability for a client to use black hole detection, and on some routers (depending on firmware), you can configure them to send back a more specific message than just that the destination was unreachable.

Power Failure

Because the router serves as the gateway from your network to the rest of the world, it is imperative that it stays up and running. Just as an uninterruptible power supply (UPS) and backup power supplies should be used with mission-critical servers, the same should be used with routers.

Bad/Missing Routes

A bad route is any that you cannot rely upon to deliver packets. This can be related to lost data, timeouts, or simply unreliable connections. When bad or missing routes are discovered, *route poisoning* can be used to prevent them from being used. Route poisoning sets the hop count on that route to a high number (16 or infinite are common values) and prevents it from being used.

Bad Modules

On routers, Small Form-Factor Pluggable modules (SFPs) and Gigabit Interface Converter modules (GBICs) are often used to link a gigabit Ethernet port with a fiber network (often 1000BASE-X). Both SFPs and GBICs exist for technologies other than fiber (Ethernet and Sonet/SDH are usual), but connecting to fiber has become the most common use.

With either an SFP or GBIC, there is a receiver port (RX) and transmitter port (TX). These devices are static-sensitive as well as dust-sensitive. Care should be taken to not remove them more often than absolutely necessary to keep from shortening their life. After a module goes bad, they can be swapped for a new one to resolve the problem.

> **Note**
>
> Cisco has a great post on the care and maintenance of SFPs at
> http://www.cisco.com/en/US/products/hw/modules/ps4999/products_tech_note091
> 86a00807a30d6.shtml.

Wrong Subnet Mask

When the subnet mask is incorrect, the router thinks the network is divided into segments other than it is actually configured. Because the purpose of the router is to route traffic, a wrong value here can cause it to try to route traffic to subnets that don't exist. The value of the subnet mask on the router must match the true configuration of the network.

> **Note**
>
> For more information on subnetting and the values that should be used, see Chapter 3.

Wrong Gateway

The default gateway configured on the router is where the data goes after it leaves the local network. Although many routes can be built dynamically, it is often necessary to add the first routes when installing/replacing a router. The ip route command can be used on most Cisco routers to do this from the command line, or most routers include a graphical interface for simplifying the process.

When you have the gateway(s) configured, use the ping and tracert/traceroute utilities to verify connectivity and proper configuration.

> **ExamAlert**
>
> Know the tools to use to test connectivity.

Duplicate IP Address

Every IP address on a network must be unique. This is true not only for every host, but for the router as well, and every network card in general. The scope of the network depends on the size of the network that the card is connected to; if it is connected to the LAN, the IP address must be unique on that LAN, whereas if it is connected to the Internet, it must be unique on it.

If there is a duplicate address, in the best scenario you will receive messages indicating Duplicate IP Addresses and in the worst scenario, network traffic will become unreliable. In all cases, you must correct the problem and make certain duplicate addresses exist nowhere on your network, including the routers.

Wrong DNS

When the wrong DNS values (typically primary and secondary) are entered during router configuration, users cannot take advantage of the DNS service. Depending on where the wrong values are given, name resolution may not occur (if all values are incorrect), or resolution could take a long time (if only the primary value is incorrect), thus giving the appearance that the web is taking a long time to load.

Make sure the correct values appear for DNS entries in the router configuration to avoid name resolution problems.

Troubleshooting Wiring

Troubleshooting wiring involves knowing what wiring your network uses and where it is used. The cable used has certain limitations, in terms of both speed and distance. It might be that the network problems are the result of trying to use a cable in an environment or in a way for which it was not designed. For example, you might find that a network is connecting two workstations that are 130 meters apart with Category 6 UTP cabling. Category 6 UTP is specified for distances up to 100 meters, so exceeding the maximum cable length could be a potential cause of the problem.

> **Tip**
>
> Carefully Look at cable distances. When you run cables along walls, across ceilings, and along baseboards, the distances can quickly add up. For this reason, carefully consider the placement of the wiring closet, and ensure that you can reach all extents of your network while staying within the specified maximum cable distances.

Determining the type of cable used by a network is often as easy as reading the cable. The cable should be stamped with its type—whether it is, for example, UTP Category 6, 6a, or something else. As you work with the various cable types used to create networks, you'll get to the point where you can easily identify them. However, be careful when identifying cable types because some cable types are almost indistinguishable. After you have determined the cable being used, you can compare the characteristics and limitations of that cable against how it is being used on the network.

> **Tip**
>
> The type of cable used in a network is an important fact and one that should be included in the network documentation.

Where the Cable Is Used

Imagine that you have been called in to track down a problem with a network. After some time, you discover that clients are connected to the network via standard UTP cable run down an elevator shaft. UTP has poor resistance to electromagnetic interference (EMI), so UTP and the electrical equipment associated with elevators react to each other like oil and water. The same can be said of cables that are run close to fluorescent light fittings. Such problems might seem farfetched, but you would be surprised at just how many environments you will work in that have random or erratic problems that users have lived with for a long time and not done anything about.

> **Note**
>
> In many buildings, risers are used to run cables between floors. A *riser* is a column that runs from the bottom of the building to the top. Risers are used for running all kinds of cables, including electrical and network cables.

Part of troubleshooting wiring problems is to identify where the cable is run to isolate whether the problem is a result of crosstalk or EMI. Be aware of problems associated with interference and the distance limitations of the cable used.

> **Tip**
>
> Never assume that the cable you use is good until you test it and confirm that it is good. Sometimes cables break, and bad media can cause network problems.

If you find a problem with a network's cable, you can do various things to correct the problem. For cables that exceed the maximum distance, you can use a repeater to regenerate the signal, try to reroute the cable over a more economical route, or even replace the type of cable with one that has greater resistance to attenuation. The method you choose often depends on the network's design and your budget.

For cable affected by EMI or other interference, consider replacing the cable with one that is more resistant to such interference or rerouting the cable away from the source of the interference. If you do reroute cable, pay attention to the maximum distance, and make sure that as you're curing one problem you don't create another.

Wiring Issues

Depending on where the cable is used and the type of cable used, you might encounter some specific cable-related difficulties. This section covers some of these problems, as well as potential solutions.

Crosstalk

Whether it's coaxial cable or UTP, copper-based cabling is susceptible to crosstalk. Crosstalk happens when the signal in one cable gets mixed up with the signal in another cable. This can happen when cables are run too closely together. Cables use shielding to help reduce the impact of crosstalk. If shielded cable is not used, cables should be separated from each other. Crosstalk can also occur when one wire pair within the twisted-pair cable interferes with the signals on other wires. Crosstalk can be a result of insufficient cable shielding, disparity between signal levels in adjacent circuits, and twisted terminations at connection points. There are two types of crosstalk interference: Near End (NEXT) and Far End Cross Talk (FEXT).

> **Note**
>
> CompTIA objectives list crosstalk as "cross-talk." The terms are synonymous, with the more common usage being "crosstalk."

Near End Crosstalk (NEXT)

NEXT refers to interference between adjacent wire pairs within the twisted-pair cable at the near end of the link (the end closest to the origin of the data signal). NEXT occurs when an outgoing data transmission leaks over to an incoming transmission. In effect, the incoming transmission overhears the signal sent by a transmitting station at the near end of the link. The result is that a portion of the outgoing signal is coupled back into the received signal.

Far End Crosstalk (FEXT)

FEXT occurs when a receiving station overhears a data signal being sent by a transmitting station at the other end of a transmission line. FEXT identifies the interference of a signal through a wire pair to an adjacent pair at the farthest end from the interfering source (the end where the signal is received).

> **Note**
>
> As mentioned, crosstalk occurs when the signals sent through media interfere with data signals on adjacent wires. Within the twisted-pair cable, each wire pair is twisted to help reduce crosstalk; the tighter the twist, the more effective the cable is at managing crosstalk. This is one reason to buy high-quality cable.

EMI

EMI can reduce or corrupt signal strength. This can happen when cables are run too close to everyday office fixtures such as computer monitors and fluorescent lighting fixtures, elevators, microwaves, and anything else that creates an electromagnetic field. Again, the solution is to carefully run cables away from such devices. If they have to be run through EMI areas, shielded cabling or fiber cabling needs to be used.

Attenuation

All media have recommended lengths at which the cable can be run. This is because data signals weaken as they travel farther from the point of origin. If the signal travels far enough, it can weaken so much that it becomes unusable. The weakening of data signals as they traverse the medium is called attenuation. All copper-based cabling is particularity susceptible to attenuation. When cable lengths have to be run farther than the recommended lengths, signal repeaters can be used to boost the signal as it travels. If you work on a network with intermittent problems and you notice that cable lengths are run too far, attenuation may be the problem. Chapter 6, "Cabling and Wiring," covers the different cable lengths.

> **ExamAlert**
>
> For the Network+ objective referencing cable problems associated with distance, think of attenuation.

Open Impedance Mismatch (Echo)

Any network segment may consist of a single continuous section of cable or be constructed from multiple cable sections attached through switches and other hardware. If multiple cable sections are used, it can result in impedance mismatches caused by slight differences in the impedance of each cable section. Impedance refers to the total opposition a circuit or device offers to the flow of a signal, measured in ohms. All media such as twisted-pair cable has characteristic impedance. Impedance characteristics for twisted-pair cable include 100, 120, and 150 ohms. UTP typically has an impedance of 100 ohms, whereas STP has an impedance of 150 ohms. Mixing these two wires in the same cable link can result in an impedance mismatch, which can cause the link to fail. To help prevent impedance mismatch, use cable rated with the same impedance rating.

Bad Connectors

One of the most obvious signs that connectors may be bad and causing a problem is when the network's problems can be isolated to one location. Depending upon how bad the connectors are, you may have no connection, or a spotty connection that comes and goes at odd intervals.

Examine the connectors to look for loose wiring, broken tabs, and other physical signs of a problem. If the connectors appear questionable, change them. If the connectors do not appear questionable but the problem is indeed isolated to one run, consider bad wiring (discussed next) as a possible culprit.

Bad Wiring

The bad wiring could be a patch cable (easy to replace) or the in-wall wiring (more difficult to replace). If you suspect wiring to be the faulty component, you can diagnose rather quickly by taking the device that is having trouble connecting to another location and/or bringing a working machine to this environment.

You can use a multifunction cable tester D to troubleshoot most wiring problems. You must check for cable continuity, as well as shorts (discussed next).

Open Short

In addition to miswiring, other problems that can occur with cables (and that can be checked with a multifunction cable tester) include open/short faults (referenced by CompTIA simply as "open short"). An open fault means that the cables are not making a full circuit; this can be due to a cut in the cable (across all or some of the wires). A short fault means that the data attempts to travel on wires other than those for which it is intended; this can be caused by miswiring or a twist in the cabling at a cut allowing the bare wires to touch.

> **ExamAlert**
>
> You should expect questions asking you what tool can be used to identify an open/short fault.

Split Cables

Most splits in a cable are intentional—enabling you to run the wiring in multiple directions with the use of a splitter. Depending upon the type of cabling in question, it is not uncommon for each split to reduce the strength of the signal. It is also not uncommon for splitters to go bad. You want to split the cable as few times as possible and check the splitter if a problem in a run that was normally working suddenly occurs.

If the split is unintentional, you are often dealing with an open/short, which was the subject of the previous discussion.

DB Loss

In the previous section, the loss of signal strength was introduced. This loss is measured in terms of decibels (dB). There will always be a difference in strength between what leaves the transmitter and what arrives at the receiver with every element (connectors, splitters/splices, and so on) causing a portion of that loss.

You can test dB loss using a power meter, or even a loopback test. If the loss is too high, look at replacing the components contributing to the problem (replace connectors with those having less loss, reduce the number of splices, and so on).

> **ExamAlert**
>
> Know that there is dB loss associated with almost every wiring component.

TXRX Reversed

Chapter 6 discussed the two types of cables that can be used in an Ethernet network: a straight-through cable (as the name implies, all wires run straight through and are the same on both ends) and a crossover cable. In a crossover cable, two pairs of the wires are reversed; these are the TX and RX pairs (transmit and receive).

A crossover cable is intended to be used in specific applications only (such as to directly network two PCs without using a hub or switch) and will cause problems when used where a straight-through cable is called for (as a general rule, in all fixed wiring).

Cable Placement

The field of cable placement encompasses using the right cable in the right location. Incorrect cable placement such as using cable outside of wiring standards (running it too close to electrical devices, for example) can make it susceptible to problems with interference, attenuation, and overall usability.

Troubleshooting Infrastructure Hardware

If you are looking for a challenge, troubleshooting hardware infrastructure problems is for you. It is often not an easy task and usually involves many processes, including baselining and performance monitoring. One of the keys to identifying the failure of a hardware network device is to know what devices are used on a particular network and what each device is designed to do. Table 11.1 lists some of the common hardware components used in a network infrastructure, as well as some common problem symptoms and troubleshooting methods.

TABLE 11.1   **Common Network Hardware Components, Their Functions, and Troubleshooting Strategies**

Networking Device	Function	Troubleshooting and Failure Signs
Hub	Hubs are used with a star network topology and UTP cable to connect multiple nodes.	Because hubs connect multiple network devices, if many devices are unable to access the network, the hub may have failed. When a hub fails, all devices connected to it cannot access the network. Additionally, hubs use broadcasts and forward data to all the connected ports, increasing network traffic. When network traffic is high and the network is operating slowly, it may be necessary to replace slow hubs with switches.

TABLE 11.1   **Continued**

Networking Device	Function	Troubleshooting and Failure Signs
Switch	Like hubs, switches are used with a star topology to create a central connectivity device.	The inability of several network devices to access the network may indicate a failed switch. If the switch fails, all devices connected to the switch cannot access the network. Switches forward data only to the intended recipient, allowing them to manage data better than hubs.
Router	Routers are used to separate broadcast domains and to connect different networks.	If a router fails, network clients are unable to access remote networks connected by the router. For example, if clients access a remote office through a network router and the router fails, the remote office is unavailable. You can test router connectivity using utilities such as ping and tracert.
Bridge	Bridges are commonly used to connect network segments within the same network. Bridges manage the flow of traffic between these network segments.	A failed bridge prevents the flow of traffic between network segments. If communication between network segments has failed, it may be due to a failed bridge.
Wireless access point	Wireless access points provide the bridge between the wired and wireless network.	If wireless clients cannot access the wired network, the AP may have failed. However, you should check many configuration settings first.

Exam Alert

Be familiar with the devices listed in Table 11.1 and their failure signs.

For more information on network hardware devices and their functions, refer to Chapter 4, "Components and Devices."

Note

The CompTIA objectives mention switching and routing loops, broadcast storms, and route problems. Although this information is discussed here, it appears in other chapters as well. Managing network loops and routing issues, for example, are covered in Chapter 4.

Configuring and Troubleshooting Client Connectivity

Connecting clients to an existing network is a common task for network administrators. Connecting a client system involves several steps, including establishing the physical connection, defining network protocols, assigning permissions, and accessing server services and resources. This section explores the requirements for connecting a client PC to a network.

Troubleshooting Client Physical Connections

Establishing physical connectivity requires configuring the client network card and connecting the system to the network medium. The first step is to select the network card. Today, selecting a NIC is simple; although, you need to consider a few factors:

▶ **Bus compatibility**: Some older systems have only Industry Standard Architecture (ISA) slots, but most modern systems have either Peripheral Component Interconnect (PCI) slots or PCIe slots. Verify that an expansion slot of the correct type is available.

▶ **Type of network**: As mentioned in the discussion of NICs in Chapter 4, unless you use a networking system other than Ethernet, you should not need to specify another type of NIC.

▶ **Media compatibility**: Today, although most NICs have UTP-based connections, some exceptions exist. Some older networks might require coaxial connections; newer networks might require a NIC that can support fiber-optic cable; and still other networks might use wireless NICs.

Besides these criteria, which dictate to a certain extent which cards you can use, the choice also depends on manufacturer, cost, and requirements. The NIC might come preinstalled in the system or, as in an increasing number of cases, the network interface might be built into the system board. In either of these situations, you do not have to install a NIC.

Connecting to Network Media

With the NIC chosen and functioning, the next step is to connect the PC to the network medium. This can be simple or complicated, depending on the type of network you use. Following are some of the factors to consider when connecting a new system to an existing network:

▶ **Connecting to a coaxial network**: The biggest consideration when connecting to a coaxial network is that it might be necessary to break the coaxial segment to insert a British Naval Connector (BNC) T-connector to physically connect the PC. Recall from Chapter 1, "Introduction to Networking," that breaking a coaxial cable segment prevents any device connected to it from working. So if you are adding a computer to a coaxial segment and you need to add a length of cable and a connector, you need to either arrange with network users for a few minutes when the network will be unavailable, or add the cable and connector before or after working hours. The good news is that you can leave spare BNC T-connectors in the coaxial cable segment as a precaution. That way, you can add a system to the coaxial segment without affecting users other than the one whose system you are connecting.

▸ **Connecting to a twisted-pair network**: Twisted pair is the easiest of all the network types to connect to. All you need to connect is a cable (called a patch cable) that connects the system to a hub or switch. In environments that use a structured cable system, the cable can be connected to a wall jack or a jack in a floor box. In a less structured environment, the cable can be run directly between the system and the hub or switch.

With the network card installed and the client system connected to the medium, the client is physically attached to the network. The next step is to configure the network protocols.

Configuring Client Systems for TCP/IP

Configuring a client for TCP/IP can be relatively complex, or it can be simple. Any complexity involved is related to the possible need to manually configure TCP/IP. The simplicity is because the TCP/IP configuration can occur automatically via Dynamic Host Configuration Protocol (DHCP) or through Automatic Private IP Addressing (APIPA). This section looks at some of the basic information required to make a system function on a network using TCP/IP. At the least, a system needs an IP address and a subnet mask. The default gateway, DNS server, and WINS server are all optional, but network functionality is limited without them. The following list briefly explains the IP-related settings used to connect to a TCP/IP network:

▸ **IP address**: Each system must be assigned a unique IP address so that it can communicate on the network. Clients on a LAN have a private IP address and matching subnet mask. Table 11.2 shows the private IP ranges. If a system has the wrong IP or subnet mask, it cannot communicate on the network. If the client system has an IP address in the

169.254.0.0 range, the system is not connected to a DHCP server and is not getting on the network. Refer to Chapter 3, "Addressing and Routing," for information on APIPA and automatic IPv4 assignments.

TABLE 11.2 **Private Address Ranges**

Class	Address Range	Default Subnet Mask
A	10.0.0.0 to 10.255.255.255	255.0.0.0
B	172.16.0.0 to 172.31.255.255	255.255.0.0
C	192.168.0.0 to 192.168.255.255	255.255.255.0

ExamAlert

You need to know the private address ranges in Table 11.2.

▶ **Subnet mask**: The subnet mask enables the system to determine what portion of the IP address represents the network address and what portion represents the node address. Table 11.2 shows the default subnet mask associated with each private IP range. To be part of the network, each client system needs the correct subnet mask, and the subnet mask must use the matching one used with the rest of the network. Figure 11.1 shows a correct IP configuration and two incorrect IP configurations on a Windows system. Using Table 11.2, can you tell which is the correct configuration?

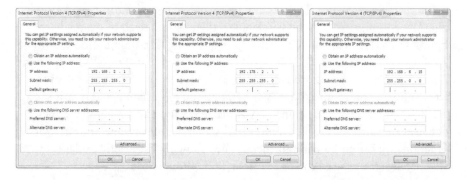

FIGURE 11.1 **One correct and two incorrect IP client configurations.**

▶ **Default gateway**: The default gateway enables internal systems to communicate with systems on a remote network. In home use, the gateway would likely be the DSL or cable modem, which acts as a router. In a business environment the gateway is the device that routes traffic from the workstation to the outside network. This network device has an IP address assigned to it, and the client configuration must use this address as the default gateway. If it doesn't, the system cannot be routed outside the local network.

▶ **DNS server addresses**: DNS servers enable dynamic hostname resolution to be performed. It is common practice to have two DNS server addresses defined so that if one server becomes unavailable, the other can be used. The client system must be configured with the IP address of the local DNS server. If a client system has the wrong DNS address listed, hostname resolution is impossible.

Exam Alert

At the very minimum, an IP address and subnet mask are required to connect to a TCP/IP network. With just this minimum configuration, connectivity is limited to the local segment, and DNS resolution is impossible.

Exactly how this information is entered on the client depends on the operating system being configured. For example, Figure 11.2 shows the Internet Protocol Version 4 (TCP/IPv4) Properties dialog box on a Windows system. As you can see, this system is fully configured for operation on a private network.

Tip

If you are adding a new system to a network that isn't using DHCP, and you're having trouble, take a look at another system on the network. You can see how it is configured and copy the IP information, including subnet mask, private address range used, DNS servers, default gateway, and more. The `ipconfig /all` command-line utility shows you all the IP information on a Windows system.

Exam Alert

If you manually enter IP information on client systems, remember that entering a duplicate IP address may prevent a client system from logging on to the network. If this happens, the second system attempting to log on to the network with the duplicate address is denied.

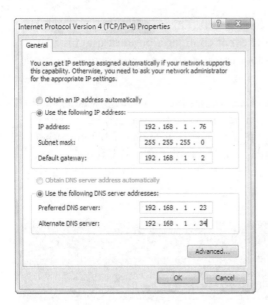

FIGURE 11.2   The Internet Protocol Version 4 (TCP/IPv4) Properties dialog box on a Windows system.

Setting Port Speeds and Duplex

When configuring a client for the network, you need to be aware of two more settings: port speed and duplex settings. These are adjusted in Windows in the Network Properties area. Figure 11.3 shows the port speed and duplex settings of a Windows system.

you have several choices for port speed and duplex settings (refer to Figure 11.3). You can choose Auto Negotiation to detect the setting that the network uses. You also can choose one of the other settings to match the network configuration, such as 100Mbps Half Duplex. If you work with a client system that is unable to log on to a network, you might need to ensure that the duplex setting and port speeds are correctly set for the network.

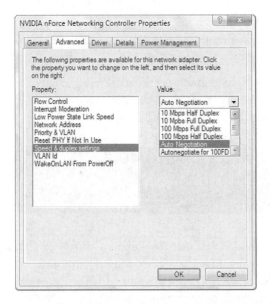

FIGURE 11.3   **The port speed and duplex settings on a Windows system.**

Troubleshooting an Incorrect VLAN

As mentioned in Chapter 1, VLANs provide a method to segment and organize the network. Computer systems can be located anywhere on the network but communicate as if they are on the same segment. For example, networks with VLANs can be segmented according to an organization's departments, such as sales, finance, and secretaries, or can be segmented according to usage, security permissions, and more.

Segmenting the network offers some clear advantages. It provides increased security because devices can communicate only with other systems in the VLAN. Users can see only the systems in their VLAN segment. This can help control broadcast traffic and makes it easier to move end systems around the network.

Problems can arise when users are moved or otherwise connected to the wrong VLAN. Administrators have to ensure that the user system is plugged into the correct VLAN port. For example, suppose a network is using port-based VLANs to assign ports 1 through 8 to marketing, ports 9 through 18 to sales, and so on. Plugging a sales client into port 6 would make that sales client part of the marketing network. This sounds simple, but if the documentation is not up to date and you work with a new network, this can be tricky to identify.

One of the keys to preventing VLAN assignment errors is to clearly document the VLAN arrangement. If systems are moved, you need to know how to reconnect them and forward them to the correct VLAN port.

> **ExamAlert**
>
> VLAN assignment is one of the troubleshooting topics you should expect to see a question about on the exam.

Another consideration to keep in mind is that membership to a VLAN can be assigned both statically and dynamically. In static VLAN assignment, the switch ports are assigned to a specific VLAN. New systems added are assigned to the VLAN associated with that particular port. For example, if you plug a new system into port 8, the user becomes part of the administrator's network. So you must ensure that you have the right port assigned to users.

Dynamic VLAN assignment requires specific software to control VLAN distribution. Using a VLAN server, administrators can dynamically assign VLAN membership based on criteria such as a MAC address or a username/password combination. As a system tries to access the network, it queries the VLAN server database to ask for VLAN membership information. The server responds and logs the system onto the appropriate VLAN network. When correctly configured, dynamic assignment reduces the human error associated with static VLAN assignment.

Topology Errors

Each physical network topology requires its own troubleshooting strategies and methods. When you troubleshoot a network, you need to know which topology is used because this can greatly impact the procedures used to resolve any problems. This section describes each of the respective physical network topologies and some common troubleshooting strategies.

ExamAlert

In one form or another, you can expect to see questions on the exam about troubleshooting the different topologies. For example, you might be asked to identify the impact on clients of a failed hub or switch on a star topology.

Star Topology

The most common topology used today is the star topology. It uses a central connection point such as a hub to connect all the devices on the network. Each device on the network uses its own length of cable, thus allowing devices to be added to or removed from the network without disrupting current network users. When troubleshooting a physical star network, consider the following:

▶ The central device, a hub or switch, provides a single point of failure. A loss of connectivity for several users might involve a faulty hub. Try placing the cables in a known working hub to confirm. You could even recycle the power to the hub or switch to see if that simple fix solves the problem.

▶ Hubs and switches provide light-emitting diodes (LEDs) that provide information on the port status. For instance, by using the LEDs, you can determine whether there is a jabbering network card, whether there is a proper connection to the network device, and whether there are too many collisions on the network.

▶ Each device, printer, or computer connects to a central device using its own length of cable. When troubleshooting a connectivity error in a star network, you might need to verify that the cable works. You can do this by swapping the cable with a known working one or by using a cable tester.

▶ Ensure that the patch cables and cables have the correct specifications and that the correct cable is used, such as a straight-through or crossover cable.

Figure 11.4 shows how a single cable break would affect only a single client system on the network.

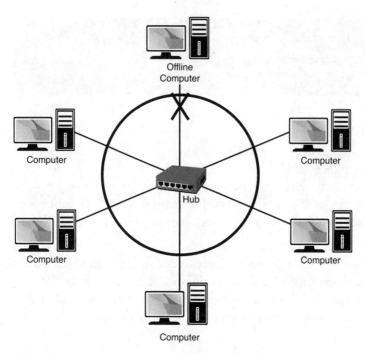

FIGURE 11.4 **Identifying cable breaks in a star network.**

Mesh Network Errors

A *mesh topology* offers high redundancy by providing several paths for data to reach its destination. In a true mesh network, each device on the network is connected to every other device, so if one cable fails, another can provide an alternative data path. Although a mesh topology is resilient to failure, the number of connections involved can make a mesh network somewhat tricky to troubleshoot.

When troubleshooting a mesh network, consider the following points:

▶ A mesh topology interconnects all devices on the network, offering the highest level of redundancy of all the topologies. In a pure mesh environment, all devices are directly connected to all other devices. In a hybrid mesh environment, some devices are connected only to certain others in the topology.

▶ Although a mesh topology can accommodate failed links, mechanisms should still be in place so that failed links are detected and reported.

▶ Design and implementation of a true mesh network can be complex and often requires specialized hardware devices.

> **Note**
>
> Most mesh networks are used to connect multiple networks, such as in a WAN scenario, rather than to connect computers in a LAN.

Mesh networks are so rare that it's unlikely you will be faced with troubleshooting one, but there will likely be questions on the Network+ Exam that focus on mesh networks.

Cram Quiz

1. Consider the following figure. Which of the following statements is true?

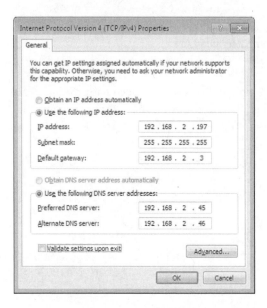

- ○ **A.** The system cannot access the local network.
- ○ **B.** The system is configured correctly and can access network resources.
- ○ **C.** The subnet mask should be 255.255.0.0 to access network resources.
- ○ **D.** The IP address 192.168.2.197 is not a valid IP address.

2. Consider the following figure. Which of the following statements is true?

- ○ **A.** The system cannot access the local network.
- ○ **B.** The system cannot access remote networks.
- ○ **C.** The system cannot have hostname resolution.
- ○ **D.** The system has the wrong subnet mask.

3. Which of the following best describes the function of the default gateway?
- ○ **A.** It converts hostnames to IP addresses.
- ○ **B.** It converts IP addresses to hostnames.
- ○ **C.** It enables systems to communicate with systems on a remote network.
- ○ **D.** It enables systems to communicate with routers.

4. Which of the following bits of IP information are mandatory to join the network? (Choose two.)
- ○ **A.** Subnet mask
- ○ **B.** IP address
- ○ **C.** DNS address
- ○ **D.** Default gateway

5. You are wiring a new network. Due to space limitations, you need to run several cables close to each other. After the setup, you find that the signals from each cable are overlapping. Which term describes what is happening?

- ○ **A.** Attenuation
- ○ **B.** Crosstalk
- ○ **C.** Near crosstalk
- ○ **D.** EMI

6. Which of the following should you consider when troubleshooting wiring problems? (Choose the three best answers.)

- ○ **A.** The distance between devices
- ○ **B.** Interference
- ○ **C.** Atmospheric conditions
- ○ **D.** Connectors

Cram Quiz Answers

1. **A.** The 192.168.x.x private address range corresponds with the subnet mask of 255.255.255.0; therefore, the subnet mask shown is incorrect. Because of this wrong configuration, the system cannot access the network. Answer D is incorrect because 192.168.2.197 is a valid IP address.

2. **B.** The IP addresses of the client system and the default gateway are the same. This error probably occurred when the IP address information was input. In this configuration, the client system would likely access the local network and resources but not remote networks because the gateway address to remote networks is wrong. The DNS, IP, and subnet mask settings are correct.

3. **C.** The default gateway enables the system to communicate with systems on a remote network, without the need for explicit routes to be defined. The default gateway can be assigned automatically using a DHCP server or can be input manually.

4. **A and B.** Configuring a client requires at least the IP address and a subnet mask. The default gateway, DNS server, and WINS server are all optional, but network functionality is limited without them.

5. **B.** Crosstalk can occur when the signal from one cable overlaps with the signal from another. This can sometimes happen when cables are run too close together. The remedy is to run the cables farther apart and use quality shielded cable.

6. **A, B,** and **D.** When you troubleshoot a wiring problem, consider the distance between devices, interference such as crosstalk and EMI, and the connection points. Answer C is incorrect because bound media (that is, cables) are unaffected by atmospheric conditions.

What Next?

Congratulations! You finished the reading and are now familiar with all the objectives on the Network+ exam. You are now ready for the Practice Exam, which follows this chapter. There are 100 multiple-choice questions to help you determine how prepared you are for the actual exam and which topics you need to review further.

Practice Exam 1

CompTIA Network+ N10-005 Authorized Exam Cram

This exam consists of 100 questions that reflect the material covered in this book. These questions represent the types of questions you should expect to see on the Network+ exam; however, they are not intended to match exactly what is on the exam.

Some of the questions require that you deduce the best possible answer. Often, you are asked to identify the best course of action to take in a given situation. You must read the questions carefully and thoroughly before you attempt to answer them. It is strongly recommended that you treat this as if it were the actual exam. When you take it, time yourself, read carefully, and answer all the questions to the best of your ability.

The answers appear in "Answers to Practice Exam 1." Check your answers against those in the "Answers at a Glance," and then read the explanations in "Answers and Explanations." You might also want to return to the chapters to review the material associated with any incorrect answers.

Exam Questions

1. You suspect that someone is capturing the data sent on your network. You want to capture data to ensure that it is encrypted and cannot be read by intruders. Which of the following network utilities can both intruders and administrators use to capture network traffic?

   - ○ **A.** Port scanner
   - ○ **B.** Packet filter
   - ○ **C.** Data watcher
   - ○ **D.** Packet sniffer

2. You have been hired to review the security of a company's network. Upon investigation, you notice that a wireless AP has been installed in a wiring closet without the consent of the administrator. The AP is actively used by remote users to access resources on the company's network. Which security problem does this represent?

   - ○ **A.** Rogue protocol interception
   - ○ **B.** Rogue AP
   - ○ **C.** Network sniffing
   - ○ **D.** Social engineering

3. You have been employed by a small company to implement a fault-tolerant hard disk configuration. You have purchased four 4TB hard disks, and you plan to install RAID 5 on the server. What is the storage capacity of the RAID solution?

   - ○ **A.** 12TB
   - ○ **B.** 4TB
   - ○ **C.** 8TB
   - ○ **D.** 16TB

4. You have been called in to troubleshoot a small network. The network uses TCP/IP and statically assigned IPv4 information. You add a new workstation to the network. It can connect to the local network but not to a server on a remote network. Which of the following is most likely the cause of the problem?

   - ○ **A.** Incorrect IP address.
   - ○ **B.** Incorrect default gateway.
   - ○ **C.** The DHCP server is unavailable.
   - ○ **D.** Duplicate IP addresses are being used.

5. Under what circumstance would you change the default channel on an access point?

   ○ **A.** When channel overlap occurs between access points

   ○ **B.** To release and renew the SSID

   ○ **C.** To increase the security settings

   ○ **D.** To decrease the security settings

6. On several occasions your wireless router has been compromised, and intruders are logging onto it. Which of the following strategies could you use to increase the security of the wireless routers? (Choose the two best answers.)

   ○ **A.** Use SSL

   ○ **B.** Disable SSID broadcast

   ○ **C.** Use MAC filtering

   ○ **D.** Use wireless filtering

7. You have just purchased a new wireless access point. You change the security settings to use 128-bit encryption. How must the client systems be configured?

   ○ **A.** All client systems must be set to 128-bit encryption.

   ○ **B.** The client system inherits security settings from the AP.

   ○ **C.** Wireless security does not support 128-bit encryption.

   ○ **D.** The client wireless settings must be set to autodetect.

8. Which of the following topology type offers the greatest amount of redundancy?

   ○ **A.** Star

   ○ **B.** Bus

   ○ **C.** Ring

   ○ **D.** Mesh

9. You need to install a network printer, and you require the printer's MAC address to finish the installation. Which of the following is a valid MAC address?

   ○ **A.** 192.168.2.13

   ○ **B.** 0x00007856

   ○ **C.** 00:04:e2:1c:7b:5a

   ○ **D.** 56g78:00h6:1415

10. You have been called in to replace a faulty ST connector. Which of the following media types are you working with?

   ○ **A.** RG-58

   ○ **B.** RG-62

   ○ **C.** Single-mode fiber

   ○ **D.** SCSI

11. Your manager asks you to recommend a secure way to copy files between a server on your network and a remote server in another location. Which of the following solutions are you most likely to recommend?

   ○ **A.** TFTP

   ○ **B.** FTP

   ○ **C.** SFTP

   ○ **D.** IGMP

12. You are setting up a wide area network between two school campuses, and you decide to use BRI ISDN. What is the maximum throughput of your connection?

   ○ **A.** 64Kbps

   ○ **B.** 128Kbps

   ○ **C.** 128Mbps

   ○ **D.** 64Mbps

13. You are troubleshooting an older 100BaseT network, and you suspect that the maximum cable length has been exceeded. What is the maximum length of a 100BaseT network segment?

   ○ **A.** 25 meters

   ○ **B.** 100 meters

   ○ **C.** 185 meters

   ○ **D.** 500 meters

14. Which of the following is a valid IPv6 address?

   ○ **A.** 42DE:7E55:63F2:21AA:CBD4:D773

   ○ **B.** 42CD:7E55:63F2:21GA:CBD4:D773:CC21:554F

   ○ **C.** 42DE:7E55:63F2:21AA

   ○ **D.** 42DE:7E55:63F2:21AA:CBD4:D773:CC21:554F

15. While troubleshooting a network connectivity problem on a Windows Server system, you need to view a list of the IP addresses that have been resolved to MAC addresses. What command would you use to do this?

   ○ **A.** `arp -a`

   ○ **B.** `nbtstat -a`

   ○ **C.** `arp -d`

   ○ **D.** `arp -s`

16. While troubleshooting a DNS issue from a UNIX server, you suspect that the DNS record for one of your other servers is incorrect. Which of the following utilities are you most likely to use to troubleshoot this problem?

   ○ **A.** ipconfig

   ○ **B.** dig

   ○ **C.** netstat

   ○ **D.** nbtstat

17. A miscreant has added a rogue access point to your wireless network. Users are mistakenly connecting to that access point instead of the legitimate one they should connect to. What is this type of attack which eavesdrops on the wireless network known as?

   ○ **A.** Evil twin

   ○ **B.** War driving

   ○ **C.** WEP cracking

   ○ **D.** DDoS

18. You are experiencing problems with the network connectivity of a Windows 7 system. You suspect that there might be a problem with an incorrect route in the routing table. Which of the following TCP/IP utilities can you use to view the routing table? (Choose two.)

   ○ **A.** tracert

   ○ **B.** nbstat

   ○ **C.** route

   ○ **D.** netstat

   ○ **E.** ping

19. Which of the following best describes the function of asymmetric key encryption?

   ○ **A.** It uses both a private and public key to encrypt and decrypt messages.

   ○ **B.** It uses two private keys to encrypt and decrypt messages.

   ○ **C.** It uses a single key for both encryption and decryption.

   ○ **D.** It uses three separate keys for both encryption and decryption.

20. Which of the following services provides name resolution services for FQDNs?

   ○ **A.** DNS

   ○ **B.** DHCP

   ○ **C.** WINS

   ○ **D.** ARP

   ○ **E.** NTP

21. You are installing a 100BaseFX network, and you need to purchase connectors. Which of the following might you purchase? (Choose two.)

   ○ **A.** RJ-45

   ○ **B.** ST

   ○ **C.** BNC

   ○ **D.** SC

22. To increase wireless network security, you have decided to implement port-based security. Which of the following standards specifies port-based access control?

   ○ **A.** 802.11x

   ○ **B.** 802.1x

   ○ **C.** 802.11b

   ○ **D.** 802.1b

23. When designing a network, you have been asked to select a cable that offers the most resistance to crosstalk. Which of the following are you likely to choose?

   ○ **A.** Multimode fiber-optic

   ○ **B.** Shielded twisted pair

   ○ **C.** UTP

   ○ **D.** Shielded mesh

24. Which of the following are considered disaster recovery measures? (Choose two.)

   ○ **A.** Backups

   ○ **B.** UPS

   ○ **C.** RAID 5

   ○ **D.** Offsite data storage

25. Which command produces the following output?

```
Interface: 24.77.218.58 --- 0x2
   Internet Address      Physical Address      Type
   24.77.216.1           00-00-77-99-a4-4c     dynamic
```

   ○ **A.** arp

   ○ **B.** tracert

   ○ **C.** ipconfig

   ○ **D.** netinf

26. You are working with a wireless network that is using channel 1 (2412MHz). What RF range would be used if you switched to channel 3?

   ○ **A.** 2417

   ○ **B.** 2422

   ○ **C.** 2427

   ○ **D.** 2408

27. What is the basic purpose of a firewall system?

   ○ **A.** It provides a single point of access to the Internet.

   ○ **B.** It caches commonly used web pages, thereby reducing the bandwidth demands on an Internet connection.

   ○ **C.** It allows hostnames to be resolved to IP addresses.

   ○ **D.** It protects one network from another by acting as an intermediary system.

28. As part of a network upgrade, you have installed a router on your network, creating two networks. Now, workstations on one side of the router cannot access workstations on the other side. Which of the following configuration changes would you need to make to the workstations to enable them to see devices on the other network? (Choose two.)

   ○ **A.** Change the IP address assignments on one side of the router so that the router is on a different IP network from the other one.

   ○ **B.** Update the default gateway information on all systems so that they use the newly installed router as the gateway.

   ○ **C.** Update the default gateway information on all systems so that they use a workstation on the other network as the default gateway.

   ○ **D.** Make sure that the IP address assignments on all network workstations are the same.

29. Which type of cable should be used to swap out a bad run in a 1000BaseT network?

   ○ **A.** RG-58

   ○ **B.** Category 5 UTP

   ○ **C.** Category 5e UTP

   ○ **D.** Multimode fiber

30. Which of the following network types is easiest to add new nodes to?

   ○ **A.** Bus

   ○ **B.** Ring

   ○ **C.** Star

   ○ **D.** Mesh

   ○ **E.** Hybrid

31. You are troubleshooting a network connectivity error, and you need to issue a continuous `ping` command. Which of the following switches is used with `ping` to send a continuous `ping` message?

   ○ **A.** `-p`

   ○ **B.** `-t`

   ○ **C.** `-c`

   ○ **D.** `-r`

32. You recently installed a DHCP server to replace static IP addressing. You configure all client systems to use DHCP and then reboot each system. After they are rebooted, they all have an IP address in the 169.254.0.0 range. Which of the following statements is true?

   ○ **A.** The DHCP server has been configured to assign addresses in the 169.254.0.0 IP range.

   ○ **B.** The DHCP server must be rebooted.

   ○ **C.** Client systems cannot access the new DHCP server.

   ○ **D.** Client systems receive IP address information from the HOSTS file.

33. Placing a node on which of the following types of networks would require that you obtain an address from the IANA (whether you do so directly or an ISP does so on your behalf)?

   ○ **A.** Private network

   ○ **B.** Public network

   ○ **C.** Ethernet network

   ○ **D.** LAN

34. You are troubleshooting a client's network. From the network specifications, you learn that you will be using the 1000BaseCX standard. What type of cable will you use?

   ○ **A.** Multimode fiber

   ○ **B.** STP

   ○ **C.** Single-mode fiber

   ○ **D.** CoreXtended fiber

35. Which of the following network protocols can recover from lost or corrupted packets in a network transmission?

   ○ **A.** L2TP

   ○ **B.** TCP

   ○ **C.** FTP

   ○ **D.** ARP

36. Your colleague decides to close all unused ports on the corporate firewall to further secure the network from intruders. The open ports are 25, 80, 110, and 53. Your colleague knows that ports 25 and 110 are required for email and that port 80 is used for nonsecure web browsing, so he decides to close port 53 because he doesn't think it is necessary. Which network service is now unavailable?

   ○ **A.** Secure HTTP

   ○ **B.** FTP

   ○ **C.** Telnet

   ○ **D.** DNS

37. You are working on a Linux system, and you suspect that there might be a problem with the TCP/IP configuration. Which of the following commands would you use to view the system's network card configuration?

   ○ **A.** config

   ○ **B.** ipconfig

   ○ **C.** winipcfg

   ○ **D.** ifconfig

38. You have configured network clients to obtain IP addresses using APIPA. Which of the following IP ranges would be assigned to client systems?

   ○ **A.** 10.10.0.0 to 10.254.254.0

   ○ **B.** 169.168.0.0 to 169.168.255.255

   ○ **C.** 192.168.0.0 to 192.168.254.254

   ○ **D.** 169.254.0.1 to 169.254.255.254

39. Your manager asks you to implement a fault-tolerant disk solution on your server. You have two 3TB hard disks and two controllers, so you decide to implement RAID 1. After the installation, your manager asks you how much storage space is now available for storing data. What do you tell her?

   ○ **A.** 3TB

   ○ **B.** 4TB

   ○ **C.** 6TB

   ○ **D.** 12TB

40. Which of the following statements best describes PRI ISDN?

   ○ **A.** PRI ISDN uses 128 B channels and two D channels.

   ○ **B.** PRI ISDN uses 23 B channels and one D channel.

   ○ **C.** PRI ISDN uses two B channels and one D channel.

   ○ **D.** PRI ISDN uses 23 D channels and one B channel.

41. Which of the following media types is used with the 802.3 1000BaseSX standard?

    ○ **A.** Coaxial

    ○ **B.** UTP

    ○ **C.** Single-mode fiber-optic

    ○ **D.** Multimode fiber-optic

42. What is the name of the bridging method used to segregate Ethernet networks?

    ○ **A.** Source-route

    ○ **B.** Invisible

    ○ **C.** Cut-through

    ○ **D.** Transparent

43. Which of the following IEEE specifications does CSMA/CD relate to?

    ○ **A.** 802.11b

    ○ **B.** 802.2

    ○ **C.** 802.5

    ○ **D.** 802.3

44. At which layer of the OSI model does a NIC operate?

    ○ **A.** Physical

    ○ **B.** Network

    ○ **C.** Data link

    ○ **D.** Transport

45. You are installing a wireless network solution that uses a feature known as MIMO. Which wireless networking standard are you using?

    ○ **A.** 802.11a

    ○ **B.** 802.11b

    ○ **C.** 802.11g

    ○ **D.** 802.11n

46. You are implementing a 1000BaseT network. Which logical topology does the network use?

    ○ **A.** Ring

    ○ **B.** Star

    ○ **C.** Mesh

    ○ **D.** Bus

47. Which command produces the following output?

```
Proto Local AddressForeign Address         State
TCP    laptop:2848  MEDIASERVICES1:1755     ESTABLISHED
TCP    laptop:1833  www.dollarhost.com:80   ESTABLISHED
TCP    laptop:2858  194.70.58.241:80        ESTABLISHED
TCP    laptop:2860  194.70.58.241:80        ESTABLISHED
TCP    laptop:2354  www.dollarhost.com:80   ESTABLISHED
TCP    laptop:2361  www.dollarhost.com:80   ESTABLISHED
TCP    laptop:1114  www.dollarhost.com:80   ESTABLISHED
TCP    laptop:1959  www.dollarhost.com:80   ESTABLISHED
TCP    laptop:1960  www.dollarhost.com:80   ESTABLISHED
TCP    laptop:1963  www.dollarhost.com:80   ESTABLISHED
TCP    laptop:2870  localhost:8431          TIME_WAIT
TCP    laptop:8431  localhost:2862          TIME_WAIT
TCP    laptop:8431  localhost:2863          TIME_WAIT
TCP    laptop:8431  localhost:2867          TIME_WAIT
TCP    laptop:8431  localhost:2872          TIME_WAIT
```

- ○ **A.** arp
- ○ **B.** netstat
- ○ **C.** nbtstat
- ○ **D.** tracert

48. Which of the following devices are specifically designed to deal with attenuation? (Choose two.)

- ○ **A.** Switch
- ○ **B.** Passive hub
- ○ **C.** DHCP server
- ○ **D.** Repeater

49. You have installed a web-based database system on your PC so that you can enter troubleshooting information and retrieve it from any location on the network. Your system's IP address is 192.168.1.164. You are not overly concerned about security, but as a basic measure, you allocate the web server application a port number of 9191 rather than the default port of 80. Assuming that you are working from another system on the network, what would you type into the address bar of a web browser to access the database?

- ○ **A.** http://192.168.1.164.9191
- ○ **B.** http://192.168.1.164/9191
- ○ **C.** http://192.168.1.164//9191
- ○ **D.** http://192.168.1.164:9191

50. Which of the following protocols maps Layer 2 addresses to Layer 3 addresses on a TCP/IP network?

- ○ **A.** ARPA
- ○ **B.** ARP
- ○ **C.** AARP
- ○ **D.** RARP

51. You have been asked to implement a server clustering strategy. Which of the following are reasons to use server clustering? (Choose two.)

- ○ **A.** To increase data transmission security over the LAN
- ○ **B.** To increase data transmission security over the WAN
- ○ **C.** To increase server service fault tolerance
- ○ **D.** To reduce network downtime

52. Which of the following is not a type of Digital Subscriber Line (DSL) technology?

- ○ **A.** VHDSL
- ○ **B.** RADSL
- ○ **C.** ADSL
- ○ **D.** XTDSL

53. You come into work on Monday to find that the DHCP server failed over the weekend. Before you can fix it, DHCP enabled client systems boot up and can communicate with each other. However, they cannot directly access the Internet or a remote network segment. Given that the DHCP server has failed, how can the systems communicate?

- ○ **A.** The DHCP service was recovered automatically using the Windows XP automatic restoration utility.
- ○ **B.** The DHCP addressing information was obtained from the client cache.
- ○ **C.** The client systems are assigned an IP address using APIPA.
- ○ **D.** The client systems are using static IP addressing.

54. Which of the following are reasons to implement a proxy server? (Choose two.)

- ○ **A.** To centrally control Internet access
- ○ **B.** To protect the internal network from intruders
- ○ **C.** To provide NAT services
- ○ **D.** To provide automatic IP addressing on the network

55. Which command produces the following output?

```
Name                    Type         Status
-------------------------------------------------
LAPTOP          <00>  UNIQUE     Registered
KCS             <00>  GROUP      Registered
LAPTOP          <03>  UNIQUE     Registered
```

- ○ **A.** nbtstat
- ○ **B.** netstat
- ○ **C.** ifconfig
- ○ **D.** arp

56. You are tasked with specifying a way to connect two buildings across a parking lot. The distance between the two buildings is 78 meters. An underground wiring duct exists between the two buildings; although, there are concerns about using it because it also houses high-voltage electrical cables. The budget for the project is tight, but your manager still wants you to specify the most suitable solution. Which of the following cable types would you recommend?

- ○ **A.** Fiber-optic
- ○ **B.** UTP
- ○ **C.** Thin coax
- ○ **D.** STP

57. Which of the following is a valid Class C address that could be assigned to a workstation on the network?

- ○ **A.** 200.200.200.200
- ○ **B.** 200.200.200.255
- ○ **C.** 143.67.151.17
- ○ **D.** 203.16.42.0

58. At which layer of the OSI model is flow control performed?

- ○ **A.** Network
- ○ **B.** Transport
- ○ **C.** Session
- ○ **D.** Data link

59. Which of the following statements is true of IMAP?

   ○ **A.** IMAP leaves messages on the mail server so that they can be viewed and accessed from various locations.

   ○ **B.** IMAP is used to send as well as receive email.

   ○ **C.** IMAP can be used only to send mail.

   ○ **D.** IMAP uses port 110.

60. Which of the address types sends data to all systems on a subnet or network instead of single hosts?

   ○ **A.** Multicast

   ○ **B.** Unicast

   ○ **C.** Broadcast

   ○ **D.** Anycast

61. A user informs you that she can't access the Internet from her system. When you visit her, you run the `ipconfig /all` utility and see the following information. What is the most likely reason the user is having problems accessing the Internet?

```
C:\>ipconfig /all

Windows IP Configuration
        Host Name . . . . . . . . . . . . : LAPTOP
        Primary DNS Suffix  . . . . . . . :
        Node Type . . . . . . . . . . . . : Broadcast
        IP Routing Enabled. . . . . . . . : No
        WINS Proxy Enabled. . . . . . . . : No

Ethernet adapter Local Area Connection:
        Connection-specific DNS Suffix  . :
        Description . . . . . . . . . . . : Intel 8255x-based PCI
Ethernet
        Physical Address. . . . . . . . . : 00-D0-59-09-07-51
        DHCP Enabled. . . . . . . . . . . : No
        IP Address. . . . . . . . . . . . : 192.168.2.1
        Subnet Mask . . . . . . . . . . . : 255.255.255.0
        Default Gateway . . . . . . . . . :
        DNS Servers . . . . . . . . . . . : 192.168.2.10
                                            192.168.2.20
```

   ○ **A.** The system is on a different subnet than the DNS servers.

   ○ **B.** DHCP is not enabled.

   ○ **C.** The subnet mask is incorrect.

   ○ **D.** The default gateway setting is not configured.

62. Your ISP account manager suggests that it might be appropriate for you to install a DNS server internally. Which of the following functions does the DNS server perform?

- ○ **A.** It performs network address translation services.
- ○ **B.** It streamlines the resolution of NetBIOS names to IP addresses.
- ○ **C.** It allows some hostname-to-IP address resolutions to occur internally.
- ○ **D.** It allows users to retrieve Internet web pages more quickly.

63. Which of the following IPv6 addressing types is associated with IPv4 automatic 169.254.0.0 addressing?

- ○ **A.** Link-local
- ○ **B.** Site-local
- ○ **C.** Global address
- ○ **D.** Unicast

64. Which of the following utilities would you use to view the TCP connections that have been established between two systems?

- ○ **A.** netstat
- ○ **B.** nbtstat
- ○ **C.** tracert
- ○ **D.** ipconfig

65. Which of the following authentication systems uses tickets as part of its authentication process?

- ○ **A.** HTTPS
- ○ **B.** POP3
- ○ **C.** Kerberos
- ○ **D.** SSL

66. Which of the following terms describes how long it takes routers to update changes in the network topology?

- ○ **A.** Poison reverse
- ○ **B.** Split horizon with poison reverse
- ○ **C.** Convergence
- ○ **D.** BGP

67. Which term describes the process of using parts of the node address range of an IP address as the network ID?

   ○ **A.** Subnetting

   ○ **B.** Supernetting

   ○ **C.** Subnet masking

   ○ **D.** Super routing

68. What network device forwards packets only to an intended port?

   ○ **A.** Hub

   ○ **B.** Switch

   ○ **C.** PPPoE

   ○ **D.** PPP

69. A user on your network can send data packets within the local subnet but cannot send packets beyond the local subnet. Which of the following is likely the problem?

   ○ **A.** Invalid permissions

   ○ **B.** Incorrect gateway information

   ○ **C.** No DNS server is installed

   ○ **D.** No WINS server is installed

70. You are the administrator for a network that uses TCP/IP. You are using a single registered Class C network address. You want to continue to use it because many of your systems are accessed from outside sources, but you also want to create more networks so that you can more effectively manage traffic and security. Which of the following strategies would help you achieve this?

   ○ **A.** Implement a 127.x.x.x addressing system throughout the network.

   ○ **B.** Use reverse proxy.

   ○ **C.** Use subnetting.

   ○ **D.** Use private addressing.

71. In a hardware loopback plug, which wire numbers are connected? (Choose the two best answers.)

   ○ **A.** 3 and 5

   ○ **B.** 1 and 3

   ○ **C.** 1 and 2

   ○ **D.** 3 and 4

   ○ **E.** 2 and 6

72. You are working with an IPv6 network, and you need to ping the local loopback address. You know that the loopback address for the IPv4 network is 127.0.0.1, and you need the equivalent for the IPv6 network. Which address should you use? (Choose two.)

- ○ **A.** 0:0:0:0:0:0:0:1
- ○ **B.** ::1
- ○ **C.** ::127
- ○ **D.** FE80::

73. Which two of the following devices can operate at the network layer of the OSI model?

- ○ **A.** AP
- ○ **B.** Switch
- ○ **C.** Hub
- ○ **D.** Router

74. A client on your network has had no problems accessing the wireless network in the past, but recently she moved to a new office. Since the move, she has had only intermittent network access. Which of the following is most likely the cause of the problem?

- ○ **A.** The SSID on the client is misconfigured.
- ○ **B.** The client system has moved too far from the AP.
- ○ **C.** The WEP settings are incorrect.
- ○ **D.** The AP is using an omnidirectional antenna.

75. You are a network administrator managing a midsized network that uses a NetWare print server, a Windows application server, and a Linux firewall server. One of your servers loses network connectivity. You type `ifconfig` at the command line to determine whether the server has a valid IP address. Which server are you using the `ifconfig` command on to see if it has lost connectivity?

- ○ **A.** The firewall server.
- ○ **B.** The print server.
- ○ **C.** The application server.
- ○ **D.** `ifconfig` is not a valid command on any of these platforms.

76. You are managing a network that uses both a UNIX server and a Windows server. Which of the following protocols can you use to transfer files between the two servers?

○ **A.** Telnet

○ **B.** PPP

○ **C.** FTP

○ **D.** PPTP

77. A user complains that access to a web page is slow. What utility can you use to find the bottleneck?

○ **A.** ping

○ **B.** Telnet

○ **C.** tracert

○ **D.** nbtstat

78. During a busy administrative week, you install a new virus suite in your network of 55 computers, a new RAID array in one of the servers, and a new office suite on 25 of the computer systems. After all the updates, you are experiencing system errors throughout the entire network. What should you do to help isolate the problem?

○ **A.** Disable the RAID array.

○ **B.** Uninstall the office suite.

○ **C.** Check the virus suite vendor's website for system patches or service packs.

○ **D.** Reinstall the virus software.

79. What utility would you use to check the IP configuration on a Windows 7 system?

○ **A.** netstat

○ **B.** nslookup

○ **C.** ping

○ **D.** ipconfig

80. Which of the following backup methods clear the archive bit? (Choose the two best answers.)

○ **A.** Differential

○ **B.** Sequential

○ **C.** Full

○ **D.** Incremental

81. You are troubleshooting a server connectivity problem on your network. A Windows 7 system is having trouble connecting to a Windows Server. Which of the following commands would you use to display per-protocol statistics on the workstation system?

   ○ **A.** arp -a

   ○ **B.** arp -A

   ○ **C.** nbtstat -s

   ○ **D.** nbtstat -S

   ○ **E.** netstat -s

82. You are working as a network administrator on a UNIX system. The system uses dynamic name resolution. What is used to dynamically resolve a hostname on a UNIX server?

   ○ **A.** TCP

   ○ **B.** ARP

   ○ **C.** DNS

   ○ **D.** UDP

83. During the night, one of your servers powers down. Upon reboot, print services do not load. Which of the following would be the first step in the troubleshooting process?

   ○ **A.** Examine the server log files.

   ○ **B.** Reboot the server.

   ○ **C.** Reinstall the printer.

   ○ **D.** Reinstall the printer software.

84. Which of the following standards uses category 6a cable?

   ○ **A.** 10GBaseT

   ○ **B.** 10GBaseSR

   ○ **C.** 10GBaseLR

   ○ **D.** 10GBaseER

85. Which of the following is a type of denial of service attack that floods a target with ping messages?

   ○ **A.** FTP bounce

   ○ **B.** Smurf

   ○ **C.** Man in the middle

   ○ **D.** Rogue access point

86. Which of the following is a distance-vector routing protocol used on TCP/IP networks?

    ○ **A.** ARP

    ○ **B.** NLSP

    ○ **C.** OSPF

    ○ **D.** RIP

87. Which of the following is a connectionless protocol?

    ○ **A.** TCP

    ○ **B.** THC

    ○ **C.** IP

    ○ **D.** UDP

88. You are upgrading the antenna on your wireless network. You need to purchase an antenna that provides a 360-degree dispersed wave pattern. Which of the following antenna types would you select?

    ○ **A.** Omni-dispersed antenna

    ○ **B.** Directional-dispersed antenna

    ○ **C.** Directional antenna

    ○ **D.** Omnidirectional antenna

89. Which copper-based medium offers speeds of up to 10Gbps and has a minimum of 250MHz of bandwidth?

    ○ **A.** Category 6b

    ○ **B.** Single-mode fiber

    ○ **C.** Multimode fiber

    ○ **D.** Category 6

90. You are experiencing a problem with a workstation, and you want to ping the local loopback. Which of the following are valid ways to check your local TCP/IP configuration? (Choose the two best answers.)

    ○ **A.** `ping host`

    ○ **B.** `ping localhost`

    ○ **C.** `ping 127.0.0.1`

    ○ **D.** `ping 127.0.0.0`

91. Which of the following network devices operates at the physical layer of the OSI model?

   ○ **A.** Router

   ○ **B.** Hub

   ○ **C.** Bridge

   ○ **D.** NIC

92. You have been asked to implement a RAID solution on one of your company's servers. You have two hard disks and two hard disk controllers. Which of the following RAID levels could you implement? (Choose the three best answers.)

   ○ **A.** RAID 0

   ○ **B.** RAID 1

   ○ **C.** Disk duplexing

   ○ **D.** RAID 10

   ○ **E.** RAID 5

93. Which of the following is a Class B IP address?

   ○ **A.** 191.23.21.54

   ○ **B.** 125.123.123.2

   ○ **C.** 24.67.118.67

   ○ **D.** 255.255.255.0

94. Which of the following is a standard for wireless that works with MIMO antennas?

   ○ **A.** HSPA+

   ○ **B.** WPA2

   ○ **C.** WEP

   ○ **D.** ICA

95. You have been called in to troubleshoot a problem with a newly installed email application. Internal users can communicate with each other via email, but neither incoming nor outgoing Internet email is working. You suspect a problem with the port-blocking configuration of the firewall system that protects the Internet connection. Which of the following ports would you allow to cure the problems with the email? (Choose the two best answers.)

   ○ **A.** 20

   ○ **B.** 25

   ○ **C.** 80

   ○ **D.** 110

   ○ **E.** 443

96. What is the default subnet mask for a Class B network?

- ○ **A.** 255.255.255.224
- ○ **B.** 255.255.255.0
- ○ **C.** 127.0.0.1
- ○ **D.** 255.255.0.0

97. At which OSI layer does TCP operate?

- ○ **A.** Network
- ○ **B.** Transport
- ○ **C.** Session
- ○ **D.** Presentation

98. Email and FTP work at which layer of the OSI model?

- ○ **A.** Application
- ○ **B.** Session
- ○ **C.** Presentation
- ○ **D.** User

99. You are implementing a new network that will use 1000BaseT with switches configured for full duplex. What is the maximum throughput that will be possible between two devices on the network?

- ○ **A.** 100Mbps
- ○ **B.** 200Mbps
- ○ **C.** 2000Mbps
- ○ **D.** 1000Mbps

100. Which of the following pieces of information is not likely to be supplied via DHCP?

- ○ **A.** IP address
- ○ **B.** NetBIOS computer name
- ○ **C.** Subnet mask
- ○ **D.** Default gateway

Answers to Practice Exam 1

Answers at a Glance

1. D	26. B	51. C, D	76. C
2. B	27. D	52. D	77. C
3. A	28. A, B	53. C	78. C
4. B	29. C	54. A, C	79. D
5. A	30. C	55. A	80. C, D
6. B, C	31. B	56. A	81. E
7. A	32. C	57. A	82. C
8. D	33. B	58. B	83. A
9. C	34. B	59. A	84. A
10. C	35. B	60. C	85. B
11. C	36. D	61. D	86. D
12. B	37. D	62. C	87. D
13. B	38. D	63. A	88. D
14. D	39. A	64. A	89. D
15. A	40. B	65. C	90. B, C
16. B	41. D	66. C	91. B
17. A	42. D	67. A	92. A, B, C
18. C, D	43. D	68. B	93. A
19. A	44. C	69. B	94. A
20. A	45. D	70. C	95. B, D
21. B, D	46. D	71. B, E	96. D
22. B	47. B	72. A, B	97. B
23. A	48. A, D	73. D	98. A
24. A, D	49. D	74. B	99. C
25. A	50. D	75. A	100. B

Answers and Explanations

Question 1

D. Both administrators and hackers use packet sniffers on networks to capture network data. They are either a hardware device or software and eavesdrop on network transmissions traveling throughout the network. The packet sniffer quietly captures data and saves it to be reviewed later. Answer A is incorrect because port scanners monitor traffic into and out of ports such as those connected to a switch. Answers B and C are not valid traffic-monitoring technologies.

Question 2

B. A rogue access point describes a situation in which a wireless access point has been placed on a network without the administrator's knowledge. The result is that it is possible to remotely access the rogue access point, because it likely does not adhere to company security policies. Answers A and C are not valid security risk types. Answer D is a type of attack that involves tricking people into performing actions or divulging confidential information such as passwords or usernames.

Question 3

A. RAID 5 reserves the equivalent space of one disk in the array for parity information. The parity information is used to rebuild the data in the event of a hard disk crash. This scenario has four 4TB hard disks. With one reserved for parity, you have 16TB total space; with 4TB removed for parity, there are 12TB of actual data storage.

Question 4

B. To connect to systems on a remote network, the default gateway address must be correctly assigned. If this address is manually entered, the number might have been incorrectly entered. Because the system can connect to the local network, the address is correctly assigned. Answer C is incorrect because IP addresses are statically assigned. Answer D is incorrect because duplicate addresses prevent the system from logging on to the network.

Question 5

A. Ordinarily the default channel used with a wireless device is adequate. However, it may be necessary to change the channel if overlap with another nearby access point occurs. The channel should be changed to another, nonoverlapping channel. Answer B is not valid. Answers C and D are incorrect because changing the channel would not inherently impact the security settings.

Question 6

B, C. Administrators can take several security steps to help secure a wireless access point. This includes disabling the SSID broadcast. This makes it more difficult for intruders to get the name of your wireless network. MAC filtering is used to accept or deny client systems based on their MAC address. MAC filtering is an example of an access control list (ACL). Answer A is incorrect because SSL is a security protocol used to increase data transmission security. Answer D is incorrect because wireless filtering is not a valid security measure.

Question 7

A. On a wireless connection between an access point and the client, each system must be configured to use the same settings, which includes the SSID, and security settings. In this question, both the client and the AP must be configured to use 128-bit encryption. Answer B is incorrect because the client does not inherit the information from the AP. Answer C is incorrect because wireless security (including WEP) does support 128-bit encryption (with WPA and WPA2 supporting 256-bit encryption). Answer D is incorrect because not all wireless clients have an autodetect feature.

Question 8

D. In a mesh topology, each device is connected directly to every other device on the network. Such a structure requires that each device have at least two network connections. Answers A, B, and C do not offer the same level of redundancy as a mesh topology.

Question 9

C. A MAC address contains six hexadecimal number sets. The first three sets represent the manufacturer's code, whereas the last three identify the unique station ID. Answer A is incorrect because the number is a valid internal IP address. Answers B and D are not valid MAC addresses.

Question 10

C. ST connectors are a twist-type connector used with single-mode fiber. Answer A is incorrect because RG-58 (thin coax) uses BNC-type connectors. Answer B is incorrect because RG-62 (thick coax) uses vampire-type AUI connectors. Answer D is incorrect because SCSI cables use a variety of connector types, none of which include ST connectors.

Question 11

C. Secure File Transfer Protocol (SFTP) enables you to securely copy files from one location to another. SFTP provides authentication and encryption capabilities to safeguard data. Answer A is incorrect because TFTP is a mechanism that provides file-transfer capabilities, but it does not provide security. Answer B is incorrect because FTP provides basic authentication mechanisms, but it does not provide encryption. Answer D is incorrect because IGMP is a protocol associated with multicast group communications. It is not a file transfer protocol.

Question 12

B. BRI ISDN uses two 64-Kbps data channels. Combined, BRI ISDN offers a 128-Kbps transfer rate.

Question 13

B. 100BaseT is an Ethernet network standard implemented using thin twisted-pair cable. The maximum length of a segment is 100 meters. When cable is run beyond 100 meters, repeaters can be used to regenerate the signal for longer transmission distances.

Question 14

D. IPv6 uses a 128-bit address, which is expressed as eight octet pairs in hexadecimal format, separated by colons. Because it is hexadecimal, only numbers and the letters A through F can be used.

Question 15

A. The `arp -a` command is used to display the IP addresses that have been resolved to MAC addresses. The `nbtstat` command (answer B) is used to view protocol statistics for NetBIOS connections. `arp -d` (answer C) is used to delete entries in the ARP cache. The `arp -s` command (answer D) enables you to add static entries to the ARP cache.

Question 16

B. The `dig` command is used on UNIX and Linux systems to perform manual name resolutions against a DNS server. This can be useful in troubleshooting DNS-related issues. The `ipconfig`, `netstat`, and `nbtstat` commands are all Windows-based commands, so they would not be used in this scenario.

Question 17

A. An evil twin is a type of attack in which a rogue access point poses as a legitimate one and eavesdrops on the network communications. Answer B is incorrect because war driving involves the act of seeking out wireless networks (usually from a vehicle, hence the name) and not setting up a rogue access point. Answer C is incorrect because WEO cracking involves breaking the WEP encryption on an existing access point and not installing a rogue one. Answer D is incorrect because DDoS is a Distributed Denial of Service attack intended to bring down a server by keeping it too busy responding to echo requests that it cannot service legitimate requests for data.

Question 18

C, D. Both the `route` and `netstat` commands can be used to view the routing table on a Windows 7 system. Answer A is incorrect because the tracert utility is used to track the route a packet takes between two destinations. Answer B is incorrect because the `nbtstat` command is used to view statistical information for NetBIOS connections. Answer E is incorrect because the ping utility is used to test network connectivity.

Question 19

A. Asymmetric key encryption uses both a private and public key to encrypt and decrypt messages. The public key is used to encrypt a message or verify a signature, and the private key is used to decrypt the message or sign a document. In a symmetric key encryption strategy, a single key is used for both encryption and decryption. None of the other answers represents asymmetric key encryption.

Question 20

A. The Domain Name System (DNS) resolves Fully Qualified Domain Names (FQDNs) to IP addresses. Answer B is incorrect because Dynamic Host Configuration Protocol (DHCP) provides automatic IP address assignment. Answer C is incorrect because the Windows Internet Naming Service (WINS) provides NetBIOS computer name to IP address resolution. Answer D is incorrect because Address Resolution Protocol (ARP) resolves IP addresses to MAC addresses. Answer E is incorrect because Network Time Protocol (NTP) facilitates the communication of time information between systems.

Question 21

B, D. 100BaseFX networks use fiber media, which can use either ST or SC connectors. Answer A is incorrect because RJ-45 connectors are used with UTP media. Answer C is incorrect because BNC connectors are used with thin coax media on 10Base2 networks.

Question 22

B. 802.1x is an IEEE standard specifying port-based network access control. Port-based network access control uses the physical characteristics of a switched local area network (LAN) infrastructure to authenticate devices attached to a LAN port and to prevent access to that port in cases where the authentication process fails. Answer A is incorrect because 802.11x is not a security standard but sometimes is used to refer to all wireless network standards, such as 802.11b/g/a/n. Answer C, 802.11b, is an actual wireless standard specifying transmission speeds of 11Mbps.

Question 23

A. Unlike copper-based media, fiber-optic media is resistant to crosstalk because it uses light transmissions. Answer B is incorrect because STP offers greater resistance to crosstalk than regular UTP but is not as resistant as fiber-optic cable. Answer C is incorrect because UTP cable is more susceptible to crosstalk than either STP or fiber-optic. Answer D is incorrect because shielded mesh is not a type of cable.

Question 24

A, D. Both backups and offsite data storage are considered disaster recovery measures. Answer B is incorrect because a UPS is considered a fault-tolerance measure, not a disaster recovery measure. Answer C is incorrect because RAID 5 is considered a fault-tolerance measure, not a disaster recovery measure.

Question 25

A. The output is from the `arp -a` command, which shows information related to IP address-to-MAC address resolutions. Answer B is incorrect because the `tracert` command displays the route a packet takes between two points. Answer C is incorrect because the `ipconfig` command displays a system's network configuration. Answer D is incorrect because there is no such command as `netinf`.

Question 26

B. IEEE 802.11g/b wireless systems communicate with each other using radio frequency signals in the band between 2.4GHz and 2.5GHz. Neighboring channels are 5MHz apart. Therefore, channel 3 would use the 2422 RF (2412+5+5).

Question 27

D. The purpose of a firewall system is to protect one network from another. One of the most common places to use a firewall is to protect a private network from a public one such as the Internet. Answer A is incorrect because although a firewall can provide a single point of access, that is not its primary purpose. Answer B more accurately describes the function of a proxy server. Answer C describes the function of a DNS server.

Question 28

A, B. The devices on one side of the router need to be configured with a different IP network address than when the network was a single segment. Also, the default gateway information on all systems needs to be updated to use the newly installed router as the default gateway. Answer C is incorrect because the default gateway address should be the address of the router, not another workstation on the network. Answer D is incorrect because for systems to communicate on an IP network, all devices must be assigned a unique IP address. Assigning systems the same address would cause address conflicts, thus keeping the systems from communicating.

Question 29

C. 1000BaseT is implemented using a minimum of Category 5e UTP cable. Answer A is incorrect because RG-58 is a type of coaxial cable with a maximum speed of 10Mbps. Answer B is incorrect because Category 5 UTP cable is not intended for use on a 1000BaseT network: it will support 10/100 but was superseded by 5e for Gigabit Ethernet. Answer D is incorrect because multimode fiber is used in fiber-optic networks. The 1000BaseT standard defines 1000Mbps networking using UTP cable.

Question 30

C. Each node on a star network uses its own cable, which makes it easy to add users without disrupting current ones. Adding a node to a bus network can sometimes involve breaking the segment, which makes it inaccessible to all other nodes on the network. This makes answer A incorrect. Answer B is incorrect because a true ring network model would require that the ring be broken to add a new device. Answer D is incorrect because a mesh topology requires that every device be connected to every other device on the network. Therefore, it is quite difficult to expand a mesh network. Answer E is incorrect because a hybrid topology requires mixing elements from at least two different topologies and is always more difficult than using only one.

Question 31

B. The `ping -t` command issues a continuous stream of ping requests until it is interrupted. A regular ping sends four requests, but sometimes this is not enough to troubleshoot a connectivity issue. None of the other answers are valid switches for a continuous `ping` command.

Question 32

C. When a client system first boots up, it looks for a DHCP server. If the server cannot be found, Automatic Private IP Addressing (APIPA) automatically assigns IP addresses to the client systems. The addresses are not routable and cannot be used to access remote segments. The addresses assigned are in the 169.254.0.0 address range. All clients configured with valid APIPA address can communicate with each other.

Question 33

B. The Internet Assigned Numbers Authority (IANA) manages the address assignments for public networks such as the Internet. Often, an ISP requests a number on your behalf when needed. Answers A and D are incorrect because on a private network or LAN, you can use any internal IP addressing scheme that is compatible with your local network. Answer C is incorrect because an Ethernet network can be either private or public. It does not directly need an IANA assigned addressing scheme.

Question 34

B. The 1000BaseCX standard specifies Gigabit Ethernet over STP cabling. Answer A is incorrect because 1000BaseSX and 1000BaseLX specify Gigabit Ethernet over two types of multimode fiber. Answer C is incorrect because single-mode fiber-optic cable is used with the 100BaseFX standard. Answer D is incorrect because there is no such thing as CoreXtended fiber-optic cable.

Question 35

B. TCP is a connection-oriented protocol, so it can recover from failed transmissions. Answer A is incorrect because L2TP is used in remote-access connections. Answer C is incorrect because FTP is a connectionless file transfer protocol and cannot recover from lost packets. Answer D is incorrect because ARP is part of the TCP/IP protocol suite that resolves IP addresses to MAC addresses.

Question 36

D. The DNS service uses port 53. If this port is accidentally blocked, the DNS service will be unavailable. Answer A is incorrect because secure HTTP uses port 443. Answer B is incorrect because FTP uses port 21. Answer C is incorrect because Telnet uses port 23.

Question 37

D. On a Linux system, the `ifconfig` command shows the network card configuration. Answer A is incorrect because the `config` command shows the network configuration on a NetWare server. Answer B is incorrect because the `ipconfig` command shows the network configuration information on a Windows system. Answer C is incorrect because the `winipcfg` command shows the network configuration information on a certain Windows system, such as Windows 95/98.

Question 38

D. The Internet Assigned Numbers Authority (IANA) has reserved addresses 169.254.0.1 to 169.254.255.254 for Automatic Private IP Addressing. APIPA uses a Class B address with a subnet mask of 255.255.0.0. None of the other IP address ranges listed are associated with APIPA address ranges.

Question 39

A. In a RAID 1 scenario in which two controllers are used (disk duplexing), one disk carries an exact copy of the other. Therefore, the total volume of one disk (3TB in this case) is lost to redundancy.

Question 40

B. Primary Rate ISDN (PRI) uses 23 B channels to carry data and one D channel to carry signaling information. Answer C is incorrect because it describes Basic Rate ISDN (BRI). Answers A and D are invalid.

Question 41

D. The Gigabit Ethernet standard 1000BaseSX specifies multimode fiber-optic cable. 1000BaseSX can be used up to 550 meters. Answers B and C are incorrect because the 1000BaseSX gigabit Ethernet standard does not specify the use of single-mode fiber-optic cable or UTP cabling. Answer A is incorrect because no Gigabit Ethernet standards use coaxial cabling.

Question 42

D. The bridging method used on Ethernet networks is called transparent because the other network devices are unaware of the existence of the bridge. Answers A, B, and C are incorrect because source-route bridges are used on Token Ring networks, invisible is not a type of bridge, and cut-through is a switching method, not a type of bridge.

Question 43

D. CSMA/CD relates to the IEEE specification 802.3. The 802.11b standard (answer A) describes wireless LAN networking. The 802.2 standard (answer B) defines the media access methods for various networking standards. The 802.5 standard (answer C) defines token ring networking.

Question 44

C. Although it provides the physical connection to the network, a NIC is considered a data link device. Answers A, B, and D are wrong because a NIC is not said to operate at any of these layers.

Question 45

D. Multiple input and multiple output (MIMO) is the use of multiple antennas at both the transmitter and receiver to improve communication performance. MIMO is used by the 802.11n standard and takes advantage of multiplexing to increase the range and speed of wireless networking. Multiplexing is a technique that combines multiple signals for transmission over a single line or medium. MIMO enables the transmission of multiple data streams traveling on different antennas in the same channel at the same time. A receiver reconstructs the streams, which have multiple antennas. The wireless standards in answers A, B, and C do not use the MIMO technology.

Question 46

D. The 1000BaseT standard defines an Ethernet network using twisted-pair cable, which would be configured in a physical star configuration. However, even in a star configuration, an Ethernet network still uses a logical bus topology.

Question 47

B. The output shown is from the `netstat` command from a Windows-based system. It is a command-line tool that displays network connections (both incoming and outgoing), routing tables, and other network interface statistics.

Question 48

A, D. Data signals weaken as they travel down a particular medium. This is known as attenuation. To increase the distance a signal can travel, you can regenerate the data signal to give it more strength. A hardware repeater regenerates the data signal as it passes, allowing it to travel farther. Repeaters typically are no longer standalones device; rather, they are included with the function of a switch. Answers B and C are incorrect because a passive hub and DHCP server are not designed to deal with attenuation.

Question 49

D. To specify a TCP/IP port other than the default of 80, simply append the port number to the end of the address, using a colon (:) to separate the two.

Question 50

D. A Layer 2 address is a MAC address. A Layer 3 address is a software-configured protocol address. Because a normal resolution is considered to be a Layer 3-to-Layer 2 resolution, the resolution the other way is considered a reverse resolution. On a TCP/IP network, such a resolution is performed by Reverse Address Resolution Protocol (RARP). Answer A is incorrect because ARPA is not an address resolution protocol. Answer B is incorrect because Address Resolution Protocol (ARP) resolves Layer 3 addresses to Layer 2 addresses. Answer C is incorrect because AppleTalk Address Resolution Protocol was used, on older AppleTalk networks, to resolve AppleTalk addresses to MAC addresses.

Question 51

C, D. Server clustering is a strategy using a grouping of servers to provide fault tolerance and failover service solutions for a network. In a clustered configuration, servers constantly communicate with each other. If one fails, the other knows, and it takes over the functions of that server, including the services that the failed server delivered. This provides fault tolerance for network services. Because the network can function in the event of a failed server, network downtime is reduced. Answers A and B are incorrect because server clustering is not used to create or increase data transmission security.

Question 52

D. XTDSL is not a recognized form of DSL. Answer A (VHDSL) and Answer B (RADSL) are recognized versions of DSL. Answer C (ADSL) is a recognized, and arguably the most popular, version of DSL.

Question 53

C. If a Windows client system cannot locate and obtain an IP address from a DHCP server, it is automatically assigned an address using APIPA. After the address is assigned, all client stations with an APIPA address can communicate with each other. However, APIPA addresses are meant for internal communication and cannot be used to access remote networks. Answer A is incorrect because there is no such thing. Answer B is incorrect because the IP address is obtained from the DHCP server, not from the client cache. Answer D is incorrect because the client was not configured to use static IP addressing.

Question 54

A, C. A proxy server acts as a centralized point for Internet access, thus making it easy to control a user's Internet use. Also, the proxy server provides network address translation services as requests are sent to the Internet using the address of the proxy server's external interface, not the system that sent it. Answer B describes the function of a firewall. Although some proxy servers also offer firewall functionality, they are separate operations. Answer D describes the function of DHCP.

Question 55

A. The output shown is from an `nbtstat` command running on a Windows system. It is a diagnostic tool designed to help troubleshoot NetBIOS name resolution problems.

Question 56

A. Fiber-optic cable provides the most resistance to EMI and therefore is often used in environments that have a risk of interference. Although it is inexpensive, UTP cable (answer B) and thin coax (answer C) have low resistance to EMI; therefore, they should not be run near high-voltage electric cables. STP (answer D) has a good level of resistance to EMI, but it is still not as resistant as fiber-optic. Not factoring in the cost, fiber-optic is the most suitable solution.

Question 57

A. Although it looks odd, this is a valid Class C address that could be assigned to a system on the network. Answer B is the broadcast address of the network 200.200.200.0. Answer C is a valid Class B address. Answer D is the network address for the network 203.16.42.

Question 58

B. Flow control occurs at the transport layer of the OSI model. Answers A, C, and D are incorrect because flow control does not occur at the network, session, or data link layers.

Question 59

A. Unlike POP3, IMAP does not directly download and then remove messages from the mail server. Instead, IMAP leaves the email on the server so that messages can be retrieved from various locations. Answers B and C are wrong because IMAP is used only to retrieve email. Answer D is incorrect because IMAP uses port 143. POP uses port 110.

Question 60

C. IPv4 broadcast addresses are IP addresses that can target all systems on a subnet or network instead of single hosts. In other words, a broadcast message goes to everyone on the network or to a specific network segment. Answer A, multicast, sends data to an entire identified group of network users. Answer B, unicast, sends data to a specific system. Answer D is incorrect because anycast is not a valid networking term.

Question 61

D. The most likely cause of the problem is that the default gateway is not configured. Answer A is incorrect because from the output it appears that the DNS servers are on the same subnet as this system. Answer B does not apply because addressing is statically configured, so there is no DHCP service. Answer C is incorrect because the subnet mask is the correct default subnet mask for a Class C network.

Question 62

C. DNS enables hostname resolutions to internally occur. In most cases, companies use a DNS server provided by the ISP. In some cases, however, it might be appropriate to have a DNS server on the internal network. Answer A is incorrect because NAT is normally a function of firewall or proxy servers. Answer B describes the purpose of a WINS server. Answer D describes the function of a proxy server.

Question 63

A. A link-local IPv6 address is automatically configured on all interfaces. This automatic configuration is equivalent to the 169.254.0.0 automatically assigned IPv4 addressing. The prefix used for a link-local address is fe80::. Answers B, C, and D are incorrect because this address falls only within the range of link-local addresses.

Question 64

A. The netstat utility enables you to view the TCP/IP connections between two systems. The nbtstat utility (answer B) is used to see the status of NetBIOS over TCP/IP connections. The tracert utility (answer C) is used to track the path that a packet of data takes between two hosts. The ipconfig utility (answer D) is used to view the IP addressing configuration information on a system.

Question 65

C. The Kerberos authentication system uses tickets as part of the authentication process. HTTPS (answer A) is an implementation of SSL. It does not use tickets. POP3 (answer B) is an email retrieval protocol. SSL (answer D) does not use tickets.

Question 66

C. Convergence is the term used to describe how long it takes routers to update changes to the network. Routing loops can occur on networks with slow convergence. Routing loops occur when the routing tables on the routers are slow to update, and a redundant communication cycle is created between routers. Answers A and B are strategies to prevent routing loops. Answer D is incorrect because BGP is a distance-vector protocol.

Question 67

A. The term subnetting refers to the process of using parts of the node address range for network addressing purposes. Supernetting (answer B) refers to the process to borrow parts of the network address portion of an assigned address to be used for node addressing. Subnet masking (answer C) describes the process to apply a subnet mask to an address. Answer D is not a valid term.

Question 68

B. A switch is more efficient than a hub because it forwards data only to intended ports. Answer A is incorrect because a hub directs data packets to all devices connected to the hub. Answers C and D are wrong because these are not network devices.

Question 69

B. If the gateway information is not correctly set, the data packets cannot get beyond the local subnet. All the other options do not prevent the user from transmitting data to remote hosts.

Question 70

C. Subnetting enables you to create more than one network from a single network address by manipulating the subnet mask to create more network addresses. Answer A is incorrect because the 127.x.x.x address range is reserved for TCP/IPv4 loopback functionality and cannot be used as an addressing scheme. Answer B is incorrect because reverse proxy is used when a proxy server protects another server (normally a web server), which responds to requests from users on the other side of the proxy server. Answer D is incorrect because private addressing might well solve the issues of security and traffic management, but without also using reverse proxy, systems on the internal network are unavailable to outside users.

Question 71

B, E. A hardware loopback plug connects the 1 and 3 wires and the 2 and 6 wires to simulate a live network connection. Answers A, C, and D are incorrect for the cable in a hardware loopback adapter.

Question 72

A, B. The IPv4 address (127.0.0.1) is reserved as the loopback address; IPv6 has the same reservation. IPv6 address 0:0:0:0:0:0:0:1 is reserved as the loopback address. The address also can be shown using the :: notation with the 0s removed, resulting in ::1. Answer C is incorrect because that is not the address for the loopback adapter. Answer D is incorrect because it is the IPv6 address for the link-local address.

Question 73

B, D. A switch can operate at the data link layer or the network layer (known as a Layer 3 switch). A router always operates at the network layer of the OSI model. Answer A is incorrect because an AP is considered a data link layer device. Answer C is incorrect because a hub is considered a physical layer device.

Question 74

B. A wireless AP has a limited range in which it can send and receive data signals. When a client system moves out of this range, client network access will either fail or be inconsistent. Answers A and C are incorrect because a misconfigured SSID or incompatible WEP settings would prevent communication between the wireless AP and client. Answer D is incorrect because an omnidirectional antenna is the type of antenna that would be used in this setting.

Question 75

A. The ifconfig command is used on a Linux system to determine the system's IP configuration. Answer B is incorrect because with NetWare, you use the config command to obtain information about network addresses. Answer C is incorrect because on a Windows system, the ipconfig command is used to view the networking configuration, including the IP address. Answer D is incorrect because the ifconfig command can be used on UNIX/Linux platforms to view the networking configuration.

Question 76

C. FTP can be used to transfer files between Windows and UNIX systems. FTP is part of the TCP/IP protocol suite and is platform-independent. The Telnet utility (answer A) is used to open a virtual terminal session on a remote host. PPP (answer B) is used to establish communications over a serial link. PPTP (answer D) is used to establish a secure link over a public network such as the Internet.

Question 77

C. tracert is a Windows command that can be used to display the full path between two systems, including the number of hops between the systems. The ping utility (answer A) can be used to test connectivity between two devices, but it reports only the time taken for the round-trip; it does not give information about how long it takes to complete each hop in the route. The Telnet utility (answer B) is used to open a virtual terminal session on a remote host. The nbtstat command (answer D) is used to view statistical information about a system's NetBIOS status.

Question 78

C. Because the system errors are over the entire network, it is likely that the cause of the problem lies with the virus suite because it is installed on all computers. To troubleshoot such a problem, it would be a good idea to check for patches or updates on the vendor's website. A problem with a RAID array (answer A) would affect only the server on which it is installed, not the entire network. Because the office suite (answer B) was installed on only some of the systems, it can be eliminated as a problem because all the systems are affected. The virus software (answer D) appears to be the cause of the problem, but reinstalling it is unlikely to help.

Question 79

D. The ipconfig utility can be used to view the TCP/IP configuration on a Windows 7, Windows Vista, or Windows Server system. The netstat utility (answer A) is used to view protocol statistics information. The nslookup (answer B) is used to query the resource records in DNS. The ping utility (answer C) is used to test the connectivity between two systems on a TCP/IP network.

Question 80

C, D. Both the full and incremental backup methods clear the archive bit to indicate which data does and does not need to be backed up. In a differential backup (answer A), the archive bit is not cleared. Sequential (answer B) is not a type of backup.

Question 81

E. The `netstat -s` command can be used to display per-protocol statistics. The `arp` command (answers A and B) is used to view a list of the IP address-to-MAC address resolutions performed by the system. The nbtstat utility (answers C and D) is used to view protocol statistics for the NetBIOS protocol.

Question 82

C. DNS is a platform-independent protocol used to resolve hostnames to IP addresses. TCP (answer A) is a network-layer connection-oriented protocol. ARP (answer B) resolves IP addresses to MAC addresses. The UDP protocol (answer D) is a connectionless protocol and is part of the TCP/IP protocol suite.

Question 83

A. In this scenario, your first step is to gather information by examining the server log files. When you have that information, you can proceed with the rest of the troubleshooting process. Rebooting the server (answer B) is unlikely to cure the problem. Before you reinstall the printer (answer C) or printer software (answer D), you should examine the log files to see if they report any problems.

Question 84

A. The 10GBaseT standard specifies twisted-pair cable of Category 6a or better. Answer B is incorrect because 10GBaseSR is a multimode fiber standard and uses fiber-optic cable. Answer C is incorrect because 10GBaseLR is a single mode fiber standard. 10GBaseER (answer D) is another single mode fiber standard and an incorrect choice.

Question 85

B. A Smurf attack is a type of attack in which a target system is flooded with ping messages that tie it up so it cannot respond to legitimate traffic. An FTP bounce (answer A) is a type of attack in which the PORT command is used to scan ports on the target machine. A man in the middle attack (answer C) is an eavesdropping attack in which the attacker intercepts messages being relayed between hosts. A rogue access point (answer D) is an access point added to a wireless network by an unauthorized party.

Question 86

D. RIP is a distance-vector routing protocol used on TCP/IP networks. Answer A is incorrect because ARP is a component of the TCP/IP protocol suite used to resolve MAC addresses to IP addresses. Answer B is incorrect because NLSP is a link-state routing protocol used on IPX networks. Answer C is incorrect because OSPF is a link-state routing protocol used on TCP/IP networks.

Question 87

D. UDP is a connectionless protocol. TCP (answer A) is a connection-oriented protocol. IP (answer C) is also a connection-oriented protocol. THC (answer B) is not a valid protocol.

Question 88

D. In a typical configuration, a wireless antenna can be either omnidirectional or directional. An omnidirectional antenna provides a 360-degree dispersed wave pattern. This provides an even signal in all directions. Answer C is incorrect because directional antennas are designed to focus the signal in a particular direction. Answers A and B are incorrect because omni-dispersed and directional-dispersed are not valid types of antennas.

Question 89

D. Category 6 high-performance UTP cable can transmit data up to 10Gbps. Category 6 has a minimum of 250MHz of bandwidth and specifies cable lengths of up to 100 meters, with 10/100/1000Mbps transfer, along with 10Gbps over shorter distances. Answers B and C are incorrect because they are not copper-based media, but fiber. Answer A is not a valid standard.

Question 90

B, C. To verify the local IP configuration, you can either ping the localhost or use the IP address 127.0.0.1. The default hostname for a system is localhost, not host, which means that answer A is incorrect. Answer D is incorrect because this is the network address for the Class A loopback address, not a valid node loopback address.

Question 91

B. A network hub operates at the physical layer of the OSI model. A router operates at the network layer of the OSI model. A bridge operates at the data link layer of the OSI model. A NIC operates at the data link layer of the OSI model.

Question 92

A, B, and **C.** With two hard disks and two controllers, you can implement RAID 0, RAID 1, and disk duplexing. RAID 10 (answer D) is a combination of RAID 1 (disk mirroring) and RAID 0 (disk striping). RAID 10 requires a minimum of four disks. RAID 5 (disk striping with parity; answer E) requires a minimum of three disks to be implemented.

Question 93

A. The first octet of a Class B address must be in the range 128 to 191. Answers B and C represent Class A addresses, which run from 1 to 126. Answer D is not a valid IP address; it is the subnet mask for a Class C network.

Question 94

A. The HSPA+ (Evolved HSPA) standard is a wireless standard that works with MIMO (multiple-input and multiple-output) antennas. Both WPA (Answer B) and WEP (Answer C) are wireless encryption protocols and not specifically wireless implementation standards. ICA (Answer D) is a networking protocol for passing data between server and client.

Question 95

B, D. TCP/IP port 25 is used by SMTP. TCP/IP port 110 is used by POP3. Because SMTP is used to send mail and POP3 is used to retrieve mail, ports 25 and 110 would need to be allowed for incoming and outgoing Internet email. TCP/IP port 20 (answer A) is used by FTP. TCP/IP port 80 (answer C) is used by HTTP. TCP/IP port 443 (answer E) is used by HTTPS.

Question 96

D. The default subnet mask for a Class B network is 255.255.0.0. Answer A is incorrect because it is not the default subnet mask for a Class B network. Answer B is not the default subnet mask for a Class B network; it is the default subnet mask for a Class C network. Answer C is the IPv4 local loopback address.

Question 97

B. TCP operates at the transport layer of the OSI model. Answers A, C, and D are incorrect because TCP does not operate at the network, session, or presentation layers.

Question 98

A. Both email and FTP work at the application layer of the OSI model. Answers B and C are incorrect because Email and FTP work at the application layer; they are not session or presentation layer protocols or applications. User (answer D) is not a layer of the OSI model.

Question 99

C. 1000BaseT is a network standard that runs at 1000Mbps. A full-duplex configuration in a switched environment gives a maximum throughput between two devices of 2000Mbps. Answer A is the maximum speed of a 100BaseT network in half-duplex mode. Answer B is the maximum speed of a 100BaseT network in full-duplex mode. Answer D is the maximum speed of a 1000BaseT network in half-duplex mode.

Question 100

B. The NetBIOS computer name is not supplied to client systems by a DHCP server.

Practice Exam 2

CompTIA Network+ N10-005 Authorized Exam Cram

This exam consists of 100 questions that reflect the material covered in this book. These questions represent the types of questions you should expect to see on the Network+ exam; however, they are not intended to match exactly what is on the exam.

Some of the questions require that you deduce the best possible answer. Often, you are asked to identify the best course of action to take in a given situation. You must read the questions carefully and thoroughly before you attempt to answer them. It is strongly recommended that you treat this as if it were the actual exam. When you take it, time yourself, read carefully, and answer all the questions to the best of your ability.

The answers appear in "Answers to Practice Exam 2." Check your answers against those in the "Answers at a Glance," and then read the explanations in "Answers and Explanations." You might also want to return to the chapters to review the material associated with any incorrect answers.

Exam Questions

1. Which utility is shown in the following figure (portions of which have been obscured to prevent telegraphing the answer)?

- ○ **A.** tracert
- ○ **B.** arp
- ○ **C.** ping
- ○ **D.** netstat

2. You are the administrator for a company that has more than 200 Windows 7 workstations. You want to prevent each workstation from seeing other network computers and devices as well as prevent people on other network computers from seeing your workstations. Which setting must you turn off?

- ○ **A.** MAN
- ○ **B.** SAN
- ○ **C.** Network discovery
- ○ **D.** CRAN

3. Most UNIX/Linux-based systems include the ability to write messages (either directly or through applications) to log files by using which utility with syslog?

- ○ **A.** scribe
- ○ **B.** master
- ○ **C.** recorder
- ○ **D.** logger

4. Which tool is shown in the following figure?

- ○ **A.** Voltmeter
- ○ **B.** Micrometer
- ○ **C.** Punchdown
- ○ **D.** Event recorder

5. At what layer of the OSI model do time domain reflectometers operate?

- ○ **A.** Session
- ○ **B.** Presentation
- ○ **C.** Application
- ○ **D.** Physical

6. Which switch is used with `ipconfig` to purge the DNS cache?

- ○ **A.** /release
- ○ **B.** /flushdns
- ○ **C.** /purgedns
- ○ **D.** /purge

7. Which utility is shown in the following figure (portions of which have been obscured to prevent telegraphing the answer)?

- ○ **A.** `ipconfig`
- ○ **B.** `ifconfig`
- ○ **C.** `nslookup`
- ○ **D.** `nbtstat`

8. Your boss returns from a conference and can't stop talking about EUI-64, which he no doubt overheard other administrators discussing. What is he referring to?

  ○ **A.** An IPv4 subnet mask

  ○ **B.** The last 64 bits of an IPv6 address

  ○ **C.** The MAC address

  ○ **D.** The conference that he most likely attended

9. You've been summoned to a small law firm to help a client with networking issues that cropped up when it added a number of new workstations. The CIDR notation appearing in the documentation kept on site is 192.168.12.0/26. What is the range of IPv4 addresses that can be assigned to workstations?

  ○ **A.** 192.168.12.1 to 192.168.12.255

  ○ **B.** 192.168.12.1 to 192.168.12.128

  ○ **C.** 192.168.12.1 to 192.168.12.62

  ○ **D.** 192.168.12.1 to 192.168.12.32

10. Traffic is not being allowed through port 53 of the firewall. Which TCP or UDP protocol is associated with that port by default?

  ○ **A.** IMAP

  ○ **B.** RDP

  ○ **C.** DNS

  ○ **D.** DHCP

11. Which command is shown in the following figure (portions of which have been obscured to prevent telegraphing the answer)?

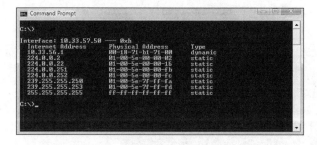

  ○ **A.** `arp -d`

  ○ **B.** `arp -a`

  ○ **C.** `arp -s`

  ○ **D.** `traceroute`

12. Which layers of the OSI model match the Network Interface Layer of the TCP/IP model? (Choose all that apply.)

○ **A.** Application

○ **B.** Presentation

○ **C.** Session

○ **D.** Transport

○ **E.** Network

○ **F.** Data Link

○ **G.** Physical

13. Which of the following are considered vulnerability scanners? (Choose all correct choices.)

○ **A.** NMAP

○ **B.** NESSUS

○ **C.** OVAL

○ **D.** BLACKHOLE

14. IPv4 has automatic private IP addressing within the range beginning 169.254.0.0. What is the equivalent addressing in IPv6?

○ **A.** There is not an equivalent.

○ **B.** FFFF:: prefix

○ **C.** 0000:: prefix

○ **D.** FE80:: prefix

15. What is the next step in the troubleshooting methodology after identifying the problem?

○ **A.** Test the theory to determine the cause.

○ **B.** Implement the solution or escalate as necessary.

○ **C.** Establish a theory of probable cause.

○ **D.** Document findings, actions, and outcomes.

16. Which of the following enables electrical power to transmit over twisted-pair Ethernet cable?

○ **A.** PPPoE

○ **B.** PoE

○ **C.** MaMM

○ **D.** EESR

17. Which of the following can be used on the Internet to capture data traveling between computers?

   ○ **A.** Registered jack

   ○ **B.** NIDS

   ○ **C.** NIPS

   ○ **D.** Packet sniffer

18. Which type of connector is used with coaxial cable?

   ○ **A.** ST

   ○ **B.** SC

   ○ **C.** F

   ○ **D.** MT-RJ

19. Which two of the following define types of wiring closets? (Choose two.)

   ○ **A.** MDF

   ○ **B.** BDF

   ○ **C.** FDF

   ○ **D.** IDF

20. Traffic is not being allowed through ports 67 and 68 of the firewall. Which TCP or UDP protocol is associated with those ports by default?

   ○ **A.** IMAP

   ○ **B.** RDP

   ○ **C.** DNS

   ○ **D.** DHCP

21. Which of the following are link-state protocols? (Choose all that apply.)

   ○ **A.** IGRP

   ○ **B.** OSPF

   ○ **C.** RIP

   ○ **D.** IS-IS

22. Which utility is shown in the following figure (portions of which have been obscured to prevent telegraphing the answer)?

- ○ **A.** tracert
- ○ **B.** arp
- ○ **C.** ping
- ○ **D.** netstat

23. Which of the following refers to the connection point between the ISP's part of the network and the customer's portion of the network?

- ○ **A.** loop
- ○ **B.** rubicon
- ○ **C.** demarcation
- ○ **D.** DMZ

24. In a traditional crossover cable, which sets of wires are crossed? (Choose all correct answers.)

- ○ **A.** 1 and 3
- ○ **B.** 2 and 6
- ○ **C.** 4 and 8
- ○ **D.** 5 and 7

25. Which of the following is a security protocol designed to provide centralized validation of users who attempt to gain access to a router or Network Access Server (NAS)?

- ○ **A.** RDP
- ○ **B.** AAA
- ○ **C.** TACACS+
- ○ **D.** ASDM

26. Which of the following is a digitally signed statement that associates the credentials of a public key to the identity of the person, device, or service that holds the corresponding private key?

- ○ **A.** certificate
- ○ **B.** record
- ○ **C.** card
- ○ **D.** ticket

27. To prevent intruders from gaining access to your live data, you have been instructed to create another server that may lure attackers in and allow you to catch them in the act. What type of server do you need to create?

- ○ **A.** NAT
- ○ **B.** DMZ
- ○ **C.** ACL
- ○ **D.** Honeypot

28. Which of the following is a collection of software, standards, and policies combined to enable users from the Internet or other unsecured public networks to securely exchange data?

- ○ **A.** Honeynet
- ○ **B.** PKI
- ○ **C.** X.509
- ○ **D.** X.503

29. Which of the following is a security protocol designed to ensure privacy between communicating client/server applications?

- ○ **A.** STFP
- ○ **B.** TFTP
- ○ **C.** IGMP
- ○ **D.** TLS

30. Which type of RAID implements disk striping with distributed parity?

- ○ **A.** RAID 1
- ○ **B.** RAID 5
- ○ **C.** RAID 0
- ○ **D.** RAID 0 + 1

31. Traffic is not being allowed through port 143 of the firewall. Which TCP or UDP protocol is associated with that port by default?

- ○ **A.** IMAP
- ○ **B.** RDP
- ○ **C.** DNS
- ○ **D.** DHCP

32. Which of the following refers to the rate of data delivery over a communication channel?

- ○ **A.** Cost
- ○ **B.** Convergence
- ○ **C.** Throughput
- ○ **D.** Latency

33. Which of the following involves the use of multiple antennas to increase data throughput?

- ○ **A.** MIMO
- ○ **B.** HSPA+
- ○ **C.** LTE
- ○ **D.** WiMAX

34. Which of the following defines specifications for the Logical Link Control (LLC)?

- ○ **A.** 802.2
- ○ **B.** 802.3
- ○ **C.** 802.11
- ○ **D.** 802.5

35. Which of the following protocols enable client systems to access and run applications on a remote system, using that system's resources? (Choose all correct answers.)

- ○ **A.** RDP
- ○ **B.** PCN
- ○ **C.** NCV
- ○ **D.** ICA

36. Which key is a nonsecret key that forms half of a cryptographic key pair used with a public key algorithm and freely given to all potential receivers?

- ○ **A.** Open
- ○ **B.** Public
- ○ **C.** Private
- ○ **D.** Restricted

37. Which of the following is true on a network that uses CSMA/CD?

- ○ **A.** Nodes can be prioritized for access to the network media.
- ○ **B.** No node is given direct access to the network media.
- ○ **C.** Every node has equal access to the network media.
- ○ **D.** Collisions cannot occur.

38. What hardware is located at the demarcation point?

- ○ **A.** AP
- ○ **B.** Punchdown block
- ○ **C.** Terminator
- ○ **D.** Smart jack

39. Traffic is not being allowed through port 443 of the firewall. Which TCP or UDP protocol is associated with that port by default?

- ○ **A.** RDP
- ○ **B.** HTTPS
- ○ **C.** SSH
- ○ **D.** SMTP

40. What is the primary purpose of PPTP?

- ○ **A.** Routes data through multiple ports
- ○ **B.** Enables you to disable the capability for traffic to pass through a port
- ○ **C.** Creates a secure tunnel between two points on a network
- ○ **D.** Looks for inappropriate activity and sends notification of any potential threats

41. Which of the following tests focus on network functioning today, as opposed to what may or may not be in the future?

- ○ **A.** Load tests
- ○ **B.** Performance tests
- ○ **C.** EGP tests
- ○ **D.** IGP tests

42. An IP address of 130.3.3.3 falls into which class?

- ○ **A.** Class A
- ○ **B.** Class B
- ○ **C.** Class C
- ○ **D.** Class D
- ○ **E.** Class E

43. Which of the following is a framework defining the procedures for authentication, creation, and management of security associations (SAs), key generation techniques, and threat mitigation?

- ○ **A.** STFP
- ○ **B.** TFTP
- ○ **C.** ISAKMP
- ○ **D.** TLS

44. What type of cable connects systems to the switch or hub using the MDI-X ports?

- ○ **A.** Plenum
- ○ **B.** ISA
- ○ **C.** Cross-over
- ○ **D.** Straight-through

45. Which framework defines a spectrum of security measures, policies, and procedures that are combined to create a secure network?

- ○ **A.** ACL
- ○ **B.** AAA
- ○ **C.** PKI
- ○ **D.** ICS

46. You try to troubleshoot telephony issues. What enables you to connect to an existing communication line and use it (makes a call, answers a call, or listens in to a call)?

- ○ **A.** OTDR
- ○ **B.** TDR
- ○ **C.** Butt set
- ○ **D.** Loop back plug

47. During what type of attack does an attacker send continuous ping packets to a server or network system, eventually tying up that system's resources, making it unable to respond to requests from other systems?

    ○ **A.** ICMP flood

    ○ **B.** Buffer overflow

    ○ **C.** Pharming

    ○ **D.** Social engineering

48. Traffic is not being allowed through port 3389 of the firewall. Which TCP or UDP protocol is associated with that port by default?

    ○ **A.** RDP

    ○ **B.** HTTPS

    ○ **C.** SSH

    ○ **D.** SMTP

49. Which of the following are distance-vector protocols? (Choose all that apply.)

    ○ **A.** IGRP

    ○ **B.** OSPF

    ○ **C.** RIP

    ○ **D.** IS-IS

50. Which of the following refers to specific access permissions assigned to an object or device on the network? (For example, wireless routers can be configured to restrict who can and cannot access the router based on the MAC address.)

    ○ **A.** GFS

    ○ **B.** DAC

    ○ **C.** RBAC

    ○ **D.** ACL

51. Which of the following refers to the mechanisms used to verify the identity of the computer or user attempting to access a particular resource (including passwords and biometrics)?

    ○ **A.** Access Control

    ○ **B.** Authentication

    ○ **C.** Authorization

    ○ **D.** Accounting

52. Which of the following protocols facilitates the access and downloading of messages from newsgroup servers?

   ○ **A.** NTP

   ○ **B.** NNTP

   ○ **C.** SIP

   ○ **D.** RTP

53. When a WAN is confined to a certain geographic area, such as a university campus or city, it is sometimes known as which of the following?

   ○ **A.** MAN

   ○ **B.** SAN

   ○ **C.** NAS

   ○ **D.** CRAN

54. Which of the following refers to the wireless technologies involved in connecting devices in close proximity to exchange data or resources?

   ○ **A.** CAN

   ○ **B.** WAN

   ○ **C.** WPAN

   ○ **D.** MPLAN

55. What protocol is used by systems within a multicast group to communicate registration information with each other?

   ○ **A.** ICMP

   ○ **B.** IGMP

   ○ **C.** NNTP

   ○ **D.** NTP

56. Which of the following connectors would you use when working with fiber-optic cable? (Choose the two best answers.)

   ○ **A.** RJ-11

   ○ **B.** SC

   ○ **C.** RJ-45

   ○ **D.** ST

   ○ **E.** BNC

57. Your manager asks you to procure a cable with a Type A connector on one end and a Type B connector on the other. What kind of interface are you most likely to be dealing with?

○ **A.** FireWire

○ **B.** USB

○ **C.** RJ-11

○ **D.** Fiber-optic

58. Which of the following wireless security protocols uses TKIP?

○ **A.** WEP-open

○ **B.** WEP-shared

○ **C.** WPA

○ **D.** WAP-shared

59. Which of the following is a valid Class A IP address?

○ **A.** 124.254.254.254

○ **B.** 127.0.0.1

○ **C.** 128.16.200.12

○ **D.** 131.17.25.200

60. You are the administrator for a network with 2 Windows Server systems and 40 Windows 7 Professional systems. One morning, three users call to report that they are having problems accessing the Windows servers. Upon investigation, you determine that the DHCP server application running on one of the servers has crashed and that the three systems are using addresses assigned via APIPA. All other systems, which were started before the DHCP server application crashed, function correctly. Which of the following statements about the situation are correct? (Choose two.)

○ **A.** Systems with an APIPA assigned address can communicate with each other.

○ **B.** Systems with an APIPA assigned address can talk to other systems that have an IP address from the DHCP server.

○ **C.** Systems with an APIPA assigned address cannot access the Internet.

○ **D.** Each system with an APIPA assigned address cannot communicate with any other system on the network.

61. Which of the following is a protocol and not part of the TCP/IP protocol suite? (Choose all that apply.)

    ○ **A.** VPN

    ○ **B.** FTP

    ○ **C.** DHCP

    ○ **D.** HTTP

    ○ **E.** DNS

62. You are attempting to configure a client's email program. The user can receive mail but cannot send any. In the mail server configuration screen of the mail application, you notice that the Type of Outgoing Mail Server field is blank. This explains why the client cannot send mail. Which of the following protocols are you most likely to enter as a value in the Type of Outgoing Mail Server field?

    ○ **A.** NMP

    ○ **B.** POP3

    ○ **C.** SMTP

    ○ **D.** IMAP

63. Which of the following is a configurable client identification setting used to differentiate one WLAN from another?

    ○ **A.** SID

    ○ **B.** WEP

    ○ **C.** SSID

    ○ **D.** Wireless channel

64. Which of the following is a valid MAC address?

    ○ **A.** 00:D0:59:09:07:51

    ○ **B.** 00:D0:59

    ○ **C.** 192.168.2.1

    ○ **D.** 2001:0db8:85a3:0000:0000:8a2e:0370:7334

    ○ **E.** 00:DG:59:09:07:51

65. Which of the following best describes 802.1x?

    ○ **A.** Port-based access control

    ○ **B.** A wireless standard specifying 11Mbps data transfer

    ○ **C.** A wireless standard specifying 54Mbps data transfer

    ○ **D.** Integrity-based access control

66. Which command produces the following output?

```
;; global options:  printcmd
;; Got answer:
;; ->>HEADER<<- opcode: QUERY, status: NOERROR, id: 17273
;; flags: qr rd ra; QUERY: 1, ANSWER: 3, AUTHORITY: 2, ADDI-
TIONAL: 0

;; QUESTION SECTION:
;examcram.com.              IN     ANY

;; ANSWER SECTION:
examcram.com.          86191   IN    A     63.240.93.157
examcram.com.          86191   IN    NS
oldtxdns2.pearsontc.com.
examcram.com.          86191   IN    NS
usrxdns1.pearsontc.com.

;; AUTHORITY SECTION:
examcram.com.          86191   IN    NS
oldtxdns2.pearsontc.com.
examcram.com.          86191   IN    NS
usrxdns1.pearsontc.com.

;; Query time: 24 msec
;; SERVER: 127.0.0.1#53(127.0.0.1)
;; WHEN: Tue Sep  18 09:07:29 2004
;; MSG SIZE  rcvd: 131
```

- ○ **A.** nslookup
- ○ **B.** nbtstat
- ○ **C.** dig
- ○ **D.** netstat

67. Which command would clear the routing table of all gateway entries?

- ○ **A.** route -p
- ○ **B.** route -f
- ○ **C.** route -g
- ○ **D.** route -r

68. Which layer of the OSI model is responsible for placing the signal on the network medium?

- ○ **A.** Physical
- ○ **B.** Data link
- ○ **C.** MAC
- ○ **D.** LLC

69. An IP address of 230.5.7.9 falls into which class?

   ○ **A.** Class A

   ○ **B.** Class B

   ○ **C.** Class C

   ○ **D.** Class D

   ○ **E.** Class E

70. Which TCP or UDP protocol is associated with port 22 by default?

   ○ **A.** RDP

   ○ **B.** HTTPS

   ○ **C.** SSH

   ○ **D.** SMTP

71. Which layer of the OSI model is responsible for synchronizing the data exchange between applications on separate devices?

   ○ **A.** Presentation

   ○ **B.** Session

   ○ **C.** Transport

   ○ **D.** Network

72. Which of the following performs the same basic function as a wire media tester, but on optical media?

   ○ **A.** Punchdown tool

   ○ **B.** Voltage event recorder

   ○ **C.** Toner probe

   ○ **D.** OTDR

73. Which two of the following protocols are commonly used to create and manage VPNs? (Choose two.)

   ○ **A.** PPPoE

   ○ **B.** SIP

   ○ **C.** PPTP

   ○ **D.** L2TP

74. Which of the following are specifically used to locate cables and track them from the patch panel to their destination?

○ **A.** Toner probes

○ **B.** Cable certifiers

○ **C.** Punchdown tools

○ **D.** Butt sets

75. Which of the following refers to the method used to determine if an authenticated user has access to a particular resource (commonly determined through group association)?

○ **A.** Access Control

○ **B.** Authentication

○ **C.** Authorization

○ **D.** Accounting

76. Which of the following is part of a strategic security solution that provides secure authentication services to users, applications, and network devices?

○ **A.** Kerberos

○ **B.** PKI

○ **C.** LDAP

○ **D.** SSL

77. Which key is the secret half of a cryptographic key pair that is never transmitted over a network?

○ **A.** Open

○ **B.** Public

○ **C.** Private

○ **D.** Restricted

78. Which of the following refers to the tracking mechanisms used to keep a record of events on a system?

○ **A.** Access Control

○ **B.** Authentication

○ **C.** Authorization

○ **D.** Accounting

79. To create secure data transmissions, IPSec uses which two separate protocols?

- ○ **A.** EGP and ARP
- ○ **B.** EIGRP and IGRP
- ○ **C.** AH and IGRP
- ○ **D.** AH and ESP

80. Which of the following defines the carrier sense multiple access with collision detection (CSMA/CD) media access method used in Ethernet networks?

- ○ **A.** 802.2
- ○ **B.** 802.3
- ○ **C.** 802.11
- ○ **D.** 802.5

81. Which layer of the OSI model is responsible for converting data from the application layer into a format that can be sent over the network?

- ○ **A.** Presentation
- ○ **B.** Session
- ○ **C.** Transport
- ○ **D.** Network

82. Which of the following is part of a network on which you place servers that must be accessible by sources both outside and inside your network?

- ○ **A.** MAN
- ○ **B.** SAN
- ○ **C.** NAS
- ○ **D.** DMZ

83. Which type of RAID offers no fault tolerance and improves I/O performance (requiring a minimum of two disks)?

- ○ **A.** RAID 1
- ○ **B.** RAID 5
- ○ **C.** RAID 0
- ○ **D.** RAID 0 + 1

84. Which type of media is used to connect telecommunication rooms, server rooms, and remote locations and offices?

   ○ **A.** PVC

   ○ **B.** Plenum

   ○ **C.** Vertical

   ○ **D.** Tracer

85. Which switch can be used with ping to force it to use IPv6?

   ○ **A.** -6

   ○ **B.** -a

   ○ **C.** -n

   ○ **D.** -l

86. What is the next step in the troubleshooting methodology after testing the theory to determine cause?

   ○ **A.** Identify the problem.

   ○ **B.** Implement the solution or escalate as necessary.

   ○ **C.** Establish a theory of probable cause.

   ○ **D.** Establish a plan of action to resolve the problem and identify potential effects.

87. What is the software-based firewall included with Windows 7 known as?

   ○ **A.** PAT

   ○ **B.** Firewall Manager

   ○ **C.** ICS

   ○ **D.** Windows Firewall

88. Which of the following is a UDP-based protocol for file transfer that does not include security or error checking?

   ○ **A.** STFP

   ○ **B.** TFTP

   ○ **C.** IGMP

   ○ **D.** TLS

89. Which utility is shown in the following figure (portions of which have been obscured to prevent telegraphing the answer)?

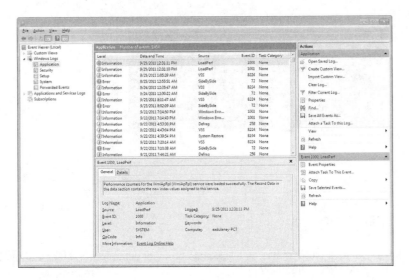

- ○ **A.** Event Viewer
- ○ **B.** System Monitor
- ○ **C.** Performance Monitor
- ○ **D.** Network Monitor

90. Which type of the following fiber connectors has a twist-type attachment?

- ○ **A.** ST
- ○ **B.** SC
- ○ **C.** LC
- ○ **D.** MT-RJ

91. You are configuring a secretary's workstation to share files with others on the network. You want anything she places in a particular location to be automatically shared with users who have access to that folder. All workstations in question, including the secretary's, run Windows 7. What feature of Windows 7 should you use to best accomplish this?

- ○ **A.** Custom folders
- ○ **B.** Public folders
- ○ **C.** File essentials
- ○ **D.** Campus foundation

92. Which utility is shown in the following figure (portions of which have been obscured to prevent telegraphing the answer)?

- ○ **A.** tracert
- ○ **B.** arp
- ○ **C.** ping
- ○ **D.** netstat

93. How does a router that uses a link-state protocol differ from a router that uses a distance-vector protocol?

- ○ **A.** Link-state builds a map of the entire network and then holds that map in memory.
- ○ **B.** Distance-vector builds a map of the entire network and then holds that map in memory.
- ○ **C.** Link-state uses only persistent links.
- ○ **D.** Distance-vector uses only persistent links.

94. Which layer of the OSI model is responsible for establishing, maintaining, and breaking connections between two devices?

- ○ **A.** Presentation
- ○ **B.** Session
- ○ **C.** Transport
- ○ **D.** Network

95. A toner probe consists of which two parts?

- ○ **A.** Tone gauge and tone indicator
- ○ **B.** Tone sine and tone cosine
- ○ **C.** Tone generator and tone locator
- ○ **D.** Tone test and tone bank

96. An IP address of 241.45.37.29 falls into which class?

- ○ **A.** Class A
- ○ **B.** Class B
- ○ **C.** Class C
- ○ **D.** Class D
- ○ **E.** Class E

97. Which TCP or UDP protocol is associated with port 25 by default?

- ○ **A.** RDP
- ○ **B.** HTTPS
- ○ **C.** SSH
- ○ **D.** SMTP

98. The CIDR notation for the network you are now troubleshooting is 192.168.67.32/28. What is the range of IPv4 addresses that can be assigned to workstations?

- ○ **A.** 192.168.67.33 to 192.168.67.46
- ○ **B.** 192.168.67.33 to 192.168.67.62
- ○ **C.** 192.168.67.1 to 192.168.67.62
- ○ **D.** 192.168.67.1 to 192.168.67.126

99. Which utility is shown in the following figure (portions of which have been obscured to prevent telegraphing the answer)?

- ○ **A.** ipconfig
- ○ **B.** nbtstat
- ○ **C.** ifconfig
- ○ **D.** nslookup

100. A colleague asks to take a measure of performance that indicates how hard the network is working and where network resources are being spent. What is this known as?

- ○ **A.** Foundation
- ○ **B.** Metric
- ○ **C.** Baseline
- ○ **D.** Control

Answers to Practice Exam 2

Answers at a Glance

1. A	26. A	51. B	76. A
2. C	27. D	52. B	77. C
3. D	28. B	53. A	78. D
4. C	29. D	54. C	79. D
5. D	30. B	55. B	80. B
6. B	31. A	56. B, D	81. A
7. C	32. C	57. B	82. D
8. B	33. A	58. C	83. C
9. C	34. A	59. A	84. C
10. C	35. A, D	60. A, C	85. A
11. B	36. B	61. A	86. D
12. F, G	37. C	62. C	87. D
13. A, B	38. D	63. C	88. B
14. D	39. B	64. A	89. A
15. C	40. C	65. A	90. A
16. B	41. B	66. C	91. B
17. D	42. B	67. B	92. C
18. C	43. C	68. A	93. A
19. A, D	44. D	69. D	94. C
20. D	45. B	70. C	95. C
21. B,D	46. C	71. B	96. E
22. D	47. A	72. D	97. D
23. C	48. A	73. C, D	98. A
24. A, B	49. A, C	74. A	99. B
25. C	50. D	75. C	100. C

Answers and Explanations

Question 1

A. The `tracert` utility is used in Windows-based operating systems to trace the route taken to reach a particular host. This same functionality is provided in UNIX/Linux-based operating systems by traceroute. `arp` (Answer B) is used for resolving IP addresses to MAC addresses. `ping` (Answer C) tests if connectivity exists, whereas `netstat` (Answer D) displays protocol statistics and current TCP/IP network connections.

Question 2

C. Toggling off network discovery prevents the workstation from seeing other networked computers and devices as well as prevents people on other networked computers from seeing each workstation on which discovery is toggled off. A metropolitan area network, or MAN (Answer A), is a network that spans a defined geographic location, such as a city or suburb. A storage area network, or SAN (Answer B), is a network of storage disks. Answer D, CRAN, is a nonexistent choice.

Question 3

D. Most UNIX/Linux-based systems include the ability to write messages (either directly or through applications) to log files via syslog. This can be done for security or management reasons and provides a central means by which devices that otherwise could not write to a central repository can easily do so (often by using the logger utility). Answers A, B, and C are nonexistent utility choices.

Question 4

C. Punchdown tools are used to attach twisted-pair network cable to connectors within a patch panel. Specifically, they connect twisted-pair wires to the insulation displacement connector (IDC). Answers A, B, and D are tools that are not shown in the figure.

Question 5

D. TDRs work at the physical layer of the OSI model, sending a signal through a length of cable, looking for cable faults. Answers A, B, and C are OSI layers above the physical layer and thus higher than that at which time domain reflectometers operate.

Question 6

B. The /flushdns switch is used with ipconfig to purge the DNS cache. The /release switch (Answer A) is used to release the IPv4 lease. The other options (Answers C and D) are not valid switches for use with ipconfig.

Question 7

C. nslookup is used to perform manual DNS lookups and is shown in the figure. The nbtstat utility (Answer D) is used to view statistics related to NetBIOS name resolution and to see information about current NetBIOS over TCP/IP connections. ipconfig (Answer A) is used to view and renew TCP/IP configuration on a Windows system, whereas ifconfig (Answer B) is its counterpart in the UNIX/Linux operating systems.

Question 8

B. The last 64 bits of an IPv6 address are known as EUI-64 (Extended Unique Identifier, 64-bit). The other choices are incorrect (Answers A, C, and D) because EUI-64 is the last 64 bits of an IPv6 address.

Question 9

C. The IP addresses available beneath 192.168.12.0/26 range from 192.168.12.1 to 192.168.12.62. With 26 mask bits, only 62 hosts can exist on a subnet. The other choices are incorrect (Answers A, B, and D) because they do not represent the correct range of IPv4 addresses that can be assigned to workstations.

Question 10

C. Port 53 is associated with DNS, by default. Port 3389, by default, is associated with RDP (Answer B), whereas port 143 is associated with IMAP (Answer A), and ports 67 and 68 are associated with DHCP (Answer D).

Question 11

B. The -a option is used with arp to display entries in the routing table. The -d option (Answer A) is used to delete an entry, whereas -s (Answer C) is used to add an entry. traceroute (Answer D) is a UNIX/Linux utility for tracing the route from one host to another.

Question 12

F and **G.** The network interface layer of the TCP/IP model matches the data link and physical layers of the OSI model in functionality. The other choices (Answers A, B, C, D, and E) are incorrect because they are OSI model layers other than those that match the network interface layer of the TCP/IP model.

Question 13

A and **B.** Both NMAP and NESSUS are considered vulnerability scanners. OVAL (Answer C) is a language and BLACKHOLE (Answer D) is a fictitious entity.

Question 14

D. Within IPv6, the FE80:: prefix is equivalent to the 169.254.0.0 range (automatic private IP addressing) in IPv4. The other choices (Answers A, B, and C) are incorrect because the FE80:: prefix is equivalent to the 169.254.0.0 range in IPv4.

Question 15

C. The next step is to establish a theory of probable cause. The steps in the methodology are 1. Identify the problem, 2. Establish a theory of probable cause (Answer C), 3. Test the theory to determine cause (Answer A), 4. Establish a plan of action to resolve the problem and identify potential effects, 5. Implement the solution or escalate as necessary (Answer B), 6. Verify full system functionality and if applicable implement preventative measures, and 7. Document findings, actions, and outcomes (Answer D).

Question 16

B. Power over Ethernet (PoE) is a technology that enables electrical power to transmit over twisted-pair Ethernet cable. The power is transferred, along with data, to provide power to remote devices. These devices may include remote switches, wireless access points, VoIP equipment, and more. Answer A, PPPoE (Point-to-Point Protocol over Ethernet) is used for encapsulating frames and does not enable electrical power to transmit over Ethernet. The other options (Answers C and D) are fictitious choices.

Question 17

D. A packet sniffer can be used on the Internet to capture data traveling between computers. A registered jack (Answer A) is a connector used with wiring. NIDS (Answer B) is a Network-based Intrusion Detection System, whereas NIPS (Answer C) is a Network-based Intrusion Prevention System.

Question 18

C. F-type connectors (which are screw-type connectors) are used with coaxial cable. ST (Answer A), SC (Answer B), and MT-RJ (Answer D) connectors are associated with fiber cabling.

Question 19

A and D. Main Distribution Frame (MDF) and Intermediate Distribution Frame (IDF) define types of wiring closets. The main wiring closet for a network typically holds the majority of the network gear, including routers, switches, wiring, servers, and more. When multiple wiring closets are used, the main distribution frame (MDF) connects to secondary wiring closets or intermediate distribution frames (IDFs). The Building Distribution Frame, or BDF (Answer B), is the superset of which both MDF and IDF constitute. Answer C is incorrect because FSF is a nonexistent entity.

Question 20

D. Ports 67 and 68 are associated with DHCP by default. Port 53 is associated with DNS (Answer C). Port 3389 by default is associated with RDP (Answer B), whereas port 143 is associated with IMAP (Answer A).

Question 21

B and **D.** Link-state protocols include Open Shortest Path First (OSPF) and Intermediate System-to-Intermediate System (IS-IS). Answer A, Interior Gateway Routing Protocol (IGRP), and Answer C, Routing Information Protocol (RIP), are examples of distance-vector protocols.

Question 22

D. The netstat utility is used to view the current TCP/IP connections on a system. The tracert utility (Answer A) is used in Windows-based operating systems to trace the route taken to reach a particular host. arp (Answer B) is used for resolving IP addresses to MAC addresses. ping (Answer C) tests if connectivity exists.

Question 23

C. A network's demarcation point refers to the connection point between the ISP's part of the network and the customer's portion of the network. A demilitarized zone, or DMZ (Answer D), is part of a network where you place servers that must be accessible by sources both outside and inside your network. The other choices (Answers A and B) are fictitious options.

Question 24

A and **B.** In a traditional crossover cable, wires 1 and 3 and wires 2 and 6 are crossed. The other options (Answers C and D) are not correct wiring choices for a traditional crossover cable.

Question 25

C. Terminal Access Controller Access Control System+ (TACACS+) is a security protocol designed to provide centralized validation of users who attempt to gain access to a router or Network Access Server (NAS). RDP, Remote Desktop Protocol (Answer A), is a presentation layer protocol that supports traffic between a Windows Terminal Client and Windows Terminal Server. AAA (Answer B) represents the authentication, authorization, and accounting model. ASDM (Answer D) is incorrect because it is a fictitious choice.

Question 26

A. A certificate is a digitally signed statement that associates the credentials of a public key to the identity of the person, device, or service that holds the corresponding private key. The other choices (Answers B, C, and D) are not correct names for a digitally signed statement associating the credentials of a public key to the identity of the person, device, or service holding the private key.

Question 27

D. A honeypot is a site created to lure attackers in and hopefully allow you to catch them in the act. Network Address Translation, or NAT (Answer A), is a standard that enables the translation of IP addresses used on one network to a different IP address that is acceptable for use on another network. A demilitarized zone, or DMZ (Answer B), is part of a network where you place servers that must be accessible by sources both outside and inside your network. An Access Control List, or ACL (Answer C), is a list of trustees assigned to a file or directory. A trustee can be any object available to the security subsystem.

Question 28

B. A public key infrastructure (PKI) is a collection of software, standards, and policies that are combined to allow users from the Internet or other unsecured public networks to securely exchange data. A honeynet (Answer A) is an entire network set up to monitor attacks from outsiders. X.509 (Answer C) and X.503 (Answer D) are standards not related to the question being asked and thus incorrect choices.

Question 29

D. TLS is a security protocol designed to ensure privacy between communicating client/server applications. STFP (Answer A) is a protocol for securely uploading and downloading files to and from a remote host. TFTP (Answer B) is a UDP-based protocol for file transfer that does not include security or error checking. IGMP (Answer C) provides a mechanism for systems within the same multicast group to register and communicate with each other.

Question 30

B. RAID 5, disk striping with distributed parity, requires a minimum of three disks—the total size of a single disk being used for the parity calculation. RAID 1 (Answer A) is a fault-tolerant standard that mirrors data between two disks to create an exact copy. RAID 0 (Answer C) requires a minimum of two disks, offers no fault tolerance and improves I/O performance. RAID 0 + 1 (Answer D) combines RAID levels 1 and 0.

Question 31

A. Port 143 is associated with IMAP by default. Port 3389, by default, is associated with RDP (Answer B), whereas port 53 is associated with DNS (Answer C), and ports 67 and 68 are associated with DHCP (Answer D).

Question 32

C. In the networking world, throughput refers to the rate of data delivery over a communication channel. Cost (Answer A) is a value used to encourage or discourage the use of a certain route through a network. Convergence (Answer B) is the time it takes for the routers to detect and accommodate a change. Latency (Answer D) is the delay induced by a piece of equipment or device used to transfer data.

Question 33

A. The use of multiple antennas to increase throughput is a part of MIMO (multiple-input and multiple-output). The other technologies given as options (Answers B, C, and D) do not apply to antennas.

Question 34

A. 802.2, the LLC sublayer, defines specifications for the Logical Link Control (LLC) sublayer in the 802 standard series. 802.3 (Answer B) defines the carrier sense multiple access with collision detection (CSMA/CD) media access method used in Ethernet networks. 802.11 (Answer C) is the standard for wireless local area networks (WLAN), whereas 802.5 (Answer D) is associated with token ring networks.

Question 35

A and **D.** The RDP and ICA protocols allow client systems to access and run applications on a remote system, using that system's resources. Only the user interface, keystrokes, and mouse movement are transferred between the client and server computers. Answers B (PCN) and C (NCV) are fictitious choices and thus incorrect.

Question 36

B. A public key is a nonsecret key that forms half of a cryptographic key pair that is used with a public key algorithm. The public key is freely given to all potential receivers. A private key is the secret half of a cryptographic key pair that is used with a public key algorithm. The private part of the public key cryptography system is never transmitted over a network. The other choices (Answers A, C, and D) are incorrect terms for the public key.

Question 37

C. On a network that uses CSMA/CD, every node has equal access to the network media. The other options (Answers A, B, and D) incorrectly state the relationship for a network using CSMA/CD.

Question 38

D. You need some form of hardware at the demarcation point: This is the smart jack, also known as the Network Interface Device (NID). An AP (Answer A) is an access point for a wireless network. A punchdown block (Answer B) is a device used to connect network cables from equipment closets or rooms to other parts of a building. A terminator (Answer C) is a hardware component used to stop a signal.

Question 39

B. Port 443 is associated with HTTPS by default. Port 3389, by default, is associated with RDP (Answer A), whereas port 22 is associated with SSH (Answer C), and port 25 is associated with SMTP (Answer D).

Question 40

C. PPTP creates a secure tunnel between two points on a network, over which other connectivity protocols, such as PPP, can be used. This tunneling functionality is the basis for VPNs. The other choices (Answers A, B, and D) do not state the primary purpose of PPTP.

Question 41

B. Performance tests are about network functioning today. Load tests (Answer A) look forward to see if performance may be hindered in the future by growth or other changes to the network. Both EGP (Answer C) and IGP (Answer D) are routing protocols and not applicable to the question asked.

Question 42

B. Class B addresses are within the range 128.0.0.0 to 191.255.255.255. The other choices (Answers A, C, and D) represent incorrect ranges for Class B addresses.

Question 43

C. ISAKMP is a framework defining the procedures for authentication, creation, and management of security associations (SAs), key generation techniques, and threat mitigation. STFP (Answer A) is a protocol for securely uploading and downloading files to and from a remote host. TFTP (Answer B) is a UDP-based protocol for file transfer that does not include security or error checking. (Answer D) TLS is a security protocol designed to ensure privacy between communicating client/server applications.

Question 44

D. A straight-through cable is used to connect systems to the switch or hub using the MDI-X ports. A plenum cable (Answer A) is used in the space between the structural ceiling and a drop-down ceiling. ISA (Answer B) is the standard of the older, more common, 8-bit and 16-bit bus and card architectures. A cross-over cable (Answer C) is used to directly connect two devices.

Question 45

B. AAA (authentication, authorization, and accounting) defines a spectrum of security measures, policies, and procedures that are combined to create a secure network. An Access Control List, or ACL (Answer A) is a list of trustees assigned to a file or directory. (A trustee can be any object available to the security subsystem.) PKI (Answer C) is a collection of software, standards, and policies combined to enable users from the Internet or other unsecured public networks to securely exchange data. ICS (Answer D) is an invalid option.

Question 46

C. A butt set enables the administrator or technician to butt into a communication line and use it. In the case of a phone line, a technician can use the line normally—that is, make a call, answer a call, or listen in to a call. An OTDR (Answer A) performs the same basic function as a wire media tester, but on optical media. TDRs (Answer B) work at the physical layer of the OSI model, sending a signal through a length of cable, looking for cable faults. A loop back plug (Answer D) has output and input wires crossed or shorted in a manner that enables all outgoing data to be routed back into the card.

Question 47

A. One type of attack is called an ICMP flood attack (also known as a ping attack). The attacker sends continuous ping packets to a server or network system, eventually tying up that system's resources, making it unable to respond to requests from other systems. Buffer overflow (Answer B) is an attack that occurs when more data is put into a buffer than it can hold, thereby overflowing it. Pharming (Answer C) redirects web traffic to an authorized server. Social engineering (Answer D) tricks individuals into giving an attacker data they would never volunteer.

Question 48

A. Port 3389, by default, is associated with RDP. Port 443 is associated with HTTPS (Answer B) by default, whereas port 22 is associated with SSH (Answer C), and port 25 is associated with SMTP (Answer D).

Question 49

A and **C.** Interior Gateway Routing Protocol (IGRP) and Routing Information Protocol (RIP) are examples of distance-vector protocols. Link-state protocols include Answer B, Open Shortest Path First (OSPF) and Answer D, Intermediate System-to-Intermediate System (IS-IS).

Question 50

D. An access control list (ACL) typically refers to specific access permissions assigned to an object or device on the network. For example, wireless routers can be configured to restrict who can and cannot access the router based on the MAC address. GFS (Answer A) is the Grandfather-Father-Son method of backup media rotation. DAC (Answer B) is discretionary access control, which is controlled by an object's owner. RBAC (Answer C) is the rule based access control method in which access to objects is given according to established rules.

Question 51

B. Authentication refers to the mechanisms used to verify the identity of the computer or user attempting to access a particular resource. This includes passwords and biometrics. Access Control (Answer A) describes the mechanisms used to filter network traffic to determine who is and who is not allowed to access the network and network resources. Authorization (Answer C) refers to identifying the resources a user can access after he is authenticated. Accounting (Answer D) refers to the tracking methods used to identify who is using the network and what he is doing on the network.

Question 52

B. NNTP (Network News Transfer Protocol) facilitates the access and downloading of messages from newsgroup servers. Answer A, NTP (Network Time Protocol) is used to communicate time synchronization information between devices. Answer C, SIP (Session Initiation Protocol) is an application layer protocol designed to establish and maintain multimedia sessions such as Internet telephony calls. Answer D, RTP (Real-time Transport Protocol) is the Internet-standard protocol for the transport of real-time data.

Question 53

A. A WAN may be referenced as a MAN (Metropolitan Area Network) when it is confined to a certain geographic area, such as a university campus or city. The other choices are incorrect as a WAN is not referred to as a storage area network (Answer B), or network attached storage (Answer C), or the fictitious CRAN (Answer D).

Question 54

C. WPAN (Wireless Personal Area Network) refers to the wireless technologies involved in connecting devices in close proximity to exchange data or resources. A campus area network (Answer A) is a WAN (Answer B) confined to a small area. Answer D, MPLAN, is a fictitious choice.

Question 55

B. Internet Group Multicast Protocol (IGMP) is used by systems within the same multicast group to communicate registration information. Answer A, Internet Control Message Protocol (ICMP) works with IP to provide error checking and reporting functionality on a network. Answer C, Network News Transfer Protocol (NNTP) is used to access Internet newsgroups. Answer D, Network Time Protocol (NTP) is used to synchronize system time with Internet servers.

Question 56

B and **D.** Fiber-optic cable can use either SC- or ST-type connectors. RJ-11 connectors (answer A) are associated with telephone cable, RJ-45 connectors (answer C) are associated with UTP cable, and BNC connectors (answer E) are associated with thin coaxial cable.

Question 57

B. USB interfaces have a number of connectors associated with them, but the most common are called Type A and Type B. FireWire interfaces (Answer A) use either a four-pin or six-pin connector; neither is referred to as Type A or Type B. RJ-11 (Answer C) is a type of connector associated with phone system wiring. Fiber-optic interfaces (Answer D) use a wide range of connectors, but none are called Type A or Type B.

Question 58

C. The WPA wireless security protocol uses TKIP (Temporal Key Integrity Protocol), which scrambles encryption keys using a hashing algorithm. Then the keys are issued an integrity check to verify that they have not been modified or tampered with during transit. Answers A and B are incorrect because TKIP encryption is not used with WEP. Answer D is not a valid encryption protocol.

Question 59

A. Class A subnets use the range 1 to 126 for the value of the first octet. Answer B is the IPv4 loopback address, which enables the IP stack functionality to be tested. Answers C and D are both addresses in the Class B range (128 to 191).

Question 60

A and C. Systems that have APIPA-assigned addresses can talk to each other (answer A), but not with any other systems (answer B). Systems with APIPA-assigned addresses cannot access the Internet (answer C) because the APIPA-assigned information does not include default gateway information. Therefore, communication is limited to the local network. Answer D is incorrect because the systems with APIPA addresses can talk to each other, even though they cannot communicate with any other systems.

Question 61

A. Of the options listed, only VPN (Virtual Private Network) is a technology and not a protocol, thus not part of the TCP/IP protocol suite. Answers B, C, D, and E are all protocols used in TCP/IP networks.

Question 62

C. SMTP is used to send email and is a protocol within the TCP/IP protocol suite. Answer A is not a valid protocol. Answers B and D are incorrect because POP3 and IMAP are email retrieval protocols, not protocols for sending email.

Question 63

C. The Service Set Identifier (SSID) is a unique identifier sent over the WLAN that acts as a simple password used when a client attempts to access an access point. The SSID is used to differentiate between networks; therefore, the client system and the AP must use the same SSID. Answer A is incorrect because a Security Identifier (commonly abbreviated SID) is a unique name (an alphanumeric character string) which is assigned by a Windows Domain controller during the log on process that is used to identify a subject, such as a user or a group of users in a network of Windows systems. WEP (Answer B) represents a form of wireless security, and the wireless channel (Answer D) is the band of frequency used for the wireless communication.

Question 64

A. The MAC address is a 6-byte address expressed in six pairs of hexadecimal values. Because it is hexadecimal, only the letters A through F and numbers can be used. Answer B is incorrect because MAC addresses are expressed as six hexadecimal pairs. Answer C is an example of an IPv4 address. Answer D is an example of an IPv6 address. Answer E is incorrect because MAC addresses are expressed in hexadecimal; therefore, only the letters A through F and numbers can be used.

Question 65

A. 802.1x is an IEEE standard specifying port-based network access control. Port-based network access control uses the physical characteristics of a switched local area network (LAN) infrastructure to authenticate devices attached to a LAN port and to prevent access to that port in cases where the authentication process fails. The other choices (Answers B, C, and D) do not describe 802.1x.

Question 66

C. The output shown is from the `dig` command. `dig` is used on UNIX and Linux systems to run manual DNS lookups. The `nslookup` command (answer A) also performs this function, but it produces different output. The `nbtstat` command (answer B) provides information on NetBIOS name resolutions. The `netstat` command (answer D) shows what TCP/IP protocol connections have been established on a system. These commands produce different output from `dig`.

Question 67

B. The −f switch of route clears all gateway entries. The −p switch (Answer A) is used with ADD to make routes persistent. The other two options (Answers C and D) are not valid switches with the route utility.

Question 68

A. The physical layer of the OSI seven-layer model is responsible for placing the signal on the network medium. The data link layer (answer B) is responsible for physical addressing and media access. MAC and LLC (answers C and D) are sublayers of the data link layer.

Question 69

D. Class D addresses fall within the range 224.0.0.0 to 239.255.255.255. Class D addresses are used for multicasting. The other choices (Answers A, B, C, and E) are incorrect because their ranges do not include 230.x.x.x.

Question 70

C. Port 22 is associated with SSH, by default. Port 3389 is associated with RDP (Answer A). Port 443 is associated with HTTPS (Answer B) by default, whereas port 25 is associated with SMTP (Answer D).

Question 71

B. The session layer synchronizes the data exchange between applications on separate devices. The presentation layer (Answer A) converts data from the application layer into a format that can be sent over the network. The transport layer (Answer C) establishes, maintains, and breaks connections between two devices. The network layer (Answer D) provides mechanisms for the routing of data between devices across single or multiple network segments.

Question 72

D. An OTDR performs the same basic function as a wire media tester, but on optical media. Punchdown tools (Answer A) are used to attach twisted-pair network cable to connectors within a patch panel. Voltage event recorders (Answer B) are used to monitor the quality of power used on the network or by network hardware. Toner probes (Answer C) are used to locate cables hidden in floors, ceilings, or walls and to track cables from the patch panel to their destination.

Question 73

C and **D.** VPNs are created and managed by using protocols such as PPTP and L2TP, which build on the functionality of PPP. This makes it possible to create dedicated point-to-point tunnels through a public network (the Internet). Answer A, PPPoE (Point-to-Point Protocol over Ethernet) is used for encapsulating frames and does not allow electrical power to be transmitted over Ethernet. Answer B, SIP (Session Initiation Protocol) is an application-layer protocol designed to establish and maintain multimedia sessions such as Internet telephony calls.

Question 74

A. Toner probes are specifically used to locate cables hidden in floors, ceilings, or walls and to track cables from the patch panel to their destination. Cable certifiers (Answer B) are a type of tester that enables you to certify cabling by testing it for speed and performance to see that the implementation lives up to the ratings. Punchdown tools (Answer C) are used to attach twisted-pair network cable to connectors within a patch panel. A butt set (Answer D) enables the administrator or technician to butt into a communication line and use it.

Question 75

C. Authorization is the method used to determine if an authenticated user has access to a particular resource. This is commonly determined through group association—a particular group may have a specific level of security clearance. Access control (Answer A) describes the mechanisms used to filter network traffic to determine who is and who is not allowed to access the network and network resources. Authentication (Answer B) refers to the mechanisms used to verify the identity of the computer or user attempting to access a particular resource (including passwords and biometrics). Accounting (Answer D) refers to the tracking methods used to identify who uses the network and what they do on the network.

Question 76

A. Kerberos is one part of a strategic security solution that provides secure authentication services to users, applications, and network devices. It eliminates the insecurities caused by passwords being stored or transmitted across the network. PKI (Answer B) is a collection of software, standards, and policies combined to enable users from the Internet or other unsecured public networks to securely exchange data. LDAP (Answer C) is a protocol used to access and query compliant directory services systems such as Microsoft Active Directory and Novell Directory services. SSL (Answer D) is a method of securely transmitting information to and receiving information from a remote website.

Question 77

C. A private key is the secret half of a cryptographic key pair used with a public key algorithm. The private part of the public key cryptography system is never transmitted over a network. A public key is a nonsecret key that forms half of a cryptographic key pair used with a public key algorithm. The public key is freely given to all potential receivers. The other choices (Answers A, B, and D) are incorrect terms for the private key.

Question 78

D. Accounting refers to the tracking mechanisms used to keep a record of events on a system. Access Control (Answer A) describes the mechanisms used to filter network traffic to determine who is and who is not allowed to access the network and network resources. Authentication (Answer B) refers to the mechanisms used to verify the identity of the computer or user attempting to access a particular resource (including passwords and biometrics). Authorization (Answer C) is the method used to determine if an authenticated user has access to a particular resource.

Question 79

D. To create secure data transmissions, IPSec uses two separate protocols: Authentication Header (AH) and Encapsulating Security Payload (ESP). The other choices (Answers A, B, and C) do not list the correct protocols that IPSec uses.

Question 80

B. 802.3 defines the carrier sense multiple access with collision detection (CSMA/CD) media access method used in Ethernet networks. 802.2 (Answer A), the LLC sublayer, defines specifications for the Logical Link Control (LLC) sublayer in the 802 standard series. 802.11 (Answer C) is the standard for wireless local area networks (WLAN), whereas 802.5 (Answer D) is associated with token ring networks.

Question 81

A. The presentation layer converts data from the application layer into a format that can be sent over the network. The session layer (Answer B) synchronizes the data exchange between applications on separate devices. The transport layer (Answer C) establishes, maintains, and breaks connections between two devices. The network layer (Answer D) provides mechanisms for the routing of data between devices across single or multiple network segments.

Question 82

D. A DMZ is part of a network on which you place servers that must be accessible by sources both outside and inside your network. A metropolitan area network, or MAN (Answer A), is a network that spans a defined geographic location, such as a city or suburb. A storage area network, or SAN (Answer B), is a network of storage disks. A demilitarized zone, or DMZ (Answer D), is part of a network where you place servers that must be accessible by sources both outside and inside your network.

Question 83

C. RAID 0 offers no fault tolerance and improves I/O performance. It requires a minimum of two disks. RAID 1 (Answer A) is a fault-tolerant standard that mirrors data between two disks to create an exact copy. RAID 5 (Answer B), disk striping with distributed parity, requires a minimum of three disks—the total size of a single disk being used for the parity calculation. RAID 0 + 1 (Answer D) combines RAID levels 1 and 0.

Question 84

C. Vertical cable, or backbone cable, refers to the media used to connect telecommunication rooms, server rooms, and remote locations and offices. A plenum cable (Answer B) is used in the space between the structural ceiling and a drop-down ceiling. Answers A (PVC) and D (tracer) are fictitious choices.

Question 85

A. The -6 switch is used with ping to force it to use IPv6; similarly -4 can be used to force it to use IPv4. The -a switch (Answer B) is used to resolve addresses to hostnames, whereas -n (Answer C) enables you specify a number of echo requests to send. The -1 option (Answer D) enables you set the buffer size.

Question 86

D. The next step is to establish a plan of action to resolve the problem and identify potential effects. The steps in the methodology are 1. Identify the problem (Answer A), 2. Establish a theory of probable cause (Answer C), 3. Test the theory to determine cause, 4. Establish a plan of action to resolve the problem and identify potential effects, 5. Implement the solution or escalate as necessary (Answer B), 6. Verify full system functionality and if applicable implement preventative measures, and 7. Document findings, actions, and outcomes.

Question 87

D. Windows Firewall is the software-based firewall included with Windows 7. PAT (Answer A) is a variation on NAT in which all systems on the LAN are translated to the same IP address, but with a different port number assignment. Firewall Manager (Answer B) is a fictitious option. ICS (Answer C) is not a valid option.

Question 88

B. TFTP is a UDP-based protocol for file transfer that does not include security or error checking. SFTP (Answer A) is a protocol for securely uploading and downloading files to and from a remote host. IGMP (Answer C) provides a mechanism for systems within the same multicast group to register and communicate with each other. TLS (Answer D) is a security protocol designed to ensure privacy between communicating client/server applications.

Question 89

A. Windows server and desktop systems such as Windows 7/Vista/XP and 2000 use Event Viewer to view many of the key log files. The logs in Event Viewer can be used to find information on, for example, an error on the system or a security incident. The other options (Answers B, C, and D) are incorrect because only Event Viewer is shown in the figure.

Question 90

A. ST connectors are associated with fiber cabling and have twist-type attachments. SC (Answer B), LC (Answer C), and MT-RJ (Answer D) connectors are associated with fiber cabling, and all three have push-on attachments.

Question 91

B. Public folders are used to share with others on the network. In Windows 7, there is a public folder available beneath each library (Documents, Music, Video, and so on). The other options (Answers A, C, and D) are incorrect choices.

Question 92

C. The ping utility is used to test connectivity between two hosts and is shown in the figure. The other options (Answers A, B, and D) are incorrect because ping is the utility shown in the figure.

Question 93

A. A router that uses a link-state protocol differs from a router that uses a distance-vector protocol because it builds a map of the entire network and then holds that map in memory. Link-state protocols include Open Shortest Path First (OSPF) and Intermediate System-to-Intermediate System (IS-IS). The other options (Answers B, C, and D) are incorrect statements.

Question 94

B. The session layer establishes, maintains, and breaks connections between two devices. The presentation layer (Answer A) coverts data from the application layer into a format that can be sent over the network. The transport layer (Answer C) provides mechanisms to transport data between network devices. The network layer (Answer D) provides mechanisms for the routing of data between devices across single or multiple network segments.

Question 95

C. A toner probe has two parts—the tone generator (or toner), and the tone locator (or probe). The toner sends the tone, and at the other end of the cable, the probe receives the toner's signal. This tool makes it easier to find the beginning and end of a cable. The other options (Answers A, B, and D) are not correct because they do not represent the two parts of a toner probe.

Question 96

E. Class E addresses fall within the range 240.0.0.0 to 255.255.255.255. Class E addresses are reserved and cannot be assigned. The other options (Answers A, B, C, and D) are incorrect because an address of 241.x.x.x would fall only within Class E.

Question 97

D. Port 25 is associated with SMTP by default. Port 3389 is associated with RDP (Answer A). Port 443 is associated with HTTPS by default (Answer B), while port 22 is associated with SSH (Answer C).

Question 98

A. The IP addresses available beneath 192.168.67.32/28 range from 192.168.67.33 to 192.168.67.46. With 28 mask bits, only 14 hosts can exist on a subnet. The other options (Answers B, C, and D) are incorrect ranges for the address and subnet values given.

Question 99

B. The nbtstat utility is used to view statistics related to NetBIOS name resolution and to see information about current NetBIOS over TCP/IP connections. ipconfig (Answer A) is used to view and renew TCP/IP configuration on a Windows system, whereas ifconfig (Answer C) is its counterpart in the UNIX/Linux operating systems. nslookup (Answer D) is used to perform manual DNS lookups.

Question 100

C. A baseline is a measure of performance that indicates how hard the network works and where network resources are spent. The other choices (Answers A, B, and D) represent wrong terms for a baseline.

Glossary

Numbers and Symbols

10Base2 An IEEE 802.3 specification for Ethernet at 10Mbps over thin coaxial cable. The maximum length of a 10Base2 segment is 185 meters (607 feet). 10Base2 operates at 10Mbps and uses a baseband transmission method.

10Base5 The IEEE 802.3 specification for 10Mbps Ethernet using thick coaxial cable. The maximum length of a 10Base5 segment is 500 meters (1,640 feet).

10BaseFL The IEEE 802.3 specification for running Ethernet at 10Mbps over fiber-optic cable. The maximum length of a 10BaseFL segment is 2,000 meters.

10BaseT The IEEE 802.3i specification for running Ethernet at 10Mbps over twisted-pair cabling. The maximum length of a 10BaseT segment is 100 meters (328 feet).

10GbaseER A 10Gbps Ethernet networking standard that can be used up to 40,000 meters.

10GbaseEW Both the ER and EW Gigabit standards deploy with extra-long-wavelength single-mode fiber. This medium provides transmission distances ranging from 2 meters to 40 kilometers. 10GbaseER deploys over dark fiber, but the EW standard is used primarily with SONET equipment.

10GbaseLR A 10Gbps Ethernet networking standard that can be used up to 10,000 meters. 10GbaseLR uses single-mode fiber-optic cabling.

10GbaseLW The 10GbaseLW Ethernet standard is over single-mode fiber. Both the LR and LW standards are designed to be used over long-wavelength single-mode fiber, giving it a potential transmission range of anywhere from 2 meters to 10 kilometers. The LW standard is designed to connect to SONET equipment.

10GbaseSR A 10Gbps Ethernet networking standard that can be used over relatively short distances, up to 300 meters.

10GbaseSW Both SR and SW are designed for deployment over short-wavelength multimode fiber. The distance range for both classifications ranges from as little as 2 meters to 300 meters. The difference between the two classifications is that SR is designed for use over dark fiber. The 10GbaseSW standard is designed for longer-distance data communications and connects to SONET equipment.

10GbE A term commonly used to refer to the 10Gbps Ethernet networking standards such as 10GbaseER, 10GbaseLR, and 10GbaseSR. 10 Gigabit Ethernet is defined in the IEEE 802.3ae standard.

100BaseFX The IEEE 802.3 specification for running Fast Ethernet at 100Mbps over fiber-optic cable. The maximum length of a 100BaseFX segment is 2,000 meters (6,561 feet) in full-duplex mode.

100BaseT The IEEE 802.3 specification for running Ethernet at 100Mbps over twisted-pair cabling. The maximum length of a 100BaseT segment is 100 meters (328 feet).

100BaseTX An IEEE 802.3u specification, also known as Fast Ethernet, for running Ethernet at 100Mbps over STP or UTP. The maximum length of a 100BaseTX segment is 100 meters (328 feet).

1000BaseT An IEEE 802.3ab standard that specifies Gigabit Ethernet over Category 5 UTP cable. The standard allows for full-duplex transmission using four pairs of twisted cable.

568A/568B standards Telecommunications standards from the Telecommunications Industry Association (TIA) and the Electronics Industry Association (EIA). These 568 standards specify the pin arrangements for the RJ-45 connectors on UTP or STP cables. The number 568 refers to the order in which the wires within the UTP cable are terminated and attached to the connector.

A

AAA   Authentication, authorization, and accounting. Authentication is the process to determine if someone is authorized to use the network—if he can log on to the network. Authorization refers to identifying the resources a user can access after he is authenticated. Accounting refers to the tracking methods used to identify who uses the network and what they do on the network.

access point   A transmitter and receiver (transceiver) device commonly used to facilitate communication between a wireless client and a wired network. Wireless APs are used with the wireless infrastructure network topology to provide a connection point between WLANs and a wired Ethernet LAN.

ACK   The acknowledgment message sent between two hosts during a TCP session.

ACL (access control list)   The list of trustees assigned to a file or directory. A trustee can be any object available to the security subsystem. The term ACL is also used with routers and firewall systems to refer to the list of permitted computers or users.

Active Directory   Used in Windows network environments, this is a directory services system that enables network objects to be stored in a database. This database can then be divided and distributed among different servers on the network.

active hub   A hub that has power supplied to it for the purposes of regenerating the signals that pass through it.

ad hoc topology   Defines a wireless network layout whereby devices communicate directly between themselves without using an access point. Sometimes called an unmanaged or peer-to-peer wireless topology.

address   A set of numbers used to identify and locate a resource or device on a network. An example is an IP address such as 192.168.2.1.

administrator   A person responsible for the control and security of the user accounts, resources, and data on a network.

Administrator account   On a Windows system, the default account that has rights to access everything and to assign rights to other users on the network. Unlike other user accounts, the Administrator account cannot be deleted.

ADSL (Asymmetric Digital Subscriber Line)   A service that transmits digital voice and data over existing (analog) phone lines.

AES (Advanced Encryption Standard)   An encryption algorithm for securing sensitive networks used by U.S. Government agencies. Has become the encryption standard for corporate networks.

AH (Authentication Header) One of the two separate protocols IPSec consists of (the other being ESP). AH provides the authentication and integrity checking for data packets.

AM (Amplitude Modulation) One of the earliest forms of radio modulation, this is a technique used in communication to transmit information over a radio wave.

ANSI (American National Standards Institute) An organization that publishes standards for communications, programming languages, and networking.

antivirus software A software application that detects and removes virus programs.

AP (wireless access point) A network device that offers connectivity between wireless clients and (usually) a wired portion of the network.

APIPA (Automatic Private IP Addressing) A technology implemented on certain Windows platforms through which a system assigns itself an IP address in the absence of a DHCP server. Addresses are assigned from the 169.254.x.x address range.

application layer Layer 7 of the OSI model, which provides support for end users and for application programs using network resources.

application-level firewall Application-layer firewalls operate at the application layer of the OSI model. Application layer firewalls can inspect data packets traveling to or from an application.

application log A log file on a Windows system that provides information on events that occur within an application.

archive bit A flag that is set on a file after it has been created or altered. Some backup methods reset the flag to indicate that it has been backed up.

ARIN (American Registry for Internet Numbers) The regional Internet registry responsible for managing both IPv4 and IPv6 IP number distribution.

ARP (Address Resolution Protocol) A protocol in the TCP/IP suite used to resolve IP addresses to MAC addresses. Specifically, the ARP command returns a Layer 2 address for a Layer 3 address.

ARP ping The ARP utility that resolves IP addresses to MAC addresses. The ARP ping utility tests connectivity by pinging a MAC address directly.

ARP table A table of entries used by ARP to store resolved ARP requests. Entries can also be manually stored.

array A group of devices arranged in a fault-tolerant configuration. *See also* RAID.

ASP (Application Service Provider) A vendor who provides computer-based services over the network.

attenuation The loss of signal experienced as data transmits over distance and across the network medium.

ATM (Asynchronous Transfer Mode)
A packet-switching technology that provides transfer speeds ranging from 1.544Mbps to 622Mbps.

authentication   The process by which a user's identity is validated on a network. The most common authentication method is a username and password combination.

B

B (bearer) channel   In ISDN, a 64Kbps channel that carries data. *See also* D (delta) channel.

backbone   A network segment that acts as a trunk between other network segments. Backbones typically are high-bandwidth implementations such as fiber-optic cable.

backup schedule   A document or plan that defines what type of backups are made, when, and what data is backed up.

bandwidth   The width of the range of electrical frequencies, or how many channels the medium can support. Bandwidth correlates to the amount of data that can traverse the medium at one time, but other factors determine the maximum speed supported by a cable .

baseband   A term applied to any medium that can carry only a single data signal at a time. Compare with broadband.

baseline   A measurement of performance of a device or system for the purposes of future comparison. Baselining is a common server administration task.

baud rate   The speed or rate of signal transfer. Baud rate bandwidth is measured in cycles per second, or Hertz (Hz). The word baud is derived from the name of French telegraphy expert J. M. Baudot.

BDF (Building Distribution Frame)
A network wiring closet typically housing wiring distribution equipment and hardware. Two common network BDFs are the Intermediate Distribution Frame (IDF) and the Main Distribution frame (MDF).

beaconing   In a wireless network, *beaconing* refers to the continuous transmission of small packets (beacons) that advertise the presence of a base station (access point).

BERT (Bit-Error Rate Test)   A test to see the number of received bits of a data stream that has changed due to noise, interference, or other distortion.

BGP   Border Gateway Protocol. Used between gateway hosts on the Internet. BGP examines the routing table, which contains a list of known routers, the addresses they can reach, and a cost metric associated with the path to each router so that the best available route is chosen. BGP communicates between the routers using TCP.

binary   A base 2 numbering system used in digital signaling. It uses only the numbers 1 and 0.

binding The process of associating a protocol with a NIC.

biometrics The science and technology of measuring and analyzing biological data. Biometrics is used for security purposes to analyze and compare characteristics such as voice patterns, retina patterns, and hand measurements.

BIOS (Basic Input/Output System) A basic set of instructions that a device needs to operate.

bit An electronic digit used in the binary numbering system. Bit is a contraction of the terms binary and digit.

blackout A total loss of electrical power.

Bluetooth A low-cost, short-range RF technology designed to replace many of the cords used to connect devices. Bluetooth uses 2.4GHz RF and provides transmission speeds up to 24Mbps.

BNC (Bayonet Neill Concelman) connector A family of connectors typically associated with thin coaxial cabling and 10Base2 networks. BNC connectors use a twist-and-lock mechanism to connect devices to the network.

BOOTP Bootp is a TCP/IP protocol used by a network device to obtain an IP address and other network information such as server address and default gateway.

bound medium Describes any medium that has physical constraints, such as coaxial, fiber-optic, and twisted pair. Compare with unbound medium.

boundless medium *See* unbound medium.

BPDU (Bridge Protocol Data Unit) Identifies the status of ports and bridges across the network. BPDUs are simple data messages exchanged between switches. They contain information on ports and provide the status of those ports to other switches.

BRI (Basic Rate Interface) An ISDN digital communications line that consists of three independent channels: two B channels each at 64Kbps and one D channel at 16Kbps. ISDN BRI is often referred to as 2B+D. *See also* ISDN and PRI.

bridge A device that connects and passes packets between two network segments that use the same communications protocol. Bridges operate at the data link layer of the OSI model. A bridge filters, forwards, or floods an incoming frame based on the packet's MAC address.

bridging address table A list of MAC addresses that a bridge keeps and uses when it receives packets. The bridge uses the bridging address table to determine which segment the destination address is on before it sends the packet to the next interface or drops the packet (if it is on the same segment as the sending node).

broadband A communications strategy that uses analog or digital signaling over multiple communications channels.

broadcast A packet-delivery system in which a copy of a packet is transmitted to all hosts attached to the network.

broadcast storm   An undesirable condition in which broadcasts become so numerous that they bog down the flow of data across the network.

brouter   A device that you can use to combine the benefits of both routers and bridges. Its common usage is to route routable protocols at the network layer of the OSI model and to bridge nonroutable protocols at the data link layer.

brownout   A short-term decrease in the voltage level, usually caused by the startup demands of other electrical devices.

BSSID (Basic Service Set Identification)   The BSSID is the MAC address of the wireless access point (AP).

buffer   An area of memory in a device used to temporarily store data before it is forwarded to another device or location.

bus topology   A linear LAN architecture in which all devices connect to a common cable, called a bus or backbone.

butt set   The butt set is typically associated with telephony systems. It is used to test and access the phone line using clip wires that attach to the phone cable.

byte   A set of bits (usually 8) that operate as a unit to signify a character.

C

cable modem   A device that provides Internet access over cable television lines.

cable stripper   A tool used to strip the sheathing from copper cabling.

cable tester   A device used to check for electrical continuity along a length of cable. Cable tester is a generic term that can be applied to devices such as volt/ohm meters and TDRs.

caching-only server   A type of DNS server that operates the same way as secondary servers except that a zone transfer does not take place when the caching-only server is started.

CARP (Common Address Redundancy Protocol)   A protocol that enables multiple hosts on the same network to share a set of IP addresses and thus provides failover redundancy. It is commonly used with routers and firewalls and can provide load balancing.

carrier   A signal that carries data. The carrier signal is modulated to create peaks and troughs, which represent binary bits.

change control   A process in which a detailed record of every change made to the network is documented.

channel   A communications path used for data transmission.

CHAP (Challenge Handshake Authentication Protocol)   A protocol that challenges a system to verify identity. CHAP is an improvement over Password Authentication Protocol (PAP) in which one-way hashing is incorporated into a three-way handshake. RFC 1334 applies to both PAP and CHAP.

checksum A basic method of error checking that involves calculating the sum of bytes in a section of data and then embedding the result in the packet. When the packet reaches the destination, the calculation is performed again to make sure that the value is still the same.

CIDR (classless interdomain routing) An IP addressing scheme that enables a single IP address to designate many unique IP addresses. CIDR addressing uses an IP address followed by a / and the IP network prefix. An example of a CIDR address is 192.168.100.0/16. CIDR is sometimes called supernetting.

circuit-level firewall A type of network security system whereby network traffic is filtered based on specified session rules and may be restricted to recognized computers only.

circuit switching A method of sending data between two parties in which a dedicated circuit is created at the beginning of the conversation and is broken at the end. All data transported during the session travels over the same path, or circuit.

Class A network A TCP/IP network that uses addresses from 1 to 126 and supports up to 126 subnets with 16,777,214 unique hosts each.

Class B network A TCP/IP network that uses addresses from 128 to 191 and supports up to 16,384 subnets with 65,534 unique hosts each.

Class C network A TCP/IP network that uses addresses from 192 to 223 and supports up to 2,097,152 subnets with 254 unique hosts each.

client A node that uses the services from another node on a network.

client/server networking A networking architecture in which front-end, or client, nodes request and process data stored by the back-end, or server, node.

cloud computing The hosting, storage, and delivery of computing as a service rather than a product. The end user accesses remotely stored programs and other resources through the Internet without the need for expensive local networking devices, services, and support.

clustering A technology that enables two or more computers to act as a single system to provide improved fault tolerance, load balancing, and failover capability.

CNAME (canonical name) Specifies an alias or nickname for a canonical hostname record in a domain name system (DNS) database. CNAME records are used to give a single computer multiple names (aliases).

coaxial cable A data cable, commonly referred to as coax, that is made of a solid copper core insulated and surrounded by braided metal and covered with a thick plastic or rubber covering. Coax is the standard cable used in cable television and in older bus topology networks.

cold site A disaster recovery site that provides office space, but the customer provides and installs all the equipment needed to continue operations.

cold spare   A redundant piece of hardware stored in case a component should fail. Typically used for server systems.

collision   The result of two frames simultaneously transmitting on an Ethernet network and colliding, thereby destroying both frames.

collision domain   A segment of an Ethernet network between managing nodes, where only one packet can be transmitted at a time. Switches, bridges, and routers can be used to segment a network into separate collision domains.

collision light   An LED on networking equipment that flashes to indicate a collision on the network. A collision light can be used to determine whether the network is experiencing many collisions.

communication   The transfer of information between nodes on a network.

concentrator   A device that combines several communications channels into one. It is often used to combine multiple terminals into one line.

connectionless communication Packet transfer in which delivery is not guaranteed.

connection-oriented communication   Packet transfer in which delivery is guaranteed.

connectivity   The linking of nodes on a network for communication to take place.

convergence   When a change in the network routing is made, it takes

some time for the routers to detect and accommodate this change; this is known as convergence.

copy backup   Normally, a backup of the entire hard drive. A copy backup is similar to a full backup, except that the copy backup does not alter the state of the archive bits on files.

cost   A value used to encourage or discourage the use of a certain route through a network. Routes that are to be discouraged are assigned a higher cost, and those that are to be encouraged are assigned a lower cost. *See also* metric.

cracker   A person who attempts to break software code or gain access to a system to which he or she is not authorized. *See also* hacker.

cracking   The process of attempting to break software code, normally to defeat copyright protection or alter the software's functioning. Also the process of attempting to gain unauthorized access to a computer system. *See also* hacking.

CRAM-MD5   A challenge-response authentication mechanism.

CRC (cyclical redundancy check) A method used to check for errors in packets that have been transferred across a network. A computation bit is added to the packet and recalculated at the destination to determine whether the entire content of the packet has been correctly transferred.

crimper   A tool used to join connectors to the ends of network cables.

crossover cable   A cable that can be used to directly connect two devices—such as two computer systems—or as a means to expand networks that use devices such as hubs or switches. A traditional crossover cable is a UTP cable in which the wires are crossed for the purposes of placing the transmit line of one device on the receive line of the other. A T1 crossover is used to connect two T1 CSU/DSU devices in a back-to-back configuration.

crosstalk   Electronic interference caused when two wires are too close to each other, and the adjacent cable creates interference.

CSMA/CA (carrier sense multiple access with collision avoidance)   A contention media access method that uses collision-avoidance techniques.

CSMA/CD (carrier sense multiple access with collision detection)   A contention media access method that uses collision-detection and retransmission techniques.

CSU/DSU (Channel Service Unit/Data Service Unit)   Acts as a translator between the LAN data format and the WAN data format. Such a conversion is necessary because the technologies used on WAN links are different from those used on LANs.

cut-through packet switching   A switching method that does not copy the entire packet into the switch buffers. Instead, the destination address is captured into the switch, the route to the destination node is determined, and the packet is quickly sent out the corresponding port. Cut-through packet switching maintains a low latency.

D

Data field   In a frame, the field or section that contains the data.

data link layer   Layer 2 of the OSI model, which is above the physical layer. Data comes off the cable, goes through the physical layer, and goes into the data link layer. The data link layer has two distinct sublayers: MAC and LLC.

datagram   An information grouping transmitted as a unit at the network layer. *See also* packet.

DB-25   A 25-pin connector used for serial port or parallel port connection between PCs and peripheral devices.

DB-9   A nine-pin connector used for serial port or parallel port connection between PCs and peripheral devices.

D (delta) channel   The channel used on ISDN to communicate signaling and other related information. Use of the D channel leaves the B channels free for data communication. *See also* B (bearer) channel.

DDNS (Dynamic Domain Name Service)   A form of DNS that enables systems to be registered and deregistered with DNS dynamically. DDNS is facilitated by DHCP, which passes IP address assignments to the DNS server for entry into the DNS server records. This is in contrast with the conventional DNS system, in which entries must be manually made.

DDoS (Distributed Denial of Service) A DoS attack that utilizes more than one computer in the attack. *See* DoS (Denial of Service).

DDS (digital data storage) A format for storing computer data on a DAT. DDS-formatted tapes can be read by either a DDS or DAT drive. The original DDS standard specified a 4mm tape cartridge with a capacity of 1.3GB. Subsequent implementations of DDS have taken the capacity to 40GB with compression.

dedicated line A dedicated circuit used in WANs to provide a constant connection between two points.

default gateway Normally a router or a multihomed computer to which packets are sent when they are destined for a host on a different network.

demarcation point The point at which communication lines enter a customer's premises. Sometimes shortened to simply demarc.

destination address The network address to which data is sent.

DHCP (Dynamic Host Configuration Protocol) A protocol that provides dynamic IP addressing to DHCP-enabled workstations on the network.

dialup networking Refers to the connection of a remote node to a network using POTS.

differential backup A backup of only the data that has been created or changed since the previous full backup. In a differential backup, the state of the archive bits is not altered.

dig On a Linux, UNIX, or Macintosh system, you can use the `dig` command to perform manual DNS lookups.

directory services A system that enables network resources to be viewed as objects stored in a database. This database can then be divided and distributed among different servers on the network. Examples of directory services systems include Novell Directory Services and Microsoft Active Directory.

disaster recovery plan A plan for implementing duplicate computer services if a natural disaster, a human-made disaster, or another catastrophe occurs. A disaster recovery plan includes offsite backups and procedures to activate information systems in alternative locations.

disk duplexing A fault-tolerant standard based on RAID 1 that uses disk mirroring with dual disk controllers. *See also* RAID.

disk mirroring A fault-tolerant standard that is defined as RAID 1 and mirrors data between two disks to create an exact copy.

disk striping An implementation of RAID in which data is distributed across multiple disks in a stripe. Some striping implementations provide performance improvements (RAID 0), whereas others provide fault tolerance (RAID 5).

distance-vector routing A type of routing in which a router uses broadcasts to inform neighboring routers on the network of the routes it knows about. Compare with link-state routing.

DLC (Data Link Control) The service provided by the data link layer of the OSI model.

DMZ (Demilitarized Zone) An area for placing web and other servers that serve the general public outside the firewall, therefore isolating them from internal network access.

DNS (Domain Name Service) A system used to translate domain names, such as www.quepublishing.com, into IP addresses, such as 165.193.123.44. DNS uses a hierarchical namespace that enables the database of hostname-to-IP address mappings to be distributed across multiple servers.

DOCSIS (Data-Over-Cable Service Interface Specification) A telecommunications standard for transmitting high-speed data over existing cable TV systems.

domain A logical boundary of an Active Directory Structure on Windows servers. Also, a section of the DNS namespace.

domain name server A server that runs application software that enables the server to perform a role associated with the DNS service.

DoS (denial of service) attack A type of hacking attack in which the target system is overwhelmed with requests for service, which keeps it from servicing any requests—legitimate or otherwise.

downtime A period of time during which a computer system or network is unavailable. This may be due to scheduled maintenance or hardware or software failure.

DSL (Digital Subscriber Line) A public network technology that delivers high bandwidth over conventional copper wiring over limited distances.

DSU (data service unit) A network communications device that formats and controls data for transmission over digital lines. A DSU is used with a CSU.

DTE (data terminal equipment) A device used at the user end of a user network interface that serves as a data source, a destination, or both. DTE devices include computers, protocol translators, and multiplexers.

dumb terminal A keyboard/monitor combination that enables access to a multiuser system but provides no processing or storage at the local level.

duplexing In RAID, a RAID 1 mirror set in which each drive is connected to a separate controller to eliminate the single point of failure that the controller created.

DWDM (Dense Wavelength Division Multiplexing) A form of multiplexing optical signals that replaces SONET/SDH regenerators with erbium doped fiber amplifiers (EDFAs) and can also amplify the signal and allow it to travel a greater distance. The main components of a DWDM system include a terminal multiplexer, line repeaters, and a terminal demultiplexer.

dynamic routing A routing system that enables routing information to be communicated between devices automatically and that can recognize changes in the network topology and update routing tables accordingly. Compare with static routing.

dynamic window   A flow control mechanism that prevents the sender of data from overwhelming the receiver. The amount of data that can be buffered in a dynamic window varies in size, hence its name.

E

E1 (E-Carrier Level 1)   An E1 link that operates over two separate sets of wires, typically twisted-pair cable.

EAP (Extensible Authentication Protocol)   An extension of PPP that supports authentication methods more secure than a standard username and password combination. EAP is commonly used as an authentication protocol for token cards, smart cards, and digital certificates.

EDNS (Extension Mechanisms for DNS)   As specified by the Internet Engineering Task Force as RFC 2671, EDNS increases the size of the flags fields, return codes and label types available in basic DNS.

EGP (Exterior Gateway Protocol)   The exterior gateway protocol defines distance vector protocols commonly used between hosts on the Internet to exchange routing table information. BGP is an example of an EGP. *See* BGP.

EIGRP (Enhanced Interior Gateway Routing Protocol)   A protocol that enables routers to exchange information more efficiently than earlier network protocols. Routers configured to use EIGRP keep copies of their neighbors' routing information and query these tables to help find the best possible route for transmissions to follow.

EMI (electromagnetic interference)   External interference of electromagnetic signals that causes a reduction in data integrity and increased error rates in a transmission medium.

encapsulation   A technique used by protocols in which header and trailer information is added to the protocol data unit as it is passed down through the protocol stack on a sending system. The reverse process, decapsulation, is performed at the receiving system as the packet travels up through the protocol suite.

encryption   Modifying data for security purposes prior to transmission so that the data cannot be read without the decryption method.

ESD (electrostatic discharge)   A condition created when two objects of dissimilar electrical charge come into contact with each other. The result is that a charge from the object with the higher electrical charge discharges itself into the object with the lower-level charge. This discharge can be harmful to computer components and circuit boards.

ESP (Encapsulated Security Packets) One of the two separate protocols IPSec consist of (the other being AH). ESP provides encryption services.

ESS (Extended Service Set) The extended service set (ESS) refers to two or more BSS sets connected, therefore using multiple APs. The ESS would be used to create WLANs or larger wireless networks and is a collection of APs and clients. *See* BSS.

ESSID (Extended Service Set Identifier) The terms ESSID and SSID are used interchangeably, but they are different. The SSID is the name used with BSS networks, and the ESSID is the network name used with an ESS wireless network design. With an ESS, not all APs necessarily use the same name.

Ethernet The most common LAN technology. Ethernet can be implemented using coaxial, twisted-pair, or fiber-optic cable. Ethernet typically uses the CSMA/CD media access method and has various implementation standards.

Event Viewer A utility available on Windows Server systems and client systems including Windows 7/Vista/XP. It is commonly used to gather systems information and also is used in the troubleshooting process.

F

failover The automatic switching from one device or system to another. Servers can be configured in a failover configuration so that if the primary server fails, the secondary server automatically takes over.

Fast Ethernet The IEEE 802.3u specification for data transfers of up to 100Mbps over twisted-pair cable. *See also* 100BaseFX, 100BaseT, and 100BaseTX.

fault tolerance The capability of a component, system, or network to endure a failure.

FDDI (Fiber Distributed Data Interface) A high-speed data transfer technology designed to extend the capabilities of existing LANs by using a dual-ring topology and a token-passing access method.

FDM (Frequency-Division Multiplexing) A technology that divides the output channel into multiple smaller-bandwidth channels, each of which uses a different frequency range.

FHSS (Frequency Hopping Spread Spectrum) A multiple access method of transferring radio signals in the frequency-hopping code division multiple access (FH-CDMA) scheme.

fiber-optic cable Also known as fiber optics or optical fiber, a physical medium that can conduct modulated light transmissions. Compared with other transmission media, fiber-optic cable is more expensive, but it is not susceptible to EMI or crosstalk, and it is capable of high data rates and increased distances.

Fibre Channel   A technology that defines full gigabit-per-second data transfer over fiber-optic cable. Commonly used with storage area network (SAN) implementations.

firewall   A program, system, device, or group of devices that acts as a barrier between one network and another. Firewalls are configured to enable certain types of traffic to pass while blocking others.

flow control   A method of controlling the amount of data transmitted within a given period of time. Different types of flow control exist. *See also* dynamic window and static window.

FM (Frequency Modulation)   One form of radio modulation, this communication technique transmits information over a radio wave.

FQDN (fully qualified domain name)   The entire domain name. It specifies the name of the computer, the domain in which it resides, and the top-level DNS domain (for example, www.marketing.quepublishing.com).

fragment-free switching   A switching method that uses the first 64 bytes of a frame to determine whether the frame is corrupted. If this first part is intact, the frame is forwarded.

frame   A grouping of information transmitted as a unit across the network at the data link layer of the OSI model.

Frame Length field   In a data frame, the field that specifies the length of a frame.

Frame Type field   In a data frame, the field that names the protocol being sent in the frame.

frequency   The number of cycles of an alternating current signal over a unit of time. Frequency is expressed in hertz.

FTP (File Transfer Protocol)   A protocol that provides for the transfer of files between two systems. FTP is part of the TCP/IP suite and operates at Layer 7 of the OSI model.

F-type connecter   A screw-type connector used with coaxial cable. In computing environments, it is most commonly used to connect cable modems to ISP equipment or incoming cable feeds.

full backup   A backup in which files, regardless of whether they have been changed, are copied to the backup medium. In a full backup, the files' archive bits are reset.

full duplex   A system in which data simultaneously transmits in two directions. Compare with half duplex.

G

gateway   A hardware or software solution that enables communications between two dissimilar networking systems or protocols. A gateway can operate at any layer of the OSI model but is commonly associated with the application layer.

Gb (gigabit)   1 billion bits, or 1000Mb.

GBIC (Gigabit Interface Converter)
A Gigabit Ethernet and fibre channel transceiver standard.

Gbps (gigabits per second) The throughput of a given network medium in terms of 1 billion bps.

GFS (grandfather, father, son) A tape rotation backup strategy of maintaining backups on a daily, weekly, and monthly schedule. Backups are made on a 5-day or 7-day schedule. A full backup is performed at least once a week. On all other days, full, incremental, or differential backups (or no backups at all) are performed. The daily incremental, or differential, backups are known as the son. The father is the last full backup in the week (the weekly backup). The grandfather is the last full backup of the month (the monthly backup).

Gigabit Ethernet An IEEE 802.3 specification that defines standards for data transmissions of 1Gbps. *See also* 1000BaseX.

GPG (GNU Privacy Guard) An IETF RFC 4880-compliant alternative to the PGP suite of cryptographic software.

guaranteed flow control A method of flow control in which the sending and receiving hosts agree on a rate of data transmission. After the rate is determined, the communication takes place at the guaranteed rate until the sender is finished. No buffering takes place at the receiver.

H

hacker A person who carries out attacks on a computer software program. *See also* cracker.

half duplex A connection in which data is transmitted in both directions but not simultaneously. Compare with full duplex.

handshake The initial communication between two data communication devices, during which they agree on protocol and transfer rules for the session.

hardware address The hardware-encoded MAC address burned into every NIC.

hardware loopback A device plugged into an interface for the purposes of simulating a network connection. This enables the interface to be tested as if it is operating while connected.

HDLC (High-Level Data Link Control) An ISO developed bit-oriented synchronous data link layer protocol used for point-to-point or point-to-multipoint connections.

hop The means by which routing protocols determine the shortest way to reach a given destination. Each router constitutes one hop. If a router is four hops away from another router, for example, three routers, or hops, exist between the first router and the destination. In some cases, the final step is also counted as a hop.

horizontal cross-connect Ties the telecommunication room to the end user. Specifically, the horizontal cabling extends from the telecommunications outlet, or network outlet with RJ-45 connectors, at the client end. It includes all cable from that outlet to the telecommunication room to the horizontal cross-connect. The term horizontal cross-connect refers to the distribution point for the horizontal cable.

host Typically refers to any device on the network that has been assigned an IP address.

host firewall A firewall system installed and configured on and used for an individual host. Contrast to a network firewall that provides firewall services for all network nodes.

host ID An identifier used to uniquely identify a client or resource on a network.

hostname A name assigned to a system for the purposes of identifying it on the network in a more user-friendly manner than by the network address.

HOSTS file A text file that contains hostname-to-IP address mappings. All commonly used platforms accommodate static name resolution using the HOSTS file.

hot site A disaster recovery term used to describe an alternative network site that can be immediately functional in the event of a disaster at the primary site.

hot spare In a RAID configuration, a drive that sits idle until another drive in the RAID array fails, at which point the hot spare takes over the role of the failed drive.

hotspot An area in which an access point provides public wireless broadband network services to mobile visitors through a WLAN. Hotspots are often located in heavily populated places such as airports, hotels, and coffee shops.

hot swap The removal and replacement of a component in a system while the power is still on and the system is functioning.

HSRP (Hot Standby Router Protocol) A Cisco proprietary protocol used for establishing redundant gateways.

HTTP (Hypertext Transfer Protocol) A protocol used by web browsers to transfer pages, links, and graphics from the remote node to the user's computer.

HTTPS (Hypertext Transfer Protocol Secure) A protocol that performs the same function as HTTP but does so over an encrypted link, ensuring the confidentiality of any data that is uploaded or downloaded. Also referred to as S-HTTP.

hub A hardware device that acts as a connection point on a network that uses twisted-pair cable. Also known as a concentrator or a multiport repeater.

HyperTerminal A Windows-based communications program that enables users to establish host/shell access to a remote system.

Hz (Hertz) Equivalent to cycles per second, hertz is the unit of frequency defined as the number of cycles per second of a periodic phenomenon.

I

IANA (Internet Assigned Numbers Authority) An organization responsible for IP addresses, domain names, and protocol parameters. Some functions of IANA, such as domain name assignment, have been devolved into other organizations.

ICMP (Internet Control Message Protocol) A network layer Internet protocol documented in RFC 792 that reports errors and provides other information relevant to IP packet processing. Utilities such as ping and tracert use functionality provided by ICMP.

ICS (Internet Connection Sharing) The use of one device with access to the Internet as an access point for other devices to connect.

IDF Some networks use multiple wiring closets. When this is the case, the wiring closet, known as the main distribution frame (MDF), connects to secondary wiring closets, or intermediate distribution frames (IDFs). *See also* MDF.

IDS (Intrusion Detection System) A software application or hardware device that monitors a network or system for malicious or nonpolicy related activity and reports to a centralized management system.

IEEE (Institute of Electrical and Electronics Engineers) A professional organization that, among other things, develops standards for networking and communications.

IEEE 1394 A standard that defines a system for connecting up to 63 devices on an external bus. IEEE 1394 is commonly used with consumer electronic devices such as video cameras and MP3 players. IEEE 1394 is based on a technology developed by Apple Computers called FireWire.

IEEE 802.1 A standard that defines the OSI model's physical and data link layers. This standard allows two IEEE LAN stations to communicate over a LAN or WAN and is often called the internetworking standard.

IEEE 802.1X An IEEE security standard designed for authenticating wireless devices. This standard uses Extensible Authentication Protocol (EAP) to provide a central authentication server to authenticate each user on the network.

IEEE 802.2 A standard that defines the LLC sublayer of the data link layer for the entire series of protocols covered by the 802.x standards. This standard specifies the adding of header fields, which tell the receiving host which upper layer sent the information.

IEEE 802.3 A standard that specifies physical layer attributes, such as signaling types, data rates, and topologies, as well as the media access method used. It also defines specifications for the implementation of the physical layer and the

MAC sublayer of the data link layer, using CSMA/CD. This standard also includes the original specifications for Fast Ethernet.

IEEE 802.4 A standard that defines how production machines should communicate. It establishes a common protocol for use in connecting these machines. It also defines specifications for the implementation of the physical layer and the MAC sublayer of the data link layer, using token ring access over a bus topology.

IEEE 802.5 A standard used to define token ring. However, it does not specify a particular topology or transmission medium. It provides specifications for the implementation of the physical layer and the MAC sublayer of the data link layer, using a token-passing media access method on a ring topology.

IEEE 802.6 A standard that defines the distributed queue dual-bus technology to transfer high-speed data between nodes. It provides specifications for the implementation of MANs.

IEEE 802.7 A standard that defines the design, installation, and testing of broadband-based communications and related physical media connectivity.

IEEE 802.8 A standard that defines the Fiber Optic Technical Advisory Group, which advises the other 802 standards committees on various fiber-optic technologies and standards.

IEEE 802.9 A standard that defines the integration of voice and data transmissions using isochronous Ethernet.

IEEE 802.10 A standard that focuses on security issues by defining a standard method for protocols and services to exchange data securely by using encryption mechanisms.

IEEE 802.11 The original IEEE wireless standard, which defines standards for wireless LAN communication.

IEEE 802.11a A wireless networking standard operating in the 5GHz band. 802.11a supports a maximum theoretical data rate of 54Mbps. Depending on interference, 802.11a could have a range of 150 feet at the lowest speed setting. Higher-speed transmissions would see a lower range. 802.11a uses the CSMA/CA media access method and is incompatible with 802.11b and 802.11g.

IEEE 802.11b A commonly deployed IEEE wireless standard that uses the 2.4GHz RF range and offers speeds up to 11Mbps. Under ideal conditions, the transmission range can be as far as 75 meters.

IEEE 802.11g An IEEE wireless standard that is backward compatible with 802.11b. 802.11g offers a data rate of 54Mbps. Like 802.11b, 802.11g uses the 2.4GHz RF range.

IEEE 802.11n The 802.11n standard significantly increase throughput in both the 2.4GHz and 5GHz frequency range. The baseline goal of the standard reaches speeds of 100Mbps, but given the right conditions, 802.11n speeds may reach 600Mbps. In practical operation, 802.11n speeds are much less.

IEEE 802.12 A standard that defines 100BaseVG-AnyLAN, which uses a 1Gbps signaling rate and a special media access method that enables 100Mbps data traffic over voice-grade cable.

IETF (Internet Engineering Task Force) A group of research volunteers responsible for specifying the protocols used on the Internet and the architecture of the Internet.

ifconfig A command used on Linux, UNIX, and OS/2 systems to obtain configuration for and configure network interfaces.

IGMP (Internet Group Management Protocol) A protocol used for communication between devices within the same multicast group. IGMP provides a mechanism for systems to detect and make themselves aware of other systems in the same group.

IGP The interior gateway protocol (IGP) identifies the protocols used to exchanging routing information between routers within a LAN or interconnected LANs. See EGP.

IIS (Internet Information Services) A web server application and supporting services created by Microsoft for Microsoft Windows.

IKE (Internet Key Exchange) An IPSec protocol that uses X.509 certificates for authentication.

IMAP4 (Internet Message Access Protocol version 4) A protocol that enables email to be retrieved from a remote server. It is part of the TCP/IP suite, and it is similar in operation to POP3 but offers more functionality.

incremental backup A backup of only files that have been created or changed since the last backup. In an incremental backup, the archive bit is cleared to indicate that a file has been backed up.

infrared A wireless data communication method that uses light pulses in the infrared range as a carrier signal.

infrastructure topology A wireless topology that defines a wireless network composed of an access point connected to a wired LAN. Wireless devices communicate with the wired LAN through the access point (AP).

inherited rights The file system or directory access rights valid at a given point as a result of those rights being assigned at a higher level in the directory structure.

intelligent hub/switch A hub or switch that contains some management or monitoring capability.

intelligent UPS A UPS that has associated software for monitoring and managing the power provided to the system. For information to be passed between the UPS and the system, the UPS and system must be connected, which normally is achieved through a serial or USB connection.

interface A device, such as a card or plug, that connects pieces of hardware with a computer so that information can be moved from place to place (for example, between computers and printers, hard disks, and other devices, or between two or more nodes on a network). Also, the part of an application or operating system that the user sees.

interference Anything that can compromise a signal's quality. On bound media, crosstalk and EMI are examples of interference. In wireless environments, atmospheric conditions that degrade a signal's quality would be considered interference.

internal loopback address Functionality built into the TCP/IP stack that enables you to verify the correct functioning of the stack. You can ping any IPv4 address in the 127.x.x.x range, except the network address (127.0.0.0) or the broadcast address (127.255.255.255). The address 127.0.0.1 is most commonly used. In IPv6, the localhost (loopback) address is 0:0:0:0:0:0:0:1.

Internet domain name The name of an area of the DNS namespace. The Internet domain name normally is expressed along with the top-level domain to which it belongs (for example, comptia.org).

Internet layer In the TCP/IP architectural model, the layer responsible for addressing, packaging, and routing functions. Protocols that operate at this layer are responsible for encapsulating packets into Internet datagrams. All necessary routing algorithms are run here.

internetwork A group of networks connected by routers or other connectivity devices so that the networks function as one network.

intrusion detection The process or procedures that warn you about successful or failed unauthorized access to a system.

IP (Internet Protocol) A network layer protocol, documented in RFC 791, that offers a connectionless internetwork service. IP provides features for addressing, packet fragmentation and reassembly, type-of-service specification, and security.

IP address The unique address used to identify the network number and node address of a device connected to a TCP/IP network. IPv4 addresses typically are expressed in dotted-decimal format, such as 192.168.1.1. A typical IPv6 address looks like 2001:0:4137:9e76:18d1: 2094:b980:a30.

IPS (Intrusion Prevention System) A network device that continually scans the network, looking for inappropriate activity.

ipconfig A Windows command that provides information about the configuration of the TCP/IP parameters, including the IP address.

IPSec (IP Security) A protocol used to provide strong security standards for encryption and authentication on virtual private networks.

IPv4 (Internet Protocol version 4) A suite of protocols used for communication on a local area network and for accessing the Internet.

IPv6 (Internet Protocol version 6) The new version of IP, which has a larger range of usable addresses than the current version of IP, IPv4, and enhanced security.

IrDA A wireless networking technology that uses infrared beams to send data transmissions between devices.

ISAKMP (Internet Security Association and Key Management Protocol) Defined by RFC 2408, ISAKMP is a protocol typically used by IKE for key exchange.

ISDN (Integrated Services Digital Network) An internationally adopted standard for providing end-to-end digital communications between two points. ISDN is a dialup technology allowing data, voice, and other source traffic to be transmitted over a dedicated link.

ISDN terminal adapter A device that enables communication over an ISDN link.

IS-IS Intermediate System-to-Intermediate System. A link-state protocol that discovers the shortest path for data to travel using the shortest path first (SPF) algorithm. IS-IS routers distribute topology information to other routers, allowing them to make the best path decisions.

ISO (International Organization for Standardization) A voluntary organization founded in 1946 that is responsible for creating international standards in many areas, including communications and computers. This also includes the development of the OSI model.

ISP (Internet service provider) A company or organization that provides facilities for clients to access the Internet.

IV (Initialization Vector) A fixed size input used in cryptography. The larger initialization vector, the more it increases the difficulty in cracking and minimizes the risk of replay.

J

jumpered (or jumpering) Refers to the physical placement of shorting connectors on a board or card.

jumperless A term used to describe devices configured via a software utility rather than by physical jumpers on the circuit board.

K

Kb (kilobit) 1,000 bits.

KB (kilobyte) 1,000 bytes.

Kerberos A network authentication protocol designed to ensure that the data sent across networks is encrypted and safe from attack. Its primary purpose is to provide authentication for client/server applications.

L

L2F (Layer 2 Forwarding) A Cisco tunneling protocol designed to specifically tunnel point-to-point protocol (PPP) traffic.

L2TP (Layer 2 Tunneling Protocol) A VPN protocol that defines its own tunneling protocol and works with the advanced security methods of IPSec. L2TP enables PPP sessions to be tunneled across an arbitrary medium to a home gate-way at an ISP or corporation.

LACP (Link Aggregation Control Protocol)   An IEEE specification that provides a control method of bundling several physical ports into one single channel.

LAN (local area network)   A group of connected computers located in a single geographic area—usually a building or office—that share data and services.

latency   The delay induced by a piece of equipment or device used to transfer data.

LC connector   A media connector used with fiber-optic cabling.

LDAP   A protocol used to access and query compliant directory services systems such as Microsoft Active Directory and Novell Directory services.

learning bridge   A bridge that builds its own bridging address table instead of requiring someone to manually enter information. Most modern bridges are learning bridges. Also called a smart bridge.

legacy   An older computer system or technology.

line conditioner   A device used to stabilize the flow of power to the connected component. Also known as a power conditioner or voltage regulator.

link light   An LED on a network-ing device such as a hub, switch, or NIC. The illumination of the link light indicates that, at a hardware level, the connection is complete and functioning.

link-state routing   A dynamic rout-ing method in which routers tell neighboring routers of their exis-tence through packets called link-state advertisements (LSAs). By interpreting the information in these packets, routers can create maps of the entire network. Compare with distance-vector routing.

Linux   A UNIX-like operating sys-tem kernel created by Linus Torvalds. Linux is distributed under an open-source license agreement, as are many of the applications and services that run on it.

LLC (logical link control) layer   A sublayer of the data link layer of the OSI model. The LLC layer pro-vides an interface for network layer protocols and the MAC sublayer.

LMHOSTS file   A text file used in a Windows network environment that contains a list of NetBIOS host-name-to-IP address mappings used in TCP/IP name resolution.

logical addressing scheme   The addressing method used in provid-ing manually assigned node address-ing.

logical topology   The appearance of the network to the devices that use it, even if in physical terms the layout of the network is different. *See also* physical topology.

loop   A continuous circle that a packet takes through a series of nodes in a network until it eventual-ly times out.

loopback plug   A device used for loopback testing.

loopback testing   A troubleshooting method in which the output and input wires are crossed or shorted in a manner that enables all outgoing data to be routed back into the card.

M

MAC (Media Access Control) address   A six-octet number, described in hexadecimal, that uniquely identifies a host on a network. It is a unique number burned into the network interface.

MAC layer   In the OSI model, the lower of the two sublayers of the data link layer. It is defined by the IEEE as being responsible for interaction with the physical layer.

Mac OS X   Version 10 of an operating system designed for Macintosh computer systems. Mac OS X represents a complete shift in Apple operating systems because it is based on UNIX code and as such can be managed using UNIX utilities and procedures.

MAN (metropolitan area network)   A network that spans a defined geographic location, such as a city or suburb.

master name server   The supplying name server that has authority in a DNS zone.

Mb (megabit)   1 million bits. Used to rate transmission transfer speeds.

MB (megabyte)   1 million bytes. Usually refers to file size.

Mbps (megabits per second)   How many millions of bits can travel across a given medium in a second.

MDF   The main distribution frame is a type of wiring closet. The primary wiring closet for a network typically holds the majority of the network gear, including routers, switches, wiring, servers, and more. This is also typically the wiring closet where outside lines run into the network. This main wiring closet is known as the MDF. One of the key components in the MDF is a primary patch panel. The network connector jacks attached to this patch panel lead out to the building for network connections. *See also* IDF.

MDI (medium-dependent interface)   A type of port found on Ethernet networking devices such as hubs and switches in which the wiring is straight through. MDI ports are sometimes called uplink ports. They are intended for use as connectivity points to other hubs and switches.

MDI-X (medium-dependent interface crossed)   A type of port found on Ethernet networking devices in which the wiring is crossed so that the transmit line of one device becomes the receive line of the other. MDI-X is used to connect hubs and switches to client computers.

media converter   Network media converters are used to interconnect different types of cables within an existing network. For example, the media converter can be used to connect newer Gigabit Ethernet technologies with older 100BaseT networks.

media tester Defines a range of software or hardware tools designed to test a particular media type.

memory address The label assigned to define the location in memory where information is stored.

mesh A type of network topology in which each node connects to every other node. The mesh network provides a high level of redundancy because it provides alternative routes for data to travel should a single route becomes unavailable.

metric A value that can be assigned to a route to encourage or discourage the use of the route. *See also* cost.

MIB (Management Information Base) A data set that defines the criteria that can be retrieved and set on a device using SNMP.

microsegmentation The process of using switches to divide a network into smaller segments.

microwaves A wireless technology sometimes used to transmit data between buildings and across vast distances.

mirroring A fault-tolerant technique in which an exact duplicate of data on one volume is created on another. Mirroring is defined as RAID 1. *See also* RAID.

MMF (Multimode Fiber) A type of fiber in which many beams of light travel through the cable, bouncing off the cable walls. This strategy actually weakens the signal, reducing the length and speed at which the data signal can travel. *See also* SMF.

modem (modulator-demodulator) A device used to modulate and demodulate the signals that pass through it. It converts the direct current pulses of the serial digital code from the controller into the analog signals compatible with the telephone network.

MPLS (Multiprotocol Label Switching) A technology designed to speed up network traffic flow by moving away from the use of traditional routing tables. Instead of routing tables, MPLS uses short labels to direct packets and forward them through the network.

MSAU (multistation access unit) A device used in an IBM Token-Ring Network. It organizes the connected nodes into an internal ring and uses the RI and RO connectors to expand to other MSAUs on the network. Sometimes referred to as MAU.

MT-RJ connector A media connector used with fiber-optic cabling.

multicast A single-packet transmission from one sender to a specific group of destination nodes.

multihomed A term used to refer to a device that has more than one network interface.

multimeter A tool used to measure voltage, current and resistance.

multiplatform A term used to refer to a programming language, technology, or protocol that runs on different types of CPUs or operating systems.

multiplexing A technique of combining multiple channels over a transmission path and then recovering or demultiplexing the separate channels at the receiving end. Examples include FDM, TDM, CDM, and WDM.

N

NaaSC (Network as a Service) A cloud computing model offered by many telecom providers provided on demand in a pay-as-you-go model.

NAC (Network Access Control) A computer networking security solution that uses a set of network protocols with the goal to unify endpoint security solutions such as antivirus, vulnerability assessment, and authentication.

name server A server that contains a database of name resolution information used to resolve network names to network addresses.

NAT (Network Address Translation) A standard that enables the translation of IP addresses used on one network to a different IP address that is acceptable for use on another network. This translation enables multiple systems to access an external network, such as the Internet, through a single IP address.

NAS (Network attached Storage) A specialized file level computer storage device connected to a network.

nbtstat A Windows operating system command-line utility that displays protocol statistics and current TCP/IP connections using NetBIOS over TCP/IP (NBT).

NetBEUI (NetBIOS Extended User Interface) A nonroutable, Microsoft-proprietary networking protocol designed for use in small networks.

NetBIOS (Network Basic Input/Output System) A software application that enables different applications to communicate between computers on a LAN.

netstat A Windows operating system command-line utility that displays protocol statistics and current TCP/IP network connections.

network card *See* NIC.

network ID The part of a TCP/IP address that specifies the network portion of the IP address. The network ID is determined by the class of the address, which in turn is determined by the subnet mask used.

network interface layer The bottom layer of the TCP/IP architectural model, which is responsible for sending and receiving frames.

network layer Layer 3 of the OSI model, which is where routing based on node addresses (IP addresses) occurs.

network operating system An operating system that runs on the servers on a network. Network operating systems include Windows Server 2008, UNIX, and Linux.

newsgroup A discussion group that focuses on a specific topic and is made up of a collection of messages posted to an Internet site. Newsgroups are useful resources for support personnel.

NFS (Network File System) A file sharing and access protocol most commonly associated with UNIX and Linux systems.

NIC (network interface card) A hardware component that serves as the interface, or connecting component, between a network and the node. It has a transceiver, a MAC address, and a physical connector for the network cable. Also called a network adapter or network card.

NIPS (Network Intrusion Prevention System) A network security system that monitors, blocks, and reports malicious network activity.

NMS (Network Management System) An application that acts as a central management point for network management. Most NMS systems use SNMP to communicate with network devices. *See also* SNMP.

NNTP (Network News Transfer Protocol) An Internet protocol that controls how news articles are to be queried, distributed, and posted. NNTP uses port 119.

noise Another name for EMI. *See also* EMI.

nslookup Windows and Linux/UNIX command-line utility used to query Domain Name System (DNS) servers and clients to obtain DNS information.

NTP (Network Time Protocol) A protocol used to communicate time synchronization information between devices on the network. NTP is part of the TCP/IP suite. NTP uses port 123.

O

OS (operating system) The main computer program that manages and integrates all the applications running on a computer. The OS handles all interactions with the processor.

OSI (Open Systems Interconnect) reference model A seven-layer model created by the ISO to standardize and explain the interactions of networking protocols.

OSPF (Open Shortest Path First) A link-state routing protocol used on TCP/IP networks. Compare with distance-vector routing.

OTDR A tool used to locate problems with optical media, such as cable breaks.

P

packet A packet refers to a unit of data that travels in communication networks.

packet filtering A firewall method in which each packet that attempts to pass through the firewall is examined to determine its contents. The packet is then allowed to pass, or it is blocked, as appropriate.

packet sniffer   A device or application that enables data to be copied from the network and analyzed. In legitimate applications, it is a useful network troubleshooting tool.

PAN (personal area network)   A network layout whereby devices work together in close proximity to share information and services, commonly using technologies such as Bluetooth or infrared.

PAP (Password Authentication Protocol)   A simple authentication protocol in which the username and password are sent to the remote-access server in clear text, making it possible for anyone listening to network traffic to steal both. PAP typically is used only when connecting to older UNIX-based remote-access servers that do not support any additional authentication protocols.

passive hub   A hub that has no power and therefore does not regenerate the signals it receives. Compare with active hub.

password   A set of characters used with a username to authenticate a user on a network and to provide the user with rights and permissions to files and resources.

PAT (Port Address Translation)   A variation on NAT (Network Address Translation). With PAT, all systems on the LAN are translated into the same IP address, but with a different port number assignment. *See also* NAT.

patch   A fix for a bug in a software application. Patches can be downloaded from the Internet to correct errors or security problems in software applications.

patch cable   A cable, normally twisted pair, used to connect two devices. Strictly speaking, a patch cable is the cable that connects a port on a hub or switch to the patch panel, but today people commonly use the term to refer to any cable connection.

patch panel   A device in which the cables used in coaxial or twisted-pair networks converge and are connected. The patch panel is usually in a central location.

peer-to-peer networking   A network environment that does not have dedicated servers, where communication occurs between similarly capable network nodes that act as both clients and servers.

permissions   Authorization provided to users that allows them to access objects on a network. Network administrators generally assign permissions. Permissions are slightly different from but often used with rights.

physical address   The MAC address on every NIC. The physical address is applied to a NIC by the manufacturer. Except for rare occurrences, it is never changed.

physical layer   Layer 1 of the OSI model, where all physical connectivity is defined.

physical network diagram   A diagram that displays the physical layout of a network including placement of systems and all network cabling.

physical topology The actual physical layout of the network. Common physical topologies include star, bus, and ring. Compare with logical topology.

ping A TCP/IP stack utility that works with ICMP and that uses echo requests and replies to test connectivity to other systems.

PKI (Public Key Infrastructure) A collection of software, standards, and policies combined to enable users from the Internet or other unsecured public networks to securely exchange data. PKI uses a public and private cryptographic key pair obtained and shared through a trusted authority.

plenum The space between the structural ceiling and a drop-down ceiling. It is commonly used for heating, ventilation, and air conditioning systems and to run network cables.

plug and play An architecture designed to enable the operating system to detect hardware devices and for the driver to be automatically loaded and configured.

PoE (Power over Ethernet) A technology that enables electrical power to be transmitted over twisted-pair Ethernet cable. The power is transferred, along with data, to provide power to remote devices.

point-to-multipoint (PtMP) A wireless connection designed to link multiple wired networks. Signals in point-to-multipoint networks travel from a central node such as a base station of a cellular system, an access point of a WLAN, or a satellite.

point-to-point (PtP) Refers to a wireless topology configuration. It identifies the communication link from one node directly to one other node. Wireless point-to-point systems are often used in wireless backbone systems such as microwave relay communications, or as a replacement for a single wired communication cable.

policies and procedures Policies refer to an organization's documented rules regarding what is to be done, or not done, and why. Network procedures differ from policies in that they identify the way in which tasks are to be performed.

polling The media access method for transmitting data in which a controlling device is used to contact each node to determine whether it has data to send.

POP3 (Post Office Protocol version 3) A protocol that is part of the TCP/IP suite used to retrieve mail stored on a remote server. The most commonly used version of POP is POP3. POP is an application layer protocol.

port In physical networking terms, a pathway on a networking device that enables other devices to be connected. In software terms, a port is the entry point into an application, a system, or a protocol stack.

port mirroring A process by which two ports on a device, such as a switch, are configured to receive the same information. Port mirroring is useful in troubleshooting scenarios.

POTS (plain old telephone system) The current analog public telephone system. *See also* PSTN.

PPP (Point-to-Point Protocol) A common dialup networking protocol that includes provisions for security and protocol negotiation. Provides host-to-network and switch-to-switch connections for one or more user sessions.

PPPoE (Point-to-Point Protocol over Ethernet) An Internet connection authentication protocol that uses two separate technologies, Ethernet and PPP, to provide a method for multiple users to share a common Digital Subscriber Line (DSL), cable modem, or wireless connection to the Internet.

PPTP (Point-to-Point Tunneling Protocol) A protocol that encapsulates private network data in IP packets. These packets are transmitted over synchronous and asynchronous circuits to hide the Internet's underlying routing and switching infrastructure from both senders and receivers.

presentation layer Layer 6 of the OSI model, which prepares information to be used by the application layer.

PRI (Primary Rate Interface) A high-level network interface standard for use with ISDN. PRI is defined as having a rate of 1.544Mbps, and it consists of a single 64Kbps D channel plus 23 T1 B channels for voice or data. *See also* BRI and ISDN.

primary name server The DNS server that offers zone data from files stored locally on the machine.

private network A network to which access is limited, restricted, or controlled. Most corporate networks are private networks. Compare with public network.

proprietary A standard or specification created by a single manufacturer, vendor, or other private enterprise.

protocol A set of rules or standards that control data transmission and other interactions between networks, computers, peripheral devices, and operating systems.

protocol analyzer Protocol analyzers can be hardware- or software-based with their primary function being to analyze network protocols such as TCP, UPD, HTTP, FTP and more.

proxy A device, application, or service that acts as an intermediary between two hosts on a network, eliminating the capability for direct communication.

proxy server A server that acts as a go-between for a workstation and the Internet. A proxy server typically provides an increased level of security, caching, NAT, and administrative control.

PSTN (public switched telephone network) A term that refers to all the telephone networks and services in the world. The same as POTS, PSTN refers to the world's collection of interconnected public telephone networks that are both commercial- and government-owned. All the PSTN is digital, except the connection between local exchanges and customers (which is called the local loop or last mile), which remains analog.

public network   A network, such as the Internet, to which anyone can connect with the most minimal of restrictions. Compare with private network.

punchdown block   A device used to connect network cables from equipment closets or rooms to other parts of a building. Connections to networking equipment such as hubs or switches are established from the punchdown block. Also used in telecommunications wiring to distribute phone cables to their respective locations throughout the building.

punchdown tool   A hand tool that enables the connection of twisted-pair wires to wiring equipment such as a patch panel.

PVC (permanent virtual circuit)   A permanent dedicated virtual link shared in a Frame Relay network, replacing a hardwired dedicated end-to-end line.

Q–R

QoS (quality of service)   Describes the strategies used to manage and increase the flow of network traffic. QoS features enable administrators to predict bandwidth use, monitor that use, and control it to ensure that bandwidth is available to the applications that need it.

RADIUS (Remote Authentication Dial-in User Service)   A security standard that employs a client/server model to authenticate remote network users. Remote users are authenticated using a challenge-and-response mechanism between the remote-access server and the RADIUS server.

RAID (Redundant Array of Inexpensive Disks)   A method to store data on multiple hard drives, enabling the overlapping of I/O operations. The RAID levels offer either fault-tolerance or performance advantages.

RAID 0   A RAID configuration that employs data striping but that lacks redundancy because no parity information is recorded (see RAID 5). As a result, RAID 0 offers no fault tolerance, but it does offer increased performance. Requires a minimum of two disks.

RAID 1   A fault-tolerant method that uses disk mirroring to duplicate the information stored on a disk. Also called disk duplexing when the two drives in a RAID 1 array are connected to separate disk controllers.

RAID 5   A fault-tolerant method that uses disk striping with distributed parity. Striping is done across the disks in blocks.

RAID 10   Also called RAID 1/0. A RAID configuration in which stripe sets (RAID 0) are mirrored (RAID 1). This combination provides the fault-tolerant aspects of RAID 1 and the performance advantages of RAID 0.

RARP (Reverse Address Resolution Protocol) A protocol, part of the TCP/IP suite, that resolves MAC addresses to IP addresses. Its relative ARP resolves IP addresses to MAC addresses. RARP resides on the network layer of the OSI model.

RAS (Remote Access Service) A Windows service that enables access to the network through remote connections.

RDP (Remote Desktop Protocol) A presentation layer protocol that supports traffic between a Windows Terminal Client and Windows Terminal Server.

regulations Regulations are actual legal restrictions with legal consequences.

remote control In networking, having physical control of a remote computer through software.

remote node A node or computer connected to a network through a remote connection. Dialing in to the Internet from home is an example of the remote node concept.

repeater A device that regenerates and retransmits signals on a network. Repeaters usually are used to strengthen signals going long distances.

resolver A system that requests the resolution of a name to an IP address. This term can be applied to both DNS and WINS clients.

restore To transfer data from backup media to a server. The opposite of backup.

RFC (Request for Comments) The process by which standards relating to the Internet, the TCP/IP suite, and associated technologies are created, commented on, and approved.

RG-6/8/58/59 Designations for the coaxial cable used in thin coaxial networks that operate on the Ethernet standard.

rights An authorization provided to users that allows them to perform certain tasks. The network administrator generally assigns rights. Slightly different from but often used with the term permissions.

RIP (Routing Information Protocol) A protocol that uses hop count as a routing metric to control the direction and flow of packets between routers on an internetwork.

RJ-11 connector A connector used with telephone systems. Can have up to six conductors.

RJ-45 connector A connector used with twisted-pair cable. Can support eight conductors for four pairs of wires.

route The entire path between two nodes on a network.

router A device that works at the network layer of the OSI model to control the flow of data between two or more network segments.

RSA An algorithm for public-key cryptography. Can be used for encryption purposes. RSA is used as a secure solution for e-commerce.

RTP Real-time Transport Protocol (RTP). The Internet-standard protocol for the transport of real-time data, including audio and video.

S

sag A momentary drop in the voltage provided by a power source.

SC connector The SC connector is a type of connector used with fiber cabling.

SCP (Secure Copy Protocol) A basic file-copying protocol that uses Secure Shell (SSH) technology to provide security to the transfer.

SDSL (Symmetrical Digital Subscriber Line) A DSL implementation that offers the same speeds for uploads and downloads. It is not widely implemented in the home/small business environment and cannot share a phone line.

secondary name server A type of DNS server that gets its zone data from another DNS name server that has authority in that zone.

Security log A log located in the Windows Event Viewer that provides information on audit events that the administrator has determined to be security-related. These events include logons, attempts to log on, attempts to access areas that are denied, and attempts to log on outside normal hours.

segment A physical section of a network.

server A network node that fulfills service requests for clients. Usually referred to by the type of service it performs, such as file server, communications server, or print server.

server-based application An application run from a network share rather than from a copy installed on a local computer.

server-based networking A network operating system dedicated to providing services to workstations, or clients. *See also* client/server networking.

service pack A software update that fixes multiple known problems and in some cases provides additional functionality to an application or operating system.

session How long the dialog remains open between two nodes.

session layer Layer 5 of the OSI model, which establishes, manages, and terminates sessions between applications on different nodes.

SFTP (Secure File Transfer Protocol) An implementation of File Transfer Protocol (FTP) that uses Secure Shell (SSH) technology to provide additional authentication and encryption services for file transfers.

shared system The infrastructure component routed directly into an internetwork's backbone for optimal systems access. It provides connectivity to servers and other shared systems.

shell An interface, graphical or otherwise, that enables a user to access the functionality of an operating system.

SIP An application layer protocol designed to establish and maintain multimedia sessions such as Internet telephony calls.

SMF (Single-mode fiber) A type of fiber that uses a single direct beam of light, thus allowing for greater distances and increased transfer speeds. *See also* MMF.

SMTP (Simple Mail Transfer Protocol) An Internet protocol used for the transfer of email messages and attachments.

SNAT (Static NAT) A simple form of NAT. SNAT maps a private IP address directly to a static unchanging public IP address. *See also* NAT.

SNMP (Simple Network Management Protocol) Provides network devices with a method to monitor and control network devices; manage configurations, statistics collection, performance, and security; and report network management information to a management console. SNMP is part of the TCP/IP suite.

SNMP agent A software component that enables a device to communicate with, and be contacted by, an SNMP management system.

SNMP trap An SNMP utility that sends an alarm to notify the administrator that something within the network activity differs from the established threshold, as defined by the administrator.

SOA (start of authority) A record of information containing data on DNS zones and other DNS records. A DNS zone is the part of a domain for which an individual DNS server is responsible. Each zone contains a single SOA record.

SOHO (Small Office / Home Office) A small network typically serving 1 to 10 users.

SONET (Synchronous Optical Network) A U.S. standard for data transmission that operates at speeds up to 2.4Gbps over optical networks referred to as OC-*x*, where x is the level. The international equivalent of SONET is Synchronous Digital Hierarchy (SDH).

source address The address of the host that sent the frame. The source address is contained in the frame so that the destination node knows who sent the data.

source-route bridge A bridge used in source-route bridging to send a packet to the destination node through the route specified by the sending node.

spike An instantaneous, dramatic increase in the voltage input to a device. Spikes are responsible for much of the damage done to network hardware components.

SPS (Standby Power Supply) A type of power supply in which the SPS monitors the power line and switches to battery power as soon as it detects a problem. During the time it takes to switch to battery power, the computer does not receive any power and may power down. This is in contrast to an online UPS, which constantly provides battery power.

SSH (Secure Shell) An application, such as Telnet, that enables a session to be opened on a remote host. SSH differs from Telnet in that it provides additional authentication methods and encryption for data as it traverses the network. SSH uses TCP/IP port 22.

SSID (Service Set Identifier) A unique client identifier sent over the WLAN that acts as a simple password used for authentication between a wireless client and an access point. The SSID is used to differentiate between networks. Therefore, the client system and the AP must use the same SSID.

SSL (Secure Sockets Layer) A method of securely transmitting information to and receiving information from a remote website. SSL is implemented through HTTPS. SSL operates at the presentation layer of the OSI model and uses TCP/IP port 443.

STA (Spanning Tree Algorithm) A standard defined by IEEE 802.1 as part of STP to eliminate loops in an internetwork with multiple paths.

star A type of physical network design is which all nodes connect to a centralized device—in most cases a network switch.

static IP address An IP address manually assigned to a network device, as opposed to dynamically via DHCP.

static routing A routing method in which all routes must be entered into a device manually and in which no route information is exchanged between routing devices on the network. Compare with dynamic routing.

static window A mechanism used in flow control that prevents the sender of data from overwhelming the receiver. The amount of data that can be buffered in a static window is configured dynamically by the protocol.

ST connector ST refers to a type of fiber connector.

storage area network (SAN) A subnetwork of storage devices, usually found on high-speed networks and shared by all servers on a network.

store-and-forward A fast-packet-switching method that produces higher latency than other switching methods because the entire contents of the packet are copied into the switch's onboard buffers. CRC calculations are performed before the packet can be passed on to the destination address.

STP (shielded twisted pair) Twisted-pair network cable that has shielding to insulate the cable from EMI.

STP (Spanning Tree Protocol) A protocol developed to eliminate the loops caused by the multiple paths in an internetwork. STP is defined in IEEE 802.1.

subdomain A privately controlled segment of the DNS namespace that exists under other segments of the namespace as a division of the main domain. Sometimes also called a child domain.

subnet A logical division of a network, based on the address to which all the devices on the network are assigned.

subnet mask A 32-bit address used to mask, or screen, a portion of an IP address to differentiate the part of the address that designates the network and the part that designates the host.

subnetting The process of using parts of the node portion of an assigned IP address to create more network IDs. Although subnetting increases the number of network IDs, it decreases the number of node addresses available for each network ID.

supernetting The process of aggregating IP network addresses and using them as a single network address range.

surge A voltage increase that is less dramatic than that of a spike but can last much longer. Sometimes called a swell. The opposite of a brownout.

surge protector An inexpensive and simple device placed between a power outlet and a network component to protect the component from spikes and surges. Also known as a surge suppressor.

SVC (switched virtual circuit) A virtual circuit dynamically established on demand to form a dedicated link. It is broken when transmission is complete.

switch A Layer 2 networking device that forwards frames based on destination addresses.

SYN A message sent to initiate a TCP session between two devices. The full term is *synchronization packet*.

synchronous transmission A digital signal transmission method that uses a precise clocking method and a predefined number of bits sent at a constant rate.

system log A log, accessed through Event Viewer on Windows Server platforms, that provides information and warnings on events logged by operating system components and hardware devices. These events include driver failures, device conflicts, read/write errors, timeouts, and bad block errors.

T

T1/E1 T1 lines are a form of T-Carrier lines that offer transmission speeds of 1.544Mbps. E1 refers to the European equivalent of T1. *See also* T-carrier.

T1 crossover *See also* crossover cable.

T3/E3 T3 carrier lines offer transmission speeds of up to 44.736Mbps, using 672 64Kbps B channels. *See also* T-carrier.

TACACS+ (Terminal Access Controller Access Control System Plus) A security protocol designed to provide centralized validation of users who are attempting to gain access to a router or Network Access Server (NAS). TACACS+ is a set of security protocols designed to provide authentication, authorization, and accounting (AAA) of remote users. TACACS uses TCP port 49 by default.

T-carrier T-carrier lines are high-speed dedicated digital lines that can be leased from telephone companies. T-carrier lines can support both voice and data transmissions and are often used to create point-to-point private networks.

TCP (Transmission Control Protocol) A connection-oriented, reliable data transmission communication service that operates at the transport layer of the OSI model. TCP is part of the TCP/IP suite.

TCP/IP (Transmission Control Protocol/Internet Protocol) A suite of protocols that includes TCP and IP. TCP/IP was originally designed for use on large internetworks but has now become the de facto protocol for networks of all sizes.

TCP/IP socket A socket, or connection to an endpoint, used in TCP/IP communication transmissions.

TDM (Time-Division Multiplexing) Divides a single communication channel into multiple channels, enabling data signals to be transferred simultaneously as subchannels in one communication channel.

Despite being only a single channel, data signals take turns sending data.

TDR (time-domain reflectometer) A device used to test copper cables to determine whether and where a break is on the cable. For optical cables, an optical TDR is used.

Telnet A standard terminal emulation protocol in the TCP/IP stack. Telnet is used to perform terminal emulation over TCP/IP via remote terminal connections, enabling users to log in to remote systems and use resources as if they were connected to a local system.

temperature monitor A device used to monitor temperature typically in a server room or wiring closet.

Terminal Services A service on Windows Server platforms that enables clients to connect to the server as if it were a multiuser operating system. All the processing for the client session is performed on the server. Only screen updates and user input are transmitted across the network connection.

TFTP (Trivial File Transfer Protocol) A simplified version of FTP that enables file transfers but does not offer any security or file management capabilities. TFTP uses TCP/IP port 69.

thick coaxial The thick cable most commonly used as the backbone of a coaxial network. It is approximately .375 inches in diameter.

thick Ethernet The IEEE 802.3 standard 10Base5, which describes Ethernet networking using thick coaxial cabling. Also called ThickNet.

thin client An application run from a back-end server system such as Microsoft Terminal Services. The processing tasks are all performed at the terminal server rather than on the client. In basic usage, only screen updates are sent from the terminal server, and only keyboard and mouse data is sent to the terminal server.

thin coaxial Cable that is thinner than thick coaxial cable but still about .25 inches in diameter. It is commonly used in older bus topologies.

thin Ethernet The 802.3a standard 10Base2, which describes Ethernet networking using thin coaxial cabling. Also called ThinNet.

throughput tester A device used to test the actual data throughput of a network cable.

TIA (Telecommunications Industry Association) An organization that, along with the Electronic Industries Association (EIA), develops standards for telecommunications technologies.

TKIP (Temporal Key Integrity Protocol) Designed to address the shortcomings of the WEP security protocol. TKIP is an encryption protocol defined in IEEE 802.11i.

T-line A digital communication line used in WANs. Commonly used T designations are T1 (Trunk Level 1) and T3 (Trunk Level 3). It is also possible to use only part of a T1 line, which is known as fractional T1. T1 lines support a data transmission rate of up to 1.544 Mbps.

TLS (Transport Layer Security) A security protocol designed to ensure privacy between communicating client/server applications. When a server and client communicate, TLS ensures that no one can eavesdrop and intercept or otherwise tamper with the data message. TLS is the successor to SSL.

token A frame that provides controlling information. In a token ring network, the node that possesses the token is the one that is allowed to transmit next.

token ring An IBM-proprietary token-passing LAN topology defined by IEEE standard 802.5. It operates at either 4Mbps or 16Mbps in a star topology.

token ring adapter Traditionally an ISA or Microchannel device with 4Mbps or 16Mbps transfer capability used to connect nodes to a token ring network.

tone generator A device used with a tone locator to locate and diagnose problems with twisted-pair cabling. Commonly referred to as fox and hound.

toner probe A network tool used to locate the ends of a run of network cable.

topology The shape or layout of a physical network and the flow of data through the network. *See also* logical topology and physical topology.

trace route   A function of the TCP/IP suite, implemented in utilities such as traceroute and tracert, which enables the entire path of a packet to be tracked between source and destination hosts. It is used as a troubleshooting tool.

tracert   A Windows command-line utility used to track the route a data packet takes to get to its destination.

transmit   To send data using light, electronic, or electric signals. In networking, this is usually done in the form of digital signals composed of bits.

transparent bridging   A situation in which the bridges on a network tell each other which ports on the bridge should be opened and closed, which ports should be forwarding packets, and which ports should be blocking packets—all without the assistance of any other device.

transport layer   Layer 4 of the OSI model. Protocols at this layer perform functions such as segmenting data so that it can be sent over the network and then reassembling the segmented data on the receiving end. The transport layer also deals with some of the errors that can occur in a stream of data, such as dropped and duplicated packets.

transport protocol   A communications protocol responsible for establishing a connection and ensuring that all data has arrived safely. It is defined in Layer 4 of the OSI model.

Trojan   A type of program that appears legitimate but performs some illicit activity when it is run.

TTL (Time To Live)   A value assigned to a packet of data to prevent it from moving around the network indefinitely. The TTL value is decremented each time the packet crosses a router, until it reaches 0, at which point it is removed from the network.

twisted pair   A type of cable that uses multiple twisted pairs of copper wire.

U

UDP (User Datagram Protocol)   A communications protocol that provides connectionless, unreliable communication services and operates at the transport layer of the OSI model. It requires a network layer protocol such as IP to guide it to the destination host.

unbound medium (or boundless medium)   Any medium that does not have physical constraints. Examples of unbound media are infrared, wireless, and microwave. Compare with bound medium.

UNC (Universal Naming Convention)   An industry-naming standard for computers and resources that provides a common syntax that should work in most systems, including Windows, UNIX, and NetWare. An example of a UNC name is \\servername\sharename.

unicast   Communication that takes place over a network between a single sender and a single receiver.

UPS (uninterruptible power supply) A system that provides protection against power surges and power outages. During blackouts, a UPS gives you time to shut down systems or devices on the network before the temporary power interruption becomes permanent. A UPS is also called battery backup.

uptime How long a device has been on and operating.

URL (uniform resource locator) A name used to identify a website and subsequently a page on the Internet. An example of a URL is www.quepublishing.com/products.

USB (universal serial bus) A type of interface between a computer system and peripheral devices. The USB interface enables you to add or remove devices without shutting down the computer. USB supports up to 127 devices. USB also supports autodetection and plug and play.

UTP (unshielded twisted pair) A type of cable that uses multiple twisted pairs of copper wire in a casing that does not provide much protection from EMI. The most common network cable in Ethernet networks, UTP is rated in categories including Category 1 through Category 6, as well as Category 5e and Category 6a.

V

VDSL (Variable Digital Subscriber Line) An asymmetric version of DSL that supports high-bandwidth applications such as VoIP and HDTV. It is the fastest available form of DSL and uses fiber-optic cabling.

vertical cross-connect The main or vertical cross-connect is the location where outside cables enter the building for distribution. This may include Internet and phone cabling.

virus A software program designed specifically to adversely affect a system or network. A virus is usually designed to be passed on to other systems with which it comes in contact.

VLAN (virtual LAN) A group of devices located on one or more different LAN segments, whose configuration is based on logical instead of physical connections. This enables the devices to operate as if they were connected to the same physical switch, regardless of whether they are connected to the same switch.

VNC (virtual network computing) Enables remote login, in which clients can access their own desktops while being physically away from their computers.

VOIP (Voice over IP) Any of a number of technologies that enable voice communication across the Internet Protocol.

volume set Multiple disks or partitions of disks that have been configured to read as one drive.

VPN (virtual private network) A network that uses a public network such as the Internet as a backbone to connect two or more private networks. A VPN provides users with the equivalent of a private network in terms of security. VPNs can also be used as a means of establishing secure remote connectivity between a remote system and another network.

VTP (VLAN Trunking Protocol) A Cisco proprietary protocol that manages the addition, deletion, and renaming of VLANs for the entire network. Information about changes to a VLAN or the addition of a new VLAN to a network is distributed to all switches on the network simultaneously and does not need to be done one at a time.

W

WAN (wide area network) A data communications network that serves users across a broad geographic area. WANs often use transmission devices such as modems or CSUs/DSUs to carry signals over leased lines or common carrier lines.

warm site A disaster recovery site offering most equipment and applications. Compare to a cold site that refers to a disaster recovery site with limited hardware and typically only a reserved location. A hot site is one with duplicate hardware and software and can be operational within minutes of a disaster.

web server A server that runs an application and makes the contents of certain directories on that server,

or other servers, available to clients for download, via a protocol such as HTTP.

WEP (Wired Equivalent Privacy) A data encryption method used to protect the transmission between 802.11 wireless clients and access points. WEP security has come under scrutiny because it uses an insufficient key length and provides no automated method for distributing the keys.

WiFi A voluntary standard that manufacturers can adhere to, which aims to create compatibility between wireless devices. WiFi is an abbreviation for wireless fidelity.

WINS (Windows Internet Name Service) A NetBIOS name-to-IP address resolution service that runs on Windows Server platforms.

WINS database A dynamically built database of NetBIOS names and IP addresses used by WINS.

wire crimper A tool used to create networking cables. The type of wire crimping tool used depends on the cable being made.

wireless channel The band of frequency used for wireless communications. Each IEEE wireless standard specifies the channels that can be used.

wireless networking Networking that uses any unbound media, such as infrared, microwave, or radio waves.

wiring schematics Network documentation designed to show the physical wiring of a network. The wiring schematic can often be used in the troubleshooting process.

WISP (Wireless Internet Service Provider) A service provider that specializes in offering users wireless access to the Internet, often including hotspot access.

WLAN (wireless LAN) A local area network created using wireless transmission methods such as radio or infrared rather than traditional wired solutions.

workstation A client computer on a network that does not offer any services of its own but that uses the services of the servers on the network.

worm A self-replicating program that can perform destructive acts to a single computer or across a network, both wired and wireless.

WPA (WiFi Protected Access) A data encryption method used on 802.11 wireless LANs. WPA is an industry-supported standard designed to address WEP's security shortcomings.

X–Z

X.25 An ITU-T standardized protocol suite for packet switching networks.

XDSL (Extended Digital Subscriber Line) All the variations of DSL available are lumped together under the label XDSL.

XML (Extensible Markup Language) A set of rules for the encoding of documents in a machine readable format.

zone transfer The passing of DNS information from one name server to a secondary name server.

Index

Numerics

O

documentation (administration), 305

hybrid mesh topologies, 21

hybrid topologies, 27

IEEE 802.3 standard, 249

infrastructure wireless topologies, 22-23

logical topologies

    defining, 16

    logical ring topologies, 18

mesh topologies, 20

    advantages/disadvantages of, 21

    fault tolerance, 21

    hybrid mesh topologies, 21

    MPLS, 21-22

    redundancy, 20

    wireless mesh networks, 25-27

physical topologies

    defining, 16

    physical bus topologies, 17

PtMP network topologies, 25

PtP network topologies, 24

ring topologies, 18-19

star topologies, 19

    advantages/disadvantages of, 20

    hubs, 19

    switches, 19

    wiring, 505

troubleshooting, 504

    mesh topologies, 506

    star topologies, 505-506

wireless mesh network topologies, 25-27

wireless topologies

    ad hoc wireless topologies, 22-23

    infrastructure wireless topologies, 22-23

    mesh network topologies, 25-27

    PtMP network topologies, 25

    PtP network topologies, 24

traceroute command, 351-355

tracert command, 123, 351-355

traffic shaping, 154, 408-409

training, administration, 304

translational bridges, 138

transmission rates (data), cabling and, 213-214

transparent bridges, 138

transport layer

    OSI seven-layer networking model, 47, 49

    TCP/IP four-layer networking model, 50

trap managers, 84

Trojan horses, 451-452

troubleshooting

    antennas (wireless), 263, 267-268, 299

    AP, 497

    AP coverage, 263-264

    bridges, 497

    buses, 498

    cable Internet access, 196-197

    connectivity

        client connections, 498

        duplexes, 502

        media connections, 498-501

        port speeds, 502

    documentation (administration), advantages of, 304

    DSL Internet access, 194

    hardware, 496-497

    hubs, 496, 505

    ipconfig command, 371

    modems, 196

    networks

        black holes, 487-488

        broadcast storms, 487

        DNS, 490

        duplicate IP addresses, 489

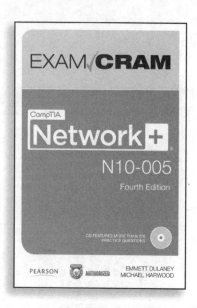

FREE Online Edition

Your purchase of **CompTIA Network+ N10-005 Authorized Exam Cram** includes access to a free online edition for 45 days through the Safari Books Online subscription service. Nearly every Pearson IT Certification book is available online through Safari Books Online, along with more than 5,000 other technical books and videos from publishers such as Addison-Wesley Professional, Cisco Press, Exam Cram, IBM Press, O'Reilly, Prentice Hall, and Sams.

SAFARI BOOKS ONLINE allows you to search for a specific answer, cut and paste code, download chapters, and stay current with emerging technologies.

Activate your FREE Online Edition at
www.informit.com/safarifree

> **STEP 1:** Enter the coupon code: EMTVFWH.

> **STEP 2:** New Safari users, complete the brief registration form.
> Safari subscribers, just log in.

If you have difficulty registering on Safari or accessing the online edition, please e-mail customer-service@safaribooksonline.com